Jap:

Why is t ... ed
two extɪ ... h?
And how did they contribute to the journey from war to peace with Australia, and within Japan itself?

This book makes available for the first time a treasure trove of hitherto unpublished documents on Japan in the war years and immediate post-war period of Allied Occupation and recovery. The documents consist of newsletters, newspaper articles, texts of radio broadcasts, and letters written by Frank William Coaldrake, an Anglican priest and pacifist, and the first Australian civilian to enter Japan after the War, and his wife Maida. Together they formed a team of participant observers in the challenge of a nation confronting its past and trying to find hope in a future while occupied by foreign powers.

This is a rare and comprehensive collection of first-hand accounts of Japan by two astute observers. The daily struggle against starvation is interspersed with issues including war atrocities, the atomic bombings, the status of the Imperial Family, and labour unions. The text is illustrated with photographs taken by Frank Coaldrake.

The documents have been compiled and edited, with an introduction and commentaries, by **William H. Coaldrake,** son of the authors and Foundation Professor of Japanese at the University of Melbourne.

Japan from War to Peace

The Coaldrake Records 1939–1956

Compiled and Edited by

William H. Coaldrake

RoutledgeCurzon
Taylor & Francis Group
LONDON AND NEW YORK

First published in 2003
by RoutledgeCurzon
11 New Fetter Lane, London EC4P 4EE

Simultaneously published in the USA and Canada
by RoutledgeCurzon
29 West 35th Street, New York, NY 10001

RoutledgeCurzon is an imprint of the Taylor & Francis Group

© 2003 William H. Coaldrake

Typeset in Baskerville by LaserScript Ltd, Mitcham, Surrey

Printed and bound in Great Britain by
TJ International, Padstow, Cornwall

British Library Cataloguing in Publication Data
A catalogue record of this book is available from the British Library

Library of Congress Cataloging in Publication Data
Coaldrake, Frank William, 1912-1970.
    Japan from war to peace: the Coaldrake records 1939-1956/compiled and edited by
William H. Coaldrake.
    p. cm.
    Includes index
    1. Coaldrake, Frank William, 1912-1970. 2. Coaldrake, Maida, 1919-
3. Missionaries–Japan–History–20th century–Sources. 4. Missionaries–Australia–History–20th
century–Sources. 5. Church of England in Australia–Missions–Japan–History–20th century–Sources.
I. Coaldrake, Maida, 1919- II. Coaldrake, William Howard. III. Title.
BV3457.C53 A3 2003
266'.3'092–dc21
[B]   2002035264

ISBN 0–7007–1721–8 (Hbk)
ISBN 0–7007–1722–6 (Pbk)

In loving memory of
Frank William Coaldrake
(1912–1970)

Contents

List of colour plates

The following plates appear between pages 306–307

Plate 13 has been used on the cover of the paperback edition

List of black and white photographs

Acknowledgements

I am indebted to many for information, guidance and support. This includes our extended family from the Izu days, Kimiyo Mutō, Ikue Kaneko, the Miyazawas of three generations, and Maruyama Akira. My cousin, the Rev. Edwin Richardson, supplied missing *Newsletters* to complete our set. Professor Kenneth J. Cable, who attended the same lectures as Dad in 1946 at the University of Sydney on Japanese history taught by Professor A. L. Sadler, gave invaluable guidance. The late Professor Manning Clark first told me that Dad tried to go to Japan in 1943. I am also most grateful for the assistance of Dr. Andrea Dale, Stephen Remington, Bishop Michael Challen, and to the Anglican Board of Mission–Australia and its National Director, Canon Geoff Smith, for permission to reprint various documents. Colleen Hodge assisted with archival searches. Many thanks also go to three generations of the Eckfeld family. The Eckfelds were part of the parish of St. Cuthbert's Church, East Brunswick, when Dad was priest there, and Dr. Tonia Eckfeld tenaciously tracked down documents and references, helped correct the manuscript and finalise illustrated materials.

I am also indebted to a number of other people who have also been involved in the production of this book at various stages over the last ten years, especially Christine MacArthur, Llewelyn Hughes, Kono Sanae and Andrew Williams, who has now gone on his own mission to Japan.

My final debt of gratitude is to my sisters, Margaret and Kimi, and most of all, to our mother.

William H. Coaldrake
Melbourne, 10 July 2002

Abbreviations

A.B.M.	The Australian Board of Missions, now called the Anglican Board of Mission–Australia.
A.S.C.M.	The Australian Student Christian Movement, also referred to simply as "S.C.M."
B.C.O.F.	British Commonwealth Occupation Force
B.S.L.	Brotherhood of St. Laurence
C.E.M.S.	Church of England Men's Society
C.M.S.	Church Missionary Society
L.A.R.A.	Licensed Agency for Relief in Asia
N.S.K.	Nippon Seikōkai
S.C.A.P.	Supreme Commander for the Allied Powers (General Douglas MacArthur).
S.P.C.K.	Society for the Promotion of Christian Knowledge
S.P.G.	Society for the Propagation of the Gospel

Introduction

William H. Coaldrake

To celebrate his fifty-sixth birthday in 1968 my father, Frank William Coaldrake, with that flair for the unconventional which characterised his entire life, gave me a present rather than just receiving one from me. It was a copy of a recently published book on the Brotherhood of St. Laurence entitled *God and Three Shillings: The Story of the Brotherhood of St. Laurence.*[1] My father had been one of the early members of this Anglican Brotherhood in Melbourne, before he ever contemplated going to Japan. He had distinguished himself controversially in the early 1940s as much for his militancy in pursuing issues of social justice as for his pacifism. His campaign against war ran parallel to his war against poverty and led logically and inexorably to a mission of reconciliation to Japan after the war.

On the flyleaf of the book Dad gave me in 1968 he wrote: "To Bill with love on my 56th birthday. Reading about myself 25 years after the events I can only ask 'What is the truth?'" At the time, of course, we did not know that Dad had only two more years to live. Subsequent events, culminating in his election as Archbishop of Brisbane on 10 July 1970 and his death twelve days later, would overtake us all. My mother suddenly had total responsibility for three teenage children, the youngest only thirteen. We had to get on with life and we did.

Dad's question to me on his fifty-sixth birthday still remains unanswered. What was the truth about Frank Coaldrake's journey from war to peace from 1939, when war broke out in Europe, until 1956 when he returned to Australia after nearly ten years in Japan? How did his personal journey contribute to Australia's national journey from war to peace with Japan? And how did Frank Coaldrake contribute to Japan's own journey from war to peace over that period? More specifically, why did he try to go to Japan as early as 1943, while the battles still raged in the Pacific War? How did his campaign for social justice in the slums of post-Depression Melbourne and his pacifism during the war from 1939 to 1945 shape his thinking about Japan and his mission of Christian reconciliation

---

1 I.R. Carter, *God and Three Shillings. The Story of the Brotherhood of St. Laurence*, Melbourne, Lansdowne Press, 1967.

after the war? What was the training, philosophical disposition and religious conviction undergirding his ten hard years of privation in Japan, his devotion to the Japanese people and to fighting the hatred of them in Australia? And what was the nature of his partnership in this venture with Maida Williams whom he married in late 1949, forming both a family and a powerful and articulate team in the mission venture? (Fig. 1) What exactly happened during these epic ten years from 1946 to 1956, still the "missing years" in the record of the life and ministry of one of the leaders of the Anglican Church of the middle decades of the twentieth century?

This book answers these questions using the actual words of Frank and Maida Coaldrake as preserved in the family records. Most are published for the first time in this book. The documents were kept carefully in numerous family files in Sydney and in boxes and filing cabinets we found in the Itō Church garage on a return visit to Japan in the mid-1970s. Above all else my intention has been to keep the focus on these original documents as written by Frank and Maida Coaldrake. They are the authors and it is their distinctive voices which are heard in answering the key questions about the Coaldrake mission of reconciliation. My approach in editing these documents has been, as much as possible, to avoid coming between the reader and the records. My role has been to assemble,

Figure 1 Frank and Maida Coaldrake on their wedding day, 3 December 1949. A.B.M. used this photograph for a fundraising pamphlet in 1950. In it the caption reads: "Our Missionaries in Japan. The Reverend Frank Coaldrake, M.A., and Miss Maida Williams, M.A., were married in Sydney last December. Miss Williams had been for four years the Youth Organiser in the Diocese of Tasmania. These two young Australians are doing one job in Japan and we must do everything in our power to give them the equipment they need. By filling in the attached form you make it possible for A.B.M. to finance the splendid plans for advance outlined in this leaflet."

select, collate, transcribe, and comment. I have been careful to differentiate clearly between the words of the authors and my comments as editor (see editorial notes at the end of *introduction*).

As the son of the authors of these documents, I have a particular and personal perspective on the events and issues involved. My earliest childhood memories are of the years immediately after the end of the Allied Occupation of Japan in 1952. Some are predictable childhood memories – of fire engines and aeroplanes, although to me of course they were *shōbō jidōsha* and *hikōki* respectively. Other memories are not so usual, either for Australians or even for the vast majority of the Japanese born and raised in more prosperous times after the war. Most of my early memories are of the Japan that was disappearing rapidly after the war: of the countryside of the Izu Peninsula one hundred kilometres southwest of Tokyo, with its thatched-roof farmhouses, smelly paddy fields and muddy lanes, and of the rugged coastline with wooden fishing vessels pulled up on the stony beaches. Of carpenters and their tools and the smell of freshly planed timber at building sites. Of a church filled with people lustily singing hymns. Of ancient Buddhist temples and Shinto shrines all around on the hillsides, to which I responded for my part from the front seat of Dad's speeding Land Rover with the words of the Christian prayer to St. Michael "... to cast down to Hell, Satan and all wicked spirits who wander through the world for the ruin of souls." This was a somewhat different approach from the one I now take to my work in Japanese architectural history and restoration! Although I did not realize it at the time this was a world in which, apart from my parents, I was the only "non-Japanese" except for occasional foreign visitors from Tokyo.

The Authors

Frank William Coaldrake (1912–1970) was an Anglican priest and the first Australian civilian to enter Occupied Japan after the war. He was one of the pioneering members of the Brotherhood of St. Laurence, the Anglican religious order working for social justice in the slums of Melbourne from the late 1930s onwards. He has been acknowledged as "the outstanding figure among Australian pacifists in the difficult years of the Second World War."[2] He combined his activities in the Brotherhood with founding the pacifist journal *The Peacemaker* on the outbreak of war in Europe in 1939. He edited and wrote much of it right through until 1946. It was to prove particularly influential in mobilising pacifists because of government restrictions on interstate travel. The first issue was sub-titled *An Australian Venture in Reconstruction*, an immediate signal of Frank Coaldrake's constructive approach to pacifism. It eventually became the official journal of the Federal Pacifist Council of Australia, which he helped establish in 1942, serving as President from 1943–46. The Council ultimately secured

---

2 Kenneth Rivett, "Frank William Coaldrake: 12-3-1912–22-7-1970. Pacifist," *The Peacemaker*, vol. 32, no. 8–9, August–September 1970, p. 5.

legislative change to allow for total exemption from military service for conscientious objectors.[3]

The journal was to be published regularly, usually monthly, throughout the war, despite government censorship, much community hostility, and Frank Coaldrake's demanding commitments to the Brotherhood of St. Laurence, the parish of St. Cuthbert's, East Brunswick, and for a time as Precentor of St. Paul's Cathedral, Melbourne. Every word published in *The Peacemaker* was meticulously checked by the censor, some of it banned.[4] This did not stop him publishing. His mail was frequently intercepted and opened, sometimes secretly.[5] Pacifists were not popular. Japanese were even less popular. Priests were expected to become army chaplains or, at the very least, support the war effort against Japan from their pulpits. A pacifist priest advocating reconciliation with the Japanese during the war was at times reviled as a traitor to his own country and a heretic to his religious vocation. He was interrogated by the security police.[6] He was equally unpopular with the ecclesiastical hierarchy of the Diocese of Melbourne, warned by Archbishop Head that if he were to have a career in the church "I don't want you pooping off on public platforms."[7] His relationship with Archbishop Head's successor, Dr. Joseph John Booth, was different only in the more moderate language the archbishop used to express the same idea.[8] Judging from the address he delivered in 1944 from the pulpit of the cathedral itself, the admonitions by successive archbishops had little effect:

3 Until then conscientious objectors were expected to render non-combatant service in the armed forces. See further: Shirley Abraham, "Frank William Coaldrake: 12-3-1912–22-7-1970," *The Peacemaker*, vol. 32, nos. 8–9, August–September, 1970, p. 5.

4 For example, see Letter to Frank Coaldrake from C. Burns, State Publicity Censor, 26 June 1940, "Frank Coaldrake Papers," Baillieu Library and Archives, the University of Melbourne.

5 See Letter from Frank W. Coaldrake to the Post Master General, Parliament House, Canberra, undated, mid-1940:

> Dear Sir, All articles of my mail addressed to me, Frank W. Coaldrake, at 65 Brunswick St, Fitzroy, N6, are being surreptitiously opened in transit, and they are also being delayed at least one delivery, frequently more. This has been going on for nearly six months, and in spite of my complaints to the Postal authorities in Melbourne it still continues and I can get no satisfactory statement as to the reason for it . . . If the mail is being opened by the Censor why is it not marked "Opened By Censor"?

6 See Letter from Frank W. Coaldrake to Inspector Birch, Commonwealth Investigation Branch, 3 March 1941 (*chapter 2*).

7 Archbishop Frederick Waldegrave Head, as recorded in Letter from Frank W. Coaldrake to his Mother, Mrs. E. R. Coaldrake, 15 July 1941. "Frank Coaldrake Papers," Baillieu Library and Archives, the University of Melbourne.

8 Letter from Archbishop Booth to Frank W. Coaldrake, 3 December 1943:

> I would suggest that you pray for guidance in this matter for you throw the Church at once into a controversy if you speak as a clergyman and, as I told you when you were ordained, you are limited by the fact that you have a duty to others, and as a very junior priest I do not think you should attempt to go [to] the press as such.

"Frank Coaldrake Papers," Baillieu Library and Archives, the University of Melbourne. Frank

If the Church pauses to reconsider its Sacred Scriptures and the ways it has known God's work it must admit that revolutionary action is very common with God. The Church must expect rather than deplore revolution... Where God does not see righteousness he wants a revolution. If God looked down on Moscow and Melbourne today it is not possible to say whether he would find righteousness in Moscow, but we know for sure that he would not find Melbourne to be a "city of righteousness."[9]

But actions spoke louder than words. For Frank Coaldrake, high principles had practical consequences, and in making this connection he proved shrewd, savvy, and selfless. He embarked on a program of direct action for social justice. In 1944 he led two "sit-in" protests in the slums of Melbourne, using Gandhi's concept of non-violent civil disobedience. The second case caught the popular, and tabloid, imagination in Melbourne. Accompanied by Tony Bishop, the Welfare Officer of the Brotherhood of St. Laurence at the time, he sat on the exposed veranda of one house in Armadale for thirty-seven days to protest against certain provisions in the Landlord and Tenant Regulations which discriminated against a widowed tenant.[10] We should remember that such actions as protests and sit-ins only became "acceptable" in the 1960s.

Frank Coaldrake felt he must go to Japan because of the combination of his priestly vocation, his conscientious objection and his commitment to practical measures, all those things which sat together so awkwardly in the estimation of his times and his superiors. He had to go to Japan because Japan was the enemy. Japanese were killing Australians and being killed by Australians. Killing was wrong. Some other way of resolving the breakdown in relations between Australians and Japanese was needed.

He had no special personal interest in Japan at first. When the war broke out in Europe his focus was on both Germany and Japan. If the course of the war had been different and Japan had stayed out of the picture, he may have tried to go to Germany instead. In February 1941 he broadcast messages of encouragement and pacifism to university students in Europe.[11] Even straight after the Japanese attack on Pearl Harbor in December 1941 he wrote in *The*

Coaldrake did attempt to separate what he saw as his "personal" views from those of the institutions with which he was associated. In *The Peacemaker* he wrote:

> A Personal Note. I should like to take this opportunity to point out with particular emphasis that The Peacemaker expresses views for which I myself am responsible, and which are not in any way attributable to the Australian Student Christian Movement, the Brotherhood of St. Laurence, or any other organisation with which I am connected.
>
> *The Peacemaker*, vol. 2, no. 1, January 1, 1940, p. 2.

9 Frank W. Coaldrake, "Do Communists Belong to God or the Devil?" St. Paul's Cathedral Address People's Service, 20 August 1944. Library of the Brotherhood of St. Laurence.

10 See further: Carter, *God and Three Shillings*, pp. 84–97.

11 *Talks by F.W. Coaldrake*: Department of Information–Broadcasting Division (February 1941), transcripts. National Archives of Australia.

Peacemaker that "we will not knowingly assist our friends to kill Germans, Japanese (or any other people); nor will we knowingly assist Germans, Japanese (or any other people) to kill our friends."[12] When it became apparent a year later, with the fall of Singapore in February 1942, that the more immediate enemy was Japan, the emphasis of Frank Coaldrake's attention shifted.

The idea of going to Japan on a mission of reconciliation started taking shape in his mind in May 1942. With the U.S. General, Douglas MacArthur, firmly ensconced in his new military headquarters in Brisbane, having been driven out of the Philippines, and the Japanese Imperial forces advancing south towards New Guinea, Frank Coaldrake wrote a prophetic editorial in the June edition of *The Peacemaker* entitled "Reaching into the future. Our approach to Japan." Because of its importance, the editorial is reprinted in full in *chapter 2*. In it Frank Coaldrake writes that "war hostilities will some day reach a stage which will permit efforts to be made in the reconciliation of Japanese and Australians." This may have seemed a trifle optimistic on the day it was issued, June 1, the day after the midget submarine attack on Sydney Harbour. The editorial is full of constructive analysis and specific proposals to establish better relations with Japan:

> The reconciliation of the people of Australia with the people of Japan bristles with difficulties. The disagreements leading up to this war; the oppositions being hardened in these months of conflict; the bitterness and sense of being wronged which will be the fruit of "Hate campaigns" in both countries; the radically different ways of life and standards of living in the two countries; the different political habits; the different religious practices and beliefs; the existence of race prejudice in both countries; these are a few of the stumbling blocks in the road to a just reconciliation. They must not be thought insuperable.

He goes on to discuss the idea of "Embassies of Reconciliation," a concept developed by the International Fellowship of Reconciliation in Europe, pointing out that Australians were already "learning Japanese and German, and are striving to equip themselves for a long stay in Japan whenever the war reaches a stage which will permit their reaching and entering the country." He notes that a similar idea had already been put forward by the Superior of the Brotherhood of St. Laurence, Father Gerard Tucker.

By April, 1943, less than a year later, Frank Coaldrake had decided to go to Japan himself. He wrote to the Minister for External Affairs, Dr. H.V. Evatt, explaining his commitment to better understanding between "our people and the Japanese people" and that "my belief is that the power of the gospel of Christ will, as nothing else can, make these enemies our friends."[13] He tells Dr. Evatt that he is "anxious to explore the possibilities of going to Japan at the earliest

---

12   "Our Attitude to the War Now," *The Peacemaker*, vol. 4, no. 1, January, 1942, p. 2.
13   Letter from Frank W. Coaldrake to The Minister for External Affairs, 21 April 1943. National Archives of Australia, Series number A989/1, Item 1943/700/48 (see *chapter 2*).

possible moment. I imagine that I should consider going only as a missionary but if there were a possibility of going in some other capacity such as that of a liaison officer with relief work or as one of a relief unit, I should be bound to give serious consideration to it." He stresses his commitment to going, if possible, even before hostilities cease.

The response, from the Secretary of the Department, reveals that the proposal was not taken seriously. Frank Coaldrake was told "as you realise there is no prospect of missionary activities from Australia being resumed in Japan until some time after the end of the war."[14] The discussions of Australia-Japan relations in *The Peacemaker* suggest that Frank Coaldrake was not prepared to accept that there was "no prospect" of going to Japan as a missionary before the end of the war. Going to Japan at the earliest possible moment was logical in his thinking and essential as the practical consequence of that thinking. He saw service in Japan, not as a soldier but as an instrument of peace, as a missionary or in some humanitarian capacity, as the positive corollary to his refusal to fight the Japanese in the armed forces. In *The Peacemaker* he was later to make a clear distinction between "passenger pacifists," or negative pacifists who simply said "no" to war, and "positive pacifists" who set out to do something directly to build the way for peace.[15]

He may have decided to go to Japan as early as 1943 but he did not receive permission from the government and the Allied Occupation authorities to enter Japan until 1947. Even General MacArthur, Supreme Commander of Allied Powers in Japan, could not speed up the process, despite a letter promising to assist.[16] By the time the authorities had sorted out the paperwork, Frank Coaldrake was already in Japan. He had "stolen a march" on them in the best military tradition. The official paperwork belatedly caught up with him many months after he actually arrived, forcing the hand of the authorities to give him official permission and sort out his status as non-military personnel. He noted in September, 1947, a full three months after his arrival, that "the B.C.O.F. [British Commonwealth Occupation Force] organisation is still catching up with myself – one section or another realises I'm here and that they should '[red]-tape' the highly irregular proceedings that have resulted from my being here ahead of schedule."[17]

Frank Coaldrake's arrival in Japan passes entirely unremarked in missionary annals. Surveying the postwar history of missionary activity in Japan, *The Japan Christian Yearbook* notes that the first wave of missionaries after the war consisted of the "experienced missionaries from the pre-war period" who came back in

14 Letter from W.R. Hodgson, Secretary, Ministry for External Affairs to the Rev. F.W. Coaldrake, 5 May 1943. National Archives of Australia, Series number A989/1, Item 1943/700/48 (see *chapter 2*).
15 *The Peacemaker*, vol. 6, no. 2, February, 1944, p. 2.
16 Letter from General Douglas MacArthur to the Chairman of the Australian Board of Missions, 7 February 1947. See *chapter 3*.
17 See *Newsletter No. 5*, 20 September 1947.

1946–47. Most were from North America, that is, the United States and Canada. A "second wave" came in 1947–49, consisting of missionaries from the boards which had "missions" in Japan from before the war as well as representatives of new American organisations.[18] According to this chronology, Frank Coaldrake's arrival in Japan coincided with the end of the first wave of predominantly North American "returnees" and the beginning of the second American wave. Like the Occupation itself, the missionary enterprise was North American dominated. So too, it would seem, have been the histories about it. *The Japan Christian Yearbook* for 1950, for example, includes no mention of Australia in its statistics for "Protestant mission boards." It lists 58 missionaries from North America, comprising 89% of the total, and 16 from Europe, making up the remaining 11%.[19] It further notes that there were 89 more "independent" missionaries, working separately from any mission boards, most of them Americans. In this analysis of Protestant missions there is no mention of Frank Coaldrake, of the Australian Board of Missions, or of Australia.[20]

He was sponsored and financially supported in the mission by the Australian Board of Missions (A.B.M.), the official mission board of the Anglican Synod of Australia.[21] He had approached A.B.M in 1943 asking the board to support his work, as we learn in his letter to Dr. Evatt.

In Japan he felt himself under constant constraints, first by the Occupation military authorities, and, after 1952, by the post-Occupation Japanese government regulation of foreign nationals. Continuing to be in Japan meant compromises. He had to keep his mouth shut, a galling limitation for Frank Coaldrake. If he had not he would have been deported and his mission would have failed. He did participate in a major pacifist congress in 1954, one of the few occasions where he felt he could contribute to public debate on pacifism in Japan without compromising his mission work. Maida Coaldrake explained his quandary in *Newsletter No. 57*: "Since we are residents of Japan at the pleasure of the Japanese Government, and though paying no taxes, have no political status, it has been difficult for Frank to understand where more than in our daily life as missionaries his contribution to pacifism may lie."[22]

Frank Coaldrake was to work for ten years as a missionary from the Anglican Church of Australia and as a member of staff of the Anglican Church of Japan (Nippon Seikōkai). He began as the former and ended much more as the latter. In the meantime his vows to serve in the Brotherhood of St. Laurence expired in

---

18   See further: Hallam C. Shorrock and Joseph J. Spae (eds.), *The Japan Christian Yearbook, 1968,* Tokyo, The Christian Literature Society of Japan (Kyo Bun Kwan), 1968, pp. 80–82.

19   Figures quoted in *The Japan Christian Yearbook, 1968*, p. 81.

20   The position and recognition of Australia in the contribution of the Roman Catholic Church was very different, with the same history duly acknowledging that appeals issued from Japan "to the entire Catholic world for missionaries and aid." Australia sent fourteen priests later in 1947. See: *The Japan Christian Yearbook, 1968*, p. 62.

21   Now known as the Anglican Board of Mission–Australia.

22   *Newsletter No. 57*, January, 1954.

1948.[23] All this was under conditions of considerable hardship and deprivation. He had to accept some level of Occupation rations, as the Japanese themselves were under severe local rationing and were eking out an existence on homegrown vegetables and anything else they could catch, including grasshoppers. "Without the privilege of buying food from their [Australian Army] canteen I would not have been able to live," he explained later.[24] His own official rations were one-half the military ration and, by his own estimation, were sufficient to last for only three or four days each month. He would not use the black market as a matter of principle. He distributed most of the food from parcels sent by supporters in Australia. He was diagnosed as suffering rickets and beriberi by late 1949 when he returned to Australia for his first period of furlough after two and a half years in Japan. By then his hair had turned completely white and he had something of the emaciated appearance of many of the P.O.W.s interned during the war. (Fig. 1 and Fig. 27)

While on furlough back in Australia, in December 1949, he married Maida Stelmar Williams (b. 1919). They had met at a summer conference of the Australian Student Christian Movement (A.S.C.M.) held at "Frensham" School at Mittagong, New South Wales, less than nine months before the outbreak of war in Europe. At the time Frank Coaldrake was one of the three national Travelling Secretaries of the A.S.C.M. Maida Williams was a member of the national committee representing the University of Tasmania. After the conference ended, committee members remained for organisational meetings, but were suddenly surrounded by bushfires, when the entire southern highlands of New South Wales exploded into fire. These were to be the worst bushfires in several generations, still talked about today in the same frightening category as the more recent 1994 and 2001–02 New South Wales bushfires. Frank Coaldrake helped organise the defence of the school and Maida Williams soaked blankets in the baths to fight the fires, which proved ineffective because the intense heat dried them out instantly. "For one terrible twenty-four hours we fought for our lives," she recalls.[25] They were to marry a decade later.

Maida Williams had been awarded the University Medal in English and the Sir Philip Fysh Prizes in English and History during the three years of studies for the Bachelor of Arts at the University of Tasmania from 1937 to 1939. She went on to complete a master's degree in Australian Federation History in 1945, in the days when masters degrees were normally the highest level of academic attainment and doctorates were only awarded for a lifetime of academic work. From 1941–43 she combined her studies with war work in the Cadbury-Fry-Pascall factory at Claremont outside Hobart. She says she was not a pacifist at that stage, but "almost everyone I knew at University did not come back from war service. I could see war was wrong but couldn't see a way

---

23 See *Newsletter No. 13*, 1 May 1948.
24 *Newsletter No. 62*, August, 1956.
25 Maida Coaldrake, 23 August 2001.

out of it."[26] In 1945 Maida Williams was appointed as the first woman on the staff of the Diocese of Tasmania, serving as Youth Organiser for the diocese until 1950 when she departed for Japan. From 1950 until the end of 1956, Frank and Maida Coaldrake formed a team of participant observers in the agonising challenge of a nation confronting its past and trying to find hope in the future while vanquished and still occupied by foreign powers.

The Coaldrake Records

The Newsletters: *Letters of Reconciliation*

During their period of service in Japan, Frank and Maida Coaldrake sent a total of sixty-three newsletters back to Australia. If *The Peacemaker* had been published as "an Australian venture in reconstruction," their *Newsletters* were a venture in reconciliation between Japan and Australia. We find this explained in one of the earliest *Newsletters*. In it Frank Coaldrake asks his readers:

> Do people want to read it (the *Newsletter*)? I fervently hope so, for the sake of Reconciliation between here [Japan] and there [Australia]. We started by sending No. 1 to 100 persons. Requests have now doubled our list and we are glad of every possible reader who will be concerned about the Reconciliation of our peoples.[27]

Both Frank and Maida Coaldrake were skilled writers and editors, Frank as editor of *The Peacemaker* and Maida as the editor of the student newspaper *Togatus* for two years at the University of Tasmania. Until 1950, the *Newsletters* were written by Frank Coaldrake. After Maida Coaldrake returned with him to Japan in that year, she took over primary responsibility, writing them in terms of what she saw and thought, with sections added by Frank. Both their names appear at the end of the *Newsletters* from 1950 onwards. The headline sometimes includes "Maida writing." To avoid possible confusion, a brief note clarifying who wrote which sections has been inserted at the beginning of each *Newsletter.*

The Coaldrake *Newsletters* are the core of this book, both in content and quantity. They amount to some 170,000 words of text in their own right. The *Newsletters* provide a more or less continuous narrative and commentary on Japan from June 1947, just days after Frank Coaldrake first arrived in Japan. They end in November 1956 shortly after he was unexpectedly appointed Chairman of the Australian Board of Missions, the executive director of the board which had sponsored his mission in Japan. They were produced almost monthly at first, tapering off towards the end as other forms of information about Japan became available to Australians and the Japanese mission became more self-reliant as Japan itself recovered from the war. We should remember that these were the

---

26 Maida Coaldrake, 10 September 2001.
27 *Newsletter No. 6*, October, 1947.

days before television and civilian airline flights between Australia and Japan. Information about Japan, as opposed to policy and polemics, reported from the ground by Australians, particularly ones who spoke Japanese, was a rare and priceless commodity.

The *Newsletters* end in late 1956, just as commercial airline flights between Australia and Japan were beginning[28] and just after Prime Minister Robert Menzies had made the first visit to Japan by an Australian Prime Minister. The next year the trade treaties, which were to establish the economic foundations of the relationship between Australia and Japan for the second half of the twentieth century, came into force.[29] At the same time the Japanese Prime Minister, Mr. Nobusuke Kishi, paid a reciprocal visit to Australia, apologising for the war:

> Although there has been a long tradition of friendship between Australia and Japan, including, in the first world war, our cherished association with your immortal Anzacs, there occurred four years of tragic interruption in that friendship. True, it is over twelve years since hostilities ceased and over six since the formal conclusion of peace. Notwithstanding that passage of time, it is my official duty, and my personal desire, to express to you, and through you to the people of Australia, our heartfelt sorrow for what occurred in the war.[30]

In the same address, he hailed the Australian Prime Minister's visit to Japan the previous year as the "first major step in the promotion of a better mutual understanding" between Japan and Australia. This statement was made on 4 December, 1957. By then it had been over ten years since Frank Coaldrake had taken his own "first step" onto Japanese soil. And it was fifteen years since he had taken his first "steps" to secure better relations between Australia and Japan in his landmark editorials in *The Peacemaker* in June 1942 and March 1943 (see *chapter 2*).

Copies of most of the *Newsletters* as well as the "carbon copies" of some of the manuscripts, have been held in the Coaldrake family archives for nearly half a century but it took several years of detective work to assemble the complete set, mostly from our relatives. Until now they have not been published, except for a number of short extracts reprinted in *The Peacemaker* at the time as a series called *Odawara Lantern*.

In May, 1948 Frank Coaldrake explained his approach to writing the *Newsletters* in an article published in *The Peacemaker*:

---

28 *The Agreement between Australia and Japan for Air Services* came into force on 27 April 1956. Australian Treaty Series 1956 No. 6, Australian Government Publishing Service, Canberra, 1997.

29 *Agreement on Commerce between the Commonwealth of Australia and Japan*. It came into force on December 4, 1957. Australian Treaty Series 1957 No. 15, Australian Government Publishing Service, Canberra, 1997.

30 Address by the Prime Minister of Japan, Mr. Nobusuke Kishi, at Parliamentary Luncheon, Canberra, Wednesday, 4 December 1957. See further: "Kishi Expresses to M.P.s Japan's 'Heartfelt Sorrow'," and "Tribute to Menzies for Leadership," *The Sydney Morning Herald*, Late edition, 5 December 1957, p. 1.

As well as the regular contributions to this "Peacemaker" column, I am sending a "Newsletter" to some friends who ask for it. There is a difference between the two. In the "Newsletter" I write in a candidly personal and subjective manner in the hope that some people will be able to see Japan through my life and work here. In these [newspaper] columns I shall try only to describe something of what I see and learn during my life and work here, and I shall sometimes achieve an objective approach.[31]

The *Newsletters* are indeed "candidly personal." At one point he signs off as "Candidly Frank," no doubt amused by the tautology. The *Newsletters* are a rare and honest first-hand account by two astute observers of Japan from a unique grass-roots perspective. They speak in an authentic and authoritative voice, informed by daily life and fluency in Japanese language and customs, and by an unshakeable conviction that the passage from war to peace for Japan begins with people and knowledge, not military victories and political vituperation.

A critically important statement of Frank Coaldrake's approach to writing about Japan in the early period of the late 1940s is contained in the original manuscript for an article published in abridged form in *The Peacemaker* in 1948.[32] In the following telling paragraph, omitted from the published version, Frank Coaldrake assesses his competence and viewpoint in writing about Japan and the Japanese:

I prefer to work from the foundation of my observations. You will wish, as I do myself, that I had a more exhaustive array of observations with which to work. But I think my material is now sufficient to justify the undertaking. Moreover, I think it is probable that no one in this country is in a position to get a better selection of material. Occupation Officials can get at statistics which are not available to me – but they lack the personal contact with Japanese citizens on the basis of partnership and friendship which I enjoy in my position. If one had been in this country longer there would be a proportionately greater number of observations, but no one has been here longer than me in such a position. A Press Correspondent would have greater facilities for moving round the country and "interviewing" people, but the formal "Press Interview" never gets to the depths reached by a parish priest with his people.

By 1948 he was already in a unique position of personal trust and friendship with many Japanese, and had been there longer than any one in such a position. To this we should also add his considerable language competence.

The *Newsletters* cover in vivid detail Japan from the ashes of defeat and starvation during the Allied Occupation into the critical period of recovery in the

---

31 Frank W. Coaldrake, "*Odawara Lantern* and *Newsletter* Relation," *The Peacemaker*, vol. 10, no. 5, May 1948, p. 3. He contributed a regular column, called the *Odawara Lantern* from the name of his first base in Japan, until March, 1949 and his impending move to Izu.

32 Frank Coaldrake, "What Defeat Has Done to Japan's Warriors," *The Peacemaker. An Australian Venture in Reconstruction*, vol. 10 no. 4, April 1948, p. 3. See *chapter 4*.

post-Occupation years. They reveal Japan on the agonising road from war to peace – people and places, tragedies and triumphs of daily life, the struggles of a defeated nation at individual and collective levels coming to terms with the legacy of war, the challenges of foreign occupation and new beginnings. The daily struggle against simple, stark starvation is interspersed with discussion of war atrocities, the war-time atomic bombing of Hiroshima and the 1954 U.S. nuclear tests at Bikini Atoll, the status of the Imperial Family, labour unions, *zaibatsu* conglomerate busting, the working of the new democratic Diet, individual rights and responsibilities. The critical choice of direction for postwar Japan becomes clear – of material well-being over spiritual and cultural values. Lofty principles of democratic rights are set against the grim realities of the American bombers flying overhead by the early 1950s on their bombing missions from nearby Atsugi airbase to the Korean war zone one hour away.

In scope and insight the *Newsletters* go well beyond what is generally understood as missionary enterprise although the fierceness of an uncompromising and self-sacrificing faith is at their core. Professor Ken Cable, recently retired Head of the Department of History, the University of Sydney, has made the following assessment of the character and importance of the Coaldrake *Newsletters*:

> The *Newsletters* belong to a well-known and long-established genre. For almost a century, missionaries in the field have been sending back newsletters to their supporters and friends at home, giving information and seeking further help. By their very nature, they are somewhat restricted. Their readers are interested in personal details and stories rather than any close analysis; failure discourages them and too much success reduces their contributions; they do not understand the background and they do not appreciate mission methodology. Long experience has made mission newsletters rigid in form and content.[33]

At one level the Coaldrake *Newsletters* fit into the missionary newsletter genre. They were written specifically for the members of the Australian church who sent supplies, financial contributions and well wishes to the mission in Japan. Maida Coaldrake confirms this:

> I was writing about topics which I thought would be of interest to the members of the parishes, womens' auxiliaries and so on who were reading the *Newsletters*, and who were sending us the parcels of food and clothes which were keeping us going because we couldn't have lived without this support. These were the sort of people I had stayed with when I had been Youth Organiser in Tasmania. I saw everything from the inside out... Until the end of the Occupation we couldn't talk about military movements.[34]

---

33 Kenneth J. Cable, Letter to William H. Coaldrake, 1 April 1997.
34 Maida Coaldrake, 16 August 2001.

At another level, the *Newsletters* go far beyond the boundaries of their genre, as Ken Cable explains:

> [The Coaldrake] *Newsletters* follow the accustomed pattern. At first glance, they seem conventional. They are not. Frank was an exceptional man, with an unusual background and a highly personal reason for coming to Japan; his later career was to be high-powered. He was perceptive and far-thinking. Above all, he had a very wide view of the Japanese situation and a capacity for seeing beneath the surface of things. His puckish sense of humour was peculiarly his own. His *Newsletters*, apparently routine, are subtle and distinctive when read with care and proper emphasis. They not only describe events but also set them against the changing background of Japanese and Anglican history. They are valuable documents.[35]

To this we should add the changing background of Australia-Japan relations and attitudes.

How were the *Newsletters* printed and circulated, and what did they actually look like? They had modest beginnings, at first simply roneoed copies of letters sent from Frank Coaldrake to his mother, Mrs. Eliza Coaldrake, in Melbourne and later in Brisbane. "I write the letter as an extra long one to Mother, being able to put all the available time into one long letter, instead of many short ones," he explained in *Newsletter No. 5* of 20 September 1947. Later he fills in more details:

> My mother had the letter duplicated and sent it to friends. From then until we reached Australia on furlough in June 1954, [printing and circulating] the *Newsletter* has always been very largely my mother's responsibility. We have written to her, she has seen to the printing, proofing, wrapping and distribution. In some cities friends have accepted the responsibility of delivering copies by hand. Circulation reached a total of several hundred.
>
> Money for the venture has always come, a lot from some, some from a lot. That, too, has been handled by my mother.[36]

One of the early *Newsletters* in this format (*No. 6*, 22 October 1947) is shown in Fig. 2. They were either *quarto* or *foolscap* in size. A technological advance came with *Newsletter No. 25* of May, 1949 when Mrs. Coaldrake had the letters type-set and professionally printed as a folding pamphlet. These *Newsletters* were usually bi-fold, allowing for four pages of text, each page 210 mm x 140 mm. They were about 5,000 words in length, the same as many of the earlier typed *Newsletters*. Some were even longer, printed as three-fold or four-fold with up to 8,000 words, each page approximately 265 mm x 140 mm. Occasionally *Newsletters* were still sent out in typescript form because of work and family pressures; during the Lake Ippeki summer camps (*No. 27*, July, 1949, and *No. 28*, August, 1949) and

---

35 Kenneth J. Cable, 1997.
36 *Newsletter No. 60*, April, 1956.

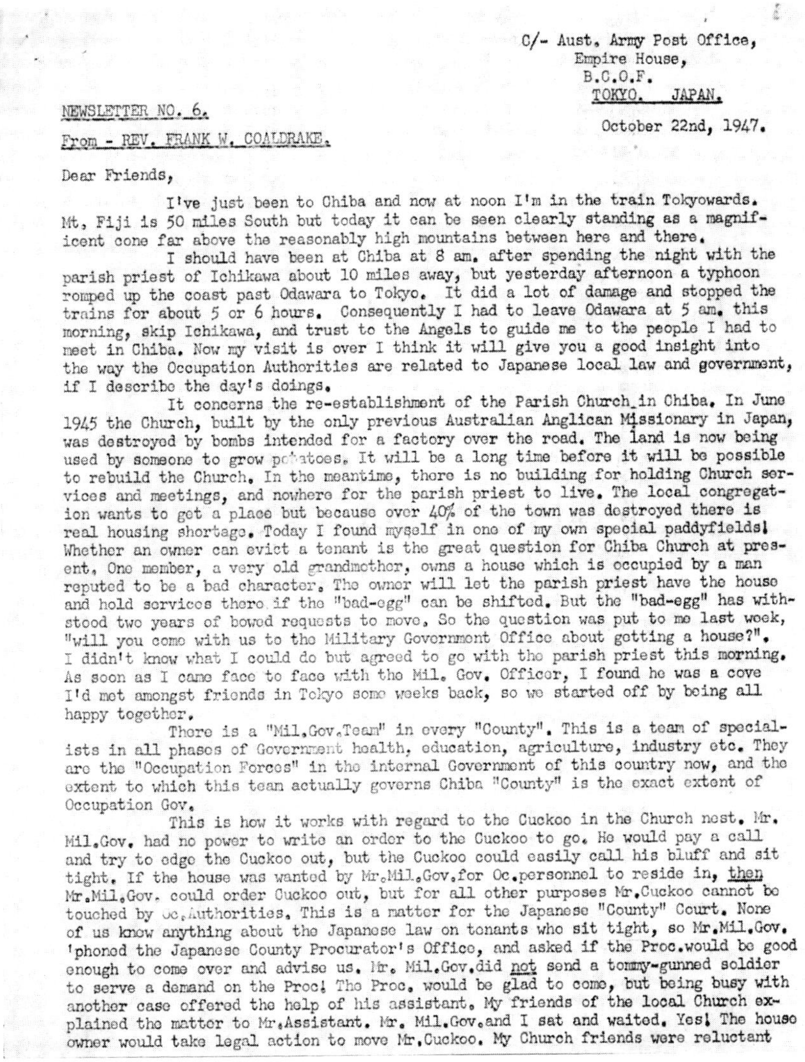

C/- Aust. Army Post Office,
Empire House,
B.C.O.F.
TOKYO. JAPAN.

NEWSLETTER NO. 6.

From - REV. FRANK W. COALDRAKE.

October 22nd, 1947.

Dear Friends,

I've just been to Chiba and now at noon I'm in the train Tokyowards. Mt. Fuji is 50 miles South but today it can be seen clearly standing as a magnificent cone far above the reasonably high mountains between here and there.

I should have been at Chiba at 8 am. after spending the night with the parish priest of Ichikawa about 10 miles away, but yesterday afternoon a typhoon romped up the coast past Odawara to Tokyo. It did a lot of damage and stopped the trains for about 5 or 6 hours. Consequently I had to leave Odawara at 5 am. this morning, skip Ichikawa, and trust to the Angels to guide me to the people I had to meet in Chiba. Now my visit is over I think it will give you a good insight into the way the Occupation Authorities are related to Japanese local law and government, if I describe the day's doings.

It concerns the re-establishment of the Parish Church in Chiba. In June 1945 the Church, built by the only previous Australian Anglican Missionary in Japan, was destroyed by bombs intended for a factory over the road. The land is now being used by someone to grow potatoes. It will be a long time before it will be possible to rebuild the Church. In the meantime, there is no building for holding Church services and meetings, and nowhere for the parish priest to live. The local congregation wants to get a place but because over 40% of the town was destroyed there is real housing shortage. Today I found myself in one of my own special paddyfields! Whether an owner can evict a tenant is the great question for Chiba Church at present. One member, a very old grandmother, owns a house which is occupied by a man reputed to be a bad character. The owner will let the parish priest have the house and hold services there if the "bad-egg" can be shifted. But the "bad-egg" has withstood two years of bowed requests to move. So the question was put to me last week, "will you come with us to the Military Government Office about getting a house?". I didn't know what I could do but agreed to go with the parish priest this morning. As soon as I came face to face with the Mil. Gov. Officer, I found he was a cove I'd met amongst friends in Tokyo some weeks back, so we started off by being all happy together.

There is a "Mil.Gov.Team" in every "County". This is a team of specialists in all phases of Government health, education, agriculture, industry etc. They are the "Occupation Forces" in the internal Government of this country now, and the extent to which this team actually governs Chiba "County" is the exact extent of Occupation Gov.

This is how it works with regard to the Cuckoo in the Church nest. Mr. Mil.Gov. had no power to write an order to the Cuckoo to go. He would pay a call and try to edge the Cuckoo out, but the Cuckoo could easily call his bluff and sit tight. If the house was wanted by Mr.Mil.Gov.for Oc.personnel to reside in, then Mr.Mil.Gov. could order Cuckoo out, but for all other purposes Mr.Cuckoo cannot be touched by Oc.Authorities. This is a matter for the Japanese "County" Court. None of us know anything about the Japanese law on tenants who sit tight, so Mr.Mil.Gov. 'phoned the Japanese County Procurator's Office, and asked if the Proc.would be good enough to come over and advise us. Mr. Mil.Gov.did not send a tommy-gunned soldier to serve a demand on the Proc. The Proc. would be glad to come, but being busy with another case offered the help of his assistant. My friends of the local Church explained the matter to Mr.Assistant. Mr. Mil.Gov.and I sat and waited. Yes! The house owner would take legal action to move Mr.Cuckoo. My Church friends were reluctant

Figure 2 Newsletter No. 6, 22 October 1947, page one. The early typed version.

immediately after the birth of Bill (*No. 46*, May, 1952). At one point things were so busy that a copy of extracts from a letter of Maida Coaldrake to Frank's mother of 9 November 1955 was circulated (see chapter 8), reverting to the procedure used in the first years in Japan.

By April 1956 the *Newsletters* were being sent not only to Australia, but America, Europe, Asia and Africa, and the production process was changed again:

Beginning with this letter we are to do things differently. The job now is too big for my mother to handle without a great deal of worry. We want to include photographs and we can borrow without charge blocks which have been used locally if we print in Japan. Chiefly for these two reasons we will print the letter here and post direct to all who want to receive it.[37]

This phase of the *Newsletters* was to be short lived – only three were produced in this format because of Frank Coaldrake's unexpected recall to Australia to take over the chairmanship of the Australian Board of Missions. (Fig. 3, *Newsletter No. 62*, August, 1956). In the last *Newsletter* we learn that:

> These *Newsletters* have gone out for nearly ten years to an ever widening circle of readers. We now send 600 copies and they seem to be passed around and read at groups so that the actual number of readers is unknown. We have written for two reasons the first being that you have so often urged us to write more. Several times it has been suggested that we publish the letters in book form. They are, however, so full of purely personal allusions that we have always put the suggestions aside. The second reason you would hardly guess. The letters have brought us wonderful sustaining encouragement in the knowledge of your interest and prayers. We have never been alone here and in times of difficulty we have been sure of being upheld by you. For this, and also for your gifts, we cannot find type that is not too cold to express our feelings.[38]

It is precisely these allusions and incidents that now give the *Newsletters* their poignant immediacy.

Other Written Records

The *Newsletters* are the main type of "reporting" on Japan in this book. They are interspersed with a judicious selection of other types of "reporting" by Frank Coaldrake. Each gives a different "angle" or perspective on events and thinking. From the pages of *The Peacemaker* we find comments of direct relevance in understanding the shaping of Frank Coaldrake's thinking on Japan.[39] Extracts from his reports to the A.B.M. include confidential analyses which were not intended for public consumption at the time but which now throw light on particular problems and issues. The text of newspaper interviews, radio broadcasts, sermons and speeches from the periods of furlough in Australia, 1949–50 and 1954–55, give clear insights into Australian attitudes towards Japan after the war. Recently discovered letters from Frank Coaldrake to Maida Coaldrake reveal more about his thinking and motivation, especially a long letter written in 1943. Selections from his unofficial, handwritten minutes of every church committee meeting he chaired in Izu from 1950 to 1956 complete the picture of his strategies and assessment of progress.

---

37 *Newsletter No. 60*, April, 1956. It was printed at the Kokusai Press, Tokyo.
38 *Newsletter No. 63*, November 1956.
39 *The Peacemaker* is held on microfilm at the University of Melbourne. UniM Baill MIC/o 6353.

日　本　聖　公　会
(Ni-　hon　Holy　Catholic　Church)

NIPPON SEIKOKAI

Church of England in Japan

NEWS LETTER No. 62   AUGUST 1956

St. Mary's Church,
960 Oka,
Ito,
JAPAN.
St. Barnabas' Day.

Dear Friends,

Today is the ninth anniversary of my first arrival in Japan.

The war was everywhere obvious as I travelled across the country that day. I was taken to see Hiroshima and marvelled at the spirit of the people even then rebuilding the city that had disappeared in a flash. The noise of countless hammers was the thing that impressed me as I stood on the top of the shell of a blasted building.

In that day I learned what most of us Australians had barely been remembering then, and will have forgotten by now. It was the extent to which the Japanese cities had been treated to old-fashioned bombing. Two cities were atom-bombed. Only one city of over one hundred thousand population in the whole of the country was spared conventional bomb raids. Every city or town I passed through that day was more than half destroyed. There's nothing so completely desolate looking as an acre or two of ashes and rubble with a great smoke-stack standing orphaned in the middle.

Japan was Destroyed

Japan in those days was battered, burnt, ragged and starving. Population had been increased in one year by seven million persons because the armies and the colonists had been brought home. To feed and clothe and house the seventy million with the resources of these four small islands would be impossible at the best of times, but with those islands pulverised the situation was hopeless. And there was a lack of hope in the people one saw standing in queues, sitting in gutters, clinging to the few trains, or feverishly padding along the streets.

American help—Australian ?

The army of Occupation was very much in evidence, and I was soon to learn that this army and the help it was bringing was really the only hope for the country. Much has been written about the Occupation but the thing I remember today is that the ordinary soldiers could not resist the sight of

Woman of five churches representing their Auxiliaries meeting at St. Mary's Ito in June. Foremost is Mrs Shimizu, one of the founders of the Home Mission Movement in Japan. Second from left, in kimono, is Mrs Harada, matron of Ito Hostel. (Cartoonists will please note that only one wears glasses.)

Figure 3 Newsletter No. 62, August, 1956, page one. Professionally printed in Japan.

Oral History

In addition to the written records, a unique oral history has been provided by my mother, Maida Coaldrake. This was recorded over a period of three years from 1999–2001 in Sydney. It explains issues which she felt she could not include in the *Newsletters* at the time she was writing them in 1950–1956:

The fact that Japan was such a tightly constructed and suffering country couldn't be explained in the *Newsletters*. That is why I have never been able to put pen to paper on these subjects – the discrepancy between what I saw and what I was instructed to believe."[40]

This oral history is particularly helpful in understanding the character of the American leadership of the Occupation of Japan, some of the tensions in church affairs, and personal hardship experienced by the Coaldrakes as Australian rather than American missionaries.

All documents included in the book are from the Coaldrake family archives, except where other sources are specifically acknowledged. Documents not written by Frank or Maida Coaldrake have been included only when they have a direct bearing on understanding particular events and issues. These include correspondence between A.B.M. and Frank Coaldrake which reveals how the Japan mission was set up – the portentous letter of 1943 from Frank Coaldrake to the Minister for External Affairs which was found in the National Archives in Canberra, and the letter from General MacArthur to A.B.M. in 1947 from the Mitchell Library in Sydney.

As a consequence of the decision to concentrate this book on the unpublished Coaldrake Records many records written by others are not included. This book would have become a multi-volume series if we had included everything we would have liked. We look forward to the results of work by other researchers in assessing all this material together, including the Japanese language documents in the archives of the Diocese of Yokohama (formerly South Tokyo), as well as Frank Coaldrake's years as Chairman of A.B.M. (1957–1970) in light of the information about his mission in Japan contained in this book.

The Photographic Record

Frank Coaldrake took an extensive visual record of the mission in Japan. Unless otherwise acknowledged, all photographs in the book are from the Coaldrake Family Records, either taken by, or taken under the instruction of, Frank Coaldrake. He began taking colour slides and movie film as soon as these media became more readily available in the late 1940s. The *Newsletters* include appeals for supporters to send him more film. Always constrained by budget, he was sparing but effective in the images he captured, whether still or moving, although a little too sparing when it came to pictures of himself.

The visual record surviving today amounts to over 2,500 black and white photographs, 850 colour slides and over two hours of 16mm black and white movie film, some of it found in poor condition. Frank Coaldrake was keen to use visual resources as well as the written word to explain Japan. The colour slides were used extensively by Frank and Maida Coaldrake for the many talks and speeches on Japan

40 Maida Coaldrake, 25 August 2001.

made during deputation work in Australia in 1954 and 1955, and after the Coaldrakes had returned to live in Australia. Some are still used in my lectures today.

These images capture a Japan that is hardly recognizable today. They challenge us to remember how much has changed so rapidly. The photographs show the keen interest in people also apparent in the written records, a desire to present "ordinary" Japanese in their daily lives and activities. Each face, sometimes cheerfully masking hardship, poses the question: "are these the feared and 'sub-human' enemy of wartime propaganda or are they just people like you and me?"

With the exception of some of the earliest photographs from 1947, the black and white photographs have been reprinted from the original negatives preserved in the Coaldrake family home. This has given them a clarity and freshness which belies their age. Because of the limitations of space the photographs included in this book have been carefully chosen wherever possible to illustrate events and people described in the written documents. Photographs were included in later *Newsletters* and these have been duly included with the *Newsletters* in this book wherever they survive. Because of cost only a few of the colour photographs could be included. Some have been selected with an eye to relevance to the text but most have been chosen because they tell a story in their own right.

The 16mm films have been transferred to archival videotape and are held at *ScreenSound Australia*, the national film and sound archives in Canberra (see *Guide to Archival Resources*, at the end of this *introduction*). The films date from as early as 1948 and include scenes of people and their activities, from church processions in streets of remote castletowns of central Japan to traditional carpenters hard at work with lumber ripsaws preparing the timbers for the church building in Itō. Today this type of saw may only be found in museums in Japan. Relatively little film of this period in Japan's history survives.

Achievements Material, Spiritual and Strategic

What were the strategies and the results, the consequences material and spiritual, of the Coaldrake mission to Japan? Ultimately the question is for others to consider but many of the immediate results, both large and small, may be gathered from the pages of the *Newsletters* themselves: people helped and lives saved at a practical level, particularly during the desperate years of starvation up to 1952; emotional and spiritual sustenance for many in the heart of despair; a strong and caring Christian witness throughout an isolated and rugged part of Japan, bringing together the people of Izu and those of the Australian church who read the *Newsletters* and who sent the hundreds of parcels and messages of encouragement; a young but growing church with its headquarters in Itō, thirteen cottage churches, and four more in preparation throughout the peninsula,[41] accorded recognition as a full parish in the diocese in October, 1956; two young priests sent to Australia for further theological studies; the experience of the

---

41 *Newsletter No. 61*, August, 1956.

thousands of young people who participated in the Lake Ippeki Camps, to discover the meaning of community and fellowship away from the bombed-out cities in which they lived, enabling them to go on to make varied contributions to Japanese society; the way the camps inspired the next generation of leaders of the Nippon Seikōkai to become its priests and bishops.

Frank Coaldrake himself summarises the progress of the mission, its achievements and difficulties, in reports and in the *Newsletters*. These summaries should be read first when considering the outcomes of the mission: in the reports from Odawara and Itō, and most particularly his broad overview, quite breathless in the vision and energy which underlies it, contained in *Newsletter No. 62* of August, 1956. This *Newsletter* was written on St. Barnabas' Day, nine years to the day after his arrival in Japan. It was written even as the official selection committee for the new Chairman of A.B.M. was meeting in Sydney, and tacitly endorsing his strategies in Japan as a blueprint for the wider community of partnership in mission for the Australian Anglican church in the Pacific and East Asia, by choosing him as their chief executive.

From Frank Coaldrake's private notes in the file called *Izu Mission Meetings. Unofficial Minutes kept by F.W.C.*, we find his personal record of what he had set out to achieve in Japan. These notes are an unambiguous declaration of what was to later become more widely known as "the post-colonial agenda." The extracts from the *Unofficial Minutes* in chapter 8 reveal the regular and orderly conduct of meetings with local church committees. Consultation, transparency and financial accountability were the basis for stimulating local responsibility in conducting the Izu mission. The basic strategies were to give the laity significant responsibility, and to make this a local church for the people of Japan. For the laity, responsibility was not to be limited to the private practice of Christian faith. Elections were held to select local representatives. This itself was not without difficulties. In *Newsletter No. 42* (December 1951–January 1952) we learn that the first elections had to be postal ballots because "we can't have a general meeting or election because our members are so scattered. Also, nobody knows everybody except myself." Even more importantly, lay persons were required to witness to their faith and to propagate that faith in deeply conservative and often isolated communities. The Ippeki summer camps were an opportunity to give the "campers" opportunities to visit local villages and learn to conduct street missions.

The ultimate objective, as set out in the *Unofficial Minutes*, was to make the church self-sustaining through "spontaneous expansion." We find this term and its origin discussed in *Newsletter No. 53* of May–June, 1953, in which Maida Coaldrake comments:

Ever since the reference in one of Keys Smith's [C.M.S. medical missionary] newsletters about Roland Allen's *Spontaneous Expansion of the Church*[42] and our

---

42   See further: Roland Allen, *The Spontaneous Expansion of the Church and the Causes which Hinder It*, London, New York, Vancouver, and Nilgiris, World Dominion Press, First edition 1927, Second edition 1949.

own reading of it, we have been much exercised over the problem of the lack of participation of the people themselves – lay and priest alike – in the evangelisation of the nation… So in the Easter Committee meeting Frank challenged our lay-people to face up to the situation of an Izu Church less dependent on the priest except for matters of priestly ministry… The resulting plan we work to today is very different from anything we ourselves might have devised. Though it has weaknesses, it is the People's Plan.

Frank Coaldrake explains that his aim was for "a spontaneously growing community of Christian locals, the title of which is 'the indigenous Church'." In this church "we must pay more attention to the one deeply concerned person than to the ten only superficially interested."[43] Behind this strategy lies Frank Coaldrake's assessment that in Japan there were two endemic problems – a danger of becoming over-dependent on foreign financial support, and too much emphasis on the priest, especially the person of the particular priest. We can wonder if this did not become the case with the Izu church after Frank Coaldrake, that he became more iconic and synonymous with the church than he would have ever wanted or allowed.

A decade later this type of thinking about the strategies of indigenous responsibility was becoming more widespread in the Anglican Communion with the concept of mission through partnership, not "conquest and conversion." In the notes of his final Izu committee meeting, held in Shimoda on 20 December 1956, just eight days before he was to leave Japan, Frank Coaldrake enunciates the central idea of this approach clearly. In his notes he asks, if there is no spontaneous expansion of local Christianity, what follows? His answer goes to the heart of the matter: "10 years no church?" he writes. Either the missionaries should achieve their own obsolescence by succeeding, or, if there is no spontaneous expansion, foreign support should be ended, and the missionaries withdrawn.

It is important to remember that, just two weeks after he discussed these ideas with the Izu Church committee in the town of Shimoda, he was chairing his first meetings at A.B.M. headquarters in Sydney. We can speculate on how this experience in Japan may have shaped his vision for the Australian Board of Missions. We do know it became a significant input at the Anglican World Congress in 1963, as discussed in chapter nine. In 1970, after a fact-finding trip back to Japan, he wrote:

No firm conclusions could be drawn but the impression is given that the Japanese church would be better left without missionaries now and helped to retain its fellowship in the wider church by being invited to offer its own people for missionary service abroad.[44]

---

43 *Newsletter No. 59*, April–May, 1954.
44 Australian Board of Missions (ed.), *Bread for Hungry Souls: Mission Workbook 1970*, Stanmore, N.S.W., Australian Board of Missions, 1970, p. 65.

For myself, I have grown up with my father and his vision reflected in the deep impression he had on so many of my oldest friends – the Miyazawa family, Kimiyo-san, Ikue-san – and in the extended family of love and faith which gathered in joy and sorrow in Tokyo on 22 July 2000 to celebrate the 50th anniversary of my mother's arrival in Japan and the 30th anniversary of Dad's death. Or in the young church worker I found myself sitting beside after mass at the new church building in Itō in 1998, and who, on being introduced, proudly produced from his wallet a photograph of Dad which he carries everywhere with him.

But there is another dimension entirely to this Australian mission of reconciliation to Japan. Reconciliation by definition involves two estranged parties. The Coaldrake mission was equally a mission to fight prejudice and hatred of Japan in Australia and, by extension, all those who shared the war and its bitter fruits. It was as much a mission of reconciliation of Japanese with Australians as it was a mission of Australians to Japan and the Japanese. This mission, the natural corollary of the first, was carried out in two ways.

First, there were the *Newsletters* themselves. These letters were, after all, addressed to Australians, as well as to an increasingly international audience, who had fought the Japanese in the war. The unhappy experiences during the war of many of the recipients were in danger of becoming a collective prejudice after hostilities ended. The prejudice was shaped by racist wartime propaganda and by a popular mood demanding "justice" after the war. It found psychological security behind the barriers of the restrictive immigration "White Australia Policy." The *Newsletters* seek to dispel fear and misunderstanding of Japan by information and analysis. The pages are full of practical experiences, real people, actual happenings, and commentary about Japan, for the readers to consider and discuss. The *Newsletters* humanised the Japanese in order to dispel the demons of the past. In a world before television and mass communication they were more important than we can ever understand today.

The second part of the mission to Australia was conducted during the two periods of furlough spent on deputation work back in Australia. This was a mission intended to inform the Australian church and the Australian public generally about Japan, the Japanese and their church. It challenged people to confront their fears and hatred. In 1950 Frank Coaldrake visited every Australian state, delivering his message of reconciliation in cathedrals and parish halls, in newspapers and radio broadcasts, the length and breadth of the land. In 1954–55, during the second furlough, Frank Coaldrake flew 7,000 miles and spoke more than 300 times.[45] Maida Coaldrake gave 65 speeches in one period of four weeks, despite family responsibilities (looking after Bill and the birth of Margaret). For this mission to Australia Frank Coaldrake was no longer a "missionary to Japan;" he was assuming an identity and a vocation defined by the new title he used for radio broadcasts – "The Rev. Frank Coaldrake of Japan."[46] As he identified

45 *Newsletter No. 60*, April, 1956.
46 See *chapter 5*.

himself increasingly with his role as a member of staff of the Anglican church of Japan, becoming less a "missionary" in the process, he became more a missionary of reconciliation from Japan to Australia.

Despite these efforts the mission against prejudice in Australia was less successful than the mission of reconciliation to Japan. On his journey by ship back to Japan in 1950 Frank Coaldrake wrote:

> The depressing thing, as I look back now, was to find that among the several thousand people I spoke to in meetings and services very few began by acknowledging the human-ness of the people of Japan. This, it seems to me, is not just the result of war with Japan. We don't find the same attitude to Germans and Italians. There must have been some special feature in our war-time ideas about the Japanese and we ought to be trying to recognise what it was, because it has warped the mind of even the Christian among us. I found that people who were quite impervious to logical argument and a reasoned statement succumbed in a few minutes to a play upon their emotions. This is, I think, because the usual Australian attitude to the Japanese is based on fear – they gave us a mighty big fright as their armies came down through Singapore on to the New Guinea mountains. Later, to this fear was added horror as we heard the stories of returning prisoners-of-war. And because fear and horror are both very strong emotions, often played upon by highly coloured press and radio reports, they overpower any attempt to size up the situation reasonably with calm thought.[47]

His declaration that the war "has warped the mind of even the Christian among us" must be one of the saddest and most telling statements in all the *Newsletters*. Even the carefully organised visit to Australia, arranged through A.B.M., for the Presiding Bishop of the Nippon Seikōkai to explain the needs and opportunities for partnership with the Japanese church failed to raise one single offer of substantial support. "Stay in Japan and save the Japanese" was the attitude.

Had attitudes changed by 1954–55 and the second Coaldrake furlough in Australia? "Everywhere there was plenty of interest, but even within the church there were also to be found prejudice and deep-seated misconceptions," Maida Coaldrake notes in *Newsletter No. 60* (April, 1956). And the last *Newsletter*[48] opens with the following statement, surely written out of love and hope, but nevertheless reflecting the deep scarring of the Australian collective psyche by the war:

Dear Friends,

Our days in Japan are numbered. We wish now that we had written many more *Newsletters* so that we might have told you much more about Japan and her people. We feel that we haven't succeeded yet in bringing you to

---

47 *Newsletter No. 31*, August, 1950.
48 *Newsletter No. 63*, November, 1956.

understand and appreciate these people who are most hated by Australians –
the Japanese. And how Australians fear them! And how ridiculous that is, how
futile.

Editorial Notes

The *Newsletters* are published in their entirety together with other relevant
documents, some of which are extracts from longer reports or articles. The
Newsletters and documents have been divided into nine chapters, corresponding to
the major phases of the journey from 1939 to 1956 in both a literal and a
metaphorical sense. A commentary has been added at the beginning of each
chapter to explain the context and circumstances of the particular period and to
highlight relevant issues. Explanatory notes have been kept to a minimum as it is
the editor's intention to allow the documents to speak for themselves. Comments
by the editor are added either as footnotes or as short explanations inserted in the
text in square parentheses [ ]. Parentheses used by the authors in the original
text are rendered as ( ). The editor has relied on two publications of the Nippon
Seikōkai in Japanese to check dates and other details of names, places and events.
One is the official history of the Diocese of South Tokyo (now Yokohama), and
the other is the official history of St. Mary's Church, Izu.[49] *The Australian
Dictionary of Biography* has been used as the reference for the brief notes identifying
Australians appearing in the pages of the documents who are not otherwise
introduced in the documents themselves.[50]

The professionally printed *Newsletters* distributed from May, 1949 (*No. 25*) were
not proof-read by the authors after they were typeset in Australia because of the
considerable delays this would have incurred. Maida Coaldrake has now
corrected minor mistakes in these "first edition" *Newsletters*. It should be stressed
that, apart from these minor corrections and attention to punctuation and
spelling, no alterations have been made to the *Newsletters* and the other
documents.

As noted earlier, the *Newsletters* were written by Frank Coaldrake until 1949.
Thereafter they were the primary responsibility of Maida Coaldrake with
sections added by Frank Coaldrake. To avoid possible confusion an editorial note
has been inserted at the beginning of each of these *Newsletters* establishing the
authorship of the different sections.

The style of the earlier *Newsletters* is less formal than the later printed ones, and
the abbreviations used have been retained as they help convey the "flavour" of

---

49 Nippon Seikōkai Yokohama Kyōku rekishi iinkai (ed.), *Mina ni yorite. Yokohama Kyōku hyakunijūgonen
no ayumi, (In His Name. A History of the 125 years of Yokohama Diocese)*, Tokyo, Seikōkai shuppan,
1998; Nippon Seikōkai Yokohama Kyōku Izu Mariya Kyōkai (ed.), *Izu Mariya Kyōkai no gojūnen
(The 50 years of St. Mary's Church, Izu)*, Itō, 1998.

50 John Ritchie *et al.*, *The Australian Dictionary of Biography*, Melbourne, Melbourne University Press,
1966–(2000).

the original documents. Most abbreviations are obvious. Of note is the use of "J'ese" for "Japanese," which avoids the pejorative "Jap" so common in war-time propaganda. The full name of organisations referred to by their acronyms has been added the first time they appear in the text. For convenience, a list has also been appended to this introduction. Japanese names are given in Western order throughout the book, with family name last, as this was the practice observed by the authors. The spelling of names has been standardised according to modern usage and made consistent throughout the documents. Hence "Bishop Mayekawa" is now referred to as "Bishop Maekawa." It is now customary for Japanese baptised as Christians to take an additional "Christian name" but these have been omitted except when specifically used in the documents, as it was not universal practice in the 1940s and 1950s.

It is normal practice in scholarly work to represent the long vowel sounds in Japanese by the addition of a macron, hence $\bar{o}$ and $\bar{u}$. Macrons were not used in the *Newsletters* or other documents in the Coaldrake Records because the immediate audience did not speak Japanese and the macrons may have caused confusion. In this book, for linguistic accuracy, the editor has included macrons in the *introduction* and commentaries, and in bibliographic citations. Otherwise they are omitted.

The Anglican Church of Japan is referred to in the Coaldrake documents as *Nippon Seiko Kwai*.[51] This romanization, with the *w* inserted before the *ai*, reflects the pronunciation prevailing in the later nineteenth century when the increasing number of foreign specialists were first systematically recording the language.[52] The official modern romanization *Nippon Seikōkai* has been adopted for the *introduction* and commentaries.[53]

Currencies used are Australian pounds (£), shillings and pence, and Japanese *yen*, which was divided into 100 *sen*. The equivalents of *yen* to Australian pounds are usually furnished by the authors at the prevailing conversion rate. There were considerable fluctuations because of the instability of the *yen* and high inflation. This is discussed further in the commentary to chapter four.

---

51 An alternate transliteration was *Nihon Seikōkwai* found, for example, in the official romanized prayer book of 1926 (Nihon Seikōkwai, *Kitōsho, Kyūshu kōsei 1915 nen*, Tokyo, Nihon Seikōkwai shuppansha, 1926).

52 Another common example is *Kwanto* for the name Kantō Plain on which the city of Tokyo is located.

53 *Nihon Seikōkai* is an alternate pronunciation of the same characters.

1 Ordinary Events, Extraordinary Outcomes: Queensland– Melbourne (1912–39)

The document presented in this chapter is of singular significance in understanding Frank Coaldrake's mission of reconciliation to Japan. It is a letter, written in 1943 in Melbourne, from Frank Coaldrake to Maida Williams. He was thirty-one years of age at the time. Some of the details not relevant to Japan have been omitted here because of its length, sixteen pages of handwriting in all.

The letter is dated 21 February 1943. It is introspective and personal, furnishing rare insights into Frank Coaldrake's thinking about himself, what he was doing and where he was going, or as he puts it "I have wanted to let you see something of what has brought me to this hour." We sense from this that momentous developments lay just ahead. Three days after writing the letter he was ordained priest at St. Paul's Cathedral, Melbourne. Precisely two months later he wrote the request to Dr. Evatt asking to go to Japan.

The letter takes the form of a commentary on a set of photographs describing his life and experiences to that time. Only one photograph survives, apparently sent later, and is included in this chapter. Despite this, the descriptions provide a clear understanding of the formation of his personality and ideas. We meet him first as a "grubby young scout" aged 12. The sequence of commentaries takes us from his upbringing in Brisbane and his growing commitment as an Anglican, through his training as a teacher to his work for the Brotherhood of St. Paul, the "Bush Brotherhood." He was Warden of the Boy's Hostel in the western Queensland town of Charleville for four years (1932–36). We are introduced to his activities as a student at the University of Queensland in 1936 and 1937; he had been a part-time student until then. We see him active in student politics, debating and sports. He was editor of the University of Queensland's student newspaper, *Semper Floreat*. In his descriptions he passes quickly over his involvement in the historic university conference in Adelaide in 1937 which saw the establishment of the National Union of Australian University Students (N.U.A.U.S). He notes visits to the Brisbane slums, speaking to the unemployed, discovering significantly that he "could 'do things' with such men." He spends more time describing his involvement in the Australian Student Christian Movement (A.S.C.M.). Through the A.S.C.M. we learn he developed a strong sense of the social relevance of Christianity, learning that "religion in practice" is "friendship." Here are the first indications of the direction his thinking was to take about reconciliation with Japan. We read about his growing desire to become a priest. Through the A.S.C.M. he meets the charismatic Chinese pastor Dr. K. Z. Koo and is profoundly influenced by Dr. Koo's views about the importance of spiritual values in a changing and challenging world. This is precisely the set of circumstances in which he is to find himself after he arrives in Japan. He is to talk about Dr. Koo's ideas in some of the early *Newsletters* from Japan. The scenes of a seaside camp for children from outback Queensland anticipate the summer camps in Japan for the children of the bombed-out Japanese cities. Finishing his degree at the University of Queensland, he is selected as one of the three national Travelling Secretaries of the A.S.C.M. in 1938. This leads him to Melbourne where he discovers the slums of Fitzroy as the letter ends.

We also see in this letter examples of his practical self-reliance and his skill with his hands. He taught woodworking at Charleville and displayed considerable ingenuity as a "bush plumber." Not surprisingly, we learn that he would have trained as an engineer if money had permitted – his family was too poor. His practical side would become "survival skills" in Japan, where priests were not expected to be practical.

All these experiences Frank Coaldrake characterises in the letter as "ordinary events but somehow working into one pattern," a pattern which was logical but in which we can now see the potential for extraordinary outcomes.

Letter from Frank Coaldrake to Maida Williams, 21 February 1943.

[Note: numbers refer to photograph numbers. Only one photograph survives.]

Maida,

Handle this bundle of photos carefully so that they do not get out of order and you will see something of the life that has been lived – an ordinary sort of life when viewed this way – that should be stressed, quite ordinary events but somehow working many things into one pattern...

4. Grubby young scout – keen as mustard – on right is F.W.C. [Frank William Coaldrake] age 12. Went to Adelaide to Scout Corroboree.

5. St. Margaret's Church, Sandgate – where F.W.C. became head server and read the lessons also. After "lapsing" from 13–17 became keen on "church" and started and ran a "Fellowship" for lads with similar gang for lasses.

6. The lads of the "Fellowship" a bit later together with Fr. Hassell – my parish priest. Should be a picture here of Rev. Cecil Edwards ... at this stage he was mainly responsible for my interest in church. He was then Head of Bush Brotherhood. Saw me on periodical visits to Brisbane.

12. House in garden suburb [in Brisbane] the Coaldrakes moved to when F.W.C. age 17 [1929]. Was teaching at Sandgate. Rode down on mo[tor] bike. Pictures later. (Fig. 4) Also rode to town four nights a week to night classes and university.

13. 14. 15. Scouting at that time. Had taken charge of backward troop of hooligans. Hard work and rough play made 'em one of top notch troops of Bris[bane]. They still make their mark...

Figure 4 Frank Coaldrake, aged 17 (1929).

16. Church at this stage very "high."[1] F.W.C. one of the gang. But mainly a spare time activity for F.W.C. the Teacher and Scout. Much work as stage manager and electrician for parish concerts & parish touring concert party. Priest an intellectual "giant," taught me Latin after church on Sunday nights, in return for which I supplied the Rectory – he was a celibate – with cake for supper – cake made Sunday afternoons by younger sister [Joyce] now age 12.

17. Twin brothers Bruce and Keith, and F.W.C. Starting for a week's camp at Christmas. Keith proud owner of broken down racehorse, eventually went bush as stockman and drover, finished up as horse breaker and left it suddenly at my request in middle of 1941 to come and help me in [the] Fitzroy Hostel [of the Brotherhood of St. Laurence]. Keith now studying at Keble House to go into priesthood [with the] view [of] joining [the] Bush Brotherhood. . .

22. 23. Scenes at seaside camp for children from far west [of outback Queensland]. F.W.C. first a helper, finally, first long vacation as resident university student, took charge of one.

25. A New Job. Having just started, at 19 years of age, as Warden in charge of Hostel for boys in Charleville, 500 miles west of Brisbane. Ran the place for the Bush Brotherhood which was centred in Charleville. We were the "boarding house" part of a "boarding school." Boys with us all time except hours of attendance at state school on week days. . .

1 High Church or Anglo-Catholic.

30. F.W.C. patent for pumping waste water away. Was always keen and adept at things mechanical. Hence the fate of this old mo'bike which I bought for £3 to do this job…

36. … So much for Charleville Days. Could write a book.

Went to the job from teaching. Must go back further. Always wanted to be an "engineer." Had skills that way; was due to start as apprentice in big "shop" after passing "Junior" Exam. (Had won scholarship of 2½ years to grammar school [Brisbane Boys' Grammar School] from State school.)

In sitting for Junior Exam, Dad, an opportunist, made me enter for Teachers' College Scholarship. Results showed F.W.C. entitled to go to Teachers' College. During the remaining week of Holiday decided to become a teacher – in order to study in spare time for the University Engineering course and save enough money to pay for the course. (Family too poor and too many of us. Things definitely too pinching at this stage.)

So I became a teacher in order to become an engineer. Did well at teaching – one of top four of five of 150 in year at college and came out of College to be a teacher because I'd been given a vision of what a teacher could do – linked up with Church work in Fellowship at Sandgate too – and scouts. Taught 2 years. Night class first year managed to matriculate. Second year passed English I on way to Arts Degree. Engineering now relegated to spare time activities. Little time for sport except irregular tennis and swimming. Much "swotting" and "handicrafts" – plaiting, fretwork, mechanics, drawing, painting, photography. No music!

At end of second year came by strange means to resign from Dept. to go out to Charleville to take charge of B'hd Hostel …

Main motive in going to Charleville was the appeal of the job and the adventure of it. Rationalisation was "want to get B.A. as soon as possible to get higher up quickly in teaching." So I went to Charleville in order to become a more successful teacher…

The work at Charleville – it was a grand "game" really – gripped me wholly. Plenty of scope to do all the things I was fond of doing. Physical work – laying out lawns, gardens, tennis courts, planting trees; mechanical work – repairs and alterations, putting in irrigation system, establishing and running "handicraft workshop" for the boys, – and myself. "Bossing" the boys – and the staff of 4. Bookkeeping too – which I didn't like. Church life which I took as a necessary but not unpalatable ingredient of the whole. Games – camping, hiking, fishing, shooting – trained cricket, football and tennis teams which eventually licked the State school teams – (we had 35 to select from, they had 250 boys). Study – pushing on for the degree.

But as an opportunity for study for B.A. it was a flop. I got 3 subjects in 4 years. Failed in 9 exams out of 12. Learned to keep on in spite of that. Got 2 of the 3 subjects in the fourth year. Gained much from reading which did not secure passes in exams.

Gradually had eyes opened to more reality in worship and religion generally. Then recognised need of men to carry on the good work of the Bush

Brotherhood. So at end of 4th year went down to university to finish degree then go to Theological College [with the] view [of] going bush to [the] Brotherhood as [a] priest.

Decided to throw myself into university life and get all possible "equipment" for job in B'hood. The B'hood members gave some financial help as "recompense" for 4 years on £65 p.a. I wanted to go to work on high pay for 2 years and "save" cost of course. Brothers agreed [it was] valuable [to] do [the] Degree before Theology course, and insisted [that I] not "waste" time earning cost of course.

As part of full university life decided should join S.C.M. [Student Christian Movement]. (Had been in it in Teachers' College. Was Teachers' College representative on Queensland State Council in 1930. Present Bishop of Adelaide was Chairman! Not least insight <u>then</u> into what S.C.M. was. [I had] Quite superficial view of religion) . . .

37. Scene at. . .S.C.M. conference which "took me somewhere" [details unknown]. The conference at which I learnt that "Religion in practice" is "Friendship."

38. Group at General Committee (National Committee of S.C.M.) 1936 August. C.F. Andrews[2] had just been in Queensland. I was secretary for his visit and he stayed in our College [St. John's, the University of Queensland]. He was responsible for what I count as my first real "conversion." Koo sharing the word [of] the "new direction" in 1937.

39. Trips south introduced me to "slums." Had been visiting Brisbane slum area during 1st year at university. Speaking to 100 men, unemployed, at Mission on Sunday evenings after they had been provided with tea. Learnt there that I could "do things" with such men.

On the trip shown in [photograph] no. 39 met the Legion of Christian Youth and got a real understanding of the social significance of Christianity. Also learnt something of technique of social action. First met "Burgie"[3]. . .

43. A broadcast debate under "Hecklers." Found feet in debating as a Fresher. Won leadership in Intervarsity team. First "fresher" to do so – though perhaps not rightly called a "fresher". . .

45. Feb. 1937. One of 2 Queensland delegates to University Conference in Adelaide. Gave birth to N.U.A.U.S.[4]. . .

48. Dr. Koo [a photograph of him] as secretary for his visit. FWC is discussing his programme with him when Press arrives and take photo. Owe much to Koo. Just after this was asked by S.C.M. chairman, Boyce Gibson, while I was at

---

2 Rev. Charles Freer Andrews (1871–1940). A Christian missionary who went to India as an Anglican priest and lecturer at St. Stephen's College in Delhi in 1904. He became a friend of Mahatma Gandhi, and may have been the source of Gandhi's influence on Frank Coaldrake.

3 Ernest Henry Burgmann (1885–1967), social activist and priest, Bishop of Goulburn from 1934. See: *Australian Dictionary of Biography*, vol. 13, pp. 300–301.

4 National Union of Australian University Students. Frank Coaldrake was to become third President. See *chapter 2*.

General Committee, if I would take job as Travelling Secretary. Flabbergasted. Consulted Head of College and Bush Brotherhood. They agreed. Arranged to start after Final Honours exam in February 1938.

49. Spent final long vacation swotting all the stuff for Final Honours I had neglected to do during final year because of being S.C.M. President, Paper Editor, Debates Leader, Union Rep., Sports Council for Rowing Club, Drama Dramatic Society play lead, College Mag Business Manager, member of College crew, and football, cricket and athletic teams and a few other things. Swotted 12 to 15 hours a day in a solid effort to get through and take up S.C.M. job. . .[5]

51. . . . It was during my first year as Travelling Secretary I discovered Fitzroy. Eventually lived there for 6 weeks in November–December 1938 – in what I discovered after two days was a Brothel. Stayed there 6 weeks!

Lived within ¼ mile of Brotherhood of St. Laurence Hostel and saw it without knowing what it was. Early next year found out about it. Then G.K.T. [Father Gerard Kennedy Tucker, Founder of the Brotherhood of St. Laurence] "blew" in to see M.H. [Margaret Holmes[6]] one day just to talk about things. Says now it was most unusual thing for him to do, first time he has ever talked to M.H. though had met her once before. Talked mainly about chance of talking to students about needs of Fitzroy. I undertook to arrange a midday address, and a few weeks later lived for a month at the Hostel while in Melbourne – July '39.

Eventually when in Brisbane in September '39 got permission of Bush Brotherhood and College and Archbishop [Halse] to turn away from Queensland Theological College [and] Bush Brotherhood in order to come to Melbourne and join the B.S.L. [Brotherhood of St. Laurence].

There is a weird mixture in the previous 15 pages. You could charge me with egotism and I'd have no answer. But I have wanted to let you see something of what has brought me to this hour. I have not set out all the influences, much less the pin-point ideas which have been the "decision moments" but perhaps you will know me better. . .

---

5 Frank Coaldrake was awarded a Rhodes Scholarship to the University of Oxford. Having turned 25 years of age in March of 1937, he was then deemed over the maximum age for acceptance.

6 The Executive Officer of the Australian Headquarters of the Australian Student Christian Movement. Everyone called her by her initials.

2 The Peacemaker: Melbourne (1939–46)

This chapter deals with Frank Coaldrake's period in Melbourne working with the Brotherhood of St. Laurence and, more significantly in terms of the later mission to Japan, with his activities as a vocal and vehement pacifist. The period in Melbourne coincides with the long and grim years of World War Two, first in Europe and then, from December 1941, with Japan.

The title of this chapter refers to the name of the pacifist journal Frank Coaldrake founded as his immediate response to the outbreak of war in Europe in September, 1939, but it also refers to his broader role during the war which was to lead him inexorably towards Japan.

War in Europe finds Frank Coaldrake as one of three Travelling Secretaries of the A.S.C.M. his focus was shifting from Queensland to Victoria and the city of Melbourne. He began working with the Brotherhood of St. Laurence in January, 1940, on the completion of his duties with A.S.C.M., combining his activities with the Brotherhood with his role as editor of *The Peacemaker*. At the same time he was completing his Master's thesis at the University of Queensland and serving as the third President of the National Union of Australian University Students (N.U.A.U.S.). In this capacity he voiced his strong views against the war, as we can see in the articles from the student newspapers of the University of Melbourne and the University of Sydney. The conference on "Pacific Affairs" he organised at the University of Sydney in January 1941 included a Japanese representative (unidentified) in a debate on the Pacific. War in the Pacific was less than a year away by then and Frank Coaldrake was including the Japanese in the debate as he turned his own mind increasingly to the issues of war and peace.

It should also be noted, as Shirley Abraham points out, that "he chaired the 1941 N.U.A.U.S. Council Meeting at which the Commonwealth Government scholarships for University students was formulated."[1]

Student politics was the initial forum for his pacifism but *The Peacemaker* was rapidly gaining momentum as the national forum for conscientious objectors, as the articles included in this chapter reveal. He was putting his experience gained

---

1 Shirley Abraham, "Frank William Coaldrake: 12-3-1912–22-7-1970," *The Peacemaker*, vol. 32, no. 8–9, August–September 1970, p. 5.

as the student newspaper editor at the University of Queensland to good use. The articles in *The Peacemaker* show his pacifism taking positive directions as he puts forward proposals about how to bridge the hostilities with understanding to create a viable framework for post-war Australia-Japan relations.

The journal also served as a vital conduit of information to pacifists around Australia, as travel and communication was now restricted because of war-time controls. We learn, for example, of the activities of the Japanese pacifist Toyohiko Kagawa in an article in March, 1941. This was the beginning of a crucial distinction Frank Coaldrake was to emphasize throughout his dealing with Japan in war and peace, that it was critical to see Japanese as individuals, some "bad" but others "good." Kagawa (1888–1960) had visited Australia in 1935 and was something of a hero to pacifists and those concerned with social justice, sometimes referred to as "the St. Francis of the Japanese slums."[2] He had founded the Anti-War League in Japan, and went on a personal mission to the United States in 1941 in a desperate last minute attempt to avert war. Frank Coaldrake was to meet this kindred spirit finally in 1947 in Odawara (see *Newsletter No. 8*, 1 December, 1947). There is also passing mention of Gandhi, whose non-violent resistance to authority inspired Frank Coaldrake's "war" against social injustice in the slums of Melbourne.

Meanwhile Frank Coaldrake was attracting the attention of the authorities. Apart from the attention of the censors, he was interrogated by the Commonwealth Investigation Bureau in March 1943, as his letter to Inspector Birch shows.

During all this he was working full-time for the Brotherhood of St. Laurence. He became a member in 1942. In the same year he received his M.A. from the University of Queensland,[3] completed the Licentiate in Theology of the Australian College of Theology and was made a Deacon in the Anglican Church. In February 1943 he was ordained a priest at St. Paul's Cathedral in Melbourne but it was as a pacifist as well as a priest that we find him turning his mind to grappling with the implications of the war with Japan. The documents included in this chapter include the letter he wrote shortly after his ordination to Dr. Evatt asking to go to Japan as soon as possible, even before hostilities ceased. He was finding that the Christian teachings of non-violence contradicted the Church's institutional support of the war. His pacifism had imperiled his candidacy for the priesthood. In the same meeting in 1941 with the Archbishop of Melbourne, F.W. Head, in which he was warned against "pooping off on public platforms" (see *introduction*), he was also cautioned against "associating with disloyal Communists" and told that:

> It is alright for you to hold these views if you really believe them, but you ought not to be passing them on to others. I am also anxious lest your reputation injure the reputation of Keble House. I think that if a man wanted to send his son

2 See further C. J. R. Price, *Toyohiko Kagawa: Christian Social Reformer*, Sydney, Assembly Hall Bookroom, 1935. This was published at the time of Dr. Kagawa's visit to Australia.

3 *A Theory of Evil (A Study in Ethics Relating to Moral Conduct). A Thesis submitted to the School of Mental and Moral Philosophy in the University of Queensland for the Degree of Master of Arts*, by Frank W. Coaldrake. B.A. 1942.

to a college now, he would look for some place like Ridley or Trinity or some other manly place.[4]

Archbishop Head advised him that if he were "seeking ordination at present... I would probably not be able to ordain you," to which he replied:

> Well, Your Grace, you have used the words "unmanly, disloyal and insincere" regarding myself, and I gather that my [pacifist] views are in your estimation almost worthless. I am, however, quite prepared to go on working for ordination, in the belief that by the time I come to ask for ordination you will have seen that there is more of truth and value in what I now say than you can now admit. I am quite happy about going on this basis.[5]

In the letter to his mother, in which he recounts these details, he adds that "the Archbishop was unfortunately somewhat annoyed and hurt by this remark."[6] Thirty years later it would have been interesting to see how an Archbishop Frank Coaldrake would have dealt with an ordinand with similar views about the Vietnam War.

"*The Peacemaker's* Policy," *The Peacemaker. An Australian Venture in Reconstruction*, vol. 1, no. 1, 29 September 1939, p. 2.

The Pacifists of Australia feel the need for unity. A common journal can be a great help. I have dared to assume that I am competent to offer this help. Please be honest in your criticism.

"Reconstruction," *The Peacemaker. An Australian Venture in Reconstruction*, vol. 1, no. 1, 29 September 1939, p. 3.

The Pacifist concentrates all his efforts for peace and justice on the task of reconstruction.

"A Personal Note," *The Peacemaker. An Australian Venture in Reconstruction*, vol. 2, no. 1, 1 January 1940, p. 2.

I must admit to some uncertainty about the immediate future of *The Peacemaker*. I am relinquishing my present position as Travelling Secretary to the Australian Student Christian Movement and am entering the Brotherhood of St. Laurence in Melbourne. Adjustment to new duties may leave little spare time for the first

---

4 Letter from Frank W. Coaldrake to his Mother, Mrs. E.R. Coaldrake, 15 July 1941, "Frank Coaldrake Papers," Baillieu Library and Archives, the University of Melbourne.
5 Letter, 15 July 1941.
6 Letter, 15 July 1941.

month or two, in which case the size of *The Peacemaker* will be reduced temporarily.

"Whither the University. Statement by N.U.A.U.S. President," *Farrago*, Tuesday 25 June 1940.

[the student newspaper of the University of Melbourne]

To the Students in the Universities of Australia:

As we gather ourselves together in readiness to answer the Prime Minister's ringing call to "all in" service we should reflect momentarily upon our duties to those who will come after us.

This is a war against Fascism – against chronic aggression on the national scale, and brutal, unscrupulousness on the individual scale.

This is not the time for spineless non-resistance. Brain and muscle and will are demanded. All, including the pacifists in our ranks, are girding their loins to resist in sundry ways the devastating forces of the new barbarism.

As we go down into the darker days of war let us cast our ideals into the future like a searchlight. There, confronting us, is the spectre of Fascism like a three-headed beast, probably inescapable. (Let me substitute for the word "Fascism" the phrase "rigid, centralized control." "Fascism" has too many meanings.)

In even one year from now Australia will inevitably be under a much greater degree of centralised control than at the moment of writing…Rigid centralised control may come. In an attempt to prevent its imposition by the foreign aggressor this war is being fought. To prevent its growth in our midst is the task of each one of us.

This is not a job that can be relegated to the future. Simultaneously with resistance of rigid control by foreigners, we must guard against the development of similar methods of control in our midst, and be ready to check the first signs of the Fascist attitude in our acquaintances…We must withstand brutality, recognise it as such, and refuse to condone or indulge it. We must discover and speak the truth in any situation. Lies and perversions of the truth used to implement policy, must be confronted with the whole truth. Above all, we can at this stage be on guard against "mob" activities. The mob, under Fascist direction, becomes the main instrument for striking fear into the hearts of people. The man in the uncontrolled mob becomes irrational, inhuman. Mob demonstrations now are preparing the psychological ground of Fascism.

Truth and Justice will survive in our community only if enough people want them, and only if these people want them keenly enough and will go after them with energy and intelligence.

It is obvious that University students owe a special responsibility to our people and to future generations at this point.

Frank W. Coaldrake

President, National Union of Australian University Students,

Melbourne, 20/6/40.

"N.U.A.U.S. Conference Begins," *Honi Soit,* **Official Journal of the Sydney University Students Representative Council. Vol. XIII, No. 1, Friday, 17 January 1941. Special N.U.A.U.S. and Camp Edition.**

DELEGATES DESCEND ON SYDNEY TODAY:
AUSTRALIAN UNIVERSITIES' VITAL WEEK

The Fourth Annual Conference of the National Union of Australian University Students [N.U.A.U.S.] begins to-day, and will conclude next Friday.

Twenty-six student delegates from other Australian universities, and a number from Sydney, will attend. Canberra University College is represented for the first time.

Public sessions in the Great Hall will include a symposium on "Pacific Affairs," by four prominent representatives of the United States, Japan, Netherlands, Indies and Australia; also addresses by Mr. Spender, Mr. Mair, and Dr. Evatt...

Unfortunately, many students will be unable to attend because of [military] camp, but it is hoped that those who can will attend and observe critically what goes on...

WHO'S WHO IN THE N.U.[A.U.S.]?

FRANK COALDRAKE, N.U.A.U.S. President, comes from Queensland, although his long and valuable association with the N.U.A.U.S. has made him truly cosmopolitan. Chairman of this year's Conference, a position he will fill ably. A sincere idealist. Takes a really practical interest in social problems. A nice bloke.

Letter from Frank Coaldrake to Inspector Birch, Commonwealth Investigation Branch, Melbourne, 3 March 1941.

> 3/3/41.
> Inspector Birch,
> Commonwealth Investigation Branch,
> MELBOURNE

Dear Sir,

It has occurred to me that one or two matters we discussed this afternoon might have been skimmed over so hurriedly that a wrong impression was left.

You asked me what conference I had attended while I was away on holiday. My answer, that I had attended the N.U.A.U.S. Conference, was correct, but I should perhaps have explained that I addressed a meeting of the Christian Pacifist Movement in Brisbane – a public meeting advertised in the daily press. The only other public utterances I made which were not directly associated with the meeting of the N.U.A.U.S. were a sermon preached at a Methodist Beach service at Currumbin, Qld., and a shortwave Broadcast to England for the

Department of Information. Privately I made contact with a great many friends whom I had not seen since I stopped travelling through those parts for the A.S.C.M. While the majority of these friends are not pacifists, a good many are and it was only natural that we spent some time talking about the matters which concern pacifists.

You asked me whether I am in the long run "For you or against you?" My answer, that I was, in the long run, against you, probably did not mean to you what I had in my mind. I am against war, and therefore am against anyone who is for a war – but that is only as far as war is concerned; more fully, I am with you in opposing the spreading movement of the new barbarism from Germany. I am with you in wanting to put an end to persecution and to give the small man and the weak the opportunity to live at peace, but I believe so fully in the futility and costliness of war as a method of solving the problems that cause it, that when you turn to war for the solution of your problems I am Not with you; and if I am not with you when you have chosen your mode of operation I guess I am against you. But that surely does not mean that I am going to give direct aid to those who are warring against you. I will not help anyone who is warring against anyone else to be more efficient in their warring; my efforts go to alleviate the suffering caused by war and to eradicate the causes of war. I might even say that I am quite "determined" about this, if that did not convey the impression of obstinacy.

The root of the whole matter is this – you did not get down to this today, but until you realise this you will probably be wondering what my "game" is – my main driving force is the religious conviction that the truth about God has been revealed to men in the person and life of Jesus Christ. My only unalterable intention is to share this knowledge far and wide. I believe that what the world, and men here and in Germany, need is the Word of God. My calling is to preach it and live it; there are countless others of the same calling. The word of God as spoken and revealed by Christ is quite definite with regard to the method of . . . [remainder of paragraph missing due to a slip of the carbon paper.]

But after all it was you who started to talk about my ideas so I must ask you to take this letter into full consideration. If you should be thinking that only a religious fanatic would write thus I would suggest that you refer to some eminent divines and laymen of the churches who both know my views and respect them; after all, these views are widely held in the churches. But I am sure that Rev. Prof. Calvert Barker, and Dr. R.C. Johnson, both of Queen's College in the University of Melbourne, Canon C.H. Murray of Christ Church South Yarra, Prof. K.H. Bailey of the University of Melbourne, Prof. F.A. Bland of the University of Sydney, Rev. Dr. W. Dumming Thom, Master of S. Andrew's College in the University of Sydney, Canon Garnsey, Warden of S. Paul's College in the University of Sydney, Rev. F.R. Arnott, Warden of S. John's College in the University of Brisbane, The Lord Bishop of Armidale, The Lord Bishop of Goulburn, and many such others whose names I will supply if necessary, would readily affirm that they know me to hold certain views which they do not themselves hold, that I hold these views strongly, and that in the course of close personal acquaintances they had found no reason to doubt my sanity or good faith.

I hope this has made the matter a bit clearer.

Yours sincerely,

　　Frank W. Coaldrake

P.S. You should come up and have a meal with us at this Hostel some evening and see just what does go on here. That is meant as an invitation.

"Kagawa of Japan," *The Peacemaker. An Australian Venture in Reconstruction*, vol. 3, no. 1, 15 March 1941, p. 8.

Late in August Kagawa and his associate, Dr. K. Ogawa, who studied at Oberlin, were seized by the military police while Kagawa was preaching at the church near his home. They were closely confined, and examined for ten days on a charge of having violated the military regulations. A dispatch from Tokyo early in September reported that Kagawa had been released, on condition that he retire to voluntary exile on an isolated island. But a letter received as this is going to press says that he has been unconditionally released and will carry on his activities with unabated vigour.

– Galen Fisher

"Speaking Personally," *The Peacemaker. An Australian Venture in Reconstruction*, vol. 3, no. 4, December, 1941, p. 2.

When I started this venture over two years ago, I little expected it to find the welcome which it did. In the face of such a strong demand for the paper, it has been exasperating to see manuscript and proofs lie waiting attention for weeks on end – and also to see a publishing fund steadily replenished by donations over and above subscriptions. But the immediate needs of wantful persons, victims of the wider war not waged with weapons, have made an irresistible and exhausting claim on my time and energy. In the contest between their visible and urgent needs, and you're so often expressed hunger of thought and will, they have generally prevailed.

But circumstances, too numerous to mention, have brought me out of the struggle – to give in order to spend some months preparing for a long-hoped for ordination to the ministry of the Church. What will follow that, God alone knows.

"Our Attitude to the War Now," *The Peacemaker. An Australian Venture in Reconstruction*, vol. 4, no. 1, January, 1942, p. 2.

We will not knowingly assist our friends to kill Germans, Japanese (or any other people); nor will we knowingly assist Germans, Japanese (or any other people) to kill our friends.

We are trying to follow Christ's way:

An indefatigable attempt to overcome evil with good, whatever the consequence to ourselves.

The Peacemaker. An Australian Venture in Reconstruction, vol. 4, no. 5, 1 May 1942, p. 1.

... Gandhi believes the Japanese are human.

Gandhi differs from the average warring patriot in that respect that he has faith in the readiness of human nature to respond to human treatment ... the majority of Australians, may think of the Japanese as a tigerish and brutal, worthy only of our hatred, and deserving only to be smashed. Gandhi and ourselves think them human, and worthy of goodwill.

"Editorial – Reaching into the Future. Our Approach to Japan," *The Peacemaker. An Australian Venture in Reconstruction*, vol. 4, no. 6, 1 June 1942, p. 2.

War hostilities will some day reach a stage which will permit efforts to be made in the reconciliation of Japanese and Australians. If this reconciliation is effective there will be no more wars between the two peoples. Projects for reconciliation are therefore of first-rate importance.

Such projects will include proposals for co-operation through Government circles, and co-operation of person with person among the masses of the peoples.

While recognising the importance of co-operation between governments we may legitimately turn our attention to the direct relation of people with people. On this will depend the success of any government projects; and out of it may come the call for more far-reaching Government action.

The reconciliation of the people of Australia with the people of Japan bristles with difficulties. The disagreements leading up to this war; the oppositions being hardened in these months of conflict; the bitterness and sense of being wronged which will be the fruit of "Hate campaigns" in both countries; the radically different ways of life and standards of living in the two countries; the different political habits; the different religious practices and beliefs; the existence of race prejudice in both countries; these are a few of the stumbling blocks in the road to a just reconciliation. They must not be thought insuperable.

They are deeply rooted in the lives of the individual persons of each nation. They will be barriers unless an attempt is made by some persons of each country to live amongst the persons of the other country in order to get to grips with each others' problems. The education of public opinion on the basis of such first-hand experience will be the only way to prevent differences being magnified into barriers.

The "Embassies of Reconciliation," fostered by the International Fellowship of Reconciliation, aim to live in foreign countries in order to interpret to their own peoples the attitudes of the foreign peoples. These Embassies are a growing organisation. Members are learning foreign languages and studying the history and customs of the countries they hope to enter. They aim to be ready to go in at the earliest possible moment.

Embassies of Reconciliation first developed in Europe, but there are already many people in Australia with the same idea. Australians are learning Japanese and German, and are striving to equip themselves for a long stay in Japan whenever the war reaches a stage which will permit their reaching and entering the country.

On very similar lines is a suggestion thrown out in Melbourne recently by Rev. G.K. Tucker, The Superior of the Brotherhood of St. Laurence. "A Christian Army of Reconciliation will be the most valuable single factor in cementing just and peaceful relations between Japan and Australia," he said. "I think it probable that the Church could prepare now to send a new type of mission to Japan immediately hostilities cease. A mission of reconciliation could try to make amends for our past failures. We have sent Japan scrap-iron and wool, and other products of our civilisation. But we have been too much engrossed in business matters to try to take the Christian gospel of love to her people. The church will fail in her duty if she does not take a lead in establishing bonds of peace and love between these two peoples."

More will be heard of these Embassies of Reconciliation and Missions of Reconciliation in the near future.

"Reports Of Japanese Atrocities," *The Peacemaker. An Australian Venture in Reconstruction*, vol. 4, no. 6, 1 June 1942, p. 4.

Fearful atrocities are perpetrated in every war. It could not be otherwise when it becomes a national function, a recognised duty, and an act of patriotism to kill and destroy to the fullest possible extent. Vengeance is let loose and cultivated; propaganda being excelled to goad the nationalities into hatred of one another. But there are many humane acts on all sides, and some have been credited to the Japanese. Escaped prisoners have told of good treatment. The Japanese dropped leaflets apologising for the bombing of a Red Cross unit in one instance, and Mr. J.A. Parker, of the Malayan Civil Service, who has arrived in Australia, was reported in the press on March 6 as saying that, from Singapore to Batavia, the Japanese did not attack the small coastal ship in which he was travelling because it carried an ambulance. "I am fairly convinced," he said, "that this was the reason they did not attack, and they should be given credit for that."

"Japan and Australia," *The Peacemaker. An Australian Venture in Reconstruction*, vol. 5, no. 3, 15 March 1943, p. 4.

It has been stated by an official of a Government Department that the government is vague on the question of Australia's post-war settlement with

Japan. It is following the line that the settlement will be dictated and implemented by Britain and U.S.A., and that all Australian need do will be to follow that lead. The government has failed entirely to realise that Australia herself has a distinct, individual and essential part to play in settlement with our nearest enemy country. She has her own relations to build up with Japan, distinct from what Britain or America do.

Little is being done by the Government to prepare for this settlement, and – what is preliminary to that – even to try to gain any knowledge about Japan in an effort to understand her. This could be done easily. There are within Australia a number of people who know the country thoroughly, missionaries, business people and journalists, who, having lived in Japan for a period, have an intimate knowledge of that country and her people. The Government should invite these people to form a consultative committee with it, drawing on their experience, to discuss and form plans for a just and durable peace between Japan and Australia.

Letter from Frank Coaldrake to Dr. H.V. Evatt, Minister for External Affairs, 21 April 1943.[7]

> 261 Glenlyon Road,
> North Fitzroy, N.7.
> 21st April, 1943.

Dear Sir,

Ever since it seemed likely that Japan would make war on Australia I have personally felt a deep concern about Australia's failure to try to understand and help the Japanese people. The events of the war so far have served only to deepen that concern.

I have been looking around for possible avenues along which a person of my age, training and convictions might work towards establishing closer links between our people and the Japanese people.

My convictions are deeply rooted in religious beliefs which have been clear and strong enough to lead me into the ministry of the Church and I am now a priest of the church stationed in Melbourne as Assistant to the Dean of Melbourne at St. Paul's Cathedral. I am, however, anxious to explore the possibilities of going to Japan at the earliest possible moment. I imagine that I should consider going only as a missionary but if there were a possibility of going in some other capacity such as that of a liaison officer with relief work or as one of a relief unit, I should be bound to give serious consideration to it. My belief is that the power of the gospel of Christ will, as nothing else can, make these enemies our friends.

---

7 Source: National Archives of Australia; Department of Foreign Affairs and Trade; A989, Correspondence files 1942–1945; item 1943/700/48.

I have already discussed the matter with the Australian Board of Missions which is the missionary body of the Church of England in Australia most likely to have any missionary interest in Japan in the future. The conditions of war make it probable that all such approaches to Japan will not be possible until some time after hostilities cease. I cannot rest content with that so I write now to ask whether you know of any way in which an early approach to Japan is likely to be possible. It has occurred to me that with the further exchange of diplomatic officers there may arise the need for someone from Australia to go to Japan for liaison work of the "Red Cross" type.

I would be glad of your advice as to the likelihood of any such avenue opening up for me.

Yours sincerely,
Rev. F.W. Coaldrake

The Minister for External Affairs,
Parliament House,
CANBERRA. A.C.T.

Letter from W.R. Hodgson, the Secretary, Department for External Affairs, 5 May 1943.[8]

PS.MS
43/700/48–2
5th May, 1943.

Dear Sir,

In the absence of the Minister, I acknowledge the receipt of your letter of 21st April concerning your desire to go to Japan. As you realise there is no prospect of missionary activities from Australia being resumed in Japan until some time after the end of the war. Even if there were any way of reaching Japan at present it is certain that a missionary, or any other national of a country at war with Japan would be immediately interned and probably imprisoned.

As for your suggestion that someone might be sent to Japan in connection with a further exchange of nationals, the position is that negotiations for another exchange have not yet been completed. In any case the Red Cross work to which you refer is undertaken by neutral nationals already resident in the Far East, and all arrangements connected with exchanges and welfare of Allied nationals in Japan and Japanese-occupied territory, are carried out by the Swiss Legation. It would not be possible for a British national such as yourself to proceed to enemy-occupied territory in connection with such work.

8 Source: National Archives of Australia; Department of Foreign Affairs and Trade; A989, Correspondence files 1942–1945; item 1943/700/48.

However, a note has been made of your desire to proceed to Japan and should consideration be given at a later juncture to the dispatch of some form of relief unit to Japan, your desire to be included will be kept in mind.

Yours faithfully,

    W.R. Hodgson

    Secretary.

The Rev. F. W. Coaldrake

261 Glenlyon Road,

North Fitzroy. N.7. VIC.

[in handwriting] (Mr. Moodie to see then file. P.S. 7/5)

"Negatives," *The Peacemaker. An Australian Venture in Reconstruction*, vol. 6, no. 2, 15 February 1944, p. 2.

Pacifists are often Negative. Pacifism is a positive attitude.

Pacifists often accept the restrictions which war brings, fold their arms, and await for peace. Pacifism is the attitude which stands out in the midst of war, and continues to act in the ways of Peace and for Peace.

Negative pacifists decline into pacifism. Positive Pacifists think, speak, write, act, pay and, perhaps, pray, for the things which belong to peace.

The negative pacifist is a passenger carried by the whole community. A positive Pacifist works his passage – he is worth his place in the community just as salt is worth its place in the stew.

The Pacifist who apologises for his views is probably being negative. If he were working his passage he would not need to apologise to anyone.

Passenger Pacifists should look for a hearse to ride in. Positive Pacifists are slowly but surely making the coffin of war.

"Our Front Line in the Pacific," *The Peacemaker. An Australian Venture in Reconstruction*, vol. 7, no. 3, 1 March 1945, p. 2.

(Script for a talk broadcast from stations 7ZL and 7NT, Hobart, on Wednesday, January 17th, by Rev. Frank W. Coaldrake.)

(After reading this, the pacifist should ask: "Are pacifists to be among those who will go for us?")

Where would you put our front line in the Pacific? Would you run it from Singapore through the Philippines to New Guinea and the Solomons? Or would you push it further north – from China through Japan to the Hawaiis? Of course, you'd have your mind chiefly on Japan when you fixed the line, and you'd be looking for the place which would most ensure our future safety against attack from Japan.

There are some people put their faith in robombs and rocket bombs. They say: "Never mind about a distant front line. We can build launching platforms in

Australia and keep a barrage of terror weapons aimed at Tokyo ready to fire off at a moment's notice." Others say: "With a strong Air Force ready, we only need a few island bases in a great curve a couple of hundred miles from Japan." Still others say: "Wipe out the entire Japanese nation and we won't need to worry about any front line."

That last seems a very simple way out of our difficulties – be butchers for a year and live happily ever after.

It is unrealistic to stand off from a neighbouring people and try to make friends from behind a barricade. It is unrealistic to stand over a conquered enemy and try to beat him into the shape of a friend. There are only two realistic things to do to a conquered enemy – one is dispose of him by killing him, the other is to give him the chance to become a good neighbour. A middle course, acting so as to keep him as a lifelong enemy is stupidity. Such a policy of unrelenting vindictiveness would ensure, among other things, that we would ourselves continue to be hampered by what the Atlantic Charter calls "the crushing burden of armaments." We must try to avoid that. The "good neighbour" policy is the realistic one.

"Cut this Out and Read it Again in 1960," *The Peacemaker. An Australian Venture in Reconstruction*, **vol. 7, no. 9, October, 1945, p. 3.**

WHAT SHALL BE DONE WITH THE DEFEATED?

REVELATIONS of Japanese prison camp atrocities have distracted attention, just as the Nazi death camp disclosures did towards the end of the European war, from the real problem: What to do with the defeated?

First, let it be clear that, whatever may be urged in explanation, nothing can excuse thrashing, starving and torturing the helpless, and the callous indifferences to or sadistic pleasure in their sufferings; deeds so documented as to be beyond doubt, so widespread and so uniform in pattern as to be obviously part of a policy dictated, or at least, condoned, by high authorities.

Don't let us lay the flattering unction to our souls that brutality is peculiar to the Japanese or the Germans. In all races there are those who will enjoy, and those who can be induced to take part in, such orgies – if they be permitted. Whether they are permitted or reprehended is a matter of growth and education.

MEN, NOT RACES

TO make a man the gaoler of others is always to bring out his least manly instincts. Race has little to do with it. Among the brutes who held Europe in terror were Frenchmen, Dutch, Belgians, Lithuanians, and Croats, when the Nazis turned them loose on their fellow countryman; many of the worst in Japanese prison camps were the Korean guards whose country the Allies are pledged to liberate. Men have been worked to death in Russian labour camps, cruelty and callousness are common in South American dictatorships.

If viciousness is to be punished, individuals, not races, will have to be sought. Races have to be taught. If brutality is to be exorcised, the climate which breeds it will have to be changed.

"Australia's Relations with Japan," *The Peacemaker. An Australian Venture in Reconstruction*, vol. 7, no. 11, December, 1945, p. 3.

(Relevance of Economic Imperialism; White Australia policy.)

The goal of present-day Australian-Japanese relations must be the eventual practice of friendship between the people of these two nations. At present, the people of each country are highly conscious of their nationality, and are exhausted by the events of a war which has exalted nationality above humanity. The Australian people suffer the subtle elated exhaustion of victors, the Japanese the more obvious exhaustion of the vanquished. Exhaustion is, however, not extinction. Both peoples will arise and build, have in fact already begun to do so.

If the rebuilding is towards a reinvigorated nationality by either or both peoples, the opportunity created by the end-of-war exhaustion will be lost. But there is a dilemma because the end-of-war exhaustion lessens in peoples the vigour and initiative essential to building a new non-national order. Fear is also a bulwark behind which people play safe with nationalism rather than venture out boldly into experiments in new people's friendships.

The history of Australian-Japanese relations on the nation level overshadows the relations on the human level.

(a) On the human level we have known good will within narrow limits. This has been especially evident in the relief ship sent from Australia after the catastrophic earthquake in 1924; in the goodwill mission led by Earl Page in 1928; in the exchange of sporting groups, culture groups, and churches. The latest of these visits, Public Relations Units from Japan, are generally discounted as deliberate espionage, but earlier visits were mutually friendly...

Pearl Harbor stands for Australian people now as a synonym for treachery, whether in fact it was so or not. Recent reports have shown that it was equally a matter of treasonable negligence on the part of U.S.A. In the interests of truth and the future relations between Australia and the Japanese people, we should insist on a balanced judgment about the Japanese action at Pearl Harbour, undoubtedly aggressive as it was.

The brutality of Japanese soldiers, especially in dealing with prisoners of war, must not be minimised – nor must it be taken as a pattern of the habits of the Japanese civilian population. If, however, the most extreme and exaggerated generalisation were true, if, that is, every individual Japanese were a sub-human brute, Australian people would still be required to adopt a positive, creative policy towards them if military victory is to bear fruits in peaceful living.

The Christian churches have an inalienable responsibility to try and catch up the lost centuries and take the Gospel of God to those in Japan who will hear it, venturing in Christian fellowship with the indigenous Japanese Christian Church which has already this century borne fruit in thousands of Japanese, six in every thousand of the population in 1938; turning from the national religious cult to the gentler living in Christian faith. The Christian Churches will go preaching the Good News of The Prince of Peace. Their witness is corrupted and weakened by the fact that they were involved in supporting in general their nation's war-time policy. So long as Christian missionaries from the Churches based in the United Nations bear any semblance to chaplains of occupation forces, or economic aggressors, they will hardly be in a position to win Japanese people into the true family of God, in which there is neither American nor British, Japanese nor Australian. The pacifist Christian has an urgent responsibility to win in his own branch of the Church in Australia recognition of the rightness of the pacifist emphasis on the way of the Cross.

The pacifist citizen in Australia has an urgent responsibility to win from his local community, and especially from governing representatives of those communities, recognition of the rightness of the pacifist emphasis on the one-ness of all human nature and the function of national policy, both home and foreign, as a means to ordering peacefully the relations of our two peoples who are one in nature.

The pacifist worker and consumer in Australia has an urgent responsibility to win from his own trades union, or federation of employers, or neighbourhood purchasing community, and especially from those who hold directive offices in such groups, recognition of the rightness of the pacifist emphasis on the right of all men everywhere to share equally the essential goods of this earth, whether the total amount available at any time be sufficient or insufficient to meet the needs of everyone if shared equally; also for his emphasis on the function of the essential goods of this earth as a means to the subsistence and security of all people, not as a means to the profit and luxury of a few at a cost of starvation and hardship to the majority.

The pacifist man and woman in Australia has an urgent responsibility to win from all Australians everywhere recognition of the rightness of the pacifist emphasis on neighbourly friendliness as the basis of national policy, and of the propriety of arranging immediately for interchange of visits between the peoples of the two countries under the auspices of schools, churches, trade unions, sporting bodies, and such organisations, together with the wide reading of the literature of the two countries.

One of the greatest obstacles to the development of sound relations between the peoples of Japan and Australia is the race prejudice which is deeply ingrained in the mind of most Australians. This prejudice is emotional rather than intellectual, and any efforts to remove it must be planned accordingly.

Australian plans for future relations with Japan must also take into account the wide disparity between the population density of the two countries. Seven million Australians are responsible for the future use and development of a much underpopulated continent in the neighbourhood of teeming millions of people who lack the basic essentials of life, and have no chance of developing the supply of those essentials within their own overcrowded boundaries. Australians cannot expect to be met with open trust so long as they jealously keep advantages which have been gained in part by industry and initiative, but in part by force and a fraud.

F.W.C. 7/11/45.

"*Peacemaker* Changes," *The Peacemaker. An Australian Venture in Reconstruction*, vol. 8, no. 2, February, 1946, p. 4.

Owing to the present editor's training and departure for missionary service in Japan, he has had to make new arrangements for the editing, publishing, printing and distribution of the journal.

Letter from the City of Brunswick, Melbourne, to Frank Coaldrake, 1 March 1946.

City of Brunswick [Melbourne]
1st March 1946

Rev. Sir,

On behalf of my Council I wish to inform you that your leaving this Municipality of the City of Brunswick has not passed without its knowledge. It learns that you have decided to journey to Japan there to render the Christian Mission Service to the unfortunately misguided people of the stricken land, and in this Holy Task may God give you his Wisdom and Strength to perform the duties of your high and sacred office as our Lord and Saviour has decreed to His Faithful. In this wish my Council is mindful of your capacity to do this because of your having already done it during your sojourn with the people of this City, especially with those folk who were parishioners of St. Cuthbert's Church at East Brunswick, and to many hundreds of others who help you to carry the Cross.

To change the outlook of worship of their present Ruler and Ancestry to the worship of the Spiritual God will not be easily performed, yet my Council is confident that your efforts will go far to achieve this purpose. No doubt it will take perhaps many generations before this can be finally accomplished and established for all time, and it wishes to congratulate you on your courage to sacrifice the fellowship of the many friends you leave behind you in Australia, particularly Brunswick, to spread the doctrine of our Christian belief.

Wishing you well and every comfort and success,

Yours in truth,

W.G. Macgregor Dawson
Town Clerk.

Rev. Father Coaldrake,
St. Cuthbert's Priory,
116 Glenlyon Rd. E.,
Brunswick.

3   Preparations in Sydney (1946–47)

Early in 1946 Frank Coaldrake moved to Sydney, the staging point for the mission to Japan. It was here that he made the preparations for the mission, and the letters to and from A.B.M. in this chapter show how he went about the task. His common sense and practical competence, shown in his early years in Charleville, come to the fore again. In one letter he has to remind A.B.M., accustomed to dealing with its long established missions in New Guinea and the Pacific, that he will need an establishment grant for the new mission in Japan.

At the same time as he was dealing with A.B.M., he negotiated with the Australian Government, the Allied Occupation authorities in Japan, and the Japanese Anglican Church, for permission to enter Japan, and to determine his status after arrival. Everyone, Japanese civilian or foreign soldier and official, was under a rationing system for food and other essentials. A foreign civilian fitted into neither category, so organizing rations was a bureaucratic nightmare. And this was only the beginning of the "paper war." Japan was occupied by a massive military force as well as by a veritable army of Allied government officials. It may have been called an "Allied" Occupation but it was entirely dominated by the United States under the leadership of the Supreme Commander for the Allied Powers (S.C.A.P.), General Douglas MacArthur. For a civilian such as Frank Coaldrake from a minor ally to attempt something unprecedented was a classic prescription for bureaucratic and political obstacles. The American missionaries were in a different position altogether, well established before the war and, from mid-1946, in the vanguard of MacArthur's pacification policy.

It is easy now to overlook the difficulties posed by the process of getting permission to enter Japan; there was no precedent or established "pipeline" for such a Christian mission from Australia. At the most basic level, it was "not permitted to write directly to Japanese citizens," as Frank Coaldrake explains in *The Peacemaker* article of February, 1947.[1]

Bishop Cranswick, at Frank Coaldrake's instigation, ultimately had to write directly to General MacArthur seeking his personal assistance. General

---

1   Frank Coaldrake, "Personal History of F.W.C., A Move in Sight," *The Peacemaker. An Australian Venture in Reconstruction*, vol. 9, no. 2, February 1947, p. 3.

MacArthur's reply is included in this chapter. His letter reveals the gloriously confused lines of responsibility in the Occupation bureaucracy, especially concerning a non-official civilian trying to enter Japan.[2]

At the end of MacArthur's letter we learn that Bishop Cranswick had also asked General MacArthur to deliver a letter to the Bishop of South Tokyo. MacArthur informs Bishop Cranswick that his letter "was delivered by an officer of my staff on 31 January 1947." This also appears unremarkable until we remember that no contact was allowed with Japanese civilians and so it became necessary for A.B.M. to go through G.H.Q. and the United States military.[3] This letter would have been the official letter from the Chairman of A.B.M. to Bishop Todomu Sugai offering Frank Coaldrake for missionary service. We can only begin to imagine the consternation which the arrival of an officer from G.H.Q. at the South Tokyo diocesan office, surrounded by the ashes of the bombed out city of Yokohama, would have caused. And the concern about how to contact Bishop Cranswick in reply.

The problem for Frank Coaldrake was not confined to the "export" arrangements from Australia. Japan presented its own difficulties on the "import" side. He had trouble finding anyone or any organisation in Japan willing to accept him for missionary service. The eventual decision by the Diocese of South Tokyo of the Nippon Seikōkai to accept him as an Assistant Priest in the parish of Odawara, spared bombing during the war, was a cautious solution of what to do with him. They were on their knees physically, psychologically, financially and spiritually, but they would not give him a full parish or allow him to speak or vote in synod, as it was to turn out.

The Sydney stopover was to stretch to eighteen months. He organised his time wisely, although his impatience as time passed becomes clear. He arranged to serve as Assistant Priest at Christ Church St. Laurence, the Anglican parish in the heart of Sydney. This paid a modest salary and gave him accommodation. He lived in a room off the parish hall at the church. At the same time he set about intensive studies of Japanese history, anthropology and language at the University of Sydney. He took the three years of the Japanese language course in a single year, a language not noted for its ease of learning with its complex writing system. He did the same with anthropology. At the University of Sydney he was taught by A.L. Sadler, a world-class historian of Japanese history and culture. His tutor was Joyce Ackroyd, who later became the Professor of Japanese at the University of Queensland. He had Japanese conversation classes with a Japanese woman who was married to an Australian and resident in Sydney.

---

2 See further: Alan Rix (ed.), *Intermittent Diplomat, The Japan and Batavia Diaries of W. Macmahon Ball*, Carlton, Victoria, Melbourne University Press, 1988, pp. 157–158 and endnote 89, on S.C.A.P./ B.C.O.F. areas of control.

3 Macmahon Ball notes in his diary (8 January 1947) just two weeks earlier, that "the Americans are the only people who operate military government teams and ... the military government teams are the only people who have direct contact with the Japanese people ..." See: Alan Rix (ed.), *Intermittent Diplomat*, p. 157.

He suspended his pacifist activities as a concession to his new commitments, although he continued to contribute to *The Peacemaker*, as we see in the excerpts from articles included in this chapter. These show him presenting information, arguing issues and attacking stereotypes about Japan with characteristic vigour.

Close to his departure he had all his top teeth extracted in "one go" at the Dental Hospital and a denture hastily made. Like the problem of rations, there was no provision at the military installations in Japan for medical or dental coverage for a foreign civilian. The authorities insisted that his top teeth had to be taken out if he were to go to Japan.

Extract from the Minutes of the Australian Board of Missions, 27 and 28 February 1946.

The Rev. F.W. Coaldrake. Resolved (1) That a letter of greeting be sent to the presiding Bishop of the Nippon Seiko Kwai, Bishop Naide, on behalf of the Board, assuring him of our prayers and of our eagerness to be of service to the Nippon Seiko Kwai, and asking him to let us know in what forms our service would be acceptable, mentioning that the Board has already received the offer of a young priest for service in Japan.

Resolved (2) That with the hope that the Australian Church may be asked to give assistance to the Nippon Seiko Kwai, the Board accepts with gratitude the offer of service from the Rev. Frank W. Coaldrake to train as a probationary candidate for Japan, with the possibility that next year a Bishop of the Nippon Seiko Kwai may be able to welcome him to his diocese as a fellow worker.

"One Way and Only One," by General Douglas MacArthur, *The Peacemaker. An Australian Venture in Reconstruction*, vol. 8, no. 8, August, 1946, p. 2.

(The following remarkable excerpts are taken verbatim from the address of General Douglas MacArthur before the opening session of the Allied Control Council in Tokyo, Japan, on April 4th, 1946. The emphasis and sub-headings are those of the editors.)

While all the provisions of this proposed new (Japanese) Constitution are of importance, and lead individually and collectively to the desired end, as expressed at Potsdam, I desire especially to mention that provision dealing with the renunciation of war. Such renunciation, while in some respects a logical sequence to the destruction of Japan's war-making potential, goes yet further in the surrender of the sovereign right to resort to arms in the international sphere.

Japan thereby proclaims her faith in a society of nations, governed by just, tolerant and effective rules of universal, social and political morality, and entrusts its national sovereignty thereto.

The cynic may view such action as demonstrating but a childlike faith in a visionary ideal, but the realist will see in it far deeper significance.

He will understand that, in the evolution of society, it became necessary for man to surrender certain rights theretofore inherent in himself in order that states might be created vested with sovereign power over the individuals who collectively formed them – that foremost of these inherent rights thus surrendered to the body politic was man's right to resort to force in the settlement of disputes with his neighbour.

OUR EXAMPLE

"In 1853, when Japan broke with the policy of seclusion and looked out upon the world, she was amazed to see floating on the opposite shores of China a number of unfamiliar flags – the Tricolour, the Union Jack and, nearest to her, the Double-Headed Eagle. If under these flags had marched an army of artists and poets, we would have emulated them and combated them in the field of art and literature. But when under the flags glistened swords and cannon, Japan had to arm herself for sheer self-defence. Militarism was thus the first suggestion given to the East in its contrast with the West. Neither the naval nor the military system of modern Japan is her own invention or innovation. They are both imitations copied from European models!"

– (From "Japanese Traits and Foreign Influences," by Inazo Nitobe, Professor in the Imperial University, Tokyo.)

Letter from Bishop George Cranswick, Chairman of the Australian Board of Missions, to Frank Coaldrake, 10 October 1946.

> The Rev. Frank Coaldrake,
> Christ Church Rectory,
> 507 Pitt Street,
> SYDNEY.
> 10/10/1946

Dear Frank,

In reply to your letter of October 7th:

1. I have passed on the account for Japanese conversation expenses and it will be paid in due course.

2. I think you should retain your membership of the Australian Clergy Provident Fund. In reckoning your expenses in Japan the cost of the premium must be included. I hope you will ask the Archbishop of Melbourne to allow your name to stand on his clergy list as "A Priest on Missionary Service." I am very anxious that this should be done with all missionaries so that a very real and useful link and relationship will be constituted between the missionary worker and the Home Church. I am sure there is great value in this.

3. I have written to Messrs. Hordern Bros to ask for their help in the matter of the suit. I will let you know the result.

In the matter of missionary equipment – when you know exactly what you have to buy please give me an estimate of the cost and I will talk to you about an equipment grant. I am afraid that I have no information here about equipment for Japan. I gather that you may have access to useful sources of information about this.

I am,

Yours every sincerely,

G.H. Cranswick

Bishop

"Looking ahead to Japan: Japanese Culture Borrowed (Sniff! Sniff!) So What," *The Peacemaker. An Australian Venture in Reconstruction*, vol. 8, no. 11, November, 1946, p. 2.

"They've borrowed everything! Admittedly they have been civilised for centuries – longer than the British, even. But they've never done anything original. All their civilisation has been built up by clever borrowing from other peoples."

In words such as those people are often heard dismissing the Japanese people as inferior to our own highly civilised selves, and even as vaguely immoral for stalking the boards of history in borrowed finery of which they are not worthy.

But, if to borrow elements of culture is to "fake" civilisation, then we are "fakes" no less than the Japanese, or if to depend on borrowed materials and usages shows incompetence and lack of originality, then we too come under those charges...

SO WHAT!

No one is either better or worse because they "borrow" elements of culture. It's the normal process. Just don't let emotion lead you, or anyone else, into accusing the Japanese of inferiority on the basis of a fact which is true of Australians as well as of Japanese, and a normal element in the life of any progressive people.

F.W.C.

Letter from Frank Coaldrake to Bishop George Cranswick, Chairman of the Australian Board of Missions, 28 December 1946.

28th December, 1946

The Right Reverend G.H. Cranswick,

Chairman,

Australian Board of Missions,

"Cherrywood"

Kallista, Vic.

Dear Bishop,

Thank you very much for the loan of the Nippon Seiko Kwai Report. It is most helpful and I anticipate valuable discussions on it with Badger. It has given me useful information on the matter of costs of living as a priest of the Nippon Seiko Kwai. I have been thinking over questions of finance and ways and means but had not been able to get very far. However the report says that the minimum required to keep a priest is Yen 500 per month (A£125 per an.). Capt. Crane has heard that U.S. Civilian officers in Japan are getting Yen 2000 per month, have access to Canteen supplies when purchasing and receive both U.S. and Japanese ration supplies (so little need to use black market), and can barely manage to live on that amount. The average Japanese working in professional service is getting about Yen 1000 per month.

On the basis of all these figures I have worked out some notes on finance which I submit for your consideration and comment. The notes are attached. In any case I expect Badger will have valuable ideas on the subject.

I am enclosing a statement of Fees due to Mrs. Crane for coaching to date. She has been most helpful.

With best wishes,

Yours sincerely,

P.S. This letter I promised you when I visited you while you were sick!

NOTES ON FINANCE

For Rev. Frank W. Coaldrake in Japan.

Stipend, allowances, maintenance, etc., might be calculated on one of the following three lines:

I. Payment at a flat rate equivalent to what F.W.C. could expect as a parish priest in a parish in Australia, say in Melbourne, this payment to cover everything.
II. Payment at a flat rate equivalent to the minimum figure stated in the Report to the Archbishop of Canterbury, i.e. Yen 500 per month, A£125 per annum.
III. Payment to meet expenses under certain headings, some sections to be variable, some fixed, and the level to be relative to the work to be done.

Considerations which influence the financial arrangements:

1. The help to be given to Seiko Kwai by A.B.M. is in effect an Australian priest equipped and maintained for the work of a priest in the Diocese of South Tokyo.
2. The Australian priest should be not unduly advantaged over his fellow priests in the Diocese.
3. The priest's efficiency should not be impaired by financial stringency.
4. That indefinable something called "prestige" or "dignity," both of the Nippon Seiko Kwai in Japan, and of the A.B.M. in the Seiko Kwai and in Japan.

Figures would therefore be something like the following:–

I. A£350 per annum.
II. Yen 500 per month. £A 125 per annum.

III. Estimates under headings (A£ per annum):

Food	100
Clothing	20
Books, stationery etc.	30
Medical, savings etc	100
Family commitment	50
Rent	a.
Travel on job	b.
Church equipment	c.
Church maintenance	d.
Total	**£300 plus a. b. c. d.**

a. Might be nil, or up to £100 per annum.
b. Might be nil or up to £50 per annum.
c. Books, pictures, textiles, furnishings and fittings, is unpredictable.
d. Altogether unpredictable.

I should have to consult you from time to time as to the items a. b. c. d. It might be best to take with me an advance against these items, (say £100), to cover them until I find out what the actual situation is. No "capital" expenditure should be included under these headings. See below.

The above "fixed" items totalling £300 could be covered by quarterly payments, half to Japan, half into my bank in Australia.

"Capital" expenditure should always be a matter for separate consultation if and when proposed. Items such as new buildings, car, or any new equipment to a total cost of more than £50 in any year, would seem to belong under this heading.

I should know before I leave what is the A.B.M.'s attitude to any such possible expenditure in Japan.

Travelling expenses are a separate item. It seems likely I shall need:

Fare by boat to Kure	£90.
Fare Kure to Odawara	x.
Travelling allowance	y.
Freight goods Melb-Sydney	£3.
1 Cabin Trunk S/H	£10.
4 packing cases s/h	£2.
1 Chest drawers	£10.
1 Filing Cabinet	£7.
Total	**£122 plus x. y.**

Equipment to be taken from here is unpredictable at present except for:

Reference Books	£10
Medical Supplies	£10
Stationery	£10
Tools	£5
Total	£35

Letter from Bishop George Cranswick, Chairman of the Australian Board of Missions, to Frank Coaldrake, 5 March 1947.

> 5th March, 1947.
> The Rev. Frank Coaldrake,
> Christ Church Rectory,
> Pitt Street,
> <u>SYDNEY.</u>

My dear Frank,

The following is the resolution passed last month by the Australian Board of Missions with reference to yourself as its first post-war missionary to the Japanese Church:

"It is the Board's custom to make a grant to the Diocese in which its missionaries work, and to leave matters of detail in the hands of diocesan authorities. This relationship should be established with the Diocese of South Tokyo as soon as possible. But that it would obviously be unjust to Mr. Coaldrake to do this at least until we have received information through him of the annual amount required under various headings.

Estimates under headings:

	A£ per annum
Food	£100
Clothing	£20
Books, stationery, etc.	£30
Medical, insurance, savings, etc.	£100
Family commitment	£50
Rent	£?
Travelling in connection with the work	£?
Church equipment	£?
Church maintenance	£?
<u>Ascertainable total</u>	A£300

Rent may be nil or it may go up to A£100 per annum.

Travelling may be nil or A£250 per annum.

Church equipment is quite unpredictable, as also is Church maintenance.

"Probably it would be best to reckon an advance against those four items of say A£100 until we have been in consultation with Mr. Coaldrake after his arrival in Japan. If this were done it would make the total estimated headings A£400.

That "capital" expenditure will always be a matter for separate consultation if and when proposed, and that the Board will never be committed to such expenditure until it has given its consent in writing.

For immediate travelling expenses from Sydney to Odawara in the Diocese of South Tokyo, together with certain necessary equipment, approximately £190 would seem to be adequate.

Taking into account all these considerations it would look as if the Board's initial outlay for the first year, not taking into reckoning either an Australian priest's remuneration or the minimum figure quoted to the Archbishop of Canterbury, might be as follows:

Estimates under headings	A£400
Travelling expenses and equipment	A£190
Total	**A£590**

Mr. Coaldrake should be instructed, that on arrival in Japan, after giving to the Board full information in detail, he should bring into effect the principle of paying a block grant to the Diocese as soon as possible."

You will recognise in the Board's decisions the fact that we gratefully took into consideration your own proposals to me. Please regard the last paragraph as an instruction to yourself. There will be no hurry about it, and much will depend upon the information in detail which you are able to send me.

Last week I had a personal letter from General MacArthur with an assurance that everything possible was being done to speed up your entry. I hope any day to hear that everything is clear.

Dominus tecum,

I am,

Yours as always,

G.H. Cranswick

Bishop

Letter from General Douglas MacArthur to the Chairman of the Australian Board of Missions, 7 February 1947.[4]

General Headquarters,
Supreme Commander for the Allied Powers,
Office of the Supreme Commander.

APO 500
7 February 1947

[handwritten notation] Received 25.2.47

Dear Bishop Cranswick:

Your letter of 4 December 1946 concerning the proposed missionary work of the Reverend Frank Coaldrake in Japan has just been received. It is gratifying to learn of the assistance which all religious groups are offering to the Japanese, and I am very hopeful indeed of the future of the Christian faith in Japan.

---

4 *Australian Board of Missions, 1873–1978*, ML MSS 4503, ADD-ON 1822, ML 196/7, in the State Library of New South Wales (Mitchell Library).

In connection with the travel of Reverend Coaldrake, I shall be happy to facilitate his movement in every way I can. The appropriate procedure is for an application to be submitted by the Officer Commanding the British Commonwealth Sub-Area in Tokyo. This has already been done, and by memorandum of 17 December 1946, British Commonwealth Sub-Area authorities were informed of certain assurances of adequate food, clothing, and shelter which should be given prior to the entrance of missionaries in order to insure their well-being in Japan. Reply to this memorandum has not yet been received; however, you may be assured that as soon as the proper application is made, it will receive prompt and most sympathetic consideration.

Your letter to the Bishop of South Tokyo[5] was delivered by an officer of my staff on 31 January 1947.

With cordial regards,
    Faithfully,
        Douglas MacArthur

The Right Reverend G.W. Cranswick,
Australian Board of Missions,
14 Spring Street,
Sydney, N.S.W.

Letter from Frank Coaldrake to Bishop George Cranswick, Chairman of the Australian Board of Missions, 13 April 1947.

Christ Church Clergy House,
507 Pitt St.,
Sydney.
13/4/47

The Right Reverend,
The Chairman,
Australian Board of Missions,
14 Spring St.,
Sydney.

Dear Bishop,

There are one or two matters incidental to finance about which it seems best I should write to you. I find, also, that I have not acknowledged, in writing, receiving your letter of March 5th advising me of the resolution passed by the Board with reference to myself going to Japan. I do so now with thanks. I note that the Board is entrusting me with quite wide responsibilities and I can only hope and pray that I will be able to come up to expectations.

---

5 The Right Reverend Todomu Sugai.

The particular matter I am concerned about just now is equipment. In its resolution the Board said "For immediate travelling expenses, from Sydney to Odawara, together with certain necessary equipment, approximately £190 would seem to be adequate." This, I think, is based on the estimates for Travelling Expenses and Equipment included in the Notes on Finance I submitted to you at the end of December. At that time it was the best basis I could find, and until recently I have regarded it as likely to be approximately right. However, I have had the opportunity to consult the Rev. Edwin Badger, the Rev. R.R. Clark, the Rev. Alan Laing and yourself, and have talked over some things with the Rev. M.A. Warren. I have also spent a lot of time scouting round shops and warehouses in Sydney pricing and buying goods. In this latter undertaking I have had the help of practical tradesmen and housewives. As a result of this I have slowly, and reluctantly, come to the conclusion that I ought to ask the Board to sanction more expenditure on Travelling Expenses and Equipment than I was able to foresee in December. At that time I listed under "Travelling Expenses" £32 to cover freighting goods from Melbourne to Sydney and purchasing trunks, cases, and chests which could be used to carry goods over and be converted into furniture on arrival. I have drawn and spent this money. But there is one additional item I did not foresee but which I now think necessary. It is insurance on my baggage. I have collected in this room goods to a value of over £500, waiting transport. There is a real risk of loss through fire, theft or damage, while they are here and while in transit. A Prudential Insurance policy to cover the lot for three months as Traveller's Baggage has cost £20/11/0. I have taken out this policy, yesterday, because so much of the property is not mine but Mission property. I hope it will be possible to receive the amount of that premium from the Board.

In my December notes I said "Equipment to be taken from here is unpredictable at present except for Reference Books £10, Medical Supplies £10, Stationery £10, Tools £5." I understand that these items are covered by the Board's Resolution. From my conversation with you in March I realise that the usual arrangement for a person going to the mission field is to make a grant of £25 to cover what is necessary. I have tried to the point of desperation to see how to keep within such a limit. Because Christ Church has paid me a generous stipend I have been able to buy a great many items of all kinds, and many good people have given specific items, some of them quite valuable. I had hoped to be able to leave Australia with a reasonable training and equipment without calling on the funds which the A.B.M. has for the work in Japan. But my own pocket and the list of willing friends is not quite equal to the task. In fact I've already gone into debt because I believe it is better to take these things and not have to call on the Japanese for them during the period of waiting for their delivery by the slow and risky procedure of sending back a request for them. I imagine that after the first brief period of "being welcomed" I will be settled into a room or rooms from which to work. Owing to the straits in which the Church is now I could easily be a burden on the local church in spite of even a fruitful ministry from the first. It would be less than the best I hope for if the Church there has to burden itself with my helping them. So I have tried to list what things I should have in order to be able to carry on under my own steam, (always allowing that offers of help can then be accepted as a free gift of fellowship not brought out under the compulsion of my own needs). This will involve taking some household effects and church effects as well as purely personal effects. I should also have enough tools to do any practically possible alterations or additions of equipment.

In the matter of tools I consulted Mr. Warren about how best to spend the £5 suggested. He helped me to make a list of essential tools and materials but it was impossible to buy more than a small fraction of them for £5 so he authorised me to spend £50 to the best advantage on items included in the list. I have now done this by going round secondhand shops and warehouses. A tradesman is satisfied that I have secured very good value considering the price of tools in the shops now.

In the matter of stationery I have not so far made any purchases, though I have ordered a quantity of duplicating paper. (One of the things I have got myself is a good duplicator because my advice is that it will be extremely useful to the Church). I think I should certainly spend the balance of £10 on typing paper, envelopes and a few sundries.

In the matter of Medical supplies I have spent nothing but have received some £2 worth of things from friends. The Sydney Woman's Auxiliary will help with this and I think it will be possible to keep expenditure here to about £5 by taking my own personal First Aid outfit which is fairly large and well stocked.

In the matter of Reference Books I have spent £7. I am advised that one way I will be able to help the Church will be to coach the priests. To do this I will need standard reference books and texts. Most of these I have already in my personal library, some I have recently got from friends, but a few remaining ones (such as Bicknell on the 39 articles) I will have to add before I go. I think the original estimate of £10 will be enough.

In my December Notes I made no provision for Church equipment, Household equipment or Personal needs. It is under those headings that I must now ask you if you could sanction further expenditure.

In the matter of Church Equipment I have been well supplied by good friends. As a result of my letter to "The Church Standard" I will have about a dozen Communion sets to take and give to the Bishop for use in the Diocese at his discretion. I have also an almost complete outfit of what would be required to equip one Church for services if I should be responsible for re-opening a Church for my own use. The remaining items will partly be supplied by friends but I estimate I would need at least £10 to complete the supply.

In the matter of Household Equipment, I have already spent nearly £20. This is one of the items on which I have run into debt. To complete my supply I shall have to spend another £10 making a total of £30 in all. (Kitchen, dining and bedroom goods have become very dear).

In the matter of Personal Needs, I have already spent the sum of £8 (Overcoat, Dressing gown and 4 shirts). If I go as I am I will have to order my first replacements within three months. To purchase clothes to cover my needs for another two years will cost at least another £20, even at the values for which the £8 has been spent.

There is one further detail which is probably covered by the offer of the Sydney Women's Auxiliary. Although I am to draw food from B.C.O.F. it seems wise to take a small supply of emergency stocks. I have made a list of specific items for emergency, and diet correction, totalling about 1¼ hundredweight and costing about £10. Miss King Kemp thinks the Auxiliary will help with this. But the balance over and above what they provide would have to bought. I do not propose to ask the Board for it yet.

Summing up: I would like my December estimates of expenses for Travelling and Equipment extended, and the provisions under the Board's Resolution extended, under the following headings:

Travelling: (Baggage Insurance)	£20.11.0
Equipment: Church Equipment	£10.0.0
Household Equipment	£30.0.0
Personal Needs	£30.0.0
Total	**£90.11.0**

I can only repeat that I am reluctant to make this claim. But I cannot convince myself that the things are not necessary and I hope that you will either agree that they are or satisfy me that there is no need for me to go into debt to get them.

With best wishes,
Yours sincerely,
Frank W. Coaldrake

[Additional letter appended]

Dear Bishop,

Attached is a rather lengthy letter on the subject of additional equipment. I have set the matter out very fully because I realise that a Board does not always reach conclusions as quickly and easily as its Chairman and you may need to place the matter before them in more detail than I would need to place it before you.

You told me that a missionary proceeding to a station usually receives £25 to buy a given list of items. I have tried to see how to approach my equipment in that light. But there seems to be a difference. Normally a missionary goes to an established station and needs to take very little beyond his own personal needs. The Mission station equipment of all kinds is provided from separate funds. The A.B.M. has so far spent no money on the provision of equipment for mission work in Japan. If I go without a basic supply of that equipment it means we are depending on the N.S.K. [Nippon Seikōkai] to provide it. Under the present straitened circumstances of N.S.K. I personally am anxious to avoid that situation. For that reason I am willing to contract debts against my stipend for the next year or so in order to take equipment if the A.B.M. Funds for Japan cannot justifiably be drawn on for this purpose. I am hopeful that they can, especially in view of the fact that any equipment which proves on the spot to be unnecessary could be sold and the money applied to essential purposes. If I buy carefully here my equipment will be worth more there than the money in a paybook. The risk that the funds would be wasted by buying this equipment seems to be practically nil.

I wait with patience hard to muster for Directorate of Shipping to advise me about a ship. The day will come no doubt.

I hope you are keeping well and enjoying yourself in the course of your work. My good friend Fr. Cecil Edwards of the Retreat House, Cheltenham, writes that he has met you recently.

With very best wishes,

Yours sincerely,

Frank W. Coaldrake

"Personal History of F.W.C. A Move in Sight," *The Peacemaker. An Australian Venture in Reconstruction,* vol. 9, no. 2, February, 1947, p. 3.

It is now a year since I took my first step towards Japan. I have spent 1946 in Sydney. My efforts have been on two main lines: First, I have tried to make arrangements for work in Japan among Japanese people. Second, I have studied the language, history and culture of Japan as a preparation for work in Japan.

The value of my studies I cannot attempt to assess objectively. In an attempt to make the most of the splendid opportunity afforded by the schools of Oriental Studies and Anthropology in the University of Sydney, I have restrained my very urgent desire to play a part in the Pacifist Movement, especially as regards its Sydney groups. While studying all the week, I have given at the weekends to the exercise of my ministry as a priest in the Church of England, at Christ Church St. Laurence, Sydney. This duty, and privilege, has added to the necessity of refraining from active interest in the Australian Pacifist Movement.

In the other matter – arrangements for work in Japan – good progress has been made. Through the Australian Board of Missions (Church of England), contact has been made with the Nippon Seiko Kwai (the Anglican Church in Japan). Delays were inevitable because it is not permitted to write directly to Japanese citizens. In due time arrangements were concluded for me to take up work in Odawara as an assistant to the parish priest there. Odawara is a city on the coast, about 50 miles south of Tokyo. It is about the size of Ballarat. The parish priest is a Japanese Christian. My duties are as yet only vaguely defined. I will live with Japanese and work among them. The food problem is not yet solved. Government authorities seem to think I should take a ton of food with me. (Very embarrassing! Where shall I store it? Under my bed, perhaps. But "bed" is a mat on the floor!)

Since Japan is under military occupation, no one is permitted to travel to its shores, let alone land and live there, without a permit from the Occupation

Authorities. Application for that permit was useless until arrangements for a place of work in Japan had been completed. Since those arrangements were completed, the application has been made. At the time of writing I am in receipt of advice from Tokyo that the permit will be granted when the Supreme Commander in Japan has been assured of three things: (a) that food and clothing will be supplied, (b) that I have a working knowledge of the Japanese language, and (c) that I have been there before or will be working with people who have been there before. Between the Australian Board of Missions and myself, those assurances can be given.

It remains now to receive the permit and fall into line for one of the not very frequent boats that sail from Sydney to Kure [the port near the city of Hiroshima]. Passport, vaccinations and the accumulation of "personal effects" will all have to be dealt with once the boat passage has been allocated by the Directorate of Shipping. (Fig. 5)

Probably the above gives two outstanding impressions: F.W.C. is a frightfully orthodox priest in the Church of England and, it's all very complicated trying to get to Japan. Both impressions would be true – provided they are not taken as the whole picture. Here are a few of the many other things which go to make up the whole:–

Chopsticks are good fun.

I find the language difficult – but not impossible.

I'll have to give up kissing – in Japan people don't kiss.

What is generally thought of as the "ingratiating politeness" of the Japanese, is not really that. It is something deeper and fine which I can sense already, but not yet define.

I outraged a Japanese doctor, who knew no English, by saying his highly-treasured antique inkstone was "Yasui" (cheap) instead of "Yoi" (good).

The [new] Editor of "The Peacemaker" is a tyrant! He always wants his copy on time. (Not that he gets it!)

I've read John Herschey's story of the atom bomb on Hiroshima ("New Yorker," August, 1946). Have you?

The Japanese combat the extreme cold of their winter by cultivating hardiness. In Australia I depend on clothes, food and fuel.

I like Australia and the Australians, right down to the last dammed one of them. I hope we're all going to "enter into Japan."

Frank W. Coaldrake

9/1/47

Figure 5 Frank Coaldrake's departure from Sydney for Occupied Japan on the *S.S. Merkur* of the China Navigation Company, 22 May 1947.

4   First Australian Civilian to Occupied Japan (1947–49)

Frank Coaldrake arrived in Japan on June 11, 1947. He was thirty-five years of age. The only surviving photograph of his first day in Japan shows a grimly and clerically garbed Frank Coaldrake flanked by Australian military personnel, sitting below a sculpture of the seated Buddha. (Fig. 6) This is an appropriate metaphor for Frank Coaldrake's first period of two and a half years in Japan, a priest caught between the Allied Occupation forces on the one hand and the apparently immovable strength of traditional Japanese beliefs and institutions on the other.

The first document in this chapter, a letter written on the ship *Merkur* just three days before his arrival in Japan, provides information about the final preparations for the mission in Japan and an assessment of his studies in Sydney. He arrived in Japan at Kure, the former naval port near Hiroshima, still filled with the sunken remnants of the Imperial Japanese Navy. The Coaldrake family records include a receipt for the fare for the journey from Sydney to Kure, which was £A90 pounds, and a bank certificate which shows that he carried with him $224 in U.S. currency.

As noted in the *introduction*, he arrived without official papers. He was followed around Tokyo by members of the American military police for his first four weeks in Japan. It was only an accidental meeting with a former parishioner from St. Cuthbert's Church in East Brunswick, Melbourne, Lew Ehrich, who was at that time working as part of the Australian government staff at the Tokyo War Crimes Tribunals, which succeeded in establishing his identity and possibly saving him from military detention.

It had been a long journey, four years from the time he had first decided to go to Japan in 1943. He found a country under total military control. Australians already in residence were either officials or staff of the Australian government, or serving with the military forces in the British Commonwealth Occupation Force (B.C.O.F), itself under the control of S.C.A.P.

Today we would describe Frank Coaldrake's status in Japan as the first representative of an Australian N.G.O. or "non-government organization." He was the first Australian civilian to enter Occupied Japan. Many of the pre-war Christian missionaries, particularly from the United States, were already arriving back in Japan. General MacArthur was encouraging more to come, as we saw in his letter to the Chairman of A.B.M. He called for "1,000 missionaries" to "place the Bible at

Figure 6 Frank Coaldrake on the day of his arrival in Japan, at Kure on 11 June 1947. From *Newsletter No. 1* we gather that the officer on the right may be Army Chaplain Laing and that the soldier on the left is Frank Davis, both of whom he knew in Australia. The photograph was possibly taken by Chaplain Mappin.

the disposal of the Japanese people."[1] His declared plan was for missionaries to come to Japan to "pacify" the Japanese using Christianity as their tool. This policy paralleled S.C.A.P.'s sweeping constitutional, political, social, educational and economic reforms which were designed to rehabilitate Japan into a nation acceptable to the international community, and at the same time to punish it for its past transgressions. The new S.C.A.P.-imposed Constitution, replacing the Emperor-centred 1889 Constitution, came into force in May, 1947, the month before Frank Coaldrake's arrival. Article Nine renounced war as an instrument of

---

1 Hallam C. Shorrock and Joseph J. Spae (eds.), *The Japan Christian Yearbook, 1968*, Tokyo, The Christian Literature Society of Japan (Kyo Bun Kwan), p. 78.

national policy.[2] The Crown Prince's new tutor, personally selected by MacArthur, was an American Quaker, by definition a pacifist.

The Occupation policies being pursued by MacArthur, however, should not be mistaken for pacifism. It was pacification. There was a blanket "non-fraternisation" policy in place between Occupation personnel and the Japanese people. We have already seen the difficulties this created for A.B.M. in communicating with the Bishop of South Tokyo. It was in this context of American pacification and non-fraternisation, and of an Australian public and government baying for "justice" for the war, that Frank Coaldrake was to launch his own "Australian venture in reconstruction." At its core was Christian fraternal love, with the objective of reconciliation between the Australian and Japanese people. How could you be "fraternal" without "fraternizing"? To succeed it was critical for Frank Coaldrake to distinguish himself from both the Occupation policies and the ubiquitous military presence. He was neither American nor military but was sometimes mistaken for both. How he accomplished his aim, while living with the obvious harsh realities of the Occupation, becomes apparent in the *Newsletters*, which begin in this chapter.

The protracted process Frank Coaldrake went through to get to Japan, and the decision to work as an assistant priest in the Diocese of South Tokyo, have been dealt with in the preceding chapter. This chapter covers his epic first years in Japan. It was "epic" in the classical sense of an odyssey. The geographic and physical journey was lengthy and gruelling. The mental and spiritual journey was to be equally long and arduous. We shall see how Frank Coaldrake, in his response to the practical as well as the spiritual challenges, drew upon his experiences in Queensland in the 1930s and Melbourne in the 1940s.

Geographically, the action in the *Newsletters* in this chapter is centred on the old castletown of Odawara, southwest of Tokyo, but includes extensive travel throughout eastern and central Japan around and beyond the boundaries of the Diocese of South Tokyo. The diocese was approximately the same size as the Diocese of Melbourne in Australia. Frank Coaldrake drew a detailed map in *Newsletter No. 14* of 1 June 1948 in which he ingeniously superimposed the Diocese of South Tokyo over the Diocese of Melbourne, and showed the location and state of each parish as a result of the war. He points out on the map that it had approximately the same population as all of Australia in 1948, or some 7.7 million people. It is now somewhat confusing visually, especially for readers not familiar with the state of Victoria. For our purposes it has been redrawn showing the geography of the Japanese diocese and omitting the comparisons drawn in the original map. (Fig. 7)

The diocese was large by any standards. It extended from the port city of Yokohama, the diocesan centre, southwards down the coast to Odawara, and westwards to Hamamatsu, more than halfway to Kyoto. To the east it did a peculiar

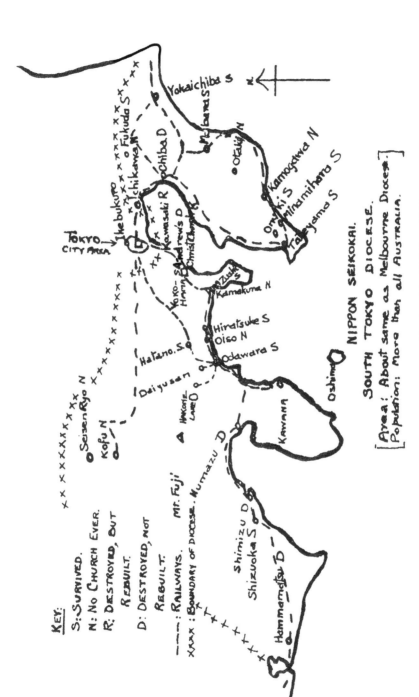

Figure 7 Map of the Diocese of South Tokyo as drawn by Frank Coaldrake for *Newsletter No. 14*, 1 June 1948

leap over the sprawl of Tokyo into Chiba Prefecture. Virtually every city in the diocese had been bombed numerous times in 1945. One of the few exceptions was the city of Odawara itself. The port city of Numazu to the west had been reduced to ashes in a single night with 90-95% loss of life and property, comparable with the destruction at Hiroshima or Nagasaki.

In the *Newsletters* we read of constant travel by Frank Coaldrake on crowded trains. This does not appear at first to be particularly remarkable. Later in the *Newsletters*, however, we learn that "none of the trains had glass in the windows as a result of the war."[3] Moreover, anyone familiar with Japan's railway system today will be appalled at the distances he travelled in a single day, even by the standards of Japan's heroic modern commuters in sophisticated trains. Traversing it in a decrepit former army jeep was to prove even more of a trial.

There was a constant struggle to obtain food. Most was rationed, except for vegetables that could be grown in the reconstituted local patches, or purchased at a prohibitively high price on the black market. There was not enough in any case – his official monthly ration, arbitrarily agreed upon by the Occupation bureaucracy, was enough to feed him "for only about 3 or 4 days."[4] In 1947 life expectancy was only 50.06 years for males and 53.96 years for women.[5] In June 1947, the month Frank Coaldrake arrived in Japan, average wage earner household expenditure on food was ¥2,405, or approximately half of total household expenditure of ¥5,027. The average wage was ¥3,893, including overtime and bonuses.[6] Not only were people hungry; they were falling deeper into debt each month, by a national average of ¥375 per wage earner. Whatever the plight of those in employment, they were infinitely better off than the army of unemployed and homeless for whom there was no government welfare. "The diet is governed by only one consideration," Frank Coaldrake remarks, "what is available to fill the emptiness."[7]

The desperate food shortages caused by the war were made worse by the sudden increase in the population with the forced repatriation of the military forces and civilians from Japan's former Asian empire. As a result, the population of the home islands jumped by nearly five million people, from 73 million to 78 million, in just over eighteen months from April 1946 to October 1947.[8] They came home to a starving populace, destroyed cities and an occupying army. This crisis is the subject of Frank Coaldrake's article in *The Peacemaker* included in this chapter entitled "What Defeat has Done to Japan's Warriors."

In terms of the "inner journey," Frank Coaldrake sensed almost immediately the struggle affecting all the Japanese whom he met in trains, on street corners, and in

3   *Newsletter No. 62*, August, 1956.
4   *Newsletter No. 7*, 1 November 1947.
5   Japan Statistical Association (ed.), *Historical Statistics of Japan*, vol. 1, Tokyo, Japan Statistical Association, 1987, p. 270.
6   The Foreign Affairs Association of Japan (ed.), *The Japan Year Book, 1946–48*, Tokyo, The Foreign Affairs Association of Japan, 1948, pp. 435–36.
7   *Newsletter No. 7*, 1 November 1947.
8   *The Japan Year Book, 1946–48*, p. 23.

shops, churches, and schools. It was to be an epic struggle between the desire for material well-being and the search for new social, political and spiritual values. He could see a choice of national direction becoming clear. The material and the materialistic were taking over from the spiritual even while there was an eagerness in the young to explore the mind as well as to satisfy the body. With poverty and starvation all pervasive it is little surprise that the Japanese took the direction they did. Frank Coaldrake's analysis in the early *Newsletters* signals the unwavering direction Japan was to take during the second half of the twentieth century, that of booming consumerism and a culture of consumption that was to continue far beyond the satisfaction of immediate physical needs.

The perversity of Occupation bureaucracy stands in stark contrast to the kindness of some Australian military personnel at an individual level. In terms of the church, the Japanese authorities seem to have been uncertain about the best way to use the services of staff coming from overseas. Frank Coaldrake was the only non-Japanese on the staff of the diocese. He was clearly capable and rapidly becoming vocal in Japanese. He could not be "contained" by a language barrier. The Bishop of South Tokyo used Frank Coaldrake shrewdly, the only non-Japanese priest in the Diocese, to embark on a program of visiting, assessing and supporting local churches throughout the diocese. This was in addition to his duties as an assistant priest in Odawara. We learn that numerous parish priests from elsewhere in the diocese spent time finding their footing, as well as food, at his farmhouse home in Odawara. He conducted a religious "retreat" for some on the meaning of "priesthood." A theological student moved in for preliminary training. The small library of theological books he had prepared specifically for this purpose was soon put to good use. There were innumerable meetings, religious services, study groups, and visitors from abroad. Homeless people were bedded down in emergencies.

There was not enough food. What he had he shared. He became a one-man relief agency, personally distributing food and clothing, and even pieces of old felt, received in parcels sent by loyal supporters in Australia, particularly the "Friends of Odawara." These he distributed throughout the length and breadth of the diocese. He managed a veritable feast (by comparison with the "normal" starvation diet) for all and sundry on Christmas Day, 1947, using jelly and canned food sent by supporting individuals and parishes in Australia, and by the personal donations made by members of the Australian army.

Even getting the first *Newsletter* to Australia turned out to be a problem. It was jettisoned from a military aircraft along with the rest of its cargo as it struggled to stay in the air somewhere over the Pacific. The re-written version finds Frank Coaldrake "seeing the sights" from the window of the train as it wound its way along the coastline of central Japan to Tokyo. The account is filled with excitement and well-informed observations: the period of preparation in Sydney was reaping its first reward, but there is a significant omission. He does not describe any of the towns and cities he passed through that day, except for an obligatory obeisance to Hiroshima. Why, we may well ask? His account of the same journey, given nine years later in *Newsletter No. 62* of August, 1956, contains the type of description of war-ravaged Japan we might have expected in *Newsletter No. 1*: "every city or town I passed through that day [in 1947] was more than half destroyed. There's nothing so completely desolate looking as an acre or two of ashes and rubble with a great smoke-stack standing orphaned in the middle." Maybe it took a number of years for him to digest the enormity of the national tragedy passing before his very eyes. Or maybe he simply did not want to alarm his mother, family and supporters, to whom the *Newsletters* were addressed.

Miraculously, one page from the first letter to his mother from Japan survives. It is located in this chapter after *Newsletter No. 1* as it would not make sense without first reading the longer, more factual account. It was retyped by his mother and circulated to friends. It is undated. The extract is strikingly different in literary style and content from the rewritten first *Newsletter*. In fact it is different from every other surviving document he was to send from Japan. It is a type of "historical fiction" in which he travels back in time to the sixteenth century and the last time there had been major war in Japan. He becomes a foot-soldier, and then a farmer, in the 1570s at the time of Nobunaga Oda and the building of the castles of Gifu and Azuchi. He has a firm grasp of historical detail. The letter becomes an existential meditation on the meaning of war and the plight of the ordinary individual under circumstances of military rule, both in the sixteenth century and 1947.

The details of where Frank Coaldrake went, and what he did and thought, all unfold in his own words in the documents in this chapter. We can see that he quickly found his feet. His own surprise is evident when he started putting his Japanese to use: "my Japanese certainly works," he exclaims.[9] Far from seeing the Japanese as the enemy, there are only a few instances where he indicates some degree of caution or concern for physical danger. By *Newsletter No. 6* of October, 1947, just four months after his arrival, he is already identifying himself with the local church, referring to Japanese priests as "our priests."

The Nippon Seikōkai was in bad shape physically and psychologically as a result of the war. Many of the church buildings had been destroyed or seriously damaged by wartime bombing, including St. Andrew's Cathedral in Yokohama. The surviving Japanese priests were dispirited, eking out an existence in secular jobs while trying to rally their decimated and dispersed congregations. To add to its troubles, the Anglican Church was deeply divided politically as a result of the enforced amalgamation with the other Protestant denominations during the war by the military government for purposes of control. Many of its leaders had been imprisoned at the notorious Sugamo Prison in Tokyo because they claimed allegiance to a foreign authority, specifically the Archbishop of Canterbury in England. The bishops who compromised were completely ostracized from the church after the war. Two bishops who had been imprisoned died soon after the war ended as a result of their imprisonment. This included the Presiding Bishop of the Nippon Seikōkai, Bishop Todomu Sugai, who died two months after Frank Coaldrake arrived in Japan. He was also the Bishop of South Tokyo so Frank

9 *Newsletter No 2*, July, 1947.

Coaldrake had met and talked with him extensively in those first two months in Japan. The life and death of Bishop Sugai is narrated with sensitivity and insight in the early *Newsletters* and in an article sent back to *The Peacemaker* entitled "Barbarian or Saint?" included in this chapter.

The polemical title and content of this article reveal one of the persistent and central themes in Frank Coaldrake's mission of reconciliation with Japan. He set out to humanise and individualise the Japanese, to put flesh on the skeleton of stereotypes, to distinguish between "good Japanese" and "bad Japanese" without in any way seeking to diminish the suffering imposed on Australians by some Japanese in the course of the war. This all seems to be a perfectly obvious approach to us now, but the "good Japanese/bad Japanese" analysis had not been used as an argument for better understanding of the Japanese before this, although it had been a common line of argument in relation to Germany.[10] We should remember that the result of wartime propaganda in Australia and the experience of P.O.W.s had been to demonize all Japanese in the eyes of the Australian public. To the outrage at wartime injustices was added self-righteousness fuelled by racism; the "White Australia" policy set out to keep the Australian nation protected against the "Asian hordes." Arthur Calwell, Australian Minister for Immigration, is quoted at the beginning of Frank Coaldrake's article on Bishop Sugai as stating: "five years of occupation is too short a time to humanize or democratize those barbarians." His was not an isolated voice in Australia at the time: "To decide on the treatment to be meted out to the Japs, we must bear in mind that they are still an uncivilized race, with a purely Oriental mentality . . . the savage remains despite the modern trappings," proclaimed one speaker at a discussion of Japan in 1948 on national radio.[11]

In sharp contrast to these expressions of opinion and vitriol, we find a perceptive, moving description of Bishop Sugai in the *Newsletters*. He was also a "prisoner of war" of the Japanese, Frank Coaldrake points out. "He suffered as so many Australian boys did at the hands of the other kind of Japanese."[12] We can hear echoes of the "war on war" familiar to us from the pages of *The Peacemaker*, but now Frank Coaldrake is tightly focusing on people in order to argue the case for reconciliation. Japanese come across the pages of the *Newsletters* and in the photographs, as fully fleshed-out people, not racial stereotypes – young "lads" eager to find new meaning in life, older women struggling to feed their families, their husbands killed in New Guinea and fearful of any Australians, old ladies bowed down under heavy burdens in crowded trains or spending their declining years in impoverished solitude. (Fig. 8) Few men are described; most between the ages of 17 and 50 had been killed in the war.

10 See further: John W. Dower, *War without Mercy: Race and Power in the Pacific War*, New York, Pantheon Books, 1986, p. 8: "There was no counterpart to the 'good German' in the popular consciousness of the Western Allies [of the Japanese]."

11 "Should we be tough with Japan?" *The Nation's Forum of the Air*, Australian Broadcasting Commission, vol. 4, no. 19, 25 August 1948, pp. 4–5.

12 *Newsletter No. 5*, 20 September 1947.

Figure 8 Old lady on verandah, c. 1947.

The financial situation in which Frank Coaldrake found himself needs to be contextualised. In the second half of 1947, Frank Coaldrake's first six months in Japan, there was a critical problem of hyper-inflation. In July, when he had been there less than a month, the government raised commodity prices sixty to sixty-five times compared with 1934–36 figures. His careful estimates for the financing of the mission, which he had compiled for A.B.M. in Sydney, were left hopelessly behind by reality. We learnt from Frank Coaldrake's letter to the Chairman of A.B.M. of 28 December 1946 (see previous chapter) that he based his budget on the assumption of an average salary for professionals in Japan of ¥1,000. In June 1947, when he arrived in Japan, the average monthly wage was already ¥3,893 for wage earners and ¥4,262 for salary earners.[13] Wages rose in an effort to keep up with inflation. Frank Coaldrake's living allowance from A.B.M. remained the same. By the end of 1947 the average for wage earners was ¥8,560 and for salary earners it was ¥10,588. By August 1948 he found he had only half the income of one farmer's son.[14] We can appreciate the problem, therefore, when we read that it cost ¥6,000 to connect electricity at the Odawara house,[15] or that

13 *The Japan Year Book, 1946–48*, pp. 435–36.
14 *Newsletter No. 16*, 1 August 1948.
15 *Newsletter No. 3*, 15 August 1947.

"one dozen each of apples, mandarins, and fresh eggs cost 582 yen altogether."[16] He was going to have to run on spiritual energy more than physical sustenance.

Letter from Frank Coaldrake to Bishop George Cranswick, Chairman of the Australian Board of Missions, 8 June 1947.

The Right Reverend,
The Chairman,
A.B.M.,
14 Spring St.,
Sydney.

At Sea, 8/6/47

Dear Bishop,

One of my pastimes on the voyage has been the sorting and valuing of equipment – on paper. The result is enclosed for your information. I shall be relieved when I find it all safely in Odawara.

The financial arrangement I made with Mr. Warren[17] in the light of my talks at Victoria Barracks, Melbourne, and with you may be summed up as follows: (and of course having regard to the Board's Resolution),

PRELIMINARY YEAR:

Grants received for, and spent on equipment and certain
travelling expenses –   A£211.11.0

AT LEAVING SYDNEY:

Advance against Travel Expenses. Kure-Odawara –	A£50.0.0
(Surplus to add to Odawara "uncertain expenses" fund).	
Allowance for certain items agreed, 1 qr. –	A£75.0.0
Agreed advance against uncertain exes in Odawara –	A£175.0.0
TOTAL	A£225.0.0

Made up as follows:

Paid to my credit with Army	A£100.0.0
Paid to my own bank	A£55.0.0
Changed to US currency	A£70.0.0
	A£225.0.0

---

16 *Newsletter No. 13*, 1 May 1948.
17 Secretary of A.B.M., effectively the executive manager.

As I understand it the present interim financial arrangements are:

Regular: Quarterly payment for certain agreed items A£75.
(Paid to my credit at Army or Sydney Bank at my discretion.)
Occasional: As necessary, reimbursement of fund to be used for Odawara "uncertain expenses."

I cannot forbear to comment – "Who wouldn't be a missionary – with the A.B.M. behind him!"

About the *Newsletter*, you will hear from Mother in due course.

About Training for Japan [for future missionaries] – I cannot say much until I have been put to the test, and then what my Archdeacon has to say will probably be more valuable. But even at the present stage the following comments seem to be valued:

1. Attitude of University Schools of Oriental Studies and Anthropology: Each school in itself took a helpful practical interest in my problems. I was not able to overstrain their willingness to let me give a special direction to work set in the general course for all students. To co-ordinate the work of the two schools was, however, left to my own initiative and judgement. Overhead co-ordination, i.e. by the professors, was haphazard and vague.

2. Sydney's resources for the study of Japan: Far greater than I was able to use, as a whole, but deficient in material about the Christian Church in recent years, and especially about the Church of England. Professor Sadler, in both his personality and his knowledge, dominates the situation – in a way that I both respect and like. He will be leaving shortly.

3. Tuition in language: I found no one who combined a thorough knowledge of the language with an ability to teach.

4. Reading lists: Those supplied by various advisers such as Dr. Maclaren and Rev. Ian Shevill were good enough, but perhaps too full and undiscriminating. A first list, to open up the subject in all its aspects, and in their contents provide reliable bibliographies for special research, would be:

Sanson: *Japan: A Short Cultural History*.[18]
Sadler: *Short History of Japan*.[19]
Anesaki: *History of Japanese Religion*.[20]
? : *Suye Mura*. (Sociological study of 1935 Japan.)[21]
Rose-Innes: *Japanese Conversational Grammar*.[22]

18 George Sansom, *Japan: A Short Cultural History*, London, The Cresset Press Ltd., 1931.
19 A.L. Sadler, *Short History of Japan*, Sydney, Angus and Robertson, 1946.
20 Masaharu Anesaki, *History of Japanese Religion: with Special Reference to the Social and Moral Life of the Nation*, London, New York, Kegan Paul International, Distributed by Columbia University Press, 1995 (1930).
21 John F. Embree, *Suye Mura: A Japanese Village*, Ann Arbor, Center for Japanese Studies, The University of Michigan, 1995 (1939).

5. Temporary Ministry: For a priest this seems to be essential, provided studies are clearly separated from ministry, in the mind of the parish clergy and people as well as of the student. Personally I found the period at Christ Church very fruitful as well as conducive to study.

You will be pleased, I am sure, to know about my final interview with the Archbishop of Sydney [H.W. Mowll]. I had sent him a wire from Melbourne telling of my departure and hoping I might have an interview. When I phoned, on my return to Sydney, he had left a message saying he would call at Christ Church to see me. He did so on the Sunday afternoon. He was altogether very gracious. He stayed for half an hour talking about Japan and our prospects. He gave me his blessing and asked me to call at the Registry next day for a letter from him as Primate to the Presiding Bishop.

Incidentally, I should perhaps have explained, when I asked for your blessing "again" in the A.B.M. Office, that I valued the Blessing at the service as from the Church at your hands, and indeed that service will long be an inspiration to me, but that I treasure, as I hope I may presume to do, a more personal strand in our relation.

Newsletter No. 1, **20 June 1947. Circular.**

NIPPON SEIKO KWAI

C/- Empire House,
B.C.O.F.,
Tokyo,
JAPAN.

Copy of letter from – Rev. Frank W. Coaldrake

Dear Friends,

Having just learnt that mail bags were jettisoned [by the Army mail service carrier] over the Halmaheras containing Air Mail letters of 14th June I now face

---

22 Arthur Rose-Innes, *Conversational Japanese for Beginners. Exercises, Grammar, Vocabulary,* Yokohama, Yoshikawa Shoten, New Edition, 1933. This book is still in the Coaldrake home in Sydney. The pencil notations in Part III ("Vocabulary of Common Japanese Words with Numerous Examples and Notes") show that Frank Coaldrake had meticulously studied the 161 pages of this section. In addition to these references he also took to Japan the 1945 American edition of *Ueda's Daijiten,* the monolithic Japanese character dictionary reprinted by Harvard University Press for use by wartime translators and interpreters. A handwritten page has been attached to the flyleaf stating that this dictionary was presented to Frank Coaldrake by "his friends at St. Linus, Merlynston, Victoria, Australia, March 1947: Edwin Badger, N.C. Badger, Ray E. Evenden, E.M. Jones, Alma Thomas, E.C., D. Gaffney, M. Rolfe, L. Hilbig, A. Drummond, P.E. Hocking, Mrs. R. Fordham, L. Thomas, M. Gibbs, Val Thomas, John Thomas, C.F. Monk, Isobel Evenden, June McDiarmid, Mrs. J. Downie, P. Blair, G. Blair, D. Spalding, T. Gibbs. A. Parker, Eileen West, Frances Marshall, R.R. Hannington." Beside this list was added an inscription in Japanese from the pre-war Japanese Prayer Book. In translation it reads: "We beseech God that in His infinite mercy he shall protect you. We ask that the Lord pray for you and preserve you."

re-writing the account of my first days in Japan from Kure to Tokyo. I cannot hope to recapture the response it all called forth on the spot, and I hope "Davy Jones" enjoys reading my lost letters.

I landed at Kure on the morning of Wednesday, June 11th. It was St. Barnabas Day and he is known as the "Son of Consolation," a good mark to aim at for my first year in Japan.

Arrangements were made for me to go on to Tokyo at midnight by the "Dixie Limited" and my crates of luggage from the Merkur's hold were to be sent under Army control to Odawara. Some days later I made urgent inquiries and located my precious crates at Yokohama port, nicely loaded all ready to go to U.S.A. They were recaptured and headed back for Odawara.

Army Chaplains Mappin and Laing[23] met me at Kure and set a hot pace in sightseeing for the day, and in spite of final smallpox vaccination troubling me, I enjoyed it all immensely. It was good to have Frank Davis[24] with us, as he had Army leave for the day and met me at the wharf also. (Fig. 6) Rex Jones, a Christ Church, N.S.W. lad, was another who turned up. He is an interpreter with the Army and was particularly helpful in the evening, when Fr. Laing took us to call on the newly appointed Anglican Rector of Kure. Fr. Yomiura is about 40 years old, and works as a clerk during the week, because his congregation is too poor to maintain him. We spent an interesting and unwearying hour with Fr. Yomiura, his wife, daughter and niece, and later on they appeared as my train was leaving, having walked the few miles to the station, to say they would "play" for me. Japanese cannot say our "R" and "L" sounds, and get them wonderfully mixed, but as I crawled into my "sleeper" I was glad to know that here in Japan and there in Australia were people "playing" for me. I felt like the first experimental rocket on a guided missile range – I'd been "sent off" from Melbourne, guided and powered to land in Japan.

It took me hours to get to sleep in a berth built for 5ft. 6in. people, but at daybreak I was at the window to see Kobe passing by, and from there my eyes were busy taking in the landscape onwards to Tokyo.

About Hiroshima there's little to be said – but a lot to be thought. It's a waste of time going there now to see the effect of an atomic bomb. The days when the damage could be seen are gone forever. The visible scars of war, even atomic war, are soon removed. In Rabaul a fortnight ago we saw jungle growth everywhere, richly green. Under it, we were told, lay the ruins of war. Very occasionally a ruin could be seen. But no imagination could picture the scene as war had left it. In Hiroshima it is impossible now to imagine just what things looked like after the

---

23 Alan Laing visited Sydney while on leave in February, 1947. He met Frank Coaldrake and the Chairman of A.B.M. and discussed the plans and preparations for the mission with them. Frank Coaldrake corresponded with Padre Laing from Sydney for advice about further preparations and equipment. See further: *Letter from Frank Coaldrake to Maida Williams, 1 August 1947*, in this chapter.

24 Frank Davis is described in more detail in *Newsletter No. 3*, 15 August 1947, as a friend who had been "a frequent visitor to St. Cuthbert's when his military wanderings allowed."

bomb. Photos, and John Hersey's superb story,[25] tell us something, but all too little. The scars are gone. The scars on people are with those people in their graves. How many have died? We didn't see a single person scarred with a weal, or crippled. The city's scars are well "sloughed over" with a new growth of buildings. The structures are only flimsy patchwork, but they're meant to be permanent – that is, until fire burns down whole blocks at a time. Rubble has been cleared away (it was mostly only very small sized pieces), and crops are growing where buildings have not yet been thrust up. There are bent bridges, a few large "air-conditioned" shells of buildings, but hurrying crowds and the bent backs of busy workers draw our attention.

Some people still live in shanties and bag huts, and the wreck of a tram-car lying in the approach to a ruined bridge is not only being used as a residence, it has electric light wires running to it. But the day of bag humpies is nearly past, for building goes on apace. Whenever we stopped to listen to the noises around us, there was an overall clatter of thousands of hammers tapping energetically. It sounded like a mighty army of woodpeckers. God and man between them have almost effaced the ruin of the bomb. Even that corner of the earth in which men most mis-used the powers of the Creation is still one of the places of which we say in the Daily Office Prayer "in His hand are all the corners of the earth."

Two years from the day of the bomb will find the bomb only a memory – a fading memory. As the memory of one tragedy fades, the door opens for a repetition of the tragedy. We can count little on the horrors of one war preventing another more horrible.

This is the Japan that has been pictured and described many times; and I suppose it will continue to be pictured and described world without end, for it has its own particular right to it. The pictures and descriptions I have seen in Australia I now know to have been true – as to the country – tho' I don't yet know about the people. "It's just like the pictures of it," a soldier next to me said this morning as I sat absorbed in the passing picture of it all. And he was both right and wrong. Where he is wrong is just what matters. It is only when you're here that you can see the all important changing detail. I wonder if pictures could be got, or stories written, to show the differences that are making it impossible to be indifferent to the charm of the place in the first days. A cluster of houses in the country, a packed mess of shanties jostling each other for a place along narrow streets and alleys in the city, a terraced hillside here or there, a patchwork of green and brown fields, a mountain mirrored in the muddy paddy waters, a shrine thrust up amongst houses and factories – the houses and workshops of men and "gods" in smelly familiarity; a river not much troubled by the sluggish movement of ancient craft; a whole family at work in the fields; children playing noisily; women carrying great bulky and heavy loads; a motley of dress revealing every possible combination and permutation of Western and J'ese items from

25 John Hersey, *Hiroshima*, Harmondsworth, Middlesex, England, Penguin, 1946. Originally published in the *New Yorker*, 1946.

shoes or geta underfoot to felt hat or sunshade overhead; some all Western, some all J'ese, but mostly all jumbled up like a paddy's market; vehicles in endless variety from the ubiquitous jeep to the motor tricycle, the bicycle with passenger "cab" attached, the horse drawn wooden wheeled wagon, or, on water, the modern speed launch, the poled barge, and even the paddle wheel barge in which the four paddle wheels are turned by men on a treadmill.

All these are seen in pictures or read about. Yet being amongst them all brings to light an infinite variety as between house and house, person and person, field and field. As days pass more and more will become apparent, and a closer walk will no doubt show ever increasing differences. I suppose if there's one thing more than any other that has helped bring about this wealth of detailed difference it is the infusion of Western ideas and things.

You should, for instance, see the footwear. Many wear the native sandal. It is wood, with two wooden bars across the sole, and a double strap that comes up between the big toe and the next, then divides so that one strap goes down over inside the instep and the other to the outside of the heel. Walking on them gives an odd jumpy movement. Many wear straight-out Western shoes or boots. Children are often bare-foot, but yesterday we saw some boys in a Buddhist Shrine garden playing baseball, and some were wearing geta (that's the sandals), and running as nimbly as those who were bare-foot. Yet the strangest sight is the boot worn by some men. It's made with the big toe separated from the other toes. The jungle kit of the J'ese soldier included such boots, and perhaps these we see now are "ex-army." It's said to be made so as to keep the toes apart for wearing the geta.

A girl in kimono with the decorative "obi," and its "back-flap" to keep it tight around her is a pleasantly colourful sight. But a girl on Osaka platform this morning wore a kind of sports tunic in white, well above the knees, and looked a bit "bold" – judging by the looks of the J'ese men, even in their eyes; and yet in the right place she would look as nice as one of our own, say, hockey players. But you'll even see the sports tunic rounded off with obi and back flap; to say nothing of clown-like checkered cloth pyjama pantaloons solemnly "geta-ing" along the street.

These are the things which must be photographed – the things that show the differences. It is said that the J'ese people are regimented in mind; I am wondering how long such an attitude will survive this infinite variety brought about by shortage. I wonder – in fact, I'm full of wonders – I even wonder if it will ever be possible to photograph the smells! It's rich! Japan, I mean. Rich in individual variety – when you get close. I suppose the problem of this present upheaval is to save the richness while making changes – if there is a truly catholic (Dictionary meaning) way that should not be impossible.

There's surely something redoubtable in the individual – as an individual I mean. This morning as I watched scores of white cranes in the fields – stately birds as they stand, but ever so clumsy as they fly – I was reminded of one of Japan's treasury of stories, about "crane soup." (It's one of the stories George Caiger didn't include in "Tojo Say No"!)[26]

A noble lord in olden times boasted that he had discovered a new way to make crane soup, and the result was delicious with a truly great deliciousness! He invited a redoubtable old retainer to partake of his rare dish. The retainer consumed a bowl of the soup, then declared loudly that he could himself produce such a bowl of soup if the noble lord and his friends would dine with him the next day. This the noble lord did, and all those present declared the soup to be equally delicious. They asked how the retainer had discovered the recipe. He, despite the risk to his living, and head, said – "It was not crane soup at all. It is made of legumes." So he called the bluff of the noble lord!

So we may wonder whether there are not such dour commoners today – they will, if they are here, call the bluff of all who claim to have the recipe for a new dish that is delicious with a truly great deliciousness. Many will swallow the guff, but we need those who will call the bluff of our nostrums, of Christianity as well as of Communism, of Buddhism and Western secularism. I suppose it is when people "call his bluff" that Our Lord becomes most convincing – and so will we be – if we do not bluff.

Awhile back I dozed as I sat looking out at waving barley tops – so close to the train that some waving heads must surely get whisked off. One thing about the richness of this country is that there's never any waste – no inch of land is wasted – they grow barley, rice, or vegetables between the sets of rails in some places!

But hold everything! We've just passed through Odawara! At 40 m.p.h. I've seen it anyway. Not much sign of these "differences." Houses look the same as all along the line; and there are trees, and rice growing by the streets, and some factories destroyed except for smoke stacks and Fuji just grand in the background; with snow dribbling down its front – and – yes! there was one difference about Odawara – a quarter mile away standing up straight, though worn, amidst the houses and factories, a red church spire topped by a solid cross. Now is that the Nippon Seiko Kwai parish church of Holy Cross, Odawara? I'll know soon. But we've gone racing on for Tokyo, $1\frac{1}{2}$ hours away. Looks like this is one of those times when a "guided missile" overshoots its mark – but it's going to land bang in the bosom of its bishop very soon.

Some hours later – I can state definitely and beyond the reach of the doubts that frequently assail me that I'm right in Tokyo – at the Marunouchi Hotel, 200 yards from Tokyo railway station, booked in for the next three days. Also have invitation for few days as guest of Mr. Macmahon Ball,[27] Commonwealth Government representative.

---

26 George Caiger, *Tojo Say No: Japanese ideas and ideals*, Sydney, Angus and Robertson, 1943. Frank Coaldrake wrote a critique of *Tojo Say No* – "Behind Tojo Say No" – in *The Peacemaker*, vol. 8 no. 12, December, 1946, p. 2.

27 William Macmahon Ball (1901–1986) was a member (with the rank of Minister) of the Allied Council for Japan representing the British Commonwealth. There were four members of the Council; the others represented the U.S.A., the U.S.S.R. and China. He resigned from the post in August 1947. See: Alan Rix (ed.), *Intermittent Diplomat: The Japan and Batavia Diaries of W. Macmahon Ball*, Carlton, Victoria, Melbourne University Press, 1988, pp. xiii–xiv.

Yesterday I went by train 25 miles down to Zushi, to meet Bishop Sugai,[28] and spent the afternoon at this home there. There were also eight (8) Japanese priests of the South Tokyo Diocese present, including Fr. Miyazawa,[29] with whom I shall be working in Odawara. It was a very happy afternoon.

I'm spending most of my time on language study with a good teacher, who was formerly on the staff of the Tokyo Foreign Language School before the war.

My address for the present will be:

Rev. F.W. Coaldrake,
C/- Empire House,
B.C.O.F.,
Tokyo. JAPAN.

Air mail takes about six days.
Yours faithfully,
    FRANK

A Page from Frank Coaldrake's 1st letter from Japan, June, 1947.

[Extract, retyped for distribution by his mother, Mrs. Coaldrake.]

Travelling from Kure to Tokyo I dozed off, and perhaps because we'd left Otsu just behind and would soon be in Owari, my mind eventually landed me in the years about 1570 with Nobunaga. For as I lost myself in barley ears and neat rows of nearly drowned rice seedlings, patchworked over the bosom of the river flats, I thought I saw an imperious Yankee with a squadron of bull-dozers come over the hills and work ruthlessly over the plain. Steinbeck in the "Grapes of Wrath" described the way the tractors changed small farm holdings into spreading acres of wheat – but what happened to the farmhouses, the cow pens, the backyard chicken coops and the children's mud pies, in the process, was nobody's business. In such a way the bull-dozers roared all day backwards and forwards levelling the mounds and ditch banks, obliterating houses and shrines, making one vast level field. When night fell on a job half done, they switched on powerful flood headlights obliterating too the homely flare of simple lamps and the faint glow of shrine lanterns. By morning their work was done and they went out over the mountains to the next plain. After them came ploughs and seeders. There was a lull, the crops sprang up, ripened, came ready for harvest. Down from the hills came a dozen harvesters. They swept the fields clean, working day and night, leaving in their wake great stacks of bagged grain, and bound stocks of hay. A valley worked by a dozen men in a couple of days – while 2,000 old hands looked on and saw their year's toil done and the fruits laid out.

---

28 Bishop Todomu Sugai, Presiding Bishop of the Nippon Seikōkai and Bishop of South Tokyo.
29 Father Kumazō Miyazawa, Rector of the Parish of the Holy Cross, Odawara. Discussed in *Newsletter No. 4*, 19 August 1947.

But in the meantime, in the way of the dreamer, I found myself treading the treads of the harvester wheel until it became a treadmill. As I slowly walked up the never-ending treads I lifted water from a canal into a ditch and from there it ran out over the fields. I trod and trod, but it seemed that each tread took me back in time till as I trod I saw a great squad of armoured soldiery of old Japan winding their way along the track that clung to the high ground through the paddy fields. This was the noble lord Nobunaga bound for his old home at Owari to his new castle at Otsu – his castle with its noble tower such as was never before seen in this land. As I trod my waters up and out he rode past on his mission of making an empire out of a race of people divided among themselves. I was a serf – with not much to call my own. Any bad season could bring me and my family to death by starvation, any movement of battle could ruin my crops; I was a serf not a samurai, so I wouldn't have to fight – but I might have to cease treading water to go and build earth-works or a castle: I was not "secure" – but yet I had my house, my shrine, my wife, children and I knew my departed parents, and their parents, and theirs were constantly watching me, expecting me to keep things going in the way they had taught us. Life was rich and warm with things I could understand, things that came close – close as the worn treads of this mill; so much a personal thing that I must always remember that one tread was slippery and another so rotten I dare not press my full weight on it; it would be replaced after the harvest when I had time to seek out the tree, when the ox could be spared to drag it in. These things were part of me. Such machinery as I had made my own interests were deeply rooted in the soil, the trees, the river...

Newsletter No. 2, July, 1947.

Aust. Army Post Office,
C/- Empire House,
B.C.O.F.,
Tokyo,
JAPAN.

From – Rev. Frank W. Coaldrake

Dear Friends,

Things have been moving since I last wrote. The week I spent with Mr. Macmahon Ball, at Commonwealth House, was very interesting and fruitful.

On Saturday 21st I went with Bishop Sugai to Odawara. We spent 6 hours there with Fr. Miyazawa. There is a well-established parish Church with a Girls' School – 30 pupils age 8 to 14 years; and a kindergarten – 60 boys and girls – bonzer kiddies. The Church building is back in a big garden block, quite attractive. The Church is reasonably large for such a centre. It seats about 50 people. Fr. Miyazawa's house is next to the Church. He has wife, sons and daughters, in-laws and grandchildren living with him in large numbers. Two houses were shown to me from which to select one to live in as a tenant. One very small and in a dark smelly corner behind a large house – the other a 400 years old "farmer's house" moved from an inland farming area to the coast, 20 to 30 years ago. Its main room is quite large. There is a kitchen-scullery along one side, and two "sleeping" rooms along the other – all of generous size. Floor is "tatami" (i.e. mats), roof is thatch, very thick, and walls are "shoji" (sliding screens). There is a narrow verandah in front, and the timber work is all "rough hewn" and solid. The whole is fittingly coloured antique.

It's on a bluff up the hill above the town, large garden area around, and many fine large trees. A Shinto Shrine is just down the hill to the right, and the front view looks across the top of a city of 40,000 people out to sea and down the coast. It is really most attractive to look at, but what it will be like to live in remains to be seen.

On Sunday 22nd, I went to Yokohama and took the services at the Church (English Language). It was very interesting.

On 24th June I moved to Fr. Viall's[30] house at St. Paul's University, Ikebukuro, which was founded by the Episcopal Church of America. While there I attended the Medical Centre for more inoculations.

The 29th found me at Odawara settling in permanently, after having a gang of men and lads of the Church to help me bring my 11 crates from the Station.

"HAJIME, IMA, YOYO" – These are the three words in the doxology here corresponding to the English: "In the beginning, now, and world without end." I like the Yoyo touch! Anyway, I find I'm thinking of my house now as "Hajime, Ima, Yoyo."

Hajime: I wound my way between the garden beds of vegetables up the steep hill and finally climbed up a flight of rough stone steps. I thought I was in a picture book. A high thick overhanging thatch covered the house and hid its interior in shadow, even the whole of the front was open. Leaving shoes on the convenient stepping-stone, we stepped the foot or so up on to the three-foot wide front verandah, and as our eyes became accustomed to the dim light, we could see the big central room stretching back for 25 feet. It is 18 ft. wide. Rush mats on the floor, two antique black camphor-wood chests, and an out-of-place European wicker chair set and table, were the only furnishings. In the centre of the room there is an open hearth sunk into the floor, and above it, just at the height of my forehead, is a 6ft square timber rack fitted with a hook of bamboo hanging down to the hearth. The rack is a relic of fish-smoking days.

The house is built of hand-hewn solid oak uprights and beams. The main beams are about a foot square. All are black with age. They are held together by fitting and wooden pegs. There's not a nail or bolt in the building. Arches and angle supports are made by the choice of appropriate pieces of bent or forked tree. Up near the top of the thatch there's a cane plaited ceiling. In one corner of the old "kitchen" there's a primitive grain-crushing "mallet." It is a beam about 10 feet long, fitted with a heavy wooden head which drops into a stone bowl let into the ground. The operator stands on the far end and levers the head up, then

---

30 Episcopalean priest and member of the Society of St. John the Evangelist (S.S.J.E.).

lets it drop. Such "machines" are still in use here. In a corner there is an old saddle. Until it has been shifted out and cleaned, I cannot say much about it. But in construction and decoration, it looks like the kind I have read were in use in mediaeval times here. The whole place is mediaeval.

First impression is that it is very like the slab-built sheds used for packing sheds on farms in the Blackall Range district in Queensland. In fact, if I'd seen a chaff-cutter in a corner, I would have thought I was back with Uncle Jack and the pineapples. But later the feeling grows that it is more like one of the old hunting lodges one sees pictured in old Europe. It certainly is a museum piece. When I unpack Prof. Sadler's *History of Japanese Architecture* I expect to find out a lot about this sort of house.[31] But from memory I can guess a lot. I'm told that it was built about 400 years ago in a farming district, over on the other side of this main island and was moved to this position about 25 years ago for use as a "Teahouse" for the booming tourist trade.[32] It would be a great attraction as a "Coffee Shop" down where the "Teapot Inn" is in Little Collins St. [Melbourne]. In fact the "TPI" is an attempt to reproduce just the kind of atmosphere found in this place. I much prefer this original to the tawdry imitation.

The space on the left of the big room is divided into two rooms 12 feet x 12 feet. The front one is floored with thick rush mats [*tatami*], and is the chief room. It has the "tokonoma," the marked off place for hanging the one picture in the house, and the very low shelf for standing sacred objects, or a vase of flowers. The rear room on the left, at the back of the chief room, is either a bedroom or a store room. In one corner is the washroom. Architecturally the building seems to be pure "aboriginal" Japanese. Its style shows no traces of the Chinese-ex-India influences which came into Japanese architecture in the 5th, 12th, and 16th centuries. The fact that it was built in a remote country district explains how, even as late as the 16th century, when it was probably built, conservatism kept it free of foreign influence.

Incidentally, that brings out one of the really prominent features in Japanese culture – that this is a land of mostly "peasants" who are extremely conservative. So I have a constant reminder of the chief factor to be faced in bringing Japan to Christianity. (Why, this building hasn't even yielded to Buddhism under the impact of 1,000 years of it. But it's now got a Christian crucifix hanging on it, and Christian prayers are said daily. Bible classes are held often, and before long the sacrifice of Calvary will be set forth in it. Perhaps people's minds and hearts will prove more tractable than building designs.) Another interesting thing about such a building as this, is that it is architectural evidence that hasn't had to be dug out of the earth. Pure aboriginal Japanese architecture is so very similar to

---

31 A.L. Sadler, *A Short History of Japanese Architecture*, Sydney and London, Angus and Robertson Ltd., 1941. One of the "classic" early Western studies of the history of Japanese architecture.

32 From the descriptions and photographs, the farmhouse was similar to the Kitamura Family House, now registered as an "Important Cultural Property" and relocated to the Kawasaki *Minka-en* building park near Yokohama. The Kitamura House was built in 1687 at Tanzawa, Yamashita, Kanagawa Prefecture.

modern Malayan architecture, that the fact of the similarity is one of the chief features in the theory now generally accepted, that the peoples of Malaya today and the aboriginal Japanese of the southern parts of Japan, were of the same parent stock. It is not that there was a migration either from Japan or Malaya or vice versa, but that both peoples migrated from the same home country, which is thought to have been somewhere in the south of China, about the north of the present-day Indo-China. But where the Japanese language comes from, no one knows. Personally, I think it is a device of the devil to make things hard for missionaries. I think it was Francis Xavier who took these words out of my mouth! Incidentally, some of the relics of the first Japanese Christian Martyrs, 1587, are to be placed in the side-Chapel of the Anglican Church at Yokohama, now being rebuilt after almost total destruction in air raids.

Ima: Living in a museum isn't so bad after all. The fact that the whole of the front is fitted with screens that can be slid back or taken right out, means that the place can be opened up to the cool sea breeze that blows every day. (Colour Plate 1) The thick thatch, and the dim light, also keep out the heat and the glare. The low door lintels and the low hanging hearth rack have bruised my head several times. I can raise the rack nearly a foot, but the lintels will have to stay. They're solid too!

Only one of my 22 pieces of luggage remains to be unpacked. It is a box of books. The owner of the house produced some of the "tea-house" furniture. The wicker furniture was part of it. Also, I now have a polished extending dining table and six chairs. A large sliding cupboard has been moved halfway back, and across one side of the big room, making a "dining-nook" just one step up from the kitchen. At each side of the back of the big room, is a large built-in cupboard. The doors are decorated with J'ese style paintings, beautifully tentative suggestions of farming activities in each of the four seasons.

In the right-hand cupboard, near the kitchen, are my bulk supplies of food. The left-hand one has stocks of books, stationery, the duplicator and the machine. At the front of the big room on the left facing in, is a small temporary writing table and my filing cabinet. Eventually there will be a study table and high desk. Across on the other side front, there is the entrance hall, screened off with two J'ese folding screens and temporarily furnished with one of my boxes in which are all my footgear. That's the handiest place, because outside footwear is taken off on entering, and put on last thing before leaving. Bare feet or sox, in the house, is the rule in order to preserve the mats. In summer time it's a jolly fine idea. I must have slippers – soft for inside, and thick wooden "geta" to slip on when going outside for a short time, and even when stepping down to walk on the dusty cement floor of the kitchen.

In the big dark kitchen, I've rigged a temporary bench just near the dining nook. It reaches across to the J'ese style washing-tray. On the bench is one Electric Stove Burner, and when kerosene or petrol are in supply, a petrol and kerosene stove. At present I'm still negotiating with every-one short of MacArthur and Hirohito to have a new transformer fitted to the area power supply lines, so I can use more than 500 watts at any one time. I hope to get this matter fixed soon. Then I'll have permanent stove-fittings made. The only water for the kitchen is a dribbling tap outside at the end of the building. An old, but clean and very large biscuit tin scrounged from the Army Stores will be put over the washing tray. Pipes will run into it from the outside tap, and so we'll have water laid on in the kitchen. (Incidentally, having the small tank will mean that all my drinking water will be easily treated for chlorination, and so prevent a recurrence of the severe attack of gastritis I've had these last three days, from drinking some of the water without boiling it first).

The pipes and taps necessary to do the job seemed likely to be unprocurable, but I found a junk shop in Odawara. I love junk-shops. In Australia they're wonderful – in Japan they're incredible. The tricks of the junk trade seem to be universal. Working them in the Japanese language is a bit of a stretch. I've found what it means to have a "working knowledge of Japanese." When I start out to do business in a junk shop in Japanese, I very soon exhaust my resources and see for myself what a funny mess I've made of it, and laugh. Then they laugh gleefully with me. We all laugh, and before I know what's happening, I've got what I want for a song; often with alterations chucked in. And when I want to travel on a train which hasn't got an "Allied Personnel" car, and the Japanese cars are jammed tight, I go along to the guard and ask him, so I think, if I can ride with him. He looks dumb, and I try again and make a howler that makes me laugh, and he laughs too, and the next thing I know, I'm in his best seat riding on to my destination, and trying to improve my J'ese by talking to him. We all laugh a lot. Probably I teach him to roll a cigarette Australian fashion, or that I am a Christian missionary from Australia, or perhaps something about Christianity and even on one occasion, to make the Sign of the Cross. My Japanese certainly "works" what I want to accomplish.

But back to the kitchen! The front end of it is the usual way of entering the house. But it is too spacious to use only for that. I've made a good solid work bench and fitted up a tool-chest. Just one corner will be curtained off for an entrance lobby, the rest will be quite a good workshop. It's dark, but with electric light will not be too bad. My tools all arrived in good order, and those I have used already turned out to be good tools. Over the next couple of months I'll be making quite a few things – a flyproof safe, a prayer desk, a study table, three sets of book shelves, a standing desk, and so on. I was fortunate to get for the equivalent of 30/- two large planks of soft wood with a nice grain. One has made the main plank of the work bench – the other when seasoned, will make a good study table. All the timber in my cases is being used too.

The tatami room is my bedroom. Don't get worried when I confirm your guess that there is no bed. I roll the sleeping bag out on the tatami and fix sheets and blankets on top of it, and sleep soundly and restfully.

Some of the old material I brought as packing has supplied the curtains for the entrance lobby, and a good table cover for the dining table and the study-table-to-be. In the tokonoma at present hangs a Japanese scroll picture of a rooster and hen feeding. It's a delightful thing, which was loaned to me to fill the vacant space of the tokonoma. In a few days' time I'll have my prayer desk in the front corner of the room, with a view out and down the coast as an inspiration. (The Odawara church building is quite an inspiration too, but there's so much to say about that, I'm going to leave it all till later.)

Along the end of the tatami room is a set of four sliding screen "windows" giving more light and air. The paper on the screens has been torn to ribbons in the last three days by the tiny kitten I've procured in the hope that she'll grow up into a good ratter. Mike is the name (Mee-keh). It means "three hairs," one black, one brown, one white. She's a very pretty tortoiseshell.

The wash room is something I'm not yet sure what I'll do about. If I could get cement or iron, I'd enlarge it and fit a shower. I've repaired most of it, but have still to make a wiped-leaded joint, as this has to be made half an inch from the wall, and the wall is a thin layer of mud-cement over two thicknesses of criss-crossed bamboo, very dry. Probably I'll get several buckets of water, the stirrup pump, and Ogata-san lined up, and hope for the best. Things are never so bad they can't get worse. In the middle of washing the other day, the water supply was cut off. That happens about twice a day, with both the water and electricity. Ogata-san washes as many clothes as I like to give her. Of course, you're wondering who Ogata-san is. She "does" for me, under two difficulties – never been in a European house before, and knows only a few scattered words of English. She's very slow but willing and completely honest.

Yoyo: I find, has been dealt with at the same time as ima.

I'd better try and clear up the matter of addresses for mail. Japanese civil mails are censored and the delay is inevitable, therefore it is better for the present to use the Army Post Office facilities. If you address as above to B.C.O.F. at the rates required for mail to B.C.O.F. personnel ($3\frac{1}{2}$ d. per oz.) it will come by air in about a week.

At present I visit Tokyo at least once each week for supplies. In Japanese the address looks frightening, but I have ordered a rubber-stamp of the address in Japanese, and send it to you so that you will be able to send Japanese mails whenever the B.C.O.F. facilities cease to be available. There is no censorship of mail to B.C.O.F. addresses. On Monday last I collected from B.C.O.F. Post Office many letters, newspapers as well as mail re-directed from A.B.M. Sydney, also several periodicals. The whole lot fills in the gap of the last several weeks.

Just a final glimpse. On the walls, the election picture of George Henderson,[33] and in the off-centre of the big room, a large cloisonne vase with five large blooms of hydrangea aptly arranged by Ogata-san. On my left, three fat dictionaries on a low Japanese table, and on my right, a clock which shows nearly midnight.

So for the present, good-bye and good wishes.

FRANK

---

33 Possibly George Cockburn Henderson (1870–1944). Research professor at the University of Sydney from 1937–44, and pioneer in the field of Pacific history. See: *Australian Dictionary of Biography*, vol. 9, pp. 254–255.

Frank Coaldrake, *Report to the Australian Board of Missions from Odawara, covering the period up to 20 July 1947.*

This report will cover my journey from Sydney to Odawara via Kure and Tokyo; my first meetings with the Presiding Bishop Nippon Seiko Kwai; the house and equipment in Odawara; Odawara city; Odawara church life and plant; the Diocese of South Tokyo; confidential comments on the Australian Bishops' impending visit; finance. All the matters after arrival in Odawara are to be taken as inconclusive.

SYDNEY TO KURE

The journey of twenty days proved to be a good rest. At Rabaul I met the Rev. F. Rowley, of the Melanesian Mission, who was there temporarily and waiting for transport to Brisbane. From the ship I sent copies of my equipment list and financial statements to the Secretary and the Chairman.

KURE

I was met at the boat by the Rev. Chaplain Mappin, who told me that the Senior Chaplain of the Forces had asked him to meet me and apologise for his own absence on duty. Subsequently the Senior Chaplain, Mayston, phoned me and said that he had been asked by Bishop Sugai, through Colonel Paul Rusch, to arrange for my reception in Kure and to ensure my safe departure by train that night. During the day I was looked after by Chaplains Mappin and Laing. At night we called on the Nippon Seiko Kwai (N.S.K.) local rector, Father Yomiura. He lives in a two-roomed hut in one of the thickly populated parts of Kure and uses one room of the hut for Church services. The congregation totals 25 Japanese. A Bible Class is held each Sunday. Fr. Yomiura had only recently been appointed. The congregation's resources are so small that Fr. Yomiura earns his living working as a clerk for the Allied Services. He is an alert man of about 35. He came to the train at midnight to see me off. He seemed to be greatly encouraged by the fact that the Church in Australia had sent me and seemed likely to send more in the years to come. My whole impression was of a faithful priest tackling a big task under difficult circumstances and needing our encouragement, help and prayers. The local Army Chaplains frequently assist him.

The Occupation Forces arranged my travel from Kure by train that night and put some of my luggage on the train with me. The heavy cases were put in charge of Army Movement Control to be sent to Odawara by Army goods train. For all travel on trains in Japan I am required by regulation, as I am a British National, to travel in the special Allied Services transport and I cannot buy a ticket. This means that my travel to Tokyo and back to Odawara was free. Meals on the train were also provided.

TOKYO

At Tokyo Station I was met by Rev. K.A. Viall, the U.S. Episcopal Church Liaison Priest in Japan. He explained that Bishop Sugai had asked him to meet me and look after me in Tokyo. I was able to book in at the B.C.O.F. Hotel and stayed there for four days. This was an irregular practice under B.C.O.F. rules, as I am merely a civilian without any official status. At the invitation of the Hon. W. Macmahon Ball [member of the Allied Council for Japan, representing the British Commonwealth] I then spent a week at Commonwealth House as his guest. Then I moved out to stay for four days at Fr. Viall's house at St. Paul's University. It had not been possible to stay there earlier because the house was only then being made ready for occupation.

The Bishop had decided that I should spend a short time in Tokyo both to meet Church people and to give time for final preparations for my move to my house at Odawara. In Tokyo I met Service Chaplains and Japanese Clergy and visited the Occupation Personnel Episcopal Church Club. This Club has raised an impressive amount of money from Occupation Personnel towards the rebuilding of Church properties. The moving spirit is Colonel Paul Rusch. Anglicans in Tokyo may attend Church services at the Episcopalian St. Luke's Hospital Chapel. Only an extremely small proportion do so. There are several thousand Occupation Anglicans for whom the only ministry of the Church is provided by two Service Chaplains – both Americans. There is no Australian Chaplain. There is an urgent need of a special ministry to Occupation Personnel in Tokyo, especially Australians. These people include civilian officials and a great many dependants. Their life is set amidst unusual surroundings and there is an urgent need of a spiritual ministry to help them keep balance.[34] Fr. Viall ministers to civilian personnel when he is in Tokyo. He is responsible for the English language services at Christ Church Yokohama. On two Sundays I took those services for him while he was at Kyoto. His duties as liaison priest keep him very busy and it seems that the appointment of liaison priests from each of the main Churches will be a valuable help to the Church here.

THE PRESIDING BISHOP

I first met the Presiding Bishop, The Rt. Rev. T. Sugai, at his office at the Central Theological College on June 17th. He made me very welcome and said how glad he was that I had arrived. I delivered to him the letters from the Archbishop of Sydney and the Rt. Rev. the Chairman of the Board. He arranged to go to Odawara with me a week later.

---

34 Much of Tokyo was in ashes and people were starving in the streets.

THE SOUTH TOKYO DIOCESAN STANDING COMMITTEE

In the meantime, I went at his invitation to his house at Zushi to attend the monthly meeting of the Standing Committee of the Diocese of South Tokyo. At that meeting there were six priests of the Diocese and one candidate for Ordination who had just returned from three years in Burma. The clergy expressed great pleasure at my arrival, and prayers of thanksgiving for both my arrival and the return of the Ordination candidate were said by the Rector of Odawara, the Rev. K. Miyazawa. By the time of the next meeting of the Standing Committee I had unpacked the A.B.M. gifts of Communion wine and bread and the clerical collars and was able to give them to the Bishop. At the same time I gave him the ten chalices and the sum of A£28. which had been given me by private persons. All these things were very gratefully received. The clergy fitted themselves out with new collars on the spot.

Communion wine and breads used by the whole of the Diocese of South Tokyo in a year total 10 dozen bottles, 10,000 people's [communion] breads and 2,000 Priests' breads. Candles total 50 dozen. The Bishop asked me whether it would be possible for these supplies to come from Australia because they are very difficult to procure in Japan as well as being poor quality and high in price. Would the Board consider making a gift of these things to the Diocese each year?

The Standing Committee tried to complete arrangements for a Youth Camp for the South Tokyo Diocese's youth to be held in August. They were very disappointed to have to cancel the camp because of shortage of food and money. It seemed to me that next summer such a camp might be possible if the Board were able to help by making finance available. I should like to keep this in mind and raise it again later.

The Bishop also asked whether it might be possible for people in Australia to send surplus clothing for Church people here. The average Japanese person now buys no clothes because of the shortage of money. With inflation increasing daily the clothing difficulty will become worse. The winter situation is dreadful to contemplate. I suggested to the Bishop that he discuss this matter with the Australian Bishops when they are here.

VISIT OF AUSTRALIAN BISHOPS

At the latter meeting of the Standing Committee, held July 15th, the Bishop announced that the Australian Bishops would be coming on a visit. The news was very happily received.

Strictly Confidential Begins Here

Subsequently I spent some time talking with the Bishop about the visit. Details for the programme were to be worked out a few days later by the Bishop in consultation with Colonel Paul Rusch. We discussed the significance of the visit and the nature of the programme. In brief, my suggestions to the Bishop were as follows:

The significance of the visit is threefold, namely –

1. to show the N.S.K. [Nippon Seikōkai] that the A.B.M. is interested and anxious to help.
2. to acquaint these Bishops with the situation of the N.S.K. as a whole in relation to Japan as a whole so that they can return to Australia and spread the information.
3. to get a close insight into the workings of a Parish of the N.S.K., if possible a parish in which the Australian missionary is working.

The programme to ensure (1) above will be well managed by Paul Rusch. In the course of that programme and in their meetings with Bishop Sugai as the Presiding Bishop, they will get a fair body of information with regard to (2) above. With regard to (3) above, I suggested that the programme might include time for the Bishops to stay with me in Odawara for a day or two.

I then pointed out that the Australian Bishops and the Rev. M.A. Warren would have one eye on the prospective Australian Mission work in the Diocese of South Tokyo. It would be an advantage if, by the time the Australian Bishops arrive, the Bishop of South Tokyo could have reached a conclusion as to the centre in which he hopes the Australian Mission Job would be done on a permanent basis. Placing due emphasis on the fact that my own personal attitude is that I will readily stay in Odawara or go anywhere else in the Diocese that the Bishop may direct, I went on to point out that if he should decide that my work in Odawara is only for an interim period of training, then probably the Australian Board would prefer to wait for the adoption of a permanent location before making any full scale effort in the provision of missionary equipment or personnel. I suggested that the Bishop might, for instance, have in the back of his mind the thought that Chiba, which was formerly the centre in which an Australian priest worked, should again become the Australian centre. As Chiba was in a highly fortified area it has been much devastated and there is a big task there for the Church. I told the Bishop that I did not expect him to make any comment to me personally on these things at this time, but that I though it would be an advantage if he could have thought them over before the Australian Bishops arrive. He seemed to understand thoroughly and I expect will be ready to talk it over.

I did not tell the Bishop just how much I am impressed by the possibilities of Odawara as a mission centre for the A.B.M. missionaries, considering that the Australian Church comes to Japan with no experience and is therefore probably going to minister more fruitfully in an area already opened up.

Strictly Confidential Ends Here

Odawara is a city of 60,000 people who are still very Japanese. Along the coast to north and south is a string of settlements with something like another 50,000 people. From Odawara, roads and rail run back into the country districts with many tens of thousands more people. In Odawara itself there are between 5 and 10 big Government schools. It is a healthy town 2 hours' run from Tokyo by train. The N.S.K. Parish Church of the Holy Cross is strongly established in a small way. The Church building, a Kindergarten building, the Vicarage and the Kindergarten teacher's residence are substantial small buildings built by the S.P.G. [Society for the Propagation of the Gospel] twenty years ago. The Parish paid one-tenth of the initial cost but now pays the total cost of maintenance. A primary grade girls' school is conducted in the nave of the church during the week, with about 40 pupils from a wide area. In the Church Kindergarten about 60 children receive a full Kindergarten course daily. There are 120 members in the Church, of whom half are communicants. The Church is small but faithful. (Fig. 9) It is a wonderfully sound foundation for future growth.

The buildings (Church, kindergarten and two residences) are all in need of repairs and paint. This is normally the responsibility of parish funds, but financial difficulties over the last few years and at present have resulted in the neglect of all but desperately urgent repairs. The walls and roofs need oil and paint, the windows need glass. Plumbing needs attention. Every effort has been made to preserve the fabric, but while Yen is spread so thin, deterioration is inevitable. I had intended writing a special report on the buildings for the Board and recommending repairs as a legitimate expenditure for the Board's Funds. Now that Mr. Warren is coming soon I am waiting for him to see the situation for

Figure 9 The congregation of the Church of the Holy Cross, Odawara, Autumn, 1947. The Parish Priest, Fr. Kumazō Miyazawa, is at centre front. Frank Coaldrake is at left rear. Ogata-san is standing beside him. Because of the acute food shortages, bales of harvested rice occupy pride of place to the right.

himself, and consider it in relation to what I have written under "Strictly Confidential" above.

Materials for Church services also need renewing, and increasing. Linen and books are particularly distressing.

I think I can best sum the situation up by saying that if I arrived at a parish in Australia to start work there and found it like this, I would place building restoration and Church materials supplies as a number one priority, because the effect of drabness and shortage on already sagging morale is very serious. The buildings are inherently sound, combining utility with beauty and dignity, and could be quite an inspiration.

The movement of church life in the parish, as disclosed by past Annual Reports and discussions with the vicar is, and always has been, slow but sure. The non-conformist churches here make and lose many converts, while we make few but hold them. The Church Schools are an asset whose value is difficult to assess. Government regulation, both pre-MacArthur and MacArthurian, in one way or another prevents instructions in Christian religion. Pupils are invited to attend Bible classes in their own time, and a fair proportion do so. There is the indefinable value in the contact of the Church with the children and their homes. I shall have more to say about the schools later.

My own work as a priest in the parish began immediately in a small way. I am assisting in the conduct of services in Japanese and conducting my own Bible Class in Japanese on the English text of St. Luke. My language studies are the key to increase of duties. With a local tutor I am working away at this. There is a difference between muddling along in conversation and conducting services or classes. But the difficulties are not insuperable. It has been well worthwhile to know something of the language on arrival, both because of the convenience and because of the impression it has had on the Church people. In September, after the Summer Holidays, I am to take over the English language lessons in the Girls' School.

The parish priest is a lovable and devout old Christian who suffers my disabilities most patiently. His fortitude and courage in the face of present day difficulties following on the different tensions of the war period are amazing, and a thing to thank God for. He has around him a band of the faithful gathered from all walks of life and all ages. I am most impressed.

My arrival in Odawara as a resident has been much noticed! I am the first "European" resident here for many years. The commonest attitude is one which includes an element of welcome as an asset to the life of the town (!) and an element of interest in my reason for coming here. ("There must be something in a religion which brings missionaries to live all alone in the far corners of the world. Can I come to your Bible Class?" – the words of a 30 year old ex-soldier now working as a clerk.)

It is evident that here in Odawara at least this is the time in which evangelism on all fronts is both our need and our peril. It will be easy to win quick assent to half truths but conversion to the love of God with body, mind, soul and strength makes a bigger demand on the truly Japanese person than it does on one brought up against a background of Christian or like-Christian, knowledge and practice. The desire for immediate relief of spiritual hunger may easily lead to satisfaction with dangerously unbalanced and superficial faith. In this matter, of course, I write as a "rookie" missionary. But I can see already how easy it is to lead the Buddhist to substitute Christian names and prayers for the Buddhist memorials for the departed, and to join in the congregational services in church in place of the observance of Buddhist Temple Rituals. But belief in the salvation of Jesus Christ is an experience in which the conservative and timid soul may be frightened to venture, and of which no need may be felt in the course of a busy attention to the details of formalities which have their own superficial satisfaction.

RESIDENCE

On Saturday 28th June I moved in to my house in Odawara. It is in the town a quarter mile from the Church. It is very old, but substantial and roomy. On my arrival it was devoid of furniture, but a few items have been put in by the owner and I am able to make others gradually. (Costs of local products are prohibitive, quality poor and design unsuitable.) The house is owned by a Church member and I am to enter into an arrangement for renting it. My efforts to arrange about scale of rent before agreeing to live here were fruitless. It has to be dealt with through a "go-between" and so far I have not been able to get any idea of the amount of rent. There is a hint that it will be purely nominal. Sanitation and power required immediate attention. After three weeks I can still only say that the matter is making progress. I am more than satisfied with the living conditions as a whole and because the place is so roomy I have asked the Bishop to send any of his clergy who need a "rest" to be my guests for a time. I must not keep so large a place to myself while round about me there are twenty people in any building half the size. It is advisable, however, to have the space used in connection with my ministry and several ways of doing this appear to be possible.

SUPPLIES

I should have been involved in much less trouble about food and fuel if I had brought everything from Australia with me. I am entitled to, and hold the paper to draw, a ration of Japanese rationed goods. These are few, and kind and quantity and are intended to be supplemented by much other unrationed food. So far, after taking two weeks and many visits to offices to get the papers, I have received my ration of foods and fuel. 10 lbs. of charcoal and 20 lbs. of pine! I have also been able to use electric current up to 1,000 watts at any time. To buy food locally is quite expensive. Eggs, e.g. cost A.1/6 d. each. Rice is rationed, but not for me, so that I cannot buy it. I am therefore dependent on supplies bought from the Army depot in Tokyo. The projected arrangement for issuing supplies to Missionaries might have been very helpful and, indeed, the individual Army personnel with whom I have dealt have gone out of their way to be helpful. But they have often received sharp reprimands from above for acting outside of, or contrary to, regulations. It took a month of constant attention to negotiations before I was able to draw any of the money placed to my credit in Australia. In the meantime I lived by borrowing B.A.F.V.S. (The British Occupation currency which is the only thing used, and with which I had to pay for supplies bought at the depot. The day I drew my first credits I was advised that in future I would not be allowed to purchase some of the most important items in my lists of supplies because of the complications about repayment. The amount of supplies available is also liable to variation without notice. I have found too many friends among Occupation personnel and among the Japanese people to run any risk of starving!) But daily attention to supplies is a distraction from more important work which I am anxious to minimise. I have asked for signals to be sent to Army H.Q. in Australia to straighten out some of the tangles. If this is not effective by the time that the Bishops arrive I will prepare a report for them in the hope that they can have it attended to in Australia. Between the top-rank Army intention to be helpful and the low-rank willing to be so, there is a gap covered, apparently, by mid-rank obtuseness (not to say stupidity) and scruple about red-tape.

I am also faced with the problem of transporting supplies from the Depot in a Tokyo suburb to my house in Odawara. At present it is a hard day's work to get a week's supplies (canned goods are disproportionately heavy).

For assistance in the house I have engaged a Japanese woman, a war-widow whose husband was a catechist in our Church but died while on war-service in the Philippines. She is very honest and willing, but quite ignorant of Western ways and slow to learn. I pay her at the rate paid to such servants in the home of Occupation Dependants i.e. Yen 1,000 a month (A£5). Her presence in the house also safeguards it and my goods while I am away during the day. (Though most of the people are completely trustworthy there are quite a few thieves about.)

MAILS

It is possible to send mail to me at this address. Such mail, however, comes by slow transport from Australia and is censored before being sent through the Japanese civilian mails. These latter are slow and unreliable also, and mail addressed in anything but Japanese script has to be delayed for translation of the address. At present I am allowed to collect and post mail at the B.C.O.F. Army Post Office in Tokyo. As I have to go to Tokyo for supplies each week it seems to be best to use this facility so long as it is available.

CONCLUSION

Am in good health, faced with plenty of the right kind of work, and in high hopes.

Letter from Frank Coaldrake to Maida Williams, 1 August 1947.

[Handwritten]
Written from "Never-an-old-man House" [the name of the farmhouse converted into the Murota teahouse.]

Odawara, 1/8/47.

It is Lammas Day – and I'm reaping the first fruits of the Japanese working man's appreciation of the return of Christian missions to Japan.

Lt. Bev Burrows, Manager of Kawana Hotel, 35 miles south, B.C.O.F. holiday rest centre, called to see me last week. His wife was on the *Merkur* [*S.S. Merkur*, the ship which brought Frank Coaldrake to Japan] as a fellow passenger with me, and I travelled up in the train with them [from Kure to Tokyo]. He told me he "used to be a preacher" and is anxious to do all he can to help me. Last week he came to find out what form his help might take. He found many ways. In my present period of interim uncertainty about supplies he is now supplying what is lacking. Fresh bread, butter and meat once a week; all supplies from Tokyo carried from the supply depot to my hill foot each week; mail brought from Tokyo P.O. in mid-week; a little paint, kerosene and petrol; and his assistant, a W/01, [Warrant Officer Class I] to do all those things, who has become a firm friend. He, the W/01, is a Brisbane lad, ex-Church Schools. We have many mutual friends. So between Lt. Burrows and W/01 John Hain the situation has changed considerably and temporarily at least the matter of supplies will be much less of an exhausting business. One thing I said would be useful was 3–5 bags of cement to make a bath. Burrows said he would send it up. John Hain later told me that when Burrows asked his Japanese building contractor to drop the cement in at my place (I'm 200 yards off the road from Tokyo to Kawana), the contractor said "I should be much displeased if the Reverend Coaldrake-sama [honorific] did not let me make the bath for him." When Johnnie told me that I had to sit down and work out location and dimensions and assemble materials other than cement...

The message from John was that the workmen would come on Tuesday. They didn't – but at 11.00 today there came the contractor, two skilled workmen and two labourers. They brought every last thing necessary, even the drainpipes! And have carried it all up the goat track. All I can do is to draw plans and keep an eye on the shaping up of things, strain my Japanese language trying to deal with technical problems, and generally try to keep cool on a disgustingly trying day. Even the sea breeze seems to be made languid by the humidity...

We're all looking forward to the bishops' visit. When Alan Laing came to Sydney on Leave in February he had lunch with Bishop George [Cranswick, Chairman of the Australian Board of Missions] and me, and it was then we thought out plans for sending out Australian bishops to visit the N.S.K. [Nippon Seikōkai]. The suggestion it should be a complementary brace of Bishops instead of any one was mine, and I suggested your Bishop as the second

[Bishop Geoffrey Cranswick of Tasmania, brother of Bishop George Cranswick], after Bishop George [Cranswick] had said he thought [the Archbishop of] Brisbane should be one But I little thought to be here myself when they came, for our plans were made to send them here for the meeting of the N.S.K. General Synod in April last! Now I'm terribly glad Geoffrey is coming. I'm hoping they'll stay here over the night of August 20th. It will be a good thing if they can take back and spread in Australia a truer understanding of things in the country and the church here. Already I'm "choc-a-bloc" with things to be written to all sorts of Australian publications. The N.S.K. is just another part of the Anglican Church and every Australian Anglican would feel very much at home in its full round of life; except for the facts of poverty; and of being a "minority" church.

I'm going to leave it to *Newsletters* to give you most of the picture – but I must tell you briefly about Minami Oka-san – my chief "mentor," who, with my landlady, Murota-san, is my "go-between" for "go-between-able" dealings, and is now my tutor in Japanese. But so much more than that. She might have come out of All Saints' [Hobart], or some place just a little short of Christ Church [St. Laurence] [High Church] practice, while sound in Catholic Doctrine, she's "Miss Minami Oka." Aged 58. Rich in Catholic Devotion; meditates and prays in English but otherwise is Japanese; a mine of information about Japan and the N.S.K. through the last 50 years; quite "Western" in liberty, for the old woman in Japan has always had liberty denied to younger people. We work over my Bible Study notes before and after; she's correcting my reading of the mass; she already brings in people, and stories about people, which give me an insight into the present. And she knows how to go home at the right time! She comes each morning at 8.30 and stays till about 10.30 or so. She has even probed into the matter of my hours of work and sleep and warned me about "Japan head."[35] She thanked me for arranging and having the St. James' Day Mass and said how she looks forward to future such. If I do nothing else but learn from her what life in N.S.K. has meant and means, and help her in it, it will have been worthwhile.

And yet I thing the most important thing about her is that she's a fruit of the Church's Ministry here in Japan and surely she's not the last...

The men are also making a concrete lid for the concrete tank down the garden where my western style "benjo" [toilet] empties into what I had fondly hoped was an equally Western septic tank but have since followed my nose and found to be just plain Japan. However a close fitting lid will make a difference.

I've said this bath making is the Lammas first fruits of appreciation. Another equally helpful "harvest" will come through from its "cultivation phase" early next week when the Local Electricity Supply Co. (Big Show with Head Office in Yokohama) connects new power lines to give me a reasonable electricity service for all my fuel needs. It took many visits to many offices of U.S.A., B.C.O.F., and

---

35 Probably a local term for "going off one's rocker" from overwork, heat and lack of sleep.

Japanese Governments to find out just why I was getting nowhere fast on this matter. Then at last it was all whittled down to the matter of getting [the] local supply company to deal with me, through a specially made S.C.A.P. loophole, as a private citizen. They could easily have put me next on the list of local citizens but the manager, when he heard that I'd like this done before winter, said "He has come to Japan on a very holy mission and we must do him our best service." So, quite quickly they've worked along to the point of connecting the newly installed transformer brought down from Yokohama. I'll have to pay ¥6,000 odd, = A£40 approx., for work which in Australia would be done at the company's expense; but I'm quite pleased to be able to do so because it helps clarify the fact that I'm here quite independently of Army & Military government. It's a £40 investment in light and liberty. . .

Ogata-san's mother [is] passing by to feed her 2 hens which are still kept where she had them when she lived here in this house, that is under the house eaves just outside the bathroom! Near enough to "in the house" – but there's no room for them in the little house they're now in, and 2 hens means eggs occasionally for the two children and eggs cost Australian 1/6 d. each in the town. So I suffer the chooks and even provide some food for them.

But the men bustled off at 5 p.m. after telling me they'd be back in a week to put the finished surface on the bath – at present it's really skid proof. I did my best to tell them how grateful I am and the contractor responded by pressing me to call at his home when I go down to Kawana shortly.

They had no sooner left than 5 hikers arrived. They were Hatano Church lads and lasses passing through Odawara on way home so called to meet me. Hatano is one of the country centres I'm to visit regularly from next month for Bible Study and services. It's very sound the way a Bible Study is made the basis of church work – and of course I love it. I'll be doing the St. Luke study in 4 centres from September onwards so my present Odawara study preparation [in Japanese] is well worth the time it takes. The Hatano folk were very shy. 2 lasses, 2 lads, and the father of one of the lads. Minami Oka-san came up with them and introduced them. That was quite a feat – getting them to loose their tongues. Then after they'd subsided again into silence for some minutes she did just the right thing. She said goodbye to them and said to me, in English, that she'd go because they'd probably be easier with me by myself. They were and we were soon having quite a lively conversation and even got as far as joking together. After they'd had tea, biscuits and cake (tinned fruit cake!) they left at 6 for a train from Odawara to Hatano. Odawara is a good centre to be in because several "routes" meet here and there are often people passing through who can stop for an hour or so. In fact, while I entertained the Hatano folk, Fr. Nosse arrived [later Bishop of South Tokyo Diocese], but stayed down at Murota-san's and had a bath before going on a bit after 6.00 to see his father in a nearby village. Fr. Nosse is another of the great souls of N.S.K. A tremendously keen Catholic. He's one of the principal people engaged in Prayer Book, Doctrine & Liturgical revision for N.S.K. just now and is making great use of my library. Perhaps later I'll tell you a lot more about him.

Mike [Mi-ke the cat] has this minute caught a beetle by swiping at it as it flew by! I've great hopes for her as a rat catcher.

After the Hatano folk had gone I had tea – what Ogata-san calls "Friday Food" – she's gradually learning to make my Friday evening dish of macaroni and fish. In a few month's time I'll teach her another one. After tea I went down to Fr. Miyazawa's to tell him no need for his son to bring me sand and pebbles tomorrow. We talked a while in the balmy evening quiet. Coming back a patter of running feet behind me made me wonder who was running me down. It was Fumio Hagihara. He's one of my "pick ups" – aged 17 & real St. Cuth's [St. Cuthbert's, East Brunswick] fellowship type. He's one of a group of 4. Last night he and another helped print photos, some of which I'll enclose. He's not very expert yet, but looks as though he might get a real interest in it. But tonight he wanted to take me to his house. So I went. It's a shop cum house and we sat on the front door step at footpath level and yarned for a while about cabbages, cats, the Buddhist funeral rites across the road for a Japanese soldier killed 3 years ago and whose fate has only just been notified; "dame desu"! (Japanese = "Poor show"! but I say it suspiciously like "Damn me" – so does Ogata-san!) While we talked half a dozen or so gathered round (Fig. 10); and his mother gave me a fan to use – which I did, as every self respecting male does in Japan. I've teemed up with Fumio and 4 others to go to see the old film "Boys' Town" week of the next at the local show and we're going [on] a day's hike in the mountains shortly. Of course, all along the line we talk about many things and they show a natural interest in the Church. [Rest of letter lost.]

Figure 10 The "neighbourhood" in the castletown of Odawara, August, 1947.

***Newsletter No. 3*, 15 August 1947.**

NIPPON SEIKO KWAI

> Aust. Army Post Office,
> C/- Empire House,
> B.C.O.F.,
> Tokyo,
> JAPAN.

From – Rev. Frank W. Coaldrake

Dear Friends,

15th July

I'm on my way up to Yokohama on business, to finalize, I hope, my arrangements about electric power for my house. I am to lunch with some fine American people and shop with them at their Army Store this afternoon for a few things our own depot hasn't got – sand-soap and "fresh" eggs, which in Odawara cost 1/6 d. each (Aust.). I'm travelling in a baggage car! It's a bit crowded, but I am sitting on a suitcase (when the other carriages are spilling people out of doors and windows they invade the baggage van). Rail traffic is terrific on this line where they run electric trains of 15 carriages every 10–20 minutes, 18 hours a day; like a suburban rail service as far as from Newcastle to Sydney and they are always packed.

Things are working along smoothly. There are more than enough decent human persons in this country no matter how many bad ones there might also be.

22nd July

Tuesday, is Tokyo Day this week because Frank Davis has to be in Tokyo on his way back to Kure after spending 5 days with me on special leave. It has been good having him here and you'll be seeing him when he reaches Melbourne for discharge in a month or two. We have enjoyed together a bit of "touring" of town and district round Odawara. The little I have now seen of the "hinterland" has whetted my appetite for what awaits me along the years ahead. It reminds me of Tamborine Queensland or Dandenongs in Victoria but so much grander and more extensive.

Over the weekend we also had as guests Ethel Lewis and an American G.I. – It was a happy week-end for all. I did a lot of work between times while Ethel typed some reports for me – she was one of the faithful helpers in my parish of St. Cuthbert's, E. Brunswick, Melbourne, during my period there as Vicar 1942–44, and is now Secretary to Col. Abbott in Tokyo, on the staff of Australian Reparations Commission.

Before Church each Sunday night I have a Bible Class of boys to study St. Luke's Gospel in English and Japanese. After Church I talk for an hour with the

Japanese Vicar and helpers about Church matters, and 3 hours of solid Japanese language leaves me fairly tired, still I get used to it as Odawara town and parish consists entirely of Japanese people. They are a bewildered people needing the helping hand of fellowship from Australian Christians. To spend all next day in the hills with Frank Davis was a good corrective, as he also was a frequent visitor at St. Cuthbert's when his military wanderings allowed.

Conveniences in the house proceed gradually. I now have a good water supply in the kitchen and bathroom. Mrs. Murota-san saw my biscuit-tin-ice-box and produced a small ice-chest made in Tokyo, steel, finished in white enamel. Ice can be bought on my way home from Church each morn for a total cost of 3/1d. (Aust.) per week.

My book-keeping is an involved business – because I trade mainly with yen and sterling, and occasionally do business with Americans on dollar basis but accounts to Australia must be in Australian figures – fortunately for me only on a small scale at present.

I look forward to my weekly visit to Tokyo mainly to collect my mail and it's good to have I can assure you. Today I had some dated 16/7/47 in Melbourne, so they are only 6 days old (by Airmail) – goodo! Am getting busier each day, so will you please accept this *Newsletter* in answer to all your kindness.

Sunday 27th July

Things in the house improve gradually as I get time to work on them. I've been here one month now and a very happy month too. Days are full of a mixture of doings. Every day is different, but to take last Saturday as an example will show you the general lay-out of life here. Up at 6 a.m. and in Church by 7 for prayers and meditation, afterwards a few words with Fr. Miyazawa. His youngest grandchild has measles and I was able to give him some fruit juice and butter [to] supplement the very inadequate diet, and later some bread and syrup. Home via the Ice Shop to get a block for my little "bachelor's" ice chest. Breakfast at 8 a.m. or a bit before, I get for myself (crispies or rice bubbles, Queensland canned pineapple and powdered milk, toast, marmalade and tea.)

Ogata-san arrives at 8 a.m. and goes about the rostered duties, Saturday is odd cleaning, mending, and looking after visitors. Minamioka-san, my tutor, arrives at 8.30 a.m. every day (except Sunday and Monday). We had just settled down to language work when my first visitors arrived. Sgt. John Haine of Staff, Kawana B.C.O.F. Rest Centre and U.S.A. friend called on their way from Tokyo to Kawana. John is an old boy of C.E.G.S.[36] Brisbane, and All Souls, Charters Towers – we have many mutual friends in Queensland. He brought a parcel of things from Kawana Store. I spent only a few minutes with these visitors, then Ogata-san served tea to go with their package of sandwiches, while I went on with my studies till Minamioka-san left at 10 a.m., after morning tea.

---

36 Church of England Grammar School.

From 10 a.m. to 1.30 I worked in the kitchen repairing the dish-washing and draining system. At 1.30 p.m. I had lunch, which Ogata-san prepared before going home for hers, (bread and cheese, honey, vegemite and tea). Work again until 3 p.m., when by arrangement a visit from Minamioka-san, Murota-san, her married youngest daughter and two boys Yasuhiro (Jonathan) aged 5, and Matahiru (Timothy) aged 10, all Seiko Kwai Christians and very fine people. I showed them the Altar Cards I'd had on the Altar here for St. James' Mass on Friday morning [25 July]. (Fig. 11) I must write to Betty Simpson[37] and tell her how much they appreciated her wonderful work on those "cards." We then looked at photos of Australian Churches and they were particularly interested in the fine pictures which are included in Mrs. Allen's *History of Christ Church S. Laurence, Sydney.*[38] Those people have a deep faith and quite an experience of the Christian life behind them, which we are gradually writing down, so that Australians may learn just how deeply the Christian faith can grip Japanese people. Of course, I expected I would find this, but finding it is quite a joy. One thing I learn, a reassurance that here in Japan, in the fellowship of the Church, we have the well of life from which to draw, just as I found in the Church in Australia. Come wind, come weather, you need have no fear for my welfare while I know this.

On August 10th (St. Laurence Day), I am to say the whole service in Japanese for the first time. Language in conversation is one thing, but the conduct of a Service in Classical Language is quite another. I am very fortunate to have found such a good tutor.

These visitors left at 5 o'clock and I was able to give them some butter and Vegemite for a cousin, 10 years old, suffering from TB. Vegemite and Marmite are the handiest things to have in full supply because many people get enough quantity of food, but suffer from defective balance of diet, and lack of vitamins.

At 5.30 p.m. more visitors came. Kunimi-san and his student brother, who is studying dentistry at University in Tokyo, and belongs to the English Speaking Society. Kunami-san is in the local Electricity Company and has been most helpful in getting my supply onto a satisfactory basis. We talked about many things including English literature, the Bible and Christianity. They stayed for an hour and after they had gone, while I was feeding the cat (I have to lock it in the bathroom like a naughty boy while visitors are here because it licks and scratches their bare feet – great fun for the cat!) I bumped my head on a low roof outside, again, but this time it was a galvanised iron edge and put a small gash in my scalp. With a handkerchief around my head I sat down to eat. Ogata-san goes home when tea is ready at 6 p.m. and it was now 7 p.m. when two more visitors came. Two lads this time, whom I met in the local Junk Shop.

---

37 A parishioner from St. Cuthbert's Church, East Brunswick, Melbourne. Later Lady Elizabeth Haddon-Cave.

38 Laura Mary Allen, *A History of Christ Church S. Laurence*, Sydney, L.M. Allen, 1939.

Figure 11 Frank Coaldrake's altar in the Odawara farmhouse, 1947.

We had an interesting talk there and they had accepted my invitation to "come and see me sometime." They had already had tea so sat and looked at books, while I ate my hot meal, which consisted of fresh beef (a luxury twice a month), fresh potatoes, tinned peas, preceded by soup yielded in cooking the beef, and followed by tinned peaches and tinned milk, with tea. (This answers many queries as to my diet). They stayed till 10 p.m. Both go to High School and neither is Christian. Their English is about as good as my Japanese, so yarning is sometimes tripped up till we call in dictionaries. Nice lads – Fukuda and Hagikara [sic] are their "given" names, which correspond to our Christian names.

After they had gone I said my evening prayers and prepared for Sunday, then to bed about 11 p.m. I generally sleep sometime between 11 p.m. and 6 a.m., more or less, as mosquitoes are plentiful, but a burning coil keeps them under control. Nights are very hot, as the sea breeze, which is a wonderful asset during the day, does not blow after sunset. The weather here is unbelievably trying and will be, after several years in Melbourne and Sydney, until I am acclimatised. Humidity is very high, even worse than Rockhampton in Queensland, but my house on the hill is in one of the coolest spots and I wear only light shirt and shorts except for Church and visiting. My umbrella has been used often on hot glaring days, also for odd showers. When you think of it – the old sun at 11 a.m. here is scorching us, while you in Melbourne are shivering in spite of the same sun shining over you at noon on the same day. In a few months our positions will be reversed and I am told to expect snow round here.

29th July

Sincere thanks to all you good people for sending stamps, newspapers, letters and other interesting items. Some of you have enquired about my "eats" – well, I have to collect rations from Army stores in Tokyo mostly and am eating well out of "cans." I was invited recently to a Japanese ceremonial meal of welcome – "supper" at 6 p.m. The meal was very palatable, except for the raw fish. I managed the chop-sticks O.K. to their huge delight, but as to "squatting" I started off in true style, kneeling position but sitting on heels. However, I was very relieved when our host said to me "sit easy" and after that I sat the way I learnt at Boy Scouts camp, legs crossed in front tailor-fashion, to eat from the customary low table. They made me very welcome, were full of questions about Australia, and quite a bit surprised when I told them what most Australians think about Japanese. I thought we should start from "tors." It was good though to be able to tell what some other Australians think along more helpful lines.

I have taken some photos I hope to send later. (Fig. 12) Also, I made a record in Tokyo, which is to be used in Youth Sunday (Aust.) Broadcast, August 3rd. It has Japanese girls as well speaking to the youth in Australia. A Girls' School uses Odawara Church building during the week, and I am teaching them English.

Whilst visiting Tokyo one is amazed at the shopping centre called The Ginza – stalls on footpaths like Melbourne or Sydney fruit barrows – attractive goods and souvenirs at daylight robbery prices – too costly to even think of buying.

I am invited to meet Dr. Evatt[39] in Tokyo next week, but doubt if I can spare time to talk politics.

5th August

In Tokyo today and busy all day – hoping to call in at Zushi on my way home to see Bishop Sugai. He is a sick man as result of war-time imprisonments and present inadequate foods. I will be helping him again 2 days this week for Japanese Clergy meetings.

Each morning also this week I am addressing at a Girls Summer School – in English, translated by Fr. Miyazawa – my subject is Australia. It's a poor way to do things and I must work harder at the language to get over it.

Will Mother please send me 1 bottle-cleaning brush, 1 Cookery book of simple recipes (including bread-making and fruit-preserving), 1 floor-mop-head (without handle) to save Ogata-san wearisome back-bending.

I am so busy with my parish work I can't do much to complete my house at present, but an Army friend arranged for a building contractor with 4 workmen to make a concrete bath in my bathroom – a great blessing! Also, my new electric supply is now hooked-up at cost of 6,000 (yen) – a local product.[40]

---

39 Dr. H.V. Evatt was Australian Attorney-General and Minister for External Affairs from 1941 to 1949.

Figure 12 Odawara "locals," 1947.

I am to try and arrange for a whole month's rations to be brought by Army Jeep to the foot of "my hill" tomorrow.

From baggage car this morning, rice fields looked beautiful to the eye, but in moist weather rather offensive to the nose.

I now have photos and material ready to write up for papers.

Hoping you are all as well and happy as I am,

　　FRANK

P.S. "Friends of Odawara" in Victoria have agreed to form a group in order to send practical help to the sick and needy of Odawara parish in Japan. Those desiring to join are asked to contact Miss Rae Campbell, Brighton Rd., Dandenong, Victoria, Hon. Secretary. One idea is to gather in clean used, or new, woollen underclothing and slippers for their coming winter.

For copies of *Newsletters* apply to:

Mrs. E.R. Coaldrake,
70 Denbigh Road,
ARMADALE. S.E.3 VIC.

---

40 As noted in the commentary to this chapter, this was nearly twice the wage earner's average monthly salary at the time, and there was no provision in the mission's budget to cover this unexpected expenditure.

Newsletter No. 4, 19 August 1947.

Odawara Shi, Jujimachi, 2 Chome, 289, Ephu, Corudoreiku

> But post to:
> C/- Aust. Army Post Office,
> Empire House,
> B.C.O.F.,
> Tokyo,
> JAPAN.

From – Rev. Frank W. Coaldrake

"Haha" Dear,

That's not just being jocular, because "haha" is Japanese for "Mother."

These are extracts from letters written by Rev. Frank W. Coaldrake to his mother and sister [Joyce], who compile this *Newsletter.*

———

Dear Friends,

Japanese civil mails are censored, therefore, it is better if you address as above to B.C.O.F. at the rates required for mail to B.C.O.F. personnel, 3½ d. per oz. and it will travel by Air in about a week.

"Odawara" is a place practically unknown in Australia except to a few students of Japanese History. In history it has fame as the site of a great castle which capitulated after a novel siege. That was in the Middle Ages. A great mound of earth and rock surrounded still by the original moat, is all that remains of the castle, since the last of it tumbled down in an earthquake forty years ago. The extensive grounds inside the moat are now used for Government schools with a total of over two thousand pupils. There was not much serious material damage done to the city during the war. It received only one major air raid, in the last week of the war.

The citizens of Odawara do not seem to understand much about what they are now going through. In this, as in many other things, Odawara is typical of all Japan outside Tokyo. Its sixty thousand citizens present in miniature a picture of seventy million Japanese. I write about Odawara rather than any other place, because it is the place to which I have come. Moving freely round the town and country, meeting people in home, office, and place of work, I have found many things which will interest and perhaps surprise many people outside Japan.

Odawara nestles on the shore of Sagami bay, forty miles south of Tokyo. The sixty thousand "Odawarriors" are crowded on a bayside flat of one mile long and a quarter mile wide. Very few buildings have two floors, none have more because of earthquake risk, so there is a heavy concentration of population. Australians who know Ballarat might try to imagine what it would be like to crowd all Ballarat's sixty thousand people into a quarter square mile of single story buildings, and put most of the factories into the houses with the people. Odawara is nothing if not congested. In the "slum" part of the city, conditions beggar description. (Fig. 13) In other parts there are fine mansions set in beautiful

Figure 13 Odawara slum. Three homeless people outside their drainpipe home, c. 1948.

gardens. We have here the Toorak and the Fitzroy neighbourhoods. I can see already many tasks of the kind I have been used to in the Brotherhood of St. Laurence in Fitzroy.

The Parish of the Holy Cross, Odawara, covers the city area and spreads out into the farmland valleys and mountain holiday resorts in the hinterland. The first Church building was opened in 1899, and served until the present buildings were opened in 1927. The buildings are substantial concrete and timber structures, designed by a Japanese architect who successfully blended Japanese detail with traditional Church architecture. The simple dignity and beauty of the Church is itself an inspiration – or it could be if there were money to spend on repairs. Much against its will, the parish had to neglect repairs during the war, and since then because the financial position everywhere, and in the Church in a particular way, has been desperate.

The Church has a roomy entrance porch in which sandals are left during the services, for it is the Japanese custom to walk on polished floors or mats only in slippers, sox or bare feet. These floors are polished wood. It is strange at first to conduct a service in one's sox, but one is reassured by a sight such as a solemn sidesman with bare feet taking up the collection. Two of the Japanese features of the building are sliding screens in place of some of the hinged doors, and woodwork finished beautifully but without paint or varnish.

The Church stands in a garden in the centre of a city block. In the same grounds are three other buildings. A large Kindergarten provides for about sixty and it is run on what we would call "normal kindergarten lines," but there is a sad dearth of materials, and many window panes are missing. Because of its garden setting it is called "Eden Kindergarten." The other two buildings are residences. One is for the Parish Priest, the other for the Kindergarten Superintendent.

Steadiness is the most noticeable thing about the life of the Church. A description of it in detail would read like the description of almost any parish in Australia, no better, no worse, but it is surprising after all we have heard about the Japanese in recent years. One of the immediately noticed differences is that at the services everybody sings. If the result does not always add the beauty of harmony to the proceedings, it certainly adds always to the sense of unity in the worship.

The other churches in Odawara are the Roman Catholic, Methodist, Greek Orthodox, and Plymouth Brethren. All have native clergy and I am the only European.

The Parish Priest, the Rev. Kumazo Miyazawa, has served the whole of his twenty-five years as a priest of this parish. He came to it after spending three years in the Mission Field in Korea. He is a scholar, well read in the Japanese Classics and has had articles on such subjects published overseas. He is an able organiser, but I must admit that the methods by which Japanese people organise things among themselves are incomprehensible to me, and often I am left standing. Overseas friends of mine who have met him have remarked on his very evident happiness – I play with the word "vivacity" to describe it. His sermons are marked by this characteristic animation. They are, moreover, pithy and short. Soon after he came to Odawara he married a local girl. With their family they are, as I have myself seen, widely known and respected in this community. He has been a faithful priest through many years of hardship and persecution. The Government put their Bishops into prison, expecting to intimidate the parish priests. He was among those who carried on in quietness and confidence. He faces the cryptic future as the pastor of a small flock. He could be pardoned if he were dismayed at the prospects of hard work amid increasing shortages. He may be dismayed, but I can catch not the slightest hint of it. Yes, I find a Light shining in Odawara.

Fuller reports on parish work have been sent to *A.B.M. Review, Church Standard* and *Australian Christian World*.

The death of the Right Rev. Todomu Sugai, Bishop of South Tokyo and Presiding Bishop of the Nippon Seiko Kwai, occurred on Thurs. Aug. 14th, 1947, at the age of 65, at his home in Zushi, 25 miles south of Tokyo.

According to the custom in Japan two services were held in the Church on the day following death, before the body was taken to the Crematorium. At a later date there will be a final service for the burial of the ashes. In the congregation were the late Bishop's wife, children and grandchildren, relatives, friends and colleagues. Many had come long distances to be present. There was not room in the Church for everyone. Among the congregation were three overseas clergy, Bishop Mann of England, Rev. K.A. Viall of the United States Episcopal Church [S.S.J.E.], and myself.

When I last spoke with the Bishop, forty-eight hours before his death, he asked me to write for him in answer to a letter which had recently come from the Chairman of the Australian Board of Missions, dealing with final preparations for the forthcoming "Goodwill Mission" from the Australian Anglican Church to the Japanese Church. Bishop Sugai was anxious to know whether plans for receiving the Goodwill Mission were well in hand. I was able to assure him they were. Then he said how sorry he was that he might not be well enough to attend their meetings. "Would you please write to the Chairman for me," he said, "and tell him we are very glad and interested in the prospect of new links with the Australian Missions." Those were to be his last words for Australia. The day after he died the Goodwill Mission landed in Tokyo by special plane from Australia. The Archbishop of Brisbane,[41] the Bishop of Tasmania,[42] Canon Warren,[43] and the Revs. L. Nash and Ian Shevill comprised the Mission.

I went from Bishop Sugai's funeral service to meet the Australians. Their arrival is most timely for they can encourage and support the Japanese Church in the hour of bereavement and loss of leadership. It is to be hoped that as a result of their visit the "links" Bishop Sugai spoke about will be made stronger and more numerous.

The late Todomu Sugai was a scholarly and saintly little man. He was consecrated Bishop for the Diocese of South Tokyo in July 1941. He was among those Anglican Church leaders who, during the war, spent some time in prison including Bishops Sasaki and Yashiro. Two of three Bishops have now died, their end being hastened by their gaol experiences. Bishop Sasaki died last December. He had been the Presiding Bishop, and it was after his death that Bishop Sugai was appointed Presiding Bishop. He has been leading a very strenuous life also as Principal of the Central Theological College in which he lectured in three subjects. The wonder is that, in his crippled condition, he did not break down sooner.

During the two months since I first met him I have seen enough of him to attempt a brief estimate of his worth. He was always quiet and unassuming. He

---

41 Most Reverend Reginald Charles Halse (1881–1962), Anglican Archbishop of Brisbane from 1943 to 1962. See: *Australian Dictionary of Biography*, vol. 14, pp. 362–364.

42 Geoffrey Franceys Cranswick (1894–1978), Anglican Bishop of Tasmania from 1943 to 1962. See: *Australian Dictionary of Biography*, vol. 13, pp. 525–527.

43 Canon Max Warren, Secretary of A.B.M., who had recently been made a canon.

did not have it in his character to lead by domination, but his leadership was real and inspiring. We have heard in Australia very frequently during recent years that it is a Japanese trait to seize upon a belief with fanatical zeal and willingly die for that faith. Todomu Sugai had a faith for which he had suffered imprisonment under appalling conditions, risked a quick death, and endured a slow dying. He had the quiet smiling eyes of a whimsical old gentleman, the heavy brows and deep-set furrowed eyes of a scholar, the slender delicate hands of an aesthete and ascetic, the soft slow hesitant speech, whether in Japanese or English, of a self-effacing man. These things were plain to the eye and ear and they left no room or need for the falsities of fanaticism. There have been Japanese fanatics. We probably cannot forget it. But let us also not forget that there have been Japanese men of serene Christian faith. These men do not die in a blaze of glory. Their death is simply the end of a life of dying daily.

It was evident at the service in St. Peter's church that people were feeling the loss of one who had upheld them because he himself had found a rock to stand on. They sang their alleluias with the intention of thanksgiving for a life of witness and service, but they sang them in a mood of solemnity which gave the music an unusually resonant quality. It was mourning in music, and mourning which was costing great effort.

(This account had been written before the words of the Hon. A.A. Calwell[44] appeared in the Japanese Press, *Nippon Times*, 18/8/47. Mr. Calwell's callous generalisation and my story cannot both be true. "Five years of occupation is too short a time to humanize or democratize those barbarians," said Hon. A.A. Calwell, Australian Minister for Immigration.)

Sunday 24th August

The Goodwill Mission visited Odawara on Wed. 20th August and Archbishop Halse, Canon Warren and Rev. Ian Shevill stayed with me that night – in fact Ian remained for 5 days to take Films for A.B.M. to show all over Australia in a few months time. We borrowed a Jeep to get around in and I'm guessing you are going to enjoy some fine pictures.

You will hear reports of the Goodwill Mission's "findings" after they return to Australia early in September – it was good seeing them here.

With best wishes to you all,

FRANK

P.S. In reply to those who have asked for suggestions about suitable parcels to send to Odawara – there is practically no soap in Japan, but it is unwise to pack it in with food. Any dried fruits are useful and vegemite or marmite, chocolate in blocks, barley sugar, peanut or lemon butter.

Films for camera – Kodak No. 120 Super XX.

---

44 Arthur Augustus Calwell (1896–1973) was Australia's first Minister for Immigration from 1945 to 1949. See: *Australian Dictionary of Biography*, vol. 13, pp. 341–345.

Please send stamps for regular copies of these Newsletters to:–

Mrs. E.R. Coaldrake
70 Denbigh Rd.,
ARMADALE. S.E.3 VIC.

Newsletter No. 5, 20 September 1947.

C/- Aust. Army Post Office,
Empire House,
B.C.O.F.,
Tokyo,
JAPAN.

From – Rev. Frank W. Coaldrake

Dear Friends,

As Friday the 15th August was the most memorable day of my first few months in Japan, I would like to add a few more "sidelights" about it in this letter.

I was up at 6 a.m. to find my bathroom flooded, because when I finished plumbing late the night before I forgot to see that all the taps were turned off tightly. In the best Heath-Robinson style I had gathered from Junk Shop and Army Store empty tins and tap to concoct a home-made shower. From the dribbling main tap over the bath, water runs through rubber tubing into a hollow curtain rod up to the ceiling where it flows into a 4-gallon Minties tin. From that reservoir a tap runs into a 5-lb. jam tin slung from the ceiling by 3 strings, and holes in the bottom of jam tin provide a refreshing shower. That morning, for the first time in Japan, I showered, with thoughts of gratitude to my Army friend and his Japanese contractor with four workmen who had built-in my concrete bath, finished with Green Glaze, a week earlier. Then off down to Church at 7 a.m. specially remembering Bishop Sugai, to whose funeral I was to go later in the day. On my way back a little block of ice cost 2/6 d. Aust. because the local supply was having a holiday and this ice came 20 miles by train. (I need ice to save losing foodstuffs.)

After breakfast for a few minutes I enjoyed the freshness and quiet of my front garden path, with the sea lying quietly in the distance and from its shore a carpet of trees dotted with housetops sloping up to my house on the hill. The sea-breeze was not yet blowing and the great Camphor Laurel tree drooped motionless leaves, while the White Hibiscus by the rock pool opened its buds to the new day. That was the last such moment of quiet in that day for me.

At 9 a.m. with three Japanese members of Odawara congregation, who travelled as my guests in "Allied Personnel" car, I was in the train to Zushi. When we arrived at St. Peter's Church the funeral service had started. This was a gathering to mourn the passing of a beloved friend and leader. The tone of the whole was in harmony with the note of joy through faith in the life after death. It was very moving. On the way to Zushi we had passed many country houses on which gay Japanese lanterns were hanging as a part of the current Shinto-Buddhist festival of O-Bon (The Lantern). At this one time in each year the old believers prepare for a visit from the spirits of the fairly recently departed. The spirits are guided to their old homes by the lanterns. When the time comes for the spirits to return they are provided with a tiny horse made of threads. After they have ridden away on this horse it is burned and the festival is over for the year. Things were different in the Church. Any Japanese who has understood the Buddhist or Shinto Faiths about the life of a person's spirit after death has a sense of spiritual, as opposed to material, values which the Christian Faith fulfils. There will be no thread horses prepared for Todomu Sugai – no Japanese lanterns will be hung to guide the steps of his returning spirit. The lights that burned around his bier were for our benefit, not his. They reminded us of the Light of the World; they spoke of the qualities of Light and Peace which he would now know. There is no hankering after the lanterns and horses because the belief in the life after death is not denied but transformed into something which rings more true.

There had been a Requiem in the Church early in the morning and those who had gathered had renewed their fellowship in the Community of Saints, knowing that Todomu Sugai was one soul who had shown in his life here that he, if any, was worthy to be found a place in that Community. These were the meditations of my heart.

What Australians are finding it hard to realise is that there are, and always have been, some Japanese who are quiet, sincere, human persons like you and me. Todomu Sugai was one. He suffered as so many Australian boys did at the hands of the other kind of Japanese. With no great stretch of imagination we can see him as one who was a "P.O.W." in Japanese hands, with the additional agony of knowing that it was his own countrymen who were acting on so degraded a level. I wish I could more effectively open to you the hearts of the fine people one meets. As to the others, they press upon one in the crowds and one cannot see much of what lies behind the facade of friendship called forth by the liberal occupation policy. There may be some truth in the assertion that most of the appearances are an assumed facade to cloak deep intrigues. If that is so it makes more urgent the task of transforming potential enemies into real friends, and no matter how you look at it the only way to do that is by the offer of friendship, taking the risk that it will be exploited. The fact that we take risks is the final instrument for winning friends.

From Zushi to Tokyo I travelled in a Jeep. It was a strange Jeep-load. There were Bishop Mann, Fr. Viall, and myself, from England, America and Australia respectively, and Bishop Makita of Tokyo. All the long hot dusty drive we held an informal conference on International Liaison of Anglican Missions. Incidentally we discovered that Occupation Authorities have given different instruction to Bishop Mann and myself. He has been told he must ride in Japanese trains and never use the special cars for Allied persons – I have been told I am liable to arrest if I travel in Japanese trains and must ride in Allied cars. I am not permitted to buy a ticket, he must have one. So, officially, I must enjoy luxury while the Bishop emulates sardines. It does not make sense.

Empire House swallowed me for the afternoon in an attempt to straighten out some more of the tangles about my supplies. The more I try to improve things the worse they get. The only reason I continue to try and clear up the Army situation is that it would be better to have the thing on a permanent basis.

The evening meal fitted in very conveniently in John Forsyth's[45] home, in one wing of Commonwealth House. A short time after I was called for by Tom Eckersley[46] and Chaplain Chase. The latter is attached to the Far Eastern Air Force of the U.S. Army. He has done a splendid job organising the details of the visit of the Australian Anglican "Goodwill Mission." They took me out with them to the Haneda Airport and we saw the Liberator land. It was good to meet old friends as they came from the plane. They had left Melbourne only four days before! Several cars took the party through Tokyo's poorly lit streets to the house where they were all to stay while in Tokyo. This car ride was their first contact with Japan. It must have been a strange experience to drop suddenly out of the skies into the midst of Tokyo's millions. Soon after their arrival at the house Mr. McMahon Ball paid a short informal visit just to see that everything was in order.

Leaving the visitors at 9 p.m. I made for Tokyo Central Station to catch an Odawara train. I just missed one, so caught a train to Yokohama, the first third of the journey, because there was a queue of hundreds already waiting for the next train to Odawara. At Yokohama, at midnight, there was another long queue – a distressing sight, these queues waiting for hours in all sorts of weather, children asleep on concrete, mothers rocking babies on their backs, and over all an atmosphere of wonder and weariness.

When the Odawara train pulled in to Yokohama I oozed my way into the front carriage and took up my stand in the passage between the rows of double seats. No description of mine could do justice to the scene in that dimly lit carriage. Through the open end door could be seen the glint of metal as the powerful electric loco. rocked along at high speed, and occasionally a lurid blue-green flash from the overhead powerline showed endless rice fields, with their waters reflecting weird lights and shadows. Inside the carriage as people get tired they sag down and many sleep on the floor, while youth finds its way into the narrow luggage racks, and the standers lean until they seem to melt among the sitters. There were as usual 15 carriages in the train and every one of them a shadowy tangled mass of hot tired people.

Near me was a middle-aged woman with a large bundle tied on her back and as she nodded in uneasy sleep I was afraid she would fall to the floor. One young mother with her babe tied on her back was sitting on her heels on the seat with her head on her arms on the window sill fast asleep. On another seat a wide awake father watched his two little girls, the elder about 10 years of age fixing a

---

45 John Forsyth was Third Secretary and interpreter to the Australian Mission to Japan. See: Alan Rix (ed.), *Intermittent Diplomat*, p. 283.

46 Tom J. Eckersley was the Australian Political Liaison Officer with the Supreme Commander for the Allied Powers (S.C.A.P.). See: Alan Rix (ed.), *Intermittent Diplomat*, p. 100.

cloth bundle as a cushion to make her little sister comfortable and giving her sips from a water-bottle. After an hour of standing and sagging I was looking for the name of a station when the alert father volunteered the information and we were soon exchanging brief personal histories. He had been a Professor of Horticulture at a university in Tokyo until 3 years ago, and was now a farmer. He knew a few English and a few German words so we were able to converse fairly well with my sprinkling of Japanese. After a while he said suddenly in English "I hate Japan" and before I thought of an appropriate reply he added "I hate America." I was wondering where the hate session would travel next when he said "but I have God." With an unspoken feeling of joy I then took the reins of the conversation and found he had learnt to hate the illusions and shadows of this troubled world with the word "hate" used in the sense of "not understanding." He is a member of the United Christian Church of Japan, and we were soon discussing the origin and relation of Sanskrit and Aryan languages. Suddenly the train jarred to a standstill and remained stationary for about 10 minutes. Someone who went to see what was wrong came back as the train started again saying calmly in Japanese – "a young woman did suicide under the train." A few people made some comment and one woman said "stupid" in Japanese, while my farmer friend said "she had not God."

I was glad we reached Odawara a short time later at 2 a.m. and I found my way through a pitch-dark silent maze of narrow streets to my home, left spick and span by Ogata-san, with one light of welcome burning and my bed laid out on the tatami mat with inviting clean sheets. The long day finished as it began with a shower and prayers.

On the following Wednesday the Goodwill Mission came to visit Odawara by car, stopping along the way to see one ruined Church, one rebuilding Church, and one surviving Church. After lunch at my place we had a busy but pleasant round of functions. For 2 hours a dozen parish priests of this area came to talk with the Australians. Enough of the Japanese could speak English to have an interpreter with each Australian. Every quarter hour I moved everyone round to make a new group. Later about 50 Church members of Odawara came and we had afternoon tea with speeches interpreted each way. My house was crowded with 70 people in it. We went down to the Church for Evensong, followed by a quiet stroll through old parts of the town. For the evening meal six Australians and twelve Japanese priests were the guests of Mrs. Murota-san. It was a joyous occasion for everyone. At 8.30 p.m. Bishop Cranswick and his Chaplain returned to Tokyo on their way to Shanghai. Archbishop Halse, Canon Warren and Rev. Ian Shevill stayed overnight with me. Ian remained for 5 days to take films which I hope you will be able to see in Australia about November.

Tuesday 2nd September

The "Duntroon" has just arrived in Kure. If I had waited for her in Sydney, as originally intended, I'd have missed knowing Bishop Sugai, and still have in front of me all the work of getting to Odawara and settling in.

It seems that some people in Australia who want to come over as Missionaries cannot get clearances and supplies arranged. The B.C.O.F. organisation is still catching up with myself – one section or another realises I'm here and that they should "tape" the highly irregular proceedings that have resulted from my being here ahead of schedule. ("Dash it, he's here! I've seen him! Why couldn't he wait until we brought him in on paper! is the kind of reaction). Last week they finally settled the tangles around the sale of supplies to missionaries. Someone just took an Army ration scale, chopped off half the items, and put the list out as the Army's supply to missionaries. Canon Warren, at present in Tokyo, is arranging for bulk supplies to be sent from Australia. We yet have to wake the Army up to give permission for the Shipping Company to carry the goods, but I won't starve because many friends among Australian and Americans help to keep supplies in my cupboard.

Wednesday 10th September

My spare minutes while train travelling offer my best opportunity for writing, and I'm now on my way to Bishop Sugai's Memorial, to be conducted from the Church University in an outer suburb of Tokyo. It will be Friday night before I get back home because a Conference is being held of Priests of this Diocese at Zushi Church for 3 days. It arises out of the need to elect a new Bishop of South Tokyo, but many other things will be dealt with. We will all live at the Church Hall, conferring and eating there during the day, and at night roll swags out on the tatami mats to sleep. You can imagine I am looking forward to it. On Friday morning there will be an Ordination Service, when 33 year old Sakurai-san will be made a Deacon. I had him for 3 days Retreat with me at Odawara – it was good for me, and I hope for him.

Ogata-san learns slowly but surely how to make bacon and scrambled eggs out of tins to my liking, and her other accomplishment is a dish of macaroni and tinned fish. The mysteries of table setting still puzzle her.

My weekly routine has added to it now a Bible Class of 25 school girls each Wednesday and a full sermon in Japanese each Sunday.

At last my shortwave radio is working after some breakages on its travels.

It was good to find a lot of letters waiting for me at the Post Office. It is an unexpected pleasure to find that people who receive the *Newsletter* regard it as a letter from me and reply to me direct. That is very good – and certainly I write the letter as an extra long one to Mother, being able to put all the available time into one long letter, instead of many short ones.

Some anonymous writer in green ink is sending me a very useful selection of cuttings from Melbourne papers. The only possible "extra" I suggest might be an "illustrated," because my visitors mostly can only read pictures!

If sending parcels the 3 d. extra for registration at Post Office is worthwhile to protect safe delivery.

Yours sincerely
FRANK

***Newsletter No. 6*, 22 October 1947.**

C/- Aust. Army Post Office,
Empire House,
B.C.O.F.,
Tokyo,
JAPAN.

From – Rev. Frank W. Coaldrake

Dear Friends,

I've just been to Chiba and now at noon I'm in the train Tokyowards. Mt. Fuji is 50 miles South but today it can be seen clearly standing as a magnificent cone far above the reasonably high mountains between here and there.

I should have been at Chiba at 8 a.m. after spending the night with the parish priest of Ichikawa about 10 miles away, but yesterday afternoon a typhoon romped up the coast past Odawara to Tokyo. It did a lot of damage and stopped the trains for about 5 or 6 hours. Consequently I had to leave Odawara at 5 a.m. this morning, skip Ichikawa, and trust to the Angels to guide me to the people I had to meet in Chiba. Now my visit is over I think it will give you a good insight into the way the Occupation Authorities are related to Japanese local law and government, if I describe the day's doings.

It concerns the re-establishment of the Parish Church in Chiba. In June 1945 the Church, built by the only previous Australian Anglican Missionary in Japan, was destroyed by bombs intended for a factory over the road. The land is now being used by someone to grow potatoes. It will be a long time before it will be possible to rebuild the Church. In the meantime, there is no building for holding Church services and meetings, and nowhere for the parish priest to live. The local congregation wants to get a place but because over 40% of the town was destroyed there is a real housing shortage. Today I found myself in one of my own special paddyfields! Whether an owner can evict a tenant is the great question for Chiba Church at present. One member, a very old grandmother, owns a house which is occupied by a man reputed to be a bad character. The owner will let the parish priest have the house and hold services there if the "bad-egg" can be shifted. But the "bad-egg" has withstood two years of bowed requests to move. So the question was put to me last week, "Will you come with us to the Military Government Office about getting a house?" I didn't know what I could do, but agreed to go with the parish priest this morning. As soon as I came face to face with the Mil. Gov. Officer, I found he was a cove I'd met amongst friends in Tokyo some weeks back, so we started off by being all happy together.

There is a "Mil.Gov.Team" in every "County." This is a team of specialists in all phases of Government health, education, agriculture, industry, etc. They are the "Occupation Forces" in the internal Government of this country now, and the extent to which this team actually governs Chiba "County" is the exact extent of Occupation Gov.

This is how it works with regard to the Cuckoo in the Church nest. Mr. Mil.Gov. had no power to write an order to the Cuckoo to go. He would pay a call and try to edge the Cuckoo out, but the Cuckoo could easily call his bluff and sit tight.[47] If the house was wanted by Mr. Mil.Gov. for Oc. personnel to reside in, <u>then</u> Mr. Mil.Gov. could order Cuckoo out, but for all other purposes Mr. Cuckoo cannot be touched by Oc.Authorities. This is a matter for the Japanese "County" Court. None of us know anything about the Japanese law on tenants who sit tight, so Mr. Mil.Gov. 'phoned the Japanese County Procurator's Office, and asked if the Proc. would be good enough to come over and advise us. Mr. Mil.Gov. did <u>not</u> send a tommy-gunned soldier to serve a demand on the Proc.! The Proc. would be glad to come, but being busy with another case offered the help of his assistant. My friends of the local Church explained the matter to Mr. Assistant. Mr. Mil.Gov. and I sat and waited. Yes! The house owner would take legal action to move Mr. Cuckoo. My Church friends were reluctant to take Church matters to Court, but at my suggestion they went on to find out what would be involved. Mr. Cuckoo should be given a written advice that the owner desired his honourable absence. The owner should then wait six months. If Mr. Cuckoo was then still in residence he should be asked to hang his honourable self on the eyes of the most honourable County Court Judge. The Judge would listen to both sides of the case, and if he saw fit, try to persuade the Cuckoo to move. But never at any stage could the Judge order the local police to elbow the Cuckoo out. The only way Court proceedings could help would be for the Church people to get the neighbours to the Court, then proceed to blacken the name and character of Mr. Cuckoo, so that he would be ashamed to stay on in the neighbourhood and quietly fly away. This whole idea rather revolted my Church friends.

Then I butted in with more questions. Supposing I bought the house, could I get the Court Order to shift the Cuckoo so I could take possession of my new property? Only by the same process already described. I asked why? Because there are so few houses, people crippled by war might be turned out to live on the street. This reminded me so much of the Australian Housing Laws that I asked – "If I find another house for the Cuckoo to move into can I get the Court to order him to move?" No, the Court could only try to persuade him that his honourable ancestors would be delighted if he were to move. I asked if Mr. Mil.Gov. could help in any way. No, there was nothing he could do. You see how the Occupation set-up lets the Japanese run their own internal affairs, even though they muddle along. The legal machinery was never required to do the kind of things we are accustomed to use it for. The rule of law, and the resort to law has yet largely to be developed.

This picture of Occupation Policy is incomplete. Another side of it came into the picture when we tried to solve another problem. The part played by

---

47 This was a familiar situation to Frank Coaldrake after his campaigns to reform landlord and tenancy laws in Melbourne.

Mr. Mil.Gov. is far more vigorous because the matter is one which very vitally concerns the development of Democratic foundations in Japan, and it is one of the spheres of Japanese national life which the Potsdam Agreement specified as requiring Occupation intervention.

In another village our Church had a large block of farm land attached to the Church. The products of the farm helped support the parish priest. The latter was sent off into the Army and was killed. The house on the farm was then taken by a real "bad-egg." (He's extra bad because he keeps two wives to the scandal of the village folk. He's not the parish priest.). Now the Church has two difficulties. It does not know how it can oust the double-wifed gent, and its about to lose most of the land.

This shows Mr. Mil.Gov. in a new role. Mr. Big-Chief-Mil.Gov. has told Mr. Big-Chief-Jap.Gov. that his land holding system will have to be altered. No one must be allowed to own more than a certain small amount of land. As a result, Mr. Jap.Gov. in every village throughout Japan has ordered owners to sell their land over and above a certain area. This is having a remarkable effect on the life of the nation. Absent landlords are having to sell their land – but they don't get rich because Mr. Mil.Gov. waits around the corner. He has told Mr. Jap.Gov. that he'll have to take 90% from them in tax. So the rich become, not poor, but less rich, and small men are becoming owners of their own land. While I think Mr. Mil.Gov. has won a lot of points by this new Land Reform Law, it cannot always be pleasant when it applies to our own back-yard. The land in question was the property of the Diocesan Church Property Board. Mr. Jap.Gov. calmly says that this cannot be so, because in 1943 the Government ordered the Diocesan to cease to exist, so it could not have any land after that. Then our Church folk remembered that the Diocesan Board had transferred the ownership to the local Church congregation, as it did throughout the Anglican Church in Japan. At last it seems clear that the real owner is the local Church Committee, so we ask Mr. Mil.Gov. if the confiscation can be stayed. Mr. Mil.Gov. says he cannot stay it because he's not doing it. He has told Mr. Jap.Gov. to get landholdings down to a small maximum size, and Mr. Mil.Gov. will see to it that Mr. Jap.Gov. carried out his order. So our question goes to Mr. Jap.Gov. who blinks calmly again and says that there's more land there anyway than one owner is allowed to have. What he thinks he will have to do to satisfy Mr. Mil.Gov. is to order the Church to sell all it owns in excess of the allowed area. Mr. Mil.Gov. nods in confirmation of this surmise.

You see the difference is between Occupation Policy on house tenancy and land ownership. The latter is reckoned to be significant at this stage of Japan's reform, the tenancy not so at present. Where the Occupation Policy makers at Potsdam decided a matter is of primary importance for reform now, they have gone further than in secondary matters. But in all cases they aim to achieve the reforms they plan by telling the Japanese Government to carry them through. So if we want to shift the Cuckoo we must use the Japanese Courts, and if the Occupation wants to stop us owning too much land they use appropriate Jap.Gov.Depts. This way has two great advantages. It invites the co-operation of the Japanese in improving their own conditions and it gives them "schooling under expert tuition" in the processes of decentralised Governments.[48]

18/9/47

At Home, and tonight the sea is thumping down on the beach with great roars, an aftermath of the typhoon which caused some damage in this district. Two bridges and several houses were washed away, while others are now propped up precariously where the ground has been washed from underneath them. The people can't do much except put up with this additional suffering as flood waters reach the plains a large area is submerged and thousands are homeless. My house has survived the typhoon and two earthquakes, and being on a hill is above tidal waves and floods.

Your parcels are arriving regularly now and the contents are gratefully accepted and distributed. The Tandaco yeast is now "leavening the lump" all round Odawara, and Glucose with Vitamin D, and Hypol, is very useful for patients. If anyone has scrap pieces of felt or feltex of any colour, thickness or condition, they'd cheer us up by posting it here to make soles for house slippers – The only kind they have now is of compressed grass and hair. Knitting wool is also very welcome, even unravelled from old garments – they can do wonders with things we'd burn.

Two very fine young Japanese parish priests work together in mountain country, tackling Japan's most difficult problem – the conversion of the Japanese country people. They both live on the meagre stipend of 500 yen per month, when by comparison a gardener gets 200 yen for one day's work. I am very concerned about this.

The Odawara Boys' Middle School have an English Study Society and asked me to visit them. I went, and they requested me to speak on Spiritual Values in Democracy. You can imagine how I welcomed such an opportunity. About 70 boys, 3 teachers and the Principal eagerly hoped I would come again. The invitation arose out of meeting a fine lad while waiting in the Ice queue a few weeks ago. The Middle School age group is 13–16 years and they go on to Higher School and later University in Tokyo. The Principal does not speak English, but reads it and is interested in philosophy. I loaned him Bertrand Russell's "History of Western Philosophy"[49] which Eric Dowling gave me when I left Sydney. If the Principal can read that with understanding he's better at English than many Australians.

Yes, I have a 'phone in my house – an extension from the main house down the hill. The number is Odawara 39 and the subscriber's name is Mrs. Murota-san.

---

48 See further: R.P. Dore, *Land Reform in Japan*, London, Oxford University Press, 1959, especially chapter 6.
49 Bertrand Russell, *History of Western Philosophy, and its Connection with Political and Social Circumstances from the Earliest Times to the Present Day*, London, George Allen and Unwin Ltd., 1946.

The addition of "San" to any name is merely a title or mark of respect and means nothing really. Some schoolgirls the other day called an American baby BEE-BEE-SAN.

Ethel Lewis has just announced her engagement to Technical Sergeant Joseph EHRIC of the United States Army. Ethel and Joe have spent two weekends here with me already and I'm hoping to see more of them. Of course, he speaks American but in every other respect he'd pass for a likeable easy going Australian. I like him a lot.

My wireless works now and I can get Australian shortwave sometimes. It brings you very near to hear a voice in familiar accent say "This is Radio Australia transmitting from Melbourne!" – and I've just heard a William Herbert session.[50]

3/10/47

This morn a passing Jeep dropped me a corn sack full of mail! There were 4 parcels of books for children and 3 other parcels with lots of newspapers and letters. All parcels were completely O.K. and I had many pleasant surprises as I opened them up. The paper wrapping was torn on one, but nothing fell out. Some old cloth sewn around not only keeps it secure but makes something useful afterwards. The old tennis ball for Yasuhiro was received with great delight, and Ogata-san and her two little girls will write to thank you for their soap. I have found grateful owners for all slippers. Remember small sizes, under size 5, are preferable – and soft soles are best for not damaging mats or polished floors.

I'm really loaded up with work and concern at present, being specially concerned about the desperate circumstances of all our parish priests.[51] I have just spent hours preparing letters for A.B.M. setting out a recommendation for help from Australia.

Next week I go 50 miles South [west] to visit Churches at Shimizu and Shizuoka to see what I can do to help them.

Tuesday also is the postponed Quiet Day, for Women's Auxiliary members, at my house. I hope to be back at midday, but it is good to know I can confidently leave home for 2 days, having arranged for Church folk to come and use my house in my absence.

Last week Fr. Miyazawa and I went with our 100 school pupils for their Picnic to Zushi Beach. It might have been an Australian picnic and was certainly hilarious. I taught them to Scavenge Hunt chasing fish, feathers, old geta and the like – by the time we reached home I had a headache from crowded trains etc. but the pupils were all still very lively. I think they must have aspirin built into their systems.

---

50 William Scott Herbert (1920–1975), Australian tenor. See: *Australian Dictionary of Biography*, vol. 14, pp. 438–439.

51 Note the use of "our," the first indication of his personal identification with the Japanese church.

Now that I have seen five *Newsletters* I'm taking stock. I'll do it on paper for you to share in the process, and comment. Several people have written that it is good to have my "first impressions" and seem to think the N/L [*Newsletter*] will stop after awhile. I guess now is a good time to ask whether to stop? Do people want to read this sort of thing? I've already got jottings which may be expanded into N/L [*Newsletter*] stuff to cover many months – and there is no end in sight of the things which strike fire from my Spirit. Do people want to read it? I fervently hope so, for the sake of Reconciliation between here and there.

We started by sending *No. 1* to 100 persons. Requests have now doubled our list and we are glad of every possible reader who will be concerned about the Reconciliation of our peoples.

Now we want to hear from those who have not already written whether to continue posting to them.

Because a friend now does the Duplicating voluntarily, postage and stationery is our chief expense. If every reader could send an average of about 3 d. per N/L [*Newsletter*] it should be self-supporting – see what I mean?

By the way, do you feel able to pass *Newsletters* round to others without apologising for them?

Gratefully yours,
    FRANK

Newsletter No. 7, 1 November 1947.

NIPPON SEIKO KWAI

Aust. Army Post Office,
C/- Empire House,
B.C.O.F.,
Tokyo,
JAPAN.

From – Rev. Frank W. Coaldrake

Dear Friends,

There are many things going on which would interest you but I can't write all about them because then I'd be doing little else. Many men and lads I meet "casually" come to talk with me. This is, of course, very good, but it makes an ordered routine rather impossible.

One Sunday I visited Hatano, 10 miles up among the hills, and from now on I am to help in the Church Service there on the 3rd Sunday each month. After the service a meeting was held to formally welcome me at which speeches were made by Church members, including one from a very old grandmother who spoke so fast I couldn't understand her, but she was very much in earnest. No one dares to even try to manage elderly women in this country, and I think they are strikingly strong and serene. The meeting finished with a meal and the "sweets" took the form of slices of cooked cold sweet potato eaten as we do cake. Corporal

Rex Jones of Sydney was on leave with me for the week-end and enjoyed visiting Hatano also. He kept asking, "why don't they salt their food?" I had to explain that they like salt as much as we do, but it is unobtainable except at a very high price. I am only allowed ¼ lb. every 2 months. I used some duplicated leaflets at Hatano and am finding my duplicator a great help in teaching at many centres.

It is raining and the clouds will probably hide the full moon tonight which will be regrettable because the Sept. full moon (or harvest moon) is by very ancient custom always admired right into the night, the whole family gathering together for "OTSUKI-MI" (moon-viewing) spending the hours reading and composing poetry. We are to have "OTSUKI-MI" on my front verandah with Mrs. Murota's family, nine of us.

My shortwave radio keeps me in touch with what is going on the world over. I can hear a U.S.A. Town Meeting, and Digest of Commentators with a dash of Moscow, Ceylon, India, China, and B.B.C., not forgetting Radio Australia, on a choice of four different wave lengths. I can hear Ben Chiffley[52] about to nationalise the banks, accompanied by static roars of acclamation on 15 metres, but on 19 metre band he seems to have lost his voice, while the 25 metre band seems to surround him with screams of liberals, bankers and parrots! Thus even the impartiality of the A.B.C. is given a bias according to which wavelength you listen to.

Japanese broadcasts include quite a lot of Talks on Australia. I hope it won't be left to Commerce and Diplomacy to interpret Australian people to Japanese people, but Australia may never be thought of creditably until she modifies the rigid exclusiveness of her immigration policy. Some sort of limited admissions at least will be needed before there can be friendship between Australians and their coloured neighbours. Of course, if we can afford to ignore them I suppose it will be O.K. to go on shutting the door on good and bad alike, just because of the colour of their subcutaneous pigment.

It's funny being a Missionary in a land where people ride in fast electric trains, have radios blaring eternally and read their newspapers as they wait for the tram to take them down to the next block. It has brought back to my memory some long forgotten words of T.Z. Koo.[53] He said he was a bridge and railway engineer in China when he realised that giving men better bridges and railways to ride over would not make them better men; he turned to dealing with the souls of men and became a Christian Missionary. But as I see it here good transport and communications are making possible a more rapid exchange of ideas – you should see the students travelling from Odawara the 50 miles each way to Tokyo Technical Schools and Universities each day, and hear the local men discussing what they've heard in the broadcasts from American and Russian Stations (both in Japanese language). These things are good if men are good. Here I can see even more clearly than I could in Australia, that the most significant factor is the

52 Prime Minister of Australia, 1945–1949.
53 Discussed in commentary to *chapter 1*.

human spirit, which determines the use to be made of modern technology. I think it is more apparent here because the human spirit at this moment trembles on the verge of a great awakening in individuals. MacArthur has set the stage for a vigorous individuality, but ancient customs and inflation-bred disillusionment combine to shackle it. And here I am in the midst of it as an insignificant missionary able to touch but few lives, when the touching of lives is now the chief thing needed to reap the fruits of all past history down to this present year. It is some encouragement to know that what I am asked to do these days is perhaps the most significant thing I could choose to do – that is to encourage and guide those whose work it is to touch the lives of many others – our own Japanese parish priests, and their Church members. They are one of the few groups who have a philosophy of life here these days. One way and another I meet a lot of other people so I can see the contrast. Some of these others I've got to know very closely. One, an ex-suicide pilot, is to stay with me over next weekend.

Some people have a desperate materialism ("accumulate all the goods possible, as quickly as possible, by any means possible"), but the prevailing spirit of Japan has <u>never</u> been materialistic. We know how the Japanese have counted more on aesthetic satisfaction than material plenty; they do not migrate to plentiful lands because the ineffable natural beauty of their own countryside holds them to shiver on an empty stomach. Material wealth satisfies a few but others are puzzled. They feel after something more substantial as a springboard of life. Among these the Churchmen I know here have the feeling their toes have gripped and now they need our encouragement if they are to launch themselves. That's where I'm trying to come in and really help them, and you to understand their urgent need.

The food situation is variously reported overseas. As I see it there is always food in the shops, usually some good food amongst a lot of what the people themselves regard as second-rate – seaweeds, cuttlefish, and chestnuts. The good things include some choice fruits in season. Apples at present would rival Tasmania's best. A few weeks ago it was tomatoes like Bowen's Beauties. There are eggs too, but these good things are to be seen because few have the money to buy them. Only a few items are subject to ration. Then rationed goods have prices fixed, but they are only a small quantity. Even the fixed price is high. I get some rations allotted to me, special "Foreigner's rations." A month's rations would feed me for about 3 or 4 days. Ration potatoes cost me 5/- per 20 lbs; 1lb. of ration butter costs 26/-; 1 lb. of ration sugar 3/8 d. The same goods on the open market would cost 2 or 3 times as much. Ration rice is about 3 times Australian price, but the extra rice needed costs about 10 times as much. Eggs, not rationed, cost 1/16 d. each; 1lb. fresh apples 4/6 d. The consequence is that most people live on cheaper second-rate foods, or what they can grow in their yard, or on the footpath! For some weeks past the main bulk of food for most people in these parts has been sweet potatoes. The diet is governed by only one consideration, what is available to fill the emptiness. (Fig. 14) S.C.A.P. has supplied some quantity of corn meal. Because there's nothing to put with it, it has been made into a saltless porridge, or scone. I have seen children coming back

Figure 14 Family in Odawara gathered around the hearth, 1947. Note the severely undernourished baby on the left.

from the fields carrying a dozen or two green grasshoppers threaded on a straw, being taken home to broil as a "delicacy." I have walked through the fields with a parish priest and observed him catch hoppers and pocket them on the quiet.

The weather has become cold very rapidly judging by the way my feet get colder than even in Sydney's midwinter. I'm glad of my old leather coat and does Mrs. Hoey remember how many birthdays it counts? These people love their Autumn, with the wonderful hues of brown and gold. They make a special effort to get out into the country, just for "maple-viewing." In such a setting the rice is being harvested, and Japan is giving her lifeblood to maintain her people. As the grain is harvested the plants are hung upside down on rails, so the whole countryside becomes a patchwork of empty paddy-mud-fields lined off with brown plant roots, but the light is so soft that nothing offends. Compared with Australia the light is unbelievably soft, as I have discovered sadly when taking photographs – 5 to 10 times longer exposure than under similar conditions in Australia is necessary, even with Super XX films. But to return to approaching winter, there's a heavy drain on electric power, and consequent rationing. I've been philosophically ruminating in darkness and recalling summer water-cuts back home, and I've discovered a sound philosophy of economy. If you turn water or power off when people need it most, you'll save more than if you turn it off when they need it less! After watching vehicles rushing madly down narrow streets crowded with pedestrians I've discovered also a philosophy of safety which might be tried in Sydney. "The more you frighten pedestrians, the quicker they'll jump – so, speed more, scare more, and miss more." But when two scared victims in the throng jump into a mid-air collision with each other, and come down in front of the rushing vehicle, that's just another statistic for S.C.A.P's Traffic Survey.

I've just been reading a *Newsletter* from Rev. Frank Whyte of India, who is set amidst rice-paddies near Calcutta. I would like to send him a pair of stilt-high geta used for walking thro' mud over here. Do you remember how Frank Whyte, Frank Engel and myself in our A.S.C.M. years were known as Frynk, Frenk and Fronk?[54] Now if only Frenk were back in Korea we could join hands and keep each others heads above the paddy-mud. Mud is a universal commodity, and perhaps that accounts for so much mud-slinging as a pastime!

Parcels from many good friends are gladdening the hearts of humble folk in my parish from grandma down to infant. Such things as "real chocolate," pastry-mix, milo, cocoa-malt, weat-harts are precious. Woollen singlets and felt slippers are always welcome. In return for my gifts I am feasted with mussell soup, shells and all in!

My visit to Shimizu and Shizuoka was typically interesting. I met local Church members and visited the State Schools to speak to boys aged 14–16, also their teachers. They are quite keen on Round-table Discussions. I tell them about Australia, usually emphasising differences, then concluding by trying to show that with all the differences there are many essential likenesses – the same human spirit tied up in different parcels, with different string, addressed in different writing, but perhaps addressed to the same place – "Tomorrow's World's Family." They seem to catch on, in spite of my J'ese(!) and I hear by unexpected means of good responses. A boy writes directly to me, in J'ese with an apology for not writing in English, and says how he has been glad to hear what I have taught; a teacher writes to say "all the teachers have been improved by your teaching;" a girl writes to a relative in Odawara to say she has found a new confidence in the help of God, and the relative meets and tells me. I can only wonder how many others find it so. Since I usually speak to about 500 at a time in the schools there must, of course, be many who have opposite reaction, and of course, one doesn't hear of them in a land of considerate politeness.

That comment about the teachers is interesting. That particular group asked me so many questions that I spent 2 hours doing nothing else but answer them. In the course of my answers I dealt with such things as trade union organisation so as to ensure responsibility with liberty to every member, discussed the pros and cons of compulsory union membership, school discipline and the relation between teacher and pupil with a good deal of attention to the problem of the "problem child" in the class, placing emphasis on our best methods which tell a teacher to blame himself for bad discipline, how to run school picnics and excursions without regimentation, how to organise vacation recreation centres in school grounds, District Schools sports competitions, appointments of School

54 All three had been Travelling Secretaries of the A.S.C.M. at the same time.

Principals, functions of parents' committees, and such like. I found myself digging up my former teaching experience and what I learnt when visiting schools of all kinds while a Travelling Secretary for the A.S.C.M. Finally they asked me "what things in Japan do you find unpleasant?" It was a sincere question so I decided to answer it, but had to spend a while thinking about it first, because it had not occurred to me to think of anything as unpleasant. That minute or two was a strange experience. I found myself, as it were, placed on an observer's platform, whereas I am usually just another person living in this teeming country trying to make the best and most enjoyable use of what there is. During my brief mental review of the Japan I had seen, the 20 teachers waited almost tensely. One thing after another had to be labelled strange or different, but not unpleasant, while ever so much rang the bell as pleasant. Yet I found one thing different and told them that – their careless public hygiene – food stuffs and sanitization in close proximity, and both open to the flies, even though covers are alongside or could easily be improvised; drainage, sanitation, and water supply carelessly allowed to mix, and I suggested that it was possible for the country's teachers to change this in one generation by teaching the children. I told them about our "Health Week" and "Kill that Rat" posters and the like. They thought at first I was objecting to their lavatory arrangements, which are different to ours, so I had to explain that I did not think Japan should convert to western style, but I thought they should learn and practice simple hygiene in the construction and use of their own-style facilities. This may sound crude, but it is one of the differences which must be reconciled for the good of all. Can you begin to see the problems of a "Mish" in a modern world?

In Tokyo a few weeks ago the time had come for the J'ese Govt. to implement the breaking up of big financial concerns. ("Smash the Zaibatsu" is the popular description of it.) You can imagine that the big shows weren't waiting for the blow lying down. The proposal was to tackle the difficult job with Cabinet Regulation, instead of bringing a Bill before the Diet, which would be a ticklish business. A few days before the matter was to be handled by Cabinet, a "spokesman" for the Occupation Authorities thundered forth in general terms on the subject of Cabinet Government. He pointed out that Japan had to learn that Cabinet could only implement what the Diet decided. There must be no avoiding of difficult issues which threatened the continuance of a party in power by dealing with it in Cabinet. The "spokesman" heavily deplored the tendency to accept the Cabinet as a law-making body instead of insisting that the Cabinet ask the Diet to make laws wherever new laws are needed. If there is no law on any matter that needs a law, the Cabinet must ask the Diet to make a law to guide the Cabinet and Government in dealing with the matter.

For a couple of days the echoes of this broadside rumbled amidst argument and lament. Then the Govt. Party leaders began to talk about bringing a "Decentralisation of Industry Bill" before the Diet. The Occupation Authority achieved its aim by leaving no room for doubt about what it wanted, while not even hinting that it would enforce its wish, and furthermore, the Party in power cannot now avoid the risk of losing power by being defeated in Parliament on this very controversial matter. The Zaibatsu "big boys" of course will use every means within their power to lobby for favourable amendments to the Bill, and even for the defeat of every Govt. that tries to pass such a Bill. We will see, I think, a long struggle which the Occupation could avert by simply issuing firm orders, but the struggle will be in a Parliament "cutting its teeth," though it might greatly strengthen the sinews of parliamentary practice. It might even deepen this nation's understanding of the scope of the Govt. by the people's representatives, and if it culminates in a reasonable accomplishment, the power of the militarists in Japan will have been permanently crippled by the people of Japan. You can guess that I am following this with great interest, for it is the back curtain to all that I do with this man and that.

Yours candidly,
  FRANK

Frank Coaldrake, *Meditation*, 18 November 1947.

RIDING ON THE BACK OF A WORKER: MEDITATIONS IN A RIKISHA

In Tokyo there are still many *jinrikisha* (literally "man-power-carriage"). In my own city there are three. I had idly watched them but had never felt inclined to use them. I found the idea repugnant. In the course of several weeks I discovered that most other Australians felt the same way. They might perhaps take one joy ride just for the fun but after that they preferred to walk if there were no other transport available. One walking soldier I spoke to said "I'm not going to ask any man to pull me round the streets" and that seems to sum up the attitude of most of us Australians. There is no race issue in it because the rikisha is used much by Japanese.

However, one day I had to travel a mile or so quicker than I could walk and with a bag heavy enough to make running impossible. The only transport available on the route was a rikisha so I bottled up my feelings and hired one. That ten minute ride provoked so many thoughts and feelings that I used rikisha on several subsequent appropriate occasions in order to continue a chain of thought which seemed to need the jogging of the vehicle to keep it moving. From time to time I have recaptured the thoughts. I think they might even be called meditations. Following are some of them.

Meditation 1

While the shafts were still on the ground I climbed backwards on to the seat. The man lifted the shafts and bent his shoulders low to the pull. I had seen a horse act that way when pulling a heavy cart I was driving. Am I asking him to do an animal's work? It was midsummer so he had taken off his shirt. I could see the muscles stand out on his back the tendons of his wrists and hands straining as he felt along the shafts for the right balance of my weight even as he pulled. My sense of repugnance made me uneasy and I shifted in my seat. This upset the balance and the man faltered is his stride. We were now well out into the street amidst the traffic but he jogged along unconcernedly. Fear of being run down by some traffic-sense-less truck driver now drove the repugnance from my mind. But the man jogged on, his feet beating a steady rhythm about the same speed as my pulse. We crossed two busy intersections so miraculously that I looked at the dashboard to see if there were a St. Christopher medal there.

The padding feet and the jolting arm-rest in my ribs soothed me and I started to think more coherently. Certainly I'm debasing this man by making him pull me like this. My toes are only an inch or two above his rump and his heels come back under my seat so that I'm literally riding on the back of a worker. Here I sit at ease while he slaves at an animal's work for my benefit. Should I say "He's only a Jap anyway, so why worry about that." It is a hot day so I ease my trousers over my knees – the sweat pours off his back. I cannot see his face but behind his ears is very red. The narrow towel knotted round his head is obviously wet.

He wears that knotted towel because he believes it is a source of added strength to him. All Japanese workmen have worn the head-towel for this reason for many centuries. When not working he tucks it in his belt. When he is about to start some ordinary exertion he puts it round his forehead knotted at the back. For extra heavy work he knots it over his forehead. And it's knotted over his forehead now. Why are we Australians such big-bodied people? Are our minds and souls bigger too?

This little man seeks a strength greater than his own. Simple faith indeed that finds it in a towel. I pray. God give this humble worker strength. Let thy power which moves him, now be shed upon him freely that he may indeed have the little extra. Let thy craft which fashioned his muscles, nerves and eyes, now give him skill to use them. Let the running sweat bring him the joy we may find in physical exertion. Let him pull honestly – and serve me well.

And serve me well – my whole prayer is not on behalf of the man but myself. How easy it is to pray for him so that I may benefit as my prayer for him is answered. If I got down and walked he wouldn't need these blessings I pray. Why don't I get down and walk praying the while for speed, endurance and patience in myself? And for meekness in facing the reproaches of the man I keep waiting. Why don't I convey myself? Perhaps I will. It's a rickety rikisha anyway. The gay tune of the current "hit" lightens my feelings. If I do get down the man won't get as much pay – and I reckon he needs the money. Why, he chooses this way to earn his living. If I get down I add to the unemployment.

With that comforting though I settle right back in my seat, and the man's feet come off the ground. He treads the air for a moment then regains the balance of the shafts. He certainly has chosen a tough job. The slightest thing his employer does for his own comfort directly affects him. I must try to remember to sit still. I can pray for him after all. God bless this worker. He has a job I couldn't do myself, but in Thy universe we each have our place. Grant to all whose place is humble the compensation of a joy in knowing thee.

Yet I cannot pray for him without realising that he is serving me even while I pray for him. How would I feel if we were fellow church members now both on our way to church? Could I travel this way in his company if we were going to kneel together to receive the Sacrament?

I should certainly be thanking God for the service I am receiving from one of his other creatures. I remember the Jewish forerunner of our Christian grace at meals. The Jews wanted the blessing of God on their food – but they didn't ask for that. They said words of thanks to God over the food – but they didn't ask for that. They said words of thanks to God over the food then partook of it as food blessed by God. How often I have done that as a Priest in the Consecration prayer in our Anglican Communion Liturgy.

God in Heaven, how often we thank you for sending your son to be man for the sake of man, not be served but to serve, now I thank you for the efforts of this man under my feet. Thank you God, I leave the man to you.

Meditation 2

"Thank you God – I leave this man to you" – "but I hope he'll get me there safely" were just about the thoughts with which I began my next ride. I feel easier at once for I see this man has his towel knotted at the back. Funny the way these coves keep up that superstitious practice. Fancy thinking a towel is the seat of strength. I can't imagine seeing an Australian transport worker wear a towel – a "wharfie" for instance. In bus, tram, train and ferry at home I see a jaunty cap or a severe hat on Australian heads. But after all, the workers I didn't see behind the scenes in Australian transport might be wearing a towel.

God, is this your way of opening my eyes? Is this how you would teach me to remember the unseen workers who sweat and toil and have their faith, and hope, and charity, and fear, like this man does now in front of me, underneath me? Have I ridden in the St. Kilda tram [in Melbourne] forgetting the men who bent their backs and tautened their thighs to lay the rails and forge the chassis? Have I never though to thank Thee for the cunning fingers that fitted the windows to protect me from the wind in the Sandy Bay "jalopies"? Or that printed the tickets and wound the armatures which take me swiftly under the heart of Sydney? Have I nattered cheerfully with C.T. in his days on conducting the East Brunswick bus and forgotten the equally cheerful man in the greasing pit at the depot, or the equally proud father sweeping out the filth we passengers leave behind?

Is that young Yankee riding in that other rikisha with a portable radio blaring as casual about the man who is pulling him as I have been about the unseen army who have dragged me round in Australia? God, why have you opened my eyes? Why have you made me unhappy about riding in a rikisha and not made me equally unhappy about riding on the backs of the unseen in trams and trains and buses? God why must I soon dismiss this man with a few yen and brief thanks without being expected to do anything more in return for what he has done for me? He is not an engine – as he plodded he has had thoughts. What can I do about them? God why have you let me see his willingness, his panting, his easy judgement in traffic, his fright when a car came too close, his peeve when people wouldn't get out of his way, his roughly bandaged elbow? Why must I have such vivid personal contact with a man when all I want is to buy his services? Why can I not have the privilege of modernity and use him at a distance without stopping to think about him personally? Have you permitted the invention of modern travel facilities just so that we can be spared the embarrassing contemplation of the work that other men do to move our tired or lazy bodies. Is the invention of "all mod. cons." your way of giving us peace of mind as we push a handle and forget the man who digs a ditch or blasts a tunnel or ceaselessly ticks dockets to make possible the whole complex operation which begins when we push the handle? When I but strike a match should I say a Litany of Labour for all the men who come before and after the flare of the chemical? And for their families? And what about the tradespeople who give them credit when matches are not being made? Should I start the Litany now as I see my destination and fish out my yen?

By the sweat and the scratches of the Carpenter of Nazareth – Good Lord deliver us from the sin of ease.

By the care of the working man for his Blessed Mother – Good Lord deliver us from the sin of forgetting those who depend on those who work for us.

By the suffering and degradation seen by blessed John from the foot of the Cross – Good Lord deliver us from unseeing of eye.

By the love which looked on Peter in his hour of denial – bring us closer good Lord to the persons who serve us unseen.

By thy judgement on Judas who thought money would even the balance – Good Lord deliver us from a money-salved conscience.

Meditation 3

It was a wet and windy day. In the rikisha I sat under a hood surrounded by curtains, quite dry. The man in the shafts was soaked. At the corner he turned right instead of left. I told him I wanted to go left. He stopped, said something I did not understand, then slowly wheeled and jogged resignedly down to the left. I thought him cantankerous. A short distance further on he stopped to roll up his trousers and then plunged forward through a sea of mud. I said sympathetically "Too bad it's so muddy." He replied quietly over his shoulder "It was to dodge this bad spot I wanted to go the other way." Once through the mud we jigged along nicely and I took out a cigarette. Three times I struck a match and the wind blew it out. Then, unexpectedly, the man stopped, put down the shafts and came round to my side. I was surprised and wondered what was to happen next. A strange fellow this: He took off his big plaited straw hat, dripping wet, and held it as a shelter so I could light my cigarette. He must have heard me striking matches. I gave him a cigarette. He took an old tin out of his pocket and I saw the cigarette put carefully among a lot of old butts. Then he bowed till his head was lower than his knees, turned and took up the shafts and started off once more. A strange fellow this!

We came to rough stony road. The right side tyre was too low. He stopped and took an old carefully wrapped pump from under the back of the seat. It was about five percent efficient and as he worked it jammed his knuckles. When he had finished the exasperating work he carefully wrapped the pump again and stowed it in the boot. I half-expected him to throw it away with a curse and a shake of his bleeding fist. Probably he will go on using the wretched thing till it, or the rikisha, falls to pieces.

A little later we came to journey's end. I paid him his forty yen with a sigh of relief, glad to be rid of this disturber of my peace of mind.

Returning I had another rikisha. I had to catch a train and was late, so I asked the man to hurry. Then I saw he was old enough to be my grandfather. He ran quickly down the streets fearlessly weaving his way through the traffic. He ran risks at the intersections. I sat there wondering whether I shouldn't rather be pulling him to the station and taking him home to give him a feed and a rest. I began to wonder what I would do if he slackened his speed and lost the train.

If he were a horse I would have a whip. Perhaps I would use it on a horse. I certainly couldn't whip a man. His chest was heaving so much I half expected him to stop for a breather. Supposing he stopped for a rest? Supposing he acted like a cart-mule and jibbed? Supposing he went on strike? Well, I couldn't blame him. He'd probably done a lot of running today before I call him out to do this extra hard job. Of course his strike would be awkward for me – strikes are always awkward for someone. I remembered a tram strike in Sydney a while back when I had to walk two miles. And then there was that most exasperating gas strike about the same time, and the never-ending coalminers' strikes which seemed to be the cause of most other troubles, and always for some foolish little reason magnified by lazy or greedy workers. But this would be different. The man would have good reason. Look at the slippery road he's trying to keep his feet on, and fancy me expecting an old fellow like him to run on and on dragging my weight. But what a pair of legs he's got. They'll get me there alright.

"The Lord delighteth not in the strength of any man's legs" came to my mind. Was there something about this that should open my eyes to God's truth, to his will? I asked. *The answer was a string of questions!*

When you denounce strikers do you remember that they might be men who work as you see this man working? You wouldn't whip this man if he slowed down – but wouldn't you tongue-lash him if he were a ferry stoker who made things awkward for you by a "go-slow" protest against his work conditions? You see this man and you'd understand if he went on strike, but when men you don't see go on strike do you always try to understand them? The men you can't see down in the coal pit don't come round to help you light your cigarette – but perhaps they stop to pick up and soothe a child that falls near them as they go home. The men you don't see working on the power lines of the trams might not want to work in the rain because of the risk – while you wait impatiently for the tram to start running again do you think of that or do you think they are cantankerous? The fettlers bruting away at sleepers and ballast don't mind a bleeding knuckle or two but if one thing after another aggravates them they might throw away their tools and tell you to walk – what would you say then?

God of Mercy, I pray, forgive me for not focusing my mind's eye on the man at a distance just because he is at a distance.

God of Love, teach me – when I see a man in danger, or injured, should I consider him or whip him? When I am discomforted by a man seeking safety or health should I be patient or angry? When I see a man being lazy, or dishonest, or greedy, or foolish, what should I do? When I don't see these men and then forget that they are human, my equals in your sight, what then will you do?

God of Love, what is man that he can be so unmindful of Thee?

God of Truth, show me when I should ride in these uneasy things.

Frank W. Coaldrake, *Odawara Mission Report to the Australian Board of Missions on quarter to 30 November 1947.*

WORK

(a) In Odawara parish:

Duties have now developed into as much work as I can handle. Each month I celebrate the Eucharist three or four times, and preach four times; conduct 11 bible class sessions; teach English for two hours each week in the church school; conduct personal interviews and individual instructions, about one per day.

(b) In the Diocese of South Tokyo:

Each third Sunday I spend all day at Hatano Church, assisting the parish priest. Two of my bible class sessions are at Hiratsuka, a church 15 miles away.

At the request of the clergy I have been visiting each parish in turn. So far I have visited 14 centres apart from those three I usually work in. On such visits I have been asked to preach at services and/or speak in local schools.

I am appointed as a consultant to the Nippon Seiko Kwai Committee on revision of Doctrine, Prayer Book and Organisation.

My house has been used for a Pre-ordination Retreat which I conducted; for a Women's Auxiliary Quiet Day; for a one day conference of Church Youth Leaders. Several parish Priests and the Bishop have stayed with me. My Library is being much used, some books being borrowed for priests in other Dioceses.

In mid-October I attended as a delegate at the Nippon Seiko Kwai conference on "Co-operation in Evangelism."

Other visitors have included Australian Chaplains The Revs. D. Beier and A. Laing.

Comments:

The visiting of other parishes has been a dominant feature of the quarter. It has involved much travel and preparation of special talks. It has meant a neglect of my duties in Odawara parish and of my studies. This "spreading" of my work seemed to me to be of doubtful value so I discussed the matter with my parish priest. He said it was a big help to the Diocese that I should do this now, but that he himself would help me to put an end to this superficial work at an early date so that I could settle down to my work as a priest in this parish. We have already planned a heavy programme from Christmas to Easter which will require me to stay here most of the time. The absence of a Diocesan [Bishop, after the death of Bishop Sugai] has also made it difficult to adopt a definite policy in relation to Diocesan work. However, the very lack of a Bishop on the job left a lack of unity in the Diocese and my visiting seem to have done something to compensate for that.

My close contact with the individual parishes has shown ever more clearly the state of the church in this Diocese. For instance, I visited five parishes in one region, and found a total of under 200 communicant members in the whole region. There are about the same number of "inquirers" and catechumens. 3 parish priests work among the five churches. Their income is pathetically inadequate but they do little side work and the congregations are growing.

The urgent need of aid to parish priests is the chief feature of the life of the church at present.

LIVING

(a) House

While in many ways admirable, the type of structure does not keep out winter cold. If fuel or power of any kind were available it could probably be made warm enough for efficient living.

(b) Food

My main concern has been the future. As a result of many gifts of foodstuffs I have been able to build up a reserve stock selected partly from the gifts and partly from purchased supplies. I had to make an interim policy decision on this point and I would like to know the wishes of the Board in the matter. As a result of the gifts I could have reduced the amount of my expenditure on supplies, and still have had sufficient for needs week by week. But, supplies are uncertain in kind and quantity, and always likely to be more so. Also, if I had to live on Japanese food, the cost in yen converted to A£ (quite apart from health considerations), would, with the inflation, be about £15 a week, even on the simplest foods. Therefore, as an insurance against greatly increased costs in the event of a breakdown or cessation of Army supplies, I decided to continue to buy the available ration of Army supplies. I now have about four hundredweight of supplies in stock, much of it stored safely in my landlady's "godown." (The gifts have come from interested and helpful occupation personnel.) Now that I have such a reserve I propose to reduce expenditure and buy only what is necessary from month to month.

The Board, however, might consider the possibility that, if gifts should continue I should buy the available ration of Army supplies and use surpluses for gifts to needy parish priests as part of the "Relief" parcels system.

Another matter the Board may wish to advise me on concerns Communion wine. I was able to purchase from a friendly Canteen Officer 3 dozen bottles of Port wine at 4/3 d. per bottle. This I distributed to the parishes for Communion wine, because the only available material is a synthetic substance at an exorbitant price. I expect to be able to get further supplies from the same source and would like the Board's approval of the policy of buying up to 10 dozen bottles in a year for the needs of the Diocese of South Tokyo. (This form of help is particularly appreciated.)

NEWSLETTER

Over 200 people have now requested to receive the *Newsletter* which my mother compiles from my letters to her. The only big expense so far has been the postage and this has been covered by many small contributions sent in response to a request for such help.

GENERAL MATTERS

On December 10th the South Tokyo Synod elected Bishop Maekawa of Hokkaido as the new Bishop of South Tokyo. Bishop Maekawa is a quiet, elderly gentleman. During the war he did not join the Amalgamation but managed to avoid trouble with the Government by continually apologising for his failure to do so.

On December 17th I am to start holding a regular Bible Study and discussion meeting at the Fuji Film Factory. There are 1,300 employees at the factory, mostly residing in the village around the factory. There is no Christian activity of any sort for the employees at present. The factory manager is not a Christian but is co-operative. So far as I know the only Christian in the place is a Seiko Kwai member whom I located with the help of the factory manager. It is a wonderful opportunity. The factory is situated ten miles from Odawara in a small out-of-the-way village.

There continues to be no end to the possible avenues of fruitful work.

The physical privations of the people are not so bad as are reported from Europe, but nevertheless are desperate. The present trend in the inflation is from bad to worse. Perhaps the worst thing for most people at present is the lack of fuel and the very small supply of electric power (each house is permitted to use 25 units a month – enough to burn only one lamp and a radio). This means much shivering in cold houses, insufficient clothes and poor diet. Temperatures are already down to freezing point and the coldest month is February. To conserve water for electric power generation, water supplies are cut off for three-quarters of the time.

Christ Church Yokohoma, one of the destroyed churches in this Diocese, has been rebuilt. It was dedicated on Sunday, December 7th. The rebuilding was possible because it is the church attended by United States Consulate personnel and is close to big Occupation Barracks. A fine job of re-building has been done. It is the only church in the Diocese on which any rebuilding has been possible.

Frank Coaldrake, *A Japanese City and Its Native Anglicans: The Church in Odawara*, unpublished typescript with handwritten annotations, excerpt from undated (1947 or 1948).

JAPANESE ANGLICANS

Steadiness is the most noticeable things about the life of the church. A description of it in detail would read like the description of almost any Anglican parish in Australia, not better, no worse, no more exciting, no more unimaginative. We need not decide whether this is good or bad but we must admit it is surprising after all we have heart about the Japanese in recent years.

In the Parish Report for the Year 1946 we find the following cold statistics:

Total Church Members, 120; Communicant members, 59; Baptisms, 7; Confirmees, 5; Catechumens, 5; Weddings, 1; Funerals, 0; services of Holy Communion in the Church, 59, in other places, 14; total Income for the year, Yen 4,742; Total Expenditure, Yen 4,720. The Credit Balance was achieved by spending only Yen 80 on Building Repairs and maintenance, and by keeping the Parish Priests stipend down to a figure approximately one third of a Japanese labourer's wages. Forty-one percent of the total income was given for purposes outside the parish. Included in this was one-tenth of the total which was given for Missionary work elsewhere. On these statistics the Parish is about the fourth largest in the Diocese.

Those cold statistics crystallise out of a warm and abiding corporate life among one hundred and twenty people living as a minority group in a city of sixty thousand. In many ways, surprisingly many ways, the parish is typical of Anglican parishes in other parts of the world. One of the immediately noticed differences is that at the services everybody sings. If the result does not always add the beauty of harmony to the proceedings, it certainly adds always to the sense of corporateness in the worship.

CHURCH MEMBERSHIP IN JAPAN

The other Churches in Odawara are the Roman Catholic, Methodist, Greek Orthodox and Plymouth Brethren. All have native clergy. Each has a membership slightly larger than the Anglican Church, the Roman Catholic being the largest. In all there are less than one thousand Christians in Odawara – and I am the only European of any category. Throughout Japan, as here, the

Anglicans are small in number. Some Churches experience the constant influx of many new members but do not hold them. This will probably be true of most of the present great increase in the number of Christians. In contrast, the Anglican Church makes few converts but has a record of astonishing permanency. Knowing this we can understand that it was a deep and abiding faith which led the Anglicans to take a stand during the war on a complicated issue with the Government which resulted in many of the clergy being imprisoned.

On any normal Sunday the Odawara Anglican congregation yields a church attendance of about forty persons. Is this another ... [one line of typescript missing] ... the community for there are all ages from infant to ancient, both sexes, professional and labourer, educated and unlettered. A small group of adolescents belongs to the Odawara Branch of the Diocese Youth Club. The chief parish activity apart from services is the conduct of Bible Classes. A good knowledge of the Bible is assumed to be essential to anyone becoming a Christian. Anyone who wishes to become a member of the Church, turning from Buddhism, or from Shinto, or nothing, will normally spend about two years in a course of preparation and testing before he finally becomes a communicant member. The grade is stiff and this acts as a deterrent upon those who are not sincere and deep in their aspirations.

A FAITHFUL PARISH PRIEST

Our final word must be about the Parish Priest, the Rev. Kumazo Miyazawa. He has served the whole of his twenty-five years as a priest in this parish. He came to it as a Deacon, after spending some three years as such in the Mission field in Korea. He is a scholar, well read in the Japanese Classics, and has had articles on such subjects published overseas. He is Chairman of the Standing Committee of the Diocese so is no doubt an able organiser. I must admit that the methods by which Japanese people organise things among themselves are incomprehensible to me and often I am left standing. Overseas friends of mine who have met him have remarked on his very evident happiness – I play with the word "vivacity" to describe it. His sermons are marked by this characteristic animation. They are, moreover, pithy and short! Soon after he came to Odawara he married a local girl. With their family they are, as I have myself seen, widely known and respected in this community. He has been a faithful priest through many years of hardship and imminent persecution. The Government put his Bishops into prison, expecting to intimidate the parish priests. He was among those who carried on in quietness and confidence. He faces the cryptic future as the pastor and priest of a small flock. He could be pardoned if he were dismayed at the prospects of hard work amid increasing shortages. He may be dismayed. But I can catch not the slightest hint of it. Whenever I try to talk about it he gives a chuckle of delight and says "It is becoming very difficult."

Yes. I find a light shining in Odawara!

Newsletter No. 8, 1 December 1947.

NIPPON SEIKO KWAI

> Aust. Army Post Office,
> C/- Empire House,
> B.C.O.F.,
> Tokyo,
> JAPAN.

From – Rev. Frank W. Coaldrake

Dear Friends,

I have met Kagawa and spoken with him![55] You can imagine how I have looked forward to meeting one who, in the days of my youth, was a hero to me. He was advertised to address a public meeting in Odawara a few nights ago, so I went along. Before making any comments I will describe what I saw and heard. Minamioka-san accompanied me as interpreter. The night was cold and wet, the hall large, unheated, bare and minus many window panes. Seating was provided and there were about 800 present, ranging from very old to quite young, with a large proportion of lads and lasses in late 'teens. There was an admission charge equal to the price of 2 daily newspapers. There was no amplification and one had to listen carefully to hear the speakers. After some brief introductions and singing Kagawa mounted the platform. He spoke for $2\frac{1}{2}$ hours, the only break being for a few moments while a candle was lighted when the electricity was cut off. Kagawa spoke with a voice not powerful enough and therefore strained, often high-pitched. But the slight weakness of his voice did nothing to weaken the impression of a strong personality and as he proceeded there was increasing warmth and dynamism. To illustrate his theme he wrote with a writing-brush on large sheets of paper hung in a frame behind him. His sight was evidently very bad because when he read quotes he used a powerful magnifying glass. His theme was that this is the time of revolution in Japan, but the real welfare of Japan depends on whether it turns out to be a spiritual, or a material revolution. He referred to many other countries in which there had been revolutions of one kind and another, pointing out gains from spiritual and losses from material revolutions. Finland and Sweden were dealt with at length. He then went on to explain how his hearers could bring about a spiritual revolution in their own lives and their community, speaking in turn to children, university students, workers and parents. He often brought roars of laughter from the audience. He seemed to be paying special attention to showing Christianity as an alternative to Communism. At the end he asked everyone to decide whether they would give themselves to Christ, and if so, to sign the paper provided, and hand it to one of the ushers. About $\frac{3}{4}$ of those present handed in the paper. Everyone had listened intently throughout the address even though it was hard to hear – and Kagawa's

---

55 Toyohiko Kagawa was one of Frank Coaldrake's "heroes." See *chapter 2.*

dialect is different to the local one. The meeting concluded with a minute of silent prayer (during which Kagawa knelt on the platform) and the singing of a hymn. After Kagawa had finished his address there were short notices from the local Methodist and Plymouth Brethren Churches announcing the times of services, the names and addresses of Japanese pastors, and inviting inquiries.

Soon after he had left the platform I was able to have a few words with him. When I told him I was an Australian and that many Australians had asked me to bring him their good wishes he was very pleased. He shook my hand till my shoulder rattled, and enquired particularly after the Archbishop of Sydney. I asked him if I could call on him in Tokyo and have a talk with him, and he readily agreed. While speaking with him I could see that he is indeed blind in one eye and the other obviously sore and weak. He was dressed in a dark suit, white shirt and black tie, all well worn.

Kagawa's approach was from current topics and politics, and one result of this is that when enquirers come to the churches afterwards, they come as often as not to learn more about politics and economics rather than about the Christian teaching on personal spiritual life. He spoke with a view to convincing us of the need of a spiritual revolution in our lives, but he did not once use the word "sin" or deal with that matter under other names. I confess I find it hard to see what a spiritual revolution from a Christian point of view can be if it does not take "sin" into account. We have often heard it said that the Japanese people have no sense of sin. In this connection it is worth quoting Bishop Yashiro, the Presiding Bishop of the Nippon Seikokwai, from his "Message of Welcome to Missionaries" given at a conference of Seikokwai members from all over Japan held last month. He said, "I often think the Japanese are the most proud nation in the world. It is beyond "pride;" it is "conceit." That is why we do not like to tell others our difficulties, neither want to confess our sins. However, to have missionaries among us, I mean people of a different race, will make it easy for us to talk to them of our spiritual secrets or to confess our sins to them. I am sure this last task is very important for the Nippon Seikokwai. Unless we have contrite hearts we cannot fulfill the tremendous task which God has prepared for us to perform. Will you be big enough ambassadors from Christ to hear our confessions as our fellow brothers in Christ and talk over spiritual matters?" I don't know if either Kagawa or Bishop Yashiro is "typical of Japanese." But they are equally Japanese, equally keen on converting Japan to Christianity, and have each suffered considerably for their faith in the past. At least it helps to underline the fact that there are such great differences amongst the Japanese that anyone who includes all Japanese under any one label is almost certainly wrong.

Of course, all I have said is about the Evangelist Kagawa. As to the other Kagawa I cannot say anything yet. I hope to have the chance to talk to him in Tokyo soon about many things. But if anyone wants to know whether Kagawa is still active and effective as an Evangelist I'd say the answer is "yes." Some of his general conclusions from his experiences are: Enthusiastic response is general, but it is least in places where the Shin Sect, the Nichiren Sect, and the Tenrikyo Sects are strong. Delay in interest is noticeable too where the Church is divided.

Interest is noticeable among officials and admittedly General MacArthur's kindly attitude has encouraged many, but on the whole Christian activity is most in evidence where the influence of the first early groups and leaders still prevails. Persecution has not ceased for members of many families; but there is a marked interest amongst Buddhist priests.

Those conclusions include some which are of the greatest importance for all of us, whether we're concerned about the conversion of Japan to Christianity or not. For instance, (1) The Nichiren Sect of Buddhists was very active in propagating the political doctrines of the militarists, many of the leaders at present on trial for war crimes being adherents of the sect. (2) Communism is a subject of great interest even while its political significance is depressed under MacArthur's frowns of January last. (e.g. a 15 year old school boy who comes a lot to talk and read and study here wants to bring his school friends with him. But because they're "reds" he hesitates, thinking I might not like the argument!) (3) Where Christianity is strongest today is where there is a heritage from Christian lives. There is no substitute for the witness of the good life, and the wide flung speaking campaign in which Kagawa himself is now engaged will, of itself, have no great permanent effect. It can only begin things which cannot develop without the witness of the good life to nourish it. (4) Persecution in the family results not only from conversions to Christianity but also and perhaps more frequently, from the efforts of the young to lead a "modern" life socially. I must wait until later to tell you of the severe strains caused by the idea that women are equal with men, and the correlated pattern of free choice of partner for marriage. The family bond is one of the really good things in the life of Japan and it would be a drastic loss if it disappeared during the present changes, which is quite a possibility. But it is integrated with many ultra-conservative tendencies which would be better discarded. Some day soon someone living here, sensitive in soul and close to the inner stresses in the Japanese soul now, will write the drama of these days into novels or plays.[56] It is a travail of the human spirit accompanied by, but more significant than, the bodily privations.

This afternoon I went once again to the hall where I heard Kagawa. It is the Assembly Hall of a local Primary School and is the only large hall in the town. This time I went to an "Autumn Music Concert" provided by the boys of the Odawara Middle School Music Society. They were assisted by a Girls' School Choir in one bracket, and by some hack concert singers from Tokyo in half the programme. I was there as the guest of the Principal. (Do you remember my reference to him a while back when I lent him my copy of Bertrand Russell's "History of Western Philosophy." He is still reading it!) The concert began at 1 p.m. on Saturday. Every one of the 1,000 seats was occupied and hundreds more were standing at the sides and back of the hall. The boys ran the whole thing, even to the taking of flashlight photographs. We all had a laugh at the

---

56 This comment anticipates the work of Shūsaku Endō in works such as *The Golden Country* (translated with an introduction by Francis Mathy), London, Owen, 1989.

antics of the flashlight photographer. When he had used his 3 flash "bulbs" he used the old-style flash-powder exploded in a frame held above his head. He had a liberal hand with the powder and nearly blew the artists through the back door of the stage – to say nothing of nearly choking them with the smoke. (As I peered through the smoke at the gasping choir, I suddenly remembered the time when in the Virginia School of Arts I was "Special Effects" man for an amateur show and had to create a flash to cover the entrance of a magician. I think you were there that night. Do you remember the result? [This is addressed to his mother.] I used so much flash-powder that the magician came on, did his piece and made his exit, before the audience recovered their sight – and there was so much smoke you couldn't see anybody on the stage for 10 minutes. I could appreciate the astonished look on the photographer lad's face today.) Another lad who took himself very seriously was the 16 year old conductor of the boys' choir – but he did a good job. The programme was mostly of the kind we'd hear in Australian School concerts of that age – good music valiantly attempted with fair success. But for 10 glorious minutes one 15 years old lad really made music on the Grand Piano with Chopin, and Liszt. (Chopin's Op 31 "Impromptu" and Liszt's "Ra Campanera" – as their programme put it.) We also had Beethoven, Brahms, Weber, Schubert and Schumann. These were bracketed with some Western-style music composed by J'ese, and some popular numbers like "My Old Kentucky Home" sung in both English and J'ese. It was an enjoyable afternoon.

Looking at the upturned faces of the thousand young people of Japan during the classical music I thought I saw part of the answer to the question being asked in places like Australia now – "Is the present amiability of the J'ese people towards the Westerners a genuine feeling or a cloak covering their real feelings, whatever they are?" I think even the "barbarism-rattlers" like Mr. Calwell would have seen in the audience this afternoon a genuine enjoyment of Western music. The Native J'ese music is basically different from the Western because they have not discarded the natural musical intervals for the artificially arranged Western scales of intervals, allowing the harmonies which have made the classical Western music of the last three centuries. Consequently when they hear the richness of music as we know it, they become "mad over music," as the lad who went with me this afternoon said of himself on the way there. But as I listen on the radio to a sandwich of boogey-woogey and native J'ese music I get the impression that the J'ese have saved themselves a lot of trouble, because the line of development our music has followed from classical through jazz to boogey-woogey seems to be leading straight back to the J'ese orientalisms. In the course of the afternoon it became apparent to me that we ought to have a choir at the church, that we could have one, and that perhaps we will. But I'll probably have to start by making a Christian out of that conductor lad.

Tucked in a pocket of headlands 5 miles down the coast from here is a little fishing village, Manazuru. It has been a fisherman's village for about 10 centuries, and looks it! It struck the headlines of Tokyo papers last month because the local fishermen registered a protest in Tokyo against some "gangster" activities in Manazuru. It seems some clever merchants had cunningly got a financial stranglehold of the fishing industry there and the local fishermen couldn't reap the financial harvest of their toil. There's a lot of this type of "gangsterism" at present. (More about it later.) S.C.A.P. is conducting a campaign to encourage the people who get caught in the toils of "gangster" blackmail and graft to organise in their own defence in the way these fishermen did. Their argument in Tokyo was picturesque. They said, "Because our families have held the fishing rights in Manazuru since they were granted by Emperor so-and-so about 1,000 years ago we ought to be holding them today – and indeed we do the fishing still, but these grafters have cheated us out of the rewards of our labours, by getting a financial hold over us and compelling us to dispose of our catch to them at a price unprofitable to us, but enabling them to make fortunes by selling at the current high prices." Did you ever see such a perfect picture of old and new?

I went down to Manazuru last week to visit a friend and view the prospects of church extension in that direction. Do you remember the ex-university Professor of Horticulture whom I met in the late train from Tokyo one night? The one who hated America and Japan but "had God." We've become good friends and I went to visit him, for he has been to my place several times. He took me to meet some of his friends in Manazuru. There is quite an "artists' colony" there with many cultured people living in cosy cottages clinging to the sides of the picturesque headlands. Among other people I met one of the old War lords of Japan. A 70 year old retired General (retired before the war) living in a little cottage which is a combination of Western and J'ese architecture. All arty-crafty and polish and chromium plating, but the view along the coast is sheer natural beauty. He did me the honour of sitting me in his own chair, which is something you cannot appreciate till you've lived here. I was a bit perturbed at accepting it when he offered, but he insisted so strongly I couldn't refuse without offending him. The Yashikuni [Yasukuni] Shrine is the shrine to which it is believed the soul of every Japanese soldier killed on war service returns. That shrine is the focal point of the religious fervor coupled with the radical militarism that held sway here for the 10 years pre-Occupation. Well, this ex-General was, in his heyday, the President of that shrine. He's still a wiry old warrior, though I mustn't give you the impression he's not a gentleman, for that would be wrong, as he was a thoroughly charming host. We talked about the difference between the Shinto Faith and Christianity. He seemed to derive a good deal of comfort from the Shinto belief that when he dies he'll become one among the Gods. I couldn't offer him anything half so attractive – to his way of thinking.

I had to leave Manazuru because of an appointment at home, but when I reached the station I found the trains were stopped by a trivial accident down the line. However, the main coast road is just across from the station, so I went over to it and hitch-hiked back to Odawara without much trouble. Waiting for me were Ethel Lewis and her fiance Sgt. Jo Ehrich of the U.S. Army. They'd been planning to marry at the end of November but had just heard that the U.S. Army was about to impose a 3 months' wait on any of its soldiers who wanted to marry. So they decided to get in ahead of the Army since they had everything ready. They had come to arrange with me for the wedding to be on the next Monday. Actually they had to be married by the U.S. Consul if Ethel were to be permitted to enter the U.S.A. when Jo returns home after service here. But they wanted to come to the church here after the consular "signing up" for prayers and my blessing. They went back to Tokyo that afternoon after we'd made the few arrangements necessary. It so happened that the day of their wedding was the day previously fixed for a 1-day conference of Church Youth Association representatives at my house. So on Monday Nov. 4th we had a mixed day. The Youth Reps. started their day with a Communion Service in my big room at 9.30 a.m., then went on with their sessions. At noon Ethel and Jo arrived as Sgt. and Mrs. Jo Ehrich and we went down to the Church, the Ehrich's, their two witnesses and me, then returned to find the Youth Reps. tucking into their lunch. We'd been able to scrape up a few things for a spot of Wedding-breakfast so the wedding group sat down on my tatami and ate while I went back to the Conference group. The Wedding-breakfast table was ornamented with some traditional J'ese Wedding ornaments which Minamioka-san lent me. My good housekeeper was most intrigued by what she saw of Western wedding ways, and after the party had left she passed the opinion that "Lewis-san" (that's Ethel Ehrich now) looked "Taihen kirei," which is, literally "very lovely." They left at about the same time as the Youth Reps. and after they'd all gone I gathered up 4 youngsters and fed them on the canned fruit salad, jelly, cream and fruit juice that was left over. We all enjoyed it – they eating and me watching. Lip-licking kiddies are always lovable aren't they?

I haven't said much about the Youth Conference, but it was apparently a useful time for all of them. There were many plans made for future work and I talked about the possibility of a revival of the pre-war summer camps for Youth. There were 40 of them between 15 and 25 years of age – the "coming Japan," and please God this place will have some influence on the coming Japan by its influence on these younguns! The "scaffolding" of the new Japan is being spread far and wide. I've come across it in yet another way here in this little town. In olden days the compulsory schooling period was for only 6 years and now it is to be increased to 9. That means a large increase in the number of students and therefore, extensive additions to buildings. Last night a meeting of parents and citizens was called to make plans for the necessary new building for this neighbourhood. The Education Dept. states what is necessary and gives the total cost at Yen 11,823,000. Of this cost the Govt. will provide 2,907,912 from Revenue and 3,624,588 from Loan money. The remaining 5,290,500 must be raised locally. The meeting accepted a plan as follows: Every citizen is to pay a total of Yen 600 in 30 monthly payments of 20 yen each. Every parent with a child at the school is expected to pay an additional lump sum immediately of Yen 1,000 per child. (But war-widows are exempt). These undertakings represent quite a burden, and this is only for the framework, the new buildings. The cost of extra teaching staff and its training will come out of Revenue, but that means tax burdens. It is all to provide the means for sounder education. With the cost so heavy on the shoulders of the individual citizen it makes a pretty fair test of the genuineness of the zeal for new things. And after all, even more buildings and teachers doesn't guarantee a better child – haven't WE got a job?

The teachers of English in the State Schools of this prefecture are planning a new supplementary text-book. They've got sub-committees working on different phases of it. One of the sub-committee chairmen has been asking my suggestions on what to include in the book. You can imagine the kind of things I suggested. He had 3 things on his list when he came, but 11 when he left. Incidentally, I found they were planning to print extracts without any thought of copyrights. Knowing that the ignoring of International copyrights was one of the things by which Japan has broken normal standards of International behaviour I set out to convince him that teachers should be especially careful about such things, if they were to develop a proper sense of International relations in their pupils. He told me later that when he raised the matter at his committee, "as we all had no idea of it, all members were much dismayed." But of course they've no need to be dismayed, if they follow the normal procedures which we can teach them.

On Monday I am to pay a "pastoral" visit to the parish of Kofu near Mt. Fuji in a rural district. Incidentally, that district is the headquarters of the Nichiren Sect of Buddhists which gets special mention from Kagawa.

I've done all this at one sitting – 5 hours. It's good to be able to paddle along without interruption, not even an earthquake tonight!

Goodnight and God keep you.

SINCERE WISHES for CHRISTMAS
   with PEACE ON EARTH
      and GOODWILL TO ALL.
         Yours sincerely,
            FRANK

Newsletter No. *9*, 22 December 1947.

NIPPON SEIKO KWAI

Aust. Army Post Office,
C/- Empire House,
B.C.O.F.,
Tokyo,
JAPAN.

From – Rev. Frank W. Coaldrake

Dear Friends,

B.C.O.F. Air Force Chaplain Dave Beier came to visit and was most interested in the doings of this centre. His Air Force lads will be glad to help in any way they can the Australian Missionary efforts. I took him to see the No. 1 Film Factory of Japan 5 miles away. He bought some films, while I talked with the manager and asked him if I might come again and talk to any of his 1,200 employees who were interested in thinking about becoming Christians. The manager was quite co-operative and leaves it to me to arrange another visit at some time convenient to myself.

Army Chaplain Alan Laing came a week later for a few days visit, with Bruce Naylor. One morning they came to my Girls' School class and Bruce played on the Harmonium "Jesus, Joy of Man's Desiring." The girls just melted under the music and both side and end doors opened while people who were working roundabout came quietly in and listened spellbound. Bruce is a really good musician, and was a little lad in St. Paul's Cathedral Choir when I worked there years ago. Afterwards he played the J'ese "Apple Song,"[57] which delighted them, and the girls sang it sweetly.

27th Nov. is "Thanksgiving Day" for all Americans, and the U.S.A. Army everywhere has a great "spree." But two "G.I." lads did a nice thing to mark their Thanksgiving. They came unannounced, bringing a large package of gifts for the X'mas party we are arranging for poor families of this district on Boxing Day. They also brought over 200 X'mas Cards beautifully printed, which will be grand for the packets from the X'mas Tree, and Church members from U.S.A. Some U.S.A. Army lads after their discharge are returning to Japan as Missionaries, altho' not very interested in Christianity before their term with Allied Occupation in Japan they now realise the fundamental importance of a Christian faith to really help in rehabilitation of Japanese.

Recently at OISO (20 miles from here towards Tokyo), a new Social Service venture of the Episcopal Church of U.S.A. in Japan was actively commenced by the laying of the "cornerstone" for the model Orphanage which is to be developed by Sisters of the Epiphany from England. This is one of the most pressing needs for post-war Tokyo-Yokohama area. Roman Catholic and Buddhist Orphanages have been fairly numerous but now cannot cope with the situation. The Social revolution now occurring here by Law, and foreign example, decrees that the supreme importance attached to the "family name" is to be discarded. Formerly many adoptions were arranged to fill family gaps to continue family prestige, but poverty is the urge now, which compels all to work for their food and shelter, so adoptions are an uncertain quantity and the problem here, as in other countries, is what to do with unwanted Orphans. As I just stop to look at an orphan lad of 5 years sleeping at night on a railway platform, or scampering round the alleys in rags, I get a picture of the stresses and strains which this new Orphanage will help to relieve in unhappy Japan. It seems likely that for a while I will be acting-Chaplain to this Orphanage in the lovely IWASAKI[58] Gardens at OISO overlooking Sagami Bay. It will be happy work for me.

Some weeks ago I went to YUMOTO, in the mountains behind Odawara, to a 3 days conference on Evangelism, 100 people were there of the Nippon Seikokwai from all over Japan. Bishops, priests, laity and missionaries! There are

---

57 The most popular Japanese song in 1947, sung by Misora Hibari.

58 The Iwasaki family founded *Mitsubishi*, the large industrial and commercial corporation. The family had a villa at the seaside resort of Oiso and allowed parts of the site to be used as an orphanage.

only 16 Anglican missionaries from overseas in Japan so far, and we were all there, from England, Canada, U.S.A., and Australia was represented by just one![59] I found myself quite at home and the conference proceeded as smoothly as any similar conference in Australia. I have a new picture of N.S.K. [Nippon Seikōkai] and can enter with more understanding into their problems, hopes and aspirations, while seeing some of its truly grand people, such as the Presiding Bishop Yashiro. He wants to see the Church alive and active in all its members.

I frequently come across people who say, "Because Australia is a very rich country, I suppose there are no poor people there?" My answer is, "There are as many wealthy people in Australia as there are barbarians in Japan." Equally true or equally false, but in any case the wealthy people and the barbarians are a factor to be reckoned with, but not to be taken as typical of the majority. Yasuhiro (Jonathan Murota) age 5 asks, "Are all Australians big?" I reply "nearly all." Y – "Are there many Australians?" "No, not many." Y – "Is Australia only a small place?" "No, it is very large." After a space of silence, Y – "Because Australia is a big place with only a few people in it, have Australians been made big to fill it?" I ask you!

I often take my life in my hands (as the saying goes) by walking without an armed guard along the streets of J'ese country towns in which I am the only European, but the "inhuman barbarians" only smile at me, and the kiddies follow me with wide-open eyes or call out "Hurro," "Gootabyoo," so I'm not exactly being heroic!

I'm quite a bit tired, but heading for Home and wishing you were there to enjoy my ramble about the doings of the last 36 hours, but instead I must put you just at the distance of your eyes from my pen, while I bake over a steam-pipe that heats the carriage attached to a Freight Express from Tokyo to the South. I've been on another pastoral tour to YOKAICHIBA, 65 miles north of Tokyo, KUJUKURI Sanatorium 3 miles from there, and ICHIKAWA, 35 miles back towards Tokyo. (See Fig. 7) I battled for over an hour on Tokyo Station yes'dy to try and enter 6 trains "going my way" towards YOKAICHIBA, but was unable to get near any of them because of struggling crowds, or tangled masses of people 20 deep on the platform between me and any trains. If I'd been dressed for football and willing to apply scrum-tactics I might have got thro', but was considering having to turn back to Odawara as 2 wrestlers with their size and weight only raised a laugh when they also could not catch their train. Just then a train pulled in with Allied Personnel "special car" attached which opened its door to show a seat for me, and I breathed a prayer of thanksgiving.

At a certain junction I was met by two parish priests and a layman recently repatriated from Manchuria. We had to wait another hour for steam-train to complete our journey, so we talked whilst we ate our sandwich tea. The layman from Manchuria has ideas about starting a farm settlement, with Orphanage, for our Church. He is a practical farmer and also a graduate of our Church

---

59 See the earlier discussions of Church representation in the commentary to this chapter.

University [Rikkyō] in Tokyo. What I knew of Melbourne Boys' Homes at Bayswater, "Tally-ho," and C.E.B.S. [Church of England Boy' Society] Farm Training School, was useful in discussion. The parish priests are anxious to learn how to produce some income in place of the funds which used to come from overseas mission societies. It's their own idea and all I can do is help by suggestions, but our "planning" carried us over the 2 hours till we reached YOKAICHIBA at 9.10 p.m. We were met by an escort of Church members and the local parish priest, who got the news by "grapevine" that we were coming on this late train. As I settled back on my heels kneeling on mats in the Church Hall (there are no seats remember) and looked around, I met 30 pairs of eyes glittering in the flicker of two candles. After speaking for 10 minutes I asked for questions but they said, "So many years since we heard a missionary we would rather hear what you have to tell us." There were housewives, farmers, students and most were Church members, with only one "post-war Christian." We talked easily, and many times I saw the spark of conviction lighting eyes around that circle. We prayed, they departed, and the visiting priests and I bedded down on the mats there for the night. Our shoes spent the night on the step outside the door, for there is no risk of thieves in this old town which was not touched by bombs. It is still "Old Japan," so there is no thieving.

Next morn we went 3 miles to visit KUJUKURI Sanatorium and Convalescent Home overlooking the beach of that name (meaning 99 miles). This Home was founded by a great act of faith and continues in the same way. There are now 30 beds and Miss Henty of C.M.S. [Church Missionary Society] who was there for many years before the war has just returned. A 70 years old J'ese lady has been Superintendent. The aged parish priest Fr. Matsumoto who founded the Home and built a lot of it with his own hands was there with me. He is a great C.M.S. worker also, and his motive was to serve the needy and demonstrate Christian love. He has the joy of seeing his plans achieved. Later in the day I visited Yokaichiba Boys' Middle School and talked to 1,000 boys. The parish priest teaches there because of not enough parish income to support him. He warned me the boys might be unruly and noisy, but I found them alert and attentive. About the only "disorder" was when my pronunciation of a word puzzled them and they turned to each other for help in recognising the word. I waited till the faces all turned back to me with lips framing the word as I should have said it, all of us enjoying the joke.

I said I hoped it would be possible for their generation to find a new level of friendship with the same generation of Australians. The key word "friendship" I said as Shimitsu,[60] meaning "secrecy," instead of Shimmitsu. When I sensed what was wrong I repeated the word more carefully. Then a great smiling light spread over that carpet of 1,000 faces. I paused to ask them if they understood? The usual answer Wakarimasu was so enthusiastic that the blast of the "Masu"

---

60 Now romanized as *himitsu*. *Shimitsu* is a more literal translation of the pronunciation in this part of Japan.

nearly blew me thro' the back of the stage where the Emperor's picture used to hang for obeisance. What can we do to cope with such an eager band of lads! Afterwards I spoke with the English-speaking students among them and they gave me 40 letters to address to Australian boys.

Then it rained, and after collecting my baggage from the Church I had $2\frac{1}{2}$ hours of crowded trains to ICHIKAWA, halfway back towards Tokyo. A short stopover here with Fr. Matsumoto Junior's study group brought me into contact for the first time with the S.C.M. in Japan. These were students of Tokyo University and Chiba Medical College. They told me the study and discussion of Marxism is the keenest interest in student life at present. The Marxists here do not soft-pedal the root-atheism of Marx doctrines, as does the Communist Party in Australia. That makes it easier to deal with here.

Yet another 200 mile journey on another day to celebrate the Eucharist with the congregation in Chiba, many of whom were baptised, instructed etc. by the former Australian Board of Missions' representative, Fr. E. Harrison. Their Church was destroyed during air-raids and the services are now held in Church members' houses. I am reminded vividly of Queensland Bush Brotherhood services when I "toured" with Fr. Leeke in 1927–28.

At St. Peter's, MOBARA, in the vestry I found a silver Chalice proudly labelled as "given in 1923 by Australian lady Korutin" which is J'ese pronunciation of and English name, probably Coulton. She gave the Chalice to Ernest Harrison, and he left it there where it is still in use.

I am sending a letter to you (Mother) from the Sec. Mrs. T. Takahashi, on behalf of the Women's Auxiliary of South Tokyo Diocese. It is a scroll 8 ft. long on very fine rainbow-tinted paper, and is typical of the customary letter between friends in Japan. The writing is done with a soft brush. Miss Minamioka has included an English translation for you. One specially happy thing in my life here is the way my Mother has become a centre of interest and affection of the women of the Church. They make me feel very welcome, but my Mother must be thanked for allowing her eldest son to come so far to help them. This shows just how deeply the idea of family life colours all their thinking, and to distil this fine quality clear into the next generations is one of the special tasks of the Church here during the present boil-up of life in general in Japan.

After the passing of some weeks I was again able to visit the Film factory, which is reached by a quaint old tram route first built to carry pilgrims to a Buddhist temple. The 1,200 employees live in the village round the factory and they had not been visited by any Christian worker before. After my previous first call the manager was interested enough (altho' not a Christian himself) to locate one of "US" in his factory and sent her to ask me to come soon to start a study group. The next afternoon I found 24 men and women, ages from 18 to 30, including the Young Men's Captain, the Young Women's Captain, and the Trade Union Organizer. Most of them had never seen a Bible, nor had any knowledge of the principles of Christianity, or a word of English! I put a New Testament (in J'ese print) in the hands of each one, and for an hour explained how it came to be written, and why, then helped them to find their way to such places as John 3–16.

It was a kind of conducted tour of the places where the central teachings of Christianity can be seen. It was rather sad to have to take the Bibles back from them, but I only have enough for the use of my various classes, and at present it is not possible to buy more. However, I left one for the men and one for the women, but could not promise to go weekly as they requested. I was sorry I could not at present arrange oftener than monthly visits. Preparing lessons in J'ese takes less time as I go on, as far as language is concerned, but contact with the people opens their minds and problems to me so that I have to spend more time pondering over each job before I start on it.

My Odawara Vicar has helped work out my schedule and timetable from now until Easter and day by day I pray for more strength, more speed, more wisdom, a larger heart, and always for the one thing these people most need in me, devotion to Our Lord Himself. They don't need us to teach science, technology, art, or even how to be skilful, and we don't really need to teach them morals, for they have high moral ideas in their age-old culture. They have been accustomed to approve the good life and frown on the bad, as the only drunkard I've seen in Japan was treated in a very hostile manner on a tram the other night, while I felt a tolerant concern for the old man as I always felt for suchlike in Australia on occasions too numerous to mention. The Occupation Army and their own moralists efficiently deal with these everyday concerns, and it is the secret of living close to God I want to share with them to deepen my own experience of living by the grace of God. Just knowing what is good is not much help to me as a philosophy of life, because it does not help me out of the bogs of failure and despair, or downright rebellion against doing what I know to be right. I guess it is knowing that God forgives that makes all the difference, and if only I can show a few people here that God has a Law of Love for us all to follow, and Himself loves us and forgives us when we fail or break His Law if we turn and ask His forgiveness, I shall not have come to Japan in vain. Christianity has this thing to bring new into J'ese life, the call to repentance and forgiveness for breaking away from what they knew to be good. That is why I wish I could be more effective in my own loving of God, and of His other creatures. Often I feel so shallow, when I need to be so deep.

6 a.m. on the nippy morn. of Dec. 22nd, and I'm on my way to Tokyo to collect 7 bags of Mail I am told are there for me. After no ship for 2 months, 2 ships have now arrived with B.C.O.F. families, and some parcels in time for our 4 parish X'mas Tree parties. There is snow on the mountains and in the valleys. When I awoke 4 days ago I thought I was in another world as I looked thro' the open shutters across my garden, across the trees and out across the bay to the gold and purple glow that heralded the coming sun. All the colours had a new velvet-softness to the eye, and all the air was hushed and still for Snow was falling, and I saw my first snowstorm. It lay already inches deep at my step and clung to leaves and rocks. But rain came soon, and by the end of the day changed the snow into mud!

Wishing you ALL the Goodwill the world needs in 1948.

Yours in God's service,

FRANK

Newsletter No. 10, 1 February 1948.

NIPPON SEIKO KWAI

Aust. Army Post Office,
C/- Empire House,
B.C.O.F.,
Tokyo,
JAPAN.

From – Rev. Frank W. Coaldrake

Dear Friends,

Now that X'mas is over I realise that it was in many ways the happiest Christmas I have ever spent. The show really started for me on the Monday before X'mas for that night the parcels arrived that came by the "Merkur." Many pleasant surprises were mine as I read the name tags, and as I opened the wrappings I wished the senders could know just how appropriate were the gifts for our needs. My room became like a Santa Claus depot. I had wondered for some anxious weeks how to provide for our four X'mas parties with 400 people. A lot of things were given by Australian and American Occupation people, but your parcels saved the situation and made all the difference. Our first party was next day, 23rd Dec., as the 120 school girls held an all-day concert, with items ranging from classical J'ese and Chinese dances to comedy dialogue. One girl did an amazing dance on high-geta (the wooden sandals used in wet weather, 4 inches high.) We provided much cordial to drink and some sweets to each child at the end of the day. On X'mas Eve the 100 Kindergarten tots had an afternoon party with their own kind of singing and games. That was great fun. We gave them peanuts and biscuits. That afternoon Mrs. Ehrich and Miss Morris of Australian office staff in Tokyo arrived to spend the X'mas helping us and brought more gifts. They slept at Mrs. Murota's house but ate with me. It was good of Jo Ehrich to let his wife come away for their first X'mas, but Ethel told me that Jo said, "If it is going to give happiness to some children, you go." Well, she certainly did that.

On X'mas Eve I conducted my first Baptism service when YUJI AKUTSU an 18 year old student was baptised. He attended Church before I came here so has completed the long period required before a person is admitted to membership. Another lad was admitted as Catechumen, and he will be ready for baptism some months hence. When I reached home two lads were waiting for me (Fumio of the film was one of them) and we listened to "Carols by Candlelight" on Radio Australia from Melbourne until the rain ended that. Then for a while Norman Banks interviewed holiday-makers at Flinders St. Station, so my X'mas was not so far from yours.

Christmas Day started with early service at 7.30 a.m., then the grand Christmas Eucharist at 9.30 a.m. when I assisted and preached in J'ese. The Church was really full and "alive," there being enough old members to carry the many who were at a Christmas Eucharist for the first time. Fr. Miyazawa said later it was the first occasion he has seen the Church full since it was built. It was a happy day in this his 30th year in this parish. After the service we made our way to the Kindergarten room and gossiped until time for X'mas dinner, which we all had together. The Ceylon tea with milk and sugar, the meat in the stew, X'mas cake and dried fruits came out of your parcels. There were many expressions of appreciation. A concert followed in the afternoon, but I had to leave early to go by train to Kawana Rest Centre[61] where I was asked to take services as no Army Chaplains were available. We had Vespers and Carols at 5 p.m. and a celebration of Eucharist next morning. Lt. Burrows and his wife then drove me back to Odawara before 11 a.m., bringing also bread and cordials for the biggest party that afternoon. Mrs. Elrich and Miss Morris had wrapped 100 parcels ready for the X'mas Tree. Our final party commenced at 2 p.m. with 60 children and 40 adults, not Church members, but mostly poor people of the district near the Church. TAKAURA-SAN, the greybeard "grandfather" in the Film[62] came as Santa Claus in traditional outfit, Ethel Elrich playing him in with "Jingle Bells" on the piano. In three groups everybody ate, after which some items of entertainment were given. The Mayor of Odawara wanted to come but was prevented by a meeting, so he sent his deputy along. It is business-as-usual on Dec. 25th and 26th in Japan, the annual holiday being New Year's Day when the nature of the festivities resembles X'mas in Australia. It was this Boxing-day party which needed a lot of things and the Menu was much appreciated, slices of bread with butter and jam or fish paste, Sao biscuits, cocoa with milk and sugar, custard specked with sultanas, and Jellies which I made on X'mas Eve. You can imagine the fun making gallons of custard from powdered milk and custard powder on a kerosene stove. It set as firm as the jelly and both were eaten from saucers with chopsticks. I explained in answer to their thanks that the gifts and food were from Australian and American friends, so they asked me to be sure to send their thanks over to you all. I do here and now, but if I were to thank you as many thanked me I'd go down on my knees in front of you and put my forehead on the mat, that being the usual custom here. "It is more than 10 years since we felt anything like this real joy at Christmas, with friends from overseas making us feel they are with us and ourselves free to enjoy it," said one Church member to me on that day. A few weeks later Fr. Miyazawa has said, "The people are still talking with me about Christmas, and we all had more of the real X'mas feeling than ever before. It means so much to us to have evidence that people in another place really wish us to have a Joyful X'mas and now we want to help our neighbouring Churches that way next X'mas, so we are planning already how we can share our joy with others."

I've just spent my first New Year in Japan. It is the greatest national festival of this country. With the land in the grip of Winter, nature's colours are very sober,

---

61 This was the Kawana Hotel, a famous pre-war hotel and golf course on the Izu Peninsula coast just south of Itō. It was commandeered for use by B.C.O.F. during the Occupation.

62 This refers to a movie film made by Frank Coaldrake which no longer survives. Later films are now preserved at ScreenSound Australia (for archival references see end of *introduction*).

but by custom the robes of women and children are extra vivid and varied. Young women have their hair dressed in a traditional manner almost as fantastic as the old Victorian bustle-skirts of England. There are many ceremonies, and ceremoniousness is the rule of the day. I do not know enough about the customs to write about them at present beyond saying that they are certainly colourful and gay, and that everyone does something special to mark the occasion. I did not go to the Odawara Beach to watch the New Year Sun rise over the ocean as many thousands of Odawarriors did, and if I had I certainly would not have gone for a swim in the icy ocean as some of the lads did. But I did spend New Year's Eve on a walk with a dozen or so of the lads to an historic mountain ridge down the coast a bit; and I did spend the hour before and after midnight at the Church in a kind of Watchnight Service with about 20 of our Church people. Before the prayers we talked about the most important, or interesting things that happened to us during the year. Five of the 16–20 year old lads told how they'd come to the Church for the first time in 1947 and what it had come to mean to them. One 17 year old who is unusually big-built for a J'ese said in a quaint way which caused much merriment, "When I first found out about Christianity 3 months ago I discovered that although I'm very big in body I'm very little in spirit." (It has just occurred to me that there's not much sign of "face-saving" in that, is there?) Although I don't yet understand their New Year Festivals I've discovered a few things during the past few days. "Once upon a time" (Mukashi) is the clue to it all I think. "Once upon a time," a soldier-monk sat against a wall for 9 years. His hands and feet gradually withered and disappeared but he went on musing. He remained cheerful throughout and nothing could upset him. He is now the "God of Happiness" and his standard effigy is an eggshaped body and head without arms and legs but with a very cheerful grin, and he is so shaped that if you try to put him on his side he always comes up smiling. He is a rich red but with pink eyeballs. Dozens of these cheerful little effigies are hung on tree branches near shrines and on the beaches. When they are hung there the "hanger" makes a prayer for happiness in the coming year. If happiness comes he goes back and draws pupils in the eyes which otherwise remain blank. "Once upon a time," the noble lord of Odawara Castle slew a rival lord, took his head to the top of the Odawara Castle Tower and threw it out into the setting sun with a mighty heave. So great was the strength of the heave that the head hurtled through the air for nearly a mile and then its hair caught in the branches of a big pine tree just down the hill from my house. As the head dangled there it terrified a wandering monk who happened to be standing under the tree. He prayed to the head to spare him and the head fell to the ground, whereupon the monk resolved to build a temple for this new deity, which he did, and the temple is there today, close enough to keep me awake with its drum beating.

"Once upon a time," a noble lord was being pursued by an enemy in the dead of night. One of his faithful retainers tried to follow and defend him. As he went he bumped into a man whom he could not recognise in the dark, so he overpowered him without a word and held him on the ground with sword poised ready to cut off his head. Then he said, "if you are my master speak to me."

When he heard no reply he cut off the man's head. Next morning he discovered that it was his noble master he had slain, and on enquiry found that his master had been suffering from a sore throat and had lost his voice. The poor retainer was much distressed so prayed to his master's spirit for forgiveness. The kindly spirit forgave him, and, moreover, communicated to him the recipe of a specially efficacious "cough-drop," which could be bought at the shrine on the scene of the master's death until the war cut off supplies. "Once upon a time," some schoolboys of Odawara came to the house of an Aust. Anglican Missionary while he was out walking on New Year's Eve. They waited till he returned then asked him to help them. About 20 secondary school boys and girls of Odawara had formed a committee to help relieve the distress of people who were still suffering as a result of having had their homes destroyed by bombs. This committee had now found a big problem in a group of 10 adults and 4 children camping in front of the Odawara Station. Would the Aust. Missionary please help them by writing a letter to an American Army Rest Centre not far away asking for waste food for these homeless people, because the hotel manager would not listen to the boys, and they believed the waste food was being given to pigs. It was no longer "Once upon a time," but 5 p.m. on Dec. 31st, 1947, with night falling cold and 10 adults and 4 children in a really miserable condition. I had already seen three of them and had visited them and asked them to our X'mas party, but they had no children and were quite old so it didn't seem to appeal to them (I suspect we hadn't understood each other). The others I had not seen because they were away foraging for food during daylight. But I went with the boys and as it was now dusk found all the homeless at home. There was formerly a big concrete building with a vehicle-bay opening off a low-level street. The building was destroyed during the war but the vehicle-bay remains with the concrete floor above it as a roof. In the "bay" live 4 adults and 1 child, and 6 adults and 3 children camp in the open on the concrete floor. I have never seen people in such a miserable plight.[63]

It has been possible to do a little to help the School Relief Committee. I did not write to the hotel manager but visited him. He follows routine American Army practice and separates edible from inedible waste, giving the edible waste to his own J'ese employees to supplement their rations. We could get no food from there. I called on the Odawara Mayor on New Year's Day (a most disturbing thing to do) and encouraged him to give the School Committee all the help possible from the Municipal Relief Organisation. He came with the chief of that bureau to see me at my place next day and I took them down to a little empty cottage that I knew about. We found that it is used sometimes to store cement. I urged them to do all they could to have it used as a house. The real work is being done by the Students' Committee. The leading lights in it are Christians, but they are all and sundry boys and girls of the local Middle Schools and High Schools. On New Year's Day and 2 days afterwards they

---

63 This comment is made by someone with deep experience of poverty in the slums of Melbourne during the Depression.

made a public collection and got 25,000 yen, mostly in $\frac{1}{2}$ yen and 1 yen notes. They are using this to provide food, clothing and medical care, but it will not go very far. Some of the homeless are quite decent people but all are very dejected and dirty. There are, too, some rogues. The students don't know much about dealing with the practical details and have asked me many questions. I am not on sure ground in these matters here for I do not know enough about the social framework, but I can encourage and appreciate their splendid efforts. They are all back at their schools now that holidays are over, but they are still at work on this relief problem. Once again I find the same general picture of the present day Japan – I see it today from the angle of the homeless person. It is a picture of many people fired with zeal for new things, keenly appreciating a new scale of values, anxious to act accordingly but ignorant of procedure and cut off from any source of training. I'm doing what I can, and am embarrassed to find so great appreciation of the little I do. This sort of thing is said – "But you are a foreigner and we do not expect foreigners to worry about our homeless ones. Because you help our homeless ones it makes us realise that we should be doing things for them." "Once upon a time" – 9 years of happy musing, cough-drops from heaven at 5 sen a packet; New Year's Day 1948 – school children with a social-conscience and practical will. The background of these people is one of distorted history (Alas! One needs to know it), the future prospect cloudy, but perhaps we can make it different with new incentives, new standards and new faith. I've been thinking about the observance of Guy Fawkes' Day in Australia. Why do we keep it up? Why does the observance survive? What does it mean to Australians? There are many observances here which are similar in nature. I cannot yet form a conclusion on the depth of their relation to normal daily life.

A few days later on my way thro' Odawara I heard a great din, then saw a god-wagon coming along the road. This is the festival day of one of the buddhist temples near here, so they had brought the god-wagon out of its shed and taken it on tour. It is a 4-wheeled wooden cage-like carriage with a covered top-deck on which $\frac{1}{2}$ doz. drummers sit, and reminded me of Wirth's Circus lion-cage or a Sandy Bay [Hobart] double-decker tram. About 50 small children were pulling it by 2 long ropes, and where the temple idol used to sit in the latticed lower-deck were 6 kiddies having a wonderful time. The schoolboy drummers on top kept a certain rhythm and everyone looked happy though dripping wet out in the rain. The children love to sing and one of our country priests has taught his villagers to sing X'mas Carols, which they now sing daily in their streets instead of crude local songs. "Silent Night" is a general favourite and I wish I had a record of Bing Crosby singing it to play for our school children to learn it.

My duplicator turned out my first issue of Parish Notes in J'ese for Christmas and I am delighted with the good work it does, thanks to Miss M. Carss[64] of Melbourne.

---

64 Presumably the donor of the equipment, or the person who facilitated its purchase.

Further light on the "homeless ones" in front of Odawara Station is appearing in 4 of Tokyo's daily papers. Two of them have come to see me before printing, the other two are going on hearsay. The Municipal Relief office found a large tent, put it up away from the station and all but two moved in. (They've probably gone to camp in front of a more "peaceful" station.) One old man is clothed in rags and I am hopeful there may be something to protect him from this bitter winter in some parcels of used clothing you have said were on the way. He asked me for a New Testament as his Kokoro (spirit) needs food as well as his body.

Air Force men have sent me 2,100 yen for whatever my work needs most, so I will buy some more J'ese Bibles. The "Friends of Odawara" have sent some very useful materials through their Sec. Rae Campbell, including illustrated Sunday-school lesson cards, Baptism cards, and special prayer leaflets. Also, a supply of Kalsomine and brushes, paper and glue, ready for a working-bee next month to repair the Church, and a large bundle of 70 skeins of knitting wool which was joyfully welcomed. Next they plan to help pay any expense likely to arise out of a youth camp suggested for later this year.

Gratefully yours,
    FRANK

Newsletter No. 11, 1 March 1948.

NIPPON SEIKO KWAI

Aust. Army Post Office,
C/- Empire House,
B.C.O.F.,
Tokyo,
JAPAN.

From – Rev. Frank W. Coaldrake

Dear Friends,

In my student days I'd have put the headline "Japanorama" over the kind of things I want to write about to you now. Our new Bishop of South Tokyo, Rt. Rev. S. Mayekawa [Maekawa], stayed with me last night and left for Hatano this morning. As he put a raincoat over his overcoat he said "This coat is a good protection from thieves," then he showed me a stitched up slit across the bottom of his hop-pocket where a pickpocket had used a razor blade to get his money out in a crowded train. Such is a common happening in crowded Japanese cities these days, and there have been some horrible crimes lately. A pseudo-health official poisoned the employees of a bank and walked off with the money. Maternity Homes have been making much money by accepting care of unwanted babies in return for cash payments and then letting the babies die of neglect. (We must hurry on with our Orphanages.) A train in the country was boarded by robbers who intimidated the passengers in one carriage and alighted at the next station with all their stolen luggage.

Perhaps these crimes are reported in Australian newspapers. They're news alright for those who prefer to hear things unfavourable to Japan. But most of the "Old Japan" people are distressed because they feel it shows a deterioration in the nation's morals. I have evidence of this distress in a letter from a countryman way up North who hopes I might be able to stem the tide. He thinks too many Japanese are "apeing" Europeans and becoming neither Japanese nor European. He hopes I will be able to appreciate the good things in the truly Japanese character and help to restore those things to prominence in their way of life. Another middle-aged man came from Tokyo to see me and his "burden" was the same. "Young Japan has gone mad in self-seeking and has thrown restraint and decency overboard." I suggested he was too sweeping in his statements, as I know many young Japanese who are acting finely even now.

Fr. Miyazawa put it in his own happy way last night – "All the Japanese associated with Occupation people are like fever-sick patients. These "feverish" folk are noisy and prominent, but most Japanese are carrying on quietly." To get his true meaning you must know the translation is from the word "shizuka" which means the opposite of anything sinister in implication. The peace of the forest is Shizuka and in our Prayer Book where we have "pure heart and humble voice" in English, it becomes "Shizuka voice" in Japanese. It is a fact that Juvenile Delinquency has increased in Japan as elsewhere, which I think is due to the same War conditions that have brought about a similar increase in other countries, but to explain it doesn't get rid of it of course. We have much work to do to overcome it.

Another letter I have is from a former P.O.W. who was interned at Murchison, Victoria. He says he was well treated and consequently grateful to Australia, and offers to help me in any way possible.

Akutsu, one of my student lads, is sharing lodgings in Tokyo during University term and he described to me just how awkward it is in a room 9 x 9 feet, with one desk and one lot of bedding. They do their own cooking and use the desk and bed in "shifts" with one studying while the other sleeps, and the shifts change at 2 a.m. This time of the year is examination study for Japan's students and they must work very hard if they are to succeed.

Tokyo public 'phone coil-slot mechanisms gradually broke down or became worn out. There were no spare parts so the 'phones were altered to allow people to use them without coins. No notices were put up and no payment asked for, but everyone using the 'phones has voluntarily poked money in the slots. Coins are scarce, so paper money and often more than the value of the call is put in. The Post Office is making money out of its unplanned "honesty boxes." Is it in Sydney that there are now Honesty Boxes in the trams, and from which the yield barely pays the cost of the boxes?

The threat of inflation becomes more serious, and in a further effort to balance the budget the Katayama Govt.[65] proposed increasing fares and postage,

---

65 Prime Minister Tetsu Katayama held office from May, 1947 until March, 1948.

but that was so unpopular they had to resign. There are many political parties and much changing of ground as the months pass, and many party members change their labels as the parties change their platform planks. Perhaps it will result in a few big parties, each with a solidly accepted permanent platform.[66] I think the present fluid state is because of the flood of new enthusiasms under the bestowed freedom which have not yet been harnessed to definite aims and methods. But as time passes the knowledge gained under the "New Constitution" will become more widespread. Tax payments in Japan have been lagging badly. Tax collectors have been instructed to proceed about their business more thoroughly. The latest development is that all Tax collectors are being allowed an extra ration of rice, so that they will be able to stand up to the strain of the work. Certainly, no one could do much on the ordinary rations. I know of one elderly person with not much money who stays in bed six days a week because it takes less food to live that way.

The Black Market is a vicious circle causing much unrest, and startling evidence is produced to prove that the Govt. scale of rationing is insufficient to sustain life for the workers. In Yokohama the magistrate appointed to try cases of alleged Black marketing decided he should restrict himself to rationed food only. He gradually starved and his death was widely reported in all the papers. It provoked many different reactions, but no change of policy that I can notice, even tho' I think that magistrate is one of the heroes of this age.

The miners of Japan made no headline when they kept a pledge, but I think it shows the right spirit is active among workers. The miners promised to produce the full quota of coal for the month of January if they were allowed to take their 5 days New Year Holiday. They were granted the holiday, then worked with a will and fulfilled their pledge.

My friend Goda-san had his home burned down last week while he was away at work, and he came at sunset to find his wife and their 3 small boys sitting in the street amid a few belongings. The fire started in a shared house because someone forgot to turn off the electric switches when all power was cut off temporarily, and they were out when the power came on again. Now Goda-san's family share a room which is used for dressmaking classes during the day.

Such privations are cheerfully endured in spite of February's bitterly cold weather. There is promise of Spring in pink and white plum blossoms now breaking into my garden landscape down the slopes "of my" hill, with a few birds chirping around too the last few days – but the temperature is lower than ever right now and they tell me March is the coldest in the calendar. Speaking of garden – we've had a fine crop of chokos from a vine climbing over the

66 The Katayama Cabinet was replaced for a few months with the Cabinet of Prime Minister Hitoshi Ashida. Then the fragmented parties and factions started to coalesce into socialist and conservative groupings. Shigeru Yoshida became Prime Minister for a second time in October, 1948, and held power at the head of the conservative party until December, 1954. Frank Coaldrake's speculation in the *Newsletter* proved accurate.

Mandarin trees. I'd like to try a Passionfruit vine, for it grows in the same conditions as chokos in Brisbane. An Army friend dropped in some lettuce and cauliflower last week. They had come from Australia by the "Quick freeze" method, and were really delicious.

A few weeks ago I stopped at ICHIKAWA for a meeting with young men of the Church there who wanted to ask how they could be more active as Christians in their community. They are full of aspirations and ideas but destitute of this world's goods, which may be a very sound foundation. This group had several possible projects in mind to work over and select one or two for definite action. The most likely are, regular contributions of their "widow's mite" or "saved-by-walking fares" to send to S.P.C.K. [The Society for Promoting Christian Knowledge] in London for the distribution of Christian Literature to Japanese held in Tokyo on trial as war-criminals. This suggestion was entirely their own. Another project considered was to start a half-day Creche at the Church for helping mothers of the district who have to work or go out in search of food. At present they carry babies on their backs, yes, even while toiling in the fields. Our little group were warm in heart and mind, even while we shivered in the bare room on a cold winter afternoon.

The parish priest Fr. Matsumoto Junr. speaks English fairly well. He said "When we see you here with us we knew many Australian Church members have a vision of the Whole-world Church (this word was in Japanese – ZENKOKWAI) but Japan Church has only worried about Japan Church. Since we saw you here our eyes are opening and we are envious a Church having many members who see a Whole-world Church. If Japan Church can look away from itself and learn to live as part of Whole-world Church how good it will be. How can we start here to spread the vision of Whole-world Church through Japan Church?" There could not be a more telling answer to those in Australia who said to me, "The Church needs man-power to do its work in Australia." In Fr. Matsumoto's spontaneous words I find the vindication of my view, and yours, which impelled me to come over and help Japanese Christians. Just my being in Japan, kept here by Australians through A.B.M., is an object lesson and a help to many Japanese whose eyes have been focused on Japan first and last. This, of course, involves a cost of hundreds of pounds per year to the Australian Board of Missions, and is therefore an expression of the will of thousands of Australians who contribute to A.B.M. funds.

Fr. Peter Shikutani will come in steaming in a few minutes. He is down at the Murota house having a hot bath in J'ese style. A huge wooden tub in a specially built little house has a fireplace built underneath. The tub holds about 50 gallons of water and it takes the little fire about 6 hours in midwinter to heat this to 120°. Then the bather dips out small buckets of water to wash all over with some soap. Finally, when all is perfectly clean the bather gets down into the tub and cooks like a little potato in a big saucepan! Fr. Peter is down from his snow-bound mountain village because he has been called as a witness to the War Crimes Trials in Yokohama. He was imprisoned by the J'ese Army in China, and also when he was brought back to Japan in 1943 with Bishops Sasaki and Sugai,

Fr. Shimizu and Fr. Takeda. Fr. Peter's health was always poor and now is worse, so I try to build him up a bit as often as he stays with me, for life is very hard for him on an "allowance" per month equal to 1 day's pay for a farmer. Water is scarce in his village in Winter as it all becomes ice, and firewood is under snow, so he cannot get a bath up there. He tells me that the X'mas goods from your parcels made it a happy X'mas for 40 of his villagers.

We had a good meal tonight with Casserole of fresh pork, potatoes, tomatoes (tinned), and stewed dried (Aust.) apricots. The pork was really fresh and was a gift worth £4 in Australian money (i.e. £2 per 1 lb. of fresh pork). Because it was a rainy day Fumio (the lad in Ian Shevill's film) came to invite me to be cheered up by a visit to his father, who is a professional hunter and was carving a wild pig he had just caught. So whilst I viewed the "carving" Fr. Peter carried on a conversation with the old man who is a very zealous Nichiren Buddhist and rather deaf. He was asking questions about Christianity which Fr. Peter answered, all in Japanese of course. There is no end to the strange situations in which the Evangelisation of Japan is carried on.

My latest request to go on our *Newsletter* list is from Mr. A. Yule, College of Chinese Studies, Peiping, China. I have had an interesting *Newsletter* from him and things in China seem to be as much worse than here, as here is worse than Australia.

Tom Inglis-Moore visited me last week. He has been lecturing on Australian Literature to B.C.O.F. personnel for the Army Education, and also trying to get an insight into conditions of ordinary life among J'ese citizens, for he is also Lecturer in Pacific Studies at Canberra University. I took him with me on some of my visits to local people, and it was his first contact with truly J'ese people in their homes during his 6 weeks' visit to Japan. It is easy enough for overseas visitors to meet those who are employed by the Occupation and also to visit their families and friends some of whom can speak English, but all these are "Occupation-conscious" or even "Occupation-happy!" However, there are millions of J'ese who accept the changes brought about under the Occupation without ever giving a thought to meeting one of the Occupiers. These are the real Japan and our judgments must take them into account, so I will be very interested to read anything Inglis-Moore writes.

Lenten addresses in J'ese are keeping me busy for some weeks, and for spare time activity I am working on odds and ends of Church repairs. My Sydney kit of tools are worth their weight here now.

Last month

A 3-day round of visits to 5 centres on the peninsula which is on the Pacific Ocean side of Tokyo Bay was filled with many incidents I know you would like to hear concerning my pastoral peregrinations. Rain followed me all thro' the 3 days and when it wasn't falling cold from the clouds it was leaping up muddy from the roads, which were really canals of mud with an occasional stone to stumble over in the dark. The many bullocks pulling wagons along with them automatically adopt the style of rhythmic lunging seen when they plough the deep mud of the paddyfields. One road [surface] we saw [only] twice in the 4 miles of it, in black darkness from the railway to the village church. Even my three Japanese companions thought it was bad enough to cancel that call, but there were people waiting at the end of that road for a meeting to be followed by a daybreak service before they went to their farm work. So I tucked my pants into my socktops and handed controls over to my feet to feel their way as other voices guided me on the track. My nostrils conveyed a "whiff to whiff" chart of the journey and I now remember it as Odour Road. To start with on the right I could not see, but could whiff the coal and sulphur smoke from the train in the misty drizzle, then on the left a paddyfield became the odour landmark.[67] That persisted until we reached the sweet scent of rain-soaked pine trees on a rise thro' a cutting. Our next odour was from the rice-milling shed with a pile of hills smouldering outside and then we bend right to pass four farmhouses, all located by combined odours of glowing charcoal, Daikon [Japanese radish] soup and stabled bullocks. So it goes on for an hour till at last we turn towards the house of the Parish Priest, a farmer among farming people. Ten Christians waiting, including one old faithful baptized 50 years ago and another of 38 years ago. The ancient one asked me a question about the status of the Emperor, himself knowing the Christian's answer but wanting the young enquirers there to hear the statement from me, a statement which would have sealed my doom 3 years ago. These believers, knowing much about the depth to plant radish seed but little about the doctrine of their faith, echo the old man's "I have known years of Joy in the Lord." The farmer-priest age 35 is helped by a loving wife in his isolated <u>KOFU</u> pasture, and his aged father of 80 years is also Priest in another parish with every inch of his Church and Rectory grounds tilled by himself to grow his food at St. Peter's, MOBARA. Next morning the walk back to the railway was no longer dark and odorous but a highway of colour and movements, busy women in nearby fields taking a crick out of their back to return the smile of the foreigner walking by!

At TATEYAMA, St. Andrew's was filled by 50 worshippers for Evensong on another wet night and they listened patiently to my $\frac{1}{2}$-hour committing atrocities on their language. All Saints [Church] ONUKI is ministered by a sickly priest who spent 2 years in prison up North for being a Communist, then later read everything Marx wrote and most of Lenin with the result he became a Christian and eventually a parish priest. MINAMIHARA has a small solid Church set back from a village street which was full for 3 p.m. service, the people dropping kitchen knife or their hoe in the fields to join us as we walked from the station. The afternoon sun came through the door as we sat on Tatami Mats and talked for an hour after the service. Then to KAMOGAWA, only a room in the Kindergarten but nevertheless part of our Church of faithful people.

I am amazed at the resourcefulness of J'ese farmers who probably acquire both the field and the peasant-lore as a family possession held thro' many

67 From the "night soil" used to fertilize the fields.

generations. The individual farmer knows how the winds of each season treat his particular field and every field is planted with old straw in low hedges, about 9" high and 2" thick to prevent the winds blowing away his few inches of fertile surface soil. The lines of straw cross and crisscross fields making attractive patterns on hill contours with no standard distance between windbreaks and only peasant wind-lore could explain the stops and starts, gaps and angles and curves of these windows of old straw.

Sincerely yours,
    FRANK

Frank Coaldrake, Manuscript with handwritten annotation "Australian Pacifist Conference. Abridged P/mkr [*The Peacemaker*], 1947/8." Published in abridged form in *The Peacemaker. An Australian Venture in Reconstruction*, vol. 10, no. 4, p. 3. [The following is the abridged version with the major deletion from the original manuscript re-inserted as indicated.]

WHAT DEFEAT HAS DONE TO JAPAN'S WARRIORS

By Rev. Frank W. Coaldrake, Odawara, Japan.

When I set out to answer our question I feel like a child playing with its building blocks. This is because I want to answer the question in terms of actual observations rather than theories. My "actual observations" are in terms of events, statements and facts. But, like a child building with toy blocks, I can arrange these things in different structures, according to my own point of view. Furthermore, another person would have different sets of blocks and arrange them differently.

1. The Blocks

(A) Japanese soldiers are still arriving in Japan. About two million or so have already returned, but tens of thousands remain in the hands of the Russians, and are now coming back at the rate of about 50,000 a month, at the most.

The repatriated soldiers I have seen arriving home reach Tokyo station packed in a third-class train. About 50 people wait to meet 1,000 soldiers. Two or three flags or pieces of bunting can be seen. A small committee waits to give addresses and advice. Some soldiers go straight to another platform and board the train for suburbs or nearby cities.

Odawara repatriates come this way. They travel the 60 miles to Odawara in an ordinary train as ordinary passengers. At the Odawara station, they will be met by a few friends or relatives. A small committee, mostly school children, waits to provide them with a cup of tea and a word of welcome. This committee also tries to help them find material needs.

Each soldier on discharge has the clothes he is wearing, and about as much ready money in his pocket as will keep him for one week. He is free of the army, and ranks entirely as an ordinary citizen subject to no more, no less controls. If he finds his house in good condition and a faithful wife waiting for him he is lucky. Often enough he finds rubble, or orphans. In any case, he must start straight away on the all-absorbing business of scratching a living.

(B) Onuki Farmers: One of my fellow parish priests is a Japanese farmer working his small farm among the thousands of other farmers in a rural district 100 miles north-east of Tokyo.

I asked him how the repatriated soldiers in his district were settling down. His answer: "They were farmers before they were 'called to the colours,' and they have come back to their farming families. With the present scarcity of food and with the parcelling out of farming lands under the Land Reforms, they are able, like all farmers, to make themselves steadily more prosperous."

I asked: "Do they have any mental difficulties about settling down to the humdrum farming life? Do they hanker after the army life?" His answer: "No. They are born farmers, and they are happy farming. They went away because they were 'called to the colours'."

"Do they have any sort of association to keep alive the old army days friendships?" – "Not that I know of."

(C) S.-san. Aged 28. Spent nine years in the army with a machine gun company, going straight from university to the army. Served in South China and Burma. Was a theological student before the war, and is now in the Ministry of the Church – was ordained three months ago. "I was a Lewis-gun expert – but I managed to evade ever having to fire a gun. Life in the army was terrible. I died so many times that this body no longer belongs to me. I must use it in the service of God and my fellow men." He is.

(D) U.-san. Lives in a mountain village in his own house with wife, mother, sister and four children. All depend on the farm for support. Farm consists of three separate patches of dry upland soil, totalling less than half an acre. Age now about 40. Served about five years. Went from farm to army. Fought at Finschafen and other parts of New Guinea. I spent a half-day walking through the country with him. As we lunched he said, with a laugh: "You know the last time I saw an Australian it was over my rifle sights." We stared at each other in silence for some time. Soon afterwards he said: "Australia is a big country with a few people. Why wont they let us emigrate to it?"

(E) G.T.-san. Was a suicide pilot. Saved by a miracle. Says it was "the hand of God, so God must want me to serve Him now." Aged 22. Went through special schooling from an early age to prepare for his service. Now studying while earning a little money in Tokyo. Often stays with me in my house. Half-starved and over-worked. By any standards is "a decent fellow." Before he knew my views on war we talked about war.

He said: "When the war ended I suddenly realised that the military had fed us on lies. Militarism is a terrible menace to the world. I want to work for peace, and I will never again think what I thought when I first went into the army, that is, that I could help the peace of the world by serving in the army. That was a great mistake. Now I want to fit myself for a great service." He thinks of going to help a friend who has opened an orphanage in the south. He is a close friend of the following.

(F) O.-san. Now aged 23. Was recalled from Shanghai commercial world to serve in the navy. Served for three years as an Air Crew Signaller in Navy Air Force. Now studying commerce. Wants to fit himself to follow in his father's footsteps in the business world. Thinks he can help Japan by being a successful trader and bringing money to his own pockets and the country. Says he "had some good fun" in the Navy Air Force – but does not want to go back to it.

(G) G.D.-san. Now aged 40. Went from office into army; now back in office and rapidly climbing up the steps of promotion in a "semi-government concern that covers Japan." Said of his four years' army service: "It was terrible. It's a terrible story, but I'd like to tell it to you." The story was a list of face-slappings and beatings he had as a private in a cavalry company in China. Always felt humiliated. Now rejoices in the freedom he finds in Japan. Especially keen to develop his powers of self-expression.

(H) A.K.-san. Now aged 18. I baptised him on Christmas Eve. As a Christmas present he gave me a small statue of an ancient Samurai warrior. With it was this letter, which I quote in full (his English is adequate though not perfect): "My dear Father Coaldrake. This is symbol of Japanese Fewdalism [sic.] and old militarism. During the war I resisted this. So I was persecuted by those who advocated militarism, but I didn't bow them. At last, Peace All Over the World! I was free from this old idea. Now I give you this little doll as a Christmas present. I am very glad to be baptised by you. I love Peace and I believe God. I will try to be a good and religious man. The grace of our Lord Jesus Christ be with us all. (Signed.)"

(I) S.F.-san. Aged 45. Lived most of his life in U.S.A. Was recalled just before the outbreak of war, but was somehow omitted from the draft when his age-group was called up. His old father was so afraid the family would be disgraced in the eyes of the village that, when the rest of the group went off to their weekly parades as "home service" men, he locked S.F.-san up inside the house till the others came back to the village. S.F.-san thought himself very lucky.

(J) Tak.-san. "When the Emperor surrendered he showed he was out of touch with the spirit of the Japanese people. The people prefer to die rather than surrender. Since the Emperor showed he is not truly Japanese in spirit I no longer believe in him."

(K) G.D.-san (again). In conversation, I said: "Some Australians say that the only good Jap. is a dead one." He [was] flustered and said: "Yes; some of our old women say that." I asked: "Why do they say it?" His answer: "No Japanese who came back from a war which we lost is a good one. The good Japanese all died on the battlefield." I tried to explain the different reason for the Australian opinion.

And again: "S.C.A.P. reports the existence of a 'hidden government' of criminals dictating the rule of the country by force of assault and by bribery. S.C.A.P. says this group will subvert the new democracy unless it is rooted out. What do you think about it?" His answer, in brief: "I think there are such men in hiding, but they won't stand a chance against the power of the new democratic spirit in Japan. Too many people have learnt to use and enjoy the freedom we now have. They won't let anybody take it from them."

(L) Tojo made his defence statement before the [War Crimes] Tribunal. It was a major event in public life. The press is currently interviewing all kinds of people for their opinion on Tojo's Defence statement. I quote from *Nippon Times*, of January 3rd [1948], on the subject. (This paper, in my opinion, after reading it daily for six months, ranks about equal with our best Australian dailies for reliability and balance.)

> There can be no doubt that Tojo's stock has risen considerably because he exonerated the Emperor from responsibility for the war and accepted the blame himself, but the vast majority of Japanese have never held, and still do not hold, any high respect for him.
>
> Most people over 40 years of age have considerably altered their views (i.e. regarding the reasons which the militarists advanced for the country's entry into World War II). But the majority of young men still believe that the war, as Tojo declares in his affidavit, was forced upon the country.
>
> The average Japanese man-in-the-street expressed more sympathy than hatred for ex-Premier Hideki Tojo, and voiced the belief that his statement made to the Military Tribunal contained the truth.

(M) Top-ranking soldiers have been "purged" – i.e. forbidden by S.C.A.P. to hold any office in the affairs of citizens.

2. Building with Blocks

This is my answer to the question: "What defeat has done to Japan's warriors."

First, it has sent them back to the ranks of citizenship as men bearing a certain measure of disgrace, certainly penniless, and mostly deprived of power. What influence they have in the community is a separate point.

Most of the ex-soldiers would again answer a "call to the colours" if they received it. Their reasons would be the same as formerly, namely, just that it was "A call to the colours." A few would resist such a call. Many would join in public discussion before the call came as to the likelihood, or need of it, and after it came, as to the rightness of obeying it.

[The following section was included in the original manuscript but cut from the published version:]

To change the outlook of the warriors S.C.A.P. seems to have depended on:

1. the morale effect of defeat.

2. the Constitution of Japan adopted this year. The constitution works on the warriors in two ways. It denies to Japan the holding of a standing army or training organisation, and it offers the attractions of American style Democracy to entice the warriors to "seek peace and ensure it."
3. the purging of the known leaders of Militarism.
4. trying to lure the old liberals out of hiding and obscurity by offering them safety and prestige, albeit, a highly unpopular job as the "Govmint" whom everybody is "agin" just because times are hard!
5. a shrewd blow at the roots of militarism through a hastily devised and clumsily executed new education programme for all children.
6. the encouragement of the Press to exercise its freedom – though this means letting publishers flood the markets with pornographic and puerile trash when there is a serious shortage of paper.
7. the encouragement of the Christian Church, both locally and from overseas, to exercise the freedom of religion now granted under the Constitution – though a non-pacifist Christian Church can be the very devil.
8. the breaking up of concentrations of industrial, financial and agricultural property holdings so that there will be no powerful combines to serve as a focus for speedy re-armament.
9. the destruction of war equipment and the dismantling of munitions factories.

The negative elements of this programme, i.e. the restricting and the destroying, have been energetically pushed ahead. But the positive sides, i.e., the creation and encouragement of the new motives and new standards, are handled more vaguely, though not without enthusiasm. S.C.A.P. is here up against a very difficult matter – the morals of a community are interlocked in a complex with its economy, technology and religion. Unfortunately there is not scope to enter into the matter here beyond reminding you that S.C.A.P. wants to change the mind of the warrior but inevitably finds it a difficult process. [End of abridged section.]

The warrior has gone back to his hoe or his hammer, to his rubble or his rush mat, to his seaweed and sweet potato. He is still consciously a Japanese, and still, as a Japanese, his chief concern is to live as artistically, i.e. with as much aesthetic enjoyment, as possible, on as little as possible.

The present is pregnant with possibilities. There is a dawning desire to live up to the Constitution, to become in fact what the Constitution describes – a country without any soldiers. A Foreign Office official said to me after I had answered his searching questions about the White Australia Policy: "Japan has a great chance to become a peace-loving nation. It would be wonderful if we could become known and understood among the other nations as the world's peace-loving nation. We need only two things to make this possible – trade, and an emigration outlet."

If Japan's leaders take her in that direction, the warriors of the past will stay at their hoes and hammers, and the men of the future will not be warriors. If the leaders head back in the direction of war, the manhood of the nation will readily, though I think not so readily as in the past, troop back to tanks, planes, machine guns and lathes – and the womanhood to their war works.

Is that likely to happen? Ultimately, the answer will come from outside Japan. Whether the demilitarising of Japan will be a fact in five years' time depends on the movements in international relations. We must always remember that the leading principle with which the Japanese people are being exhorted is "Be democratic," and that being "democratic" does not of itself, connote restraint from war. On the contrary, it was often argued in democratic countries during the war, that the more democratic the people were the more efficient they would be as a fighting nation. Horror of horrors! If a fascist Japan was a terrible enemy – what would a democratic Japan be?

A democratic Japan would be a potent ally and her recent warriors would be easily revitalised. The Japanese have few fears of the hardships of war because they ordinarily live on the borderline between hardship and desperation.

Newsletter No. 12, 1 April 1948.

NIPPON SEIKO KWAI

> Aust. Army Post Office,
> C/- Empire House,
> B.C.O.F.,
> Tokyo,
> JAPAN.

From – Rev. Frank W. Coaldrake

Dear Friends,

Our *Newsletters* are proving to be all and more than I hoped for as they become a Prayer-link around the globe. My old friend Rev. C. Leeke, formerly of Bush Brotherhood, Queensland and now Vicar in Spalding, England, has sent me the address of Miss Ruth Wordsworth who was a missionary in Japan some years ago, but now lives in London. Also I received the address of Miss E.G. Phillips, who was in Tokyo 1901–41, but now is in Surrey and she kindly sent us the address of Mrs. Harrison, Vancouver, Canada (widow of Rev. Ernest Harrison, the only Australian Missionary in pre-war Japan at Chiba, north of Tokyo). We would be glad of any early issues of *Newsletters* that you can spare for new readers coming along. Please return to Mrs. E.R. Coaldrake. No. 70 Denbigh Road. Armadale. S.E.3. Victoria.

The need for clothing of any description is urgent for the homeless widows and children of South Tokyo Diocese and parcels up to 11 lbs. may be posted for 1/9 d. to me C/- B.C.O.F. Aust. Army P.O. 214, Empire House, Tokyo. Among my parcels have come two from an anonymous sender – a fine book and a child's colourful outfit. Thanks very much to "anonymous."

Yesterday there came a large case of tinned foodstuffs from Air Force men in the south of Japan which I can hold for the projected Summer Youth Camp. Also, at long last some bulk kerosene was landed at my gate and solves my fuel problem for many months to come.

I think this is the appropriate occasion to say something about prayer and to encourage those who pray to make their prayers for our work here their chief contribution to it. Things often happen quite unexpectedly to solve difficult situations. They happen in unpredictable ways and very effectively. I am convinced that my daily steps are guided and protected in answer to the prayers of many friends. Here is one of the things I mean. Back in December it was very cold and this house a wind tunnel. Electric power was rationed so that I was allowed to use only 20 units in the month. I had a pint of kerosene and a quart of petrol left from previous gifts; charcoal enough for cooking for a fortnight and none of these things, nor wood, accessible except by black-market. As the days passed I was preparing for a grim month or two and reckoning I'd be able to "take it," though efficiency would be low. Then one thing after another happened; a "GI" came down specially with 5 gallons of petrol; a Japanese visitor who shivered went away and talked to his friend the Electric Supply Co. manager – the final outcome was permission to use 100 units in February, and 200 a month afterwards. Finally came a letter from a missionary organisation asking if I wanted to join in a group-purchase of kerosene or fuel oil which the U.S. Army was prepared to sell us just once. So I was included in the group and the kerosene has now been delivered. That's what I call my "fuel bracket" of other people's prayers. There are many other such "brackets" which make me always conscious of the fact that my hands and tongue are implementing the prayers of a great many people. And that's why I'm so often saying people help most who pray most.

But yet it's not easy to know what to pray is it? I've been praying that my open house of things invaluable on the blackmarket would not attract thieves. My prayer in fact is that I may use everything here always unselfishly in God's service. If I am so doing I know that anything He needs me to have will be left here. But two houses within 100 yards of me have been robbed recently. The last was the small home of a widow with 4 young children. They took all the clothes (the police have recovered them a week later). But are the thieves being deflected from the purpose of robbing my house and turning on my poor neighbours? I don't think so. But praying is a humbling business, especially when one sees the effects of prayer.

This is the season of Marathon Relay Races in Japan. They had one between 8 Tokyo Universities from Tokyo to Hakone Lake and back, a distance of 80 miles each way with Odawara one of the "changing" points. Each man ran about 20 miles. There have been others, one being High School boys starting from Odawara Station finishing in Tokyo and it was a very wet day. But they're tough and everyone seemed to enjoy it, even the runners.

I haven't told you about the time I went to see the National Kabuki plays. It was a fascinating day but I felt I had better not say things which would be inconclusive. When I've seen some more I'll tell you about it. It's a very contentious matter from some points of view.

Several people have written saying they liked my Christmas Card and asking what it is made of? If you're rich enough to buy meat from the butcher he wraps it in that stuff. If you buy a hash of rice balls from a railway station peddler it's wrapped in that. It is a very thin veneer of pine, each piece being 20″ x 5″. With its grain and glint it is so much "nicer" than paper – that's why they like to use it. I simply stuck 2 pieces together for strength, after writing on one side of each. Now that it has been admired I can point to it as a sample of that pleasure in beauty of common things which is an outstanding feature of life here. This stuff is a little more awkward than paper in the using but we put up with the clumsiness because it is more artistically satisfying.

I tread from the road to my front door along a line of awkward stepping stones. A concrete or gravel path would be less clumsy but not half so much a feast to the eyes, nor calling for nearly as much artistic touch in the laying. I have to turn a tea-cup round to use one part of the brim from which it is possible to drink cleanly because the rest is bulged or lipped or gapped, or the glaze has been daringly blobbed or skimped. Awkward, but individually artistic and alive with a vigorous life quite absent from a smooth thin circle. In the middle of the guest chamber there's an old block of wood looking as though it might have spent a century or two at the bottom of the woodman's pile, always passed over because too knotty to split. But now in one end is a hollow lined with sheet copper and it serves as a charcoal brazier. A thing of natural beauty, attracting the eye, more awkward to handle than an electric radiator, but entirely different in the way it gives character to the room. By my front door there's a big old moss covered rock (10 ft. long, probably weighing 3 tons) with a natural cupped hollow on one side near the end. It holds water that trickles into it from an old bamboo pipe. It overflows into a bath-size pool from which one cups water to rinse one's fingers. (The J'ese word for garden NIWA means literally "cleaning place.") That rock looks as though it "grew there" and had the garden made around it, but it was carried from several miles away just to do what it does so well. What an eye it must have been that picked it out among the thousands of rocks in a gorge.

26.2.48

It was Ogata-san's birthday, on her day off fortunately. I used some "Pastry-mix" from one of your gift parcels and blackcurrant jam and tinned cream from the same source, to make her a jam tart with whipped cream, and took it down to her house just before tea tonight. Hope it hasn't make them sick. I was glad to have a good excuse to learn the tricks of a little "biscuit-tin" oven I bought from the junk-shop this week. It sits over the element of an electric heater, or the flame of a kerosene stove. Once we understand it we will be able to make better bread than we've been making in the frying pan. (Ogata came next morning full of thanks for the tart. Her children said it was the most delicious thing they had ever tasted.)

7.3.48. *Mothering Sunday*

I wish I knew more about feeding an infant. I fed it slowly with a spoon but after a while it gave me back most of it. The mother usually feeds it the invalid dish I make, but she didn't come for it today, through some misunderstanding. I took the food down and found the mother away and the babe lying shivering and whimpering, so decided to feed it. Now I've left the food by the straw palliasse so the mother can feed it when she comes back. The infant is one of the "homeless ones" I've mentioned before. The child was knocked down by a bus sometime ago. The mother is a decent woman borne down by such circumstances as being widowed and having constantly to be with the sick child and so being unable to work, nor even to go begging food. The infant when I saw her first was just a skeleton lying in dirty rags on a heap of straw. Now the mother keeps her "corner" of the shelter as clean as possible, but it's a losing fight. After trying for some weeks to get a doctor to see the infant he advised that it was a hopeless case. A week later the mother sent for me to tell me her little one had died and the Municipal Bureau had taken the body for cremation according to Buddhist rites. She was grief-stricken as any mother would be, and had gathered the child's few possessions, including the glass jar in which I had sent the food, before an improvised altar on which burned a few bits of incense. This child died of malnutrition brought about by the adversities following on the father's death a year ago, and there are other children dying for the same reason. Food is a problem but I am unable to help where I can with such things from your gift parcels as cornflour, barley, tinned milk, wheat hearts, glucose and Vegemite.

The Municipal Relief Office seems to have shot its bolt by putting up a crude shelter of straw "bagging." The school children are still supplying some things with their money, but they're in the middle of their annual exams at present, so I'm keeping in closer touch with the 14 people in the shelter. Last week another man dropped into Odawara from somewhere and found his way to the front of the station. He is the only new one in 2 months, despite the Japan-wide "advertisement" of Odawara's care for beggars. But he really was a sight – just black with dirt, sick and too weak to stand. The others in the shelter didn't want him because he was so dirty and he spent some nights in the open. The Municipal Bureau wasn't doing anything for him so the students came and told me about him and asked if I could do anything. I gave them soap to wash him, some good food to tempt his stomach. He seems to be doing O.K. now.

The Church's Mothering Sunday strangely enough has never been observed by the Anglican Churches here, though the community at large knows something of the modern commercial Mother's Day. I have happy memories of Mothering Sunday in Australia and must talk to our Bishop here about the traditional observance of it in Japan now as it would have particular point.

Odawara it seems is famous for its plums and the blossoms have been a picture for some weeks. I've been living on a postcard! KIKU is the local name for Chrysanthemums. There have been some magnificent flowers during the last few months. I had a large bunch given me by the High School students whom I helped with their Play, and the blooms remained beautiful for over a month in my large vase.

2.4.48

We had an inspiring Easter as the culmination of an earnest Lent. Church was full at the Easter Service, many young people being in the congregation. After the chief service of the morning the congregation went to the Kindergarten Hall and spent a couple of hours pleasantly in eating lunch, talking and singing. In the evening a young woman was admitted as a Catechumen and 3 Catechumen lads were baptised. I suppose we can say that each such event marks a growth of the Church, but we must not overlook the other kind of growth – that growth in an individual Christian which we call a deepening of Christian experience. I think Lent has been that for many.

From *The Church Standard* – "The Australian Board of Missions through its State organisations, has undertaken regularly to send parcels containing food and clothing in order as far as possible to liberate the Japanese Clergy from their secular duties, and enable them once again to give their whole time to the service of their parishes. It his hoped that Church people far and near will warmly support this action. Japanese Clergy themselves are likely to do far more for the evangelisation of Japan than any foreigners can, and therefore the most useful thing the Church in Australia can do at the present time is so to improve their economic position as to enable them to give their whole time to their pastoral functions. Amongst other things that the Board is hoping to do as gestures of fellowship and help in Japan: bicycle tyres are to be provided for the Japanese Clergy, as these cannot be secured in Japan at the present time; it is also hoped to make it possible for Bishop Yashiro, the Presiding Bishop, to secure a much needed car for his long journeys."

The parcels sent by the Australian Board of Missions' office from Sydney are now reaching each of the 23 parish priests in this diocese. A parcel a month to each of them is not very much but represents a considerable expense to the board. There is no doubting the value of the parcels is psychological more than physical. The parcels are made up by either of two lists according to whether there are children in the house. For special personal needs we can get particular things and in that way came a Greek Grammar for Fr. Endo.

Costs of goods and services here continue to rise so there is little prospect of improvement in local church finances for the present. There are times when it looks as though our church in one centre or another is just about ready to "fold up." That is the reason the Bishop has asked me to go round visiting all the centres as much as possible and make it my chief work for a long time to come. There is no end to the things that can be done to encourage, uphold, advise and relieve the parish priests. The Bishop cannot travel very much because of expense. The priests rarely see any of their colleagues, and never have any break in the round of Sunday ministry and week-day working for a living. I can at least give them a spell for a few hours and perhaps a few new ideas. For a scholar to have all his books burned and be unable to buy new ones must be like wandering in a desert. That is the case with several of them. I'm not clear yet what my work will be, and in fact I suppose it will not be possible to forecast or plan very much.

I'm just a Missionary to South Tokyo Diocese. One very pleasant way of being such is to have the parish priests as my guests at home. I've just had Fr. Shimizu and his 14 year old son to stay with me for 3 days. It is school holidays at present so he, as a teacher, could come. He rested, walked and talked. His English is quite good so we could talk about almost anything by combining his English and my Japanese. We spent one of the days in Hell (!) talking about sin, repentance, guilt, shame, responsibility and such things. In the Hakone mountains is a weird valley of geysers and craters and smoking sulphuric slopes. Its name is OWAKUDANI which means "Big Hell." We walked round the mountain road to the top of the pass enjoying a wonderful view of Fuji and Lake Hakone on the way. Then from the top of the pass we followed the narrow winding track down through the valley. Anyone who had seen Queenstown (Tasmania) would see the similarity of scene, but Big Hell is alive, moving, and smelling. Water everywhere but not a drop to drink because it is hot sulphurous deposits. The track winds along the face of bluffs of slowly-sliding sulphurous deposits. Except in the valley there was still much snow lying around in the mountains. It was quite unpremeditated that we should discuss sin and the like in walking through Big Hell, but perhaps not unnatural.

Fr. Shimizu returned home on Thursday and on Friday he was to go on up to Shizuoka to a 1-day meeting of the four parish priests of that region. They are to meet for the first time since the war and talk over their work.

Yours sincerely,
FRANK COALDRAKE

Newsletter No. 13, 1 May 1948.

NIPPON SEIKO KWAI

Aust. Army Post Office,
C/- Empire House,
B.C.O.F.,
Tokyo,
JAPAN.

From – Rev. Frank W. Coaldrake

Dear Friends,

If I throw away any sheets of paper with one side unused, Ogata-san is scandalised so I write this on the back of Minamioka-san's translation of an address I gave to mothers at the Kindergarten at Kamakura. When I'm short of time I give my English script to Minamioka-san and it comes back in Japanese-English which I then type, and work out just what she has done with my English (but thankful for her patience).

In Odawara I think the hardest Lenten discipline was my series of weekly addresses, finishing with one every night in Holy Week. They were a double burden, to myself in preparing hour-long addresses in Japanese, and to the congregation in hearing them with all the atrocities of my accent. In the course of the preparations for Lent I reached what is for me a new level of failure to understand this difficult language. It comes about when two people use the same word but with different meaning in their minds, yet thinking they mean the same.[68] For instance, Church and Dictionary alike translate the English word sin as "tsumi," but if I speak to a man in the street who knows nothing of Christianity and use the word "tsumi" he thinks I mean "crime." Then the trouble begins, and I have only just learnt to anticipate a deeper difficulty even with the Christian Japanese who does not understand the doctrine of sin. I hesitated to reach such a conclusion but have talked to Japanese scholar-priests and older missionaries and find it is a fact to face up to. The implications of this are, of course, very significant. How shall a person find the full joy of knowing the Love of God if he has not realised to the full the nature of forgiveness? And the secondary considerations for social and political life are equally disturbing. How shall a people with no understanding of individual responsibility become a "free democratic" people? How shall we learn to respect the responsibly exercised freedom of others when we do not understand it in ourselves? Then to pursue our logic still further we must ask how can this understanding be introduced into Japanese customary thinking and reckoning except by the Christian Church? Politics and Economics can provide the institutions while Education may provoke the exercise of latent powers, but how shall we regenerate this generation? So my thinking runs and I am still far from my conclusions as my train covers the last mile into Tokyo for my monthly-rations visit.

April 13, 1948

I'm at Chiba Station now waiting for the steam-train to take me onwards a couple of hours into the country to YOKAICHIBA where I'll stay tonight. The occasion is a 36 hour gathering of members of the Women's Auxiliary from all over the Diocese and some will have travelled hundreds of miles to get here. I'll tell you about the Conference later.

Recently whilst Fr. Shikutani was my guest he assisted me to celebrate the Mass of St. Laurence, which was by way of being my official "farewell" as a member of the Brotherhood of St. Laurence, Melbourne. I joined the B.S.L. in 1940 so it is not a little thing to come to the end of my membership. I knew when I decided to do so that it would be strange to find myself alone as a priest, for I was ordained whilst a member of B.S.L. Now I find myself aware of great help received amidst an almost frantically busy life while in Melbourne. I think of Fr. Tucker as he carries on with the work of the B.S.L. and I have a tremendous respect for his great-heartedness about his crusading for better things for the under-privileged in that city.

---

68 This is not an uncommon problem in Japanese language usage even among the Japanese themselves.

Lunch with an elderly couple around the foot of the hill from my house last week was full of pleasant surprises. This is the year of their golden wedding. They have travelled the world and were in Australia for a month in 1923, and loved it. With a lively memory of Australia and Australians Mrs. Kadono had taken the trouble to get a bowl of golden wattle (called Mimosa in Japan) from a friend at OISO and in front of their gate stands a 40 ft. blue gum tree. It is the season of cherry blossom in Odawara, a season of breath-taking beauty, but the wattle has a beauty all its own. Even more pleasant was to make acquaintance of another guest, a Mrs. Kishi, who lives nearby. Her husband was a Vice-Consul in Sydney "before the bridge," i.e. 1928–30. They all speak English and are Christians. Mrs. Kishi knew Prof. and Mrs. Sadler[69] very well, and we found another bond in a common friendship with that uncommonly cosmopolitan Sydney identity – Mr. Archie Ranclaud. They recall many delightful evenings spent in his amazing lounge.

I have to specially thank Miss Ida Thompson for 2 sugarbags full of felt hat pieces which delight the clever-fingered mothers who make cosy infant shoes out of them. The Kindergarten teachers are also glad of any strips left for their children to make into useful articles which are then sold to help raise funds for the church.

Our friend, Miss A. Fieldsend of Sydney has hit on the bright idea of sending the N/L. *[Newsletter]* to a friend in Essex, England, who is Sunday School Superintendent. Thank you. Without the kindest friend of all in Sydney there would be no *Newsletter*, so how many thank-yous do we owe her.

We've started up towards summer heat with as much speed as we left it in October. Ice starts tomorrow and I'll be glad of those precious jellies you sent. Inquiries at the Shipping Office in Sydney revealed the fact that the Merkur was due to leave for Japan on April 24th and about every 8 weeks after then, so you can guess how long some parcels take to reach us with a month added for the sea voyage.

Next day

What shall we think about as we stand with eight other people in the short narrow passage between the toilet cabins at the entrance to a carriage in a country train? The ceiling against my hat seems to forbid lofty thoughts; the elbow jabbing my floating rib prevents composure; my own elbows pressing the head of an infant tied to its mother's back prevents relaxation; the two-feet long carrots sticking dirtily out of a rucksack into my face prevent, repel, hunger; a glance back over heads at men riding on the buffers at the end of the carriage, their lot is worse than mine, prevent discontent; a glance ahead into a carriage packed with people swaying amidst rucksacks of precious vegetables being carried from country to kitchen prevents complacency. Food is the key to Japan's future. S.C.A.P. has effected one major improvement in the food situation this

---

69 Professor of Oriental Studies at the University of Sydney, who taught Frank Coaldrake in 1946.

last three months. It has made the flow of rationed staple food regular. The ration or calories have not been increased but last year's delays have been cut out. There are no days or weeks of waiting for "behind schedule" rations. When the ration was 24 days late it meant that for those 24 days one had to buy everything on the "black" or starve. But the ration is now up to date and delivery dates announced for the next month. The collection of the full quota of rice from last November's crop seems to have made all the difference. So the uncertainty and its haunting fear of starvation is pushed into the background. But rations are not enough to sustain life so the search for other foods continues. People flock into the country to buy vegetables direct from farmers. On the return journey they run the gauntlet of train-riding inspectors whose job it is to stop this blackmarket on the farms.

Ah! The carrots have gone and a young school-teacher has taken their place. He tells me there is yet half an hour's ride and my sleepy feet protest. An hour and a half of this so far! And this morning for 40 minutes I stopped their circulation by squatting on heels on the floor in the sanctuary of Holy Trinity, YOKAICHIBA. The Bishop was preaching at the Eucharist so we three priests went to where the Se . . .[70] (seat) might be and sat in local fashion. My legs took a long time to wake up after that. But pins and needles didn't matter much then for it was a great occasion. Forty members of the Women's Auxiliary of the Diocese had gathered for the Annual Business meeting and this was the act of worship in which the whole meeting centred. Those from a great distance had arrived the day before and the rest had arrived at 9.30 a.m. this morning just before the Eucharist began. Five of them had left their homes in SHIMOFUKUDA at 4.30 a.m. on a long walk to the train. One really ancient old dear had braved the two hours' "crush" from Chiba on this journey.

I'm now returning after the service. We sat down to lunch or breakfast or something, but had to wait about half an hour before eating – because speeches come first. During the speeches the Parish Priest, Fr. Matsubara, made mention of the old lady from Chiba, Yoshida-san, and as he spoke of her long years of work in the church he broke down and wept. Many of the company wept with him. I have never seen that before, and of course in Australia we don't let our feelings get hold of us like that. When the speeches reached the point of welcoming me I was asked to reply but said I couldn't do so because in Australia I had been trained to make speeches after the meal. That idea seemed to catch on and we were soon eating. One of the titbits presented to me was a plate of "asparagus substitute" – cooked bracken-fern tips – WARABE – a poor substitute for asparagus but a good adjunct to sweet potatoes.

What can I do about my sleepy feet? As we wait on a loop for another train to pass, the teacher consults his watch and says still 20 minutes to go. One good thing about this crush is that I can't fall over if I get a leg cramp. Better think about other things.

---

70 One word indecipherable.

Mrs. Sugai was re-elected President at the end of the meeting, and Miss Minamioka, Vice-President. Old Yoshida-san, busy counting votes over the rim of her spectacles, was quite a picture. The Women's Auxiliary is a very keen body. Before the war they maintained two women missionary workers. Now they can't do so much because it is not so easy to make money. But they are aiming to present 1,000 yen to each of the nine burned Churches in the Diocese especially for the restoration of the altar. They have already done this for four and are planning how to complete the job. Also they want to help provide a temporary kindergarten in a farming parish during the farmer's busy seasons. (I've told you before about farmer's wives with infant on back.) And how shall they get the money for these things? It must come from outside the Church's ordinary sources. The word "BAA-ZAA" is common parlance in the Japanese Church – and much has been done with Bazaar profits – but first get the goods to sell. Mrs. Sugai is a rapid talker and she keeps the business moving along – in fact she does the business till occasionally someone else decides to have a say. As I listen I hear Mrs. Sugai talking about some felt scraps I've given to the Auxiliary. With these they can make many things which will sell at good prices. In fact it seems as though a parcel of felt scraps put into clever fingers in HATANO or HIRATSUKA can produce articles worth thousands of yen – slippers, floral decorations, animals, hats, caps, and almost anything. By all means let us have a hundredweight of felt scraps and build a new church, laying the foundations with needle and cotton. And in between my reflections on the value of "waste" I hear them planning to send my mother a present for next Christmas. It would be nice to bring my mother to meet them – but I'm glad she doesn't have to travel like this.

By now I'm sort of punch-drunk and remain propped up in a fog till we finally tumble out at Chiba. The 50 yards walk along the platform is blessed relief, then we enter another train for the hour's run to Tokyo. This is not half so bad. I can even read a book occasionally as I hang on a strap, and the constant movement of passengers in and out of each suburban station keeps us milling round the carriage. The book, by the way, is one I'm reducing to a 5,000 word outline for translation and Duplicating. That way I'm trying to give our bishops and parish priests some contact with recent thought overseas. They can't read the English even if we could get the books, and to translate and print the whole book is out of the question. This is the second book treated this way. I hope to do one every few weeks. This is one of the ways I've hit on for carrying out my "mission to a Diocese."

I had a short visit last week from two Australian soldiers, Laurence Topp of Christ Church, Sydney, and a friend. I met them accidentally on the train, so dragged them off to stay the night with me, and rang their C/O. to say I'd return them in the morning. We had quite a yarn. They bought some fruit at a shop on the way to my place. I was a bit alarmed at the extravagance. One dozen each of apples, mandarins, and fresh eggs cost 582 yen altogether, that is £3.12.9 Australian!

I've lately come on several instances of one of the jobs of a parish priest in this country. They are frequently called in to act as "go-between" in arranging marriages. The father of a marriageable bachelor normally asks a "go-between" to approach, and perhaps even to locate first, a marriageable young woman and approach her parents. So now in Christian families it is often the parish priest to whom they turn. The bachelor's party suggest the kind of things they want to find in the wife – money, intelligence, housekeeping ability, good health, good looks, good family, Christianity – any of these in any order of preference. The priest, if he is asked to locate, generally starts by consulting other parish priests. So it happens frequently that Christian lad marries Christian lass. The only unusual thing in this is that Christianity should be the deciding factor in the arrangement. In all such marriages, and they are the only kind of marriage known here for centuries, love, if it comes, is a by-product of marriage. Yet the traditional loyalty and devotion of the Japanese wife seems to be a fact. There is of course a Divorce question, but I'll have to leave that till I know more about it.

Yours sincerely,
    FRANK

Letter from Frank Coaldrake to Canon M. Warren, Secretary, the Australian Board of Missions, 20 May 1948.

20/5/48
The Secretary,
Australian Board of Missions,
14 Spring Street,
Sydney.

Dear Canon Warren,

In preparing an estimate of expenditure for the coming year [Australian Financial Year, July 1948–June 1949] there are so many uncertain factors to be taken into account that there is a temptation to allow a good margin. However, I have not done this. I have prepared the estimate on the assumption that conditions will average out the same as during the past year, and on the further assumption that the Board wants this "factory" to be in "full production." Subsequently I have prepared a smaller estimate based on the idea that if the previous amount is too high the work and expense could be reduced at certain points [figures in parentheses on right of Estimated Budget Expenditure, below].

The conditions which I have assumed will remain the same are as follows:

1. Occupation Authority supplies will continue to be available at the same cost. Travel will continue to be the same negligible item – (though Government rail fares are being quadrupled next month, also Post Office charges).
2. Inflation in Japan will not become any worse than at present – though there is no sign of stability yet.
3. The Exchange Rate will remain the same – though a change would result in a reduction of real costs of things and services purchased in this country unless the alteration of the exchange accentuated inflationary trends.

4. The work of this centre should continue to be aimed at the whole diocese and especially its priests, instead of just in this district.

5. I make no provision for expenditures on things like car, stove or refrigerator, or new water service.

6. If the amount of food available to be purchased is more than I need for this centre it can be used for helping priests and their families or others.

ESTIMATED EXPENDITURE FOR ODAWARA MISSIONARY CENTRE

For 12 months 1948–49

Food, fuel and power	A£200	(120)
Rent and Water	60	(60)
Housekeeper	104	(104)
'Mission work expenses and travel. Repairs and		
Maintenance	200	(105)
Sundries	50	(25)
Personal items, Insurance, family etc	200	(200)
Total	**A£814**	**(614)**

Therefore, my estimate for the cost of full scale work is £814, with no provision for capital expenditure.

I hope this is the kind of thing you are wanting.

> With very best wishes,
> Yours sincerely,
> Frank W. Coaldrake

P.S. The "factory" does not contemplate any extra charge for overtime.

Newsletter No. 14, **1 June 1948.**

NIPPON SEIKO KWAI

> Aust. Army Post Office,
> C/- Empire House,
> B.C.O.F.,
> Tokyo,
> JAPAN.

From – Rev. Frank W. Coaldrake

Dear Friends,

I'm in a luggage van en route through Tokyo to Ichikawa where I'll work with a study group this evening and stay tonight, then go on to Chiba early in the morning to take the service there. Then I'll head back for Odawara arriving in time for the Evening Bible Class and sermon tomorrow night. I'm well into my travels again now and they become less of a strain as everything becomes more familiar, but they do use up a lot of time and energy. As I write I can see out of the windows the vivid green of springtime Japan. The weather is perfect after recent rains. Cherry trees are now an incandescent green. The blossom season is over leaving a keen desire to see it again, and again. One sees it for only a couple of days, then it falls. Nothing I have read, and no picture I have seen, had prepared me for the overwhelming effect of massed beauty. The blossom is silvery pink in colour and each flower a thing of exquisite line, delicately fragile. The mass of it breaks upon the country-side still slumbering in the browns and russets of winter. In our district it met the eye at every turn, and it was not for nothing that people came in thousands from Tokyo to Odawara to see the Cherry blossom. One hardly comprehends the sweeping delicacy when it is gone – spring breezes stir the branches and all the air is full of petals floating reluctantly to earth. The occasional butterfly mingling in the petal-shower becomes as one of them and the earth resembles a carpet. Then the rains came and one sadly recalls that it will be a year's span to the next second week in April!

Now everything is green and the trees have their new leaves. The wheat which has stood ankle high through the long winter has suddenly become waist high and crowned with grain. When I see it golden ready for harvest I will know I've been here the full round of the calendar.

Going to Ichikawa is always a time to wonder "what now?" for it was the parish priest there who led his people to think out some means of turning their hands and eyes and prayers outward on people outside the local Church group. They have moved to some purpose and the time is not far ahead when they will open a Baby Clinic. There are 80,000 people in the town and no kind of baby centre at all, so it will be a great boon.

One of the young women of the parish was married early this month to the recently ordained Deacon, Sakurai-san (who spent his Retreat with me last September). They were married at Christ Church, Yokohama. It was, of course, the kind of Christian wedding we see in Anglican Australia, the only notable difference being the presence of many guests in beautiful red-toned kimonos. The bride wore a white frock – spare the details!

The following weekend Fr. Matsumoto came to stay with me. He wanted peace and quiet to write the introduction to a translation of a book he has just handed over to the printer. He did the writing and we had quite a yarn about many things. Visitors are very frequent these days – that means steady work is possible only at night. The Presiding Bishop Yashiro, of Kobe, called in for a couple of hours on his way to Tokyo last week. He is going to England for the Lambeth Conference, leaving early in May and two others of our Bishops are also going. Under MacArthur's new policy of allowing selected Japanese to travel for special purposes three permits were issued to our Bishops. Of course, it will be no use the Australian Bishops inviting them to visit Australia when returning because the Australian Government has announced that none of MacArthur's "permitted" travellers from Japan will be allowed to visit Australia. Perhaps you in Australia will be able to see a reason for that? For the life of me I can't from here.

Bishop Yashiro had come to talk about a couple of matters, and ask my help in regard to some of his needs for the journey to England. It's too late to get things from Australia, but he's just the right size to wear my winter-shrunk things.

The same day I had a quite unexpected visitor who has long been a respected name to me, but whom you [Frank Coaldrake's mother, Mrs. Coaldrake] met in Melbourne in 1944 – Harry Silcock. He has been in China for 3 months on a personal round of visits to various people, to do what he can to maintain a sense of community amongst scattered groups. My friend the Reformatory Superintendent brought him to see me after he had lunched with him. Harry Silcock had with him Lindsay Crozier, a New Zealand lad who is in a Friends' Ambulance unit in China. He had come back this far with Silcock to have a bit of a break. Between them they gave a very interesting picture of conditions in China. One thing Crozier said stood out as a commentary on the whole situation – "We're in a war area[71] and it is our work to help the Refugees – I've never seen Refugees fleeing <u>into</u> the Communist areas!" Also with them was Ayuizawa-san [sic.], whose father is now in the U.S.A. as one of MacArthur's permitted travellers. He has gone to study labour conditions and Relations there. He is a Quaker and the Newspaper says of him that when the war broke out he took the Quaker's Pacifist stand, and soon went into hiding till the war was over. His son is a fine type of young Quaker.

Our Orphanage at Oiso is developing gradually. The Sisters of the Epiphany found they were too few in number to undertake the management, but other staff has been found. I've been appointed to the Board of Directors and will be there for meetings, and to take the service on Sunday morning next weekend. The Chalice and Paten sent by St. Cuthbert's, East Brunswick, are now in use at Oiso.

Another centre I've been to twice recently and will henceforth go to once a month is Numazu. It is about 40 miles South [west] of Odawara and is a fairly large town by the sea. It was wiped out in one night's air raid in July 1945. The Church, Day Kindergarten, Hall and Vicarage all went. The only thing standing is a small concrete Repository for Ashes of the dead. It is a forlorn sight. (Fig. 15) But the congregation has reassembled and the Church is alive amidst the ruins. Timber for a new Day Kindergarten has been obtained (Govt. building permits come more readily for Kindergartens than for Churches!) and it is hoped to have the Kindergarten in operation by next month. There are several congregations scattered around the countryside in little villages but it will be some time before I can get to all of them.

When I was at Numazu last Thursday I worked with a study group of students. Instead of giving a formal address I invited their questions right from the beginning. The first two were "why do you believe in God?" and "I am not a believer but I want to be – I find I am not able to believe, what can I do?" You can imagine from those questions the kind of youth they are, and what we talked

---

71 The war between the Kuomintang and the Communists.

Figure 15 Fr. Yamazaki and his family at the site of the bombed church in Numazu, June, 1948. The Repository for Ashes of the Dead, the only part of the church which survived, can be seen behind Fr. Yamazaki. The entire family is sitting proudly on the recently acquired timbers for rebuilding the Church kindergarten. See *Newsletter No. 14.*

about. I look forward to future visits. In the meantime the parish priest, Fr. Yamazaki leads them, but he is very fatigued because he works 6 days a week for a living. He was working as Accountant to a company, but the company eventually made him its Manager. The Church, of course, feels the loss of his time and energy, and even his company-manager salary is hardly enough to live on. He very much appreciated the recent relief parcel sent by the A.B.M. from Sydney. With such practical help in a small way, and whatever I can do to encourage and help him, we might perhaps have him back on his feet being a real parish priest and evangelist in a few year's time. I take it as part of my job here to aim at doing that in every one of our parishes. Just think what it would mean if all our 24 centres had a full-time ministry instead of just the 3 which have it now. To liberate the ministry for its true work – that's a bit of a job, but I find myself warming to the task.

I had to stay in Tokyo overnight last week, so I took the opportunity of staying with Jo and Ethel Ehrich. They've now got their own house in an Occupation Personnel Housing Settlement in an outer suburb of Tokyo. The settlement is still building and Jo has been moved in as Mess Sergeant for the Engineers, Medicoes and Management. They are very happy and find it no end of a relief to be able to live in their own house at last. I hadn't seen them since I visited Jo while he was in hospital and we had much to talk about.

I arrived from home from one of my recent journeys at 10 p.m. to find Padre Alan Laing[72] and a friend bedded down for the night. They'd arrived at about 5 p.m. and Ogata-san had done all the right things to make them comfortable. Fr. Laing was a welcome "sparring partner" for many problems I had on my mind. He went off to Tokyo next morning but I joined him on the train that evening as he came through on his way to the Kawana Leave Hotel and went with him. I stayed the night and came back home next afternoon. The friendliness of the manager, Capt. Burrows, and his wife, is unending. The brief stay with them made a welcome break. Fr. Laing told me he had bought a dinner set for my house while he was in Tokyo, as a gift from the "boys" in his Units at Kure. It is a 92 piece set, and weighs about a hundredweight, so I haven't been able to get it home from Tokyo yet. I will be very glad of it because I haven't enough crockery to entertain more than four visitors. All I hope is that I can get it home in 92 pieces!

When I reach home tonight I will not find an empty house waiting for me, as for some months at least I have a companion living with me. Bishop Yashiro has asked me to look after a young student who wants to enter the Theological College next year to study for Orders. In the meantime I am to direct his studies and give him various practical duties which will, at the same time, help his experience and "Testing." Hiroshi Kominami is just 20, about 5′1″ and slightly built. He was baptised 5 years ago and confirmed later. His father is dead. His mother is in charge of one of our Church Homes for homeless boys, his sister is the wife of one of our Deacons, and his elder brother is studying philosophy at Keio University in Tokyo with the hope he will be at our Theological College next year. He comes from Kobe, which is Bishop Yashiro's Diocese. He will get the usual individual Japanese rations but this will not be enough to keep him in full health and vigour, so I will have to find some extra food for him as well as the Yen to pay for his rations, but I am very glad to have him.

I am attaching a map of South Tokyo Diocese which I hope will help you to follow more clearly my travels to and from Odawara. [Redrawn in simplified form in Fig. 7.]

Yours sincerely,

FRANK

P.S. To "Friends of Odawara" – the last wool parcels arrived and have been distributed. Apart from the gratitude for warm clothing it has two very important effects. When the Japanese are hearing only confirmation of previous impressions that the Australians are "hard" and "vindictive" toward the Japanese, this is tangible evidence that some Australians are friendly. Also it is evidence of solidarity of the Christian fellowship and really is worthwhile. This month we sent off 6 parcels of Putty and Linseed Oil to repair the Churches, also 20 lbs. of Macaroni and 36 Puddings for the Christian Youth Camp at the end of July. Please do pray about this.

E.R.C. [Mrs. Coaldrake]

---

72 One of the two Australian Army chaplains who had met him on arrival at Kure in 1947.

Frank Coaldrake, Odawara Mission Report to the Australian Board of Missions, as at June, 1948.

ODAWARA MISSION REPORT. AS AT JUNE 1948

[Notation in Frank Coaldrake's handwriting] Printed in full in *A.B.M. Review* – August 1948.

This is the nature of an Annual Report, covering my first year in this country.

My role in the diocese has been somewhat changed since my arrival. The late Bishop Sugai asked me to settle down to work in Odawara and district. After the election of the Rt. Rev. L.S. Maekawa as Bishop of South Tokyo my function was reviewed and he asked me to visit other centres in the Diocese as much as possible. In this capacity my contribution should be to help and encourage all the parish priests in their work. It is not difficult to find ways of doing this, but because there are twenty-five widely scattered centres it is difficult to make visits frequently enough. I have so far visited every centre at least once, and some very often. In addition to irregular visits I have regular classes, study groups and services to conduct. These include: 2 school Bible classes and 1 Church Bible Class in Odawara weekly; Factory study group fortnightly near Odawara; Bible class in Hiratsuka fortnightly; Bible Class and service at Hatano monthly; Study groups at Ichikawa and Numazu monthly; Services at St. Andrew's Yokohama and at Chiba monthly. I teach English six hours each week in two Odawara schools, one the Church school, the other a Christian High School for Girls.

My house is used as a "Refreshment" centre by the parish priests and my library books are widely loaned. Conferences and meetings are also held at the house. I have a postulant for Holy Orders living with me for a year's training and testing. He was sent to me by the Presiding Bishop. If all goes well he should go the Theological College in Tokyo next year. With materials brought and sent from Australia I am gradually carrying our repair and maintenance works at the Odawara Church.

9 of the 23 Churches in the Diocese were completely destroyed during the war. Of these, one only has been properly restored – Christ Church Yokohama. At Kawasaki, a semi-permanent residence has been built in which services are held. A similar building is nearing completion at Hamamatsu and a third will shortly be built at Chiba. The kindergarten building has just been completed at Numazu. All this building is of low quality but extremely expensive.

The women of the Diocese are organised in a Women's Auxiliary and work effectively to raise money for Church needs. They have been much encouraged by messages and materials received from Australia.

Each of the parish priests has now received three Relief Parcels sent direct from Australia by the Board, and also some various items sent to me to distribute to them. Expressions of appreciation have been manifold. In my opinion it should be possible to find a way to make this help of more permanent value and I am discussing the matter constantly with priests and the Bishop. The difficulty is that there is little conception of "strategy" as we know it. Instead there is a mighty hunger and suffering and even a little immediate alleviation is too real a blessing for the mind to be able to think beyond it to the further future.

Plans are well in hand for Youth Camp this summer for youth representatives from each Church in the Diocese. This has been made possible by the food which I have been able to collect and am receiving in parcels from Australia. It will be the first Youth Camp of the Church since before the war. We are planning to make it a worthwhile experience in Christian Community living.

The N.S.K. [Nippon Seikōkai] has founded an orphanage for unwanted children at Oiso, near Odawara, and I am one of the Board of Directors. The first 6 infants are all children of Occupation soldiers. As soon as official formalities have been completed the number of infants which the House will be allowed to keep will be greatly increased.

I have started the publication of "Theological Papers" every month or two. Each paper is an outline of a recent important Theological book which will benefit the priests but which it is not feasible to translate and publish. The Papers are issued to any N.S.K. priests who want them. Nearly one half of the 300 priests have asked for them. They are issued free, being roneoed on my machine.

The general situation in Japan is worth noting. The people generally are avid for recognition as one of the world's nations once more. In this respect the N.S.K. has gained no little respect from the fact that its three Bishops were the first Japanese to be granted permission to travel abroad. The daily papers carry reports of their movements.

I have found no sense of shame at defeat in the war, but many have expressed a shame at the moral deterioration which they declare has taken place since the end of the war – as evidenced by what they call the mad scramble for money, food and American favour.

Inflation continues to become worse. The extent of blackmarketing is a big factor in this and the blackmarket is revealed to have drawn a large quantity of its goods from illegally acquired ex-Japanese Army goods. There is not a little corruption in high places, almost everyday bringing fresh news of officials arrested. In spite of such handicaps Occupation-inspired and directed reforms, and the rehabilitation of industry, move forward steadily. Civilisation in this country has had many loose ends but the Occupation is fast tying these up. The final result looks like being a civilisation cast in the Christian mould but without the Christian faith, for the Churches are still a negligible proportion of the people, and what counts in re-organisation is democratic politics, free-enterprise economics and humanist sociology.

The freedom of religion granted under the New Constitution together with the cessation of State Shinto has had an interesting effect. Both Buddhism and Sect-Shinto are reported to be effecting a "Counter-Reformation" within themselves. War destruction and loss of official status have been a heavy blow but sincere priests and believers have been sufficiently numerous to stage a quite impressive "comeback." The Christian Churches are making good use of the present unprecedented opportunities. The Roman Catholic Church has been particularly effective in starting new social service works, building new churches, publishing new books and journals, and making new members. Their activities follow the pattern common in Australia. The Protestant Churches are of numerous kinds and their activities likewise. The nature of their impact varies considerably but is bearing great fruit. The Nippon Seiko Kwai has taken more of a beating than either of those groups and is still groggy on its feet. The matter of the Bishops consecrated within the Amalgamated Church [during the war] is much discussed and there are frequent references to this or that war-time development. The impact of Missionary help from U.S.A., Canada, England, (and Australia!), has been very noticeable. But help in the form of personnel, supplies or funds is always in the nature of co-operation with a self-conscious indigenous church.

Newsletter No. 15, 1 July 1948.

NIPPON SEIKO KWAI

> Aust. Army Post Office,
> C/- Empire House,
> B.C.O.F.,
> Tokyo,
> JAPAN.

From – Rev. Frank W. Coaldrake

Dear Friends,

I'm sitting on the roof of the vicarage in Shizuoka as I write this. In an hour I shall be called for and taken to a Boys' Technical School to speak to the boys, then lunch and a yarn with the teachers for a couple of hours until my train leaves for Hamamatsu. I was down here for a short visit last October but could not see much of the place. Yesterday I arrived at noon and had nothing to do till the evening so we went for a walk to the top of a nearby hill. This city of 200,000 people lies cramped in a corner of a mountain edged plain about 10 miles long by 5 miles wide with the sea along one end. The city covers about 2 miles, the rest being farmlands, stretching from the sea up to the city. It is quite an important place, being the capital of the Prefecture and historically famous as the home city and country of the first of the Tokugawa Shoguns [1603–1868]. In the days before modern communications one could have lived in this little plain and thought it the whole world – but for two things – the Tokaido, the main highway from Tokyo to Kyoto, and the cone of Mt. Fuji hanging in the distant clouds. Since those days the Tokaido hasn't changed much and Fuji not at all. It's out there in front of me as I write. The horizon line of the nearby mountains is etched ruggedly against the sky. The eye is caught by white streaks higher up in the sky, and through the mists and shadows they all converge into the snow-capped Mt. Fuji on the eastern side as it reflects the morning sun. Perhaps that cone awoke the restless spirit of Tokugawa IEYASU [the founding Tokugawa shogun] and led him out of this valley to see and conquer the whole of the land on which that eerie cone rests solidly through the mists, and after he had conquered, ruled, and retired in favour of his family line, he came back here to live in retirement till death. His castle stood within a moat and its walls are all that remain now. Within the moat was a military barracks until recently. Now it is mostly occupied by schools and the public buildings.

About three-quarters of this whole city was burned down in one night in 1945. From a hilltop yesterday we could see the isolated patches of buildings that survived. The only new buildings that are large are the schools, and as everywhere in Japan, they are mostly very long two-storied barracks, each housing probably a thousand children. I counted 14 such schools lying within one quarter of the city. Providing schools for Japan's multitudes of children is quite a contract, and of course, providing able teachers is an even more difficult job.

Our wooden Church was one of the few buildings to survive. It is quite a good place in size and atmosphere, reminding one of the better kind of wooden parish Church in many Australian towns. But the important thing is the active and growing congregation, in which are many young men and women. I told you last year about the interesting evening I spent with them in informal conversation. When I left them I had "thrown them the ball." Last night we had another such gathering of 35. I found them on their toes ready to throw the ball back to me. I suppose one could say the subject of discussion was "what should the Christian's life be like," but we were guided by their questions, so covered a wide field. One man who had been very vivacious last time, was silent last night, so I asked him why he was so quiet. He said he was worried because he had just been told that his house is in the area which is to be cleared and made into a park. He will be given another piece of land, but because his house was built out of post-war scraps and without license, he will get no compensation for the building. How will he move the building, pay for labour, and get time off from work to carry the job through? Civic improvement is necessary and a good thing – for the next generation! In Shizuoka they use manpower for haulage. It is a common sight to see one man slowly hauling a two-wheeled long wagon heavily loaded and one I noticed had 20 bags of cement which, with the wagon, would weigh more than 1 ton.

When I opened a tin of butter at Fr. Nakano's to eat with my bread and cheese, I gave him some. He went through the actions of a formal greeting to a long absent friend. "Mr. Butter, it is a long time, many years, since I have seen you."

Whitsunday. 16/5/48

I've escaped from the narrow plain of Shizuoka through a tunnel under the Hakone mountains and had a most interesting visit to Hamamatsu, two hours journey southward [southwest]. It is exactly mid-way between Tokyo and Kyoto, just 200 miles from each. It is the most southerly [westerly] of the South Tokyo Diocese centres. This has been my first visit. Last Whitsunday I was on the "Merkur" off Townsville, and all that has come and gone in the meantime does nothing to lessen the effect of entering a city that has been almost completely wiped out, and hurriedly replaced by a temporary shanty-town. To see the blasted shells and foundations of buildings is to realise acutely that war has an insatiable appetite for good things as well as bad, good lives as well as bad lives. Hamamatsu had 27 separate air raids. One reason seems to have been that factories which before the war supplied the orient with all kinds of mouth-organs, were changed over to supply all the aeroplane propellors for Japan's Air Force. Now the people are picking themselves up amid the ruins. They seem to be well into the second stage of rebuilding. The first temporary "lean-to" type of bag and iron hut is being replaced by tiny wooden houses properly constructed.

My host Yamanaka-san apologies profusely for the small house in which he had to entertain me. He now uses the "lean-to" which he put up soon after the air raids for a kitchen, and his new "house" is the eating, living, and sleeping room. It is just one 12 foot square room, compact, you might even call it crowded, but still showing that refinement I've spoken of before. Yamanaka-san is an old man now and has no teeth, but he still has plenty of "bite." He's making a wonderful job of a really big undertaking he'd bitten off.

There were "homeless ones" in front of Hamamatsu Station, as in Odawara. Yamanaka-san had a 20 year old Christian conscience about such things. Moreover, he was one of the city's "Social Welfare Bureau" officials. But he hadn't any money, he hadn't even a house, and the congregation of his Church was scattered, houseless and virtually lost in the mists. His parish priest was so ill with T.B. that he was in hospital, shortly to die. The Government was offering a yen-for-yen subsidy for monies raised for welfare institutions, so Yamanaka-san persuaded a wealthy Buddhist Sect to raise money and establish the Home for the Homeless. They raised a considerable sum which the Government doubled. Now there is a fine block of several dormitories housing something like 10 widows with their 21 children, and 20 really ancient men and women, and there are no "homeless ones" living in front of Hamamatsu Station. I've seen many good and many bad institutions in Australia and Yamanaka-san's "Yoroin" [Home for the Homeless] finds its place among the best. The able-bodied work in their own rooms making cardboard boxes for a local mouth-organ firm. The Government gives a meagre pension to widows. To raise the money to run the place is Yamanaka-san's responsibility. The Government and Buddhists did their bit in the building. From the Japan-wide "Community Chest" he has received 10,000 yen for a year. He was loud in his gratitude to L.A.R.A.[73] for many relief gifts of food and clothes. But quite often they all eat little because the money is short. There is a large hall in the centre of the quadrangle where it is hoped all work will be done, as well as recreation held. But it cannot be used at present because thieves stole the glass sliding screens that made the walls on three sides. But on all

---

73 Licensed Agencies for Relief in Asia, a consortium of U.S. relief agencies which sent $400 million worth of relief goods to Japan between 1946 and 1952.

the floors there is a good thick tatami, an item so costly in Japan today that Hamanaka-san has not been able to afford it for the floor of his own new 8–mat house. As I think of the miserable bag hut so far provided for the "homeless ones" in Odawara I hang my head in shame before Yamanaka-san, and those 21 children love him. I think they know he's not just the gruff old grandfather he appears to be.

Yamanaka-san's work is, shall we say, the individual work of a man who lives by the faith he found in the Seiko Kwai. I'm thinking now of another way that same faith is reaching out to bring love and succour to needy people here in Japan. Among those at the service this morning was a young woman who had walked for 3 hours, and ridden for 2, in order to be there. She used to live in Hamamatsu and at that time became a communicant. The family's house was destroyed in the raids and they now live in a distant village. This is her nearest Church. She has heard about the Orphanage at Oiso and wants to go and work in it. (I think it will probably be arranged). I haven't told you about the growth of the Orphanage. Last time I was there six infants were in residence and a nurse in charge. Since the "baby-farming" scandals of a few months ago, there are additional regulations to be complied with before such an institution can effect registration and take charge of more than 10 infants, and until that is done there are no rations or relief goods or infant foods available. So the 6 infants have been taken only because they were foundlings who must be taken in or left to die. For foods the Orphanage depends on what the "ravens" bring. I have been made a member of the Board of Directors so I know pretty well what's happening. Once registration is effected we will be in a position to appeal for funds for the expansion which is contemplated.

The difference from Yamanaka-san's effort is obvious isn't it. He persuaded the Buddhists and Government to build an institution and let him run it. The Orphanage will be built as well as maintained by the Church. There's need of both kinds of effort I'm sure.

But I mustn't take you right away from Hamamatsu yet, though this train is now rushing me through tunnels across the Shizuoka plain back to Odawara in time for my Bible Class and the service tonight. We said Whitsunday Mass today in a "first stage" type of temporary building, quite full with 18 of us. The foundations of the blasted Church stand amid rows of potatoes. The simple foundations of the "second stage" building all in place waiting for the carpenter to turn up and use the materials which have been procured. (Just down the road there is a fine large Buddhist temple, brought from 50 miles away to replace the one burned when our Church was burned.) The new Church building will be a 25 foot square room in which services will be held on Sundays and the parish priest lives for the rest of the week. But this morning we worshipped with rain beating on, and often through, the bark roof. We prayed for our three Bishops now flying to England to attend the Lambeth Conference. In the background was a photograph of the faithful parish priest who died six months ago. His widow and small son and daughter were with us. There were Yamanaka-san and his good wife, the 5–hours travelled lass, and others of the same kind. As I stood with my head not far from the roof waiting for the moment to begin I was remembering my Whitsunday on the *Merkur*. What a contrast. I arranged for an early celebration of the Eucharist and had it included in the official announcements – but not one person came! There were many Anglicans on board. But there are truly faithful souls among the debris and distress here in Japan.

Now perhaps we'd better leave Hamamatsu – for we can do so without forgetting its faithful ones – and head for home. Shizuoka has slid past the window, and Shimizu. They are two of the four places this express stops at in the 140 mile run to Odawara. Next will be Numazu where Fr. IIDA will leave me. He is the regular visiting priest for Hamamatsu and has guided me round on this my first visit. He wears in his lapel the badge of the Teachers' Union to which he belongs because he teaches to earn a living. I think one will never tire of seeing this countryside, especially as one learns to know what goes on in the minds behind the fingers that are shaping the terraces, plucking the new green tea, and bagging the loquats as we pass. "Bagging the loquats" is a quaint process. A paper bag is tied over each cluster of the young fruit to protect it from fruit-fly. In the end the tree looks rather like one of those ladies back home who, when we called unexpectedly on our parish rounds, met us at the door with hair being "permed" in squiggles of rag.

The wheat stands everywhere now with a heavy golden crown and some patches will be cut next week. Then we will see plainly what we can only glimpse now – the sweet-potato and pumpkin vines already planted between the rows of wheat. In those fields the wheat stubble will stay. In others it will be dug in to prepare for transplanting the rice seedlings now springing green through the water in their special beds. Rice seed has been planted during the last fortnight. Any mud-pie loving child would love to plant rice seed. The chief requisite seems to be run water into the patch until it has stood 6 inches deep over the soil for a week. Then you run the water off, puddle the mud into long narrow level beds, sprinkle the seed on top, then switch it into the mud with a fly-swatter kind of twig bundle. Finally, you run the water in again and mount an array of scarecrows, old tins, and red-cloth streamers to scare the birds away. From those beds the seedlings will be taken in June and transplanted out into the paddyfields. In that work everyone who is able to stand has to help. Mothers have to neglect their infants unless they can stand the backbreaking strain of bending over the rows all day with an infant on the back. In our mountain parish at Seisen Ryo a new venture will be undertaken this year during the 3 weeks' planting time. The Church will conduct a creche and kindergarten in the village for some 200 of the farmers' infants who would otherwise be neglected. Dr. Matsumoto will go up to supervise the welfare side of the work. There was a difficulty. From where could the locals get food for the doctor for three weeks? That's one way I'm going to be able to help. My plan for a hitchhike includes Seisen Ryo.

Our plans for a Youth Camp this summer are taking shape. We made a big move forward at our Diocesan Youth Conference held at Odawara. There were

80 present from far and wide throughout the Diocese. We started at 9.30 a.m. with the Mass. Afterwards until lunch time we listened to the testimonies of some of the new Christians in our midst. (Among our readers are some who care a lot about "High" and "Low" Church matters. They will be interested, perhaps amazed, that I should say we followed "Mass" with "Testimonies"! But those are the words used, and the things done, all quite happily in this community which now has its own life, though its roots are in different kinds of Church soil.) The rest of the day was spent in reporting and planning many things.

By carefully guarding a 10-day period and cramming things in before and after, I've been able to arrange a break from June 2–12. I'm going hitchhiking North-west direct across the main island from Odawara. I've got plenty of the right kind of food to carry, thanks to your parcels, and a good supply of films also.

Yours sincerely,

FRANK

Newsletter No. *16*, 1 August 1948.

NIPPON SEIKO KWAI

Aust. Army Post Office,
C/- Empire House,
B.C.O.F.,
Tokyo,
JAPAN.

From – Rev. Frank W. Coaldrake

Dear Friends,

What a fellow does on his holidays is always a most boring tale for others to listen to, so I won't expect you to do more than skim lightly over the mountains, roads, and rivers of back-country Japan with me. To mark the end of my first year here I have hitch-hiked from Odawara in a great circle round Fuji, then across the Northern Alps.[74] I've been in country where the people have not seen an Occupation soldier except 2 or 3 times as a Jeep rushed through. This was the country and people I hoped to find, the true Japanese upon whom the Occupation is having its influence indirectly, but they still live the way of life which has persisted for centuries. If only you could have been with me to share it all. To walk across the gently arching match-work suspension bridges, to rest in the wayside houses and village shops – oh but your feet! and it would be impossible to do it by car or train or bus. Perhaps if I drag you like I've dragged my pack from the first day to the last you'll get a picture of this Japan.

---

74 This "great circle" encompassed most of the central Japan Alps, Yamanashi and Nagano prefectures.

Heading north-west at Midday on Wednesday, I started out across the Hakone Mountains. The rain pelted down so there was nothing to see but muddy road and dripping trees. I had to carry all my food for 10 days because I'm not yet immune to the wogs in locally grown foods – also, it costs a fortune. The dried fruits, chocolate and biscuits you sent were a great asset. The country I was heading for had an epidemic lately causing the death of hundreds of people. The J'ese Health experts didn't understand it but the Occ. Health Section said it was due to unhygienic preparation of food, so I reckoned I'd be O.K. with my own food. With tent, clothes, camera and food, the weight was 70 lbs. The first night I spent at Gotemba, 26 miles along the way, after two lifts in American cars and one in a J'ese truck, but I walked half the distance. I found my cape and jacket were not keeping the rain out, so I took refuge in the Inn instead of camping for my first night out. I had my own food but for the use of a room paid £1 Aust.

Thurs. morn. still raining, I started towards Kofu, 48 miles away. At the first village rice planting was in progress so I spent an hour watching, talking, listening and taking photos. Rice planting is a wonderfully dirty job. After the field has been under water for 2 weeks the mud is churned up with implements drawn by man, woman, bullock or horse. Then a string is stretched from side to side at one end, and planters, mostly women, line up along it with a bundle of seedlings in hand, and push the roots of the plant into the mud at spaces of 6 inches all along the line. Then the cord is moved down the field 6 inches and again the planters bend their back and fill their portion of the line. They stand knee deep in mud and get mud thick to the elbows. In their old clothes and big hats they're quite a picture. Under their hats the women wear a towelling veil around the head, so that all you see is the face, with its brown eyes and sparkling teeth. It takes quite an effort to realise that these are the belles of the village who at other times saunter in gay kimono. The owner of these fields was in the mud with his workers. He was an Army Captain in Batavia during the war. His offsiders told me these facts with a noticeable respect, and he himself seems to preserve something of the status of his former rank. They thought at first that I was a soldier, but when I told them I was a Christian Missionary and nothing to do with the army they became noticeably more at ease and free in conversation. When I took photos the planters were very shy of the camera, generally trying to hide behind their big hats.

The rain began to clear as I moved on up through the ranges. At midday came a U.S. Army truck which carried me forward into the Fuji National Park amongst the Five Lakes. This is an Occupation Leave area so the roads are in good order and Occ. traffic numerous. However, as I walked they ignored my signals, due to the fact that from inside a Jeep one does not see much, and in company with walking J'ese they probably didn't realise I was a hitch-hiker. In one village as I stood by the roadside talking to about 15 people, a sight-seeing bus came along. It stopped and the American staff asked me if I'd like a lift? But they were going the wrong way! From this village to the next I was accompanied by a squad of a dozen boys on bicycles. As I walked they talked. They didn't realise I could understand them at first, and their speculations were most interesting. At length I spoke to them and put them right, then we went on our way talking together. This brought me to Kawaguchi – the loveliest spot I'd seen in Japan up to that time. It is a small lake surrounded by mountains, and Mt. Fuji towers above it. (Fig. 16) When the water is still, there is a wonderful reflection of the mountain in the lake. In winter the lake freezes and is a good skating rink. The weather was now quite fine and there were many pleasure boats on the lake. I spent an hour in one of the lakeside tea-shops getting some boiling water for my tea and sharing it with the proprietor. It was not difficult to find a camp site around the lake beside the mountain stream that keeps it filled. A tent was not necessary. I camped in amongst the trees surrounding a little shrine. From my sleeping bag I could see Fuji's snow-cap fade into the darkness, and later come pink and gold in the dawn.

An early start up the road to the Pass soon had me perspiring, so I stopped to take some photos. (Fig. 17) Then came a J'ese truck and in 2 hours its charcoal-gas had lifted me over the Pass and down the other side to Kofu. Sitting on top of the load in a truck moving slowly through the country is really quite the best way to see things, and there are invariably a number of fellow-travellers who can point out places of interest or explain things being done. That ride up to Misaka Pass was a feast of clear views of Fuji. This was the opposite side to that which we see from the Odawara-Tokyo region and I was seeing it for the first time. In my usual view of Fuji it is a cone of perfect shape, without a flaw in line or surface. I have always felt vaguely that such perfect line is not quite fitting in nature. From Misaka one sees a cone of broken symmetry with jagged nicks in the side and to me it is entirely pleasing – an aesthetic feast presented on a vapour salver of enveloping mists.

Turning our backs on Fuji we passed through a short tunnel and came out on the other side of the range. There in the distance, 50 or 70 miles away, were the snow-capped jags of the Northern Alps which I hoped to reach.

It was now Friday, and I spent from 11 a.m. to 4 p.m. with our Kofu parish priest Father Uemura. He is now teaching at the High School. We made plans for my visit later in the summer. His infant son, born in Feb., died in May as a result of pneumonia and malnutrition. He helped me find maps at the local Travel Bureau. Maps are a problem. No two are the same, so I bought every map I could find and worked on the average. At 4 p.m. I set out from Kofu for Kiyosato and Seisen Ryo. I had great difficulty in persuading Fr. Uemura not to come along the way to carry some of my swag. But it was already growing lighter and I had given him some of the food which I had decided I'd not need. I also left with him the Guide Book and dictionaries I had started with. I had expected to find them necessary but was pleasantly surprised to find I was getting on quite well without needing to refer to them.

Kofu is the outer limit of active movement of Occupation personnel so I was now in the kind of country I was looking for. From here on the journey became more interesting and the lack of "hitching" was no handicap. Kiyosato is not on the direct road from Kofu to the Alps. In fact, it's not on the road to anywhere,

Figure 16 Mt. Fuji and Lake Kawaguchi, photographed during Frank Coaldrake's hiking holiday in the Central Japan Alps, July, 1948.

Figure 17 Frank Coaldrake. Rest stop, hiking holiday, July, 1948.

lying high up on the side of a great 8–peak mountain, Yatsugatake. It is reached by rail and road, the station being the highest in Japan. To get to and from it promised to be a long and tedious journey of about 40 miles, but I was anxious to call there. Just above the village our Church has a young and growing "Rural Community Centre." I have often told you about the 2 young priests, Frs. Uematsu and Shikutani who are working there. This was my first opportunity of visiting them. Also, a special 3-weeks Kindergarten and clinic for the children of the farmers was to be run during the rice-planting season. It was to start the next day, so I made for Kiyosato. The sun was fierce and the road rough and dusty so I hailed a passing truck, and climbed up on top of his load of bricks. He wasn't going far on this road but he'd gladly take me along. In fact he went further on this road than he should have and took me to a bus-terminus from which I could catch the bus to the next town. I tried to explain I didn't need a bus. Then he suggested running me half a mile across to the railway station. I said I didn't want a train, or a bus. He didn't seem to understand anything but the cigarette I offered him. He went off, the bus came. I let it go. Then suddenly, the truck roared off after the bus, stopped it, and the truck man signalled me frantically to come and catch the bus. I ran up and told the bus-driver to get going, I didn't want him. Then I tried to make my peace with the truck man. We were understanding each other's J'ese quite well, but he just couldn't get the idea of hitch-hiking, and when I said I was on a holiday and taking a walk, he looked at me as though I were quite mad, then graciously accepted another cigarette, and drove off with an "It can't be helped" air. This was, in fact, only one of the most amusing instances of what I met all along the way. Hitch-hiking is a practice unknown. Moreover, to the eyes of a J'ese I'm like an "American," and if an American is walking he must have suffered some ghastly misfortune!

I spent my time trying not to be led to a railway station, or police station. First of all they'd try to take me to the train. When I said I didn't need that, nor a bus, they'd look at my swag, decide I was a bit simple in the head, and therefore should best be placed under the kindly care of the local policeman. It was one of the quite unexpected delights of the trip to observe the curious inability of most people to grasp what I was doing.

Anyway, the mad foreigner set out to walk. Many trucks were passing, but I was enjoying the walk. Finally I decided to hail one. He stopped and I joined him in the cabin, with my gear on top of the building material in the back. I told him I was going to Kiyosato. His reply, "Boku Mo," (me too) was sweet music, and almost the last of his speech I could understand – his clipped accent and local variety of colloquialisms were beyond me. He was in fact, carrying materials for the new Church building and Kiyosato, and I spent most of the 2 hours keeping two windows safe on the seat between us. His antidote for a rough road was to drive so fast you spent only half your time on the ground. My head jerked up and down so fiercely my clerical collar was near cutting my throat, so I took it off. But I couldn't take my heart out of my mouth as we roared up and down narrow mountain curves.

We reached Kiyosato an hour before sunset, and in the thin mountain air I panted up the slope to the cabins. I stayed till Saturday midday, saying the Mass in the Chapel at daybreak. I'm not going to stop to tell you more about it now, because I have to go back there to a conference on Rural Evangelism. At that time the Kindergarten will be in full swing. The only way to get out of Kiyosato without retracing my steps was to walk down the railway. This took most of Sat. aft'n. Part of the way I walked with a group of Kofu High School Geology students on an expedition with their teacher. That night I camped in a gully 1,000 ft. above the highway along which I must travel to the Alps. It was raining so I put up my tent. Of course, there were always people watching me from near or far as I moved around. Once as I was sitting on a bank by the road reading the Daily Office, I became aware of watching eyes and I looked up to see a school-boy's cap above a bank 20 yards away and his two eyes peering at me. When I spoke his head disappeared and he was running away behind a hedge. Then as I fixed camp a youth came up the road, and after standing watching me, answered my greeting and came over to talk. "Sunset" (I called him), is now 23, country born and bred. During the war he was a fireguard in the local village. He helped me find good fire wood and, while I stewed some fruit, he used my tomahawk, greatly admiring it. We talked about the life of a farmer's boy in Japan now. He was interested in my boots (ordinary labourer's boots, bought in Sydney for £1), my tomahawk, (7/6 d. in Melbourne), my tent (made it myself for 30/-), my wind-jacket, (bought second-hand in Melbourne for 4/-), these things had him thinking I must be wealthy until we worked out our income in Yen and found his to be twice mine. (Incidentally, he was no yokel. He could work Exchange sums in his head quicker than I could ... which is unusual, for most J'ese are tied to their abacus for even the most simplest calculations.) To earn his wage he works in the field from 5 a.m. to 8 p.m. He wants to become a village fireman. We know all about each others families now of course, that being the inevitable first matter of interest. Once he learned I was not a soldier, but a missionary, he became friendly. His first question about Australia was "Why won't you let J'ese go to Australia?"

Next morning as I walked along the Highway, I spent some time taking photos. Then "Sunset" came along. He was walking the 8 miles up to Fujimi so we walked together. As we sat to rest on the stone base of a roadside shrine the locals gathered to gaze at me and I heard him tell them all about me. Then down a side track came a girl with a bundle of newspapers on her back, walking so lightly she was a pleasure to watch. "Sunset" told me she walked every day from Fujimi to his village and back, delivering the paper, in a round walk of nearly 20 miles. "Sunset" continued on to the far end of the bypass. By lunch time I reached the top of a long rise and as I ate, could enjoy a glimpse of the now far distant Mt. Fuji. Then a truck came – with a driver who thought I should wait for the bus! He was a surly coot, the first and last I met on the whole journey. If I had insisted he would have carried me, but I preferred to see some more of Fuji. The next truck that came took me 2 miles, then turned off to go to the railway, so I got down and walked. The next bend of the road took me into the main street

Figure 18 Village street in the Central Japan Alps, photographed during Frank Coaldrake's hiking holiday, July, 1948. This scene and its significance is described in *Newsletter No. 16*.

of a really ancient village stretching for $\frac{1}{2}$ mile along both sides of the road.[75] (Fig. 18) I spent a couple of hours there. I stepped into a shop to buy some fruit and finished up making tea with their boiling water, sharing the tea, and being invited to join the master in his parlour just off the shop. This I declined, but sat on his step in the shop, and talked. Meanwhile the village youngsters gathered outside to peep round the door at me. When I looked at them and spoke they nearly fell over in fright. As I walked through earlier that day, the street suddenly emptied itself before me and then filled up behind me with people gazing after me. I felt a bit like Zane Gray's "Lone Ranger" walking down the street with gun at his hip and wondering where the first shot could come from. Not that I feared any such thing – but it is weird to walk alone down a street, with hundreds of people watching from behind their doors, and children scampering away in fright. Three 10-year old boys playing in a wagon did not see me coming. Hearing my steps they looked up and quickly shut their eyes, took off their hats and bowed their heads over their knees. So I was anxious to try to make friends with the youngsters of this village.

I was talking to the shopkeeper and his son about the children, when a youth came panting in and spoke in Tokyo-student English. He was home for the

---

75 Scenes of this type of "ancient village" are included in the Coaldrake films now preserved at ScreenSound Australia.

weekend. Tokyo is 6 hours by train from this village. In Tokyo he works as a baker during the day and goes to school at night. Between us we worked out that the children were chiefly moved by the fear that attaches to a strange sight. They had seen Americans ride through in a Jeep but they'd never seen one sitting in their village. He told them I was not an American, nor a soldier, but an Australian Christian Missionary. Finally we had quite a yarn, and they all sat down to have their photo taken. When I left, three of the boys walked with me till I told them it was time they turned back. A little girl persisted in keeping up with me, chattering away, till I took her back to her old grandmother who was hobbling along behind. In that village and in most of the places I've been, there are no Christians, and though the name of Christ is known, the meaning of Christianity as a faith is not understood. There are many shrines and temples of Buddhism and Shinto, some well cared for, others dilapidated. In the really rural areas the shrines and temples seem to be much used and many had newly placed offerings of flowers, rice or dolls. The shady areas round the bigger ones are generally the children's play-grounds.

The other half of my Hike will have to be "continued in our next." I had a wonderful time but it's good to be home and Odawara is really home to me now. I'm very fit after losing my winter-fat climbing those mountains between hitches.

A week later

I stopped off at Takenogawa, just outside Tokyo to visit another of our Church's undertakings. It is a school for subnormal children – the only non-govt. one in Japan. There are 65 boys and girls of all ages. Feeding, clothing and washing them is a great problem. The principal, Seki-san, is a member of the Church in Odawara. The school was founded over 50 years ago by his uncle, as a Christian venture, and at his death Seki-san took over the reins, even while continuing his business as an electrical engineer. Such places can fill one with sorrow – but there is such a happiness among staff and children that my sorrow was lightened.

While I was there the children were being given their daily drink of milk received from L.A.R.A. Relief agencies in U.S.A. – yet another unlooked for proof that relief contributions are finding their goal.

I stayed the night at nearby Kokubunji, our Church's Liaison Mission House, then next morning went on to Tokyo. This was my first visit in 3 weeks and I found lots of mail waiting for me – 40 letters! and some asking why I haven't answered earlier letters. I'm sorry not to be able to give myself such pleasure, but if I did there'd be less of these *Newsletters* to all of you, or else so much less work done locally, and I must beg people to be content with this apology.

Yours sincerely,
FRANK

***Newsletter No. 17,* 1 September 1948.**

NIPPON SEIKO KWAI

Aust. Army Post Office,
C/- Empire House,
B.C.O.F.,
Tokyo,
JAPAN.

From – Rev. Frank W. Coaldrake

Dear Friends,

A 5-day camp for Sunday School teachers was held in the mountains behind Odawara last month. 100 came from Tokyo and district. The site was an old Y.M.C.A. Conference House, ideal for the purpose. Most of the teachers were 18–20 years of age (there are older teachers but they can't come to such a camp). (Fig. 19) It was a Youth show, and was arranged and run by the J'ese clergy. Fr. Arnold of S.P.C. and Fr. Merrit, a young American, and I were the only others present. (Fig. 20) We worked as "advisers" and Fr. Arnold gave the chief addresses. He has been here and in Korea for 15 years and speaks J'ese very fluently – but with a delightful Oxford accent! Of course, we climbed mountains and had camp fires, and a quaint session when a neighbour visited us. He is Prince Chichibu, the younger brother of the Emperor. It was, of course, a democratic function. I was glad to have such a chance to observe the attitude of J'ese youth in the presence of one who has been for them surrounded by the aura of divinity. It was exactly like a crowd of admirers gazing at Laurence Olivier in the flesh. The people who arranged the visit couldn't understand my attitude when I said I wasn't in the least anxious to meet a Prince.

S.S. [Sunday School] Teachers' gatherings in Australia deal with lesson preparation, teaching aids and methods. Here the problem is much more elementary. The teachers have to be taught the things we would teach our 10-year old scholars. They're so young in the faith and shallow in experience that they really shouldn't be teaching. But there's no one else, and certainly no one to take the lead in a teachers' camp such as we know in Australia. What a wonderful thing it would be if one of our Australian Diocesan Youth Organisers (or Sunday School Organisers) could be let loose here. The camp was at Gotemba, one of the chief starting points for climbing Fuji. One of my Odawara lads and two of his Tokyo student friends met me in Gotemba after the camp was over and we climbed together. To climb Mt. Fuji is an exhausting but exhilarating event. There is a J'ese saying that one is a fool if one has not climbed Fuji once, and a fool if one climbs it more than once. Well, I'll probably be the second kind of fool eventually. The mountain in its many moods provides an infinite variety of experiences and all so "un-twentieth century" once you leave the bus. I've read many brief accounts of the climb but never anything which opened out the details that make it so worthwhile. I'll take you with me out of the sultry summer at the foot up into the midwinter snows at the peak and back

Figure 19 Sunday School Teachers' Camp at Gotemba, August, 1948. Practicing hymn singing under the guidance of a young Fr. Matsumoto (centre).

again, all in the course of 24 hours. (But we'll have to put off your "climb" till next month.)

Now shall we finish my hitch-hike from Kiyosato? While I rested by the roadside a farmer came to talk with me and the first question was "are you alone?" They seemed to find two things to marvel at in my travelling alone – it must be very lonely and risky. The most fearsome thing was the fear that people tried to implant in me. In a year of living in Japan I've found nothing half as fearful as the ideas I imbibed in spite of myself in Australia. Now, as I talked to this farmer, I was able to laugh at his worries. Then came a truck and in an hour I was on the shores of Lake Suwa with an 8–mile walk around the lake to Ohaya which I wanted to reach in time for Evensong in our Church there. I just did it –

Figure 20 Sunday School Teachers' Camp at Gotemba, August, 1948.

stopping to rest at one beautiful place by the water. As I sat, the whole family came out of the nearby house and joined me. They fed me on luscious cherries from the fruit-bearing cherry tree we know in Australia, but which is rare in Japan. There is a U.S. Army Rest Centre in one town on the lake. I saw two Jeeps – one was a poor sight – full of rowdy soldiers. I suppose soldiers on leave must have their fun, but such demonstrations seem to be particularly unfortunate in this region.

Evensong in the fine Church building at Ohaya was a joy. Instead of a sermon, the parish priest used a Paper-Theatre series of pictures to tell the story of an old time Christian heroine in Japan. I'd learned the story from Prof. Sadler, and as the details came up in J'ese I found myself recalling his telling of the facts of the Lady Hosokawa. Finally, there was a lesson in Church music. The Vicar showed Holman Hunt's "Light of the World" and explained about the door. Such hinged doors are not very common in Japan – most doors slide. Then two hymns on the theme of the picture were learned.

Next morning with the Vicar's son for company I set out for "anywhere along the road." He had many questions and as we walked I tried to fill some of the gaps in his knowledge. We found a House-factory where silk thread was being wound from Cocoons. It was illuminating to see the primitive conditions under which a beautiful result is achieved. I hope my photos will turn out clearly – you'll see a row of hot, tired looking old women sitting in front of old battered tin wash basins full of steaming water in which dozens of Cocoons dance a jig as they yield their precious thread. The old women sit over the haze stirring the basin with chopsticks, looking like fabled witches.

Four miles up we sat on the roadside, ate our lunch and boiled the billy. After being most interested in the purely Australian habit of "boiling the billy" my companion became perturbed at my failure to move on. I tried to explain the hitch-hiker's philosophy. There hadn't been a truck going our way all morning and that increased the probability that one would come soon. It did, and then another short walk, another truck, and in 2 hours we were at the town he was to stop at, 2 days walking from his home. He began to understand! We have a Church in Matsumoto and he guided me through the quite large city to it, and then to the Rectory. On the way we passed by the 150 year old Feudal Castle. In the grounds inside its moat are now some schools, and right beside the castle a baseball match was being played, complete with a great crowd of fans. I thought I had seen the last of baseball, for in the country regions the last few days I hadn't seen the boys pitching and catching which in the towns is a great craze.

It was 5 p.m. by the time I set out, once more alone, now within a day's walk of the Alps riding sheer along the skyline under the setting sun. Camp that night among Acacias was very cool and pleasant. In the morning I met a woman member of our Church in Matsumoto who had supplied the strawberries I had eaten at the Rectory the day before. She pressed me to spend the rest of the day eating strawberries and cherries and wait for a truck which she knew was going up tomorrow, but the good weather was too precious to miss, so I left her and wandered on. A truck soon came and took me 20 miles up a road winding steeply. Then I walked 4 miles and stopped to boil the billy. As I munched biscuits and cheese children came up the road, school-bags on their back. The road was only a narrow ledge high up on a cliff so they had to pass quite close to me. They stopped, eyed me, spoke to each other, and stood still. I called to them as reassuringly as I knew how, and they came on, rather bravely I thought, but keeping out on the far edge of the road and keeping an eye on me. I couldn't help feeling sorry to be giving the kids such a fright. Ten minutes later a workman came down the road. He was expecting to see me. The children had talked, no doubt. He stood off and spoke aggressively. "Are you alone?" "Yes." "Where are you going?" and "Why?" and all the rest of it. As I sat and sipped tea from the old black mug and told him quietly who and what and why I was, he relented and tried to be unobtrusive in putting away the hunting hatchet he had been carrying bare in hand. He was a telephone linesman. Later, others came down and they joined me in smoking a pipe of peace before they went on downhill. After more walking another truck came. It was a relief because the going up was steep and hot. A 20-year old local riding in the truck was full of conversation, and as I was from Australia could I tell him if it were true that no J'ese is allowed into Australia although it's a wide rich land with few people. I could tell him it was true, and so we talked on as the truck climbed up into breathtaking grandeur. From where it stopped was an 8–mile climb to where I wanted to camp that night, so I had to keep moving. It was 7 p.m. when I reached the "Sprite River Bridge" in the heart of Kamikochi, some 5,000 ft. above sea level, surrounded by mountains 8, 10 and 11 thousand feet high. There was snow by the roadside. I found a few hunters in the glen. The holiday resort life is suspended at present because the road is blocked 5 miles from the top. Most of the Inns and the great European style hotel are closed.

The stream coming straight from the snow was too tempting to resist and I filled my billies and drank it without chlorine tabs. It was a relief to the palate, for throughout the journey I have had to be careful to use only water chlorinated with the tablets I carry. Perhaps over the years I'll build up an immunity against the wogs in most of the water. Then I ate bacon and absorbed the rugged scene. Fading into sleep I have dreamed – but remember trying to discern the cosmic formula for the formation of this land. Take a God's handful of mountains, a God's bucketful of water, with the power of earthquakes to mix and churn for an aeon or two, sprinkle liberally with trees and garnish with human hundreds and thousands, giving to both the power to procreate. Then by A.D. 1948 you have the Japan and J'ese I'm seeing. And so to sleep! Up at dawn, more snow-water, more bacon, more and endlessly more mountains, then off early to cross the range on a 12-mile trudge under the shadow of an active volcano. On the way a party of High-school boys overtook me. Their young legs and light loads made quicker pace than me, so I soon sent them on ahead. But as we rested together after a steep pinch, they tried to raise echoes among the mountains and I taught them the Australian "Cooee." Then they went on up the very steep short-cuts while I ambled on the longer, quite steep enough main track. Then I came to a fork, obeyed my map, ignoring the very difficult J'ese signpost, and went merrily on. Suddenly, from high up on the mountainside I heard a many voiced "Cooee." Looking up I saw the lads on a bluff and two of them clambering down to me. I was on the wrong track. They helped me up the mountainside, one of them lending me his alpine-stock. We boiled the billy and I noticed again their strange reserve. Thinking about it I realised I hadn't told them I wasn't a soldier. I was telling them my house in Odawara had come from their home district, and they were puzzled at my living in a J'ese house. One of them asked – "Are you a soldier?" When I explained I was nothing to do with the Army they became at once more at ease.

I went on 5 miles up to the pass before I camped at sunset. That was quite a climb over the main range just below the summit of Mt. Abo. This peak is the same height as Kosciusko, but is one of the lowest in this range. From it the track goes down and down to the Hot-spring resort, Hirayu. In this out of the way place I sat with my feet in one of the many fish ponds, watching the golden carp in the Iris bordered pools. The village children stood off, till one of the men came to talk to me, then the youngsters gathered round to gaze and listen. The second ascent, 5 miles, and up 3 or 4 thousand feet in 3 hours, left me exhausted but amazed at the daring of J'ese road engineers. This whole region is alive and on the move. A road is built. A week or a month, or a year later, a whole hillside moves. The road is once more delicately traced across the new hillside, and a notice board erected saying "slide area." Even as you walk you hear the rattle of stones or the roar of a rock, or see dust rising from behind a shoulder where a slide is moving. Near the top I met a road-mender. It seemed ludicrous to have puny men trying to mend this plaything of Vulcan, but he was most concerned about me. Where was I going to spend the night? It was 10 miles down to the first village. Hadn't I better come back and spend the night in his cottage? But I had no need to worry him, and eventually found my camp site just below a flock of sheep (a rare sight in Japan), on a shoulder of Mt. Norikura, beside another snow-fed stream.

Next morn. started a 20-mile descent, down to Takayama in Gifu Prefecture. At first it was the land of huntsmen and woodmen, then gradually came level terraces laid out in fields. The people are true "backwoods" people, dressed according to the much pictured dress of Tokugawa period of 200 years ago. They speak a quite peculiar J'ese which I could not well understand, though they could understand me. And I thought their voices had a pleasant musical ring I hadn't heard elsewhere. On one curve of the road I came suddenly on four timber-getters at work on a log. Their quaint old costume captivated me, and I stood watching and listening. Then I took out my camera, and they moved off into the trees. A camera is often a nuisance. There is an old superstition that you will die soon after your photo is taken. I always waited until the end of a conversation to ask if I could take a photo. It is only a sense of owing it to you to send you pictures that makes me carry a camera at all. For myself my mind's eye is full of vivid recollections. Further down the road I stopped to watch the working of a primitive water-powered grain crushing hammer. The owner came out to talk and soon I was at his hearth having lunch and making tea for all of us. This included several neighbours waiting at his door for the bus from Hiraya. The High School boys were among the sardines in the bus. They thought I was having the better journey – so did I.

The remaining 12 miles to Takayama was mostly walked, but a truck took me the last couple of miles. It was of particular interest in this region to notice the houses closely. My own house at Odawara came from this district. It was built in the days before the saw was known. The great hewn timbers bear the working marks of a tool that experts say was superseded 700 years ago.[76] It was moved from the Takayama district to its present site about 20 years ago to be used as a house for Tea Ceremony. A guidebook says that these Tea-Houses are placed "built for aesthetic enjoyment," "not for residence." Present-day Takayama houses are two storeys with a flat shingle roof. My house is one storey with a steep thatch roof. To trace the change through the centuries would be interesting. It probably has something to do with the need of a second storey for keeping silkworms. Inside my house are some low beams close together which are meant to carry the racks of leaves and worms. Another difference is that present day roofs abound in the curves of Buddhist, or the spikes of Shinto influence, while my roof has neither. I go back to my house with a deeper appreciation of its antiquity and simplicity.

For 10 miles I walked with a man who had been a farmer in Korea. He knew something about Christianity – thought it was a code of conduct based on

---

76 The adze, used for smoothing beams until the adoption of the two-man frame-saw from China, probably in the fourteenth century. See: William H. Coaldrake, *The Way of the Carpenter, Tools and Japanese Architecture*, Tokyo, Weatherhill, 1990, pp. 93–95, 130–137.

abstention from Sake and tobacco! As we walked and talked he said that many people now living in this mountain region fled here at the end of the war because they were afraid of the coming of the conquering army.

In Takayama I went to the station to arrange my return by train. One of the station men told me, "Yes! There is a Christian Church in Takayama. I will take you to it." So I found myself at a 50-year long established Presbyterian Church. They would not hear of my going out to camp, so I spent the night there. After being a very small body for many years the Church has greatly increased in numbers in the last 2 years. The carpenters are at work enlarging the building. It was a very happy evening. I left early next morning by train for Gifu city and then up the Tokaido line to Odawara.

So ends a 10-day holiday, travelling over 250 miles of "back country" Japan. Three quarters of Japan's people live in the kind of country and conditions I've been seeing. They are hard at work, taking about as much notice of the fact that there has been a war and a defeat, as they would if there were an earthquake. The beauties of nature are all pervading, but nature is unrelenting in her rejection of man's efforts to tame her.

The Christianity Community is small, and scattered.

After my 10 days in truly rural Japan it was interesting to go back to the mountainside "Pure Spring" camp (Seisen Ryo), and attend a Church Conference on Rural Evangelism at nearby Kiyosato, the village in which a Rural Community Centre is established and being developed by The Brotherhood of St. Andrew, an official organisation of the Laymen of our Church throughout Japan. The scheme is extensive, and owes its inspiration to the vision of Paul Rusch, an American Episcopalian who has been long years in Japan. (You can meet him by reading the John Morris, Penguin, *Traveller from Tokyo*.) The scheme started in 1938 with the opening of the Seisen Ryo Camp on the mountain slopes above the village. More than 2,000 young men had attended vacation camps there when war broke out. These men remembered the experience, and after the war set to work to revive the great project. In July 1947, the movement was granted a J'ese Govt. Charter, and now development goes on apace. The fine stone church has just been completed. Camp cabins are being multiplied. A Rural Health Clinic is being erected. Funds are being provided by Churchmen throughout Japan and as funds and material become available there will be added a Vocational School and Public Library and the Experimental Farms will be developed. The aim is to bring to life a coordinated program of Christian action. In this setting last week there were two simultaneous activities from which I have just returned. The "Farm Children's Kindergarten" was conducted in the rice-planting season. Two Sisters of the Epiphany and Dr. Matsumoto, (all three J'ese women), conducted the Kindergarten. They had 40 children and had done wonders in teaching them to sing, pray, and recognise pictures in the Christian story. They had learnt to work and play together, also to wash hands and face before meals – with soap and towelling I had been able to provide from parcels.

The other event was the Conference of 10 leaders from the country to make the "First 5-Year Plan" for a Rural Evangelism drive by our Church. They had invited me to go and tell them about Bush Brotherhoods in Australia. This I did though the contrast in conditions could not be more complete. I also told them about Australian Bush Church Aid and Church Mail Bag School. Out of all this they drew several practical ideas.

I made the discovery that the 10 days I spent recently was regarded by these men as a most important experiment, and they suggested I should do the same thing often, as it's good for Japan to see a non-Occupation Christian fellow strolling at ease through the country. To follow their advice will be a pleasant experience – except in winter.

I've had a break this week because I've had Laurence Topp staying on leave from Kure. He brings the fresh air of Christ Church [St. Laurence], Sydney, and it is invigorating. He has also spent some time cooking and has proved that he's a first class chef. He brought a box of rations with him to teach her [Ogata-san] to cook Christmas Dinner! Yesterday he dressed in a man's bathrobe and wooden clogs and with Fr. Uematsu and me went for a stroll round the town. There's a taboo on comments! This morning we said the Mass of St. Mary Magdalen and he departed for Kure.

Talking of Christmas! The Odawara people have just given me about 40 locally made toys to send to appropriate places in Australia as a Christmas gift. They have other things ready to send to some of our neighbouring Churches here. Perhaps you remember that they said to me in February, "It has meant so much to us to receive gifts which show us that we are part of a great family, that we want to sent gifts to other Churches next Christmas." They're well on the way to doing it. I will divide these toys and send them to Australia. Here in Odawara they're not expecting any gifts such as they had last year, but I guess it would be a great joy to them if some came, so if anyone in Australia wants to give them a surprise at Christmas they could send a parcel to me sometime before the end of October. The best things to send would be jam, soap, cheese, sweets, chewing gum, cocoa or milk. There'll be the school and Kindergarten breaking-up parties on Christmas Eve, the gathering of Church members after the Eucharist on Christmas Day and some sort of Christmas Tree for neighbourhood people on Boxing Day. That will make a total of 500, and it will be mid-winter.

Yours sincerely,
    FRANK

P.S. In order to help anyone wishing to share in sending jam, soap, etc. for Christmas I will gladly accept stamps towards the cost of buying and dispatching parcels.

E.R. Coaldrake,
70 Denbigh Rd.,
ARMADALE. S.E.3 VICTORIA.

Regular boat leaves Sydney about Sept. 17th
    next   "   "   "   "   Nov. 17th

[Added in Mrs. Coaldrake's handwriting.]

Newsletter No. 18, **1 October 1948.**

NIPPON SEIKO KWAI

> Aust. Army Post Office,
> C/- Empire House,
> B.C.O.F.,
> Tokyo,
> JAPAN.

From – Rev. Frank W. Coaldrake

Dear Friends,

About Mt. Fuji – the things I've never seen mentioned are the spice of maintaining the climb – the fleas, the all night climbers, the jig-stepping porters, people fainting high up, the children crouching round their fires on the summit before sunrise, the steep sandy "ski" track to run breathlessly halfway down the mountain, the echoes and re-echoes of an Australian Cooee shouted at dusk from an eyrie above the clouds, the predominance of clouds as a feature of the outlook – but I'm jumping about like any Fuji Mt. flea. Let's get going from the point where we leave the bus, and start on foot.

We walk, very hot, up a wide steep track for half a mile to the old "Send horse back" place. A cup of tea is pressed upon us (at a price) and we pass the souvenir gift shop thinking we might buy something on the way down. We are over 4,000 ft. above sea level. As we walk, we are part of a procession of climbers, and another procession passes us on its way down. It is as busy as a Collins St. footpath. A tinkling bell marks a white clad pilgrim returning from devotional exercise on the mountain. The lad wearing wooden clogs for such a climb must be one of these "Studentish" students. We drag our 5 foot climbing stick, and wonder if it is worth the trouble. It becomes a record of our journey because at each "Station" we get it branded with a hot iron stamp (at a price). Thick tree foliage shades the track and keeps out the breeze. We pass Station 1 and at Station 1½ we each lunch, paying well for the water and a brand!

At 1 p.m. we start again, soon reach Station 2, then toil up and up towards Station 3. It seems miles, the track is steep, the zeal at starting is well and truly punctured before we sight it. More tea, more brands, the prices already being double what they were at starting. We find that there is no Station 4 so start off briskly for the fairly close Station 5 and move up towards 6. The trees give place to low alpine shrubs and the afternoon sun has at its mercy whenever the clouds break.

Through the break we catch glimpses of white clad climbers on the track winding high up above us. We're very glad of the big straw hats we bought at the bottom. They're becoming quite well decorated with duplicates of the stick brands too. The sticks are more important as a climbing aid than as a totem pole now. At 5 p.m. we reach Station 6, about 9,000 ft. up, and stop for tea. Many climbers make this the end of the day's climb, spending the night in the Inn at the Station. But we push on, aiming to reach Station 8 before dark. The track now is always steep, usually narrow, but never dangerous. We find we are overtaking many people and no one overtakes us, so we must be moving quite well. In fact, our 3 student companions often sing old folk songs of the mountain as they climb. At my age, climbing is more than enough for the breath I can get at this height. My rucksack is on one of the young fellow's backs, and I'm only the Gunga Din of the party, carrying 4 waterbottles. There is no water except what we pay for at the Stations.

We pass all kinds of people, young and old, all finding it heavy going. A small child says his age is 7. We reach the tail of a long line of 14–15 year old school girls with their teachers. One has fainted. We give her a little stimulant, instruct her how to breathe, stretch her out to wait for the teacher to come back, and move on. We see, in the party of girls, something that is unbelievable – a man carrying about 20 of the girls rucksacks fixed on a frame that starts from his hips and towers 4 ft. above his head, its weight about 150 lbs. I hear his breathing as I come alongside – he is human after all – in fact about 40 years old, and can smile cheerfully. I pace him step for step and hear him breath in and out with each short jumpy step. The baggage sways. He seems to be doing a jig up the mountain track. The sun sets under clouds and we pass 10,000 ft. and I have a spasm of breathlessness. I copy the porter's method of breathing and all is well. Our companions sing less frequently now. I find there is no Station 7, and Station 8 is in sight, just 5 zigs and 6 zags up the track. It is too cold to stop more than a minute or so to rest. We walk at the pace of a lovers' stroll and breathe like a marathon runner. We reach Station 8 where the Inn is a low stone cabin built in the manner of Chinese castles of a thousand years ago. For $^3/_4$ of the year it is buried under snow and even now there are some great banks of snow nearby. We look in to see about staying the night but our companions are surprised that so many people could be packed into such a building and there are yet 50 school girls to come! So we go on through the dark up to Station $8^1/_2$. We are the only guests and share the fire of mine host and his wife. We huddle at one end of the one long dark room. A cup of tea and some raisins and chocolate gives us the energy to prepare food and beds, and we go outside to see what we can see. (Get out your map please.) [The sketch map included in *Newsletter No. 14*.] There is much cloud a way below us. Through breaks in it we see widely scattered points. The great Island Oshima on the horizon in front of my house lies like a pancake at our feet. Closer in are the lights of the town next to Odawara which is itself hidden by cloud. Mt. Oyama near Hatano, and the Hakone Mts. push their peaks through the clouds. Away round the shoulder on which we stand, in the middle distance, the lights of Kofu twinkle. Fr. Peter Shikutani's "8 peak mountain" stands gauntly against the western sky behind it.

Fr. Endo's peninsula beyond Tokyo Bay [the Bōsō Peninsula of Chiba prefecture] is all under cloud except its highest mountain, which we can see plainly. Sweeping away round to the right and south we see the mountains near Shizuoka. We are seeing the greater part of the Diocese of South Tokyo. (It is like standing high above Melbourne looking at Warnambool, Philip Island, and Sale with the Baw Baws tucked in under our toes.) I Cooee, 6 Cooees come back on the echoes. Our companions try to cooee but they haven't learnt the trick. A cloud window slides open and we see the glint of Lakes Yamanaka and Kawaguchi. We are frozen so go to the fire again for a short time, then prepare for bed. We get a hearty welcome from the fleas. They never cease to ply us with their attentions. They are so many and so vigorous that if all their jumps happened to coincide in time and direction I'm sure they'd lift the cabin off its narrow shoulder and send it hurtling into space. Fitful sleep. A voice at the door and 2 more guests come in. Mine host calls to good wife and she gets up and pulls quilt like mattresses (cotton filled) off the stockpile and the newcomers go to bed amongst them on the floor. It is 11.30 p.m. At 1 a.m. come four more lads, and in 5 minutes they are snoring! We all sleep in our clothes. From now on there are climbers passing along the narrow track in front of the door all the time. These are they who start climbing in the evening and aim to reach the top by sunrise. We all do, and the fleas make sure we will be awake for the 4 a.m. rise. A friend suggests that fleas are extra bad here tonight because the whole company of fleas have only so few visitors to work on.

By 4.30 a.m. we stumble out into the dark and join the file of climbers, many sit beside the track, many sing the mountain songs. The eastern sky pales.

We breathe our way through the Torii stone arch of Shintoism that bestrides a flight of steps and at the top of the flight we roll on to the level ground that is the summit. We are in the one and only street of a village of about 20 buildings, all built with local stones. There are Inns and souvenir shops and a shrine. We come to the end of the street and a stone wind break flanks a narrow level strip. Against the wall huddle groups of weary climbers. Smoke from their fires rises straight upwards till it clears the wind break, then it gets blown sharply away. We clear the end of the wind break and nearly go with the smoke. The wind is cold. A little rise with a pole at the top marks the highest point of this part of the top. From the pole we look back across the pinnacle. In the middle is the vast crater, snow still lying on it. The track around its rim would be about a mile in length. At two points there are weather instrument stations. We turn to the east and give our whole attention to the horizon. The clouds there are golding. A sea of cloud covers the land but stops at the coast. Mountain peaks rest on the cloud base and catch the new light. In the far distance around to the left I can see the Alps where I walked not long ago. We are 12,500 ft. above the sea, we freeze but the sky warms to red. About 1,000 people are spread out along this eastern arc of the crater's rim. Some stand stiffly to attention. Most are casual. On the sea just this side of the horizon we see the red reflection of the sun. The sun itself is still out of sight under the horizon, but in a moment it lips the sea, grows, and comes clear and round and red. We have taken photographs and I have looked, but failed to see anyone bowing in prayer. We turn eventually and scramble round for a while, then go into the shrine and pay the price for the brands and rosettes, which declare that we have this morning worshipped the sun from this sacred spot?? It's all very easy, so many yen for this and that!

At 6.30 a.m. we start going down. It is quite an event to be going down after coming up to 12,500 feet at the rate of 1,000 ft. per hour, per mile, of walking. In fact, we're so pleased about it we run. There is just room to pass the late comers, still toiling towards the top. In a few minutes we reach our Inn, eat breakfast and pack up. Other people are buying eatables at the window beside the track. The favourite article is the Squid – a repulsive looking dried cuttlefish complete with tentacles. Each one is a leathery flat object about 1 ft. long. If we must eat Squid we chew the tentacles as we walk. We leave the Inn and follow a different track, steep, direct, and with a surface of loose sand.

We run, and taking long strides we can skate a couple of feet each stride. We run right to bottom of the bare cone and at the snowline, as we enter the trees, we stop to take the sand out of our boots. The track is lined with thousands of pairs of discarded grass sandals which have been used to save ordinary footwear from the wear and tear of the rough track. From here down it is plain sailing, but we find the heat stifling. Back at Gotemba little more than 24 hours after leaving we catch the train for Odawara.

The Youth Camp has really been a great thrill.[77] I started preparations for it a year ago when the Camp at that time had to be cancelled for lack of food and facilities. There were many anxious times, when it looked as though it would again be impossible, especially when, 3 days before starting date, long-promised tents failed to materialise. But constant "backing up" by groups back in Australia, and a disposition to be helpful on the part of many Australians and Americans, carried us through to the end of a tip-top week.

We had 80 campers from 21 centres, aged between 15 and 25, lads slightly fewer than lasses, and an amazing mixture of farm peasantry, factory workers and students. 80 per cent were communicants and the basis of camp life was the early morning Eucharist offered under a giant trellised wisteria. We lived in 5 tents scattered round the crown of the high hill in the grounds of the Elizabeth Sanders Home at Oiso.[78] (That's our new Babies' Home.) For eating and meeting quarters we put tarpaulins over the skeleton of a large workshed. Each camper brought this own "ration" for the period, either rice or potatoes. From the camp fee they paid we bought fresh vegetables. The rest came out of my saved up stores, Australian parcels, "Friends of Odawara" gifts, and a last minute arrival of goods seized by Army M.P's from blackmarketeers and handed over to me through Air Force Chaplain Geoff Parker. For bread I gave 300 lbs. of flour to the Odawara baker and paid him to bake it. Cooking gear came on loan from the Australian Army, and tents from the U.S. Army. Cooking was done by a staff of 6 volunteers under capable Saito-san, one of St. Andrew's, Yokohama, Church women. Since the bulk of the food was European I had to be at the kitchen to teach the methods of cooking. I had also been made Hygiene Officer, and spent some effort inculcating principles of public hygiene. Large quantities of soap in the ex-blackmarket goods made it possible to provide a cake of soap per person.

---

77 This success was to lay the basis for many more such camps, described later.

78 The Elizabeth Sanders Home run by Nippon Seikōkai for the illegitimate children of Occupation soldiers and Japanese women.

Despite primitive sanitation and water facilities, we had no sickness. We kept the multitudes of mosquitoes at bay be using Repellent I'd cadged from the Australian Army. The tail of a typhoon hit the area one night but only the dining room tarpaulin roof failed in the test.

Our programme for each day proved to be too heavy. It is my role to help and advise the local leaders, and my fate to see advice ignored, and lessons learned the hard way. By the end of camp we were doing several things in the manner of camps in Australia, America, or England. I've pressed for a "post-mortem" meeting of staff and campers to reap the benefits of our experience and store it up for next year.

Judging by what the youngsters were saying, and by what one could see going on, the camp life together as a Christian Community, embracing both sexes and different home backgrounds, was a very enjoyable experience quite undreamt of. They started by being very lonely in the midst of each other, but finished as a very lively fellowship. A school of Music run during camp by Prof. Suji of our University in Tokyo, achieved marked results, and on the second last morning we had a fully choral Eucharist under the wisteria. For many it was the first time they have known such Beauty in Holiness.

Many of the campers spent hours helping the staff of the Babies' Home, and after camp I gave the surplus food to the Home.

On the lighter side, the flummery puddings sent by "Friends of Odawara" made the most popular dish of the camp – but it took 4 days to set, and finally I had to put in cornflour to thicken it. After the fifth making it was quite a dish! For the final campfire stunts the kitchen group made a "wild duck" soup, into which, for lack of a wild duck, they put a real live Coaldrake, and won the prize for the best stunt. The camp was next door to the Bishop's palace so we saw quite a lot of him. He was, in fact, the father of the family. His "Palace" is the former gardener's cottage on the estate – just two small rooms.

"Carried through" – Perhaps I should say I had to spend 12,000 yen (A£15) in various items and services for the camp. I had been saving up yen donations for many months but was a bit short when there came a 5,000 yen gift from God, through Laurie Topp and his Army friends just the day before camp. You see what I mean when I say we were "carried through."

Later, a few days in the mountains beside Lake Nojiri [in northern Nagano prefecture in central Japan], tussling with Theology in four languages. Two young American priests and myself with a dozen young Japanese priests from North and South, have met in the cottage of one of the Americans. It was his father's house for years before the war, as his father was Missionary too, and Fr. John Lloyd spent his boyhood there. Fr. Dick Merritt spent 4 years in Japan before the war as an "Exchange Student" from his U.S.A. University. They are very expert in the Japanese language. I tagged along. We used Japanese mainly but the local priests know German and Greek as well as English, so all four languages took a battering. My impression is that the Japanese lack only the reading material that's been missing for 10 years. They're the thinking spearhead of the Japanese Church in the next generation, so we take it as our duty to encourage and advise.

The lakeside setting was very pleasant and cook, with swimming, boating and walking. Before the war Lake Nojiri Settlement was run as a Cooperative Community.

By the end of September we start on the rapid plunge into winter cold. If anyone is thinking of sending old warm clothing, now is the time to parcel and post it. The "Changte" will be sailing about mid-October from Sydney.

Yours sincerely,
FRANK

Newsletter No. 19, 1 November 1948.

NIPPON SEIKO KWAI

Aust. Army Post Office,
C/- Empire House,
B.C.O.F.,
Tokyo,
JAPAN.

From – Rev. Frank W. Coaldrake

Dear Friends,

In answer to queries, in the photos I sent, the J'ese priests had their own stoles. The newest is 10 years old, but that doesn't show in the photo,[79] nor the patches in surplices and cassocks, and their rusty colour! The Robe sent to Canterbury was made of beautiful silk which survived the war. It was a more costly gift than people realise. They wanted to show their real appreciation of help from England. It was presented by members of the Brotherhood of St. Andrew which is the C.E.M.S. [Church of England Men's Society] of Nippon Seiko Kwai. In that are many Occupation American Episcopalians, and that's where the bulk of the money comes from. The J'ese members add their mites. That also is the Brotherhood who are building the Church and Rural Community Centre at Kiyosato, and the money for that comes the same way. In Fuji photos, the neatlooking white sox of the other fellows are O.K. for photo, but in actual practice I put my long khaki sox down over the tops of my boots, to keep the small gravel from getting in. Result – they empty gravel out every mile, I do it only at nightfall.

I've just taken in a "heartful" of distress as a result of the damage done by Typhoon Ione while I was away at Oiso Youth Camp. It is much worse in this area than last year's "Kathleen" – but I'll write about that separately later.

During the recent school holidays four parish priests from Shizuoka region came to stay with me from Tuesday to Friday. We spent the first half of the time in recreation, walking, talking. Then for 2 days and nights I conducted a Retreat

---

79 This photograph does not survive.

for them. My experience at a so-called "Retreat" for all of us last year determined me to explain the fundamental purpose and method of a Retreat. The subject followed was "Priesthood." I found the language a burden, but the others expressed their great sense of gain and renewal. For one it was the first Retreat ever, for the others the first for 9 years. It is our plan to follow with two more for the priests of the remaining regions in the Diocese. Because so many are at work in jobs it is not easy to get them together during the week and if some are to lose their salary by being absent from work, then I shall have to make good the amount so that their families do not suffer. Add to that the necessity of providing railway tickets and all food, and you'll see it involves an outlay of quite a bit of A.B.M. money; what better way could money be used? As if to prove it, I found when I visited one of my recent guests at his home a few days ago, that he is reading again *My Priesthood* by Carey. Such results are what we need more than anything else, that we should renew our vision and take hope to pursue it.

Last week I had a visit by Fr. Muruoka, priest at Kawasaki, between Yokohama and Tokyo. He is one of the "grand old men" of the Diocese. His church was reduced to ashes during the war and in March this year a present-day style Hut was built as his residence, and Church. It cost a fortune, mostly of English money, but a significant portion locally provided. Now just 5 months later, the roof is leaking badly. There are no tiles to be had by the honest poor, and the substitute is a shingling of small pine veneer shingles, which quickly crack in the weather. I couldn't give him a new roof but managed to dig out several other things he was needing. I have not yet visited his parish but am to go there on Advent Sunday.

The dispersion of city population during the air-raids has scattered some of our most faithful members far and wide in isolated places. The ministry to them is a responsibility we aren't able to handle properly. Then marriage takes many faithful members, especially women, to distant parts where they are quite cut off from Church and friends. I've imitated Australian Bush Brotherhood methods in a small way, and ministered to some of the dispersion-by-marriage. Mrs. Kuwahara is a friend of Miss Minamioka and it was through her interest that I made the arrangements. They used to be Kindergarten teachers in Numazu.

Aiming at Kofu for a week-end visit I left Odawara on Thurs. by train for Gotemba and bus to Yoshida. The K. family lives in an old-style village surrounded by rice fields, rejoicing in the name of Asumi, meaning "see tomorrow." It nestles on the very lowest slopes of Fuji and consequently the regular cloud bank blocks the view of the peak which you can always hope to "see tomorrow!" I saw it at daybreak through Autumn cloud-skirts, as I was getting ready to celebrate the Holy Mysteries in the family Parlour. It was for that purpose I had come and what a great joy it was.

This is a silk weaving village, every house a factory, every factory a house. The cheerful clatter of the looms is as ever-present as the roar of traffic in Sydney. In the evening 15 of the village youth club came to talk and "to see" – for we foreigners are rarely to be seen face to face in such villages as this. Also they had a good reason for coming to thank me for the felt scraps I had sent them some weeks earlier. I learned that they had made articles and sold them at a bazaar. The good result is only part of the fun and they're using the money now to provide comforts for the really old folk of the village. The total population is 8,000 and the whole crazy patchwork of cottage-factory thatches, water-wheels, and shrines, would fit inside the Caulfield racecourse. They belong almost entirely to the same "great family" with its roots traceable way back through the mists of Feudalism. This is the kind of village in which, we are told, the old Feudal type of life survives. The picture comes usually from the pen of communists with highlights on long hours of work, mere pittance of wages, dark and unhealthy work places, and severe restrictions of liberty. "Slave labour" it is called, and if it is the local commos doing the publicity, the claim is made that only communism can right it, that the workers know this and strain against their bondage looking for revolution.

As I sat on the mats with these 20 year olds who may be "slaves," I tried to see if this village is one of that type. Complexions and figures speak of enough food and fresh air and workroom space. Clothes, old style silk kimonos in new brightness such as we rarely see in the cities suggest a standard of living much better than we could call slavery. The "bazaar" venture of youthful effort on behalf of age, and their early farewell to me so they could go on to an evening-school class in modern music and indoor sport, these bespeak some liberty in fact, and spirit. My visits to cottage factories confirmed the general impression that this village cannot be accurately described as a centre of feudal slavery. Of course, there are economic factors needing improvement, but the purpose is to provide the needs of a healthy happy creative life. Perhaps this village is not typical, but whatever the condition of its economic machinery, the outcome in terms of healthy living is far more significant. But that's the field of Economics and Technology, into which we guardians and promoters of things spiritual and creative are, curiously enough, hardly allowed to venture. There is no interest in communism in this village, but around herself Mrs. K. has gathered this group of searching young souls. I am invited to go back again, and how I hope I may. The silk cloth they weave, at the rate of 12 yards per loom per working day of 9 hours, is suit lining and umbrella covering. They wonder whether Australians need these materials as much as they need Australian wool?

Another 3 hours "rough-ride" on Friday took me over the high mountain pass at Misaka, with views of Fuji and Lake Kawaguchi, and down into Kofu. This is the chief grape-growing centre in Japan, and it is harvest time. The city is literally bulging with grapes! That's an annual event, but I found another and a better kind of "bulging" – our Church bursting with new members. I believe Fr. Uemara has turned the corner. Since my first visit a year ago I've been deeply concerned about his special difficulties, but there's a new "bounce" in the life of the Church now. Many enquirers of high school age he is well able to cope with for he is well educated (holds the B.D.), and a constant reader of good works in English, and he certainly knows the fires of suffering as a faithful priest. It seems as though our Australian interest in him plays no small part in keeping him full of hope and endeavour. His courageous little wife mourns the loss of their child last January through malnutrition. I was able to take a trunk of clothes and food to them, I had filled gradually as parcels came from Australia. They'll have some warm clothes for the bitter Kofu winter. Their 10 year old girl is suffering from T.B. and the 2 year old under-developed. I had milk and glucose and Vitamin D in the trunk. It will last about 2 months I think.

On the Saturday morning I spoke to 500 boys at the High School. Just before me, Miss Greenbank, a Canadian missionary teacher in the local Methodist Mission School, spoke on moral Rearmament. I set out to answer the questions I now know this kind of lad wants to ask, it all hung together as the story of an ordinary "Australian Life," from cradle to adult. It was rather good fun to venture into an hour's talk without notes in J'ese for the first time. Judging by questions that followed they got the gist of it. The first question reveals quite a lot – "Why did you change your mind and become a priest instead of an engineer?" And afterwards, one of the teachers, "Why, if Australians think badly about the J'ese, did you come here?"

In the afternoon 25 of the Church youths gathered for a Question and Answer session. After sitting on our haunches for a time we continued the session as we walked up the mountain side to the shrine of the old Feudal Lord of these parts – Takeda Shingen[80] had first come alive for me as I sat at the feet of Prof. Sadler in Sydney. I found that a lad I walked with was proud to be a descendant of the chivalrous old tyrant. But the lad's foundations during the war had crumbled. He came out eventually with one of these "Thought-frontier" questions which merely to ask is a venture. "Who do you think our Emperor is?" My answer "A man. Is he not a fine, but human person?" is more than he would dare to say, but I think is relieved to hear me say. In the course of our talking there were many questions about life in Australia, and the difference between religion in Japan and Australia. I wonder if you will think the following illustration accurate? I discovered it in the cottage-factories, and it seems to explain the matter to their minds. I'm only anxious about how far it may be misleading? In a J'ese loom the warp is called "standing thread" and the woof "moving thread." I suggest that the pattern of life in Australia is woven with Christianity as the "standing thread" and "freedom" as the "moving thread," adding that Christianity is for many Australians a heritage received from the past but not much thought about. It is woven into our laws and customs, and there is nothing else which could accurately be called the "standing thread" of our Australian life; and when one looks at woven cloth the standing thread is inconspicuous. The pattern is the result of the shuttling backwards and forwards of the moving-thread, and I suggest it is the liberties we have in Australia, and the way we use them, that give the final pattern to our life. Liberty alone, which so many J'ese are striving for, is as useless as a moving thread shuttling merrily on a loom with no standing-thread to hold it. In Australia we hold ourselves in check by the standards set by Christianity, though of course

---

80 Takeda Shingen had fought for power in the civil wars of the mid-sixteenth century. His home base was Kai, which became the city of Kofu and prefectural capital of Yamanashi.

many uphold the standards without acknowledging their source. Now if that is a reasonably true picture of Australia – what about Japan? I asked that question but there seems some difficulty about selecting the standing and moving thread counterparts. I imagine that the standing-thread is Family, descending through many generations and holding the pattern together. But just what are the one or more moving-threads? It is certainly not liberty, for the newly acquired liberties are as yet so little understood and used that they play no great part in forming the regular pattern of life.

One of the High School teachers came to the rectory to talk about my answer to one of the morning's questions. I had explained that Australian people thought that treatment of P.O.W.s by J'ese guards was cruel where there could be no excuse for cruelty. He wanted to ask me to assure Australians that J'ese people are not cruel, that in spirit they are kind, and quiet. I led him through his own literature and history, and some of the things I'd seen for myself, to convince him that we cannot make the generalisation that the J'ese people are kind and quiet. My endeavour was to give him a new sense of purpose as a teacher, so I went on to talk about the J'ese who are quiet and kind. I told him how most of the J'ese people I know are, by our standards, very kindly, homely people, but my own apprehension is that these are constantly dominated by the few unscrupulous cruel ambitious J'ese. In his school and in the city, was it not a fact that the quiet kindly personality is not called out into prominence, certainly not into leadership? Where shall we start to change J'ese life so that it is not dominated by hard cruel ambition or greed? Why is it that J'ese newspapers will splash any utterance of any Westerner, but won't give any space to the words of the nobler spirits of their own country?

After a long time of this and such he took his leave. But he did tell Father Uemura that the boys had commented on the difference of atmosphere between our session this morning and the times when some Occupation Person has come to address them. It seems that they felt I talked "with" them, whereas others have talked "at" them. I think there is a difference of attitude in themselves as well as in the speakers. It is curious how we who do not come here specifically to further the work of the Occupation may nevertheless be more effective in achieving its ideals.

Sunday morning was a great joy. The tiny 12 x 10 Church was packed, and twice as many people in the Rectory rooms and passages outside. (The Church is a room built into one corner of the Rectory.) There were two such assemblies. First the Sunday School, Mrs. Uemura at the organ leading them through singing "Jesus Loves Me" in English. Then the older people at Mass. Afterwards a hurried meal, then off to the station with a large company who stood on the platform to sing farewell in pouring rain.

That was the beginning of the long journey down to Kure for a brief visit to Padre Laing at B.C.O.F. headquarters. At Shizuoka I dropped off the train for 3 hours to attend Evensong at our Church. I found Fr. Nakano rejoicing over that morning's service when he had baptised six adults, and two infants. Back on the train and all night run brought us to Osaka, and on to Kure arriving at 5 p.m. Monday.

Now enter "Kumazo," one who I expect will be a faithful servant. He is a Jeep which I have bought from the Australian Army. (Fig. 21) It is to collect him and drive back to Odawara that I have come down to Kure. He's going to be a treasure – as anyone who reads this *Newsletter* will readily understand. Treasure? Well he cost a lot of money. Once again I realise, and think you will, just how much my working here depends on the Australian Board of Missions. They have paid the whole cost of the Jeep and its overhaul, and they will pay the cost of its running.

But why the name Kumazo? It is a favourite name for J'ese men, because it conveys the idea of great strength. It is a combination of the words "ninety-thousand" and "elephant"! It is in fact Fr. Miyazawa's name, so I hope to flatter him! I owe it to him for he recently told me my face would stop a tram. It did too! He wanted the Odawara city tram to restore a pre-war stopping place near our Church. His visits and appeals were fruitless, so he asked me to go along and show my face. Sure enough the tram stop was restored. I haven't yet succeeded in explaining to him the English saying connecting faces and trams!

Yours sincerely,
FRANK

Figure 21 The jeep "Kumazō," purchased from the Australian Army, November, 1948.

Letter from Frank Coaldrake to Canon M. Warren, Secretary, the Australian Board of Missions, 30 November 1948.

Odawara 30/11/48

The Secretary,
Australian Board of Missions,
14 Spring St.,
SYDNEY.

Dear Canon Warren,

I wish to advise the Board in detail about a development in my work which is of some importance because it is the beginning of what is to be my permanent long-term job in this Diocese. There is very little detail to report because I am appointed to undertake an entirely new work for the Diocese and details will depend on circumstances yet to be discovered.

The Bishop of this Diocese has appointed me to be Priest-in-charge ("Kanri-cho") of Izu Peninsula. The peninsula is a mountainous area 80 miles long by 30 wide, completely isolated by the rugged mountains that stretch from Odawara to Numazu, these two cities standing at the only entrances to the region. It is famous in history as the area to which troublesome people were banished! Though it should be added that two of them burst out of exile to effect far-reaching reforms. Our Bishop says that the Diocese is shaped like a fan with the peninsula as the hub – which is true enough.

All this is relevant, for to my own mind, when the Bishop first asked me to think about the appointment, came the thought that there are other unworked areas of the Diocese which should be opened up before Izu. This and other points I discussed with Frs. Viall and Arnold and with Bishop Mann as the Liaison Representative of the Australian Church. Bishop Mann advised me to emphasise this matter in discussion with the Bishop, but to remember that in the end it was a matter for him to decide, and if he was convinced that this was the right time to tackle Izu I should accept his judgment. In this matter I have done as Bishop Mann advised.

It should be noted that the Bishop desired to start this new work and appointed one of the priests of his diocese to it. In fact that priest happens to be the Australian Missionary. No doubt that had something to do with the Bishop's selection of the priest. But the Diocese preserves the new post-war principle of not assigning particular Overseas Mission societies to a particular distinct area of Japan. This is a most important principle from the point of view of strengthening the unity of the Nippon Seiko Kwai as a national Church. I had some doubt about this appointment in relation to that principle so it was one of the matters which I discussed with Bishop Mann. His opinion was that there was no conflict because it is an appointment made within the Diocese without reference to an overseas Mission Society.

My final major doubt was about the wisdom of appointing an inexperienced missionary to such a work. The people of the region are farmers and fishermen, notoriously conservative and proud of their well-remembered roots in rich traditions. My advisers all agreed that, provided the Bishop were able to carry out his plan to appoint a Japanese priest as my assistant, the probability of failure would be greatly reduced!

I also satisfied myself that it was my Bishop's intention to leave me at this work for a long term and I begged him to have the Diocesan Administration rest content to leave me at it until I have had time to build up something that will produce results. This I felt to be necessary in the light of what I have seen of Diocesan Administration in action in the last eighteen months.

The appointment has been made, both of myself as Priest in charge of Izu, and of the Reverend G. Iida as my assistant. I have delayed sending this report because I have asked the Bishop to write me a letter about it so I could send you a copy and I have been waiting for the letter. It has not come yet. He has personally told me that I am appointed, and has written Fr. Iida that he is appointed as my assistant and we have together done our first small work in the peninsula, but there is as yet no letter of which I can send you a copy. I asked the Bishop about it again on Sunday last and he said he would be writing it.

So much for the appointment. Now for the work.

Our first step, and in fact the only step so far clearly planned, is to make contact with about ten church members living in isolation in different parts of the area. They have moved in there after having their homes destroyed in air-raids elsewhere. We plan to visit them and minister to them and try to use them as "growing points." One lives in Ito and we will start at once to hold regular Sunday Services at his house. The others we will seek out during a three-day journey round our parish at the end of December. It is our hope that we can build up small groups around most of these members by regular rounds of visits in much the manner of Australian Bush Brotherhoods.

Fr. Iida will do as much of this as he possibly can, and indeed, the ministry to persons must for some time to come be his rather than mine. I will have to depend on him for deep digging and cultivating. My own activity will be largely limited by the amount he is available to do. Prior to this appointment he has been in charge of the church at Hamamatsu. There has been no house there and he has lived in one of the church cottages at Numazu where he has a full-time job as a school-teacher. He has visited Hamamatsu once a month. Lack of money has been the trouble. Now he has finished the Hamamatsu work and handed over to another priest he is available for our work for just as much time as is left after he has done his "bread and butter work." He has a wife and two sons, aged 10 and 12 years. I think you will see that we cannot extend our work very much, and I myself cannot do much, in the peninsula until I can find an income for him which will enable him to give up his teaching job. He is anxious to do so. The foreseeable income from Izu itself will be very small during the first stages of work at least. I have therefore told Fr. Iida that, although I will be trying to arrange an income for him, he must reckon on continuing his teaching job for several months, at least until July next year.

Fr. Iida is my "bottleneck!" While my activities in Izu are limited I am to continue with the work I have in hand at present. In any case I will be staying in Odawara until we reach a much more definite plan and development than we can foresee at present. But Izu is now my centre of gravity and as I cease other work to take up Izu work there are some items of expenditure in the budget of this year which will not have to be paid. I can see the possibility of saving perhaps £50 on expenditure from now till the end of the May in that way, but certainly less rather than more. At the same time we reckon that the cost of living for his family for the year from June next year will be about £A150. It is because of this discrepancy I have told him I do not know when I can provide an income for him. When I can see an income of £150 spread over a year, with a reasonable likelihood of its continuance, then I can ask him to resign his job. (A part of this could be in goods if that were to prove more economical.)

My present hope is that it will be possible to have provision for this included in the budget for the next financial year when the Board is considering the matter. Could you give me your opinion on that? The effect would be that my budget estimate for my work would be wholly cast in the light of my responsibilities in Izu, with a considerable reduction of expenditure for other purposes, but one explicit item, "Stipend for Assistant-priest, Japanese." I cannot say now, but it might well be that the total would be no more.

I do not contemplate any capital expenditure until we have explored the situation pretty thoroughly and formed some idea of what we should aim at doing in Izu. One aspect of it is that the peninsula is the strategic and geographic centre for a Diocesan Summer Camp establishment able to be used for Retreats and Conferences all the year round. It is my dream that this may be done, for then we can continue to grapple with the spiritual needs of the whole Diocese. The headquarters of our work in Izu could well be combined with such a centre. My advisers were all very keen on the prospect of making a missionary's work in a local area a matter of example and inspiration for impact on the clergy and people of the whole Diocese. Izu has the natural features to make it easy to attract people to it from all over the Diocese. Also, in the matter of capital expenditure, I rather feel the need of an effort being made to build by local effort and I have already spoken in those terms to the Bishop and Fr. Iida. But perhaps that is the optimism of the "rookie." Anyway, there is no question of capital expenditure at present.

Izu is a Rural area and it is significant that the new work of the Diocese is to be located in a rural area rather than in a city. This is a distinctly post-war feature of the Nippon Seiko Kwai. We are realising our failure to grapple with the baffling problem of converting the peasantry who comprise over 70 percent of the people of Japan. Before I came to Japan I had reached the conclusion that the conversion of the peasantry was a crucial task. I have therefore been thinking it is probably the calling of God to me that the Bishop should suddenly ask me to undertake this quite unthought-of work in the rurality of Izu. I've raised all possible objections and none of them seems to be very strong so I am now very wholeheartedly rolling up my sleeves.

Need I say that the jeep will be a most important piece of equipment. It would be impossible to do anything significant without our own transport – despite what Tourist literature says about transport offering to tourists.

This letter is rather long, but I hope not confusing.

Frank Coaldrake

Newsletter No. 20, 1 December 1948.

NIPPON SEIKO KWAI

Aust. Army Post Office,
C/- Empire House,
B.C.O.F.,
Tokyo,
JAPAN.

From – Rev. Frank W. Coaldrake

Dear Friends,

Yesterday I visited the home of an 18 year old girl student. The farmer family is of long-standing in Buddhism and daily Buddhist practices. The reality of a daughter's freedom is always problematical, so I went to meet the family and ask the father if she could become a Christian if she desired to do so? The answer was "she is free to decide." We spent the afternoon talking and eating fruit from the garden and I found myself bogged down in an explanation of the words "transcendent and immanent" in J'ese. I think the thing to notice about this visit is that a father could say his daughter was free to decide for herself!

I have with me today the five members of the Committee of the South Tokyo Diocesan Women's Auxiliary. We are having a Quiet Day. They came early this morning to start the day with Mass and continue in silent meditation and prayer until late afternoon. If they can understand my J'ese, I have explained to them about Consecration, using as my outline that excellent little "Litany of Personal Consecration" by Mowbray which I think you know. We've been thinking about what it means to give into God's hands everything you've got, everything you are, then live as possessing what you have in trust to use for God. For people who haven't got much, the "everything you are" is more significant. Minamioka-san is their Vice-President and has translated that Litany into J'ese for me, no easy task for it is expressed in ideas common to our Western minds, but often quite foreign to eastern minds. If you think over that phrase we all know, "The beauty of holiness," you'll realise that it has a quite distinctive meaning, and that is lost if we simply translate the words literally. We used that Litany at noon after intercessions, Minamioka-san saying it. Mrs. Sugai (the President) is here, and Mrs. Takahashi, who wrote you the poem of remembrance; and Miss Tanaka, who grows most beautiful flowers in Hiratsuka and "put the lid on me" in the kitchen staff stunt at the Oiso Camp, and Ogata-san with tea towel and soap in the kitchen, keeping the material side of things going smoothly. We've all been shivering because it has turned quite cold, and they have pulled out my blankets and wrapped them round their knees and shoulders. At the end of the day they said very nice "thank-yous" and gave me things to send to you.

On Wednesday last week it was "Culture Day," a Public Holiday In Japan [November 11]. We had a gathering of the Youth Groups of this prefecture's Churches up at Hadano. It was a grey day with some drizzle, so the ardour for the projected mountain climbing cooled off and everyone spent the day in the Church hall having fun and games. I couldn't resist the lure of a small mountain in the fascinating misty weather, so after lunch I made my way to the top. It was worth it. I think there is a special mystic beauty about Japan's hills and valleys, trees and fields, in such weather.

The rice has been gathered again now and the fields are lying in freshly turned brown mud germinating the seeds of the new crop which must be hurried up before the snow comes. The rice crop now being delivered from farms to distribution centres is the biggest for some years. Every year's crop is reduced by toll of earthquakes and typhoons. On the basis of the crop increase, daily food issue to the J'ese citizens has been increased by 10% in quantity; the price increase has jumped 50%. The new level of basic ration supplies, which is what the honest citizen is dependent on, is still far too low. Official statements say that it provides 1,400 calories daily. Workers in heavy industry get 500 calories a day more, and of course farm-dwellers do better than city dwellers. But 1,400 calories a day is about half the recognised minimum and a third of the average Australian's diet. The way that it strikes my eyes and ears is that 9 out of 10 citizens are hungry at any time, but they keep in fair health. The other 1 in 10 usually has gone downhill to T.B. if an adolescent with malnutrition, or just plain starvation, if any infant. I could name 40 or 50 people among my friends and acquaintances who have T.B., some very far advanced. Of course, there's the occasional 1 in 10 who is thriving at the expense of others. In any country such people are able to exploit their weaker brethren, and Japan on 1,400 calories a day is no exception. Talking of food and sustenance, our Theological students hoe a hard row. They hoe it every afternoon between morning and evening study, trying inexpertly to grow something to raise the level of the pot. When I get a chance I bring them in here for a solid meal.

On Sunday afternoon last I baptised the infant grandchild of Fr. Miyazawa. He is born into an established Christian family and Paul is his name. He's a chubby little squeaker, and your parcels have played a part in the chubbiness.

Kumazo is pulling his weight. One really great advantage proves to be that I can drop in on people and priests who live along the way of my travels. This means I have already come into closer touch with our Babies' Home at Oiso, 10 miles along the road to Tokyo. Then I'd never been to our Church at Kawasaki, between Yokohama and Tokyo. The train from here always goes express through there and the Church is some distance from the station; but it's only 200 yards off the main road so I have visited the parish priest three times in the last month. He was wondering if I had a grudge against him, as I'd not been there before. Now I've found the way Kumazo carries things like a roll of bitumenoid paper to mend his leaking roof, and glass to fill gaps in his windows.

Another one of the Jeep's early burdens was felt scraps in large bundles. I hadn't been able to spread it around to all the people who were wanting it. But now every scrap I've received is out under the needles. One Church has a new fence, repaired seats and windows and a general overhaul, all derived from sales of worked up felt scraps. Please note that I haven't any more at present to meet the constant enquiries.

I've indulged in a little play with tools and built a "bark humpy" as a garage for Kumazo. Many houses now being built are roofed with this bark so I thought it good for the garage in the garden under the pine trees. I didn't know that one of disadvantages of the bark is that it cracks apart as it dries. I'll have to do the roof again, and I wonder how people live in houses roofed with it. It is only a makeshift "reconstruction."

Autumn tones in red, brown and gold provide a rich accompaniment to the cold wind prelude to winter. The sun has moved over into your part of the world, and we go into the long wait to welcome him back in April next year.

The Film Factory Study Group has been carrying on steadily, meeting once a fortnight. A dozen or so attend regularly and others come when they can, as all have to work in the fields after factory hours. Last night I had eight of them come to tea with me and stay for a talk afterwards. Fr. Miyazawa and Miss Minamioka came too. This marks a definite stage in the group. They came ready to ask questions about the right things.

To take them further requires a closer knowledge of the language than I possess, but as we continue our studies I hope to have some pass out of my hands into Fr. Miyazawa's. I am thankful to have brought this group of 8 new young people to him.

Today I have been up to Oiso Babies' Home. There was a money-raising function which attracted many Americans from Tokyo. With 27 babies on our hands now our expenses are high. One little son of a B.C.O.F. father is a very bright one year old.

After collecting the Jeep from B.C.O.F. [at Kure] on Thurs. Morn. we started out for Odawara having to reach here so that I could take services on Sunday. I had Sgt. Laurie Topp with me to share the driving and it took 2½ days to do the 582 miles. That is very slow – but the road is rough, winding and narrow, and during the daytime crowded with all sorts of traffic which knows no rule, not even self-preservation. We covered most of the distance at night because the roads are empty then. On the way we called at several Church centres. The Jeep performed well and as he has pulled a heavy load and a trailer over rough mountain roads he has earned the name Kumazo! On Monday the Jeep did its first job. Three of our school girls were injured when a tram ran off the end of a bridge washed away by Typhoon floods. They live in the country near the Film Factory so Fr. Miyazawa and I went out to visit them. An all-day job (without the Jeep) only took us 3 hours and when I called on the senior member of the Factory group I found her home sick also. Roads and bridges are in a temporarily repaired state and bridges are so narrow that the Jeep wheels have only a couple of inches to spare. I am very fortunate to have Laurie to initiate me into the mysteries of the Jeep, as I'd never driven one before, but he has driven them a lot in the Army. One good feature about the Jeep is it has wonderful 4-wheel brakes.

Laurie's description of our "Jeepish Nightmare" from Kure to Odawara includes this: "At Hiro, 5 miles out of Kure, one tyre gave out and after 50 miles of mountains further on we discovered a main leaf of rear spring broken. We drove for 1 hour each through the night and stopped for dawn wayside breakfast. A few more hours and we reach Kobe, where we visited St. Michael's Church and School which is a great credit to Miss Lea and her staff. It has grown from a small group started in war years (under J'ese military police supervision) to an International School of 200 pupils. Miss Lea graciously entertained us at luncheon and we met her parents Bishop and Mrs. Lea. St. Michael's Church has a beautiful Altar and Reredos made by Bishop Yashiro. We also met Bishop Mann, Archbishop of Canterbury's personal representative in Japan, who went with us to visit St. Michael's Orphanage, and then we set out for Osaka where Bishop and Mrs. Mann reside in the grounds of C.M.S. [Church Missionary Society] Poole Memorial School for Girls. After two hours' sleep and a meal, we drove continuously thro' the second night and arrived at Hamamatsu where St. Andrew's Church and residence were completely destroyed during the war. The work is being carried on in a temporary house, and a permanent building awaits 20,000 yen (£20 Aust.) to complete it. Next we came to Shizuoka where Fr. Nakano and family have a beautiful Church and house. Later we called at Shimizu where St. James' Episcopal Church and residence were destroyed and they now use a small house for services. The beauty of the scenery along the way by the Inland Sea I'll never forget. We arrived at Odawara exhausted after 582 miles of rough roads, much of it done in 1st gear over cart tracks of 12 ft. widening to 16 ft. in spots to allow vehicles to pass. Twice we got lost, and once ended on a wrong track in someone's backyard. Have you ever tried to back a Jeep with a trailer? However, after a few hours' sleep I revived to enjoy the rest of my week's Army leave. One day we drove around Odawara to see the extensive damage caused by a recent typhoon, when bridges, houses, roadways and crops were all ruined, but in the usual Eastern manner temporary houses and bridges were being built, and new crops were already 2 inches above the ground. Another day we climbed the steep road bordered by magnificent cryptomeria trees to view the Buddhist monastery at Diuysan, where the Abbot entertained us at a traditional J'ese Tea Ceremony, and we saw the monks at their evening devotions."

I hear from Mother that many Christmas parcels are on the way, and to all those friends who have helped our work in Japan we say Thank you.

Stop Press

50 parcels you told me to expect have just arrived, and now I'm having a happy time sorting them ready for our Christmas parties. What a joy they will spread.

May the Christian Peace which you have shared go round the wide world and return again to rest in your hearts and homes.

Yours sincerely,
    FRANK

Newsletter No. 21, January, 1949.

NIPPON SEIKO KWAI

> Aust. Army Post Office,
> C/- Empire House,
> B.C.O.F.,
> Tokyo,
> JAPAN.

From – Rev. Frank W. Coaldrake

Dear Friends,

During December we prepared seriously for Winter with unpacked last year's woollens,[81] and I was thankful for each and every parcel that arrived with warm clothing to distribute. In our little sleeping-room, Kiroshi-san [the theological student?] and I prepared for bleak nights with layers and layers of newspapers and corrugated cardboard flat on top of the ceiling. This will stop, we hope, the air <u>we</u> warm rushing away through the many wide curtains, as it did last Winter.

I can't attempt to write now the thanks that will come to you for all those wonderful parcels I have opened and sorted ready for our Christmas "Surprise" parties. What surprises! A few days ago I took the Jeep to Tokyo to collect my Santa Claus load of parcels. At Ebisu, collecting rations, I ran into a Queensland pal, Bill Cuppaidge, and lunched with him before he hurried back to his work as Associate to Sir William Webb at the War Crimes Trials. Later, at Kawana, I met the Chief Justice just before he returned to Australia. My Jeep was as good as any "launch" for the very rainy ride home, but my old Queensland leather coat keeps me fine and dry.

Life is full of everything pleasant except a plentiful amount of time. I have started on my Izu work, which is the Peninsula South of Odawara. Yesterday the Jeep took me over the Hakone Mts. down to Numazu where I picked up Fr. Iida and Fr. Yamazaki, then cut across the Peninsula to Ito midst rain and bad roads. I'll have more to tell you later about Izu. Time has been so full I hardly know where to start. It is just a matter of this and that to be got ready for Christmas, and already we have started meetings, parties, or services with isolated groups for

---

81 This is Japanese sentence construction. Frank Coaldrake's immersion in a Japanese environment is affecting his English expression.

their Christmas observances. When it is all over I shall have more time for writing I hope.

Now I want to tell you just one thing (Mother). You will have received the letter I posted last week from Minamioka-san. It will be the last you will have from her. Quite suddenly and without any signs she suffered a cerebral haemorrhage on Sunday the 19th and died within 3 hours. I had been at Zushi for the morning service and arrived home at 2 o'clock to find her on a stretcher in our Odawara Church, with a doctor in attendance, and death very close. I learned she had gone to Church with the family and received her communion. Afterwards she had played the organ while the young people practised the Christmas singing. At the end of it she felt a dizziness and the others realised it was serious, so a doctor was called, but she did not recover consciousness. We would all wish to die that way I think – in our Church just after receiving the Sacrament. It was, we think, the reward of a life spent in faithful service to Our Lord. Minamioka-san was just 60. She was educated at Girton College, England, 40 years ago and had been a Mission worker.

I do not know what was in the letter she wrote you for Christmas – perhaps a few home truths about your rough and rowdy son! But perhaps something you could quote, which would show better than my words can do, what kind of a woman she was.

I think you will have caught the atmosphere of serenity always about her and her patience was proof even against my crude stumblings through those first months in Japan. She has (how can I put it), yes, she has been the mother of my childhood in the J'ese life. How I shall miss her if it were not for the Communion of Saints. We meet on earth such choice spirits from time to time, don't we, and usually briefly. There seems to be a kind of spiritual growth which starts deeper down in human nature than nationality and of skin and blossoms to a fullness which belittles man's divisions.

A year ago I should have been lost without her. Now I shall often wander and stumble for lack of words and understanding. I cannot say, except in prayer, my deepest feelings at the moment.

Her equally rare but quite different companion in semi-retirement, Mrs. Murota [in whose grounds the Coaldrake house is located], you also know. If I am sad at this time, it is for the gap that has opened in her household. They were as close as right hand and left, and lived together in a quite closeness that had qualities I've never seen before. The youthful Yasuhiro Jonathan will miss her too, but not sadly for he sees at once and simply that Harubachan (which was her name to the children) has gone to live with God and the Angels, where he too hopes to go some day.

(Yes, her letters were a joy to receive and I shall always treasure them, just such as any dear sister could have written to me with homely understanding. Her last page of perfect English described for me the Women's Auxiliary Communion Service in Frank's House Chapel a week earlier, and the picnic lunch which followed. She said also – "Looking through the windows of Fr. Coaldrake's house, out over the beautiful sea. I thought again how wonderful a

gift from Australia was the coming of Fr. Coaldrake to help us in Japan."
E.R.C.)[82]

Our Christmas parties were all very happy affairs. The things I received for Christmas distribution exceeded my wildest dreams, both in quantity and quality. For a start I was able to take quite a large box of food and clothes to the Bishop, and each of our 24 parish priests and their families, and the 6 Kindergarten teachers. Because the parcels had arrived early it was possible to deliver these Christmas Boxes during the ordinary course of my travels from the very beginning of December.

On Christmas Eve there was a staff dance and party out at the Film Factory. Several hundred factory workers were to be there. For an hour beforehand my study group held another kind of Christmas party. They had set up and decorated a tree and about 50 workers came. We sang Carols and I told them about the origin and meaning of Christmas and explained Christmas customs and symbols.

After an hour at home making jelly and custard by the gallon for our Church Christmas dinner I set out for St. Peter's, Zushi, where we had midnight Mass. About 40 people were there – despite pouring rain and bitter cold. After the service we drank your cocoa and ate your biscuits and a cake from an American friend, then at 3 a.m. Kumazo set out on the 35 mile run back to Odawara, quite undaunted by the rain. Minamioka-san had intended going with me to Zushi because for many years she worked at that Church, but her nephew came instead. After a couple of hours sleep we had the first Christmas Mass at Odawara, then a little later the second. The Church was filled to overflowing, even more than last year. There has been a steady increase in membership in each parish throughout the year. We had 70 communicants in Odawara on Christmas Day. After the service we had our parish Christmas dinner followed by a concert and party. The supplies of food stood up to the demand and there was cake and candy too!

As well as the parcels from Australia I received things from friends in America and from Australians and Americans serving in Japan. In fact, as I pointed out to the party, our stomachs that day became a meeting place of many nations! Fr. Miyazawa was a bit overwhelmed and stammered out something about Odawara being a centre for making strong links of fellowship between ordinary people in Japan and other countries.

The two earlier parties at the Church, for the Kindergarten children and the Girls' School, had also been very cheerful occasions. The fourth and final party was on Boxing Day. We gathered about 60 social service workers of the district and entertained and fed them. They are the voluntary workers who get little recognition for their continual service of the community. I found among them people who seek out the sick poor and arrange for their treatment, those who

---

82 Added by Frank Coaldrake's mother as she prepared the *Newsletter* for duplication and distribution.

collect funds for charity or who undertake the care of the needy, and many other such workers. The last of the jelly and custard was finished at this party. Imagine eating jelly and custard with chopsticks.

I was in a cave late on the night of Boxing Day when I realised that my Christmas was over. Perhaps it was because a Mother and Child in a cave-stable were the beginning of all Christmases. However, there was not much likeness between the Bethlehem cave and this one. The mother is a widow and the daughter a 5 year old. Their house was burned during air raids, and now the mother works chopping blocks of firewood into little pieces from daylight to dark. The cave was dug into the side of a hill as an air raid shelter. It is just earth and there are no props. I cannot get right into it because the entrance tunnel is too small. I was there on Boxing Night to take some food. It was some of the good given me for such a purpose by our Church members in Odawara, and I had taken some to each of 20 people sleeping out in the open spaces. The food from our people was just little bags of sweet potato slices, or hard biscuits, rice, or mandarins. To it I was able to add things I'd kept from your parcels, so that each person received a day's food and a few sweets.

You'll be interested in the story of the Church members' food gifts because it shows an age old Japanese custom still being rigidly observed which requires the recipient of any gift, whether of things or help, to make a "return gift." Consequently whenever I take anything to a person there is a strong desire to bring me a present in return. This makes it a problem taking relief goods to needy people. They're likely to deprive themselves of some much needed article in order to express their thanks properly. It makes my work quite complicated at times, for if I visit a family in an ordinary "pastoral" way they often consider I have done them a great honour by entering their house, and feel bound to express their thanks. If I visit a sick person he will get up and greet me with the customary low bow, kneeling with forehead to floor. This has been done by a man recovering from a major operation, even if I try to prevent it. One has to think twice before dropping in on pastoral visits. Back of it all is also the attitude to a Westerner of the ordinary J'ese homely men and women. It is difficult to meet with them on the level proper to a parish priest, because they start by expecting me to be "the Sahib." But that is all a problem much wider than the Christmas season.

It was a natural part of this tradition that made our Odawara people want to "return thanks" to the Australian friends who had given them things for Christmas. We must not think that this is an insincere formality. You and I say "thank you" usually with sincerity. I explained here that we do not understand the "return present" custom, and might even be a bit offended, thinking it cast reflections on the generosity of the givers. We have another way, much more indirect. I cannot hope to repay all the people who have given me things or helped me. I can only say thank you and try to be similarly kind and helpful to other people, hoping that they in turn will be kind to others, and so on. With that in mind I told them how I was hoping to be able to take some Christmas cheer to the beggars of Odawara and suggested they should try to bring some gift of food from their own table. They were very glad to do so. Perhaps they will have learnt something about extending their Christian love and social responsibility outside the circle of their family and immediate friends. Such concern for people with whom there is no direct personal link is a marked gap in Japanese social life.

Boxing Day was a Sunday this year, so we had the usual Sunday services. It was after the evening service that I took the food gifts around and came eventually to the cave. And so Christmas was over 1948, and we are grateful to all those friends who shared in our Japanese Christmas – and we hope yours was happy.

Yours sincerely,

FRANK

Newsletter No. 22, **February, 1949.**

NIPPON SEIKO KWAI

Aust. Army Post Office,
C/- Empire House,
B.C.O.F.,
Tokyo,
JAPAN.

From – Rev. Frank W. Coaldrake

Dear Friends,

Between Christmas and New Year I was able to make a 250 mile journey round and about in the Izu Peninsula. This is only the first of what I hope will be many years of travel in the Peninsula, for it has just been given to me as my own district. During my year and a half of being assistant priest in Odawara with other duties ranging over the whole Diocese I have no doubt been "on the balances" of the Bishop's judgement and now he has asked me to take this appointment. With a Japanese priest (Iida) to be my assistant, I am from now on Priest of Izu. This large peninsula, 80 miles long and 30 wide, is actually in the very centre of the Diocese, but no work has ever been undertaken in it because it is very effectively cut off by sea and mountain. (Fig. 22) On our *Newsletter* map you'll see it with the word "Kawana" written right across it, for the B.C.O.F. Kawana Rest Hotel is on the east coast; but I'll probably draw a map of Izu only shortly. (See Fig. 7) The place simply reeks with history. For centuries it has been the practice of governments to exile troublesome reformers to Izu because it is so inaccessible. More than 700 years ago 2 such exiles were Nichiren and Yoritomo. Both came out of exile later and effected far reaching reforms. Nichiren started what is today the most vigorous of the Buddhist Sects, and Yoritomo laid the foundations of government by militarism. We know of ten families at various points who have been Christians and for some reason have moved into Izu. My first job has been to locate them and take the ministry of the Church to them. With Fr. Iida accompanying me we found many people wanting baptism and confirmation, and we have taken the Christmas Communion to families who have not received it for 10 or 15 years.

Figure 22 The rugged coastline, fishing village and farm land of the Izu Peninsula, 1949 or 1950.

The second purpose of this initial journey was to get a picture of the whole territory, and the kind of people who are our charge. As we went from one of our families to the other we looked around and often stopped to talk, or explore. This is not the time for details but I can describe it briefly as a part of Japan little affected by the Occupation, with fishing villages right round the rugged coast, and farmers, timber-getters and hunters in the mountains, and wherever we go the Jeep proves a wonderful draw-card to gather a crowd for us to talk to.

During these initial stages the work is very like that done in Australia by our Bush Brotherhoods. The differences however, are often striking. For instance, we had to carry a small folding table for use as an altar, for nowhere is there a table more than 1 foot high. Another difference is that the Australian Bush Brothers in their journey from one family to the next see no other homes. As we went we saw thousands. It is our hope that as time goes on we will know people all along the way. This first visitation was a short and quick one, though I was surprised to find my speedo showed 250 miles at the end of it, making a total of 2,100 miles travelled in the month of December. It may be years before I am able to go and reside in Izu.[83]

At one place while we were running after dark on a very narrow road banked up between the paddies, the edge of the road on one side gave way and we were bogged down for 2 hours. The Jeep's 4-wheel drive couldn't get into action because the engine and chassis were sunk in the soft edge of the bank. The local farmers gathered around and were very willing to help. With great levers they started to pry us up and back on to the road, but this threatened to wreck steering and brake gear. As a joke I suggested there were so many they could lift me back onto the road. No sooner said than done, with a chorus of Yoi! Sho! for each heave they picked up the Jeep, its luggage and me and put us back on the road – about 8 of these "Yoi-Sho!" I've heard it from fishermen hauling their nets; windlass men winding a load; farmers loading a wagon; and Ogata-san lifting a basket of clothes. In the course of our efforts in the mud we had to completely destroy 10 yards of bamboo fence. The owner would not hear of my paying for repairs, and it was with difficulty I prevailed on him to take some tinned food for his children – a tin of syrup and one of stew. Cigarettes to each of the lifters were not quite so slowly accepted, then they went off home with their paper lanterns bobbing, as we went on our way.

In the last days of December everyone was busy with preparations for observing the New Year in the age-old manner. Special dress, special food and special doings mark the occasion. The chief item of food is a cake made of ground-rice [*mochi*]. It is ground wet in a large wooden mortar with Dad swinging a large wooden mallet to powder the meal while mother deftly turns the gradually pulping mass between blows. The final result is a doughy lump which is flattened ½ inch thick and spread in the sun to dry. For some extra special cakes, some of it is coloured pink, the rest remaining white. It is cut into matchbox slices. These dry out in a day or two and are usually dealt with in the way we use crumpets; they are also submerged in a soup made of very sweet red beans, this being a special delicacy. The New Year cakes, O-Mochi, are served on every possible occasion during 5 days from Jan. 1st. They prove palatable enough in my mouth, but very heavy down below. Where streets are narrow, and kitchens too small for the swinging mallet, the Jeep must dodge between swinging mallets of couples making O-Mochi in the roadway. The chief idea deciding the food for the New Year seems to be that it must be prepared in quantity. There is a special kind of dish made by piling high small portions of several kinds of food; as the

83 The move to Izu was to come sooner than he expected.

day progresses the mountain is gradually eaten away. This New Year Festival, O-Shogatsu, is said to be the only holiday the womenfolk have in the whole year. With much food prepared they forget the kitchen, and dress themselves in their finest gowns. The long sleeves, full-length tight skirts, and thick constraining waist-bows, make kitchen work out of the question.

Perhaps the most intriguing thing of all is the hairdo of the women. In the same general mode as the wedding fashion, but now the decorative paper and symbols are distinctive. Women use their hair to express their mood at special times. The mourning mother wears her hair hanging straight down, unbound and unadorned. But for weddings and the New Year she makes it an ornate crown built up and bedecked with colours, that artistically complete the lines and colours of her gown. First you must have the hair long enough to fall below the shoulders. (It will, of course, be jet-black and straight.) You should then dip the head in a bucket of thick starch. After a few minutes it will be nearly set, so take a coarse comb and run it down the length of the hair dividing it into long strands like black bootlaces. Next divide the hair into quarters, front, back and sides. The front strands roll up and up and inwards till you have a roll across the brow in the position of a fringe. Get the comb out somehow, then take the lower ends of each side quarter, one in each hand, and with a quick movement sweep each up and out and over to the centre top, leaving a great rolling bulge over each ear; while doing this you will have taken the back quarter in another hand and whooped it up to the top, leaving a bulging roll well above the neck. All that remains is to weave the ends of the 2 sides and one back bulges together so they'll lock, then hang garlands on the corners and put coloured papers to rest in the bulging nests. At least, that's how it looks to me. But you wouldn't have to trust your head to my imagination for you could simply hire a headdress at a wiggery. Laurie Topp sported a wonderful display of jet black hair dressed in this fashion at a New Year party in the Sergeants' Mess, the Mess which has just subscribed 25,000 yen for our Babies' Home at Oiso.

The business of the New Year Festival is to walk the streets in order to meet friends. Greetings are exchanged with elaborate bowings. Thanks are spoken for all gifts and help received during the year, and wishes for a Happy New Year are smilingly exchanged. Letters of greetings are sent to distant friends and calls are made on relatives. Houses and shops, buses, cars, trams, factories, are festooned with symbolic decorations. In quite a few places Christmas trees have stood through from Christmas and take a central place in the New Year decorations. The exploitation of Christmas by commerce is already well developed, for it is only a matter of advancing by 2 weeks the vast organisation already developed to exploit the New Year Festival customs. The New Year is "run in" with the bells of every Buddhist temple – in no sense could one say of the sound, "Ring out wild bells" for the note is a deep solemn boom. This merges with the thunder of hundreds of drums beaten by small boys in specially constructed huts of bamboo branches or great wooden wagons by the roadside. As the sun rises from the ocean horizon on Jan. 1st people gather on beaches, and the hardy young men bathe in the midwinter breakers. On every beach are set up clumps of bamboo with the comical plump red "Daruma" swinging. Daruma is a fellow you simply can't upset; squat and round with no arms and legs and no matter how you knock him he always bobs up again. He was a soldier who many centuries ago met with bad fortune so he simply sat down and smiled his way cheerfully through the years. In the process his arms and legs gradually withered away, but he still faced the future with a smile. Today he expresses the resolution of the average Japanese about to start on a New Year, smiling and hopeful in spite of what might come, be it earthquake, fire, typhoon, taxes, war or peace. So as Daruma bobs about on the beach bamboos the New Year dawns and great is the celebration. The point of it all? Why it's everybody's birthday! On the first of the year everyone takes another year to his age. The anniversary of his birth is perhaps observed quietly, but it makes no difference to the counting of his age. To understand the Japanese method of stating a person's age we must remember this. Deacon Sakurai's wife had a son born on Dec. 22nd last. From then until Dec. 31st, the Sakurai babe was "aged 1" but from Jan. 1st he is "aged 2." Capt. & Mrs. Burrows of Kawana Hotel are rejoicing in the birth of a son on the same day and reckon his age now as not yet 1. So that in this case the Japanese age is 2 years ahead of ours. However, New Year's Day is the birthday party of everyone – a Nation's "birthday party." With everyone rejoicing becomes a community festival.

Yours faithfully,

FRANK

P.S. Will readers please note my new address. I will be glad of any old *Newsletters* returned to me, as I find the supply is not equal to the demand at present. Cost price is 3/- yearly posted. Mrs. E.R. Coaldrake. Francis St. Blackburn, Victoria.

Newsletter No. 23, March, 1949.

NIPPON SEIKO KWAI

C/- B.C.O.F. Aust. Army P.O. 214,
Empire House,
Tokyo,
JAPAN.

From – Rev. Frank W. Coaldrake

Dear Friends,

Please take note that B.C.O.F. is not ending – it has only been "reduced." I wish all those who have sent parcels to know how grateful is each and everyone who receives their share of the warm clothing, or food. I would still like to know who was responsible for sending from Sydney the very welcome butter in calico (and tins). That was a rare treat! To lend variety to my breakfast table Mrs. Murota has lately organised a working-party of four women to pick and pickle from her one Dai-dai orange tree a supply of enjoyable marmalade. I was able to supply the sugar from your parcels. Another clever friend in Frankston, Vic. discovered a useful little booklet of soap-paper-leaves to send me, which I shall save for my next "hitchhike" in May. Dishes are not usually washed in hot water during winter round here, because knobs of charcoal are scarce and must be saved to cook rice and vegetables.

The calendar tells me it is now nearly 2 years since I started towards Japan, but the time has been so interesting and happy it seems to me like only 6 months gone. On Friday March 25th is the Festival of The Annunciation, and that is the day I have chosen for my Induction as Priest of Izu, by the Bishop at Ito. Please remember me and my assistant, Fr. Iida, in your prayers, as we start out on our new adventure to witness for Christ and His Church in the tourist mountain regions where no Church at present exists. Odawara is the door at one end, with Numazu (and Fr. Iida as the doorkeeper) at the other end of a barrier of mountains, over which there is not even a walking path in some places. Izu parish has to be developed from nothing as it were and we hope for great progress.

The Hatano Women's Auxiliary of St. Luke's Church in another direction, have written to express their appreciation of help in repairing their Church, and include these words – "We Christians have a great responsibility upon our shoulders in reconstruction and Peace in our country."

With the new camera provided by "Friends of Odawara," Melbourne, I am able to take many better photos. A very interesting group was snapped at Kofu recently, after the baptism of an American baby by Fr. Uemura, when a wonderful demonstration was given of Occupation Co-operation with Japanese native Clergy as mentioned in recent U.S.A. visiting-Bishop Bentley's Report. Many Americans were in the happy group. I plan to have sets of 10 of my photos printed by a local J'ese who does good work cheaply, for sale and distribution to spread the good news of our Mission abroad – the cost will probably work out about 6 d. per picture.

I was at Ebisu Camp last week to see about buying old tins from B.C.O.F. salvage disposals, to use for roofing the shed I plan to build for our Youth Summer Camps. While there I met a former S.C.M. pal newly arrived from Goondiwindi, Queensland, Capt. Lofts is now an Army Medico, and he enquired about my Jeep's general health? I had to explain how badly we needed a Jeep Manual with charts, diagrams, and general maintenance instructions. He soon produced the Manual, so now I no longer need to take apart to bits to see how it works, or doesn't.

Already my speedo shows 7,000 miles consumed, and tomorrow I go to Ichikawa to report on the development of our Baby Clinic there in charge of Dr. Joji (Georgie in English) Matsumoto. The Baby Scales were provided by Comrades of Christ Church, Sydney, and the medicines are provided by A.B.M. Women's Auxiliary, Sydney. They are doing a grand job.

Another interesting day for me was at Kawana when I met the Australian Mission in Japan's representative, Mr. Pat Shaw, with whom I was acquainted in Melbourne. Kawana's manager, Bev. Burrows, also had a message for me from

Gen. Robertson,[84] to assure me of his interest in my Mission and offering any help he could give. Yes, I can use it all! You see Burrows has a collection-box on the Inquiry Counter at Kawana Hotel (B.C.O.F. Leave Centre) labelled "Odawara Mission," with a painting of me with very long legs waving a Bible at a line of very small Japanese children.

Don't forget please, my Clergy friends, any simple theological books are welcome for Japanese Clergy who can mostly read English though they can't speak it! – – And Ogata-san loves Mystic Mits.

Six of the old sheets you sent were used to recover kneeler and seat pads in Odawara Church falling to bits and ready to be scrapped. This will save them for another 10 years. Yes! Spotlessly white because no shoes worn in Church and you could eat off the floor.

The Clergy clothes sent by Miss Slade arrived a few days before an old-timer parish priest from N. Tokyo arrived to visit me in "rags." I was able to send him away happy with a complete outfit, even to shoes and cassock.

A parcel of Weeties and milk arrived from a Melbourne friend to gladden Fr. Uemura's family at Kofu just after their newest son arrived.

We are very grateful to many Readers who have sent "returns" of earlier issues of *Newsletters*, but what happened to No. 18? Are you all learning how to climb Mt. Fuji?

My plans for Izu will take shape at greater speed when Spring comes. I warned you that I would have less time for writing when I rather joyfully changed from crowded train-travelling to "Jeeping," so if this letter is scrappy blame the Jeep.

One of those doubtful compliments was voiced by my passenger peering through the night at the road ahead, winding, rough and slippery in the rain. He appeared anxious, so I asked if my driving worried him as there was not time for slow travel. He replied, "No, it would be a joyful honour to arrive in heaven with you?" Then he asked if a Jeep's brakes were good? For answer I braked suddenly and as he peeled himself off the windscreen he said "Sa!!"

I have antifreeze in the Jeep radiator now, so I don't have to worry about slowly draining and refilling the radiator every time we stop anywhere for a few hours. We had some snow and our waterpipes are sometimes frozen. As I write now I hear the water trickling into the tin on the ceiling above my shower-bath. It takes the best part of a day to fill the 4–gallon tin because the pressure is bad up to our hill. Don't worry it will be a warm shower as I am "permitted" to use an immersion heater, though my ration of electricity does not permit me to use a room radiator.

Yours sincerely,
FRANK

---

84 Horace Clement Hugh Robertson (1894–1960), Australian, Commander-in-Chief of the British Commonwealth Occupation Forces in Japan. See also *Newsletter No. 29* and *No. 33*.

Newsletter No. 24, April, 1949.

NIPPON SEIKO KWAI

C/- B.C.O.F. Aust. Army P.O. 214,
Empire House,
Tokyo,
JAPAN.

From – Rev. Frank W. Coaldrake

Dear Friends,

It's hard to realise that today makes 3 months since, figuratively speaking, the stilts on which I'd walked since my arrival in Japan were suddenly taken away from me. That's the feeling I have as I join in today's third monthly Commemoration of Minamioka-san. Perhaps I think of it that way because this is the time of the year when schoolboys play on bamboo stilts – their name for them is "Bamboo-horse." They're very adept, often using stilts which put their feet up near the level of my head. Perhaps it was seeing this that prompted the top-rank Economic Adviser to MacArthur (J.B. Dodge) to say recently that the Japanese economy is walking on two stilts – American aid, and Japanese Government subsidies to industry. It struck me as a very apt illustration, especially when he went on to point out that as one walks on stilts one likes to make them longer and longer. Anyway after 3 months of having to walk on my own feet I'm more than ever grateful for all that Minamioka-san had done to hold me up and help me on. Did I ever tell you about one simple question she asked me? I had showed her a report from our Mission in Papua saying that the Papuan Christians had decided to send a gift to our Church here. The report spoke of "the barbarian enemy." I explained why the Japanese were referred to as barbarians. Then she asked quite simply, "Do you also call the Russians barbarians?" I said I had not heard it and asked her why she asked. "Well our men now coming back from prison camps in Russia tell of being treated in that way by the Russians."

Today marks, as far as I understand it, the end of the period of close remembrance. There is a strong reflection of Buddhist practices in the way we carry out burials and mournings in Japan. The Buddhists have always made such a big thing of the observance of deaths that the Christians seem to have felt it was the naturally religious thing to do. Also those who had been accustomed to receiving the comfort of Buddhist observance would have felt that they were left comfortless if there were not similar rites in the Church. At the time of a death there are therefore many little rites of which we know nothing in Australia. The underlying feeling is one of loving remembrance in close familiarity. When the body is brought to the home there is a short rite of preparing it for peaceful repose. That evening family and friends gather in the room around the bier, and there are prayers and psalms and hymns. (In Buddhism this service goes on all night, in fact all the time the body is in the house until it is enclosed in the casket.) Our service at this time lasts about 1 hour. When the time comes for placing the body in the casket, the whole family and close friends, from the youngest to the oldest, gathers in the room and there is another short service. Then everyone helps place the loved one in the casket, even if it be only by holding of the fringe of the white kimono. After arranging everything appropriately within the casket the space is filled with paper bags of fragrant leaves and herbs. The Bible and Prayer Books of the departed person are placed on top of all and then the cover is put on. But I mustn't forget to tell you about Yasuhiro. The kid was just one of the family group in all this, but last thing before the cover was placed in position he went over and placed a little note he had written in his childish scribble, within the folded hands. I'm not sure, but as far as I've been able to make out it was a sort of "kind regards" to God and the Angels.

The cover is left unfastened until the Burial Service proper. This took place on the following day. In the meantime, we said a Requiem Mass in the early morning. The Burial Service was conducted in my house chapel for it was there she had loved to worship. It was Mrs. Murota's suggestion that the service be here instead of in the Church and Fr. Miyazawa agreed. The last thing before the casket is carried out to the hearse, everyone files slowly by the casket for a last farewell look on the beloved face. Some drop a flower into the open space. Then the cover is nailed on, the chief mourners again taking part by giving the nails a final tap with a small stone held in the hand. The hearse is, unfortunately for us Christians, ornately bedecked with Buddhist symbols. There are few, if any, undertakers able to provide a hearse seemly for Christian funerals. I am considering the possibility of having an appropriately simple but dignified fitting made to put upon the top of my Jeep trailer for use on such occasions. It would not be odd to people here to see a trailer-hearse for many of the hearses are little carts drawn by a couple of men dressed as we are accustomed to see grave-diggers dressed. My trailer was the 2nd mourning coach on this occasion, the women riding in the Jeep, the men in the trailer. So we came to the Crematorium at Odawara. Again one is struck by the "candidness" with which death and burial are regarded. Cremation has been the chief method of disposal in Japan for over 1,000 years. As we entered the building I noticed Buddhist symbols and burning incense. Again it was a family action to push the casket through the opening. After bowing in prayer before the closed doors everyone goes away to a waiting room where the next 3 hours are spent quietly waiting for the time to receive the urn of ashes. For the next month the urn is kept in the chief room of the house in the alcove of honour with many flowers most beautifully arranged. A photograph stands in front of the urn. The presence of a cross in the central position and the lack of burning incense are the chief things which distinguish the Christian home from the Buddhist at this time. At some time convenient the ashes are taken away to be deposited in a public vault and there is a special service for that. The monthly anniversaries are kept by a gathering for "remembrance talks" on the night before, and a Requiem in the early morning. Finally, as has been done today, some small particles of bone kept apart when everything else was placed in the urn, are deposited separately in a vault provided for this purpose in Christian cemeteries. I was able to say the Requiem this morning but couldn't go to the vault in Tokyo because of duties here, so that part of the service was taken by others.

How does it strike you? Perhaps as you read my description you fall a victim to my words. I only wish you could know the refreshing sense of temporariness in the parting, the candid acknowledgment that the body has served its good purpose, and above all, the extraordinarily real sense of survival.

It was rather a different kind of thing that kept me in Odawara today. In fact, my ears are still ringing with the noisy chatter of 100 16-year old girls at their school graduation ceremony and party. Our Church School has run its course of 3 years. It was a unique kind of graduation ceremony really, for the School has been of an unusual kind. 3 years ago there were many girls, mostly farmers' children, who had qualified to enter a Girls' High School here in Odawara, but could not be accepted because of lack of accommodation. Fr. Miyazawa turned the Church building into a classroom to use on weekdays and these girls were formed into 2 classes. There have been no newcomers during the 3 years for we also could not accommodate more than the 2 classes of 50 each. They have now completed the 3 year course and today has been both a sad and happy occasion for the school, as it has now come to an end. Most will go on up to a Higher School and do a 3 year course there. We will continue our own school with about 30 of them in one group, on a syllabus as near as we can provide to the Higher School. Our pupils will be those whose parents cannot afford the expense of the ordinary High School, and some of the smartest girls will continue with us. We will not have to prepare them for standard examinations, so hope to be able to give them something rather more in the nature of a "sound, higher education." I look forward to it for these country girls are a delight to work with. I was only sorry I couldn't go with them last week when they followed the strange custom of this land – just <u>before</u> their final exams. They went off as a school group on a 5-day trip to famous places in the south. This "End of School Trip" is the customary last corporate activity of a class. One frequently hears people say that they visited such and such a place when on their "End of School Trip." In the old days it was probably quite a sound alternative to the "swot-vac" spent in cold towels and black coffee or benzedrine as done in Australia. Our girls had a typical trip and were away 5 days. Boarding houses are very few, because of bombings, and very expensive, so they spent each night in the train travelling to the next attraction. Theoretically that's where they had their night's rest, but trains are always crowded so in fact the only sleep they had was the kind of coma that comes with exhaustion. Bath of course is simple for there are always public bath-houses in which one can get a hot bath for a few yen. And, of course, on such a trip, places one visits are bound to include a hot spring or two where one really does have a bogey in a big way.

Either Fr. Miyazawa or myself had to go with the party. Although I wanted to spare him the pain of it, I couldn't see myself adequately carrying the responsibility of 100 school girls on such a trip. They're up to all the tricks of course, and anyway I never could understand schoolgirls. I reasoned I'd better be the one to carry on the duties here. Anyway the old chap was bound to enjoy visiting the famous centres round Kyoto and Nara. He did too!

After they returned everyone sat for the Final Examination. This seems to be a short and sharp tussle with the result known almost immediately because only 2 days later plans for the future are all completed.

We held the formal ceremony in the nave of the Church today. Very formal it was. The pews were round the walls for any parents able to come. About 10 were there. The students squatted on cushions in orderly array in the centre. We sang a hymn, then a teacher solemnly called the name of each girl in one class. They stood and bowed in answer to their call until finally the whole class was standing. Then the prefect of that class was called. She walked to the front, bowed to the Principal (Fr. M.), to the group of teachers, then to me, each of us bowing appropriately in return. She received the certificates for the whole class, stepped back, held the bundle of certificates head high, bowed as before, then returned to her place. The same was done for the other class. There were short formal addresses by the Principal and myself (although I'm not sure how "formal" mine was). They all looked so lugubrious I couldn't but try to make them laugh a bit. They did once "at" me and my Japanese, but mostly "with" me as we thought of graduating students' worries and joys the world over. The kind of think they find very amusing was the play on my name as it's pronounced in Japanese. I pointed out how before graduation we students are slaves to our books, afterwards books are our slaves. The word for slave is most prominent in the centre of my name.

The Principal of the High School I mentioned earlier had written, and his letter was read. The Head Prefect then read an address of thanks and appreciation to the Principal and staff, a final hymn was sung and the formal ceremony was over.

What followed was as different as could well be. Quite a "beano," including sweets which John Forsyth sent last November from Bathurst for our Christmas parties. They arrived only last week, seemingly just for this purpose. To cap it all the teachers took turns to sing for the entertainment of the pupils – perhaps I should say "amusement." I was requested to sing songs of my student days. Of course no one understood a word (I hope).

In Tokyo for language lesson tomorrow, then on Friday to Ito for our Great Day! The official inauguration of the Izu Mission. The Collect for that day is the central prayer of the "Angelus." Perhaps the time will come when on the fields and beaches of Izu people will stop their work for the minute of prayer at noon.

Yours sincerely,
FRANK

Newsletter No. 25, May, 1949.[85]

NIPPON SEIKO KWAI

C/o B.C.O.F. Army P.O. 214,
Empire House,
Tokyo,
JAPAN.

From – Rev. F. W. Coaldrake

Dear Friends,

You'd have tired feet and a happy heart if you'd been with us today, for we've been tramping round a mountain side, and standing on "the hill tops of praise and aspiration!" How I have wished you might have been here in fact as I know you have been in spirit and prayer. At Ito, at the house of our one and only Church member there, we had the first service of Holy Communion in that town, and the Bishop of South Tokyo formally inducted me into the charge of the Izu Peninsula, giving me the Bible and Prayer Book as tokens of my duty to call new people into the Church and minister to them. (Fig. 23 and Fig. 24) The form of Service actually includes the key of the Church building, but there is no Church. Perhaps we should have used the key of the Jeep?

At the time for bidding people to pray for specific things, I explained our hopes and plans for the great new work and bid them pray for us. It went on something like this: – "Ye shall pray for. . . ." What an "authoritarian" way to request prayer! Yet, this is my personal responsibility, this Izu work, and it is for me to decide the lines of approach. As we prayed at the mass, it was my responsibility to give point and intention to the prayers which people were going to offer.

So: "Ye shall pray for the eight known families of the faithful Church members scattered through the Peninsula." Nosse-san and others at Mishima; Takahashi-san and family at Chinno; Endo-san and family at Ikadaba; Dr. Kawai and family at Ose; Osawa-san and family at Shitura; and Miyazawa Ichijiro and family at Ito: that these faithful Christians may now have deepened the Faith that has held them true through difficult years in isolation from the Church and contact with other Christians. That they may be witnesses in their districts, showing Our Lord to others by word and deed. That they may, in St. Paul's words in Ephesians 5.16, "buy up the opportunity" that is now theirs.

Then for all the other people of Izu (half a million more or less) who don't know God and the Christian Faith, who worship stone foxes, and put pebbles of prayer at the base of crude stone pillars, whose religion is only the enjoyment of something like "the fun of the fair," who don't know the incalculable worth of their next door neighbour; who don't know the freedom they find who give themselves over to the service of Our Lord. For these ye shall pray; and for us,

---

85 The *Newsletters* were professionally type-set and printed from *No. 25*.

Figure 23 Inauguration of the Izu Mission and Commissioning of Frank Coaldrake as Priest-in-Charge by Bishop Maekawa (left). Bishop Maekawa is holding the Bible and Prayer Book he presented to Frank Coaldrake as a "token" of his new duties (see *Newsletter No. 25*). Fr. Iida, the new Assistant Priest of Izu, sits on the right. The Service was conducted on 25 March 1949 in the home of Hisashi Miyazawa at Kameyama in Itō.

Iida Masao and Frank Coaldrake, priests upon whom has been laid the burden of the ignorance, superstition, and fear, the suffering, the circumscribed aspirations, the goodness, deep but not well-rooted, of these people.

For us, as we fan-out from village to village, from Ito, Mishima and Shimoda: for us as we follow the tracks of the sower described by Our Lord – scattering seed far and wide, wastefully scattering so as to be sure that no good ground is missed. The seed is scattered wastefully, but whatever falls in good ground is not wasted. Pray that we may have the courage to go on scattering the Word thus, far and wide, making sure that no person ready for it shall miss hearing it; ready to go on scattering even when so much is obviously waste of effort. Pray too, as time goes on, for those people who are "the good ground" and gradually begin to show in their lives the fruits that come from the Word.

Then pray for our special work of which the purpose may very easily be forgotten in the good fun it is going to be. Pray for our Camp at Lake Ippeki, which is intended to be a place for training people (especially young people) how to set about making themselves effective **witnesses** in their daily circumstances.

Figure 24 Commemorative photograph of representatives of the Diocese of South Tokyo and parishes, Izu representatives and families taken after the Inauguration of the Izu Mission in Itō, 25 March 1949.

Back row (left to right): Frank Coaldrake, Ikuko Iida (wife of Fr. Iida), Chieko Miyazawa (wife of Hisashi Miyazawa of Itō), Fr. Yoneo Muraoka, Fr. Katsuhiko Iwai (later Bishop of Yokohama), Bishop Shinjirō Maekawa (Bishop of South Tokyo), Fr. Gorō Hayashi, Fr. Kumazō Miyazawa (from Odawara). Middle row: Naotada Hattori (layman from Zushi), Fr. Shūji Toyoda, Kazuo Watanabe (layman from Odawara), Nobuko Yamada, Yasushi Miyazawa, Motoko Miyazawa, Hisashi Miyazawa (Lay Evangelist for the Izu Mission from Itō). Front row: Fr. Masao Iida (Assistant Priest, Izu Mission), Moto Takasaki, Ikue Yoneyama, Takeshi Miyazawa, Tadashi Miyazawa, the daughter of Fr. Iwai (name unknown).

Except for Fr. Iwai's daughter, the young children are members of the Itō Miyazawa family. The three young women at the centre were students from Itō or its vicinity who were being taught by Frank Coaldrake at the Anglican girls' school (Shōzan Joshi Gakuen) run by the Odawara Church.

Pointing them so they will be the wedge of the Church as it drives into the great mass of the people. Pray for them that they may be the kind of Christians the grandparents of many of you were – always talking about the Christian Faith and always ready to let their faith be obvious to others; always regular in the witness provided by walking along the street and entering the Church.

Remember that in this country no one takes Christianity for granted, and nothing will be done the Christian way just because that's the customary way.

Many things are done in a way so obviously contrary to Christian ways that the Christian must be very obvious in those ways in which he is different. Pray that our Camp will be able to train people in that courage which is required if they are to break obviously with accepted customs and ideas. Pray that the Camp may be the life and soul of a great campaign in all the villages round and about it; a place where people "learn by doing," not merely "learn about." Pray that the Camp campaign may put a belt of faithful peasants and fishermen around the nearby town of Ito, within which, as you pray, will be a growing band working outwards from Miyazawa's household. (This family is not related to Fr. Miyazawa of Odawara).

If you can't come with us to see the Camp site as we did to-day, try to imagine 5 acres on a wooded mountain side, stretching down from the summit where we'll have our Chapel tent, to within 300 yards of the gem of a lake where we'll swim and row. Try to stand under the pines up there and look out and around across miles of rising hills and backdrop mountains; try to feel the silence which we will often shatter; try to see the smoke rising among the hills, from the villages into which we will go. Try to see the distant peasant villages from which campers will come, and the shanty-towns in bombed areas from which city youth will come; and the tiny bare Churches, mostly jammed in the backyard of many houses, which are all they know; or the shanty on the ruins of bombed out Churches, where there's not a vestige of beauty, and Worship is an almost dry well for those who look for the Living Water. Try to roll your week's ration of half enough food, and your one spare shirt, and your Bible, in the broad old handkerchief that serves as a kitbag, and come out of those ruins to drink in the unsurpassable beauty of God's own handiwork spread far and wide at your feet and over against your eyes. Start to be obvious in your differences from your fellow countrymen by resolutely turning your back on Mt. Fuji's distant gleam in the West, and face Eastward with all your fellow Christians as you stand in the Chapel to say the few words of Belief which mean so much to so many.

And pray, for God's sake, that this may soon pass beyond the dream stage and be as real as the beauty of the Camp site.

Pray, too, that this Peninsula which juts out into the Pacific Ocean in the direction of Australia, may be the centre of a work in which the One Church, in Australia and Japan, may be brought together as a "bridge" of conciliation between antagonistic peoples. Pray that we may be bound in the Fellowship of the Gospel – and pray that you in Australia may not leave it all to me.

So we prayed – and so, I hope longingly, will you, perhaps more than once.

Have another look at the Collect set for March 25th, The Annunciation [the day of his induction as Priest of Izu]. That collect is the central prayer of the short prayers of "The Angelus." Remember how European peasants through the ages have stopped their work at the chime of the distant Church bell, morning, noon, and evening, to stand bowed in prayer. That is the prayer of millions three times a day. Will it be possible, I wonder, to have a customary noon-tide pause for prayer by all the faithful in Izu? I intend to try. I'm pretty sure that you can vividly recall the immortal painting of the two workers standing in a European field with heads bowed in prayer, but I'm also pretty sure you don't know the prayer they were saying, so here it is: "We beseech Thee, O Lord, pour Thy grace into our hearts; that as we have known the Incarnation of Thy Son, Jesus Christ, by the message of an angel, so by His Cross and passion we may be brought unto the glory of His resurrection; through the same Jesus Christ our Lord."

There's a mountain to shape into a Camp before summer hits us 2 months hence, and much of the work depends on the supply of money for materials. Money, incidentally, which I've set my heart on raising from within Japan. However, we can proceed with the erection of 30 ft. x 24 ft. Hall for use as a store shed, and only wait the carpenters' pleasure. They're still the busiest people in the land.

The long awaited opening of the cherry blossoms begins today. There is a faint touch of pink along the path to my door. Four days from now it will be a glimpse of splendour in the heavens, then on the fifth, sixth and seventh days it will be a poignant carpet under rapidly greening trees.

This morning "Ten No Heika" (that's the generally used title for the Emperor) passed through Odawara to spend the day viewing the blossoms in a famous glen in the Hakone Mts. In an excited voice one of my factory group spoke to me on the 'phone from the station telling me that he was to arrive shortly, and wouldn't I like to see him? I took Mrs. Murota round and we joined the circle of about a thousand people ringing the open place. At noon he could be seen in the distance as he came out of the station and entered his car. His wife was with him. There was a cheer to which he waved his hat, and the car sailed off. I watched particularly the line of people the car was passing. A wave of cheers ran along the lines with the passing of the car. Happy cheering, not wild, not subdued. There was one Japanese flag waved and one university student carried a yellow silk school banner (one can be sure it is a university student when one sees shabby clothes, long black cloak, heavy wooden clogs, and black peaked cap bedecked with a great metal badge). The youngsters frankly peered at Their Majesties, even while waving and cheering. The only people I could see do anything else were women folk of middle age. They gave a slight bow like one of our curtsies to Royalty, with eyes riveted on the car. I could see no sign of anyone going through the formal obeisances which used to be required. There were about a dozen local policemen controlling traffic and half a dozen American M.P.s doing the same. Today his coming and going has aroused almost no interest, for the crowd was little more than normally comes and goes at the station during the half hour. The visit had been announced in the papers but few people waited along the streets. Shopkeepers were at business as usual. Rubbish and empty baskets lined the kerbs as usual. Make what you can of it!

Our goat had two kids on March 31. All are going well and the kids are particularly quaint. When I told Mrs. Murota that they were both "girls" and therefore destined to increase the milk herd, she said, "O kage Sama de," which is literally "By your honourable shadow," and is the usual way of thanking a person for kindly help or interest! If you ask after my health I will say "Thank you. By your honourable shadow, I'm very well." In the early days I put my foot in it properly. I was not feeling very well, and when someone asked after my health I replied, "By your honourable shadow, pretty crook." The horrified start showed me quite plainly I still had something to learn about the use of that phrase. Down the slope at this moment, I can see two of our schoolgirls closing in on the goat and kids. They're evidently on their way to see me, but can't resist the pets of kids. They'll come up soon, we'll probably say a few words, then they'll freeze, so I'll send them off to play with the goats. They'll come back half an hour later to say goodbye and raise the subject they have really come about. I know them now!

I went down to Hamamatsu the other day to take a big bundle of clothes for the Old People's Home, some invalid food for the T.B.s at the Vicarage, and an organ for the new Church. On the way I called and left things, especially Communion wine, at each Church along the way. Shimizu now has another little room added to the original one. In it is a little Altar. That is a great improvement on the stack of boxes covered by a sheet that has done service for three years. At Hamamatsu itself a shack has been built alongside the foundations of the ruined Church, and Fr. Peter Shikutani is now in charge.

If I get a chance I'm going to use the Cine-Kodak movie camera given me by "Friends of Odawara" to film the story of Fr. Peter's life, but how I'll get him into a Chinese prison near Peiping I don't at present know.

Laurie Topp is to stay a week with me from May 2nd, and we'll go over through Kofu to Kyosato.

Yours sincerely,
FRANK

Letter from Frank Coaldrake to Maida Williams, 26 April 1949.

[This letter was written after the preceding *Newsletter*. "May" is the date the *Newsletter* was printed in Australia, not the date it was written in Japan.]

It would be a great asset to you if you could drive a car (in preparation for coming to Japan.) Learn on a car, then a jeep is easy. Any chance of your father teaching you? As a final schooling for Japanese conditions you should do 3 things – 1. drive up and down the hair-pin bending road into Queenstown [west coast of Tasmania, where Maida Williams was born] all day at 30 M.P.H.; 2. drive nonchalantly around and about the Queen Victoria Markets in Melbourne all one Saturday morning [the busiest time]; and 3. drive down the track to Port Davey [wild, virtually impenetrable countryside and narrow tracks]. After all, it's for conditions under those three headings your learning will be … budget will be deficited by about £50 for the year – local will be about £900 Australian exclusive of capital cost of jeep. But the A.B.M. says ok. Difficult to estimate. And now I've got a real headache – how to make an estimate for the 12 months from June 1. Not only my possible absence – but also I must include the cost of living of Father Iida so I can get him out of school teaching and on to my job [during my absence in Australia.]

Yesterday the Exchange Rate was altered again, and once again things in the local market became accessible to me. An egg is now 3 d., and fruit likewise reasonable... Sent out our letter introducing "Ippeki-ko Camp" to clergy youth leaders of Tokyo and South Tokyo Diocese last Friday and already have 4 applications for camps this Summer. That is from 4 groups of varying numbers and kinds. They're all a bit scared of one of the two prerequisite conditions for all campers. One is reasonable and to be expected, "that <u>all</u> shall share reasonably in the work of the camp." That's because I've seen enough of camps <u>in the church</u> here to know that without a good deal of stirring up the boys and lads will sit on their heels while the girls and women work. But that's not the troublesome condition. The other one is that every camper shall join with Father Iida and I in our evangelism campaign in the district around the camp. They're scared stiff and say they don't know how, and must first learn and practice at home; and a camp is for play etc. etc., all of which seems to vindicate my guess that training in the life of Christian witness is the one major lack in church life here. If they weren't worrying about it I'd be worrying about the necessity of it...

Newsletter No. 26, June, 1949.

NIPPON SEIKO KWAI

C/o B.C.O.F. Army P.O. 214,
Empire House,
Tokyo,
JAPAN.

From – Rev. F. W. Coaldrake

Dear Friends,

I found myself with some "hot" charcoal on my hands the other day. It all arose out of the need for some means of warming the room at the Ichikawa Church Clinic so the kiddies wouldn't catch cold when stripped for examination by the doctor. The doctor's brother is living just down the coast from me. He told me he had bought fifteen bales of charcoal and asked if I could take it across to Ichikawa in the trailer, a distance of 80 miles. All kinds of fuel, but especially charcoal, are very scarce in the cities but can be got out in the country. I went down and collected the charcoal. It filled the trailer and for the next three days it waited in my garage. Then in the newspaper I saw a picture of the inside of a passenger carriage that had just arrived in Tokyo from the country. There were piles of charcoal on the floor between the seats. The story was that people were going into the country to buy charcoal and bringing it back in rucksacks. On this day blackmarket inspectors had boarded the train, but they had caught only a few, because all the rest had emptied their bags on the floor as soon as they realised what was happening. That picture woke me up. There's no such thing as non-ration charcoal these days, and therefore my 15 bales must be blackmarket charcoal.

Can you imagine my thoughts? First of all, we must have warmth for the children. But next, I'd made it a rule not to do anything on the blackmarket. I must go back and ask if it is ration charcoal – or if it's "black" what must I do? All along the roads there are check points where vehicles are examined for black goods. My registration plate is Japanese, and I'm a Westerner in a jeep, so when I stop at the Japanese police checkpoints they wave me on. I've never been examined even when there's a trailer load bulging under a tarpaulin cover. I could certainly get through Ichikawa without any difficulty, but that very fact affects me with a special sense of responsibility.

Therefore, if it's "black" charcoal I must return it. But here's where the matter strikes deepest. If I don't take this charcoal they'll have to buy local blackmarket at twice the price. Am I to wash my hands and leave my colleagues and friends to dirty theirs? Which is the greater offence, to carry black goods or to stand aloof and know that they must therefore go on the black? It looked like a "choose the lesser of two evils" situation such as was so keenly portrayed during the early war years. "The devil's alternative" was the way it was headed up in many Christian journals round about 1940. The Japanese have a saying for such situations – "Shikata ga nai" – "There's nothing can be done about it." But I've always felt that the Christian's course is never brought to such a point. There always is something to be done which brings God's Providence into play.

This may seem to have been a lot of worrying on a few bales of charcoal, but it was in my sight an important issue. When I asked old Fr. Miyazawa he was most concerned and most anxious I should not become involved in the black market. If I were going to use the "black" why stop at charcoal? I could sell half a dozen tins of this or that and the money would buy twice as much charcoal over in Ichikawa.

But as I drove back with the charcoal I was pretty sick at heart. It was like giving the good fellow a blow under the belt to ask him if it was blackmarket or ration charcoal? Yes – it was not rationed charcoal. So I off-loaded it and fled, chewing over what I could do on the level about the Church Clinic – doing a bit of praying, too.

I decided to take some kerosene over. I can buy it with my petrol and use it in my mission centres, but it is not available to Japanese. But where could I get a kerosene heater? I'd searched before – I searched again all the way to Tokyo without success. When I told them at Ichikawa about the charcoal they came to light with some fresh information. The brother down near my place is a doctor. He's got T.B. and is resting in the country for some months. Occasionally he treats sick people among his neighbours. One of these happened to be a charcoal burner and he offered to pay in charcoal. (It's no use asking why the doctor himself hadn't told me that? That's just another of the mysteries of the life here.) I told the Ichikawa people they should go to the Ration Office and ask for a permit to procure this 15 bales of charcoal. If they had the permit I'd willingly carry it over. A fortnight later I heard the result. At the Ration Office the official heard the story then said, "No, I won't give you a permit to do that. But I'll give your Clinic a special ration of 3 bales of charcoal a month from now on. Here's the ticket." So they could buy all they needed at official prices locally. This was a quite unexpected turn of events and no one would have thought of asking for such a special ration for it is an unheard of thing. I was very thankful when I learned this – it's just another instance of the way things turn out unexpectedly to solve apparently insoluble problems, if we'll only refuse to choose a devil's alternative and go as far as we can along the way of our Lord.

The Clinic itself is also born of faith. These are the people who wanted to find a way to serve the community and turn their eyes out beyond their own Church confines. They planned the Clinic, and I asked some help from Australia. The Sydney Women's Auxiliary sent a large case of medicines and bandages, and the Christ Church Sydney Comrades a baby-weighing scale. Some other things turned up in a "scrounge" around Australian army establishments, and the local parishioners put up a lot of money to buy remaining essentials. With Australian gift money I bought some chairs. The Vicarage daughter had just graduated from medical college and the sick doctor brother hoped to be well enough to work after April, so they put up notices and started in a small corner room in the Vicarage at the beginning of January.

At the end of the first ten weeks they reported to me on their activities. 150 separate patients, with a total of 660 treatments have been dealt with in 10 weeks. 73 came with children's complaints, ear, nose and throat were 21 cases, internal 35 cases, skin 17 cases, and others 4. The number of daily callers at the clinic was only 4 or 5 the first week, but soon it was over 40. The original room had to be opened out along two verandahs. The dispensary is in another room.

The reason for this rapid growth is that St. Mary's Clinic is meeting a real need – treatment and medicine and instruction at cost or less. A few people in poor circumstances pay nothing at all. The cost to the others is set at the rate allowed for Government Compensation Sickness payments – this is so low that ordinary doctors invariably demand additional payment. St. Mary's Clinic expects only the Compensation payment offices, and they deduct 10 percent, saying, you are a Social Service.

The Clinic is the only place specialising in children's treatment in a city of 90,000 struggling working people. The doctor also visits cot cases in their home at night. Occasional public lectures supplement the personal advice given in the course of treatment. Hygiene and Motherhood are two special subjects of instruction.

It is a very happy place. The only really difficult matter now is that income is all used in buying medicine and equipment. There's not so far anything to keep the doctor in food! But parishioners are subscribing to subsidise the Clinic income. It is a real "Church Community" project and as an act of witness to Christian love it is invaluable. One of my promises was that I'd keep them supplied with soap. The way it turns up in parcels when it is needed means there are people in Australia joining in this work.

We have now passed Easter and look back on a time of well filled Churches and happy parish meetings. My own Easter was spent here and there. For the Good Friday 3 Hours service I went down to Shizuoka, and at night we had a lantern talk on the events of Holy Week and Easter. On Easter Eve the jeep zoomed back over the Hakone Mountains in time for the baptism of five people at Odawara. Grace, Agnes, Monica and Makoto are all girls from our Church school. The other was an elderly man. Saturday night was spent with the faithful preparing for Easter. After the Easter Eucharist at Odawara I had to drive to Zushi, where the congregation at St. Peter's waited for my arrival. We took the Sacrament out to a T.B. Sanatorium 15 miles away at Kurihama on the point at the entrance to Tokyo Bay. There is a group of members and [Christian] Inquirers in the hospital who meet fortnightly. It was a joy to give the Sacrament to one man, and then baptise his friend in the next bed. They've been there 3 years and seem likely to stay for a long time yet. It was 5 o'clock when I got home to prepare for the evening service in Odawara.

Monday morning saw us on the road early headed for Ito where we said the Easter Mass at Mr. Miyazawa's house. By the time we'd planned future activities in Ito, and made some calls at offices and the Ippeki Lake Camp site, it was afternoon. With Joji[86] as companion we headed for Shimoda and beyond. We stayed the next two nights with Dr. Kawai at Ose. The ministry to the few faithful in this centre of little fishing villages is a great joy. We had meetings for enquirers and Joji entertained about 60 children with "Paper Theatre" [*kamishibai*] Stories. This is the "Punch and Judy" of Japan and is a great favourite with the children. It is used by the Church as a means of spreading Christian stories. Such stories as the Prodigal Son and the Good Samaritan are very easy to tell by this means. You'll see the "Paper Theatre" usually fixed on the carrier of a pushbike, here, there and everywhere, especially in the late afternoon when the schools are out. The storyteller bangs a drum, or rings a bell, or claps two sticks together and heigh-ho, twenty or thirty children drop from the skies! He sells each one a little sweet for a small coin. That's the way he makes his living, but it seems to me he doesn't do it only for that, as he seems to enjoy pitching his tale in a way that will enthrall the children. When everyone has the sweet the "curtain" goes up, and the kiddies raise their lolly sticks in the right hand towards the "Theatre" and shout something. Up to this moment they haven't started to eat the sweet, but down it comes pop into their mouths, and the story starts. After that their wide eyes are fixed on the succession of vivid poster pictures, each with its appropriate portion of the story recited by the storyteller. I only know one thing capable of distracting them and drawing their eyes from the pictures – that is a jeep! If I walk up and join the group no one notices. If I drive up in the jeep and stop, nearly all eyes shift and the jeep becomes the centre of interest. Fr. Iida is to use a Paper Theatre on the jeep in

86 Jōji (John) Matsumoto, one of two of the Youth Leaders selected for the Ippeki Camp (see next *Newsletter*). He later became a priest.

future. He was to have come with me on this Easter visiting round the peninsula but could not get leave from his school teaching duties. How we look forward to the day when he'll be able to give up the teaching and do his parish work.

We left Ose on Wednesday morning and went up the west coast of the peninsula looking for people vaguely heard of and calling on the Takahashi Family at Chinno. That night we had a long "planning" session in Numazu at Fr. Iida's house. Among other things we had to work out the details of the plan to incorporate a series of Summer Youth Camps at Lake Ippeki into our work in the district. Joji is to be Camp Manager so it was necessary to have the three of us together. It was 2 a.m. when we finished so we decided to go on home to Odawara rather than sleep the few hours in Numazu. It is always far less nervewracking to drive Japanese roads at night. We did the journey without seeing a single child (in the day time they bob up out of holes in the road it seems to me) and gave Joji another driving lesson up the [Hakone] range in top gear, down in second.

It will give you some idea of the difficulties of working with the Japanese language if I tell you our late session was due to the time it took to draft a circular letter about the Camp plans. Three of us back in Australia working in English would have taken an hour to draft the letter. In Japanese it took 6 hours. I think it is well nigh impossible to match a Westerner's thinking with Japanese language. (Let treaty-makers take note.) There doesn't seem to be any normal method for coping with the unstated implications of words, and those implications are different for Japanese and Western minds, even though the latter be "thinking in Japanese." If I say in English, "The three permanent camp leaders, and other sub-leaders chosen as necessary from among the campers, will cooperate in running the camp according to the previously arranged programme," I think you'll understand pretty clearly how we're going to do things. But it took over an hour to get just that one sentence into Japanese. The word "co-operate" went through many changes with the result that we were in danger of handing the camp over to the fancies of leaders chosen on the spot, or putting it under the iron rules of the permanent staff in every detail.

Perhaps the best example of the headaches and tangles that derive from this language is what happened the very first time I arranged a meeting with Fr. Iida to make plans. He understands English a bit, but not reliably, so to make sure of detail I sent a Japanese letter saying I'd call on him at his home in Numazu on a certain day. He was to let me know if it would be convenient. He replied in meaningless English in which was the sentence "I will be going," so I thought that was just a mistranslation of the one word which can mean "come" or "go" or "stay at home." When I arrived at his house I found he'd gone up to my place and we'd passed in the trains. When we looked at the Japanese letter we found that it had the perfectly normal polite phrase "Oide ni narimasu ka?" which means both "will you come?" or "will you be at home?" and he assumed that I, his chief, was calling on him to attend on me.

Perhaps some day I'll have acquired that degree of mental telepathy which seems to lead two Japanese to an understanding of each other by means of what appears to us to be a very clumsy language. If ever a missionary needed the "gift of tongues" he needs it here.

———

Circulated by Mrs. E.R. Coaldrake, 35 Francis Street, Blackburn, Vic.
Printed by T.J. Higham Pty. Ltd., Blackburn.

Newsletter No. 27, July, 1949.[87]

NIPPON SEIKO KWAI

C/- B.C.O.F. Army P.O. 214,
Empire House,
Tokyo,
JAPAN.

From – Rev. Frank W. Coaldrake

Dear Friends,

I am still living at Odawara, but spending much time on the road to Izu Peninsula and Lake Ippeki Camp site, preparing for our Youth Camp this month. Izu work must be developed from practically nothing, and my own output of work must be geared to my Japanese assistant, Fr. Iida. Till I can find him a living wage, he has to continue teaching to earn a living.

We have selected two Youth Leaders, Joji (John) Matsumoto for the lads the Michiko-san for the lasses. They are tackling their share of the preparations very well and working keenly – in fact they have now reached the stage where they'll put up ideas of their own and try to knock mine out. It's great fun drawing them out into a sense of responsibility. Camp preparations include electric light and water in process of being brought in, but probably not ready for first Camp though many apparently insurmountable difficulties are already behind us.

Many B.C.O.F. and U.S.A. Units have helped Mission funds since early in the Occupation. They realised that Christian Japanese were in want, and hungry children needing food and clothing. Recently Mrs. Pat Shaw, wife of an Australian Government official, issued a neatly printed appeal in Tokyo on behalf of the Anglican Mission Youth Camp at Lake Ippeki. The response was good and sufficient supplies of food are now assured for the opening Leaders' Training Camp.

Camps will be held for two kinds of groups, each camp for about 50 persons for one week. Some groups will be for children from inland villages and towns, and from the industrial and burned out areas of Tokyo and Yokohama; others will be for Youth of both sexes between the ages of 15 and 25 years. These campers will be selected from groups associated with Mission Centres, School, Factories, and families regularly in contact with the Churches.

———

87 This *Newsletter* was in the typed and roneod format.

A B.C.O.F. Public Relations Officer spent two days with me getting material to send to Australian newspapers, and after tagging along with me on my usual rounds he dropped out with fatigue, and lack of more time. I'm trying to be as philosophically calm as the traditional Eastern, with a full day ahead in Tokyo and rain pouring down, something has now gone wrong with the Jeep ignition, so here I wait in Yokohama for a mechanic who has been called to fit it.

There is much I want to write down for you but it will have to wait till next month I'm afraid.

The sets of 10 photos representative of my Mission work are now in circulation at 6 d. per photo – cost price – and can be obtained from Mrs. E.R. Coaldrake, No. 35 Francis Street, Blackburn, Victoria.

A mixed marriage

One of our Church members married his daughter to a non-Christian and the ceremony had perforce to be according to the faith of the husband. Later Church members gathered at the house for the parish priest to give the Church's blessing on the wedding. Since one of the couple is a member of the Church it only requires that the non-Christian partner shall be willing. The bridal couple dressed once again in their wedding clothes. The bride wore kimono – I won't attempt a fashion-column description, but I can say it was a very beautiful gown in pink with silver and blue pattern.

After the prayers, which were said in the Western style sitting room, we all went round to the usual style main room for the "wedding breakfast." Presumably this was also a second effort. The menu included rice boiled with red beans so that it was red in colour and sweet to taste; fish, boiled, fried in batter, and raw; mussels floating nicely in thin soup; a morsel of meat, boiled; carrots, radish, turnip, beans, and peas, all boiled; two slices of ham loaf; omelette; raw-fish paste cake; peanuts, roasted; soy-bean sauce. The rice was served separately in a plain pine wood box. In another box were vegetables, meats, fish, and omelette, all arranged in a design pleasing to the eye. The mussel soup came separately in a covered bowl; the raw fish sat menacingly in its own capacious bowl. The chopsticks, new for each guest, lay inside an envelope decorated with emblems of happiness.

We sat for two hours over it, or rather we squatted on our cushions. Legs go to sleep of course, but as long as one doesn't have to stand up in a hurry it's all right. The bridal couple are seated at the lowest end of the table away from the Alcove of Honour [*tokonoma*], and the seat nearest the Alcove is given the guest to whom it is desired to pay most honour. I was embarrassed to find myself appointed to this seat. You remember what I told you a while ago about the difficulty of getting one's self treated on the proper level. There were at least two other people present, notably Fr. Miyazawa, who should have been in that seat instead of me, but for the fact that I'm a Westerner. It seems that, if on such an occasion I were to decline that seat, I would be imputing bad judgement to my host, so it isn't possible to do much about it.

Even after two hours we had a good deal left in our pine boxes and dishes. The pine boxes are a concession to post-war shortages, as formerly everything would have been in dishes, but the pine boxes have a special use at the end of the meal. We put everything left over into them and wrapped them up again as we found them when we sat down. When we left for home we carried the packets with us. In the days of dishes we would have produced little folding boxes from our sleeves or pockets and put the left-overs into them. It is an insult to leave anything in one's place when one leaves. Also, one takes most of the feast home anyway, so that the younger people at home may eat it and share in the happiness of matrimony.

When I come home on leave you may save on furniture for me, as I have learned to live on the floor here – no bed and no chairs necessary, and a couple of pine splinters to eat with! I may be home for Christmas.

Yours sincerely,
FRANK

Newsletter No. 28, August, 1949.[88]

NIPPON SEIKO KWAI

C/- B.C.O.F. Army P.O. 214,
Empire House,
Tokyo,
JAPAN.

From – Rev. Frank W. Coaldrake

Dear Friends,

My only regret during the last 6 weeks has been lack of time to sit down and write you all the interesting highlights of my work and travels to and from the lake on Izu Peninsula. From June to September I am spending about one day per week in Odawara and the remainder at the Youth Camp on the banks of Lake Ippeki, which is now well established and has already been used by over 200 selected campers, in groups of 50 fresh recruits each week, during the month of July. Even typhoons can't upset things, at least not the one that has come so far. When the really big ones reach us we will have to take the tarpaulins off the frames of our large Dining and Chapel tents but the smaller living tents are as secure as any house in a storm.

I have only been able to visit Tokyo and collect mailbags once in the last 6 weeks. Now at Odawara a great stack of parcels in the corner of my room await my opening and listings and acknowledging – then distributing your generous gifts to our grateful Japanese Christians and Parish Priests and their families.

---

88 This *Newsletter* was in the typed and roneod format.

I am glad the 20 sets of photos I sent were well received, but am afraid there won't be time for more at present.

Before I go on leave there are plans to be worked out as nearly as possible to assist in the carrying on of my work here while I am away. I am tremendously happy in it all and don't like leaving even for a few months. Meanwhile I must cram some extra effort into the intervening months until a boat consents to ferry me across the Pacific Ocean. Please keep the parcels coming if you can as our Christians here will need your help and encouragement more, than less, during my absence.

Tonight I have tuned in on shortwave to Australia and right now I am enjoying my pal of Queensland years the Rev. Evan Wetherell, giving an Epilogue on the theme of "The Angelus" picture. Again I feel how much that is the message Japanese country workers need this summer. Work to be done; love to enrich it; and God to bless and direct it. Christ made of work a noble thing: Men could serve God at a carpenter's bench just as in a glorious building. Work must be enriched by love – love of man and love of God.

I can only promise you more news as more spare time permits,

Yours sincerely,

FRANK

Newsletter No. 29, September, 1949.

NIPPON SEIKO KWAI

C/o B.C.O.F. Army P.O. 214,
Empire House,
Tokyo,
JAPAN.

From – Rev. F. W. Coaldrake

Dear Friends,

The "Uncle Jim" we used to sing about when I was rather younger has been strong in my memory during recent months. Do you remember how he was "under water swimming against the tide?" It was the end of July when I sat on the hillside up here and looked around a camp teeming with active youngsters that I felt I'd been with Uncle Jim for weeks and weeks, but had at last come up for air. You needn't worry, the feeling has completely gone now for the camp "works." I mean it really functions as a youth camp should. Now we're rather in the thrill of riding a breaker to the beach. It's really good fun and fast movement. Such good fun, in fact, that I've been longing for a decent chance to sit down and write you about it. Tonight I give up waiting for the "good" chance and start in now, at midnight, to try and sketch the outlines of it.

The camp "works." Just try to imagine sitting in the trailer behind the jeep and jolting two miles down the road from the heights above the lake to the little village of T– which snuggles in a pocket in the mountains. It's just after dark and there's a fair moon. Through the dust that rolls from the jeep wheels straight to your eyes, you and the five young'uns with you can see the rice paddies which lie flat in the centre of the village. The 40 or 50 houses form a ring on the lower slopes of the mountains. Frogs croak in the paddies but their voices are out-boomed by a gramophone in the first house we come to. A scratchy record wails a popular folk-song about the moon. That house, like all the others, is wide open. The gramophone's electric speaker blares around for the whole village to hear. Half a dozen young men are in the house, dressed in the light cotton kimono that men like in the summer. This is our first visit to T–, though we have spied out the land when we passed through it. We stop the jeep near the gramophone. This is the likeliest spot for our purpose. The six of us from the jeep get out, and six more stagger up out of the trailer. We are a team and we get right on to the ball. Some this way, some that, all spread out around the village announcing as loudly as possible. "Come, Come, Everybody come. We're going to talk Christianity." That gramophone is a menace so I go to the house and explain politely what we hope to do. They don't have to be asked to stop the machine. They shut it off and come out to the jeep. Then as a final rallying effort I stand out in the light of the jeep and lift my voice up to the hills inviting everyone to "come and hear the Christian Faith."

The team gathers in the jeep light, around our Cross, we pray together for the blessing of God on our efforts – I for the "gift of tongues!" – then we sing a hymn, in three part harmony, which sounds very beautiful above the booming frogs in the valley. People have gathered, from the very old to the very young, perhaps fifty in all. Others can be seen watching and listening from their houses. (There are practically no walls or windows in the houses in summer – the sliding screens are out and the house is virtually a roof and a floor with a few uprights in between.) We take it in turns to speak, always trying to get our words away over to the farthest house. We've done some stiff preparation for this evening's meeting, so there is no dragging. But everybody is very shy. This is the first time they've ever been at a roadside meeting – let alone speak about their Faith to strangers. Some stammer, but are convincing; others perhaps glib but shallow. It's my job to "compere" for the others are between 15 and 25 years, and at that age they flee from responsibility. One of the qualities of the average Australian youth I've learnt to appreciate since I left Australia is the way in which they are able to assume individual responsibility. That's a precious asset which I hope will never be lost from the Australian way of life.

It was 9 o'clock when we arrived and we carried on till 10.30 p.m. Those are the best hours for evangelism during the summer in the country here. People get home from the fields just after dark (about 8 o'clock), bath and eat, then from 9 till about 11 they just sit around and talk and read, or listen to the wireless. The evangelising band easily captures their attention. I've found during the summer that I can get an audience of 30 to 100 people any evening if I simply stand in the midst of a few houses and lift up my voice. Among the listeners are many troubled and worried older people, and many deeply puzzled youth.

We always pass out addressed postcards which they can fill in and post to us if they want to hear the Christian Faith in more detail. (They have to pay the postage.) We've been getting a steady return of postcards, and naturally make a special effort to develop that first contact. Tonight in T–, as we are getting into the jeep to return to camp a woman in the thirties with a youngster strapped to her back comes and tells us she is eager to hear more. In Tokyo, as a child, she went once or twice to a Christian Church. Then during the last war, while her husband was away – he has not returned – her house was burnt and she came to live here in T–. We will call on her within the next week. When we come again to preach we will find others who want to be taught.

We reach camp to find the three teams from O– village already having supper. But four other teams went in to Y– village and only three have returned. They tell us that the fourth team was invited into the village Youth Club and were last seen at 10.30 engaged in a discussion with the locals. From Y– to camp is a long up-hill walk so I go down and fetch them up in the jeep and trailer. By 11.30 p.m. all are home, brief reports have been made, and everyone simmers down to silence and sleep. On that Sunday evening 8 teams each of 10 or 12 youths, lads and lasses, took part in the Campaign. The 45 who are communicants all did something in the way of speaking.

————

I'm sorry to hear that you've been so worried at not hearing from me for six weeks. I evidently did not make it clear enough that this "Summer Camp" was not to be just a one week show. We are at it continuously from mid-June to mid-September with a new group of campers coming every week. We've already had over 400 campers and will finally get well over 500. The youngest age is 8 years and the oldest 27 years. With every group we start from scratch to teach them how to live in a community based on freedom and faith. At the same time we train them and lead them out to tell other people about it. This camp is the spearhead of our peninsula campaign. Of course, the camp life is a full round of games, sports, work, study and worship, but it is all related to the final purpose of the camp so that our happy days in camp are an example of real Christian fellowship into which the local people can enter – which they do.

Let's take last Monday for an example. We started as usual with the early morning Communion in the Chapel tent on the hill-top by the pine forest at 6.30 a.m. We had 30 boys and their leaders from Tokyo in camp for the weekend and 25 of them came to the morning Offering. You see it's not only voluntary but a bit difficult to come to that service each morning. General rising time for the camp is 6.30, so that those who want to come to the service have to get up extra early. Sometimes it means one or two out of a tentful get up and come. We make it that way because that's the usual conditions in their own house. The one or two communicants have to get up and leave home before the other members of the family are stirring. Anyway, on the Monday morning we came "offering" whatever we might have achieved in the outdoor campaign the night before. Also we came thanking God for the experience of being used by the Holy Spirit as witnesses to the Christian Faith.

It has been clearly noticeable that everyone who has come into camp this summer has come rather dreading the prospect of having to help in outdoor evangelism. Of the 400 only the clergy have ever done such work before. But everyone knows when they apply that it is expected they will help, so it's fair enough to take them along, don't you think? Invariably they come home after village evangelising saying to me "Mo ippen" – which is just plain "once again." We aim to get as close as we can to the Church of the New Testament and we find much of the experience of the Church of those days. Our preaching is moulded to the pattern of the New Testament and gets much the same response (I say it quite humbly). I knew it would be so. This generation of young Japanese Christians has never been led out into the open so they haven't had the chance to taste of the fruits of a life of open witness. Before they reach the street-side meeting place they have to think out what they ought to say, what they can honestly say, and then how to say it. I'll tell you later on about the terrific handicap of shyness that is imposed on them by their home and school training. We've had to devise special ways of curing that.

Straight after the morning Mass we come down for breakfast. Everyone must be up, dressed, bed made, and ready for the day before breakfast call at 7.15. Then in the Dining Tent we have general morning prayers – which take about ten minutes. (Fig. 25) It's the usual practice over here to have the long formal service of Morning Prayer from the Prayer Book for morning prayers in Camps. But I've scrapped that

Figure 25 One of the first Lake Ippeki camps, Summer, 1949. Morning Prayers in the Dining Tent. (See *Newsletter No. 28.*)

idea because that service was never intended for such an occasion. Instead we have a simple Bible reading and comments on it, then say the Creed. After that some informal prayers related to the coming day and the camp's purpose.

Then we eat. How much? We are serving approx. 25 per cent above the fixed ration scale and that seems to be plenty. Some eat more, some less. If we serve just the ration scale there is a general shortage and tightening of the belt, but no complaints. In order to serve the extra I had to import rice and buy milk from U.S.A. This I was able to do because Mrs. Patrick Shaw, wife of the head of the Australian Mission in Japan, collected quite a lot of money to help the camps. With Mr. Lou Border as Treasurer she asked for direct contributions of money and the result was astonishing– the equivalent of £300 Aust. The contributors included Australian, English, American and Indian people.

Gen. Robertson[89] helped in other ways and came over to see the camp. If it hadn't been for his personal help we would have been in real trouble over our water supply. He saved us having to carry all our water up by bullock cart. Once or twice I thought I would have to ask him for permission to buy some extra foodstuffs from B.C.O.F. but many parcels from Australia and money to buy local vegetables and fish, as well as American imports, provided just enough. Of course, everyone who comes brings the appropriate "staple ration" for the period.

Well Monday's breakfast is like every other meal – everyone has a hand in the preparation of it and everyone washes their own dishes – in hot soapy water, a striking innovation in this land of no soap and little fuel. Then for one hour everyone joins in "Camp Social Service." Once during each camp we go outside and do some act of social service in the district, of no benefit to ourselves. It is generally something quite humble such as picking up rubbish along the paths and beaches and round the other camps. But "Camp Social Service" includes scrubbing tables, bathrooms, and lavatories, collecting wood, cutting new paths, levelling new tent sites and such work.

From 8 to 9 a.m. everyone is busy at that. Then from 9 to 10.30 we have the morning study and discussion session. In the middle of it some visitors from a nearby village come. They sit and listen till it's over. Then for a few minutes I can talk to them while everyone is getting on to the job of packing up. On the last day of a camp it's always packing-up time from 10.30 till noon. Other days that is swimming and boating time. When it's swimming time I have to be down on the beach keeping a general eye on the gang, although the lake is as safe as any swimming pool.

Just as I pass the villagers over to Fr. Iida along comes another visitor. The villagers came asking to see the camp and hear "Christian-talk." This man has come about a piece of land in Ito. I've started looking for a suitable site for the Headquarters of our Peninsula Church. For a foreigner to buy land here is quite a complicated business and land values don't seem to be fixed according to our scale. I think I'd better know something about it before I get back to Australia.

This businessman raises a knotty problem – he thinks he is the owner of the piece of land I've been looking at. He certainly has been the owner for many years past, and he still pays the taxes. It is farmland and he isn't a farmer and doesn't live on it, so the Government Land Reform Board has advised him that they have resumed it. They have not yet paid him the purchase money, even though it is only about one per cent of the real value of the land. He therefore says the land is still his and wants me to discuss "sale" with him.

There is a farmer working the land. He has been a tenant on it for over ten years. He has now bought it from the Land Reform Board, but he also has not paid any money and has refused to pay taxes on it. He also wants to discuss "sale" with me, because he wants to move to a new site out of the city and start a dairy farm. Before he can sell he will have to get the approval of the local Farmers' Representative Council; and before I can buy I will have to get their approval of the change of farmland into building land. Then the whole transaction will have to get the approval of the Prefectural Farmers' Council, and finally the Government Bureau and S.C.A.P. In Australia we have our "Closer Settlement" schemes and this Land Reform works out the same way. This comes crashing into the middle of Monday morning's programme. We have to wait for Fr. Iida to finish his "Christian Talk" to the villagers, so that he can help me to understand the technical language involved in a discussion of land sales. The last stages of our talk have a background of community singing. Matsumoto-san has a crowd of the boys and the villagers making harmony according to our Camp-Song Book.

Just before lunch my ears throb to a different sound – Australian boys' voices! A patrol of Australian Sea Scouts has arrived for five days. I must write more about the Aussie boys, but just at this stage all we did was welcome them and make them at home in their tents. (Fig. 26) It was sheer delight to hear their chaff and chatter. The Japanese youngsters arrive in a polite silence which it takes hours to break.

Over lunch we say goodbye to the Tokyo boys and remind them to take special notice of what is written on the back of the Notice at the camp entrance. As they come in they read "Nippon Seikokwai Youth Camp," but as they go out they see those horrible words from Revelation 3: 16, "Because you are luke-warm I spew you out of my mouth." We explain it is not that they have been luke-warm in camp, but that if they are luke-warm in the future God will have that feeling about them.

They go – and we watch them go. They are going out with the possibility of being leaders in the making of a new Japan. We have put all we know into giving them a life in camp which will help them to be just that. We have talked to them especially about the standards of "good behaviour" by which they have been trained. In some respects the well-behaved Japanese youth cannot be a good Christian. Of course, in most respects we endorse the general standards, but the well-behaved young man or woman is expected to be "hazukashii" (shy, embarrassed), in the presence of others, unless they are younger, and they are expected to "enryo" (hesitate, be diffident) in a situation where they might influence the thoughts or actions of others. We have tried to give practical

Figure 26 Five day visit by Australian Sea Scouts, Lake Ippeki Camp, August, 1949. A pioneering example of rebuilding Japan-Australia relations at a "grassroots" level.

instances of where they must, as a Christian, not "enryo," where they must discard all thought of self and shyness, and thinking only of Christ, speak as a witness to the power and wisdom of God.

We have factory workers, office workers, farm workers and students so there is a wide field of practical situations to choose from. On a very personal level, as a priest to his people, I have talked to them about the relation between pride and shame, and the Christian counsel to "be a fool!" In the village streets they've had the chance to cap their learning with expression work by actual active witness – of the word in preaching; of the deed in street cleaning. In the camp life they've had actual practical experience of being a leader in one sphere and at the same time a follower in other spheres. The lad who has "bossed" the food serving has had to do what he's told about wood chopping.

We are very sorry to see them go. They've just been shaped up into a team. Now we must start all over again with a new group of raw recruits. These Tokyo boys have been very keen. On the Sunday night they used a slide projector in the village street, with an electric light lead by courtesy of the nearest house. About a hundred people gathered at that meeting. Afterwards the boys dramatized in the simplest possible form the story of the Good Samaritan. You can imagine the boy playing the man who was robbed and beaten. The actual dusty road was a better setting than any stage could provide. He really took a beating from two very willing robbers (who then ducked round the back and donned a blanket to become the Good Samaritan's donkey). As he lay in the dust there was some real feeling in his cries of pain and his calls for help. The well dressed priest and respectable gentleman treading very carefully through the dust were obviously not going to get all dirty trying to help him, let alone risk being caught themselves by the robbers. They beat a dainty retreat. Then the Good Samariboy came dragging his donkey and played the "good neighbour" to perfection.

We plan to do more of that sort of teaching. It is especially necessary because the Bible is in literary Japanese. If our Bible were in Chaucer's English we'd understand it about as well as the average Japanese understands the Japanese Bible.

The boys are well on their way home now and we start in on the many odd jobs that have to be done to get ready for the next batch. There's a broken front spring on the jeep and it's a holiday in Ito, so I have to patch it up for the journey I must start after tea. Because it is a public holiday we have several young men from two nearby villages call on us during the afternoon. As usual they want to see the camp and hear Christian talk. Also they invite us to go down and dance with them the Bon-odori that night. It is the Festival of the Departed Spirits and the dance was originally intended for the consolation of those spirits. That traditional meaning is now completely lost. It is simply good fun for everybody. In fact the evening's dancing is mostly old English and Scottish Square Dances. The Square Dance in Japan has caught very quickly during the last year, and this village is no exception. One of the many things I'll be writing more about later is the Youth Club down in this village. Our camp has evidently already made a great impact on them and in the three years that lie ahead of us we can, it seems, expect some tangible results.

After tea – it is still the same Monday! – Hostess Michiko and Manager Joji sit down with Fr. Iida and me for the usual reports, and business arising out of the camp just ended. After that there are the plans and orders for the camp about to begin. By 10 p.m. I am free to get into the jeep and start on the 35 mile journey home to Odawara. On the way home we stop for a few minutes at the Festival Dancing. The open space in front of the village Temple is brightly lit and an electric pick-up provides a good volume of recorded dance music. About 200 are doing the second figure of the Alberts! In kimono! But it is too late to stay for the fun, so we go on. Sonota-san is with me. He is a theological student who is one of the camp helpers. He has to go to the hospital in Tokyo for an injection next day, and I have to go also on all sorts of business, including another round of Shipping Offices to try and arrange for my leave passage. All the shipping schedules have been upset by the strike in Australia. We reach home at 1 a.m., spread our mats and sleep.

That was Monday. Every day is much the same. Just when I think I've got an hour to go on writing letters there's something crops up which I cannot avoid handling, even if it is only for a few minutes till I can hand it on to someone else. On the whole my own particular responsibilities have now been reduced to those associated with my real position on the camp staff, that is, Chaplain. In a camp like this, of course, that is a busy key position, but the rest of the staff have by now learned a good deal of what I have wanted to teach them and they carry their responsibilities pretty well. There's only one thing I haven't really got over yet – when a Japanese feels sleepy he just drops everything and sleeps!

My kero lamp is burning out: it's 2 a.m., and I'm sleepy so right now I'm dropping everything, too!

Good night and God bless you.

    FRANK

Circulated by Mrs. E.R. Coaldrake, 35 Francis Street, Blackburn, Vic.
Printed by T.J. Higham Pty. Ltd., Blackburn.

Letter from Frank Coaldrake to Maida Williams, 11 and 13 September 1949.

[Handwritten in pencil.]

11.9.1949 in Camp at the Lake [Ippeki]

Trinity XIV

Better not worry mother with the enclosed photos![90] (Fig. 27)

Darling, I suddenly find myself possessed with an extra hour of time by favour of the Government. In camp, we're rather oblivious of outside events, we didn't know that "Summertime" ended at midnight last night until we heard the radio at breakfast this morning. How to use the hour is no problem – for me. Take a pen and paper and spend it with you...

This is our last Sunday in our Camp for summer and the rain is pouring down. That means difficulties for the big final open-air Evangelism Service we have planned for the village tonight. Rain or not we can go on with it but the locals won't be inclined to come out in the rain. It's astonishing how Japanese love to fly into their houses and stay there when the rain is falling. But actually our work is done. The meeting tonight is only a kind of joyful "rounding off." We've made wide contacts, started much thinking, entered into the life of the district, and gathered groups for steady Bible study and preparation throughout the Winter...

13.9.49

Now I'm in [the] jeep outside P.O. in Tokyo about to post this. Have just met agent for *S.S. Changte* and he says letter on way to me at Odawara advising a berth held for me and pleased to confirm by return.

---

90 He was noticeably emaciated in appearance through the effects of malnutrition at this stage, and did not want to worry his mother.

Figure 27 "Better not worry mother with the enclosed photo." (See *Letter from Frank Coaldrake to Maida Williams*, 11 and 13 September 1949.) Frank Coaldrake at Lake Ippeki, August, 1949.

"The First Editor's Old Thoughts About War and New Thoughts About Peace," Frank Coaldrake, *The Peacemaker. An Australian Venture in Reconstruction*, vol. 11, no. 11, p. 3, November, 1949.

AFTER 10 YEARS – "A LAMENT FOR PEACE"

Imagination run riot couldn't have worked it out. Ten years ago when I wrote the first *Peacemaker* copy, I was sitting in the Sydney to Brisbane Express. Now I have a polite request from the Editor and I'm sitting in a tent in Japan waiting for the Muse and meanwhile drinking black coffee. The Editor asks for an article for the "Tenth Anniversary Number." It's easy enough for him to ask. He's hopping around trying to keep warm in the Melbourne winter. But when it comes to the writing, why, over here, its mid-summer with tropical mugginess and rain hanging like a mist in the air...

A Creative Militarist's Posthumous Triumph

Here, in this very district in which I now sit writing, but some eight hundred and thirty years ago, lived the most creative militarist of all time. He didn't devise new methods of warfare. He devised an original form of government which flourished in Japan right up to the present generation – and in this generation is fast coming into its own as the accepted form of efficient government in most nations of the world – government based on "Sovereignty vested in the Army."

Yoritomo had his own Feudal Army to wield the sovereignty. Today, we have "Armies of Righteousness," or "Peoples' Armies," or "Armies of Liberation." When "Peace" comes the armies play war games and the people play self-government. It's all very jittery...

New Thoughts About Peace

But about peace I think differently. You see, I've now lived two years in a country with a constitution which abrogates war as an instrument of national policy. There is no national army and no military training. Of course, there is an "Occupation Army," which it is expected would resist an invader. That army has ruled the country, but is rapidly reducing its sphere of control. Authority is being handed back to the people and their government. At the present rate of change, it will not be many more months until the "Occupation Army" is filling the role only of a "Protector" standing by.

If you want to see a people without an army, look at Japan. Of course, militaristic thinking and habits have not been eradicated. But in Japan now the surest way to condemn anything is to label it "militaristic." (I'm not at the moment considering whether or not there is likely to be a swing back to militarism). In this country, we may look to find a society living under the conditions of peace. If a person is intent on establishing "The Peaceful Society," let him look at this Japan as the first attempt to do so by a nation on a national scale. The motives behind this attempt must be examined – some other time...

Newsletter No. 30, November, 1949.

NIPPON SEIKO KWAI

C/o B.C.O.F. Army P.O. 214,
Empire House,
Tokyo,
JAPAN.

(Address now till April: 35 Francis Street, Blackburn, Vic., Australia)

From – Rev. F. W. Coaldrake

Dear Friends,

It is just after 10 p.m. and I've been listening to the Australian National News that goes to you at 11 p.m. Our Summer Time ended in September, so our clocks are now back at one hour behind Australian Eastern Standard Time. It is early autumn and the nights are cool.

There's a quite unforeseen number of people coming to wish me "bon voyage." So constant was the interruption that I put a notice on my gate stating that "I decline to interview visitors until next Monday." By means of this polite device I have managed with only one interruption today.

Tomorrow I must go down to Ito to inspect the Quonset Hut[91] we have put up as a Temporary Church. It should have been finished, but heavy rain for three days held up the work. It was, however, sufficiently finished for us to hold the Dedication Service in it on Sunday morning, October 9th. Bishop Maekawa dedicated it and preached the sermon to 30 people present. It was great to have Laurie Topp there. He has left the Army and is now Brother Laurence, Custodian of the Theological College in Tokyo (Episcopal). Another very welcome group were the six who came in from Yoshida, the village near Lake Ippeki Camp. At the luncheon after the service some of these reminded us it was just four months since they first heard the word of God when we preached at the roadside in their village.

We have divided the building into two sections, the larger for meetings and services, the other for a vestry and living quarters. Until I get back next April Fr. Iida will live there each week from Friday to Tuesday, conducting Bible Classes, Sunday School, and the Services. Miyazawa-san will conduct Morning Prayer one Sunday each month. The Bishop has given a special approval to this for it is quite without precedent over here. In Australia, of course, it is common enough to have Lay Readers. I look forward to telling you more about these two men, Iida and Miyazawa. They are very different – but a good combination and I have no hesitation in leaving them to push on with our programme while I am away.

Owing to shipping delays no parcels arrived for a few months, but I collected 80 in Tokyo during September, which meant a few days of sorting and acknowledging, before distributing as I go on my round of farewell visits to the parishes of South Tokyo Diocese, preparatory to my few months of home leave to Australia. In the last fortnight I have distributed all the goods which came in recent parcels, and with the approach of winter the warm clothing and good food were very welcome. I must take this opportunity of mentioning that several parcels have arrived with no name of sender. I can only hope the anonymous friends will read this and know how grateful we are. I have made arrangements for the suitable distribution of parcels during my absence, so please do not

91 Prefabricated semi-circular-roofed multi-purpose building used by the military.

hesitate to continue with practical help if you are able, as usual to my B.C.O.F. address. A rough tally shows that approximately 750 parcels have come to me since I arrived here 2½ years ago. That is a remarkably fine voluntary effort and I can assure you it has had a really beneficial effect on the health as well as the outlook of a great many people.

The parcels of food from Singapore Sunday School children sent by Dr. Keys and Cath. Smith were much appreciated by some of our Japanese children during Camp weeks, and they were greatly impressed by the fact of it coming from Chinese children.

This will be my last letter to friends in general until I get back here in April, so I want to say a very humble thank you to all who have been content to accept this poor substitute for personal letters, also I must say how much it has meant to me to know of so many people taking a close personal interest in the "doings" over here.

The "Friends of Odawara" have by regular contributions provided a surprisingly large amount of help in goods and cash. They really have been friends, and their efforts have proved a vital witness of Christian co-operation, proving that reconciliation is not only necessary, but possible, between former enemies. The Hon. Sec., Miss Rae Campbell, C/o. Mrs. Shaw, Fitzgerald St., Balwyn, E.8, Victoria, will continue sending contributions and parcels regularly as the need will remain even though I am on furlough.

One of the things I was asked to do before leaving was to visit all the churches in the Diocese. It proved impossible in the time available, so I have only been to the Church in the chief city of each of the four Prefectures, that is Kofu, Shizuoka, Yokohama and Chiba. It was well to do so and reflect on the progress of the two years since I first visited them. It was also good to meet an enthusiastic band of ex-campers at each place. The Camp has had some of the effect I hoped for. I learned that in one region a Saturday Youth Convention was called by Campers, and 80 came from seven centres. Under the leadership of those who had been at the Camp they divided into two groups, and went round the town to hold streetside evangelistic meetings.

In another place High School student Campers invited other student Campers to their school and conducted meetings. In another centre the returning party of campers stayed at the Church Hall for two days and cleaned the building and grounds from top to bottom and east to west.

It is good to know that our efforts have borne fruit in the Campers as well as in the district. Perhaps one way to explain the scope of the Camp this Summer is to give a few statistics. 503 different individuals spent some time in the camp. The total number of meals served was 6,000, the turn over of money involved £1,000.

There is still no end of things I want to write about, but the pressure of work waiting to be done has mounted steadily. One interesting feature is that my local "inside-Japan" correspondence has become fairly large and takes up an increasing amount of writing time.

All things considered I'm taking quite seriously the suggestion made by many here when they have heard about my return to Australia. They urge me to bring back a wife. There is so much, they say, which a wife might do to help. One was heard to comment that I'd better bring four or five. Of course, the way marriage is arranged here, it would be a simple thing to select an appropriately able missionary worker and ask someone like the Chairman of the Board to act as "go-between" and arrange the marriage. When I try to explain that our customs require something else, and that a Christian marriage is something more than a working partnership, it doesn't seem to sink in. At all events, if I can manage to bring a wife she will be assured of a warm welcome. I came prepared to find that Japan needed me in bachelordom. I find to the contrary, so will see what I can do about it. Then "heigh ho" for double barrelled *Newsletters* next year.

Ship news is that the *Changte* leaves Kobe on October 27th, so that the earliest I can reach Sydney is about November 25th.

Kumazo's gearbox lost several of its teeth last week, so I am in the luggage van making a 900 mile journey to say au revoir at Yokohama and Chiba. How I happen to be in the luggage van is rather curious, because usually on Sunday evening the carriages are not crowded and I easily found quite a good seat. Then the guard came along and said it would be better to ride in his cabin, explaining that "it is very risky in the train late at night." I asked why, and he replied, "many bad people travel." Now that is a judgment which I have seen little to substantiate, but I think it is specially interesting for the reason it is heard so often over here. Things can't be so bad with the state of this nation when the presence of a few rogues brings such a generally widespread feeling that rogues are so predominant.

Recently another completely honest man I know very well said to me almost bitterly, "you told me when you came that many Australians think all Japanese are very bad people. At that time I objected and said we were not bad, but now I know differently and we Japanese have become very bad I have lately discovered." I know many such honest Japanese and they all say much the same thing to me.

My conclusion is that the rogues are only in a very small minority, and that so small a proportion of rogues can make such a general feeling of humiliation is to me rather significant.

What do Australians want to hear about? What questions am I going to be asked? Please write and tell me C/o. 35 Francis St., Blackburn, Vic. It will be a big help in preparing my "talks" with you.

May God Bless and keep you all,

FRANK

P.S.: Would subscribers to our *Newsletter* please let me know if any stamps or postal notes have not been acknowledged. I have tried to send receipts and keep my books in order. I have sent over 100 parcels to include your many gifts of food, soap and clothing.

Thank you sincerely,

E.R.C.

———

Circulated by Mrs. E.R. Coaldrake, 35 Francis Street, Blackburn, Vic.
Printed by T.J. Higham Pty. Ltd., Blackburn.

Maida Coaldrake, Oral History, 25 August 2001.

In 1949 Frank had Summer camps and then he was planning to go straight on to deputation work in Australia, and he fell ill. Can you imagine going from Odawara to Kobe on the ordinary *donkō* [slow train, approximately 12 hours] and then turning around and going back the next night because he had a couple of extra days in Kobe – he couldn't waste time waiting for the *S.S. Changte*. And then, when he got back to Kobe a second time, the boat had already gone. He hastily boarded the next boat out, caught up with *S.S. Changte* in Hong Kong but by then was so ill that he had to be transferred by stretcher ship-to-ship in the harbour. He spent the rest of the return voyage to Sydney confined by illness to his cabin.

5 The Campaign Against Prejudice: Australia (1949–50)

This chapter covers the period of Frank Coaldrake's first "furlough" back in Australia, from December, 1949 until July, 1950. During these eight months he married Maida Williams, lectured throughout Australia, and prepared for the next phase of the mission in Japan. The return to Japan was delayed by the problems of obtaining shipping passage with the outbreak of the Korean War in June, 1950, which was disrupting all Australian shipping to Asia.

This period is important for two developments. First is the campaign against prejudice. Frank Coaldrake's campaign for better understanding of Japan throughout Australia reads more like the final stages of a desperate political campaign than a period of rest and recuperation. For example, the schedule for 22–27 April 1950 in Queensland, and his letter to Maida Coaldrake about it, is exhausting to read let alone to fulfill. He drew enormous crowds – Brisbane Cathedral was packed for his speech on 23 April. As he was to remark in *Newsletter No. 31*, written on the ship back to Japan at the end of the stay in Australia:

> There seems to be a catch in the word "furlough." Many people seem to think that when a missionary is on furlough he is on holiday. Nothing could be further from the truth, especially for a missionary from Japan. To put it briefly:– Our work in Japan is to convert heathens to Christianity. The chief thing that hampers us in this is the lack of resources which can only be supplied by the Home Church – men, materials and money. When I am in Australia I am in the one place where it is possible to bring about more interest and practical help from the Home Church. No opportunity to do so must be missed. When there is no opportunity for such work, then we have a holiday, visit friends, seek better health and make preparations for return.

The comment about "seeking better health" is significant. Frank Coaldrake was in failing health when he arrived back in Sydney in December, 1949, suffering from the effects of malnutrition, as we saw at the end of the previous chapter. By the time he arrived in Sydney he was having difficulty walking. He was eventually diagnosed with beriberi and rickets by a doctor who had been imprisoned in a Japanese P.O.W. camp during the war. Despite the illness, Frank Coaldrake carried out a frenetic speaking schedule of sermons, speeches and newspaper interviews, from cathedral to country parish hall, from metropolitan newspaper to regional radio station.

The furlough coincided with the official visit to Australia by the Presiding Bishop of the Nippon Seikōkai, Michael Yashiro of the Diocese of Kobe. The visit had been organised by A.B.M. after the visit by the Australian Bishops to Japan in 1947. The Coaldrake records mention this visit only in passing, with Frank Coaldrake concentrating on his own hard task of debate and discussion, leaving the Japanese Bishop, accompanied by Canon Warren, to make his own case for support and understanding of the Nippon Seikōkai.

Seen from the perspective of fifty years later, it is striking how consistently Frank Coaldrake anticipated issues and policies across a broad spectrum by at least a decade in his speeches, sermons, and newspaper interviews. For example, he called for exchanges of Japanese and Australian university students while Japan was still an Occupied country. Such exchanges did not become a commonly accepted practice between Australian and Japanese universities until the late 1970s. In the same newspaper interview he points out that the Japanese were producing manufactured goods "up to best world quality." He concludes that "this was the truer Japanese standard," anticipating the coming of Japanese world leadership in industry and electronic goods.[1]

The period of furlough is important for a second development. A week after arriving back in Australia in December, 1949, he married Maida Williams, whom he had first met a decade earlier at the A.S.C.M. conference at Mittagong during the bush-fires of 1939, as we learnt in the *introduction*. (Fig. 28) At the time of their marriage she was Youth Organiser for the Diocese of Tasmania. Maida Williams had nearly five years' experience in diocesan youth work. She ran the youth clubs, visited the parishes (some 62 in total), organized all the education programs for Sunday School teachers, and other camps for the Church of England fellowships, as well as sitting on the National Fitness Council as a representative of the church. She had already distinguished herself academically at the University of Tasmania before becoming the first woman on the management staff of the Diocese of Tasmania. But it had not all been plain sailing, as the first document in this chapter reveals.

Maida Coaldrake, Oral History, 29 September 2001.

In 1947 the World Council of Churches Youth Department decided that it would mark the end of the war by conducting a World Council of Christian Youth with representatives from each of the Christian countries. Bob Dann, Graham Delbridge[2] and I were nominated from Australia and we were

---

1 "Friendlier Line to Japan Plea: Visits Urged," *The Herald*, Melbourne, 30 January 1950, p. 8.
2 At the time these were Maida Coaldrake's opposite numbers in Sydney and Melbourne: Rev. R.W. Dann was Youth Director for the Diocese of Melbourne and later Archbishop of Melbourne. Rev. Graham Delbridge was Youth Director in the Diocese of Sydney and later Bishop of Gippsland.

Figure 28 Wedding reception for Frank and Maida Coaldrake, 3 December 1949. Seated at left are Bishop Geoffrey Cranswick (Bishop of Tasmania), Corinne (Maida's sister), and the bridal couple. Standing behind Maida are her father (William Henry Williams) and her mother (Kathleen Marie Williams).

planning our travel by boat. At first the Diocese of Tasmania was very honoured to have me nominated but when the moment came for confirmation with the Oslo committee, they withdrew the nomination. They felt a young woman was not a suitable representative as there would not be much working life afterwards because of the likelihood of marriage! Bob and Graham considered withdrawing themselves but eventually did go. No-one was sent in my place. I had got to the stage of buying a new suitcase, two seersucker suits, because they would not crush, and a travel rug. I think one of the problems was that some of the diocesan clergy were wary of me as I was by then far better educated than most of them; most only had a Th.L. [Licentiate of Theology] and I had a University Degree.

Letter from Canon J.H. Lansdell, Diocese of Tasmania, to Mrs. F.W. Coaldrake, 1 February 1950.

Telephone 871
St. George's Rectory,
98 Invermay Road,
Launceston.

1st February 1950.

Mrs. F. Coaldrake,
Diocesan Youth Organiser,
Church House,
HOBART.

Dear Mrs. Coaldrake,

At the last meeting of the Diocesan Youth Committee I was instructed to write to you for the purpose of tendering to you the Committee's Congratulations on your Marriage and to wish you every happiness for the future, and to express our most sincere and grateful thanks for all that you have done for the Diocese in your position as Youth Organiser.

The Committee feels that you have done a wonderful work during your term of office, beginning with very little and a great deal of inconvenience and putting the youth work of the Diocese in such a sound position, in a most efficient and satisfactory manner.

We are at a loss to understand how that you really brought it all into being, except for the fact that we realise your sense of vocation, your great personal gifts, your perseverance and enthusiasm and charming personality; all these you have given generously to your work and it is very pleasing to review the scene as it was when you came and to compare it with what it is today.

We very sincerely regret your departure from us, but we are consoled by the fact that your services are not being lost to the Church, being confident that you will give just as generously in the your new sphere of activity as you have done with us.

> We pray that God's abundant Blessing will rest upon you.
> With kind regards and best wishes.
> On behalf of the Diocesan Youth Committee,
>   Yours sincerely,
>   J.H. Lansdell

It was resolved that the following minute be recorded:

> The Diocesan Youth Committee desires to place on record its deep appreciation of Mrs. Coaldrake's four years of untiring work as Youth and Sunday School Organiser. She pioneered the organisation of Youth work and leader training in the Diocese. Her outstanding ability coupled with enthusiasm and spiritual zeal have been the means of laying solid foundations on which to build in the future. Not least has been her work on the Associated Youth Committee of the National Fitness Council, in which the influence of the Church of England is now an important factor.

Maida Coaldrake, Oral History, 16 August 2001.

When Frank got back to Australia finally he looked absolutely terrible. In addition to whatever he had contracted before his departure he had beriberi from lack of nourishment. The first time I saw him I almost did not recognize him. His hair had gone completely white and he looked cadaverous – his cheeks had caved in so that you could put your hands in the hollows. He could barely walk. So in this condition he presented himself at the church, Christ Church St. Laurence in George Street, Sydney, for the wedding as arranged on December 3rd, 1949. But, after only a few weeks, he went on an arduous Australia-wide deputation campaign, between the middle of December and the end of May. He called on most of the Anglican parishes which had supported his work, talking, preaching, giving radio broadcasts, and newspaper interviews.

"Friendlier Line to Japan Plea: Visits Urged," *The Herald*, Melbourne, 30 January 1950, p. 8.

Australia had to consider seriously the need for a new policy in Japanese-Australian relations, the Rev. Frank Coaldrake said today. "I hope the Menzies Government will tackle this important issue as soon as possible," he said.

Well-known social worker, missionary and pacifist, Mr. Coaldrake has spent $2\frac{1}{2}$ years in Japan, and is now home on six months' furlough. Today, he urged:

Exchanges of Japanese and Australian university students;

Visits to Australia by selected Japanese educational, religious, industrial and trade union leaders; and

Reconsideration of the non-fraternisation ban as applied to B.C.O.F. troops.

Such measures, said Mr. Coaldrake, would aid mutual understanding and greatly help liberal political leaders in Japan.

"The United States has already set the way," he went on. "But when, for instance, the Chifley Government was recently sounded for a permit for a Japanese bishop to visit Australia, the reply – from the highest quarters – was 'No.'

"If some of the decent liberal Japanese could visit Australia, nothing but advantage could result for the whole Pacific area.

UNETHICAL

"There is something shockingly unethical about trading with Japan while refusing any personal contact to get at the truth about the people making the goods we buy from them.

"The Americans' new policy of close fraternisation between their troops and the Japanese, adopted last September, is proving successful."

Mr. Coaldrake said the Japanese were exporting two grades of manufactured goods. One was the cheapjack stuff so well known before the war.

The other was a high-grade article up to best world quality. This was the truer Japanese standard.

The Department of Commerce should tell Australians more background about Japanese goods and the human story behind them.

Frank Coaldrake, Script for Radio Broadcast, 19 February 1950.

Script for a broadcast from 5KA, Adelaide at 5.30 p.m. on Sunday February 19th, by Rev. Frank W. Coaldrake of Japan.

F.W.C.:

Good afternoon Listeners. Did you know that when three hundred or more Bishops from the Church of England all over the world gathered at Lambeth in 1948 there were among them three Japanese Bishops? Many who saw the public functions in connection with the Lambeth Conference said that one of the most impressive sights of all was to see the Presiding Bishops of the Churches in China and Japan walking side by side in moccasins. In that act of a Chinese Bishop and a Japanese Bishop we may see at a glance the wider significance of Christian Missions for the world.

The impression is deepened when we realise that at the final service of the Conference the Archbishop of Canterbury wore a cope and mitre which he had just received as a present from the laymen of the Church in Japan. It was a beautiful robe of costly silks and many have wondered how the impoverished Church in Japan could have managed to send it. It should be remembered that there are many Anglicans among the American Occupation soldiers and these American Laymen are in every way co-operating with the Japanese Church. The result is that the Americans among the laymen give the largest proportion of the monies subscribed for such a purpose as this gift, but the Japanese laymen, giving each his little, far outnumber the Americans.

It is one of the remarkable things about the Occupation of Japan that the Christians among the Occupation soldiers, and the people under Occupation, are meeting together in the Churches as brothers in Christ.

Another instance of practical co-operation in this way is the Church of St. Andrew in the mountains in mid-Japan. This fine stone Church was dedicated at the beginning of 1949. It cost several thousands of pounds. Most of the money was contributed by the Americans, but most of the contributors were Japanese. It is the Headquarters Church of the Brotherhood of St. Andrew, an organisation of the Laymen of the Anglican Church in Japan which corresponds to the Church of England Men's Society in Australia. It has undertaken a long-term project in the mountain villages and the new church stands as the centre of a growing Rural Community Centre. Two Japanese Parish priests work full time in the villages gradually bringing the light of the Gospel to the poverty-stricken mountain homes.

Another common happening was seen once again at Christ Church Yokohama on Christmas Day just past. The Japanese Bishop of South Tokyo confirmed seven adults of whom four were Japanese and three American soldiers, one a Lieutenant Colonel.

The Church of England in Japan is very aware of its links with the Church in America for it never forgets that the first Anglican missionaries came from America [in the nineteenth century]. But English and Canadian Missionaries were not far behind and there are today many parish churches which owe their origin to the work of S.P.G. or C.M.S. missionaries from England.

The day of separate Missionary society work in Japan is however over. That is of course the necessary first stage in the development of the Church in a country but it is always preliminary to the final independence of that country's church as a Province within the Anglican Communion. Our Church in Japan reached that stage just before the last war [1914–1918]. In fact it was the policy of the Japanese Government to sever all dependence of Japanese institutions upon parent bodies in other countries and this policy hastened the completion of a process that was already well advanced by 1920. But the Government which insisted on the autonomy of the Japanese Anglican Church also insisted on establishing further controls over the Church [with the onset of World War II]. As a result of this policy our Church came into conflict with the Government. Many members of the Church suffered suspicion, oppression and some went to prison. Two of the Bishops and at least three of the priests spent some time in Sugamo Prison in Tokyo.

So it came about that the Japanese Church in the very first days of its independence as a Province of our Communion met a sore testing. It survived, faithful but scarred, and is today tackling the task of spreading Christianity in Japan.

In this work it has asked for and is receiving the help of the parent Missionary Churches in America, England, Canada and Australia. This help takes the form of missionary workers, and money and materials. But despite its dependence on our help the Japanese Church is autonomous. It has its own Bishops and priests ministering to its own people. Because it thus stands erect and on its own ground it is able to provide the ministry they need to soldiers of the Occupation who are unable to receive it from their own rather scarce Army Chaplains.

How big is the Anglican Church in Japan? The latest figures show 25,000 baptised members among whom are ten thousand communicants. Looking for comparison at other Christian bodies we see that there are 130,000 Roman Catholics and the same number of members in the United Protestant Church, (i.e. mainly Methodist, Presbyterian, Baptist and Congregational). There are also 14,000 Eastern Orthodox members and a few thousands in various smaller churches. There are a total of 300,000 Christians in the 82 million people in Japan. That is one third of one percent. Or, to put it another way, in any group of three hundred Japanese there will be one Christian.

Our 25,000 Anglicans are scattered over the whole country – a pretty thin spread? We have 8 Dioceses, each with its Japanese Bishop and its staff of Japanese Priests. There are about 210 Japanese Parish Priests spread through the 8 Dioceses. Working with them today are four missionary bishops, 8 missionary priests, of whom I am one, and about 45 other missionary workers – doctors, nurses, teachers. There are also 3 Sisters of the Epiphany from Truro in England.

We missionaries are welcomed as co-workers with special tasks for which there are no Japanese workers. We all of us depend entirely on our Home Church for financial support. But in all other respects we are on exactly the same footing as the Japanese workers. I, for instance, have the same relation to my Japanese Bishop and twenty-four fellow priests in the Diocese of South Tokyo as I would have if I were a priest in a parish here in the Diocese of Adelaide.

When we think of the Anglican Church in Japan we must think of it above the level of a particular missionary society. It is truly a sister church. But it is a very young and weak sister, shall we say a "convalescent" church, needing our sympathy and help as it faces its present task in a weakened condition because of its suffering through the war years. Remember also that the task it faces is a particularly difficult one. It is 400 years since the first missionaries went to Japan. Yet today, despite the deaths of countless martyrs and the sufferings of many confessors, there are only three hundred thousand Christians altogether. This is not due to the weakness of the efforts of the missionaries in the country. It is due to the difficulties in the ordinary outlook of Japanese people and the sharp contrast between what Japanese religion asks and what Christianity asks of its converts. But it is also undoubtedly due in part to the failure of Churches in the Home countries to take Japan seriously enough.

Think for a moment about what we in Australia have done. In 1914 we sent a missionary priest and his wife – the Rev. Eric and Mrs. Harrison. They went to the Diocese of South Tokyo and worked very effectively for twenty years. But towards the end of that time we in the Church in Australia lost interest in Japan and our support of them dwindled away to nothing. Rather than leave Japan Eric Harrison moved into the Canadian Mission area and until his death by accident a few years later was supported by the Canadian Church. I have spent a lot of time in the area in which Eric Harrison worked and have found, twenty years after his death, a strong memory of him and an abiding love for him. In fact the people there expected and hoped that when I arrived from Australia I was going to renew the work that he had begun. In fact I was at the disposal of the Bishop, and he has seen fit to appoint me to another new work in another part of the Diocese. But the point is that we started a new work in Japan from Australia then lost interest in it. In the succeeding years all we sent from Australia to Japan was scrap iron which came back as bombs and bullets. Now, after two and a half years in Japan I'm back here for a few months to tell you about the needs of our little Japanese Anglican Church and to ask you if you won't renew your help. The way to do it is to increase your support of the missionary activities of the church in your own parish. More directly, the funds to support the work I am doing for the Bishop of South Tokyo come to that Diocese through the Australian Board of Missions, so it is best to send help for the Japanese Church, marked that way, to the A.B.M. office, or through your local church.

Of course my main concern in Japan is to bring Japanese to the Christian faith. And believe me that keeps me busy. The only justification for leaving it at this time was the desire of my Bishop that I should tell the Church here about his needs over there and try to persuade you to increase the support that has been given in a small way since the end of the war.

You see, from Australia we've done nothing at all about rebuilding any of the churches that were destroyed during the war. 73 out of 271 were completely destroyed. Already 50 have been rebuilt. Our churches in England and America have co-operated to provide the sum of £500 for each Church that had to be rebuilt. It is a glorious achievement to England and that she has paid in full the amount she undertook for this purpose. The Church in America and Canada is as yet short of the total and the rebuilding is delayed to just that extent. But we in Australia have done nothing. Now you can't tell me that we in Australia have no concern about Japan. What is the greatest fear in Australia with regard to the future? Doesn't it concern Japan? Isn't it a probability that Japan among the other Asiatic countries will be aware of Australia? We are virtually concerned about the Japan of the future. No matter how far MacArthur may have succeeded in providing new laws on a democratic basis in Japan during the Occupation, he cannot really make a new Japan by reforms imposed from the top down. Bishop Bentley of the American Church spent a long time in Japan recently and at the end of his visit uttered the warning that the democratisation of Japan must wait upon her Christianisation. I cannot take the time to substantiate that here now, though I am doing so in many other places this week in Adelaide.

The fact is that the future of Japan depends very largely on what use the Christian Churches make of their present opportunities. Now in Japan nearly everybody wants to hear what Christianity has to say – they also want to hear what the Communists have to say. Just how many hear the Christian Gospel, and see it in action in the Church, depends partly on the Church in Australia. There is a field in which we are the only overseas mission at work – the peninsula which the Bishop has put under my charge. The missionaries from England, Canada and America have each their own full work. We all would echo the words which came to me in a letter from Japan last month. My assistant, the Rev. Francis Iida, is carrying on the work in our peninsula during my absence. He has to maintain the works we already had under way. He was to take on new work only if there was time left. And he was not to go searching for new work. But new work lies all around him. And he has written to say "My hands are too few." That is the experience of all of us over there.

There never has been such an opportunity in such a difficult country. Already since the end of the war the number of communicant members of our Church has trebled. My own little district is a very conservative rural area with a quarter of a million people in it. In October last we dedicated an Army Hut as a Church. Now, in these months there are more than fifty people at every service so that the hut is overflowing. That means the people are standing in the street for land is so precious that the only place we could find to put up the hut was a man's front garden. Children are coming to the Sunday School in such numbers that they have to be turned away.

Our hands are too few. Our buildings are temporary little huts. Now is the time to establish a strong permanent mission there and strengthen the hands of the Church in Japan before it again faces the winds of opposition. If we can act fast enough we might yet stifle those winds at their source. You cannot escape a share in the responsibility for what happens in Japan in the future.

Letter from Frank Coaldrake to Archdeacon C.S. Robertson, Chairman of the Australian Board of Missions, Sydney, 14 April 1950.

The Venerable,
The Chairman,
A.B.M.,
Sydney.

Sydney, 14/4/50

Dear Mr. Archdeacon,

In connection with the Board's decision in February last to make a grant from the Centenary Fund for the Izu Mission in Japan there is a matter on which I would be grateful to have the Board decide.

My question is whether a portion of the grant might be available fairly soon. I realise that there is an appreciable income by interest on the monies held but certain expenses for rentals and travel would be saved once the money were available in Japan. It is possible that this saving would about equal the income from interest. Perhaps the present inflationary trend is also a consideration.

Until at least a portion of the grant is available I must continue to pay the following rentals, viz:

   i. House at Odawara – A£60 per annum;
   ii. Church land at Ito – A£50 per annum.

Also, while living at Odawara, whenever I go to my work anywhere in the peninsula I must cover an extra distance of 35 miles each way from Odawara. Even if done only once a week this extra travel involves approximately A£50 per year, possibly much more.

Continuing on the present basis, which I must do until some of the grant is available, involves approximately A£160 a year additional expenditure. Another consideration is that until I can move my Headquarters to Ito I must delay full scale operation of our Mission programme. Therefore if the Board could make some of the grant available fairly soon it would be a great help.

If the Board agreed I should like to inspect land in Ito as soon as I return and then advise the Board of the lines on which we are ready to proceed. It would probably be October or November of this year. If at that stage we could receive at least enough to pay a deposit on the purchase and provide for the removal of the Church it would be ideal.

Before I could start these enquiries and negotiations I would have to know when, and to what amount, some of the grant would be available in Japan.

Yours sincerely,
   Frank W. Coaldrake

"Symbol Of Jap. Repentance," *Telegraph*, **Brisbane, 22 April 1950.**

A Church of England missionary in Japan arrived in Brisbane this Saturday carrying with him a plaque symbolising the repentance of Japanese Christians for the murder of Australian missionaries in New Guinea during the war.

The missionary, Rev. Frank Coaldrake, formerly of Sandgate, also carried 10 bamboo crosses which will be placed in five New Guinea churches and five Queensland churches in memory of the missionaries.

Rev. Coaldrake, who has been in Japan for two and a half years, said that the plaque would be hung in the cathedral at Dogura, New Guinea.

Its symbolic meaning was repentance towards God and reconciliation towards man.

The plaque was carved in wood by a young Christian member of Rev. Coaldrake's church at Odawara.

It bears a crucified Christ on a background of Mount Fuji, symbolising the hope that the Japanese will become Christians; drooping wisteria, meaning repentance; and the mountain raspberry, which grows in inaccessible places, meaning reconciliation.

The Anglican Archbishop of Brisbane (Dr. Halse) will bless the crosses and plaque at a special service tonight...

His first service in Queensland since his return will be at Sandgate – his boyhood parish – for the Office of the Comrades of St. George at 7 p.m. tonight.

Rev. Coaldrake will also tell of his missionary work in Japan at the following services:

Sunday [23 April 1950]: Holy Trinity, Valley, 7.30 a.m.; Holy Trinity, Wooloongabba, 9.30 a.m.; St. John's Cathedral, 11 a.m.; St. John's Cathedral (children's service), 3.30 p.m.; St. Paul's, Ipswich, 7.15 p.m.

Monday [24 April 1950]: St. James, Toowoomba, 7.30 p.m.

Wednesday [25 April 1950]: St. Paul's Cathedral, Rockhampton, 7.45 p.m.

Thursday [26 April 1950]: National Missionary Council luncheon, McDonald's cafe, 1 p.m.; A.B.M. rally, Bible House, 8 p.m.

Friday [27 April 1950]: St. Peter's, Southport, 8 p.m.

Letter from Frank Coaldrake to Maida Coaldrake, 26 April 1950.

[This describes the activities that are advertised in the preceeding newspaper article.]

It is mid-afternoon and mid-way to Rockhampton. The flight is smooth and the weather beautifully clear... On Saturday the Archbishop [Halse] came with Eric and Pat and me [Rev. Eric Hawkey, then the Queensland Secretary of the A.B.M.] to Tugnell[?] Home Fete and on to Sandgate [Frank Coaldrake's original parish church]. Comrades of St. George had gathered, and Sandgate parishioners, and St. Francis theologs [theological students]. We sang the Comrade's Office with full ceremonial. The church has been lovingly cared for and the sparkling brass, well polished red-brown woods, red-blue bricks, all glinting in the lights made an exactly right rich setting for red and gold copes, and red servers' cassocks and white collars. And one of the server's cassocks the very one first made for me when I was head server 20 years or more ago. And the music of chanted canticles, the incense and the swaying banners and bobbing lights – my it was good. . .

The blessing of the Bamboo crosses for martyred missionaries' parish churches was the centre of the service. (Fig. 29) The Archbishop did it with incense too!. . . We spent a short night at Bishopsbourne [Brisbane] and 7.30 a.m. found us at Holy Trinity, Valley to present one of the crosses, then breakfast at the rectory during which I said "Good morning Mrs. Rector" to the Housekeeper! Then to dear old Holy Trinity Woolloongabba for 9.30 a.m. Mass to present another cross. This church also is well preserved and a place whose material beauty is forgotten in the evident spiritual beauty of the worship there. In the congregation several old friends, Lydia and Sid Ware and others. And Joyce, Carl, Edwin and Rosemary too [Frank Coaldrake's sister, her husband, and their children]. Bob Moreson is now the parish priest. The side chapel here was my place of morning worship during my John's days [St. John's College, University of Queensland] for we had Mass at John's only every second day. . .

Figure 29 The Archbishop of Brisbane, Dr. Halse, blesses the bamboo crosses sent by the Nippon Seikōkai for "the martyred missionaries' parish churches," 22 April 1950.

A bit of a rush to get to the Cathedral [St. John's Cathedral, Brisbane] for 11.00 a.m. but I had time for a few words with Joyce and others. But Joyce and the two kids [Edwin and Rosemary] came to Cathedral too. It was "University Service" to begin Commem Week and I had the rare experience of preaching to my old profs and teachers – quite a roll up of profs, lecturers, grads and undergrads... The 3.30 p.m. Cathedral service was I think the best hour of service I've been at so far this trip. The Cathedral was packed, nave, aisles, transepts and little chapels – over fifteen hundred. Sunday school children had come to present their Lenten Self Denial offerings and I had the pleasure of talking to them. The service was well planned and ran smoothly – took just 1 hour and finished with procession and clergy and choir round ambulatory and aisles. (Over £400 handed in. They had to rush for additional alms dishes and people to carry them.)

We had just nice time for tea and to get away up to Ipswich for 7.30 p.m. and presentation of a Cross. There was a nearly full church, about 300, but I reacted strongly to the genuine atmosphere of the place, including a block of members of "Royal Society of St. George" and got launched into one of my hitting sermons, perhaps even "snarly" so that I was wondering whether I was possessed by the Holy Spirit or the Devil. We stayed at the Hotel and slept in in the morning... My bed was hopeless so I put the mattress on the floor. It was cold. About 3 a.m. Eric brought his blanket and joined me and we put the floor mat on top for extra warmth and woke up at 8 a.m. It was a warm sunny day on Monday and the drive to Toowoomba was a real picnic jaunt... (We've started down for Rockhampton already, we were very high, it is bumpy and I'm chewing a Minty.)

"What goes on in Japan?" *The Peacemaker. An Australian Venture in Reconstruction*, vol. 12, no. 5, May 1950, p. 3.

The Rev. Frank Coaldrake, *Peacemaker's* founder, told a crowded meeting of the Christian Pacifist Movement, in Melbourne, what he had seen and heard and learnt since he went to Japan as an Anglican missionary (he is back on furlough).

War brutality and war trials (seen through Japanese eyes and ours), Japan as a nation made pacifist by a law imposed by the victors, Japanese puzzled and groping toward some kind of political and industrial democracy – Frank dealt with all these in a brilliant 90–minute extempore exposition.

His picture was very different from that given in press and broadcasting, deeper and more understanding – from a man who had lived among them not as a visitor, but as a friend and helper.

Here are some of the things he said:

He was asked by a Japanese: "Why is the Australian heart so hard?" His reply was: "Some Australian hearts are so hard because of the things done in prisoner-of-war camps."

The Japanese asked: "Was it necessary to burn old women and children to death? And what of the atom bomb?"

Then Frank told of cities reduced to ashes by one air raid, cities where half of the population had been wiped out – and of a 24–mile forest of reinforced concrete smoke-stacks, where once factories had lined the road from Yokohama to Tokyo. A fire raid and roaring wind had done that – and some estimates of death went as high as 250,000.

We had said brutality to prisoners was not a military necessity; a Japanese asked why we dropped the atom bomb, which we now admit was not a military necessity. . .

PACIFISTS

The Japanese are, by their new Constitution, bound to a belief that war is a mistake, and to depend on peaceful procedures.

Article 9 says that war is renounced and Japan is committed to defencelessness.

The ordinary man is relieved at not having to go into the army. A few people think that the idea is an idealistic one; many more say it is false to the spirit of Japan, the soul of the patriotic Japanese cannot consent to the renunciation of war.

For that matter, how many people of any nationality consent to war's renunciation and a state of defencelessness and dependence on peaceful procedures? . . .

Frank Coaldrake, *Report to the Australian Board of Missions*, undated carbon copy, early 1950.

Agenda No. 6

ADDENDUM TO THE CHAIRMAN'S REPORT

The Most Reverend the President, and
The Venerable the Chairman,
Australian Board of Missions,
SYDNEY.

Sirs,

An outline of what the Bishop of South Tokyo hopes will be undertaken by the Australian Church follows in accordance with your wishes expressed to me upon my arrival in Australia.

I should just say, without attempting a detailed report of my early work in the Diocese of South Tokyo, that the Bishop appointed me to the charge of the Izu Peninsula at the beginning of 1949. He described it as pioneering rural work in difficult country. The Church had long wanted to undertake it and he hoped that with the backing of the Australian Church it would now be possible. He reminded me that the Japanese General Synod meeting in 1946 had resolved to make a special effort to spread the church into the rural areas. (The Nippon Seiko Kwai is so far confined almost entirely to cities and towns.) He hoped that I would be able to establish the church while making our mission an example in rural evangelism for the whole church.

Situated in the geographical centre of the Diocese and of Japan, the Izu Peninsula is a rugged, mountainous area of about 1,000 square miles, with a population of a quarter of a million farmers, fishermen and woodsmen. The Roman Catholics and United Protestants each have small congregations in the area. *Total 500 of ¼ million* [people].

The Reverend Francis Masao Iida, twelve years a priest, was appointed as my assistant. Together we made a survey and some experiments. We then discussed the Bishop's hopes with him again in detail and the plan of campaign is now as follows:

Plan of campaign

With Coaldrake and Iida maintained by the Australian Church £1,250:

1. To visit regularly the six Church families scattered over the Peninsula, making each home the centre for regular services and an outward expansion in that district. To maintain these centres and aim at establishing new ones as new families are won, the Izu Mission church to be very largely a "church in the cottages;"
2. To buy land in Ito city as the permanent site of the Mission Headquarters. To erect on it a temporary church hut to be dedicated as the parish church of the Peninsula for the time being;
3. To lease land at Lake Ippeki near Ito for Summer Camps for the youth of the Diocese, the camp to be the spearhead of our village evangelism, the campers all helping to build up a congregation in Ito and its surrounding villages;
4. To continue living in Odawara for the present, but as soon as possible make my own permanent residence on the land, in Ito, Iida and his family to live in his present cottage on the other side of the Peninsula;
5. To establish in conjunction with my own residence in Ito a Hostel to be used for
   (i)   Children of our church families who have to leave home to attend secondary schools, of which there are several in Ito, and
   (ii) Young laymen being trained by us in Rural Evangelism, the men to live with us for about two years, then return to their own districts;
6. To build on the site in Ito a permanent Church with Hall and Kindergarten incorporated, the Church building itself to have a distinctively Christian atmosphere to stand over against the very religious atmosphere of many fine temples and shrines in the district;
7. To establish a Mission School in or near Ito.

Progress during 1949

During the year of our ministry in the Peninsula we have:

1. Maintained the original 6 cottage centres and started 4 more;
2. Rented a site in Ito and erected a Quonset Hut bought from Army Surplus, fitted the Hut as a church and had it dedicated on October 10th, 1949. Services are now conducted there each Sunday and congregations and Sunday School classes are growing so rapidly that Iida has written in mid-January to say it is "overflowing;"
3. Bought camping equipment mainly from Army Surplus, and held Summer Camps for 500 youth of the Diocese, conducting with their participation, a widespread evangelising campaign in the villages;
4. Enquired into costs and sites with a view to moving to live in Ito;
5. Found children and young men who are wanting to come to our Hostel and Training Centre;
6. and 7. Nothing done.

All our work is made possible by the grant from A.B.M. The £900 for the current year supports Iida and myself. The fall in exchange rate in September was a 30% drop in income. All the camp expenses and the cost of buying and erecting the Hut Church were raised in Japan quite independently of the A.B.M. grants.

Estimated cost of plan

Capital expenditure required to establish the plan proposed is estimated as follows:

re (2.) Land in Ito, 1–1½ acres	£2,000
re (2.) also, Transfer of Hut Church with Improvements	£200
re (3.) Camp extensions and equipment	£500
re (4.) Residence in Ito – build or buy and renovate	£2,000
re (5.) Hostel and Training centre – addition to residence	£1,000
re (6.) Church, Hall and Kindergarten	£5,000
re (7.) Mission School	??????

My own personal comment is that the Mission School need not be considered until the present Mission Schools are proving more effective than they are now. The Church, Hall and Kindergarten should also wait until we have gathered enough church members to warrant it and the cost should then be partly undertaken by the local members. Nevertheless, it would be a wonderful thing if the Australian Church should give the Japanese a Memorial Church dedicated to the Prince of Peace.

The other items are in order of importance and really should be taken as a whole, £5,700, for then the Mission would be permanently established and equipped to do all it can handle in the next four or five years.

My Bishop has sent me back to Australia for these few months so that I might consult with the Board about how far we can go with this big undertaking.

Additional workers from Australia

The Bishop would gladly receive more missionary workers from Australia provided their maintenance is undertaken entirely by the Australian Church. He has spoken to me about a priest for Chiba and a Kindergartener for the Kindergarten when it is established. He is even more keen to receive financial contributions to the "Clergy Stipends Subsidisation Fund" which the Diocesan clergy have themselves started as a Self-Help towards financial stability. However, the Bishop's first hope with regard to Australian help is that the Izu Mission will be established and maintained.

Extraordinary incident

After seeking a campsite for months, I found my way into Lake Ippeki, lying among the mountains near Ito. There I leased a block of land we set up our Camp. One day with some of the campers I was in a village for evangelising, and as I spoke at the roadside a Japanese man spoke to me in English and joined in our meeting. He was a Christian doctor visiting a friend in the village. Afterwards he came to the camp and when he saw it, and heard about the campaign of which it is the centre, he told us excitedly of a day 28 years before when he had come to this out of the way beauty-spot with the Rev. Todomu Sugai [later Bishop]. They had stood just below our camp site and Sugai had prayed that this lake might become the site of a great mission to convert the country areas, spreading out from Izu into all Japan. Sugai became Bishop of South Tokyo and Presiding Bishop of the Nippon Seiko Kwai. It was in that capacity that he welcomed to South Tokyo Diocese in 1947. He died and Bishop Maekawa took his place. He appointed me to Izu and gave me only general instructions about the work. When he heard this doctor's story, it was the first he had known of the Bishop Sugai's hopes about Izu and Lake Ippeki. We believe that it is surely in the Providence of God that Bishop Sugai's prayer is being answered after 28 years.

Can the Australian Board of Missions make it possible to carry out the Bishop's hopes and plans? If the Board is not sure of this, it would be better to continue to help Japan only in the present temporary, easily terminable basis, lest the Nippon Seiko Kwai again have cause to feel let down by the Australian Church.

It is my hope that I might have a chance to talk to the Board about these plans.

Yours sincerely and respectfully,
    FRANK W. COALDRAKE

6   The Team in Japan: Odawara and Izu (1950–54)

The first *Newsletter* in this chapter summarises the results of the Coaldrake campaign against prejudice and the visit by Bishop Yashiro to Australia. Frank Coaldrake's message for the Australian Church is blunt: hatred and prejudice have compromised the fundamental Christian qualities of love and forgiveness. He concludes that his mission of reconciliation of Australians with Japanese is only "one-tenth completed" as a result of the deputation work of the first half of 1950.[1]

The focus of this chapter is the four difficult years back in Japan for Frank Coaldrake, the first four years in Japan for Maida Coaldrake. In terms of the mission of reconciliation to Japan, we see the shift of operations from the parish of Odawara to the rugged and isolated Izu Peninsula; in terms of Japan we see the transition from an Occupied and defeated country to the beginnings of prosperity for an independent nation. Real national income in 1951 recovered to the levels of 1934–36. When Frank Coaldrake had first arrived in Japan in 1947 it had stood at only 61.1% of the pre-war levels.[2] At the same time mining and manufacturing reached 116.9% of the pre-war levels, compared with a mere 37.8% in 1947.[3]

In 1952 the San Francisco Peace Treaty came into effect and the Occupation ended. Politically, the years 1950 to 1954 are separated by what is seen as the "great divide" of post-war Japanese history – between the end of the Occupation in April, 1952, and the immediate post-Occupation era. In reality there was not much difference on the ground for the Coaldrakes and for many Japanese. The Americans were still very much in evidence in Japan. There were the first protests against the continuing U.S. military bases in Okinawa, despite the official end of the Occupation. In March, 1954 a Japanese fishing ship, the *Lucky Dragon*, was contaminated by "death ash," radioactive fallout from one of the series of U.S. hydrogen bomb tests in the vicinity of Bikini Atoll in the north Pacific.[4] This resulted

1 *Newsletter No. 31*, August, 1950.
2 Hidezō Inaba, "Problems of Economic Recovery and Self-Support," *Japan Quarterly*, vol. II, no. 2, April–June, 1955, p. 156.
3 *Japan Quarterly*, p. 156.
4 Shinjirō Tanaka, "'Death Ash' Experience of 23 Japanese Fishermen," *Japan Quarterly*, vol. II, no. 1, pp. 36–42; Ralph E. Lapp, *The Voyage of the Lucky Dragon. The true story of the Japanese fishermen who were the first victims of the H-Bomb*, Harmondsworth, Middlesex, Penguin Books, 1958.

in contaminated fish being sold at the Japanese fish markets and entering the domestic food supply. Some of the seamen from the *Lucky Dragon,* and the people who ate the food, died. Throughout the Occupation period there had been a total ban imposed by MacArthur on discussing the atomic bombing of Hiroshima and Nagasaki. With the Bikini Atoll incident, the entire population of Japan was made dramatically aware of the dangers of atomic radiation for the first time. Hiroshima and Nagasaki suddenly took on fuller and more sinister meaning. The atomic age was no longer synonymous with the optimistic animation hero "Astroboy" who had become so popular at this time.

We find this and other issues of the day reflected in the *Newsletters*, now for the most part being written by Maida Coaldrake with sections added by Frank. The home port of the *Lucky Dragon* was Yaizu, not far away in the same prefecture as Itō. These issues form the background for a struggle for survival and stability in Izu during these four long years.

Four years represents an unusually long period for uninterrupted missionary service in any country. By contrast, A.B.M. usually brought its missionaries back from the field in New Guinea on at least a biennial basis. A decision was made to leave the Coaldrakes in Japan for twice that length of time, possibly due to expense, as they were the missionaries posted farthest from Australia. This decision now seems counter-intuitive given the distance and the hardship of the posting. The major cities of Japan like Tokyo were booming because of the continuing American military presence but conditions in the countryside had not significantly improved from the years immediately after the defeat. In Odawara and Izu people were still suffering from near starvation and related problems of illness and high infant mortality. Mothers were often unable to breast-feed their infants because of dietary insufficiency. Dysentery, cholera and typhus were rife. And another major conflict in Northeast Asia was breaking out in the Korean peninsula just as the Coaldrakes returned to Japan in 1950. This turned Japan into the major staging area and strategic bastion for American and United Nations forces. The Coaldrakes returned to Japan in mid-1950 on a ship which was stalked by hostile mainland Chinese planes in the Taiwan Straits. Through much of the rest of 1950 they spent in Odawara, bombing missions to Korea flew out every evening close overhead from the nearby Atsugi Air Base.

In many ways material conditions became more trying for the Coaldrakes because of the withdrawal of Occupation rations, although material prosperity for the Japanese population was improving. We see this in the shortages of food and failures of infrastructure described in this chapter. The usually optimistic tone of the *Newsletters* makes way for valiantly disguised near despair at times. The parcels of food and essential goods sent by supporters in Australia dried up with the end of cheap army mail services on the Australian side, and with the imposition of prohibitive duty and regulations on overseas parcels on the Japanese end. The black market was such a scourge that foreigners, including the Coaldrakes, were suspected of profiting from it. Medical facilities were inadequate for the Coaldrakes in Itō. Frank Coaldrake was injured seriously as a result of a domestic accident while repairing equipment. He was blind for several months as a result. During this period no money, not even the regular stipend, came from Australia because of mishandling by the banks, unused to the new procedures for transferring money between Australia and Japan. Maida Coaldrake ran the parish as well as commuting between Itō and Tokyo every second day to deal with a desperately sick husband in hospital there.

We can see these problems reflected in the letter from Bruce McCall, a priest originally from the Diocese of Tasmania whom Maida Coaldrake had known from her days as Youth Organizer. By then he was working on the Home Mission staff at A.B.M. headquarters in Sydney. "It is very hard to get news of Japan," he writes. "Nobody in this office [A.B.M. Headquarters, 14 Spring Street, Sydney] co-operates very much in those things but I am gradually cultivating Canon Warren and he has been very good lately in passing things on to me." The Coaldrakes were mostly out of sight and out of mind.

The major development in terms of the Coaldrakes' responsibilities in Japan was the establishment of the Izu Mission *(Izu dendō mishon)*. This marked the beginning of the second phase of Frank Coaldrake's ministry in Japan. We saw in the documents in the last chapter that he had been given the job as "Priest-in-charge (Kanri-chō) of the Izu Peninsula" by the Bishop of South Tokyo in late 1948.[5] He reports his formal induction by Bishop Shinjirō Maekawa on 25 March 1949 in *Newsletter No. 25* of May, 1949.

After the return of "the team" to Japan in 1950, the Izu Peninsula was visited on a weekly basis by Frank Coaldrake, usually accompanied by Maida. Her first visit around the entire peninsula is described and analysed in two of the *Newsletters* in this chapter. The Coaldrakes set up their Izu headquarters in the second storey room of the house in Itō of the lay evangelist Hisashi Miyazawa, who later became a priest as well as one of Frank Coaldrake's closest friends. (Fig. 30) Shortly after, the centre of operations was moved from Odawara to Itō. Temporary lodgings were found in a house on a block of land in the centre of the town of Itō that was bought with A.B.M. money. The first months in Itō were not without drama, a typhoon blowing away part of the roof of the temporary rectory and financial dishonesty marring the purchase of the land, all of which is described in detail in the *Newsletters* and confidential reports in this chapter.

Rural evangelism was the new strategic priority for the Diocese of South Tokyo. Until then the focus had been almost entirely on the cities and towns, reflected in the name of the diocese. The shift in Japan's population from rural to urban was about to happen but in the early 1950s close to half the total population still lived in farming and fishing villages.[6] The evangelization of the farmers and fisher folk of the Izu Peninsula was a bold new direction for a hitherto urban-centred diocese.

---

5   Letter from Frank Coaldrake to Canon M. Warren, Secretary, the Australian Board of Missions, 30 November 1948.

6   In the national census of 1 February 1954, 43% of the total population, some 37,600,000 people, lived on farms. Ichirō Hidaka (ed.), *New Japan*, vol. 9, 1956–57, Tokyo, The Mainichi Newspapers, 1956, p. 63.

Figure 30 The Lay Evangelist Hisashi Miyazawa, later priested, in his home at Kameyama in Itō which served as the first headquarters for the Izu Mission, 1949.

Moving Frank Coaldrake to serve as priest in charge of Izu may have addressed the strategic objective of rural evangelism but it was also an expedient way for the Diocese of South Tokyo to solve the problem of the placement, status, and authority of an experienced foreign priest on its staff. There was a limit to how long such a priest could be expected to serve as an assistant in a parish. The foreign mission board, financially underwriting the enterprise, might ask questions. He was allowed to attend synod but neither speak nor vote. Izu offered the diocese a splendid opportunity to solve both problems – the mission and the missionary. The historical irony was not lost on Frank Coaldrake; he remarks wryly that "for centuries it has been the practice of governments to exile troublesome reformers to Izu because it is so inaccessible."[7] The mission needed someone unconventional, as well as practical, who could define his own role but be conveniently isolated by geography from the rest of the diocese, in a manner reminscent of the Buddhist Saint and revolutionary Nichiren in the thirteenth century. Frank Coaldrake was probably even more suitable for these challenges than the diocese realised.

7 *Newsletter No. 22*, February, 1949.

Frank Coaldrake was already considering the challenge of rural ministry in 1948 and 1949 as he travelled, by jeep and by foot, around the villages and countryside of Izu and central Japan.[8] He knew how impoverished these areas were, how desperate the physical and spiritual needs. In 1948 he had participated in a conference on rural evangelism at the experimental farm and church at Kiyosato in the Japan Alps.[9] As we saw in the previous chapter, in the summer of 1949 he ran the first of what were to become landmark summer camps for city children at Lake Ippeki, just outside Itō.[10]

Frank Coaldrake's strategies for the Izu Mission were influenced by the rural evangelism carried out at the Ōmi Mission in western Japan half a century earlier. The evidence for this influence is provided by one of the books preserved in the Coaldrake Sydney home. It is Dr. William Merrell Vories' *The Ōmi Brotherhood in Nippon*.[11] This is a history of the work of the Ōmi Mission, founded by the Canadian evangelist (and architect) Dr. Vories in 1905 in the province of Ōmi (now Shiga prefecture). Ōmi was the ancient province surrounding Lake Biwa to the east of the old capital of Kyoto. On the fly-leaf of the book Frank Coaldrake has written in pencil "Frank W. Coaldrake from Murata-san, Omi 24/10/49." K. Murata was one of the three founders of the Brotherhood.[12] In his travels around Japan Frank Coaldrake must have visited the town of Ōmi-Hachiman in late 1949 and had discussions with Murata about the Brotherhood, its philosophies and mission methods. There would have been a strong resonance with Frank Coaldrake, whose own ministry had developed through the Anglican Bush Brotherhood and the Brotherhood of St. Laurence. Like the Brotherhood of St. Laurence, the Ōmi Brotherhood was conceived of as a self-sustaining Christian community. In addition to a church and school ("academy"), it ran an architectural firm, orchestra, publisher, infirmary as well as a sizeable farming cooperative. In addition to the main church centre in the town of Ōmi-Hachiman, it established "cottage churches" (*katei kyōkai*) throughout the farming villages of the region. Frank Coaldrake drew a pencil line beside Dr. Vories' description of the powerful impact of being taken to a church in an ordinary house just days after he first arrived in Ōmi in 1905:

> On that first Sunday, we entered the meeting place – a small ordinary house, not much different from the one in which I lived. There were five or six people present, besides my fellow teacher and myself; all sat in a circle on the matted floor, and waited for time to begin the service. After a few minutes a middle-aged man, who appeared to be a leader among them, turned to my friend and

---

8   See *Newsletter No. 22*, February, 1949.

9   *Newsletter No.16*, 1 August 1948.

10 *Newsletters No. 26–29*, July–September, 1949.

11 William Merrell Vories, *The Ōmi Brotherhood in Nippon: A Brief History of the "Ōmi Mission" founded in Ōmi-Hachiman, Japan, in 1905*, Ōmi-Hachiman, Japan, The Ōmi-Hachiman Brotherhood Book Department. Fifth edition, June, 1940. First published in 1934.

12 Vories, p. 69.

said something in Japanese. "They are asking if you will please preach to them," he interpreted. This was rather short notice![13]

This may have been the prototype for the "cottage churches" Frank Coaldrake was to establish throughout the length and breadth of the Izu Peninsula. By August, 1956, there were thirteen such cottage churches and four more in preparation.[14] They were to function not only as centres of worship but of Christian witness by laity in the heart of conservative rural communities.

The Ōmi experience also anticipates the initiatives Frank Coaldrake was to take in Izu in creating a new "cottage industry" as the practical counterpart of the "cottage churches" – sheep stocked from sheep stations in Tasmania, to provide wool for "homespun" clothing. The warm clothing was to clothe cold people and to act as a source of income to supplement income from subsistence agriculture in the barren soil of Izu.

The Ōmi Brotherhood may well have inspired this, but we may also see something of the influence of Gandhi's efforts, going on in India at the same time, to create cottage industries such as spinning as part of his defiance of British rule and industrialisation. The objectives in Izu may have been different but the methods were similar. Gandhi's tactics of civil disobedience had worked for Frank Coaldrake in Melbourne with the verandah "sit-in" for social justice. Why not try some of his other practices in Izu?

Newsletter No. 31, **August, 1950.**

NIPPON SEIKO KWAI

C/o B.C.O.F. Army P.O. 214,
Empire House,
Tokyo,
JAPAN.

From – Rev. F. W. Coaldrake

[written by Frank Coaldrake]

S.S. Changte, en route to Japan

Dear Friends,

The Chinese sailors have been letting off crackers and now they are chattering excitedly as one after another they haul in a fish. Their lines are over the side all along the deck outside our cabin porthole. Some of the passengers are up on the promenade deck listening to the radio and trying to persuade themselves they might dance despite the heat. Others are down along the side watching the

13 Vories, p. 33.
14 *Newsletter No. 61*, August, 1956.

fishing. We're almost as still as the poet's "painted ship upon a painted ocean." We're anchored off Cairns waiting for the high tide. I'm sitting between two fans trying not to get clammy and Maida is doing the washing.

That's the great new fact that has come into my life since I last wrote to you through this *Newsletter*. The "fact," I hasten to add, is not that I now have someone to do my washing. There were always kind ladies or a housekeeper to do that. The fact is that I now have someone I love to share the whole of this life with me. There's no need for me to try to explain in detail what it means. But I think I ought to ask you to try to imagine what it involves for Maida to leave the more or less settled and very secure life in Australia for a life of almost complete isolation in a strange land. Eventually she will, I'm sure, find many true friends in Japan, but for some time to come she'll be very much alone except for me. She has yet to learn the language and until she does she will hear only what I translate for her and be able to say things to others only with the same limitation. Though I make grim jests about having her completely under my thumb during that period, it really is no laughing matter. There will be some small mitigating factors such as an occasional meeting with other missionaries or Australian Army people. We will hear the A.B.C. on shortwave at night whenever we care to tune in. There will be the fellowship in faith with our church people, especially in worship. But if anyone cared to press the point I would have to admit that she's bound to have a lot of loneliness, especially when I have to travel to distant parts on my work. I've got my reason for reminding you of all this. One of the best antidotes to loneliness is to get lots of letters from home and friends.

It is hard to believe that I have spent just on eight months in Australia "on furlough." I seem to have been able to do very little of all that should have been done. One thing in particular I regret very much having had to neglect – renewing old friendships and acquaintances, looking up people who have helped me, some very generously, while I have been in Japan. There seems to be a catch in the word "furlough." Many people seem to think that when a missionary is on furlough he is on holiday. Nothing could be further from the truth, especially for a missionary from Japan. To put it briefly: Our work in Japan is to convert heathens to Christianity. The chief thing that hampers us in this is the lack of resources which can only be supplied by the Home Church – men, materials and money. When I am in Australia I am in the one place where it is possible to bring about more interest and practical help from the Home Church. No opportunity to do so must be missed. When there is no opportunity for such work, then we have a holiday, visit friends, seek better health and make preparations for return.

I spent some months visiting centres big and small to talk about Japan and our work here. In the course of visiting all States I met many to whom this letter goes. Where that was possible it was a great joy to me. The depressing thing, as I look back now, was to find that among the several thousand people I spoke to in meetings and services very few began by acknowledging the human-ness of the people of Japan. This, it seems to me, is not just the result of war with Japan. We don't find the same attitude to Germans and Italians. There must have been some special feature in our war-time ideas about the Japanese and we ought to be trying to recognise what it was, because it has warped the mind of even the Christian among us. I found that people who were quite impervious to logical argument and a reasoned statement succumbed in a few minutes to a play upon their emotions. This is, I think, because the usual Australian attitude to the Japanese is based on fear – they gave us a mighty big fright as their armies came down through Singapore on to the New Guinea mountains. Later, to this fear was added horror as we heard the stories of returning prisoners-of-war. And because fear and horror are both very strong emotions, often played upon by highly coloured press and radio reports, they overpower any attempt to size up the situation reasonably with calm thought.

We don't need even to try to disguise the badness of the worst of the Japanese people, but we do have to make an effort to recognise the goodness of the best of them. Sir Thomas Blamey[15] has said lately that we had better make sure that Japanese are our allies rather than our enemies if there is going to be another war. For much better reasons than that we should be true to our Australian heritage and give credit where credit is due. When I was a boy we learnt in Australian schools that you "don't kick a man when he's down," and after a fight you were always expected to "Shake [hands] and be friends." When quite young I had learnt in Sunday School that a Christian is to follow our Lord's teaching to "Love your enemies." Did anything unique happen during the years 1940–45 to make things that had been recognised as Truth for centuries no longer important?

I'm telling you all this now because the difficulty and strain of meeting that attitude and trying to change it has left me time and energy for little else on this furlough. Nor is the task one-tenth completed. I must leave it to you and hope that what you will read in these letters from time to time will encourage and help you.

The visit of the Presiding Bishop of our Church to Australia made a lot of Australians sit up. Bishop Yashiro said and represented many deep and provocative things. But perhaps the most striking thing about his visit was that it stirred up many hitherto silent champions of justice and Christian fellowship to speak openly in favour of good relations with **good** Japanese. The Press reported a few instances of people saying "Bishop Yashiro should be so busy trying to Christianize his nation that he shouldn't have time to come to Australia." That was clever enough comment but it should have served to highlight the Bishop's frequent plea for more help from Australia so that he could cope with the task at home in Japan. Australia will I think face her judgment for the fact that she has let the Bishop go back to his task with not one substantial offer of help as a result of his visit.

---

15 Thomas Albert Blamey (1884–1951), Australian General, Commander-in-Chief of the Australian Military Forces from 1942 to 1945. He was promoted to Field Marshall in June 1950. See: *Australian Dictionary of Biography*, vol. 13, pp. 196–201.

On a different scale I have a different result to report. I go back with several cases of clothing and food sent through me as gifts to Japanese people. Also I have some much needed equipment, either supplied by the A.B.M. or given by individuals or small groups. I am especially glad to be well equipped for visual education among the rural people. Queensland A.B.M. people have given me a Cinevox portable "Talkie" projector and the Friends of Odawara have provided a fine projector for still films. We haven't got much film yet, but that will come. Incidentally, my own Movie of my work in Japan has been copied and will be shown here and there by the A.B.M.[16]

You'll be wondering what difference the war in Korea will make to us in Japan. It is hard to say. Various authorities endorsed my own opinion that it should make little difference and at this stage was certainly no reason for not going back. In fact I'm so eager to get back that even these few hours standing still off Cairns seem to drag on indefinitely.

In a few weeks we will be able to write you from Odawara again. We go back to the same old house and will stay there for the present. Of course, there will be changes all around and I'm not expecting change in one thing – the keenness of the people of our Church.

Maida will no doubt have much to say off her own bat in future letters. As far as this one is concerned she joins me only in this last word–goodbye for the present.

Yours sincerely,

FRANK

P.S.– Maida has just read the third last paragraph above. She comments "I LIKE standing off Cairns. It's probably saving my life to have this smooth still spell between rough sailing." – F

A few notes for readers [from Frank Coaldrake's mother]

This *Newsletter* is compiled from letters to his Mother written by the Rev. Frank Coaldrake and his wife. It is sent to anyone interested in Frank and Maida and their work.

It is expected that all who get this letter should do their best to pass it round for others to read.

It is hoped that all who receive the *Newsletter* will send something now and then towards the cost of printing and postage. This amounts to roughly 3 d. per copy.

As far as possible the *Newsletter* is sent out at the beginning of each month, but when letters from Japan come irregularly this is hardly possible.

Friends of Odawara please note that your Secretary Miss Rae Campbell's address is now C/o 17 Wellesley St., Mont Albert, E.10, Victoria.

---

16 Preserved in the collection of ScreenSound Australia, *Coaldrake Movie Collection: The Anglican Church in Japan as Seen by the Australian Missionary Frank Coaldrake*, title number 526742.

After September, mother's address will be, Mrs. E.R. Coaldrake, C/o A.B.M. Office, Church House, Ann St., Brisbane, Queensland.

***

[Added to the end of *Newsletter* after arrival back in Japan.]

August 22nd, 1950.

Back to the old address, C/o B.C.O.F. Army P.O. 214, Tokyo. It was a very happy day when we reached Odawara, and found our various friends had cared well for everything during my absence.

They prepared for our coming with loving attention to details. All our luggage has arrived safely as well.

I came up to Tokyo by train this morning to go through the process of official registrations, permits and the like. All has gone smoothly and I am now due to catch the train back to Odawara.

The weather is extremely hot, sticky and unpleasant, but otherwise everything makes for contentment, and a big job started has now to be continued. All goes well.

I have just met George and Val Yule, missionaries evacuated from Korea, now working temporarily in Tokyo.

I hope to be in Tokyo again next week and post you a real newsletter from Maida as well.

Sincerely yours,
    FRANK

***

Circulated by Mrs. E.R. Coaldrake, 35 Francis Street, Blackburn, Vic.
Printed by T.J. Higham Pty. Ltd., Blackburn.

Newsletter No. 32, October, 1950.

NIPPON SEIKO KWAI

C/o B.C.O.F. Army P.O. 214,
Empire House,
Tokyo,
JAPAN.

(Address: E.R. Coaldrake, Hamilton Road, Nundah, Queensland.)

From – Rev. F. W. Coaldrake

[written by Frank Coaldrake with an addition by Maida]

Odawara.

It is now one month since we arrived here and you have had only one short letter from us so far. We have been once to Tokyo in the jeep and were delayed in Yokohama on the way for the registration of the jeep. When we reached Tokyo we found Rev. George and Val Yule about to board ship to return to Australia, so we gave up some hours to farewell them. Afterwards we had quite a rush to buy our month's supplies, and visit the Sisters with things to deliver from Australia, and collect others sent to them from England for our mission work. Also I had to see Bishop Viall (U.S.A.) at the Theological College to discuss several matters, which meant it was evening before we set out for Odawara.

During our first month back here we have been twice to Ito for three days at a time, twice to the Babies' Home at Oiso, and twice to Atami. We have attended two official welcomes in Odawara and two in Ito area, plus innumerable visitors to see us, and visits to others in Odawara. It has been strenuous but interesting, and sometimes exciting.

We've had several earth tremors, one very severe and alarming, and two typhoons in the south, with another coming, but none actually reaching here yet. The summer weather has been very hot and trying, with mosquitoes voracious. The jeep is jibbing at having to work again after its long rest, and stopped last night on our way home from Ito. It was raining, and a passing truck driver kindly towed us home.

This old house is bulging with unpacked luggage, mostly food and clothing to be given away. Several parcels have arrived, and more in five boxes sent from A.B.M. Melbourne Office. I'll write directly to the senders where their names and addresses are attached, but in many cases there is no visible evidence of person or place of origin. Perhaps some puzzled friends reading this will realise that their parcel is one of these unknown but very much appreciated packages.

It was a great joy to find so many Church members on Odawara [Station] platform to greet us when we arrived from the south by train on the day of our "Journey's End." It was perhaps the most pleasant part of the whole journey as we travelled 2nd class in Japan's "super" train – the Osaka-Tokyo express. It is called the Swallow (Tsubane) [also transcribed as Tsubame] and earns the title by swooping smoothly over the 400-mile run in nine hours. This train compared favourably in every respect with the Newcastle Flyer, in which I rode a few months ago in Australia, with the added advantage that Japan's 2nd class equals Australia's 1st class in room and comfort, but is very much cheaper. There are 1st, 2nd and 3rd class in Japan, the 3rd being quite alright for short journeys.

One of the most noticeable improvements during my absence was the better railway services now in Japan. All carriages are now completely fitted with seats and glass windows. The days of jampacked trains have passed, because of many new carriages and engines and improved supplies of coal and electricity, enabling more trains to be run. Whereas three years ago every train was crowded inside and out, one now rarely sees a train with people standing. Perhaps one reason is that people are travelling less because money has become scarce and fares are higher than ever before.

Also, food supplies have improved so much that it is no longer necessary for people to travel in search of food. Previously there was a ceaseless stream of hungry people from starving towns out into the country areas to buy vegetables and grain. These improvements led me to remark to some friends that with regard to food, clothing, housing and travel, things had become much easier for ordinary people. One man replied, "Yes, it's easier now, if you have the money."

That is a good clue to understanding life in Japan today. The ordinary wage-earner has been put back by financial controls and conservative government policies into the position where he is content to do a full week's hard work for barely a crust, a roof and a shirt, but poverty-stricken workers are numerous and unemployment has greatly increased. In recent weeks there have been serious riots of unemployed in Tokyo. One does not have to look far below the surface to realise that shops full of food, textiles and building materials is a sign that most people cannot afford to buy them. Because people cannot buy what they need the shops remain full of necessities.

Inflation has been held in check, but the value at which money has been levelled out is about one hundredth of its value five years ago. Tax collections are more effective than they were, but at the same time we read that people are not putting as much into savings, and telephone accounts in arrears total nearly one million pounds in Australian figures.

Another change that was in progress has now become full circle. The Occupation Army has moved aside and stands as watchful policemen and helpful adviser, while everything is done by Japanese Government or civic officers. At our port of entry we saw it at work in the saloon of our ship. Some occupation staff sat smoking in the background while we were "progressed" by Japanese Customs, Immigration and quarantine officials.

For our travels and baggage, for citizenship registration, jeep registration and all such things we dealt entirely with Japanese personnel. We are classified as "Semi-permanent Resident-Missionary." That status entitles us to draw rations of bread and other bare necessities from Japanese sources, and to have bank deposits of money originating from overseas.

As Australians we have still the distinct advantage of being allowed to purchase also a ration of supplies from the B.C.O.F. Canteen in Tokyo. If we did not have that privilege we would be able to buy some similar things of American origin, but at about twice the price.

The present exchange rate between Australia and Japan causes us to think twice before buying many things which the ordinary Japanese person buys as he needs them. On the other hand fruit and vegetables in season are about the same as present Australian prices mostly, but in Atami yesterday we thought to buy a bunch of nice grapes, about 1 lb., only to find the price was 10/-, so we hurried off without them.

The whole country feels more "solid." I used to have the feeling that things were on the verge of exploding or "folding up." There was a kind of frenzy in the daily rush to work which has gone. There is still suffering and hardship, but hope has been revived.

The Korean war is a matter of constant conversation, and one effect is that prices which had been actually dropping during the earlier part of 1950 have gone up again. Discussion about the meaning and significance of the "No War" clause in Japanese Constitution goes on in all circles and the Press carries articles on the subject. The general trend seems to try to find a way to keep the clause, but make loopholes in it. There is not much sign of war in everyday life in provincial Japan.

Such is life! **A week later,** and we are off to Tokyo to attend a Memorial service to Fr. Arnold (U.S.A.). He died suddenly of heart trouble six weeks ago while travelling for a series of summer Conference addresses. He will be a great loss, for he had been in Korea for many years, and in Japan since the war. There are now only two pre-war Anglican overseas missionaries, Bishop Viall from America and Bishop Powles from Canada. Bishop Mann has just retired and gone home to England.

Something Ogata-san told me tonight sets up some strange reactions. She has been looking for another job because we are thinking we will not need her help when we move to Ito in a few months' time. One job she enquired about was painting the faces of very small doll souvenirs. Ogata-san is quite a talented artist and could do it well, but there are seven people working in the "house factory," and the most skilful can do 500 dolls in 15 hours of hard work for which she gets 200 yen. That is 5/- Australian, which means that 30 days of 15 working hours would give less than the Government scale of wage for an unskilled labourer. That is much the same picture of pre-war as well as post-war Japan; the difference being that now the workers are very angry because the factory owner's daughter is taking expensive lessons in dancing, painting and piano. She is becoming a lady by the sweat of their brows they say. In pre-war Japan the workers would not have questioned the right of the owner to make big profits and spend them for the benefit of "the little lady."

We have already inspected about twenty properties in Ito, hoping to find a suitable site for our Izu Mission Headquarters and our new home. Several of the places inspected were suitable, but the stumbling block in all cases is the basic value of land in this little overcrowded country. Ito is a small provincial town with big ideas about its own future importance as a Spa resort. There are 600 hot springs in the town area and most of the places we have inspected so far have their own spring. The result is that land sells in the business part of the town at £1,900 (Aust.) an acre. Within one mile of the Post Office the cheapest price is about £3,000 an acre. It is rather disheartening to meet this obstacle whenever a good site comes into view. We now have two quite good sites under consideration and will likely have to choose between one which is centrally situated, and the other with beautiful views and quiet surroundings on the edge of the town. Either may be a possibility under the terms of the Fund which the Australian Board of Missions is collecting for a Building Grant.

With that complete tally of the moans of a missionary, I can now add that they play but a small part in the whole life of these busy days. We are making preparations for the baptism of our converts in the Izu Peninsula. These will be most of the "regulars" now attending our services and instruction classes in different centres. I also had the joy of being back in time to assist at the Baptism of a 63 year-old gentleman who has attended Odawara Church and my Bible Class for three years. He had delayed because of honest doubts that he "couldn't believe," but at length conviction came after new aspects opened up, and now he is one of us. He is to be confirmed shortly.

At Lake Ippeki we were "welcomed" at a sort of Civic Reception with an arch over the roadway and little kimono-clad boys and girls to dance for us. There are three more Welcomes just ahead and invitations to visit other Churches of the Diocese. It will probably be many months before we can complete the round of "first visits."

Quite remarkable improvements had been made to the old Odawara house by Capt. Bev. and Ruth Burrows of Kawana before we arrived back. The bathroom especially has become a place of sparkling white porcelain. They also fitted a neat little water heater outside, with an astonishing dog-leg chimney to take the sparks away from our thatched roof. The chimney roused the wrath of a neighbour, not because of its smoke, but because it reared its ugly head into the middle of his view! He will be pleased when we take it with us in a few months to our new home at Ito maybe. Bev. and Ruth also arranged for us to borrow some necessary furnishings until we know what we need to buy after we move. Ruth returned to Australia just after we arrived, and Bev. is to return in a few weeks also. They have been wonderfully understanding of us and our difficulties.

Laurie Topp brought the mails from B.C.O.F. Tokyo last week-end, which saves my going up for them.

Maida adds observations and "findings" thus:

Odawara at last, safely and happily midst heavy rains and humidity. A group of such happy people to meet us, who did their best by smiles to show what they couldn't say. (Fig. 31) The house is really a gem even though I had predictions in plenty of what to expect. (Fig. 32) Our living room is beautiful now the days are so hot. The whole of our southern wall is open, sliding screens all out, and a basket of white lilies, red dahlias and carnations hanging on the huge oak beam.

I'm not isolated on a hill, for in the midst of the thick bamboos, crepe myrtle, and hibiscus there are other houses. I can hear a wireless up the hill and little Megumi Ogata playing scales down-hill.

My first Sunday was very happy and in spite of a tropical deluge of rain all day the Church people turned out wonderfully. The same joy on everyone's face was a loving welcome to me, even if I could only smile and smile, and mop up perspiration! Frank is very much a man back on the job, with an amazing grasp of the language, and very good at manual tasks. While I'm having to build up my own new world slowly and a little painfully, everyone is very kind and very thrilled to have me here; and tho' I miss you all and long for a yarn with my Youth pals, this life holds immense possibilities, not only as a life of Service within the Nippon Seiko Kwai, but unexpectedly as one's own way of development of the Inner Life.

Ogata-san I loved for her sheer goodness and willing ways, and our priceless cups of tea together with dictionary on either side, and numerous bows to cover up my many mistakes.

Figure 31 Maida Coaldrake shortly after she arrived in Odawara with Ikue Yoneyama, a member of the group which met the Coaldrakes at Odawara Station, August, 1950.

Another impression is of Fr. Miyazawa, incredibly like a little old round Japanese teacup, antique style. Also, everywhere I find such adorable babies, with straight fringes and delicious smiles.

Although I haven't told you anything about the fascinations of Manila or the wonderful few days in Hong Kong, I expect I should react a little to this Japan where I am destined to spend a part of my life. My first reaction when I was told we were in the Inland Sea, and that there were lights of the fishing villages along the shore. The islands of the Island Sea are some conical, some like fans, most of them with terraces and fir trees all over. In the water surrounding, Japanese junks with outboard engines were much cleaner than Chinese junks we noticed earlier in our travels.

We were far too busy during the morning repacking our trunks and cases, after being on *Changte* for over a month, to do much else but watch the skyline outside our porthole but at morning tea time we watched Hiroshima pass at a distance, and by lunchtime we were at Kure. Kure is very much a military and naval depot and like Manila, war wreckage is still in evidence. On deck we waved

Figure 32 Maida Coaldrake and the 600 year old Odawara House, August, 1950.

greetings to Fred and Margaret Parkes, and Padre Alan Laing of B.C.O.F., and then Customs and Immigration officials were on board – same routine, passports, vaccination certificates, visas and so on. S.C.A.P. has drugged the Japanese with American methods and so we ploughed through piles and piles of printed forms and signed here and there. I am landed as Miss. Dep. S.P.R. – translated means Missionary dependent, semi-permanent residence, so I'm pretty harmless.

A few days in Hong Kong has proved to me that there is very little similarity between Chinese and Japanese.

After two days at Kure we travelled north and stayed at Kobe, Frank with Fr. Rex Clarke of N.Z. and me with the most interesting Miss Leonora

Lee.[17] The next break at Kyoto produced a Buddhist festival and a ride in a bicycle chair.

Fr. Iida met us at Numazu and the joy on his face as he ran to meet us, in one moment wiped away all the ship rolls (and there were many after Hong Kong) and hours of unbearable warmth in trains.

Japan is a land of contradictions! Beneath all this seemingly modern Western culture, fast trains, splendidly distributed electricity and luxury hotels, their women are still in a position of near-slavery in their houses and in the fields or farming areas.

From our windows we can see a glorious curve of sea and Oshima island, with its active volcano, which obligingly turned on a display as we sipped coffee a few evenings after I arrived in Odawara.

With good wishes to you all.

Sincerely yours,
FRANK & MAIDA

———

Circulated by Mrs. E.R. Coaldrake, Hamilton Road, Nundah.
Printed by Brisbane City Printery, Edward Street, Brisbane.

Maida Coaldrake, Oral History, 19 June 2000.

At first at Odawara we lived in the teahouse, a former farmhouse from the mountains, of Mrs. Murota. She was a Tokugawa shogunal family scion. The farmhouse was typical but high quality, brought down from the mountains, possibly from the Central Alps, to form a teahouse to which had been added a laundry and kitchen area. The floor was wood and tatami mats.

Mrs. Murota was in her mid-sixties. Her family had a proper *kura* or storehouse in which there were family treasures. Like so many families at this time, they were having to sell their household treasures and objects to the Americans to buy food. The objects went into traders' hands who acted as the middle-men in the sale. The Americans were the only ones with money.

The Odawara area was one of the big centres of the Occupation, immediately adjacent to the region in which major American bases were located – the naval base at Yokosuka, and the army and air bases at Yokota and Zama, and then down as far as Atsugi, just up the road from Odawara.

Oiso, the next town up from Odawara, had been the place for escape from Tokyo for wealthy families. It was there that Sawada Miki, a member of the Mitsui family, ran the Elizabeth Sanders Home with which we were involved. She was an Anglican. There were many nice two-storey houses along the seafront there. They did not seem to have been damaged during the war.

---

17 Miss Lee was the daughter of an English S.P.G. missionary to Japan before the war. She was brought up in Japan and was Secretary to Bishop Yashiro.

By contrast Izu was not a wealthy area. Atami was visited for hot springs. It was only later that Itō became so popular.

Even when we were living in Odawara, Frank was going to Mishima and Numazu for visits to churches and out-centres.

Maida Coaldrake, Oral History, 23 and 25 August 2001.

The destruction and death of the civilian population of the Pacific seaboard from U.S. bombing at the end of the Pacific War were everywhere apparent when I got to Japan. People were still poor and hungry and the towns along the seaboard of the western half of the diocese, such as nearby Numazu and Shimizu, had been 90–95% destroyed in a single night by American bombing.

Every night as I lay in bed in my first home, the 600 year old thatch-roof farmhouse in the castletown of Odawara, I wondered why all the screens in the house were shaking and where the planes flying overhead were going. The shaking was caused by eruptions of the volcano of Mount Mihara on Ōshima, just across the bay, and the planes were the U.S. airforce going over to bomb the Korean peninsula from nearby Atsugi airbase. Nature and man were both fighting at the same time and both were uncomfortably close. Itō, later to become our permanent home, was on the fault line from Mount Fuji to Ōshima. Mount Fuji was visible from just outside Itō and Ōshima was the large island with a wisp of smoke trailing off into the wind just across the water halfway to the horizon in the sparkling Pacific.

Pacific it was not. Although the Pacific War was over Asia itself was still in a state of war and instability and this influenced the character of the American presence. Times were still desperate. The Occupation created a very tense situation in Japanese society with the war trials and the executions. With the Korean War at its height there were troops there on rest and recreation from active service on every train from Itō and Odawara up to Tokyo. This gave the foreign armed forces the feeling of ownership of Japan, even after 1952 and the end of the Occupation.

We resented the soldiers everywhere, even into the 1950s. If we felt like this, what did the Japanese think – all these soldiers just using our land to go on fighting their wars. I sometimes wonder why the Japanese were so nice to us as we'd killed a lot of their fathers, brothers and uncles. We were sent from Australia on a holy mission with the blessing of the church. We got to Japan and found we were in a country being run by the Americans and being bossed around by American M.P.s. Non-fraternisation was the strictly enforced policy. "You mustn't go near the Japanese," or "You must not sit in the train carriages with the Japanese." We were forced to sit in the Armed Forces waiting room at Tokyo Station while waiting for the Odawara train. I began to wonder why the Japanese wanted us there at all.

For Frank this was a real problem. The only places you could stay were on army bases and everything you ate was army food there. Taking rations from the army from time to time, as there was little or no local food, presented Frank with a real moral dilemma. As a pacifist he wanted nothing to do with the Armed Forces. I had never heard Japanese spoken until I arrived in Japan. The first Japanese I learned was "Amerikajin ja nai [I'm not American]." It was very useful, especially in my first year in Japan.

I was very isolated at first. Ogata-san was quite frightened to work in the house with me. At first I didn't have Japanese language at that stage. And her husband had been killed in the fighting in the Pacific War. She had been taken into the household of Murota-san at Odawara and then she found herself looking after people who had been on the side of the soldiers who had killed her husband. This is the sort of thing we couldn't say in the *Newsletters*.

Maida Coaldrake, Oral History, 25 August 2001.

The American Episcopal missionaries had a firm base and precedent for work in Japan, and its pre-war staff returned to take up the work again after the war. They had the Episcopal church of St. Alban's in Tokyo, as well as St. Luke's International Hospital, which became one of the official Occupation hospitals and later a major centre for treating casualties evacuated from the Korean War. The American missionaries themselves had an inter-missions service which "civilianised" U.S. military rations and supplies after the end of the Occupation. Frank did not have access nor wished to use it, at least until the mid-1950s.

We would go to Tokyo for church meetings and see all the American missionaries with station sedan cars and even refrigerators, and Frank was still driving a battered old jeep discarded by B.C.O.F.! I used to be furious. I was living in a thatched hut in someone's backyard, and here were American missionaries with appliances we did not even have in Australia – and food, groceries and clothing in abundance from the "PX" from the military bases. Half the problem for us was that A.B.M. had never had a firm mission in Japan before us. Half the time the Americans didn't even know where Australia was!

Newsletter No. 33, November, 1950.

NIPPON SEIKO KWAI

C/o B.C.O.F. Army P.O. 214,
Empire House,
Tokyo,
JAPAN.

From – Rev. F. W. Coaldrake

[written by Maida Coaldrake]

Odawara, Japan.

IZU JOURNEY

As so many things do, our Izu journey began the night before. The jeep had been having one of its endless refresher sessions at the local garage in preparation for its week's run, so Frank decided to train to Ito 30 miles down the Peninsula, for the final instruction class of Catachumens who were to be baptized the following Sunday. It was a night of the high moon so that I thought nothing of the few hours alone in our hill top house, though I am not quite used to being alone and unarmed, linguistically speaking, when all sorts of visitors come clicking their geta by the frog pool and up our stony path. Some hours after his departure, I made suitable Japanese noises at the neighbour's friendly dog who comes visiting each night, prepared supper, set the Heath Robinson hot-water system working, and went to bed. Four hours later, the time then being 1 o'clock, I was agitatedly wondering, were I to begin to sound the alarm, which of my twelve [Japanese] words would be the most useful when trying to discover Frank's whereabouts.

The road from Odawara to Ito, I might add, is one of the most beautiful in the world. It winds along the coast of the Izu Peninsula, diving through tunnels dripping with ground water, flinging itself suddenly through villages packed between cliff and sea, skating over corners still half repaired from the ravages of last year's typhoon, panting up steep mountains and then falling into towns of which the biggest is Atami, with its tourists and great buses and packed play areas. Nowhere is it wide enough for a jeep and a bus to pass unless one stops and pulls into the side of the road, or slows to a crawling pace and eases through with an inch to spare (I know, as a jeep is left hand drive and I sit near the bus!), and along much of its length the new telephone cable is being dug in.

At 1.30 a.m. I didn't remember much of the beauty of that road – its cherry avenues and fir forests and thatched cottages – and especially I didn't dwell too long on the glorious cliffs with their view of fishing fleets and silver bays. In the bathroom the sudden noise of splashing water called me to a general flood in which a dripping tap had become a waterfall and a lake. What with mopping up I was quite busy for a while. When the jeep engine music began to throb around our hills I was almost as badly in need of repair as the tap! After no less than eleven breakdowns in some quite impossible places, and cranking sessions sufficient to make and break blisters, Frank wasn't much use for anything except the bath, and bed.

The next morning, being Saturday, the day we began our first journey around the area which is known to A.B.M., as well as the South Tokyo Diocese, as the Izu Mission. The jeep went for another refresher while we packed such things as might be required – chopsticks and rice, to clothes and a sleeping bag. We also smuggled in a special case with Frank's best black suit and my pink organdie [dress], with the prospect of a beautiful dinner of fresh meat and fresh vegs., and people to speak English to, at Kawana Hotel, which is the magnificent rest hotel of B.C.O.F. with its two golf links, swimming pool, tennis courts, view of the sea and a real live volcano, not to mention its 290 servants. Captain Bev. Burrows, a friend of ours who is in charge, is leaving shortly for Australia, and this night a party had been arranged to farewell him.

Jeep and trailer loaded with food, the Queensland A.B.M. "gift" movie projector, films, books, and all that makes our travelling Church, we set off in time for that dinner, 35 miles away down the Peninsula, but at 9.45 p.m. we were sitting in Bev's suite, having a steak and an ice. It somehow suffered from lack of dining room noise and companionship. Official dinner time we had spent at a road police station, Frank coping with the jeep's innards under the fatherly eyes and helpful hands of three policemen, and I sitting in a nearby house waiting for a phone connection. "Fatherly" doesn't quite describe the eye of the Japanese policeman, for without exception he looks like a high school boy in cadet uniform. On point duty he presents the most efficient exterior of his American model, and with flourishes and clicks controls traffic such as Australia never sees, but at night, like all the contradictions of this amazing country, he has to be seen to be believed. Standing smart on his little box in the centre of the road he waves on the traffic with a paper party lantern complete with pink painted characters and a tiny candle flame inside.

While Frank worked with spanners and interested spectators my time was not without interest. Before me was a modern telephone, beside me was a ginger cat, around the door were all the townsfolk who were not busy watching Frank, and with me in my vigil were three nice young women, dressed in Western style skirts and blouses. You might see such young women anywhere in any country town at home. But did they behave like it? Oh, no! Unashamedly intrigued by this foreign woman, they lifted her skirt to see how the seams were sewn, they smelled her scarf, they studied her hair and head from several angles, and said what they thought in conversation with each other and with her. Fortunately I couldn't understand much, but behaved as I thought a film star would in those circumstances, remembering how much the Japanese girl had absorbed of Western culture from the film, and how keen she was of absorbing a great deal more. They wore our type clothes but they haven't quite got the slant on how to wear them, and go clattering off down the street on their noisy awkward geta, hatless, gloveless, stockingless, wondering why they lack the finish and the carriage! No one could have any carriage, it seems to me, when four wooden stilts tied to your feet by your big toe push your stomach alternately in and out.

We felt very frustrated at missing that farewell dinner, mostly because along with everyone else, we wanted to pay our respects to Bev., who is a grand person. But when we arrived two hours late and found that General Robertson[18] had asked for me to be placed next to him at dinner, I had my own feminine frustrations. However, we made our bow and apologies in the ballroom (on empty stomachs) and all was well. Later, fed and refreshed, we were able to be in on some of the more informal farewellings and were glad to slide into comfortable beds after brushing our teeth in our own private bathroom.

18 See *Newsletter No. 23*.

We greeted Sunday from the balcony overlooking sweeps of lawn and silver bay with the fishing fleet coming home, and shortly afterwards were packed up in the jeep swinging around the drive en route for Ito. Kawana Hotel is only four miles from Ito which is the rail terminal. So it was a short run to St. Mary's Church. We passed the usual number of great gas-producer buses, and "Honey" carts on their way to fertilise the fields, and the same number of shoppers at street stalls and bicycles and school children as one passes any day of the week, which reminds me that we are in a heathen country. People who attend our church services often have to miss a day's work to do so, or can only come in the evening.

Round the corner into the Church street down near the fishing village part of the town (Ito is the size of Launceston with regard to population), we waved to the owner of the ice shop and bowed to some of the congregation already walking down the street. Little boys and little girls with smaller girls on their backs, stood around while the jeep was parked and various bits unloaded from the trailer. An important day today – some baptisms, five of them our first group of catachumens. (Fig. 33) I find myself godmother to them all – by request. The baby – Kimiko-chan [visible at the rear of Fig. 33] – is the daughter of two communicant members of the Church [Mr. and Mrs. Miyazawa] who are frequently our host and hostess in Ito. We feel as if we belong in their upper room on the hill behind the town. The others are girls of 16 to 18, and following the

Figure 33 An important day for the new Church in Itō: Maida Coaldrake's first visit and the baptism of the first group of five catechumens, Summer, 1950. "Honey carts" outside contributed to the atmosphere and melting blocks of ice were placed inside to reduce the heat.

practice of the Nippon Seiko Kwai they have all chosen a western "Christian" name in addition to their own. We have Agnes and Prisca, Cecilia, Maria and Frances. I made the responses in English for that service, which was completely in Japanese, having quite a time as usual counting the Amens to be sure I was at the right place. It takes me so much less time to read the prayers and readings than it does to say the Japanese. Moreover, the Japanese always requires more words to express the same thought as does the English. Since that Sunday, a week ago, I have been godmother again, on this occasion to the new baby grandson in the Odawara Rectory whom we called Henry after my father when we were asked to name the young man.

Adult baptisms are often the only reminder we have that the church here is very young and very missionary. Otherwise the pattern we find in so many Anglican churches is repeated so exactly that we forget its short life, and shorter history. Baptisms are always very great occasions because the church is growing; the babies important because they mean established Christian homes, the adults because they mean people stepping aside from their former life against the stream of their national custom and thought, into a new and larger life as Children of God. But it is more solemn than that, as catachumens are told plainly during their classes. During 250 years of the 400 years of the existence of a Church in this country Christians have been persecuted, many thousands of them dying for the Faith. During the last war something like this happened and there is no reason to believe that it will not happen again. A beautiful red lily, which blooms everywhere at the moment, reminds us of it again and again. Legend has it that the first lily sprang from the blood of Christian martyrs as they were marched down the length of this Island on their way to destruction more than 300 years ago – an interesting legend, for this is not a Christian country.[19] When I go outside my kitchen door to hang tea towels in the sun I remember this, for the lilies are blazing between the ferns all over the high bank behind the house.

After the baptisms there was Church service and talkings with people. It is much more comfortable staying around in the Quonset Hut now that the worst of the hot weather is over. I shall never forget my first Sunday there, with the huge blocks of ice placed on the tables to cool the air smoking away like minor volcanoes, and the need for smelling salts and a fan during the services. But now Autumn has set in and the temperature drops 10 degrees [Fahrenheit] a week, so that it is quite bearable in the Hut which serves as a Hall, Rectory, and Church at present. After a late and much-needed dinner, we climbed into the jeep again, and [drove] around the sites offering for our new Mission centre. All spare time

19 These are the first chronicled Christian martyrs when Christianity was prohibited in the seventeenth century. 27 Japanese Christians were crucified hanging upside down on the hills above the site of the Martyrs' Roman Catholic Church in Nagasaki. It is firmly believed that, as they were marched from Kyotō in Honshu to Nagasaki in Kyushu, the footprints from their bleeding feet blossomed into nerines or red lilies.

in Ito to date has been spent that way, but by now all save two have been eliminated, and we divided our time and our enthusiasms exactly in half. From the higher ground near the station we had the most wonderful view of the town tucked away under its hills near the sea shore, and the beautiful valleys which slice through the mountains behind.

The mountains in Japan are unlike anything I have ever seen. There's none of the softly rounded curves of the hills and mountains round Hobart, nor of the angles and firm corners of the mountains in the west [of Tasmania]. So many of them look like fans (some open, some closed), flung line after line against the lovely sky, and all of them are embroidered in unbelievable patterns with their terraces and fir groves and swaying bamboo patches. And the valleys – why they are like great rivers with their green waves fixed forever in set patterns and curves, though the green waves are turning gold now with the rice harvest, and along the edges of the fields there is the red frill of the lilies.

We turned down into the heart of the town and stood on another block which will probably be ours by the time I write again, and looking up at the hills (though the Japanese usually call all their hills *yama* – mountain) I thought it might be best to live in the town so that you could always look up at the hills and along to the sea. On the stones of the street behind the hedge, geta were clattering along and the late afternoon was already a little chill.

After Evensong Frank showed movie films – *Bushland Symphony* is a great success, with its wonderful shots of kangaroos and koala bears, Australian birds, and rivers and great open spaces. I love it myself (and would need to, the times I have to see it!) Then comes the story of rice growing in Australia, a never ending source of amazement to the folk here who can't believe that such machines can do the job or are necessary or possible even in Japan. It is a film in beautiful colour of farming methods around Griffith in New South Wales. Third comes our own film – lovely colour shots of Hobart – family, Bishopscourt, Church House and Miss Henslowe and Rae [Townsend],[20] Echlin's cottage at Howden,[21] aeroplanes, Bishop Yashiro [in Australia], Corinne [Maida's sister] at Bundeena, 35 Francis Street [the house of Frank Coladrake's mother, in Melbourne], Little Frankie [White, Frank Coaldrake's nephew] and finally ships and seas – what seas![22] **They** soon cure any tendency towards homesickness just to look at them. Pixie [another member of the Coaldrake clan?] and Little Frankie [White] share honours as No. 1 film star and our wedding shots are a huge success. Finally we have the film of the Diamond Jubilee of the Community of the Holy Name at Cheltenham, Victoria, with its lovely shots of Sisters and Bishops and the Retreat House and the Processions on that great Day. It gives

---

20 Dorothea Henslowe was the A.B.M. Secretary in Tasmania and Rae Townsend was her assistant before entering the Community of the Holy Name.

21 Major Echlin was the Registrar of the Diocese of Tasmania.

22 Preserved at ScreenSound Australia: *Coaldrake Collection Compilation: first consignment*, title number 41366; and *Coaldrake Movies Collection: compilation second consignment*, title number 43548.

people a most inspiring glimpse of the Church in Australia – to begin with there are 19 Bishops in copes and mitres walking across the screen looking as if they have stepped straight out of an unexpected shot of Henry V film or an old English frieze.

Finally we go home to a bath in approved Japanese style, soap and throw water over oneself outside the bath, and then ease yourself into the staggeringly hot water and sit and stew. We stagger upstairs wondering why Japanese stairs always have such an angle that they tend to tilt you backwards, and so to bed – or rather "futon" spread on the floor. My last memory is of a mosquito buzzing.

Imaihama[23]

Monday was to be a special day. It was the Feast day of the Holy Guardian Angels which seemed a very auspicious day to set off on the next stage of our journey. As little Kimiko-chan [the recently baptized daughter of Miyazawa from Ito] had been given the name of Angela the day before, we felt the Holy Guardian Angels would be smiling. And they were. With Miyazawa-san [of Ito, not to be confused with the rector of the Odawara church] in the back and the trailer bowling along behind, we bounced and rattled over an impossible road around the superbly beautiful coast. Getting further down the Peninsula which hangs out into the sea below Tokyo we began to command views of ocean and rugged coastline more beautiful than anything I have seen anywhere else. We were making fine pace, no groans from the jeep, with a 10 a.m. meeting of the key laymen of the Peninsula in mind.

Half way to Imaihama we encountered a whole school out for a day's outing. Children in Japan seem to have no fear or understanding of road traffic, especially jeeps. Higher on the hill, we met the big boys, then big girls and so on down to the foot of the hill where we drove through lines of little ones crowding in so close they could almost touch the jeep. Suddenly from nowhere sprang the inevitable dog and for a split second there didn't seem much choice between knocking down the nearest children and killing the dog before their eyes; but somehow or other Frank kept the jeep straight, the dog got off with a bad knock, and the children were untouched.

So we swept on, waving to the boys and girls who always waggle their hands in a sideways wave and say "good-bye," down into a valley with its rivers of rice, and thatched cottages packed in amongst the trees.

At Imaihama we came to the house of Harada-san[24] after encouraging the jeep up what looked like a very bad footpath. It is a beautiful house, two-stories high, tucked into a hillside, with a glorious view of the bay through the surrounding pine trees. The roof is partly thatch and partly tile. We are shown

---

23 Originally spelt in the *Newsletters* by Maida Coaldrake as "Imainohama." This was an older usage which was disappearing by 1950. The name is standardized as Imaihama in this book.

24 She was the caretaker for a wealthy family which owned the house but lived in Tokyo.

Plate 1 Interior of Coaldrake Odawara House, looking over Sagami Bay towards Ōshima. Watercolour by S. Ishigai, 1949.

Plate 2 The rugged Izu coastline and fishing village, c.1951.

Plate 3 Frank Coaldrake and two children looking over the town of Itō, 1952.

Plate 4 The congregation of St. Mary's Church, after Sunday Mass, in the new church grounds, summer, 1951.

Plate 5 The village of Ōse, near Irozaki on the tip of the Izu Peninsula, home of Dr. Kawai and his "cottage church," c.1951. In *Colour Slide Talk Commentaries, 1958*, Frank Coaldrake notes that "over 40 people are in regular touch with the services, bible classes and meetings at this cottage church."

Plate 6 Tokyo, Nihonbashi, November, 1950. This part of Tokyo is now unrecognizable because of the overhead expressways built in the 1960s.

Plate 7 Children at Lake Ippeki Summer Camp, July or August, 1951.

Plate 8 Lake Ippeki Camp, 1951. Rest-stop climbing Mt. Ōmuro. Communion with nature and the "Buddhas of the Fields."

Plate 9 Baptism of William Howard Coaldrake, Itō, May, 1952.

Plate 10 St. Mary's Church, Itō. The reconstituted Quonset hut with new sanctuary and vestry, 1952.

Plate 11 View from new Rectory of Shimoda Highway and Amagi Foothills, 1954.

Plate 12 Cherry blossoms at Itō. Maida Coaldrake with Bill on his first birthday, April 5, 1953.

Plate 13 War and Peace at Nikkō, September, 1953. Disabled returned soldiers begging for alms outside the entry to the Tōshōgū Shrines while students on a school excursion pass by. At right, Maida Coaldrake watches a young Bill Coaldrake asking the soldiers: "itai? itai?" ("Does it hurt?")

Plate 14 Frank Coaldrake preaching in St. Mary's Church on a return visit as Chairman of the Australian Board of Mission in 1959.

into the airy upper room, with its easily moved walls, and balcony catching the sunlight. There is the inevitable drinking of Japanese tea – pale green in colour, bitter and luke warm to the taste – and the nibbling of impossibly sweet biscuits. All the rooms are very beautiful, with flowers arranged in best Japanese style, most interesting and absorbing.

Harada-san and her daughter are two of the few Christians in the Peninsula, having come some four or five years ago to live there. Since then Harada-san, who is a teacher of the ancient Tea Ceremony and of Flower Arrangement, has made her home a centre of Christian influence and gathered together a little group of people who studied and prayed together until such time as we heard of them and their keenness. Now regular services are held in her home; she is one of the advisers on the panel of lay people who are planning the evangelisation of the whole Peninsula, and twice a month a celebration of Holy Communion is made in her home.

While I rested upstairs, an important discussion was in progress in the room below and from it came all manner of information and suggestions which will shape the Mission in that area.[25]

In the afternoon we made up our minds to go looking for a jeep spring, having broken one on our way down in the morning. Now jeep springs are rare even in the big garages of Tokyo or Yokohama. What chance had we of finding one down the Peninsula, let alone of finding a mechanic who could put it in for us! The alternative was a rough patching up job and the prospect of the rest of the week bouncing over bad roads on bad springs. Down the road and into the next village with the fascinating name of Mine [pronounced *me-ne*]; the first little garage had a jeep spring, yes, and yes, he would fix it for us. The Holy Guardian Angels were surely caring for us. Frank could scarcely believe the evidence of his eyes, or even his feet, when he jumped on the spring to test it.

So before us was a delightful village and a free hour to see it. The whole valley, like much of the Peninsula, was alive with Hot Springs (Spa). Through clumps of trees and along the riverbank we could see the steam from the pumping stations. Iris gardens we came to, hurried into blooming for early city markets, by pouring hot water over the beds. Inns advertised their special hot baths. Here and there as we walked through the fields we stepped over bamboo pipelines tucked around with matting which carried the hot water to various points. When we came to a bore the hiss and steam was amazing, and the water we were assured was well over boiling point. In a wide shed, various salts were being dried out of it. As we walked along the road by the river, followed by our usual gathering of shy youngsters (when we stopped the jeep I counted 56 standing around) we could see plots of carnations being grown in an intricate system of wiring and string. It was the first time I had seen decorative flower-growing in this country – always so hungry for rice and vegetables that every tiny clear space must be given to

---

25 Frank Coaldrake's handwritten notes of this "important discussion" are preserved in the Coaldrake Records. See next document in this chapter.

food production. Everywhere women came to their doors to see the two foreigners go by, and they smiled shyly at our greetings. They were completely taken aback at Frank's easy flow of Japanese, as so many people are.

Back to the garage we found everything ready for us and we set off for Harada-san's as evening came on. Just up the road and round the corner in the hopelessly narrow village street a little boy darted straight out from the side of the road in front of our wheels. After the brakes had gone on, neither Frank, I, nor the lass in the back seat, nor especially the little boy's mother who had him safe in her arms, were capable of movement for several seconds. My knees shook all the way home. We had every reason to believe the Angels were working overtime. I think had that Japanese mother known about Angels she would have thought so too.

Then, Evensong by candlelight, due to a fuse in the main electricity supply, and such a nice gathering of neighbours and friends. When the fuse was connected, it was a joy to show them our films. It was also a very great joy to stand up again. From squatting my knees were creaking and groaning to such an extent that my neighbour took pity and sent me an extra cushion. But I learned to ignore the creaks and groans, this being the usual state of Australian knees anywhere else except in the house at Odawara.

With these beautiful tatami covered rooms of Harada-san's and the exquisitely arranged flowers, I felt I had discovered the real Japan for the first time. To add the finishing touches, Harada-san with some of her students performed the "Tea ceremony" for us. There is not space enough here to describe it in all its intricacies of movement and rite, but suffice it to say that it is very beautiful.

And as if to complete my picture of the unspoiled Japan, next morning we decided to take a hot spring bath and sailed off down to the nearest Inn armed with soap and towels. We were shown into a private bathroom out of concession to our Western origin (Japan generally baths as a community gesture!) and in between much splashing and groaning at the heat of a "luke-warm" bath, we had a lengthy discussion on the make-up of a nation which washes its greasy pots with cold water, even in a hot-spa area, yet thinks of a blazing hot bath as the summing up of heaven on earth! We had only sufficient strength to dress and felt if we didn't soon get outside, our fate would be similar to the top of the soap dish which had already floated down the outlet pipe.

Shimoda

Our next appointment was at Shimoda. Before we left we had filled a thermos flask so that we could picnic on the way. Fr. Iida was now travelling with us. We left the coast and climbed across a rib of mountains, getting further into the country which had been completely untouched by western influence, [country] which scarcely seemed to know there had been a war and an Occupation. Up an endless hill we climbed watching the road dip and curve below us. The jeep was hot with the effort. Suddenly at the side of the road we saw a large notice in English – HILL – and straightway we flattened out at the top. It was too much – we wondered just what we had been pulling up for some time!

Shirahama[26] is the most beautiful beach I have seen since I came to Japan. It is the first white beach I have seen, too, for most beaches have grey sand and are very rocky. We pulled up, climbed along the grassy bank, and with a salt breeze blowing in our faces, drank Nescafe and ate a slice of Mrs. Millar of Blackburn's fruit cake. With great foamy waves tumbling out of the indigo sea, and sand dunes behind the beach, we could have been anywhere in Australia. On a slight rise amongst some trees there is a burying ground. With its southerly aspect we think it would be a lovely place to have a family vault – everything is so like Australia and the ocean makes home very close.

Holding the jeep against the strong wind we set off into Shimoda. Most people know about the Open Door Policy and the setting up of a treaty port and an American Consulate in 1856, and how Commodore Perry and Townsend Harris opened Japan once more to Western influence. But you have to visit Shimoda to see just how slight a concession that granting of a treaty port was. A tiny harbour thrust into a rough and wild Peninsula, direct roads to which have been opened only 25 years, could scarcely be an auspicious opening to great trade and political agreements. As in those days, most of the townspeople are directly or indirectly involved in the fishing industry.

We called at the home of a Christian school teacher who formerly played the organ at St. Paul's University College in Tokyo and who is anxious to be used by us to start a church in Shimoda. After working our way past a narrow doorway and screen in a dark passage, we ascended some stairs and found ourselves in two rooms above a shop and just beyond a teacher of Koto (a thirteen-string harp) gave lessons during our visit. Attempts had been made to make the rooms pleasant and livable but nothing could disguise the dingy roofs outside, the noise and the festoons of washing across the windows. But there was a little alcove with a cross and a clean white cloth, together with much used prayer books. The school teacher was a pleasant, intelligent young man who coupled the teaching of physics with that of music in the big Middle School nearby.

———

Circulated by Mrs. E.R. Coaldrake, Hamilton Road, Nundah.
Printed by Brisbane City Printery, Edward Street, Brisbane.

Izu Mission Meetings. Unofficial Minutes kept by F.W.C. [handwritten].

MEETING AT IMAIHAMA ON 2 OCTOBER 1950

2. Relations between Izu Dendo [Evangelism] Mission and Diocese

F.W.C. constantly comparing [Izu] with Bush Brotherhood of St. Paul in Diocese of Brisbane, from out of which Brotherhood District already Roma has been

---

26 The name means "white beach." It refers to the astonishing white sand in a country characterized by black or grey volcanic sand or pebble beaches.

made into a separate parish in the normal manner. So Izu Mission aim is to build congregation which will eventually "hive-off" as separate self-sustaining parish churches...

Newsletter No. 34, **December, 1950.**

NIPPON SEIKO KWAI

C/o B.C.O.F. Army P.O. 214,
Empire House,
Tokyo,
JAPAN.

From – Rev. F. W. Coaldrake

[written by Maida Coaldrake with an addition by Frank]

MAIDA'S IZU JOURNEY (CONTINUED FROM NOVEMBER)

I am always staggered at the schools wherever I go. They are the dominating building of every town and village and, as towns become smaller, somehow the schools seem to grow larger. But I am still working out on what kind of a timetable children attend classes, for wherever you go, on lonely mountain roads or in the cities, there are always groups of children walking home from school.

At the school teacher's house we drank hot condensed milk, very sweet, and chewed very sweet little cakes made of rice and sweet potato flour, decorated with pink icing and little flowers, and talked about the Church – at least everyone else did, while I sat on my aching knees and meditated on the odd music of the Koto, and listened for words I understood of the many that were being flung around.

Outside the shopping area and away from the port, we stopped the jeep and picked up a nice schoolgirl of 17 and said a few words to her equally nice sister. They were two of the daughters of Dr. Kawai, a Christian doctor who has lived for 40 years in the tiny village of Ose ministering to the people of that area. His home has become another of the cottage churches to which Fr. Iida and Frank go regularly to give Holy Communion and take classes.

The road to Ose was even more amazing and rougher than any other roads along which we had come, but as beautiful. We crossed a wide, deep river, passed wooden ship building yards, saw fishing fleets, and diving girls going home. At jetties masses of seaweed, which later in the season will be sent to Hokkaido to be treated and finally made into isinglass, were drying. A portion of the road was still as the last landslide had left it; another portion was being repaired. As usual we edged past buses between cliffs and sea wall. Near Ose we called on a church member who keeps bees, fowls, and grows special plants. He proved to be very sick and it was great encouragement to his wife and to him that we were able to stop to see him and make arrangements for his Communion the next morning. Our exit from that home was very rapid as the jeep was completely blocking the "main" highway and a bus was tooting to pass. The jeep wouldn't start until the co-operative bus driver, encouraged by the whole child populace of the district, had urged the engine along with a crank-handle and much energy.

Ose at last – at the end of the Peninsula and surely at the end of the world. A gallup poll (or some such) names it as the most conservative village in the whole of Japan. With its 6 foot wide main street running alongside a creek and its 125 families of fisher folk, I can well believe it. (Colour Plate 5) The good doctor was out to meet us. The jeep was unloaded well away from the house so that all parts of the movie projector, our food box, sleeping bags and luggage had to be carried up to the house. There was a veritable chain gang at work greatly admired by the collection of villagers. We felt like the old style travelling circus – and indeed a jeep in Japan is a greater attraction for the young and old than ever the circus elephant was.

The Doctor's house smelt strongly of seaweed, antiseptic, and cooking fish, together with the peculiarly pungent aroma of new tatami. Tatami is woven of a certain kind of grass straw and is strongly scented when first woven. Came the usual green tea and friendly talk, the setting up of the projector with the help of the village electrician, family prayers and hymn singing, and then the arrival of more children and friends to see the films and hear a Talk.

That night the floor seemed even harder than before and the primitive pump and washing arrangements even worse. I went to bed making feeble flapping noises at the mosquitoes and thinking fondly of our "Heath Robinson" hot water system at home.

Early the next morning, our "futon" being rolled up and the table prepared the night before as an altar set up, Frank celebrated the Mass with Fr. Iida serving. There is something very conducive of devout worship in these homes where there are no pews or chairs to distract one and only a large flat cushion as a rest. There was so much contrast between the Mass at Ose and the Mass we had at Harada-san's. At Harada-san's all was beauty, the room, the sea through the pine grove far below clear in the rising sun, the three or four autumn crocuses on the altar – though I understood not a word of the service the whole Mass went in and through me and I was completely with the small congregation there. In Ose, that crowded little village, in the doctor's house, we seemed in the midst of all the sweat and toil of wresting a living from the sea (hurried footsteps outside on the cobbles echoed through the room), and amidst all the pain and troubles that flow in and out a doctor's surgery. Yet the Mass was never more real nor more urgently needed.

Here in Izu we are very interested in the whole system of a Cottage-Church in its own right, not just as a half-way house until we build a fine church building, nor even as a means of evangelisation only, which it undoubtedly is – but in its own right, as a cell in the whole Living Church; the church living in the life of the people, in their homes, in the pattern of their hurried, hard-working lives, lifting the sweat and toil into beauty and meaning, and harmony with God's Purpose.

Before we left on our way to Shuzenji [in the centre of the Peninsula], we went to Cape Iro – that magnificent cape on the edge of a terrifyingly rugged cliff

– on the accuracy of whose lighthouse many ships depend for safety. Right on the edge there is a tawdry Buddhist shrine where on stormy days prayers are offered for the safety of those at sea. A high wind was blowing and slight rain was falling. Below the sea gurgled and rose and fell against the black crags. I was glad to be gone.

Winding down the impossibly steep road to the village below, we overlooked a Scandinavian-like fjord, with great high cliffs heavily wooded with firs, and deep blue water sheltered from the ocean by a bar across the narrow opening, outside which the waves thundered. Along both sides at intervals were deep caves, used now for the drying and storing of fishing nets and tackle, used not very long ago for the storing of midget submarines. The quiet village has known very much busier days.

Shuzenji

Shuzenji is noted in tourist books for its wonderful hot springs (one of them even emerges out of the depths of the very cold river) and for its wonderful Buddhist Temple. But I shall remember it for its inn – our first stay in a real Japanese inn, and the difficulty of getting there. There was a moment on our journey when we thought never to see it.

We left Ose in the drizzling rain and began almost immediately an ascent into the mountains which are the backbone of the Izu Peninsula. No words can describe the beauty of the mountains in the rain – the thick forests, home of deer, wild boar, rabbits and many game birds, luxuriant green tipping off into pale gold with the maples, and brown with the autumn cherry. Here and there patches of bamboo with its fragile leaves and delicate bending trunk, lighted up the fir green. Along the banks among the ferns white and mauve daisies, known to us as Easter daisies, were blooming in great masses. I leaned out of the jeep as we went along, and tucked a little spray into the windscreen. What with our St. Christopher medal and the daisies, we felt quite jaunty despite the increasing slush and rapidly closing-in evening.

Coming up towards the Amagi Pass through the valley, we encountered a small road blockage, with one great charcoal supply lorry half over the steep drop, two others looped on trying to pull it out, and ten buses and other lorries waiting to get by. Tourist parties were wandering all over the road. There were two or three great logs down where they had been trying to raise the lorry up, and everywhere clouds of smoke were issuing out of the charcoal burning units [in cars] as drivers took the opportunity to stoke their [own] engines. We joined the interested spectators and pretty soon had our own special group! Then the three of us, Fr. Iida, Frank and I retired to the jeep and opened a tin of pineapple juice and biscuits. Nicely involved in precariously balanced tumblers, half eaten biscuits and opened tins, we suddenly found that the lorry had been moved, the queue was moving and that everybody coming down the mountain was waiting for the little jeep to slip on up. I think you do not need to be told that the jeep wouldn't start. . . .

That was really the beginning of the end. When we did get away and made up the steep gradient, things promised fair. We stopped a big school party bus and spoke to Dr. Kawai's young son who had been in Tokyo for a few days, and then faced the mists and loveliness of the higher regions. Mt. Amagi itself is over four and a half thousand feet high and the Pass well over three thousand, so we had a good climb ahead. It was increasingly beautiful, waterfalls, green glens, colouring trees, and the daisies everywhere. We rounded over the Pass and stopped to admire a lovely bridge and river. Not long after that, the three of us with macs buttoned and trousers tucked in our sox, were running along in the mud and squelch with the rain dripping off our ears and noses, giving the jeep a little help. A man with a huge paper umbrella and geta lifting him high above the mud, passed us walking the other way. A sudden incline and we leaped aboard, and we were off again. It was all down hill fortunately – sometimes we ran with the engine, sometimes without, as the mood took it. Sometimes Frank had to get out and crank, sometimes we got out and pushed. It grew darker and a good deal wetter. The jeep began to find some holes in its hood to let the water in. Through some villages, violently down a slope, on to a flat and then, ten miles from Shuzenji, stop for good. Frank cranked and got wetter and wetter. His "mac" was really only a cotton driving coat. We produced another piece of Mrs. Millar's cake and a slice of apple each, cold comfort but very good to eat. Buses passed with a great splash and went gaily up the hill on their own rather despised producer-gas. Various things were done to the innards of the engine. It got quite dark. We had given up all hope of warmth or finding a roof for the night, when with a little purr and splash we were off again. I think Fr. Iida and I drove every inch of the next few miles as well as Frank. By dint of doing unheard of things with the choke, revving wildly when the engine was about [extinct, and racing madly through] the villages now safety tucked up for the night, we finally saw the lights of Shuzenji through the rain. We were on a nice flat road between rice fields.

When the jeep and trailer finally pulled up outside the very clean and modern Inn, it was hard to distinguish jeep and trailer from its passengers, so uniformly muddy and wet were we. On the doorstep of the inn stood a beautifully kimonoed lady (the mother of one of our Tokyo theological students) waiting to greet us; around us bowed six or so nicely gowned and giggling room maids, who removed our outer garments, bore off cases, food box, shoes and us to the first floor, where a suite of three rooms were waiting for us. In the special alcove for such things hung a picture of a duck. All pictures, and the flowers for the occasions, are always chosen with great care and special reference to circumstances. We expect the duck had something to do with the weather – but we are not sure it didn't have a cross reference to our name [i.e. Coal*drake*]. Kimono – two in fact, one cotton and one padded – were provided, so we sauntered off to the hot spring bath feeling already much more normal. Back again, the fluttery little maids had arranged a table and two charcoal braziers for our tea kettle and heating of food. In Japanese Inns one always eats in one's room with suitable attendants to care for one's needs.

Inside it was warm. Outside, just below our balcony, the swollen river rushed and roared. It took us nearly 30 minutes to bring our kettle to the boil for our much-needed tea. We fried our rice on the brazier, mixing it with oil and fish (needless to say only Fr. Iida used chopsticks). We heated tinned meat and peas, made tea, ate bread and butter, and had pineapple, and tinned milk. We felt much better, then went to sleep.

In the morning we were able to admire the rooms more carefully – being in the new wing we had opportunity to examine the lovely woods and the new tatami, and the structure of the sliding doors and the balcony. At present, with [plans for] building at Ito looming, we are very interested in Japanese craftsmanship. After breakfast during which I consumed an amazing quantity of rice in lieu of porridge, we regretfully took off our kimonos. We had rather fancied a stroll down town in them.

I have been amused by the practice in these hot springs and holiday centres, of Inns turning out all their guests in kimono of the same cut and colour. At Atami any weekend you will encounter dozens of young and old men and women, strolling around the beach and the street stalls looking like members of an orphanage, when actually they just happen to be staying at the same inn. Though intended for resting and the bath, these kimono are always worn in the street. It is a sort of cult. We rather anticipated the fun of joining the cult. Only Fr. Iida wore his with an air – Frank's legs were too long, and I spoilt my appearance by insisting on wrapping the folds the wrong way.[27]

Refreshed by such kind hospitality we were prepared to move on and even cope with the jeep which we did at the nearest "parts" shop. But before we left Shuzenji, I was taken to see our first shrine [temple] – and I am still breathless. Pagan, perhaps, but beautiful, dignified appearance and lay out not unlike a Christian church with side aisles, sanctuary, subdued brass, and polished floor. The real atmosphere of worship could not be disputed. The final touch came with the chanting, in high shrill voices of Buddhist morning hymns coming from somewhere nearby. Fr. Iida told me it was a Buddhist kindergarten!

It was all most impressive. It was borne in on me again how precise must be our teaching of the Faith and how beautiful and dignified must be our ceremonies, and the celebration of the Sacraments. Japanese religion at its best sets a very high standard.

With jeep soaring like a bird, we swooped and swayed down a valley and over a mountain, and near noon stopped on the height above Ito for our final meal. We had jeep-eating down to a fine art – hot water from thermos for the coffee, on one tin plate each we have slices of bread, meat, cheese, jam and a piece of apple. Outside the rain continued so we put out our plates at the end of the meal to be washed by Nature. At 2 p.m. we were in the Government Town Planning Office in Ito examining the location of the site which the Bishop and Standing Committee

---

27   In Japan men and women do up coats and kimono strictly by rule, women left over right and men right over left.

were coming with us to inspect that afternoon. After three hours discussion the Bishop and Committee prepared for their journey back to Yokohama. Two hours later we were eating our dinner in the vestry at the back of the Quonset Hut [Church], St. Mary's, and at 10:30 p.m. we were back in Odawara to find the carpenters had that day been busy placing a new pine floor in our kitchen. Also, on our front terrace stood our new little sunroom, 9 x 6 [feet], of glass and tex, to catch the winter sunshine for long hours of writing, reading and sewing. It is made like a movable bungalow so we can take it with us when we move to Ito.

Autumn is with us and already the thermometer is mostly on the 50 degrees or 60 degrees mark.

Frank adds:

The five teachers from Melbourne A.B.M. and many other parcels from friends have arrived in good condition (except for some of the lollies melted into sticky lumps, and a leaking tin of syrup!) Bundles of wool were very welcome and gratefully accepted by our Japanese friends who sent gifts last year to Australia. The tins of Teddy Bear biscuits opened up well, and are a treat for our Church schoolgirls or other picture parties. The "Rins and Dry" machine from Sydney is most useful on damp washing days.

The jeep developed all sorts of little complaints and was very troublesome, often making us late for appointments, so now we have made a loan venture which meant selling the jeep as first instalment on a "used" Land Rover station wagon that is a big improvement for our many travels. It carries all our luggage inside, and has windows and doors to keep out rain and snow. Snow on the mountains with cold winds tells us Winter has arrived. Right now we are huddled over a charcoal brazier for an hour of letter writing before bed at midnight. We plan to be up at 5:30 a.m. for early start to Tokyo for our month's rations. [There has been] a shortage of tea, coffee, and milk at B.C.O.F. Canteen for two months, but Kawana has come to the rescue with tea, and we have reserves of coffee and tinned milk.

Today we visited the Fuji Film Factory and met again our Bible Study Group there. Because of Izu work I won't be able to see them regularly but Ota-san of Hatano will carry on the good work. Work, if that's what it's called (tho' I enjoy it so much), plentiful than ever, with much travelling around Izu peninsula. Several of our outer centres are really flourishing. At one, started a few months ago, we now have 80 in attendance for our fortnightly visits. We look forward to getting over to Ito to live, tho' we would like to take this old thatched farmhouse with us.

May the Peace that you have helped to spread bring Peace to you at this Christmas Season.

With good wishes to you all,

Yours sincerely,

FRANK and MAIDA

———

Circulated by Mrs. E.R. Coaldrake, Hamilton Road, Nundah.
Printed by Brisbane City Printery, Edward Street, Brisbane.

Izu Mission Meetings. Unofficial Minutes kept by F.W.C. [handwritten].

IZU CHURCH PRELIMINARY COMMITTEE MEETING AT ITO,
3 DECEMBER 1950.

The first meeting of the Committee appointed as a result of the discussions at church members' meeting at Imaihama 2/10/50...

3. Overall Plans.

F.W.C. recalled original strategy: F.W.C. living in Ito working down east coast [of Izu] and [Fr.] Iida living in Numazu working down west coast, and decided to continue on those lines so Iida to move back as soon as possible from Ito [where he had decided to live during Frank Coaldrake's absence in Australia] to live in Numazu and concentrate on Mishima, Shuzenji and west coast, leaving east coast work except as necessary to fill gaps...

Letter from Canon Warren, Secretary of the Australian Board of Missions, to Frank Coaldrake, 4 August 1950.

The Rev. F.W. Coaldrake,
C/- B.C.O.F.,
Empire House,
Tokyo,
JAPAN.

4th August 1950

My dear Coaldrake,

In your letter of the 14th April you asked whether the Board might make available portion of the grant from the Centenary Fund for the Izu Mission in Japan in order that you might arrange for buildings &c. in Ito.

I am pleased to advise that the Board has agreed to this request and it was resolved:

That so much as is needed of the amount of £5,700 from the Centenary Fund as is now in hand for Japan be made available to Mr. Coaldrake as soon as he is able to advise the Board as to the exact amount required.

This makes the way clear for you to proceed, and we shall be glad to hear further from you on the matter as soon as you have anything to report.

We hope that you and Mrs. Coaldrake have had a good passage on your return from Australia.

With kindest regards and every good wish.

Yours sincerely,
M.A. Warren
SECRETARY

Letter from Frank Coaldrake to the Chairman and Secretary, Australian Board of Missions, 11 October 1950.

The Venerable the Chairman and The Reverend the Secretary,
Australian Board of Missions,
14 Spring St.,
Sydney

Dear Mr. Archdeacon [Robertson] and Canon [Warren],

After inspecting fourteen blocks offering for sale in Ito at present we have finally selected the land we want for the Church. Everyone thinks it will be a very good site. I will enclose a full description and a map with this letter. You will see that the site is near the centre of the city. There is a vacant small Japanese style house on one corner of the block which could be used as part of the Hostel and Training Centre. There are no other buildings on the block and it is all under cultivation.

The fact that it is "farmland" in the Lands Department Registers is the one stumbling block to its purchase. Under the post-war Land Reform Law land under cultivation cannot be taken for any other use without the express permission of Agricultural Land Control Bureaux at the local and Prefectural levels. Further, such land cannot be sold except to a farmer.

The owner has recently decided to sell because he needs money quickly. He was a Diet member but was defeated at the last election and plans to stand again at the next. It is in connection with his political career that he urgently needs money! He has applied to the local and State Land Bureaux for the re-registration of the land as residential land so that he can sell it. The matter should be finalised at the end of October and he is confident that his request will be granted. He will then be able to sell at the prices prevailing for land in that part of the city, about 5,000 yen per tsubo. (1 tsubo is 36 square feet.)

He has given special consideration to our enquiries about the land because he has a young son about whose future he is concerned. This concern is a very real feature of post-war family life and I believe it is a valid argument for a Japanese parent considering the sale of land adjoining his own residence. He would like very much to have us next door. He is a Waseda University Professor who spent twelve years in the United States as a student and knows what the church is without being himself a Christian. He has cut the price to us to the minimum to meet his own financial needs and has offered the land and the small house on it to us for Yen 2,500,000. (A£3,200). This is a price per tsubo of Yen 2,800, which is about half the price at which land in that part of the town has been sold in recent months. Sales have been effected recently of land within a quarter-mile of here at Yen 20,000 per tsubo, by Australian standards a fantastic price.

I have had the Bishop and Standing Committee of the Diocese inspect the block and have consulted Bishop Viall in Tokyo. There is no question that it is a very suitable block in a good position and offered at a very cheap price. I have reached the conclusion that it is the block we should buy. Mrs. Coaldrake agrees with me. Of course the re-registration of the land as a residential block is a pre-requisite to any sale.

In thinking about the purchase of this block at this price I have remembered that in my report to the Board in February I estimated £2000 for an acre or more of land. Detailed inquiries into building costs show that there has been a big drop in the last year. The price per square is now little more than half what it was. As to the size of the block, the Bishop and others have said that it is more than large enough for our needs. While I do not agree with that I have reckoned that because it is level there will be no unusable portions. I enclose a plan of the block showing one way in which the buildings could be placed.

In balancing increased land values and decreased building costs I find that the result for the whole project works out at about the same total. I consider that the amount of £5700 promised by the Board should now be used in the following way:

Item	Previous estimate	Present estimate
Land in Ito 1½ acres	£2,000	—
" " " ¾ acre and small house	—	£3,200
Transfer of Church and Improvements	£200	£400+
Camp extensions and equipment	£500	£200
Residence in Ito	£2,000	£1,200
Hostel and Training Centre	£1,000	—
" " " additions to house now on block	—	£300
Mission Office and Garage	—	£200
TOTAL	**£5,700**	**£5,500+**

Increased because enlargement necessary to cope with increasing membership.

I would have liked to put the matter up to you at the stage to which I have now brought this report. But the owner was pressing for an answer to his special offer to us and there was not time to consult you. Also I have been in Tokyo only once in the last seven weeks, when I sent my preliminary report to the Chairman. I have relied on your letter advising me of the Board's decision in July and the information given me at the Board meeting in February that there was then already £3,500 in hand and have said that we will buy the block as soon as the registration is effected. That is, I have closed with the offer. This letter is both a report of the results of enquiries and an application for funds to make the purchase.

I am conscious of the fact that I have pushed ahead in this matter but the chance to get this particular block was too good to be missed. I have gone ahead on the assumption that it would neither embarrass the Board nor be contrary to their own judgement of the matter. The only immediate need is for the purchase money £3,200. The payment of further portions of the grant will be the deciding factor in our use of the block and it can of course lie idle for some time. I will wait your advice on what the Board can do about the building items. Our first move would be to put the Temporary Church on the block (Estimated cost is £400).

Transfer of money will no doubt require Government approval. Canon Warren may know a better way to do it but I suggest that one way would be to let me handle it through the banking channels I have established for the regular transfer of funds for working expenses. I will enclose a letter to the Commonwealth Bank Manager which can be used for that purpose.

My enclosed note on Purchase Procedure will explain what will be done with the Land Purchase money when it reaches my hands. I hope you will agree to the inclusion of the condition I have proposed whatever else you may want to include regarding the wishes of the Board.

I expect this will find you both very busy with the visit of the Archbishop of Canterbury. I hope everything will run smoothly in that matter and that the Centenary Celebrations will worthily commemorate the century of wonderful work.

With our very best wishes,

Yours sincerely,

Rev. Frank W. Coaldrake

NOTE ON PURCHASE PROCEDURE

In connection with the purchase of land for Headquarters for the Izu Mission I have made enquiries at Government Offices and consulted Bishop Viall and the Bishop and Standing Committee of the Diocese.

Under Occupation Regulations and Japanese Law the purchase of land by a non-Japanese national for any purpose other than his own private residence is an involved and almost impossible undertaking.

Under Japanese Taxation Laws any sale of land involves both the vendor and the purchaser in the payment of sales tax at a very high rate, but religious bodies recognised by the Government do not have to pay the Land Sales Tax. Coaldrake and the A.B.M. are not such a registered religious body. The Nippon Seiko Kwai Corporation is.

The lands of churches, rectories, schools and other church institutions throughout Japan are held by this Corporation. The unification of the Dioceses of the N.S.K. is still in the course of completion and the Landholding Corporation is still a group of individual Diocesan Corporations. The Nippon Seiko Kwai South Tokyo Diocese Corporation is the landholding body for this Diocese. It was originally the S.P.G. Corporation but has been changed to the Diocesan Corporation and lands not originally S.P.G. are now in its hands. This is part of the overall plan of development adopted by the Bench of Bishops and General Synod. The Secretary of the South Tokyo Diocese Corporation is the Reverend Y. Muraoka of Kawasaki.

Bishop Viall has expressed complete confidence in Muraoka's competence and reliability. The procedure proposed by the Bishop and Standing Committee of the Diocese is the same as that outlined to me by Bishop Viall. It is as follows:

The land should be the subject of a contract of sale made between the vendor, Fujii Shinichi, and the South Tokyo Diocese Corporation, Muraoka acting as its representative. The purchase money paid at the time of the contract could be paid directly by Coaldrake to the vendor, but the receipt by the vendor would be made to the Diocesan Corporation.

At the same time the A.B.M. should give the Diocesan Corporation a statement of the gift and its purpose. At this point I personally wish to make a strong recommendation. It is that in the statement of gift there should be included a condition in something like the following terms:

> The A.B.M. hereby gives to the Nippon Seiko Kwai South Tokyo Diocese Corporation the land in Ito described as blocks 960, 961, 962/1, 963/1, 964/1, 965/1, to be used for the N.S.K. South Tokyo Diocese Izu Mission Church and Headquarters, with the condition that the land is to be used only for and by the Izu Mission and shall not be sold or in any way alienated from the work of that mission without the explicit approval of the A.B.M., and this condition shall apply even should the direct connection between the A.B.M. and the Izu Mission cease. This statement of gift and conditions is to be permanently affixed to the Title Deeds of the land.

I am making this recommendation as a result of statements made to me by Bishop Mann, Bishop Viall and Fr. Arnold on different occasions, and as a result of my own observations. Personnel of corporations and staff can be completely changed within a few years and Japanese Church leaders have given proof that they do not regard a financial trust in the way we do and do not realise the continuing responsibilities of a corporation. I hope to see established an Izu Mission which will outlast Coaldrake and which will be capable of extension beyond his particular plans. The basis of any such permanent expansion will be the possession of a block of land such as we are now buying. The Japanese think it is bigger than we need. They might easily decide a few years from now to put a Clergy Rest House or a Diocesan Mission School or some such institution on the block with no relevance to the Izu Mission. Or they might sell part or all of it at an advantageous price and buy a small cheap block somewhere else. It is to prevent any such action by the Corporation that I propose the above condition.

DESCRIPTION OF THE BLOCK

The area is 900 tsubo, i.e. three-quarters of an acre. There is a slight slope across the whole block with a total drop of about one foot. A small two roomed house, vacant and in good order, stands in one corner. The rest of the block is under cultivation, vegetables, mandarins, and rice. On the east and south the block is hedged and bounded by a narrow road. Entrance to the road on the east is from stone stairs so no vehicles use it. Road on the south is to be widened in the future according to Town Planners. On the west the boundary is a hedge with a field two feet lower down on the other side. On the north the boundary is a stone wall dropping down to the garden and residence of the owner of this block. The whole piece lies on a level shelf reached directly from the main street of the town by a fifty yard side street and thirty stone stairs. The main street winds round a short curve and climbs to pass level with the back of the block. Entrance for vehicles is at this point with a twenty foot run along the narrow road already mentioned as on the south side. The height of the block puts it above the roofs of two and three storeyed buildings in the shopping centre of the town immediately below, in a northerly direction. To the south the slope runs away up to the mountains. To east and west there is a small area of the shelf before the slopes run down to the flat. The block is readily accessible from all parts of the town and in plain sight of the whole town. There are good views of sea and mountain. It is well situated with regard to Secondary Schools which Hostel boarders would be attending. The station, being on the edge of the town, is fifteen minutes walk.

Of the two blocks mentioned in my letter to the Chairman on 20/9/50 the hilltop near the station was withdrawn from sale. This is the other.

Confidential Report from Frank Coaldrake to the Australian Board of Missions, January 1951 [document undated].

REPORT ON LAND PURCHASE

On October 5th, 1950, the Bishop of the Diocese, the Chairman of the Diocesan Property Trust, my assistant, Rev. F.M. Iida, my chief layman, Mr. H. Miyazawa, and myself, met Professor S. Fujii and discussed the purchase of a block of land from him. After the Bishop and Chairman had expressed their approval of the block, we discussed price with the owner and agreed on the sum of 2,500,000 yen. I then signed a promise to purchase the land when the money had arrived from Australia. At the same time the Bishop signed the Japanese equivalent of my undertaking which was written in English.

December, 18th, 1950 was eventually appointed as the day of settlement. I took with me a highly recommended lawyer from Odawara as my legal adviser to watch the interests of the A.B.M. Muraoka as Chairman of the Diocesan Property Trust, was to have negotiated the purchase on behalf of the church but at the last minute we heard that he could not come because he was ill. My assistant Rev. F.M. Iida was also present.

I refused to make full payment of the money until the registration of the sale at the Lands Office had been made and this could not be done without Muraoka present. The owner pressed for payment of a large proportion of the money and as payment was already overdue I agreed to pay sixty percent then, and the balance on completion of the registration. My lawyer having assured me of the validity and reliability of the re-classification of the land as a residential block, and having explained that the payment of a deposit and deferment of balance until registration was a usual contract upheld by law, the preparation of the documents was undertaken.

Usual custom was followed in having a clerk from the Lands Office to write the documents. While he was writing, the owner asked my lawyer to go outside with him so that he could "make an explanation." When they came back I asked my lawyer to tell me what had been said to him. At that the owner objected but I insisted so the lawyer took Iida and myself outside and recounted what had been said to him. It was that no mention of the price should be made in the presence of the clerk, no money should be paid in his presence, the price should be written into the document later, and the price to be reported should be 410,000 yen.

I asked the reason for this and was told that it would save the vendor paying a huge tax on the transaction. (We ourselves, as the church, do not have to pay tax on land purchase). I objected to being a party to such a procedure, and discussed the matter with the lawyer and Iida. They both assured me that it was the usual practice and that the Government realised it was always done. The lawyer assured me that he had never had anything to do with a land deal where it had not been done. When I asked him "But is it honest?" he answered, "Well, it is not honest, but it is custom." Iida assured me that both Muraoka and the Bishop knew that this was to be done and the lawyer reminded me that since Muraoka would be making the transaction it was out of my hands. Somewhat staggered by the whole business, I returned to the room, and after the clerk had been asked to go outside for a while, I paid sixty percent and the lawyer signed the interim documents on behalf of Muraoka, January 8th being agreed on for the final transaction.

Christmas and New Year activities and sicknesses prevented my discussing the matter with the Bishop or Muraoka until the latter arrived in Ito for the final meeting.

On January 8th, 1951, before going to meet the Vendor, I met Muraoka and discussed the matter with him and Iida.

I asked Muraoka if he knew that it was intended to report the selling price at 410,000 yen. He said he did not know the actual figure, but had agreed with the vendor on the principle. (The actual figure is the Government assessment of the value of the land). It had to be discovered by indirect enquiries, and was not known at the time of the discussion between Muraoka and the vendor on October 5th, 1950. It should be noted that this assessment is not fixed as a maximum price for the sale of the land. There is no control on selling price of land at present).

Muraoka gave as the vendor's reasons for requiring this that it would save him a huge tax on the sale and also that it would avoid bad feeling among neighbouring landowners whose land would be revalued for rates if the sale were registered at such a price. I reminded Muraoka that the vendor had on October 5 given as his only reason for refusing to reduce the price below 2,500,000 yen that neighbouring land owners would be angry with him for cutting down the value of their land.

In the course of a long, and sometimes heated, discussion Muraoka assured me that this practice had always been followed because it is "a Japanese custom." He declared that it had always been done in any Church land deal he had been a party to whether the money had come from C.M.S., S.P.G. or America. He constantly referred to "Coaldrake's special honesty," so that I had to remind him that it was more than that, our responsibility as stewards of the Church. He urged upon me that he would give me the receipt for the whole 2,500,000 yen to send to the Board, and that the responsibility for the fraudulent statement would be his, so that I need not worry. He said that the custom was so strongly established that if the sale were to be reported as 2,500,000 yen, the Government would assume that this was something less than one third of the actual figure and tax accordingly!

Eventually I told him what I proposed to do and we went to see the vendor.

I first asked the vendor to write the selling price into the documents as 2,500,000 yen. He refused to do this, insisting that it must be written in as 410,000. I then told him that I refused to be party to such a lie and asked him if he would write a vague but not untrue statement such as "410,000 yen and other valuable consideration" – though in Japanese it becomes rather "410,000 etc. etc.!" He asked me what I would answer if anyone asked me what the "other valuable consideration" had been, and I told him I would say "2,090,000 yen." He thereupon refused to write that. I then said that I would not pay any more money, called the whole deal off and asked him to refund what I had paid him.

Muraoka had urged me not to do this saying that I would never afterwards be able to buy land in Ito. The vendor then produced the undertakings signed on October 5th, 1950 and said that before he signed he had been told by the Bishop and Muraoka that they would agree to the Registration of the Sale at the figure set by the Government assessment of the land. He therefore expected the Seiko Kwai to keep its promises and Coaldrake to pay the money.

I asked Muraoka if the matter had been discussed in my absence and before signing the contract and he said that it had been.

It appeared to me that I had not only been tricked, but trapped, that I had to honour the undertaking given to this non-Christian, and that my dispute really lay with my colleagues. I stated this and paid the money and the registration of the sale was made at the Lands Office at the figure 410,000 yen. Two receipts were written, one for 410,000 yen for the land which was exhibited at the Lands Office, and one for "2,500,000 yen for the land, house, fences, trees etc. etc." which may be sent to the A.B.M. In addition, the Bishop and Muraoka have signed a receipt for the sum of A£3,115 from the A.B.M. for the purchase of the land.

The thing that I found particularly disturbing in this whole business was that the Church was expected to conform to local custom even though that custom was plainly dishonest and recognised as a bad custom. No matter how strongly I expressed the thoughts of the people back in Australia who contributed the money, I was told that the Church in Japan could not be expected to break with the usual custom. Because of this, and because it was stated that monies from other Mission Boards and Societies had been used in the same way, I brought the matter before the Anglican Missionaries' conference in Tokyo on January 11th and 12th, 1951, at which over forty of our missionaries and all Japanese Bishops and National Church Council officials were present.

I asked particularly if I could be assured that it had not been usual practice to make fraudulent returns, and asked for a consideration of the necessity of breaking away from national customs that were contrary to basic morality and Christian faith. After some rather desultory conversation and discussion the matter lapsed till a later session when I moved:

That this meeting of missionaries affirms the principle that honesty and openness in financial dealings is implicit in the Christian life and recommends that the Nippon Seiko Kwai take every opportunity to alter local customs which involve financial dishonesty.

The motion was seconded. The Presiding Bishop then rose and said he thought it better not to pass the motion because "there would need to be a hundred" other such motions. Bishop Viall then said he thought the motion should be rejected as inopportune. He thought it expressed the convictions of the meeting, but doubted if such a conference was competent to make such a recommendation. He also thought we would have to start making similar recommendations to our Boards back home. No one else was prepared to speak and on being put the motion was rejected by about 30 votes to 2.

Because I have been handling the A.B.M.'s money, I would like them to know what has happened. I feel a personal responsibility for having failed to ensure an honest transaction, and cannot say how deeply embarrassed I am at the thought of building our church on land got by these means as the headquarters for our work of converting the people of that area.

Over and above that, I am puzzled as to what had better be done, or not done, about the standards of our church. Though nobody would publicly say so, at a session of the Missionary conference, yet several missionaries said to me privately that they were very glad to hear me tackling the matter because they had known much dishonest dealing, both before and since the war. These private statements were made by missionaries from America, England, Canada and New Zealand. I would be very glad to have your counsel in this matter.

Newsletter No. 35, February, 1951.[28]

CHRISTIANITY IN JAPAN

C/o B.C.O.F. Army P.O. 214,
Empire House,
Tokyo,
JAPAN.

From – Frank and Maida Coaldrake (Maida writing.)

Odawara, Japan.

Arrival at Kure

We were tying up at the wharf at Kure – the centre of the B.C.O.F. Occupation Area in the south on the main island of Japan. The hot dusty collection of

---

28 The first part of this *Newsletter* is out of chronological order with the preceding documents in this chapter because it is a review of the first six months in Japan by Maida Coaldrake.

wharves and buildings lay in a hot dusty hollow of hills, surrounded by oily water.

Perhaps, I had been victim of a too-efficient wartime propaganda; perhaps the pleasant round-faced, white-shirted, half-western Chinese of Hong Kong were too recently in mind. Whatever it was, when the Customs officials came aboard at Kure armed with sheaves of paper to set our landing in progress, I felt in myself an instant recoil.

They looked too like the pictures of their fellow-countrymen who had overrun the New Guinea forests. In their anxiety to carry through the new American official routine of duty, they were too brusque – until they smiled and wiped the perspiration from their heads. Then they were just ordinary rather harassed men doing an unfamiliar job to the best of their ability.

But the impression lasted. The streets, still lined with the rubble of war destruction, were untidy and rough. The houses, mostly shanty, the street stalls and shops, unkempt. Everything was hot and dusty, including the people. You had to remember firmly that soap was an unknown luxury and that the poverty and shortages were the legacy of a war that was five years passed, before things came into perspective.

An influx of business men into our carriage on the journey north didn't do much towards helping me adjust myself to this new country. Forty of them poured in, chose seats and having first taken off their shoes, they stood on their seats and divested themselves of all their outer garments settling down for a journey of eating, spitting and snoring in a varied collection of striped underpants and athletic singlets.

A greater spur

I was glad that I did not find the Japanese entirely pleasing on first acquaintance. I had come prepared to love him and spend the rest of my life working alongside him.

The strange, the unlovable characteristics and habits are, so many of them, fruit of a pagan society, that I have all the more spur to my intent to live the Faith out, change the community which produces him, into a Christian community. For over and over again you see proven the thesis that you cannot superimpose on one culture another alien culture without corroding the very heart of that culture, unless at the same time you understand completely and absorb also the spiritual basis, in this case Christianity. Western civilisation, for all that it often fails abysmally to live up to its Christian origins, is rooted and grounded in the Church, and so much of its culture is understandable only if this is remembered. Yet here in Japan we have a nation which in a short space of time changed its whole life and outlook to meet a new world, adopting with great skill that which seemed good and useful, and leaving out that which seemed unessential.

So now everywhere you find contradictions – in the status of women who by law have everything we have at home, but by custom are still slave to their husbands, their households and their kitchens; in the conducting of business; in the use of such amenities as electricity; in the education system.

Lovable individual

But whatever one feels about the man in the street and however one exercises Christian charity over him, one does love the individual. Sometimes one loves him so much that inability to do something for him, or inability to express oneself in an incredibly difficult language, makes one nearly burst with love.

I feel that way about the scrubby children who hang around the car when it is parked outside the church. I feel that way about the old women we pass on the roads, burdened down by their huge loads of wood and vegetables.

I feel that even more about the nice girls of 17 or 18 who this year are at school and next sweating in the fields from dawn to dark, all day, every day, or groping in the black holes of kitchens with which every house is plagued.

Every now and then you see in the editorial columns of the press, or in letters to the editor, a plea to women to take advantage of the new laws, to make more system in their homes, to read more, take an interest in things outside the home, attend the lectures and the classes in arts and crafts which are now available to them.

At the same time there are pleas to men to help their womenfolk enjoy life more – for there, seemingly lies the crux of the matter. For until a woman attains a ripe old age, becomes "Obasan" the grandmother, the unquestionable authority in the home, her development, her leisure, her thoughts and aspirations, are given as little consideration as any of the useful but unbeautiful kitchen utensils.

Poor little housewife

From the little I have seen already it is obvious that the routine of any household is such that it makes a slave of somebody, whether teeny maid or wife. It is so unmethodical, so cumbrous.

Apart from the endless fanning of charcoal and the chopping of vegetables in the dark kitchen, I think it is the washing which hangs most heavily around the housewife's neck. Whatever she does, whether it be work in the fields all day, or work in the house all day with children under foot in the crowded rooms, the washing must be done.

In cold water by the pump or in the running water of the gutter outside the kitchen door, which also serves as a garbage carrier, sometimes in the bath water after the whole family has had its soak – but always the eternal washing, rub, rub, rub, with little or no soap to help it along. And everyday, the bamboo pole of washing slung outside the house....[29]

---

29 These dots do not indicate an omission but a literary device by Maida Coaldrake to indicate "and so on."

In one household I know well, five children and two adults make enough washing to keep the nice little wife going at it hard at 10 o'clock at night, squatting on the bathroom floor surrounded by wooden tubs of soiled clothes.

You can imagine what my weekly wash-day has done for the neighbours! Thanks to the Rins-and-dry, my most faithful servant, my whole washing blowing in the wind by 10 a.m. …and sometimes we have seven sheets. All the washing on one day!

An opportunity to help

My first opportunity to do something concrete about this household routine, this kitchen situation, has been given me and I seized upon it joyfully.

A young and able woman, a catachumen of the Church in Ito, has a dressmaking school and wants, now that she has moved into a new and well appointed building, to turn it into more than a school for young women who wish to learn the art of "Western-style" dressmaking. She wants her students to learn something of the household and life of the western woman whom they know only through pattern books and the film.

In addition to the ancient Japanese arts, she wants them taught how to behave in a Western world of which they have already adopted many customs.

She wants me to help her. At present I am very limited by my scanty vocabulary but Frank has been a willing interpreter going to great lengths to make sure the class of forty grasps the point. There was one morning when he had me standing in stockinged feet on the teacher's desk to demonstrate some point which I was sure I had already made clearly. …

But the whole project has great possibilities for the future.

The White Season

Snowflakes drifting across the hills outside remind me of the White Christmas that we nearly had. The real "White" season fell on us unexpectedly a few days later when we were in Tokyo to attend a conference of Anglican missionaries from all over Japan.

Our house at Odawara, being 600 years or more old, is allowed the privilege of changing its position every now and then. In winter with the intense cold, the lovely, highly polished floorboards shrink and leave little gaps. The sliding doors relax and leave spaces for draughts, the levels of the floor alter. An earthquake now and then shakes the foundations – so, in winter, it is very hard to keep an even temperature and by January we have given up the fight.

We just open up the house, encourage the sun, wear many woollies, eat hot food and live quite happily and very healthily.

But white or not, a missionary's Christmas has its moments – and for a novice at the game, this Christmas had almost too many! Frank went down with aches and pains and a cough on Friday, right in the midst of wrapping of parcels and gathering of a multitude of things to take to Ito, 35 miles away.

We patched him up sufficiently to get away on Saturday afternoon, the vehicle loaded down with food presents, flowers, and a tree or two we collected on the road!

At the Church there was a message to say Fr. Iida, the assistant priest, was also down with the ache and pain and cough and couldn't do his field trips for Christmas Communions.

We had just begun a grand-sized spring cleaning of the Quonset Hut made especially necessary by the recent evacuation of Fr. Iida and his two boys after a six months' stay. Little gangs of people were beginning to nibble at jobs – but as ever, we were up against the old attitude to work displayed by people who do not earn their living by manual labour, and we had to plunge into every job head foremost ourselves, to inspire them.

Miracle of Christmas

Nativity plays and Christmas parties or no Christmas Communions for our widely scattered family was the heart of the matter – so at 7 p.m. I found myself alone in Ito, Frank having left to cover half the Peninsula by Evensong on Sunday.

My twenty or so Japanese words worked overtime. I almost stood on my head demonstrating.

But the Hut-Church began to shine. The Crib was finished. A tree decorated. Silver and brass polished. Flowers and candles ready to put in place for Midnight Mass as soon as Sunday's Evensong was over. And arranged neatly in position were piles of towels (striped), from the Coaldrake linen press, curtain material, from the Coaldrake sewing box, a doll, a lamb, pins and ribbon and string ready for the Nativity Play.

When a very dusty and tired priest arrived back in Ito, he found an exhausted but triumphant wife organising the last stages of the cocoa making. . . . When you remember that most of the helpers were very new Christians. . . .

Perhaps, because of that, the children's party was quite wonderful for us all, the Nativity scenes and the carols, very real, and the quiet of Midnight Mass in the shining church a very beautiful Christmas.

Outside in the fishing village the cold wind was blowing dust and scraps of paper along the dirty streets, and some loud-voiced youths shouted to each other.

We wanted the whole pagan town to share the miracle with us.

"Just an earthquake"

Not long after Christmas we spent the night in the vestry of the Quonset Hut Church in Ito, curled up in sleeping bags. At half past three a.m. I was raised on my elbow trying to steady down the beating of my heart and the swaying of the bamboo couch on which I was lying.

"Just an earthquake," said Frank turning over.

But "just an earthquake" lasting sixty seconds is a very long earthquake. The buildings around us were rumbling and cups on the vestry shelves rattling in an ominous way. The newspaper next day was very scientific about it –

"considerable strength, lasting for about a minute rocked the Kanto region at 3.32 a.m. Tuesday. The epicenter of the quake was in the northern part of Tokyo Bay. Vertical rocking was slight but horizontal shaking was severe. Power lines in Yokohama were broken in nine places.... Frightened residents ran outdoors and clocks stopped."

I went to sleep finally consoling myself with the thought that we are "strangers and pilgrims here," a phrase which always springs to mind when we have a quake. There's such an uncertain feeling clutching you when the very earth sways underfoot.

To glorify his Church

And that thought is very much in mind again as I finish off these reflections. Last night from Radio Australia we had news of the Papuan tragedy – the tragic eruption of Mt. Lamington and the consequent disaster to life and property on our mission station at Sangara.

We did what we could, commending the native church and the souls of our missionaries to the prayers of the little congregation gathered this morning at Odawara for the Feast of the Conversion of St. Paul, and ourselves praying to God Who is All-Good that He will use even this moment for the strengthening and glorifying of His Church.

Circulated by Mrs. E.R. Coaldrake, Hamilton Road, Nundah.
Printed by the Daily Examiner Pty. Ltd., Prince Street, Grafton.

Newsletter No. 36, March, 1951.

NIPPON SEIKO KWAI

C/o B.C.O.F. Army P.O. Ebisu,
Tokyo,
JAPAN.

From – Rev. F.W. Coaldrake

[written by Frank and Maida Coaldrake]

March 1951

REFLECTIONS IN A *KOTATSU*

Maida writes:

Each season in this fascinating country produces its own special fascinations and peculiarities. Driving through town at the beginning of the winter I was staggered and alarmed to see a number of people moving about the streets wearing white nose and mouth masks, such as we see only in operating theatres in Australia. I closed my eyes and remembered the many vaccines which had been poured into me in Australia with grateful thanks and asked in a trembling voice what was the matter. The matter? Why nothing was the matter. People were just hoping to protect themselves from the common cold, or else, with a cough on them, were protecting their neighbours. I brightened. A splendid idea, I thought until I discovered that the masks were rarely washed and that when they were, it was in cold water! Since then I have become accustomed to the muffled voices, the strange appearance and the consequent sniffing which must go on in Winter. The hairdresser's assistant this morning smiled over such a mask slung from her ears and every second man, woman, and child is now disguised.

A Kotatsu is another seasonal outcrop. In prospect, Japanese Winters held no terrors for me, brought up on cold Tasmanian weather, but I have since decided that anyone arriving in Japan for the first time in Dec. or Jan. would be shocked. The cold may be equalled elsewhere, but I think it would be difficult to find houses which more nearly resemble ice-boxes. Every door, sliding wall and window fits badly, due to the common practice of building quickly with unseasoned timber. In our ancient house, bamboo slats are the only apology we have for a ceiling, and away beyond the slats soars the thatched roof. The result is there are only two places one can be warm in any house – in the bath where you gradually boil away altogether, 114 deg. F. being the correct temperature, or in bed, where if you accept usual hospitality you are flattened out under the weight of huge eiderdowns. There is one other place you can seek only in moments of leisure, under a Kotatsu. Yesterday, while snow and sleet drifted past the window of a room in Ito, I had my second experience of a Kotatsu.

Most of our cooking and heating is done by charcoal. The Kotatsu is a small charcoal stove with a wooden frame like a chicken coop over the top. On top of this is placed a blanket, then a great thick eiderdown. Under this you slide as much of your frozen body as you can, draw in a back rest, fold your hands and relax. Of course you could do the family mending or write letters, but the steady warmth creeping into your bloodstream has anything but an urge about it. The inclination is to let the world slip by and just stay there sipping tea, and meditating.

And so I did. . . . It is five months since I arrived in Japan for the first time, six months since we left Australia. What are the most lasting impressions of these months?

We berthed at Cairns on a steamy, hot Sunday morning and walked up the wide streets to the Church of St. John. It is a high, cool church, with a cloister open down one side, and palm trees rustling in the garden between the church and the Sunday School. The Sunday School on its stilts and lattice-work, buzzes with voices and singing. Our communion hymn, "Let all mortal flesh keep silence. . . ." with its memories for me of youth camps at Collinsvale and chilly early mornings over Collins Gap, brings the whole known and loved Church close. After Mass we go to the Rectory with the Parish Priest, Fr. Copp, and breakfast in the airy house whose shutters are already drawn against the blazing morning sun. To me, Cairns, with its brilliant greens, dazzling white streets, houses without fireplaces, and the great red poinsettias, was a surprise. But here was the Church and the Faith, news of people we know and snippets of parish progress.

Many days later we slip into Manila Bay. We are to be given landing permits for the few hours we are in port, so I rush down to the cabin to change ship wear for dress and sandals. The ship is suddenly still, and I look up to find we are inside the breakwater. Is this a graveyard for ships? As far as one can see are the shattered wrecks of ships of every kind. It is a sad, depressing sight. It is my first encounter with the devastation of a war we are too easily forgetting. More than 400 ships were sunk in that harbour by American bombs. We get ashore finally through the crowd of sweating coolies, and walk into the city. Overhead a helicopter whines. Policemen patrolling the streets bristle with guns. Each cafe and eating house we pass, has some such notice as "Please leave your firearms here." The new city rising out of the ruins has some magnificent modern buildings, but all around are the ruins of greater and more beautiful buildings, riddled with machine-gun shot, blackened and burnt. We post some letters in the huge, half-built post office, having first counted out the small money allowance and keeping enough for an emergency taxi fare. Then we make our way to the Episcopal Church which is in the care of the American Missionary Societies. Fr. Swifte opens the door of the Rectory. "Do come in. We have just had a party and supper will be late." We have a lovely supper. American style – iced water, bread and jam with our meat course, chilled vegetables, cold sliced meat, custard. The Church is new and temporary, but well built for that hot climate and beautifully furnished in light oak woods. The vestry and kitchenette would be the envy of most rectors and their wives. It is the kind of high standard of building and convenience which I have since learned to expect from the Americans.

In the cool evening we call on Bishop Binstead. Bishopscourt is a Spanish-style mansion in white stucco, with iron grilles over the glassless windows, and palm trees rustling in the garden. The Bishop and his wife receive us with fans set at convenient intervals on the floor in the manner in which we use radiators at home. The Bishop is very interested in our plans, having himself spent many years in Japan.

It is a very unsettled country we learn as we drive out to the Theological Seminary. Despite the fact that the vast majority of the people are nominally Roman Catholics, and their great institutions – hospitals, convents, schools are everywhere, there is no security for life or personal property. Bandits swarm the country roads and hills. Citizens must bar their doors and windows against robbers. Graft in the Government and dishonesty in business is beyond description. Most people carry firearms – hence the notices which so intrigued us on our walk from the port.

The Theological Seminary has the most beautiful garden I have ever seen. It is like the most carefully tended of Botanical Gardens and when it is suddenly floodlit for our benefit I catch my breath. The buildings themselves are temporary, having once housed a mental asylum! This accounts for certain odd features such as the low ceilings and the carefully wired verandahs. But it is admirably suited for its purpose as a college and has a surprisingly cool and quiet atmosphere about it. We met the pleasant American Fathers who are in charge of the training. Compline was in the Chapel with rows of small black men in white or black cassocks, according to their year of status. Among them were some members of the Aglapayan Church (priests) who were undergoing refresher courses before being received into the ministry of the Anglican Communion. This Church with its membership of two million, has had a chequered history since its secession from the Roman Catholic Communion and is now in communion with our own Church. The students sang Compline in English Plainsong which seems to suit their native musical ability so well.

Back to the city. We see the Chapel at St. Luke's Mission Hospital in slum town. We drive through crowded China town. Despite the late hour the whole world seems to be out and about with his family, visiting his neighbour. All the houses are open, so we have an excellent view of Manila's home life. In a brightly lit barber's shop on the corner we see an immaculately coated and smooth-haired barber's assistant shaving a customer. The chromium plated atmosphere is rather spoiled by the yellow swimming trunks which are his only lower garment.

At the wharf amid much rush and heat and many officials and police, we say goodbye to the American missionaries who have been so kind to us. It is difficult to believe we didn't know them until 5 p.m. I finally fall asleep in the oven-of-a-cabin listening to policemen on duty chattering below us on the wharf.

Nothing I had read or heard had prepared me for Hong Kong. The excitement of seeing the brilliant green hills, the harbour crowded with junks, and the Peak springing out of the city with a suburb on its back, completely amazed me.

For the four days of our shore stay, it never ceased to fascinate me. Riding on the top of a tram on our first night, we ran into a Chinese wedding celebration, complete with catherine wheels of flowers and cracker display. We took a tram trip up the Peak, and it was only Frank's restraint that kept me from falling out when I discovered that the tram rose by cable at such an angle that the tram stations and the modern blocks of flats on the side of the Peak passed us at right angles! We saw fireflies in the dusk; we had a wonderful picnic supper in the soft dark near the notorious Stanley Camp site, where many missionaries and English people, including our host and hostess, had been interned for three years during the war. We explored Flower Street and the waterfront. We counted ships up to sixty on the misty harbour in the early morning. We balanced on the edge of jetties getting photographs of junks and odd craft. We saw over the L.M.S.[30] Nethersole Hospital, in whose staff quarters we were staying as guests of Dr. Frank and Betty Ashton, friends of Australian Student Christian Movement days. We paid 2/2 d. for a lemon squash! And so hot was it that we used to go into the air-conditioned Hong Kong Shanghai Bank to cool off.

All the Chinese menfolk wore such brilliantly white and beautifully laundered shirts that I spent most of my time at the flat doing Frank's shirts and shorts up to competition standard. The girls were very beautiful, but must have been very hot in their high-necked, close fitting dresses in bright silks, with split skirts. A goodly sprinkling of British army and naval men reminded us that this was a strategic point in Eastern Asia.

---

30 London Missionary Society of the Congregational Church.

The beautifully proportioned Cathedral is only now beginning to recover from war damage and the stripping which followed the Japanese occupation. A pleasantly spoken Chinese priest with an Oxford accent found us wandering around and explained some of the lovely woodwork to us. He urged us to come to the parish breakfast after the early Celebration the next day, which was the Feast of the Transfiguration.

And there it is again – the Church family, the home feeling. The congregation was part English, part Chinese. The huge fans turning overhead kept us a little cool. Halfway through the service a priest slipped into the sanctuary and administered the chalice. As he turned towards the altar I saw khaki socks. It must be Bishop Ronald Owen I thought, having spent some hours on the ship studying his book, *The Missionary as an Artist*, and finding it wholly inspiring, wise and unconventional. It was the Bishop, and in the parish room, over tea and sausage, bread and marmalade (what other menu could you have for a parish breakfast anyway?), he moved about the room chatting with the people and making us all feel at home. Hong Kong is very much the sorting out place for the East, so we met many interesting people on their way to and from jobs all over Eastern Asia as well as those living in Hong Kong itself. They wished us luck and said, "We'll meet in Hong Kong again some day."

That blazing hot Sunday morning in Hong Kong which suddenly melted into a tropical downpour of rain, wetting us through on our way home, seemed a long way removed from the wintry scene outside the window as I thawed out in my Kotatsu.

And as far removed was the East of the Englishman and the tourist which so fascinated me in Hong Kong, from the East which met me at Kure – the centre of the B.C.O.F. Occupation Area in the South of Japan.

All night we had been slipping up the Inland Sea. Villages blinked on the water's edge and fishing fleets passed us on their way out for the catch. By midday we had seen many beautiful islands, patterned with terraces, fields, often crowned by firs, twisted into fantastic shapes. Now and then we had seen fair sized towns and factories. At lunch time people waved towards the shore and said "Hiroshima." Then suddenly we were tying up at Kure wharf.

Hiroshima is recovering. Wide streets have been laid out. Buildings restored and much new building is in progress on the side of the city that was annihilated. Over the hill, another section of the town was untouched. The Church is rebuilding too. We met a Canadian missionary the other day who is stationed at Hiroshima, and a new church kindergarten is to be opened in March. We are particularly interested in this because Ogata-san, Frank's faithful friend and housekeeper who is also a trained kindergarten teacher, is to be in charge.

The impression of Hiroshima on a burning hot afternoon will last as long as I live, as also someone's casual remark that there was the bank where all that remained of a person who was sitting on the steps when the atom bomb exploded was a shadow blown into the granite of the building.

Frank writes:

Letters haven't been getting a look-in lately. In fact, since I wrote that first sentence there has been a break of about twenty minutes while I acted "millionaire" and transferred a million yen from one foreign bank to open an account in another (local) bank. The building grant from A.B.M. has arrived in Tokyo this week, and we have come up hurriedly to get things moving. We have been able to do that in between Tuesday and Friday in offices, banks and shops; looking into, and ordering, building operations. First to start will be the small house into which we will move as soon as it is finished. When our own permanent house is done, we will have the small one for hostel use – but we will put up a small temporary Church[31] between finishing one house and starting the next. I should have said that the very first job will be the septic tank and sewerage.

Yet another interruption. I'm sitting at a table in the bank private consulting room to add a little to this as the bank officers go away to take business a stage further.

About life as we live it these days. The chief thing is that we live 32 miles away from our nearest point of work so we seem to be always travelling. We hope it won't be long before we can move down to live in Ito. I suppose a 32 mile journey on a main road in Australia is barely a 32 minute incident – but the Odawara to Ito main road must be one of the world's finest examples of a high-road whose only redeeming feature is its scenery. It has mountains that play ball with you between sea and sky, truck and bus drivers who allow two inches to spare, and children who seem to hide in the holes in the road and pop up to pat this shiny pet of a car. With the Land Rover instead of the Jeep, we don't have roadside breakdowns any more, and rain and cold don't alarm us.

Food supplies are all right and Maida does some very interesting things with the kerosene stove and pressure cooker.

Maida is now on firm ground with the language. Someone said the other day that she is keeping pace with a year-old infant who spoke his first word on almost the same day as Maida spoke hers in Japanese. It's quite alarming to hear a whole phrase correctly issue from her lips spontaneously in the right situation, although she hasn't reached that particular stage in formal lessons yet. I think I must look a bit like Balaam on those occasions!

As to work. There is no lack of people who want to learn, and many of them come again and again with questions. There are, of course, some who come wanting to learn English only. As usual, I refuse to use English, but nowadays the smarter ones wait till I'm not about and tackle Maida who, for lack of Japanese, is a willing victim to their practice of English. It is a good thing for Maida actually, because it's her only way of meeting people.

---

31 The "temporary" Church building constructed by Frank Coaldrake was to remain in service until 1995.

There is much sickness about. Mrs. Iida has gone into hospital in Tokyo and is being operated on for tubercular infection of the lungs. The bearded "grandfather" of Ian Shevill's film has nearly succumbed to appendicitis, but is on his feet again, thanks to penicillin. This drug is being made in Japan now, and is in great vogue. Injections of all kinds seem to have a great fascination for people, as well as all the usual ones we are accustomed to: there are some quite "fancy" ones, such as vitamin and hormone injections when one is weary and worn. Chooks get their share too, to extend their laying period, or to make their combs bright.

It is my impression that the menace to health caused by very poor public hygiene is by-passed by nicely calculated "C & C" of immunity. The needle prevents the vital statistics tables becoming too alarming, so nothing is done to improve public hygiene. In everything to do with public safety, Japan is just about where England was 50 years ago. I was musing on that fact while in the local barber's chair last time – and Maida says after similar treatment, she is about ready for a dandruff-correcting needle.

Last time we visited Tokyo we looked up Muriel Lester, of England, who was staying at The Friends with Esther Rhoades, who is [a] tutor to the Crown Prince of Japan. Muriel had been lunching with the Rev. Stanley Jones, a visitor from U.S.A. She is a remarkable woman, known internationally as a peacemaker.

Sincerely yours,

FRANK AND MAIDA

P.S. Would readers please signify their desire to continue receiving our *Newsletter* by contributing to the cost of printing? We are grateful to many who have generously remembered that printers must be paid.

———

Circulated by Mrs. E.R. Coaldrake, Hamilton Road, Nundah.
Printed by Brisbane City Printery, Edward Street, Brisbane.

Newsletter No. *37*, **May, 1951.**

NIPPON SEIKO KWAI

C/o B.C.O.F. Army P.O. Ebisu,
Tokyo,
JAPAN.

From – Rev. F.W. Coaldrake

[written by Frank Coaldrake]

Dear Friends,

It is one of our now rare 4-day stretches home in Odawara. We anticipate a visit by the architect, but apart from that have kept these days free so we can catch up on some work which needs to be done here, me at my study table and Maida in laundry and house. She has just done the first washing for a month and everything we had was on the lines. Having been away constantly since March, and having had two visitors with us at different times meant that all our reserves of linen have been put into use. Now the washing is dry and ready to be ironed.

Ogata-san used to be able to plod along with washing in our absence, but she left our service in February and spent six weeks preparing for her move to the South at Hiroshima, where she is to open and run a new Day Kindergarten established by the Church. She has not done any kindergarten teaching for 15 years and is rather nervous at the prospect of starting again, but it is a good thing for her to have such worthwhile work. We were able to give her only simple housework to do and it was rather dull for her here. She sparked up no end as the day of new work drew near.

Her two girls, Megumi and Shinobu, are growing up very quickly into nice girls. Her old mother, Ogata-san senior, has returned to her pre-war work as an Evangelist in another district and is said to be doing a very effective job.

Mrs. Murota, our landlady, who lives in the big house nearby, is in good health. In fact I have never seen her looking better since she has taken to wearing "western" clothes, including jacket and slacks when working round the house. Also, she has her hair cut and permed now! We both think she is one of the brightest and nicest of people we know anywhere among our Christian friends. She thinks now about moving into our house when we have gone, and selling her big house. Her daughter Ayako, with her three sons, aged from 5 to 12, come from Tokyo frequently to visit her. The boys are growing rapidly and get into their share of scrapes, about which their mother is inclined to worry overmuch. She is a faithful Christian and loves her Church.

Our own building programme is moving now, but slowly. This morning's mail brought bills for cement, galv. iron, flooring and 3-ply, totalling £600 Australian. These materials cannot be obtained in Ito, except of very poor quality, so I have had to search them out in Tokyo. Three hundred sheets of 3-ply in nine bales arrived on Odawara Station yesterday, although addressed to Ito, so I had to send them on. That is typical of the unforeseen muddles that crop up all along the line. Our first building needs only doors, windows, and paint to finish it now, but it is only the garage! That went up first in order that it can be used to store other building materials. Next stage is moving the present house (bought with the land) and enlarging it to suit us as a temporary Rectory. Later still this will be used as a Training Hostel, after our new Rectory is built and ready for us to occupy.

Meanwhile the first stage includes septic tank, water, electricity and drainage to be done.

It is rather a headache trying to get the best possible value for our money. The main trouble here is the variable standard of building, which allows the very best at £60 a square, or you can have anything less down to £10 a square, all in timber, but the different rates in the quality of timber and varying standards of workmanship. We are aiming at good work and materials, which limit the size of building accordingly.

Our original estimates were all upset by the effect of the Korean war. Prices have soared during this year, though they are still actually lower than building costs in Australia.

It looks now as if we will move from Odawara to Ito permanently during May, provided no further delays crop up unexpectedly. We have started a small vegetable garden already in our anticipated backyard at Ito, with peas and tomatoes, while a box of lettuce seedlings is at Odawara ready for our migration. This is one of the many pleasures of everyday home life we expect to quite early fit into our permanent settlement in Ito. At present the Land Rover is as much our home as either house here or there. (Fig. 34)

We all enjoyed having as visitor Miss Gladys Smith for 10 days over Easter. She is a newly arrived young Englishwoman working as a teacher in a Mission School at Kobe. Maida especially enjoyed having another English-speaking companion for a while. Then another English visitor was Mrs. Hammer, whose husband [Raymond] is a Missionary Lecturer at the Theological College in Tokyo. She was with us for two enjoyable days last week. Their home is a converted Quonset hut in the College grounds in Tokyo.

The cherry trees have again blossomed, and petals carpeted the ground, and now the country everywhere is clothed in the fresh green of spring.

The blossoms were as magnificent as usual and they came out 10 days earlier this year and lasted longer. It was Maida's first cherry season and she has been, as we all are, amazed at the massed beauty of it all. The trees in our Odawara garden have put on a specially beautiful display.

A note from Rev. E.A. Leaver, Secretary of A.B.M. in Melbourne, about other things last week included the news that Keith and Sheila [Coaldrake, Frank's brother and sister-in-law] were in his office as he wrote. We hope they are enjoying

Figure 34 Maida Coaldrake putting into practice Frank Coaldrake's advice about driving on a typical Izu "road." Near Itō, 1951. (See *Letter*, 26 April 1949.)

their furlough and the "taste" of civilisation again for a while after their three years of Missionary work among the Natives of North-west Australia, at Forrest River.

Next week I am to take Bishop Maekawa round Izu Peninsula for our first Confirmations. We make slow but sure progress in gathering together a group of sincere practising Christians, and every day makes the need of Christianity in this country more apparent.

News of the New Guinea disaster struck an immediate response in the Church here and from all over the Diocese have come contributions in money, also silk or cotton handkerchiefs and towels. I have already sent over £20 Aust. and four parcels of goods, which is a matter for great joy you will agree.

The Land Rover (English manufacture) is running very well, but I have broken a front spring going over a great hole in the concrete road through Atami city, which was not there when I passed through three days earlier. Quite a problem about repairs, because no spare parts are in Japan. We have done 6,000 miles now, and I used to break a Jeep spring about every 2,000 miles.

Maida is getting very expert results from pressure cooker and kero[sene] stove. She even produces cakes from the latter, when there is not a strong wind blowing through the cracks in the walls to prevent the stove getting hot. She has also made three lots of marmalade from various local citrus fruits. One of our local visitors was so impressed with the marmalade that he wrote about it in the local newspaper! Now you know why it has been left for me to provide your *Newsletter* this month, seeing Maida is rather overtired with too much travelling, combined with overtime as housewife. We are all well and hope you each and all are likewise.

Yours sincerely,

   FRANK AND MAIDA

P.S.: A sincere thank you to those friends who promptly and generously responded to our March PS. reminder about printing costs.

———

Circulated by Mrs. E.R. Coaldrake, Hamilton Road, Nundah.
Printed by Brisbane City Printery, Edward Street, Brisbane.

Newsletter No. 38, June, 1951.

NIPPON SEIKO KWAI

C/o B.C.O.F. Army P.O. Ebisu,
Tokyo,
JAPAN.

From – Rev. F.W. Coaldrake

[first half written by Frank Coaldrake, second half by Maida]

Dear Friends,

It has been sad necessity that prevented both of us from sending you the news you need to fill up pages for June. We have each had "seedy" turns in the midst of very busy weeks, and the lack of Fr. Iida's assistance now makes the days doubly full. Constant supervision of building plans, and preparation of removal to Ito are adding up to an extra strenuous month for us.

There's an old saying in Japan which comes into English like this – "It took an ox and a washtub to lead me to Church." The story is that an old lady who had been very negligent about going up to her Church to pray was one day doing her washing. Suddenly an ox appeared in her garden and got its horns tangled in the clothes on the line. Taking fright it raced away with the laundry flapping from its horns. The old lady chased it up the road hoping to recover her clothes. The ox at last came to a standstill and she gathered the remains of her garments. Then she noticed that the ox had stopped right opposite the steps of the Church she had so long neglected, whereupon she entered and said her prayers, then turning to a bystander made the historic remark quoted above.

Miyazawa-san reminded me of it in Shimoda last week. We have a small, rather uncertain group of Christians in Shimoda village, and very vigorous determined groups in Imaihama and Ose on either side of it. The man in charge of the Shimoda group recently moved and I had only vague directions about finding the new organiser. For some weeks I had moved backwards and forwards through Shimoda between the other centres, neglecting the rather vague possibilities in Shimoda.

Last week Miyazawa-san was with me as we zoomed over the mountains through Shimoda and on out to Ose. We must have looked rather like a rocket going along the straight stretches at high speed with a great trail of dust spreading out beyond us. Then the clutch broke and we had to be towed back the 10 miles into Shimoda by a motor cycle, passengers and driver all having to get out and push up the hills. It was an inglorious return! By the time we reached the service station it was evening, and we stood in half-light watching the removal of the Land Rover engine, so that the clutch could be repaired. (Fig. 35)

One of our previously uncertain group suddenly appeared and shouted: "Hello! Hooray! You've come at last, I'll go and get the others." Which he did, and within an hour they all appeared, specially bathed and brushed up for the occasion and ready to take Miyazawa-san and me away to the new meeting place.

It proved to be right opposite the filling station where I usually bought petrol on my way through the village in recent weeks. That's how easy it is to be misled, or carelessly over-busy with lesser routine matters!

We had Bible study and discussion till 11 p.m., then went back to find the car repairs nearly done. As we completed arrangements for subsequent meetings and said goodbye, Miyazawa-san remarked, "It took a breakdown and motor-bike to lead us to Church in Shimoda." Yes, and we eventually reached his house back in Ito at 2 a.m. Maida was at home alone in Odawara expecting me there about 10 p.m., so I hoped she wouldn't worry about my non-arrival. As a matter of fact, she was so tired and slept so soundly she did not know till morning that I had not come home. Just as well that in broad daylight possibilities are never so fearful as at midnight.

Figure 35 The disabled Land Rover in the dusk at Shimoda, May, 1951.

There are hundreds of places like Imaihama in Japan today. It is a very mountainous area where agricultural land is very scarce. There are no secondary industries. The only product with a surplus over local requirements is fish. The struggle for existence has always been grim, but the already heavy population has been nearly doubled since the end of the war, mainly by the return of soldiers and "colonials" from other countries. It is a place where the relentless pressure of person upon person in daily life is very noticeable. I am often asked what chance there is of getting away to work for a living in Australia?

It is an uncomfortable situation, because no matter how cleverly I may answer the question, there still remains the fact of too little food, clothing and housing for too many people, not only here, but in the next village too, and the next, and the next! If "population pressure" means anything, it means hungry people who have nowhere to grow the food they need, be they ever so willing to try and grow anything. They have a blind and desperate desire to move outwards from here to anywhere, where there are a few square yards of unused land. It comes to me here not in cold tables of statistics, but in the bleak eyes and querulous voice of a mother who had sat through an hour-long service with a hungry 2 year old infant constantly at her insufficient breasts.

For me to find at home a few hours later some more generous parcels of food from Australia which can be brought to such people on my next visit is a wonderful help. Not a permanent solution of the problem of course, but enough to nourish that 2 year old.

Was it your parcel? Then thank you with the almost unutterable thanks of that mother. You can perhaps send parcels. What else, what more? What else, what more? That question seems to be written on the walls of every one of the hundreds of tumbledown huts we pass in that village.

Another story. "Little Cosette" she might be called if we remember our school reader. She is aged 11. Her mother died four years ago at the birth of her brother. She has since then kept house for the family, just their father and the two children. Water has to be carried in buckets from a well 200 yards from their shack, and it is the sight of this little girl in rags stumbling along with two buckets of water that reminds me of "Little Cosette." Their father was a ship's engineer in the merchant marine until the end of the war, but now he is one of the crew of four-oared fishing boat on Imaihama beach. He must be away with the tides, so the family life is very irregular. Just lately we found the boy of four was not at Sunday school, although they are both usually regular in attending. On looking them up I found the boy was pale and sickly, so I suggested a visit to the doctor. The trouble was located as a severe attack of intestinal worms, and it takes years of careful treatment to effect a real cure. Meanwhile, some good food from your parcels, and fresh clothing (second-hand anyway) from the same source has helped improve things generally.

Our first food gift was taken home by the girl and put on their table for tea. Later, she told her Sunday school teacher that her father would not say a prayer of thanks himself when she suggested it, but he waited quietly while she herself prayed.

The 4 year old boy was at Sunday school today. When the collection box came along from hand to hand as far as himself the little scallywag took charge of it. He had nothing to put in, so he went from child to child receiving their collection into his own hand and then himself dropping it into the box, in the course of which he dropped the box on the floor and scattered the contents, to his huge delight as he dived around everyone's feet to pick it up again. After completing the round he came all perspiration and smiles to hand the box over as the offering of the day.

And so we cheerfully go on our interesting journeyings. Sometimes when things seem tough Maida reduces us both to laughter by starting to sing somewhat wryly a hymn she recalls having sung with great gusto at the age of ten. The first line goes "Chosen to be soldiers, in an alien land," etc., etc. By the time my voice has cracked on the high note of each line, we've at least enjoyed ourselves, even if we haven't jacked up our enthusiasm. Amazing how, when enthusiasm has evaporated faith remains all the stronger. That's all I can offer for this session, but Maida will add her contribution to fill in the gaps.

———

Maida writes:

It always happens just when I want most to write; interruptions come along. Last week I came home from Ito to make various jams and cakes, to unpack some parcels, and write letters, when down in Odawara I met Michiko-san (one-time

"Cinderella" of a Tokyo girls' school pageant) who used to write quaintly beautiful letters to Frank during his furlough in Australia. I brought her home for lunch, and soon after she left three other vocal Japanese school-girls arrived. When they had gone, another visitor appeared who stayed until 9 p.m. And so the days go on, very full of many things to be done. Now we have Laurie Topp with us for four days.

I am managing better now with the Japanese language and some regular study should give me more confidence. I wish you could know just how much your appreciative letters mean to us, and I am truly sorry I have not been able to write more news lately.

Parcels have been coming regularly from many generous friends. I opened and unpacked the 60th this year a few days ago. Had you come walking along the path to the front of our house you may have been as surprised as were the little girls from down the hill near here, for our large front room looked like a mixture of railway station, grocery store, and clothing parade. Seven big chairs stood around labelled Hiakawa [Hayakawa], Oiso Babies' Home, Imaihama, etc. I went around in circles adding shoes here, a coat there, butter in the next one, and so on, all the while keeping in mind children here and there, or sick people needing food. In two days I prepared and despatched the seven cases for distribution to our most needy parishioners, and I can assure you they are very thankfully received. We can use all the clean (even if old) warm clothing of any description you can find to send us ready for next Winter, which comes at the end of the year. A.B.M. office in each State will be glad to forward parcels to us.

There's a glorious scent of blossoms around our home since the mandarin orchard is in bloom next door at Mrs. Murota's place. In fact, the whole country is blossoming and beautiful, while the harvesting is on, and the young rice plants are nearly ready for transplanting season soon. The heat and humidity suggests the rainy season is nearly on us, which will be my first of its kind over here.

Two weeks ago we had the great joy of attending the dedication and opening of the new Chapel and House of the Sisters of the Epiphany, an English community whose sisters were with the Community of the Holy Name in Melbourne during the war.[32]

It was a hot morning when we left before 6 a.m. for Tokyo to be present at the celebration of Holy Communion in their new Chapel, with Bishop Viall[33] officiating, assisted by Japanese priests and the Bishop of Tokyo presiding.

The Chapel has the window frames and altar which were all that remained of the old Chapel that was burnt out by Allied bombing raids during war years. The cream and palest pink roses and carnations matched the lovely cream brocade and Tudor roses of the vestments. The singing was sweet and high in a beautiful

---

32 Film of the construction and completion of the Chapel and House of the Sisters of the Epiphany
is included in the Coaldrake films held in the collection of ScreenSound Australia.
33 Fr. Viall had been consecrated as Bishop by this.

plain-song. To be present in such a place on such a day, and know how much prayer and devotion, and life, would flow out of these walls, was indeed a deep experience for me. I had quite an English breakfast afterwards with the Sisters, but Frank eating in the Refectory with the priests enjoyed his garnished with Japanese conversation!

Just below the new Chapel and House of the Epiphany it was wonderful to see also the other large house soon to be occupied by the Japanese Order of Nazareth. It means that a number of young Japanese women who have waited for years to test their vocation need wait no longer.

Please remember us in your prayers – we need them all.

Yours sincerely,

FRANK AND MAIDA

———

Circulated by Mrs. E.R. Coaldrake, Hamilton Road, Nundah.
Printed by Brisbane City Printery, Edward Street, Brisbane.

Newsletter No. 39, **July, 1951.**

NIPPON SEIKO KWAI

C/o B.C.O.F. Army P.O. Ebisu,
Tokyo,
JAPAN.

From – Rev. F.W. Coaldrake

[written by Maida Coaldrake]

MORE REFLECTIONS

With only the last coat of paint to come and the sliding doors and windows to slip into place, our move into St. Mari-ya House is a matter of days away. Then we shall be living in Ito, at the centre of our Mission area, and the hours of buffeting on the rough roads which lie between Odawara [and Ito] will disappear out of the weekly programme. During these months of waiting for buildings to be completed and at the same time building up the work in each of our Cottage Churches round Izu Peninsula, Frank has been theoretically still on the staff of the Odawara Church. In practice, of course, it is months since we spent a Sunday in Odawara and the most that we have been able to do is to put in an occasional appearance at the Girls' School Bible Class. But it is a characteristic of the Japanese mind that it finds difficulty in making a clean break. When Frank pointed out the anomaly the Bishop said that the arrangement may as well stand, until such time as the termination of our residence in Odawara put an end to it.

And now the time has come and our undivided attention can be given to Izu. Frank, more than I, will be sorry to leave this ancient house with its uneven floors, lovely wooden beams, trees and quiet. But even I, with not quite a year against his four, have grown very attached to its beauties and oddities, although I must confess I am glad to be going before the Summer is really at its height again. I found it difficult to be absolutely friendly to the dinner plate-sized frogs which used to sit on my back door step while I was preparing dinner at night, or to the multitudinous insects and moths which stream in when the lights go on. Recently with the coming of the wet season everything has become so green and lush, and the growing tree tips such lovely bronze and red, it would be difficult to find a more beautiful hillside than that to which we open our eyes each morning. And with the blossoming of the mandarin trees which grow right up to the house, the scent of orange blossom has made me think I have strayed into a church aisle by mistake when I go out to hang the tea towels in the sun.

I have often been told as I look around for the best ways of serving the Church and the people, that I have no need to look far. Frank has told me, the senior missionaries have told me and the Japanese people have told me. The thinking people are terribly worried about their sons and daughters. Everybody is worried about the "loose" morals that have become the fashion, and the decaying social standards. Young people, no longer taught the rigorous code of the ways of pre-war Japan, and without the guidance of Christianity, learn about the new democracy from films and cheap magazines, and from the flood of foreign literature, often in very bad translation, which is flowing into the country. Tokyo is full of Japanese style bobby-soxers, nice youngsters who for all their jeans, and t-shirts, and saddle shoes and long hair haven't quite got hold of the idea that juke-boxes, hand-holding in public, and baseball are not democracy in action. Beside the alive young Americans we see around the Occupation Housing Areas, the Japanese are a very pale and bodiless imitation.

That's in the larger cities where the Western influence is strongest, but even in the remote and conservative country districts, there's the same unrest and dissatisfaction. Months ago at one of our welcome meetings, an elder of the village said how glad they all were Frank had brought back a wife for more than anything else they wanted their young folk to see a Western Christian man and woman living and working side by side. They want the witness of a Christian home in their village. When I heard it first I understood the point he was making but now I understand it much more deeply.

This fact has made living in our old Japanese house something of a demonstration, and it has added quite a thrill even to the tussles with the kero stove and the laundry arrangements.

Only last week the "laundry arrangements" really did turn into an authentic demonstration. I've told you before we've often laughed about the consternation my large weekly wash causes among the neighbours. As some neighbours live six or eight feet above me on the next hill terrace they have plenty of opportunity to observe the strange things which go on in the foreigners' back yard. In Japan, the sheer drudgery of the daily wash has to be seen to be believed. Huge heavy dishes, carried outside to the nearest tap or running water, the endless squatting before a funny inadequate board, the endless rinsing – and the results such as you or I would be ashamed to put on a suburban Monday morning line. Well last week, Mrs. Murota, landlady and friend of long standing, asked Frank if she could come up and see me do the wash. She said that all the neighbours considered my wash a "miracle" – how there were no clothes on the line for a week, and then in two or three hours flapping in the breeze was a wash sufficient to keep the ordinary Japanese housewife busy for a week. She had heard we had a wonderful machine that did all the work. So outside in my laundry, which consists of a bench running the length of a wall, a copper in a petrol drum, and a tap, plus my much valued £6 worth of "Rins-and-Dry" machine, Frank and I put on a demonstration. We showed how boiling water eliminates most of the rubbing, how proper rinsing and blueing maintains colour without six waters, and how finally the machine merely whisks out surplus water and defeats our worst enemy – humidity.

It was great fun, and Mrs. Murota went away quite convinced the ordinary housewife could do a miracle wash without a miracle machine, although a "Rins-and-Dry" was a highly desirable servant.

Mt. Mihara on Oshima, an island 25 odd miles off Ito, continues to erupt from time to time. Quite apart from its scenic attractions, camellias, and conservative peasants and the like, this island has been the destination for a pleasant trip by sea from Tokyo or Atami, and has been most popular of late.

But recently one sightseeing party was badly injured by falling rocks and pumice, and night by night the residents are disturbed in their slumbers by the growls of the mountain, which has come to life after fifteen years.

The other morning I had to wash pumice and ash out of the bath before it could be used and glanced out the window across the water to see a great plume of smoke rising from the crater. We don't look on Mihara as a scenic attraction. Our New Guinea friends are too close to our heart.

But as we look at our own volcano and remember Lamington, we can also rejoice that the hearts of Christian people all round our Diocese have been touched. More than £35 Aust. has been subscribed – over 30,000 yen in Japanese money, and we have packed gift parcels of silk and cotton goods from every parish in the Diocese. One good lady brought 50 yards of beautiful white silk to us. Our own parish gave its Lenten offering, feeling it small offering against that of the lives of two generations of martyrs.... We are proud of these Izu people. They are very, very poor. Six thousand yen a month would be good pay for a man with a large family.

Last Sunday we had our last services in the Quonset Hut Church in the fishing village of Ito City. Some of the churchfolk say they will have a nostalgia for the little Church. We leave it – or rather start it on its elevation to the new block and a new appearance, with nothing but joy. It has been so hard to keep clean and tidy – with dust and rubbish blowing in off the street, lorries drowning the singing on Saturday nights, and awful smells offending our nostrils. We have had beautiful services there, and made many advances, and had lots of fun. "Saturday nights," beginning during Lent as a time of instruction and meditation for any who might come, have become quite an institution. If you dropped in any Saturday about sunset you would be greeted at the front door by clouds of fine gravel being swept out, and at the back door have your entrance blocked by Ikue-san carrying two buckets of water for washing the seats and doing the flowers.

Once the dirt has been banished and the seats put in place in the main section of the Hut, then the sliding doors of the altar cabinet are taken out and we prepare the altar for Sunday's services.

Meanwhile in the vestry cum study cum kitchen, cum kindergarten, Frank has started instruction – perhaps the two or three policemen friends of one of our Christian boys have dropped in. They sit down easily on the cane settee in their brand new American-style uniform of Special Reserve Police, and listen to the Bible study session, alongside some of our nice High School student lads and girls from the local shops. Or tonight it might be that some of our more advanced people have been able to come, and then you might find them pouring over an excellent map of Palestine, or studying the structure of the Holy Communion service. Sometimes there are ten crowded in the back room, sometimes three. But Frank is always there, and people have taken to dropping in and having a talk.

Out in the main Hall we have rubbed up the light wooden candlesticks, polished the brass, dusted the books and turned our attention to the vases. This is where my fun always begins. To the Japanese the art of flower arrangement is sacred, and the tendency is that unless you have made a special study of it, you dare not touch a flower. If you have made a study of it, then you will prepare a vase for the altar which may, by its arrangement of stem, leaf, and perhaps one blossom, have deep significance for the initiated, but for ecclesiastical purposes looks extraordinarily awkward and ugly.

So I am running what is virtually a renegade school of flower arrangement week by week doing the vases, or one vase and having a girl copy it, showing that colour mass with due respect for seasonal colour, and symmetry, are the particular ends we serve. But I do have some embarrassing moments when I find a lady of the congregation kneeling before a vase I have finished, gazing for about five minutes at it, obviously seeking its inner meaning or when a whole row of giggly girls (giggly only because they are shy), watch every movement I make as I pick up a vase.

But they are learning, and already they are loving to learn about the altar, and its care. All these things we have done from a very early stage. It's a joy to pass them on.

After our chores and instruction, it being already dark, candles are lit, kneelers are got out and we have a quiet preparation for Sunday, singing perhaps our Communion hymn for the next day. Because so many people work as usual on Sundays, our Saturday night "Holy Hour" is beginning to loom quite large in the week's programme.

Sundays begin anything but quietly as very early in the morning children arrive for Sunday School. To such an extent has the idea of Christian Church and Sunday School become synonymous in the Japanese mind, that we have the greatest difficulty in convincing people that our permanent presence in Ito is not for the purpose of opening a kindergarten.

We never have any difficulty in getting children for the Sunday School we run. Threatened with a deluge of the infant population of Ito, who come for years to "Sunday School" and are once more reabsorbed and forever lost in the pagan community, we took drastic measures last Sunday and called together the parents of our own School. Not many came, but later we shall try again by letter to point out that the school must be (so long as we are limited by space and staff), the training class for the children of Church families, or of families which themselves are anxious to learn about the Gospel of Christ. We shall have plenty of them. It is a drastic step, but it is a drastic situation.

All over Japan for more than seventy years, good Christians have been labouring in the Sunday Schools teaching children year by year about Our Lord and His Church. Less than one per cent of the present Church membership came through Sunday Schools. The reason? Children were allowed to come year after year with no word said about Baptism, Church membership or obligation – and so they went away.

In this city of Odawara, [where I am currently writing,] with a population of over 60,000 and a church that has been established for years, most people only know the Church because it is attached to a Kindergarten! Yet for twenty-five years, year by year, up to 110 children have been passing through the Kindergarten. Any Sunday morning in Church there are never more than thirty people. It seems that the Sunday School and Kindergarten are not the best ways of evangelising Japan's millions.

But we have had good and happy hours with the little flock we have collected, and while elder brothers and sisters are learning with great enthusiasm to say the Creed and sing "Holy, Holy, Holy," which comes out as "Sei naru, Sei naru, Sei naru," in the Japanese. We have a tiny "Babies Class" in the backroom. Here I am constantly amazed at the lack in the government education system demonstrated, firstly by the inability of a lass with a first-class brain and High School education, to make anything of teaching a picture story, and secondly at the inability of any of the five year olds to express themselves with paper and crayon.

At home most kiddies [in Australia] can draw, at least satisfactorily to themselves, ships, and houses and people, by the time they are four. Moreover, they can colour with gusto. But here the children have neither had the medium nor the opportunity to express themselves in a way that delights our children for hours. So to the echoes of the Creed from the big school, our babies are experiencing for the first time the huge joy of putting purple ships on a yellow sea, and drawing donkeys standing round the manger.

It has been a great joy to us that Frank's first call to administer the Sacrament of Unction came from one of our very dear and active church men who is also himself a doctor, with sons and daughters in the medical profession. Dr. Kawai of Ose Village, in whose house we have a "cottage church," was seriously ill and getting worse. His doctor son was already with him bringing all that modern medicine in Japan could offer. Frank drove many miles over terrible roads to reach him as soon as his desire was known. A few days later we had a long distance call – "Thank you, the Doctor is very much better, even getting up for a short time each day. And, could he have some of your soup, please? It is just what he fancies." We gave thanks and sent the Doctor his soup.

This year I have unpacked and repacked for distribution to our needy people over 80 parcels from Australia. Every mail brings six or seven, and sometimes the officer in charge of the Australian Post Office says – "You need a 7–ton truck today."

We are immensely grateful to all our friends and church people at home for keeping these relief goods coming. For the poor are always with us and most Japanese families live out to the limit of their income every year. The farmer still lives and eats well only when his crop is good or in the good season of the year – for every year has a lean season, and then the diet is mostly sweet potatoes, and there is no extra money for clothes or shoes. And if there is sickness or other expense, or more babies...?

When we get an S.O.S. from such folk as Dr. Kawai or the widow of a priest, who herself has the dreaded scourge of T.B., we are very thankful to be able to turn to our store and take milk and soup and tinned butter and so on. And now our Summer Camps at Lake Ippeki are nearly on us. I have the happy thought of dozens of jellies and packets of custard put away against that "special tea."

One group of young people – Heralds of the King – in Launceston, Tasmania, have posted 26 parcels, which have all been received safely, with others on the way. And from A.B.M. Office in Hobart, parcel after parcel of warm, used clothing. If you could come with us on just one of our round trips, you would have your thanks, but as you can't, please accept this as thanks from the Coaldrakes, the Izu Mission, and many Japanese people.

A business letter in English from the Tokyo Electric Power Co. opens with these words:

"May 1st, 1951.

Dear Sir,

Greetings of May with its freshness of joyous spring. Everything around us seems happy with renewed life and vigor, and we sincerely hope that you and your family too, are well and happy."

It then proceeds to give details of new electric power rates!

The Coaldrakes hope this finds you as it leaves the Electric Power Company.

Yours sincerely,

FRANK AND MAIDA

—

Circulated by Mrs. E.R. Coaldrake, Hamilton Road, Nundah.
Printed by Brisbane City Printery, Edward Street, Brisbane.

***Newsletter No. 40*, August–September, 1951.**

NIPPON SEIKO KWAI

C/o B.C.O.F. Army P.O. Ebisu,
Tokyo,
JAPAN.

From – Rev. F.W. Coaldrake

[Maida Coaldrake initially with the rest by Frank]

Dear Friends:

You will be interested in these quotations from this morning's press – *Nippon Times* – one of the English language newspapers which we have proved often is sane and balanced in its judgments.

Quiet will mark treaty's signing. Historic event at San Francisco to be observed modestly by Japanese people

> The signing of the Peace Treaty will be observed quietly in Japan, with only modest commemorative events scheduled in limited parts of the nation...
>
> Commenting on these plans, the Chief of the Information Section Foreign Office, said the Government wants the people to refrain from gala celebration in view of the delicate attitude taken by Soviet Russia and Asian nations on the Japanese peace.

———

So the man in the street forms his own opinion if he is the thinking type; otherwise he just wonders what it is going to mean to him in terms of price of rice and freedom to express opinions. The foreigner, missionary included, can't help but give some thought to how it will affect his living conditions – for we have all enjoyed certain privileges in the buying of food and the sending of mail. As we paid 180 yen (Aust. 4/9) for a decent loaf of bread the other day here in Ito, because the sour, badly baked Japanese bread, costing 62 yen for the same size, was upsetting our stomachs, we can't help being a little anxious about future living costs.

On the whole, except for scattered tree-planting ceremonies and a few "prayers for the war dead" at suitable shrines, life during this momentous week goes on a usual. As I write I can hear the familiar whine of the sawmill up the street, the clod-clod of the pick in the field next door, and the rumble of buses and rear-carts on the Shimoda Highway outside the block.

Frank has just handed his contribution across.... This is the day of starting our University students' camp at the lake. We are to centre our studies on Temple's *Christianity and Social Order*, which has just been published in Japanese. Our hope is that we will be able to develop a Student Conference on the line of the Australian S.C.M. Conference, something not so far accomplished in Japan because of the entirely different student characteristics. Our Organising Secretary approached his task with great diffidence because he will be having to tell students senior to him in status what to do in camp. He is alarmed at the prospect of joining issue in discussion with senior students. This has nothing to do with thoughts about the subject. It is a matter of rank in the Educational Hierarchy.

The Peace Treaty Conference is going on in San Francisco as I write about prestige of rank among students. About the Peace Treaty everyone who has a chance is saying as much as he can. It really is a significant Treaty Conference, but whether we will come more to regret it than to rejoice in it is not difficult to foresee. My own idea is that it is too soon to put what there is of democratic freedom-loving leadership in Japan on to its own resources. Leadership of the old style is still far and away the most able leadership in Japan. Its methods are understood and approved by the people. For instance, in every school, and at all conferences and meetings, great bellowing loudspeakers are used. In the little backward village of Ose last month I found the latest instance of individuals wishing to be treated as a "block group." On the hill at the edge of the village a huge speaker had been set up. The microphone is in the village office. The sound penetrates every room of every house. While staying there with Dr. Kawai I found it so distracting that I asked various people what they thought about it. The answers could all be put in the words of a sixteen-year old: "It was everybody's wish." It starts at 6 a.m. with a 15–minute session of National Radio Eurythmics. The great voice blares: "HEEP-HOOP; HEEP-HOOP," and here, as everywhere else in the land, groups stand in the street and do the identical monotonous swinging of arms and swaying of body. This is not "regimentation" of unwilling masses. It is a great number of people who like the feeling of "belonging" to a great unified body. I could write several pages of further instances of the same desire to be submerged in one's proper status in the orderly array of a great host.

The embryonic individualists begotten by the Occupation are very numerous – more so than ever before, I should think. But when thinking about these individualists we must remember that there have always been "outcrops" of rugged individualism in Japan's massive populace. They have often been notable persons. But ordinary, non individualistic people, while perhaps admiring them, have never shown any inclination to follow them. Nor do they now.

On that basis the Japanese leaders are standing ready to sign whatever Treaty they can get out of the wrangles between former allies [especially the United States and the Soviet Union].

It is not historically pretty. It suggests that a "New Japan," if it were possible, should have been developed on entirely different lines.

Economically speaking, the U.S.A. seems to have achieved the gigantic task of restoring the Japanese economy to pre-war levels. It is not economically pretty, because it has restored the former unbalance of economic strength. On the one hand a few wealthy who are extremely wealthy – and not heeding the needs of others; on the other hand, a frightening number of very poor, who just manage to exist – fortunately for the peace of the nation at present not heeding the excessive luxuries of the few. If anything should bestir them to awareness, there would be a great upheaval. But the present leadership is well practised in maintaining and satisfying the desire of the individual to be submerged in society at his appropriate present status.

Politically speaking, the big question has been: "Whose ally will Japan be?" The only question at the moment is whether she will be more closely tied to Britain or America. Economics show a trend towards the sterling area, but public interest is undoubtedly attached to America. For anyone who is chiefly interested in Japan as a future enemy or ally the important thing is, as Macmahon Ball put it in the last words of his 1948 book:[34]

> If we want Japan as our ally, the way to succeed is not by subsidising reactionary governments, or resuming trade relations with a disguised Zaibatsu, but by giving firm friendship and effective help to the Japanese people. At present the Japanese masses lack political consciousness and experienced leaders. They are still sunk in the past. But when they are without food or clothing or shelter, they want radical change. Those who help them achieve this change will be their friends; those who resist the change will be their enemies.

This has been proved in part by the popular response to American relief in the years since it was written. But the end is not yet.

"Giving firm friendship and effective help to the Japanese people" is one of the corollaries of the missionary enterprise. The Australian help channelled through Odawara and Izu has not been insignificant. But it is, after all, not our main undertaking. It is the expression of the faith and love we hope to help them to catch. Given that, the individual Japanese enters into a much more brightly illuminated world. But Japan is, as before, a most difficult place in which to achieve visible results. Time and again we find people unable to move over to join us because they are bogged down. The inertia of their own emotional attachments to the social mass makes them afraid of loneliness if they take an individual line.

Our LONG SILENCE – during which generous parcels and many letters from friends all over Australia have had to remain unacknowledged – has been due to several factors, which could be summed up as: MOVING; VISITORS; CAMPS; TEACHERS' CONFERENCE; and, by no means least, WEATHER.

Any one of them could well occupy a letter in its own right.

Of **moving,** my most vivid memory is of rain, rain, and more rain. The day we moved the "wet" season began, and the lovely green hill in Mrs. Murota's garden was so slippery that the workmen had to tie pieces of straw rope around their rubber "tabi" or boots to prevent them sliding the whole way. Household effects were complicated enough, but to move a library, projects, tools, relief goods, food stores, and so on in the deluge of rain, 35 miles down the coast and

34 W. Macmahon Ball, *Japan ... Enemy or Ally?*, Melbourne, Wilke and Co., 1948, p. 208.

into a house with glassless windows was a nightmare. Our little Land Rover proved its merit beyond question in the final stages of our move by pulling a four-ton truck, fully loaded, up the muddy slope on to the Ito block after it had become bogged. It was ironic to find when we did start unpacking that the water main had not been connected and there was no water for household use. However, there was a celebration of Holy Communion in our big room at 10 a.m. the next day, and other services as usual. We now use this house as a church until a temporary church has been erected on the block.

Of **visitors,** nothing but joy. In the five weeks of our occupation our tiny three-mat spare room has been full most of the time, and in addition we have had someone else bedded down, Japanese style, on futon or the floor in the living-room. David Chamberlain, ex-Hobart and latest A.B.M. missionary to arrive in Japan, had a few days in Kobe to settle his luggage and books, and then made the nine-hour rail journey north [east] to us.

He will be teaching at the Church's International School in Kobe, commonly called St. Michael's, whose Principal is our New Zealand friend, Fr. Rex Clarke. Kobe is Bishop Yashiro's home [the Presiding Bishop of the Nippon Seikōkai], and David had already seen something of him before he came to Ito. Some of his three weeks' stay was spent at Lake Ippeki under canvas as Summer Camps were in full swing. In fact, we must confess we whisked him straight from the train to Ippeki, and there, in a very familiar atmosphere for us, we welcomed him, and our 75 campers sang a song they are very fond of – part English, part Japanese, to say how pleased they were to see him. His stay was a great pleasure and overlapped with that of Gladys Smith, an S.P.G. missionary, who shared our Easter adventures. She also teaches in Kobe, but is staying on long enough here to help at our final camp of 1951 for University students, beginning today. Gladys, an S.C.M.-er like ourselves, attended the last Study Camp at Swanwick before leaving England, stayed with the Hobsons at Penang, met the Keys-Smiths of St. Andrews, Singapore, and brought us most welcome first-hand news of both.

Of **Camps** there will be much more to say later. But for now the feeling I have is of walking in a world I have already known because I [Frank] showed the Ippeki film so often in Australia.[35] The scene has changed a deal though, with all sorts of improvements, a permanent roof on the dining pavilion, a permanent chapel shelter, new paths, an adequate water system and so on. Except for the Middle and High School Camp, which was literally "washed out" by rainstorms, we have had wonderful camps and missions, with the young people going out to the villages and in great voice speaking of their Faith and its answer to the needs of Japan. We have lived on a kind of shuttle service between the Lake and Ito, coming home for a day or two between camps. Biscuits, bathing suits and jelly and custard have been some of the happy ways our Australian friends have participated in the camps. As before the young people are coming from all over

---

35 Scenes from the camps are in the films preserved at ScreenSound Australia.

our own and other central Japan dioceses, and those from the cities especially are loving the beauty and coolness of the Lake country. (Colour Plate 7)

[Maida writes:]

Of the **Teachers' Conference,** held at Bessho Hot Spring resort, some 200 miles from Ito, I can only say it was an exceedingly interesting experience. From all over Japan came Sunday School teachers and others interested in the work of Religious Education. I was greatly intrigued by the attitude of even young people to such conferences; their lack of any conception of joy of community living; of the proper arrangement of a day's programme; their readiness to accept everything said in lectures and addresses without question; and their willingness to sit for hours and hours listening to other people talking.

I had been asked to give a lecture on Audio-Visual Aids to Memory in Education, and had had great fun preparing posters, collecting material, and generally working along the lines we do at home. My one session extended to another, by request, and the whole group was delighted and enlightened by the simplest aids to teaching. There is a great deal to do here, and I was glad to add my bit. I had to work mostly with an interpreter, but posters, etc., do speak for themselves. And I have been convinced posters with Japanese characters are twice as eye-catching and telling as our own.

The journey to and from Bessho through big cities, lovely mountain areas and river valleys, was fascinating. We had two nights for visiting other diocesan parishes, on one of them having a grand evening with the Uemuras at Kofu, meeting the people, showing films, and generally getting to know folk who had been only names before. The other night we spent in the mountains, and drove down into the hot plains very early in the morning. Fuji-san – the beautiful, the unbelievable – swam slowly out of the pink mists, a dream of perfection, standing high above us. Later, as we tore down dusty roads, encountering army convoys to remind us of the "civilised" world, we passed pilgrims returning from their all-night climb. Thousands and thousands of people are making the climb at this season, as the snows have melted. With their pilgrims' hats and stamped staffs they are quite a tourist attraction in themselves.

And, lastly, of the **weather,** I don't think I am capable of writing much. As the Winter was bitter, with snow and winds and rain, so the Summer is beyond description with its smells, beetles, insects, humidity and heat. There are times when, with the wind blowing first across the fish market and then across the newly fertilised fields over the lane, one doesn't believe survival is possible – until the wind changes and blows across town garbage and pigs and more fields, and then we wish it around. But there's no boredom here. . . .

Yours sincerely,

FRANK and MAIDA

––––––

Circulated by Mrs. E.R. Coaldrake, Hamilton Road, Nundah.
Printed by Brisbane City Printery, Edward Street, Brisbane.

Izu Mission Meetings. Unofficial Minutes kept by F.W.C. [handwritten].

MEETING AT DR. KAWAI'S HOUSE, OSE, 17 SEPTEMBER 1951.

<u>Present</u>: Miyazawa-san, Dr. Kawai, Mrs. Harada, Fukuo, F.W.C.
Opened with prayer 1p.m.
<u>Minutes</u> Meeting held at Imaihama 2/10/50 read.

1. Committee: Subject to Bishop's approval to hold a postal election for 4 members, and F.W.C. to select 3 others to act for 1952. All communicants to be notified of this proposal and opinion asked – re. method of election in December. The Committee to meet monthly in various centres and report to absent members (no connection with Ito church if formed). [Frank Coaldrake was trying to establish committees in each regional centre.]

... Meeting closed with prayer at 4.30 p.m.

Newsletter No. 41, October–November, 1951.

NIPPON SEIKO KWAI

> C/o B.C.O.F. Army P.O. Ebisu,
> Tokyo,
> JAPAN.

From – Rev. F.W. Coaldrake

[written by Maida Coaldrake]

> [Address written in Japanese.]
>
> Our Japanese address which reads in English:
>
>> Ito-shi
>> Oka-ku
>> Shimo-uchi, 960.
>
>> St. Mary's Church House,
>> 960, Shimouchi,
>> Okaku,
>> Ito,
>> JAPAN.

Dear Friends,

The house seems strangely empty this afternoon, although Meyoko-san is sitting beside me doing some sewing, and Maruyama-san is close by in the study working over the Lenten Bible studies with Frank. The house seems empty because one hour ago we were standing on the Ito Station saying, "please come again" to Muriel Lester, World Traveller, Writer, Christian gentlewoman. Last

Spring for a few moments we drank tea with her in Tokyo. We talked of many of you at home in Australia; we talked of our work in Izu, of Miss Lester's intended visit to America, of India and of the Kabuki Theatre in Tokyo. She said: "I hope to come to Japan again in the Autumn; if I do I shall come to see you." To Frank that brief meeting was as the coming together of old friends, but to me the beginning of a wonderful experience. All the way back to Odawara that night I pondered on the spiritual energy and depth and love of a woman who could draw you close in such a brief encounter.

A few weeks ago we had a postcard. Miss Lester was back in Japan. She would be coming to Ito. Nobody who knows Miss Lester, or her writings, can fail to enter into the joy we felt nor the way in which she lighted with her interest so many routines of life in this "Church house." The way we have continuous classes on Saturdays in the big room, switching over suddenly to dining from study table, and then back for evening meeting and instruction; the moving in of the Altar and the preparations for Sunday services, which require us to eat in the narrow kitchen or on a tray in the bedroom, all reminded her of her London East End days. Her delight in the changing expressions on people's faces (for she knows no Japanese), made us delight in them too; her sidelights on six weeks non-stop travel from Hokkaido in the north, to Hiroshima in the south, made us get our maps and enjoy the country, and see the desperate spiritual straits of so many of its people all over again. But perhaps her delight in the simple routine of family life, the meals and the books, and our grand-sized Japanese style bath, did most to colour the two grey wet days she stayed with us. Only a great person can do that, and she is a great person. In a week she will be on her way to Hong Kong, perhaps into Communist China. Later in the year Rangoon, Africa, Palestine, Italy, and not until May will she see the cottage in Essex, whose address she left in the Visitors' Book.

———

You will be wondering about the new names – Meyoko and Maruyama. Today it is very much "hail and farewell," as Meyoko has been with us two weeks, and Maruyama leaves us on Wednesday. During the three months of his work here he has been kept very busy. (Fig. 36) A Psychology student from the Peers' University [Gakushuin] in Tokyo, and a keen young member of Kofu church, he gave up his summer vacation and part of his term to work with Frank during the camps, and later on to do such jobs as the drafting of a whole year's Bible Study notes for the people of the Izu Church. There's no intellectual snobbery about Maruyama, and I've seen him turn his hand to everything, from changing a blown-out tyre on our very first day together to levelling ground near this house, or swinging on the beams of the big shelter at Ippeki Camp in the pouring rain, helping fix the tarpaulin. But he's equally at home in the study and his no mean ability in English has made him an invaluable right hand man for Frank during these difficult days of no assistant priest. It is now more than six months since Fr. Iida's appointment was terminated, and as yet, the Bishop can see no relief in sight within the year. This diocese has still vacant parishes and not enough candidates for Holy Orders.

Figure 36 Akira Maruyama's "Leap of Faith" at the Lake Ippeki Camp, July, 1951.

But that is quite another matter and for now we are sorry to see Maruyama return to his University for our own sakes, but very glad for his. One day we hope he will get a University teaching appointment as he plans (for he has the mental calibre), and go abroad. We have even thought so far ahead as an Australian College! Who knows?[36]

As for Meyoko-san, all I can say is "may she go on forever!" She has come to share the work of the constant stream of visitors, the callers who pop up at any of the three legitimate entrances and at other odd places besides, and the routine work of a house that is at present also a Church, and the centre of a busy parish. A young married woman whose husband works away from home, she has already proved a treasure, showing fruits of the excellent training the Japanese staff at the B.C.O.F. Kawana Hotel receives. With work there, and for a while in an Occupation household in Tokyo, she has absorbed the strange ways of the Western household, while work in a Japanese restaurant from 8 a.m. to 11 p.m. every day of every week in every month has given her a willingness to "bend her

36 Akira Maruyama was to become an editor for Kodansha, one of Japan's leading publishers. He took charge of the "stable" of brilliant *manga* artists who were to change the world's popular culture. They included Osamu Tetsuka, creator of "Astroboy."

bones" to please us. After dear Ogata-san's slow-moving, slow-thinking ways, I am often hard put to keep up with Meyoko-san. Certainly after nearly a year of doing everything myself and still trying to put my hand to parish affairs, stores, parcels, letters, and language study, I am ready to "bend my bones" to be sure she stays. As I listen to other missionary wives tell hair-raising stories of domestic crises with their house girls – and they have many – I count my own blessings!

With Camps over, everything else happened with a rush. In Meyoko's first week we were serving morning and afternoon teas to as many as fourteen workers round the property with lots of extras to meals as well. Two lads were living on the block in a tent we brought in from the camp. At 7 a.m., six or seven gardeners arrived. When they all, and Frank, got to work an amazing transformation took place. In less than two days 150 yards of hedge were removed to a new location and grew as green and bright the next day as if in the place planted; two short lines of bushes skilfully placed began a new era of privacy for the Coaldrakes, and most amazing of all, garden beds full of blooming chrysanthemums and marigolds appeared around the white walls of the house. Two hundred strawberry plants were in, rhubarb and parsley started off on a useful career, timber for the next groups of buildings stacked. In one week so much happened on St. Mary's Church property.

What would be quite a miracle in Australia is more of an everyday occurrence in this country. Japanese gardeners have a remarkable skill and an equally remarkable knowledge of the art of moving fully grown trees, hedges, flowers, and so on. Overnight you will see a fine rock garden of shrubs, and ferns and pine trees overshadowing it, put in outside a new inn or house.

The result of that week's work has been the appearance of order around the Church house and garage-store, and with a layout of paths and garden beds you can see some promise of the pleasant place we hope to create during the next few years. (Colour Plate 4)

I began to write this letter while I could see the orange globes of persimmons on the trees across the road, but sudden autumn dark has descended, and continual blackouts mean that I now type by the light of a candle. Typhoon "Ruth" – all typhoons are distinguished each season by girls' names given according to date order, so that we trust "Ruth" will be the last of the season – did her best to repair the damage a long, dry spell has done to the country. She was, to be sure, equal to millions of tons of coal for electricity production, but this has scarcely balanced the loss of life in the south and the millions of yen worth of damage to crops and building all over this main island of Honshu. Even Ito was in the grip of raging winds and floods of rain for two days, and we spent daylight hours in a kind of twilight because it was necessary to have all the wooden shutters up to the windows. But now days are calm and bright and the temperature is dropping at the rate of 10 degrees [Fahrenheit] each week.

We often comment on "seasonal outcrops" – the interesting and different things which occur only at certain times of the year. With Autumn, we are once more in the midst of "school field days," and it is a constant source of conversation in this household as to how the school lesson programme is ever covered.

Everywhere one goes one meets hundreds of school children with their food boxes and water bottles. In the cities there are thousands, emptied out of huge buses. On the mountain roads one passes further streams of great buses. In the country the city children walk in endless lines to a lake, or a forest or some shrine of special interest. Younger children enjoy day excursions, but sometimes we suspect that "enjoy" is not the right word. For they might leave home before 6 a.m., take a long train journey, walk 10 miles, and return home near midnight. The middle and high school students often go on two-day trips, spending two consecutive nights in a train journey, and the two days trekking round historical spots. Without doubt they see and learn to appreciate much outside the range of their every day life, but we doubt the wisdom of the organisation which necessitates a day off school, the next day, to recover from the effects of fatigue and stomach upsets. However on they go, and any early morning you can stand at our windows and watch hundreds of little ones clatter in their wooden "geta" up the hill on their four mile walk to Lake Ippeki.

———

Autumn for us has meant a swing into a work programme in the Peninsula which residence in Odawara had made very difficult, and we find already in the "callers" and in the regular classes in Ito a feeling of coming to grips with a widely scattered Mission area. Our "Cottage Church" centres are growing and all being within three hours' driving to Ito, special visits outside the time-table are possible. Perhaps there is an anniversary of a death or some great occasion – the Shinto and the Buddhist [believers] keep many anniversaries – and it is good to show that the Christian Church through the centuries has had provision for every need of the individual. So Frank leaves early in the morning and celebrates Holy Communion in some quiet house miles away from home. On All Saints' Day, after an early celebration in Ito, there will be another in Imaihama.

With the assistance of Miyazawa-san, Rector's warden and first lay reader to be commissioned in this diocese, every centre has two visits a month, and some more. Not only services are conducted and pastoral visits carried out, but Bible classes and other instruction given. It is going to be a wonderful help when our Bible Study Series are ready for each season, beginning with Advent, for there will be regular, intelligent thinking and praying going on in all our Christian homes all over the Peninsula.

On the first Sunday of each month Frank is in Ito for two services, after beginning the weekend with boys' class, teachers' group, and everybody's discussion group on Saturday. But early Monday finds him speeding over the rough mountain road to Mishima and all the little farmhouses by the way where isolated Christians live. It is often two o'clock on Tuesday morning before the Land Rover whirs to rest again in Ito and the smell of coffee and cooking eggs and toast puzzles the neighbours, who keep very regular hours.

A confirmation class after the Parish Communion always pushes time rather hard on the second Sunday [in the month], for a hasty meal has to be eaten mid-morning to last over until evening. Then Miyazawa-san says Evensong in Ito, and Frank is already many miles away. Down this side of the Peninsula there are many interesting folk to visit, one with a market garden which sometimes provides us with a rare treat of celery or some fine plant for the garden; another – a plant experimental farm – actually grows passion fruit and Australian trees under glass! Ose village streets don't get any wider though, and the Rover is still a tight fit in the main street. At the Bible class there, some of the members were lately rejoicing because their summer work had for the first time in years brought them a profit. They are diving girls who bring in the harvest of seaweed, later to become gelatine. Two of them are thinking about baptism. Little by little the church grows.

Before Frank returns home again he visits Shimoda as well. In this ancient town, one of the five "treaty" ports granted to Admiral Perry in the middle of the last century, our Cottage Church occupies the second floor of a museum which contains all kinds of interesting relics of the days when the first U.S. Consul Townsend Harris lived in the old temple nearby. In those days the granting of a treaty port was a great triumph for the Western world, but the Japanese Government knew how to keep controls in its own hands. Even now, with a fine new road opening up, Shimoda is still the edge of the world with its close bay and high wooded hills, but then – with only sea transport, and the densely forested hinterland – it must have been almost out of the world! It is though, a very busy port, and small vessels load fish, stones, charcoal and timber continually destined for the great cities. I love the old stone houses with their tea-cake icing exteriors, but the usual street smells seem only to have improved with age!

Once more the early hours of a morning are cheered by boiling kettle and toast browning – for we have found such times very good for electricity supply.

We call the third Sunday "the quiet one," with all day in Ito, lay reader in Imaihama, and other centre visits confined to weekday services and discussions. But after the fourth Sunday comes such a round of visits, with so much eating of Japanese food and talking that it takes a full day to recover from a three-day trip. Last week a new centre was opened up in the particular [Ose] district in a room under the brow of rugged Cape Iro [Irozaki] which overlooks a rock-infested sea.

And this scattered area will be drawn together not only by shared thought and prayer; at the end of November we are to have a "teaching mission" for church people. The conductor, Fr. Sakurai, of the Society of St. John the Evangelist, is a Japanese priest wonderfully skilled and experienced in the conduct of retreats and missions, and is the author of many simply written but profound booklets on church teaching. He will be in Ito for a week and people from outcentres will travel in by bus as they can, and those who are free to come full-time will be offered hospitality in the homes of our Ito parishoners. We all look forward to this week as the beginning of a new life for us all.

Back to the more material things, press reports of high prices at Home have no reflection in the generous food parcels we are receiving. As we repack for distribution I particularly appreciate the notes and letters I find attached to little luxuries; and bits of parish papers, glimpses of your life at home. Fats, meats and milks, with jellies, are still way up on the preference lists and we continue to be most grateful for used woollens and men's clothing, so long as Army Post keeps postage within your pocket limits. At the moment there is one packing case in the store that is my particular joy and pride. All the year we keep new clothes and such things as will make "special" presents for Christmas. During the last unpacking this box received a grand fillip with more than two dozen pairs of lovely new wincyette pantees and more than that number of the most wonderful animals and rag gollies – animals such as no zoo has ever seen but which will delight the kiddies of Hiakawa. This village had a beautifully decorated tree last Christmas, standing the full time in the corner of a room – but there were never any presents on it! There is no reason to suppose that this Christmas would have been any different had it not been for your generosity and imagination.

––––––

It never rains, but etc., and on the side of material things we have had a downpour in the last few days. After weeks of bad Japanese bread and conscientious skirting of the "black" shop, a soldier friend going on extended leave had his bread ration made up for us. One afternoon there arrived on my doorstep, fifteen loaves of warm fragrant Australian type bread – fifteen 2 lb. loaves. I sat by the box for some time just sniffing before I could get down to practical details of what to do with it. The next day 34 eggs arrived – and eggs at about 19 yen – i.e. about 6 d. Aust. each! The Coaldrakes and friends have been living in luxury.

––––––

Talk of peace treaties and the possible effect of the cessation of hostilities in Korea on the Japanese economy, and perhaps more importantly, the control of rice scheduled for April next year, occupies the thought and talk of people in the towns, in factories, trains, offices. But the Japanese man or woman, at the table or in the home, is pre-occupied with other, deeper problems. What is to become of the children as they grow up in this confused society in these confused days? How can I, a Christian, continue to be a Christian and go to worship God and receive His Sacraments in His Church, when in my work from day to day, in the very practices of the society on which I am dependent for my food and my family's good, I must sin to survive? It is the old, old, question but always in a new form. We ourselves have already encountered it in land dealings and purchases. Corruption and bribery is so rife and an accepted thing in every kind of business and government dealing, that provision is made for it officially. For example, it is taken for granted that no one fills in his taxation forms for the total amount of income and possessions, so in assessment, tax is levied on an income a fixed percentage higher than that acknowledged in one's form! That is the problem the man who is honest by Christian standards is up against. Everywhere we hear "no, it's not honest, but it's custom." The tension is becoming acute. That is good. It means that Christians are thinking. The Church must teach more and more deeply on man's nature as a sinner and his place in the

Redeemed Society. This truth seems understood even less in Japan than in other countries.

We do appreciate your letters and your parcels. We are constantly aware of the support and strength your prayers give us. We do not need the 6 a.m. drums at the nearby Buddhist shrine to remind us that we live in a pagan society – a society as pagan, and civilised and conventional, as the society of St. Paul's day. But we do need your help to withstand its subtle inroads and to lay the foundations of a new Christian community.

We plan to write again before the end of the year but should like to send you our best wishes for a blessed Advent season.

Yours very sincerely,

FRANK AND MAIDA

P.S. Until you hear to the contrary, we still enjoy the benefits of B.C.O.F. mails. Our postal address is therefore –

C/- Aust. Army P.O., 214,
B.C.O.F.,
Tokyo, JAPAN.

We receive the usual B.C.O.F. concession for letters and parcels (1/9 d. per 11 pounds).

For those who care to pay the extra, please remember that an air mail letter (1/6 d.) addressed to our Ito address comes direct in less than a week.

———

Circulated by Mrs. E.R. Coaldrake, Hamilton Road, Nundah.
Printed by Brisbane City Printery, Edward Street, Brisbane.

Newsletter No. 42, December, 1951–January, 1952.

NIPPON SEIKO KWAI

From – Rev. F.W. Coaldrake

[written by Maida Coaldrake]

[Address written in Japanese.]

Ito, 19th Dec., 1951.

Dear Friends,

Bless you for all your encouragement and support. It does give both us and the cause of peace and love in a very shaky world a tremendous push along.

Once more Frank, with the Rover laden down with relief goods which we have been sorting and packing for two days solidly, has gone off on pastoral work. He has days away every week, which does so cut down on time for jobs and writing home. Today he will visit about five different centres and get back at midnight a very exhausted man.

I'm always particularly glad to be about then to urge him to the bath, and stand over him while he takes hot food. He usually thinks he's too tired for both, but we've proved over and over again its worth more than an hour's sleep to bath and eat properly. Well, letter writing is one thing I can do which doesn't need great proficiency in Japanese, and you'd laugh with me over the corn on my writing finger!

We do realise we failed to get you your Christmas message, but since writing last more than 200 letters have gone out to our friends. We hope to give you a New Year thought as well as lots of thanks and summing up for 1951, or advice for 1952!

It is getting very difficult to get parcels and boxes in safely. I will be telling you more of the sad story of our three day argument with Customs in Yokohama, and also of the arrival of a completely empty box whose contents were valued at £7/7/-. Of course, we are filing a claim.

The whole matter is in a very fluid state and will need much thought.

[One much appreciated parcel] has arrived safely, with great rejoicings. I purred over the nice black sox and the precious white baby wool.

We are looking forward to the arrival of our first-born in April, to establish an Australian Christian family of Izu Peninsula. Gathering a stock of Nestle's "Ideal" evaporated milk is one of our problems. Canteens have to ration us at six tins per month at present. We have a "pusher" stored in the garage already, given to us by the Forsythes who returned to Canberra. They also gave us feeding bottles.

We have a set of concrete tubs made on the premises, a Sydney "Rins an' Dry," a Wood-burning Copper, ex. Aust. Army Cooks, and a Rotary Clothes Line we made from galv. piping and sundry bits and pieces, made or picked up. It works well.

I'm much better, thank you. Our doctor discovered my particular trouble was smells – and so we now keep food where it belongs, by a splendid system of Airwicks, an American scientific discovery based on chlorophyll, which clears the air of any smell very quickly, or if you can beat the smell by opening the wick first it stops it altogether. A miracle indeed. I defy anyone either to imagine or better the smells in this country.

You know we shall be thinking of you at Christmas, both in our prayers and at our festival board, at which David Chamberlain will join us. We shall be carving a home-grown chicken too! But whether that will be before, or well after Christmas, depends on Frank's travel programme.

Frank writes: I've just come in from a full day in some distant villages. I took two Ito church members with me on my rounds. They were at the early morning celebration and had breakfast with us before we set off. I like to take Ito members out to visit village members because it helps develop a sense of unity throughout the Peninsula and also, they add weight to my impact. They find it full of interest and always enjoy joining in whatever goes on.

Some day perhaps you or some Australian friend will be able to spend a day with me on a journey such as I've made today.

It starts, as I've said, with the quiet refreshment of prayer in the early morning. If you're here we'll say it in English and the Japanese people will say their portions in Japanese, while we use English. They know their way well enough now to be at home before the altar whether it is north, south, east or west of home. Of course we use Japanese as the regular medium of our prayer, so perhaps this morning you would have been a little astray sometimes.

We have breakfast next, with the Autumn sun slanting through the windows to warm our feet as we do our best to hurry through what always threatens to be a prolonged act of almost tiresome politeness.

Once on the road I can let my foot on the accelerator work out a compensation for any over politeness.

There is nothing gentle or gracious about our bounding along over badly washed-out roads. We have an appointment for a service 25 miles away and an hour to get there. If, perhaps, we had Ian Shevill with us he'd be recalling what he wrote in "A Man's Job," price 6 d. Describing the work of the bush priest in Australia, he said, "He is provided with a car and usually has one hairbreadth escape per month."

We do, too! But "near-misses" are a regular part of any day's run. For instance, if you'd had your elbow over the door ledge as we ran through Inatori this morning, you'd have had it knocked on the roadside door post when I had to swing in to clear a coming truck. Such things are so commonplace that I no longer notice them, but the gasp of my visitor passenger at that point this morning gave me quite a start.

Arriving at Harada-san's "Katei-Kyokai" [cottage church at Imaihama], we waste no time about setting up the altar and once again celebrate the sacred mysteries, this time to the accompaniment of waves booming on the beach below. The widow and her daughter were simply teachers of flower-arrangement and tea ceremony two years ago. Church members for many years, they were doing a little to spread the Faith even then, but now their influence has spread up and down the road. They put everything they have into our campaign now. Today, after the service and sandwich lunch, we went to call on several people. One is a sick woman, mother of a school teacher, who regularly attends the services and instruction at the widow's house. Others were families of several children in poor circumstances, to whom we took clothing and food from Australian parcels. Another was an elderly shopkeeper and farmer, whose wife and daughter were the first of Mrs. Harada's friends to be baptised.

With one parcel of gifts we got out of the car right beside the sea. After watching a flock of domestic ducks swimming in the sheltered water of the fishing boat harbour, we turned to ask a rapidly gathering crowd of the curious, which was the right track to our man?

Following instructions we turned into a narrow street, which was really a long stone stairway, and climbed up the steep hillside. Stone walls held up six square feet of vegetable garden for a house on the left. A bend in the lane was matched by a bend in the outer wall of the house at that point, and the bending accomplished by using the sides of wrecked fishing boats for the outer boards of the house. The well seasoned timbers of wrecked or worn out boats are always in great demand for the outer walls of houses. Usually they are straightened out on the wall, but in this case they had just the same bend as the road, so they went on in their original shape. There is a house down in Ose built entirely from old fishing boats. The storms of any year can be counted on to provide timber enough for several walls.

A little further up a family patching its bay fishing net stops to watch us file past. Nearby a woman swinging a hoe in her sweet potato patch (three square yards), leans on the handle and chirps between her only two teeth to ask where we want to go.

She turns us off the stairs onto the narrow terrace that is the front garden of a fisherman's house. We know he is a fisherman because, as we pass along the front, we see his fishing gear on the verandah – a pair of gumboots, a long lance, a landing net and an underwater electric lamp with wire leads for clipping to battery terminals. We don't see his catch but salt crystals on everything tell the story of his rough night in the storm just over. He catches squid and octopus with that gear. The light attracts and illuminates them and he waits leaning over the side of the boat until he can spear them with the long lance.

At the end of this terrace we find a ten foot square cottage on a shelf of the cliff. Those of "the curious" who have followed us up crowd around and ahead of us as we greet the mother and tell her why we've come. She is somewhat overcome to have a parcel of such necessary but unprocurable things dropped into her lap from an unknown person in distant Australia. Standing at her door after coming out from teaching her how to mix powdered milk, I can point straight out over the sea to where far away Australia lies.

On the way down to the main road we spot two of our Sunday School lads and try to discover why one hasn't been coming very regularly lately.

We leave Mrs. Harada to walk back the mile to her home, while we carry on along the road back to Ito. At a suitable spot we back down to the beach and pick up a heavy load of round stones for our garden paths. With this five hundredweight of rock in the back we ride much more smoothly on the way home.

At a village we usually pass through in two great bounds we slow down and turn up a side street. It leads us past the houses and out across the paddifields into the mandarin orchards on the lower slopes of the hills. We call on a very isolated family of three daughters, the elderly mother being away in Yokohama for a few weeks. We want to interest them in getting our Daily Bible Reading Notes, so we leave a few copies of the leaflet with the sixteen year old, who has just come home from school and is about to cook the evening meal. We decline the invitation to stay for tea and set out on the last fifteen miles to home. It is rice-harvest time and everyone is very busy until late in the dusk.

We see a funeral starting off headed by the Shinto priest. It had to be delayed until dusk so that the day's fine harvest weather might not be wasted. The casket, wrapped in gorgeously patterned pink and red kimono cloth, is barely two feet long, and is slung from a bamboo pole carried by two men. About twenty people walk along behind the parents, whose infant has died.

We reach Ito at six and find Kubota-san waiting. He has come to take Maruyama-san's place as my helper for the next few months. We make brief plans for his first day's work tomorrow and our own day's work is done.

We are conducting a postal election of a Mission Committee at present, which will be the first of its kind in Izu. We can't have a general meeting or election because our members are so scattered. Also, nobody knows everybody except myself, so we must use the postal method.

We have nearly completed the distribution of clothing and foodstuffs out of a great many parcels which have arrived during the last few months. The warm woollen clothes are a great blessing.

Our 24 trees planted last week are doing well. No rain meant care about watering them. Our gardener is also a volunteer fireman and he solved the problem on Saturday afternoon by turning his brigade out for practice, and turning the hoses towards our trees.

Yours very sincerely,

FRANK AND MAIDA

P.S.: The time has come to address your letters to our address at – 960 Shimouchi, Okaku, Ito-Shi, Japan. The British Commonwealth Forces' duties in Korea may end in Peace any day now we hope.

――――

Circulated by Mrs. E.R. Coaldrake, Hamilton Road, Nundah.
Printed by Brisbane City Printery, Edward Street, Brisbane.

Newsletter No. 43, **February, 1952.**

NIPPON SEIKO KWAI

From – Rev. F.W. Coaldrake

[written by Maida Coaldrake with addition by Frank]

> [Address written in Japanese.]
> St. Mary's Church House
> 960 Shimonouchi,
> Okaku,
> Ito-shi,
> JAPAN.

15th January, 1952

Dear Friends,

Yesterday we put away the [Christmas] Crib and turned over some pages in our hymn books. So before we roll our sleeves up and get on to the business of preparations for Lent I can't resist the suggestion that now is the time for a long letter to you.

Christmas was altogether delightful and we had the joy of seeing the year's work reflected in the biggest congregation we have had. Some of the church people from other centres made the trip to Ito for the 9 a.m. service on Christmas Day, making a congregation of 53, which considerably taxed the capacity of our living room, which becomes the church, meeting hall or dining-room as the case may be.

Christmas began at 5 o'clock on Christmas Eve when a working-bee descended on us. Flowers and berries had been arriving all day so we had the loveliest decorations – white and gold chrysanthemums, carnations from a church family way down the Peninsula, a few delicious smelling early spring bulbs and the glossy bronze leaves and red berries of the "nan-ten," a wonderful shrub which boasts the name of Southern Heaven.

Someone had remembered that in Australia poinsettia blooms are favourites and four lovely sprays turned up straight from hothouses. They certainly couldn't survive in the chilly outdoors of Japan at Christmas. In between polishing and decorating, we slipped off to the Ito Station to collect David Chamberlain from the Kobe train and he had his "saved-up" Christmas dinner sitting in the kitchen out of the way of buckets, cloths and berry bushes.

We had eaten our home-grown chicken with all the trimmings, and plum pudding (made possible by generous parcels from Australia), earlier in the day, knowing full well that at 5 p.m. the Coaldrakes' private life was over for a season. To understand that you really must pay us a visit some time. This present house is built in the shape of a T with the big room the stem, the bedrooms to one side of the cross bar, and the kitchen, store and bathroom on the other. Normally a long polished passage or "roka" with large windows and our little used front entrance opening from it connects the rooms. But for services the Altar is set up in the "roka," the sliding wooden doors into the big living room opened back, and there you have a most effective church. The small two-[*tatami*] mat room which during the week is used as an oratory, and by reason of the splendid habit of having removable sliding doors in most rooms in the house, can be used for week-day celebrations of Holy Communion, now becomes the vestry. That leaves us with a three-mat room for guests and our own room accessible only through the "church," and on the other side a long narrow room, the kitchen, which though never built as a dinette, often has to provide snack bar service for all and sundry. So – we had our Christmas dinner early . . . on Xmas Eve.

It was a lovely clear, cold night and people were already assembling for Midnight Mass, even more special than usual this year because there were to be First Communions made by girls confirmed the previous Sunday. Suddenly a clatter of geta running fast was heard inside and just as the outer doors were flung back and an agitated voice cried "Fire – Kameyama," the dreaded sound of the fire siren wailed out. Several church families live on the hill behind the town called Kameyama and we were acutely conscious that, with only five minutes to go to midnight, no member of any of these families was yet present. A red glare was spreading rapidly across the sky and later a family from the hill arrived. Their whispered conversation told us they were alright. "The fire was in a village four miles away behind the hill. No, they didn't know how bad. No, there was nothing to be done, the fire engines were already there." With a sigh of relief we settled down to sing "Mitsu kai no" (*Adeste Fideles*), and join our worship with that of the Angels and all our friends at home at the Crib of the Holy Babe of Bethlehem.

But to return to the fire: the strained faces around that room brought home to us more than any number of newspaper reports, the terror of fire there is in this country. Only two or three weeks before Christmas 400 homes were swept away in an hour or two on the outskirts of Odawara. Every day you hear of disastrous fires in this or that town or village.

Recently hospitals and schools have been burned down all over the country in the first wave of fires that seems to follow the onslaught of winter. No amount of education in fire prevention weeks seems to make any impact on the general negligence with regard to use of open hibachi [charcoal braziers] or the proper inspection of electrical wiring. That is responsible for more than half of the fires that take terrible toll of life and property every year. Only a couple of days ago a high school lad we know came to pay us a visit. When asked how it was that he wasn't at school in Osaka, many miles away, he said that his New Year holidays had been extended indefinitely as his school had just been burnt down. We continue to hope and pray that the terror of fire might soon be translated into positive action.

————

After the 9 a.m. celebration the next morning, 35 stayed to a festive meal together. For tables we had the wooden shutters off the windows, standing on big biscuit tins and swathed in sheets. That makes a 15' x 15' table, the necessary foot high and everybody but Frank can fold up quite happily at it. Frank folds up alright but as his legs are almost twice as long as those of an average Japanese, he isn't quite so happy. After everyone had eaten their fill, came introductions and speeches without which any parish gathering is incomplete. There may be strangers in our midst, but whether or not, we must all introduce ourselves by name and church, and should we feel so moved nobody will protest if we make a half hour speech on any theme uppermost in our minds. After a meal this is as may be, but I have sat hungrily in front of an appetising hot meal, watching my tempura (a pork chop fried in batter), soup and rice grow greasily cold before everyone was through with their speeches of welcome [before the meal].

We scrambled to what was left of our feet about noon and made hasty preparations for the children's party at 2 p.m. Once more, thanks to parcels from many friends at Home, I had been able to make dozens of jellies in the small round Japanese tea cups, and these, with a fancy iced animal biscuit on top, made the table very gay. It was the children from our Saturday afternoon church school and from Christian families who crackled biscuits and consumed piles of bread rolls and jam.

After everyone had eaten their fill, we gave out the Christmas cards and calendars, and to the three "babies" delightful kangaroo toys which had come from a church in Adelaide. What with "food," cards, many carols and some films the time passed so quickly that it seemed only one hour instead of two when we were finding the right shoes at the entrance for the kiddies, and at the same time handing out food and bedding for David and Frank as they set off to "do" the Peninsula and take Christmas Communions to our cottage churches. They had several more parties to arrange too, so as the Land Rover streaked off into the dusk I didn't exactly envy them, and went inside to a good cup of black tea. A gang of nice girls helped set the house to rights, and even if their idea of setting a house to rights is to put all the furniture as close to the walls as possible, who cared? It was Christmas.

At 7 o'clock, with the shutters once more doing their job to keep the cold and dark out, I switched on Radio Australia, and to the tune of Carols from Home set out some more of the lovely greeting cards we had just received.

———

Early in December the Parish Teaching Mission, conducted for us by Fr. Sakurai of the Society of St. John the Evangelist was all and more than we hoped. For a week daily services were conducted and instruction given on the life of the Christian within the Church. We hoped that in this way those who are already keen church members would be strengthened in their Faith and ready to help us evangelise the Peninsula. Ito folk offered hospitality for those coming from Ose, Shimoda, Imaihama and other centres, so that on Monday, after we had all gathered together for Sunday services, we were able to have a grand day of shared meals, talk and instruction. The children had their special sessions, too.

One of the best aspects of the week's programme, and one which delighted both Frank and the Father equally, was the number of church members who went to them for advice or discussion on their problems. We feel very much the lack of a Japanese priest on the staff, and this week in some small measure compensated for it. The most unexpected outcome was the delight we ourselves could take in the company of Fr. Sakurai and the pertinent and wise comment he had so often for many of our own problems. Four years' training in the United States has given him a background from which he could see both our problem and the true answer in this situation. And for a mere housewife, his appreciation of meals and his ability to disappear just when cleaning or some domestic crisis was imminent, ranks him high on the list of perfect guests.

———

This Teaching Mission to church people led to the confirmation later of four of our girls. Three of them were baptised shortly after our return to Japan and are my goddaughters – Asako-san, in the office of the big Middle School nearby; Kimura-san, a High School student whose growing interest in her kindergarten class of the Church School has inspired the thought of some such work as a full-time job after graduation; Arai-san, the third daughter in a family whose widowed mother has done a grand job of upbringing; and Motoko-chan, the daughter of our Rector's Warden and lay reader, Miyazawa-san. Motoko-chan is one of the few in the whole of our huge parish who has had the privilege of growing up in a Christian home and she was the youngest of the group. The Bishop of South Tokyo, Bishop Maekawa, came down from Yokohama on Saturday, and the Confirmation Service took place before the usual 9 o'clock celebration of Holy Communion on Sunday. We thought the singing of the congregation had never been so joyful. Now the girls are anxiously setting about ways and means of serving the Church which has given them so much. They are fine examples of the wisdom, in this fluid time, of making the preparation for Baptism and Confirmation a long one. In 18 months or two years the chaff flutters away very easily.

———

Into the already overcrowded month of December we managed to pack another session of "overnight" gardening. In a way this had more spectacular results than the last, for between dawn and dusk on a short winter day, 24 trees were planted around the house and up what will one day be a gently curving drive to the church door. I used to associate tree-planting with "Arbor Days" at school when we stood around and watched a senior prefect or other august personage plant an eighteen inch potential oak tree. Not so in Japan. Trees between 14 and 20 feet [in height] grace our land, and the ever-useful Land Rover and trailer was plying between the Lake Ippeki Camp site and Ito at the rate of a trip every two hours, carrying trees twice its combined length. And joy of joys, the next week not only were tiny buds swelling on the trees but birds had come to stay; certainly only our common or garden sparrow, but birds are a rarity in this country where so much of the life of the land depends on the safe harvesting of a good grain crop. I used to stand on our really lovely hillside at Odawara, amongst maple and plum and cherry and pine trees, and long for the sight or sound of a bird. Now busy little sparrows in their legion pick crumbs and young grass, and fluff up against the bitter westerlies, on the branches of our trees.

———

[Frank writes:]

It is an old Japanese custom to spend the last week of the year in a grand clearing away of dust and dirt and a balancing of the year's money figures. If we take stock of our Izu Mission's first year we can write all sorts of statistics, but perhaps the most revealing one is that 160 people used the special envelopes to make a Christmas offering. Of these 35 are on the roll of communicants and all these have made their Christmas Communions, and 33 of them exercised their right to vote for the election of a Mission Committee for the coming year.

The other very promising figure is that 58 people have enrolled for the correspondence course of notes for daily reading of the Bible. We are having to prepare these notes ourselves so that they will meet the needs of people who have no religious background and often very little education.

We might add another hundred or more people who are in regular contact with the church.

We are a small church in the midst of a [district with a] quarter of a million people who are proving to be easy to interest superficially, but hesitate at anything involving a change of traditional habits! Don't we all?

I am missing the help of my Japanese assistant who is training now in Tokyo Theological College for Holy Orders. Here is the polite note I found after returning from a round of Parish visiting. He was a treasure while here.

"I found your letter on my desk Tuesday morning. All appointed works are finished, but Bible reading plan requires much time and I have just crossed the Red Sea.

As I have spoken of the other day, I have an examination tomorrow morning. One of my friends was kind enough to send me the notebook of the subject. So I wish to go to school and have the examination.

I have been wondering if I could go or not? I thought I should not do so without your permission while you are absent. But when I spoke of exam before you allowed me to go and it is a pretty loss for me not to have it.

Please excuse me to go and stay away from my work tomorrow.

[from] MARUYAMA AKIRA"

———

Recent alterations in mailing and import proceedings have made it difficult and costly to get gift parcels of food and clothing into Japan. The steady flow of parcels of useful things has been something to marvel at. During these years of recovery they have meant the difference between life and death in a few cases, and between despair and hope in many others. The people in need of such help are much fewer now. Recovery has reached the stage where necessities are available to anyone with money to buy them. A salaried worker, for instance, can get along safely if he is careful. There is still much poverty, and people in small villages, especially those burned out during the war, or repatriated from abroad after the war, are still having a struggle. It would be good to be able to go on helping with discretion those who are in need.

But new policies mean that you will have to pay about 1/- postage per pound of parcel and we will have to pay import duties between 20 and 80 per cent of the value of the goods – even though they are for free distribution to needy people. It is cock-eyed, of course, and I have not been able to refrain from saying so in various government offices. The only apparent result of my impassioned oratory was to make the officials bow very low and refer me to the next table, and then the next, on up the official hierarchy. The sheer number of tables beats you! I've never got as far as the glass-topped one at the far end.

It all adds up to this – there are people who need help but the Government seems determined to secure revenue from foreign charity.

So with the end of postal privileges we have enjoyed through the now finished B.C.O.F. service, letters at airmail rate of 1/6 d., or 7 d. air letter forms, to our Japanese address reach us very quickly, some times in six days, and surface mail at ordinary foreign mail rates takes perhaps six weeks.

As for PARCELS, the best thing to do will be to put the cost of contents and postage into open Postal Notes and leave us to buy such things as Japanese processed Australian wool for those who need it. That way your Australian pound will produce more goods in the village here – it may be wool, or rice, or fat, or anything!

Second-hand clothes sales at home and the result in Postal Notes might be a practical way of continuing help to those who need it.

Of course, what underlies all this is that it is the funds of A.B.M. which keep us here and you can't go wrong in adding to A.B.M. funds for Japan.

May we take this opportunity of thanking all who have been sending us parcels, particularly several small groups of people who have kept up a steady flow month by month – I think the "prize" would go to the Launceston St. Peter's group and Mrs. Brook's group in Bathurst.

——

Against your news of heat and bushfires we can only place cold and more cold, with every variation of it. Across the bay, the range of mountains blue in the clear light is so ribbed with snow that it looks like the beginning of a sub-arctic continent, and certainly the winds which blow off it would suggest it to be so. Every morning the common frost raises the earth around the house some two or three inches, and while in Tokyo last week for rations and mail, and a retreat arranged by the Sisters of the Epiphany, we awoke one morning to the first snow fall of the year.

It was a great joy to be in touch with so many of you by letter and card. We hope 1952 will be full of good things for you.

Yours sincerely,

FRANK AND MAIDA

——

Circulated by Mrs. E.R. Coaldrake, Hamilton Road, Nundah.
Printed by Brisbane City Printery, Edward Street, Brisbane.

Maida Coaldrake, Oral History, 1 October 2001.

The Occupation finished but in some ways things became harder. Until then we received large parcels from parishioners from the various churches that were supporting us. The parcels came via the military post and cost only about 2/6 d. After the end of the Occupation we had to do everything through the ordinary channels. People from Australia largely stopped sending parcels, perhaps because it was more expensive, but probably more because they did not see the need to support the Japanese and Japan mission in Japan now that Japan was an independent nation again. By this stage the monthly payment to support the mission in Japan from A.B.M. was being sent directly to the parish in Odawara and then later in Izu, not filtered through the Japanese diocese.

The American-dominated Occupation may have ended but we didn't notice much difference in the American presence. The Americans were still there but now using Japan as the main base to fight the war in Korea. The nearby Kawana Hotel in Ito was still full of American soldiers. It was still poverty and hardship in the countryside. Tokyo was prospering but I had terrible trouble with Frank because he had the greatest of difficulty accepting any sort of army rations in the first period 1950–52. For him to accept the rations due to an Australian civilian was unacceptable. He did at first give it all away and that left him worse off in terms of living standards because he did not have the access to local Japanese sources and household networks that the Japanese were using. We were giving away our rations to the Japanese. I had to fight to keep the rice ration. In addition no financial provision was made for the fact that Frank Coaldrake had married and therefore the cost of living had increased. In fact the budget provided by A.B.M. was decreased by £200 p.a. because it was considered that it was no longer necessary to employ Ogata-san as a housekeeper.

Newsletter No. 44, March, 1952.

NIPPON SEIKO KWAI

From – Rev. F.W. Coaldrake

[written by Frank Coaldrake]

> [Address written in Japanese.]
> St. Mary's Church House
> 960 Shimouchi,
> Okaku,
> Ito-shi,
> JAPAN.

Dear Friends,

It was a great pleasure to get a large swag of mail and parcels in Tokyo at B.C.O.F. Post Office mid-February, as we had no letters for nearly a month. For some reason they had not been forwarded to us as usual. Properly speaking, the privilege of using B.C.O.F. Post Office has been withdrawn, though they still handle them for us under protest.

Our address now is at top of this letter, and the postage rates are same as to any foreign country. Surface letter 1 oz., 7½ d.; air mail ½ oz., 1/6 d.; or air folders, 7 d. each. Printed matter, foreign rates 3 d. per 4 oz., 2 d. extra 4 oz.; newspapers, 2½ d. per 6 oz., 2 d. extra 6 oz. The Japanese Post Office is now just about as reliable and prompt as the Australian.

We have received gratefully many generous gifts of baby clothes and equipment, and have ordered a crib basket to be made locally. Japanese infants are outfitted so differently to the usual Australian infant, and though there are a few Overseas Suppliers shops the prices are ruinous.

Maida is to stay with Mrs. Neil Currie in Tokyo during the days of waiting to go into hospital, and it is a great relief to be able to count on that help.

We were visiting Mr. Neil Currie, who is secretary at the Australian Legation, when we heard the sad news of the King's sudden passing. Mrs. Currie was Geraldine Dexter, daughter of Padre Dexter, of Melbourne, and I married Neil and Geraldine in Tokyo last year.

I was requested by the British Ambassador, Sir Esler Dening, to conduct the Memorial Service for the King in Tokyo on February 15th. To complete details of the service I was called again to Tokyo a few days later, which meant leaving Ito at 5 p.m. for the 100 miles drive, and it was 2.30 a.m. before I was home again. Sir Esler is a son of a former Anglican missionary in Japan, and his mother was an Australian of Bacchus Marsh, Victoria. He had been an active layman of the Church also.

The Service was arranged by the British Ambassador and 200 officials attended, including members of the Japanese Imperial Family, Prime Minister Yoshida and members of the Diet.

Army representatives included Gen. Ridgway (USA) and Col. Hodgson (Aust.). India and Canada also were represented.

I am writing now from Ose, and where I sit in the second storey of Dr. Kawai's house I can see a new thatch roof has been put on a house down the street from here. (Colour Plate 5) The men are at work with hedge clippers trimming the ends of the straw to make the roof neat. Village houses still have straw thatched roofs, though grey tiles are becoming more common. Tiles are continually slipping or shifting so that a tiled roof needs attention every few months, but a straw roof needs no attention except to be completely renewed every 50 years or so. A communal levy system is still in use for such works in the villages of Japan.

In this fishing village on the coast there are about 100 straw-roofed houses, so two have their roofs renewed each year. Every family is expected to provide a volunteer for the necessary work on a community basis.

The women go up the mountain and cut the bales and bales of the particular long dry grass and carry it down. They also bring in the necessary bundles of bamboo rods. The men do the laying and trimming of the straw on the roof while the women carry it up the ladders to them. The fire risk with a straw roof is great, of course.

Another village "levy" job has just been done at Osawa-san's village, where 50 villagers and 50 State Roads Department labourers have built a road from the village along the valley through the fields. It is a good road and wide enough for a truck to pass for a mile into the hills, but the start of it is in the old village street along which even the Land Rover is too wide to pass. The day will come when the narrow part will be widened, but probably not for many years. In recent times there have been many improvements on main roads, mostly the widening of bottlenecks, but the surfaces are still as rough as ever.

Mention of fire risks reminds me to tell you about the great fire in Odawara recently, where 400 buildings went up in smoke in a couple of hours. There was a strong gale blowing at the time. I saw the area 10 hours after the fire had been put out, and already the frames of new buildings were being erected and some even had roofs on. It was the fishing village area of the town, with the poorest people, and some distance from our church and the old house we lived in for some years. Last Sunday I went to Odawara again, this time to take the morning service while Fr. Miyazawa took my place in Ito. It was a great pleasure to be back there and to meet many old friends. As a special welcome there was a fall of snow.

Every week similar fires occur, because buildings of light wood are crowded against each other in very narrow streets. Once a fire starts the whole block burns in a very few minutes. Fire is the ever-present fear in the daily life of everybody, but yet one sees much of a very stupid carelessness. All night long the "firewatch" goes around in town or village, which again is a rostered volunteer duty. They ring a bell or bang a drum, or clap boards as they go. When there is a high wind bands of schoolboys are sent around calling such slogans as "one match can start a big fire."

We saw quite a sight the other day while driving along a country road with some committeemen as passengers. A man was stoking a blazing fire under an upended petrol drum on the road outside his house. Almost lost to sight in the smoke and flames was his wife sitting inside the drum with just her head showing, and she did not look at all agitated. Into my mind flashed the traditional picture of cannibals boiling a missionary, but it was only a Japanese village family taking a bath.

———

We are up against age-old conservative parents again. This time it is the 35 year old father of three children, whose own old father won't permit him to come to Church and be baptised as he wishes to. However, the young man still makes it his business to go out and place logs over a wide drain for me to cross every time I am due at the Church up the road near to his place. I wondered who was kindly placing the logs there, but never saw anyone doing it, until another person told me who does it.

Another young man school teacher wants to be instructed, but his mother is a zealous Buddhist and prevents him coming to classes.

In yet another village the Town Council has asked us to build a chapel on village ground. They fear for the future of their 8,000 villagers because there is now no positive religious or moral teaching there. The land they offer us is alongside the entrance to an ancient Buddhist temple.

Also on the ground lie the ruins of a Soldier's Memorial, broken down by MacArthur's orders, presumably to counteract any influence of the Shinto doctrine which glorifies war. One of the stated reasons for wanting to place the chapel on that particular spot is to forestall any movement to restore the monument when the Peace Treaty is completed. It is a difficult situation, and I would like to seize the chance, but at present there is no way I know of getting the £200 it would cost to build the little chapel there.

Recently a letter came from our old friend of Queensland Bush Brotherhood years, the Rev. Christopher Leeke, who is now vicar in the parish of Surfleet Spalding, England. He refers to the tour of English parishes by Bishop Viall who was on leave from Tokyo, where he has been the U.S.A. Episcopal (Anglican) Representative for many years. Bishop Viall speaking on aspects of life in Japan described the extreme poverty of the masses who are underfed and insufficiently clothed.

———

"Aunty" is fun. I call her Aunty because she brings her little niece to church with her, but she is an 18 year old student who would qualify in any country as a "good student type" – bright, vigorous, assertive, and talkative. She has been baptised and confirmed and is now fairly well established in the Communicant life. It is three years since she first came enquiring to the Church. This week she finishes High School. What she is to do now has been the subject of lively and varied debate for many weeks past.

The parents' ideas, more especially father's, have been quite the opposite of what she wants.

He has insisted that she spend the next few years quietly at home, learning the gentle arts of flower arrangement, tea-ceremony and Japanese style dress-making. All this he says will prepare her for the day when he will send her out as a bride. He has the money necessary to enable his daughter to do all this.

In response to all this Aunty has burbled about her father's funny old feudal idea, or blubbered on the floor in front of him in protest. She has wheedled and stormed and moped, all expressly for the purpose of wearing him down.

Her greatest hope is that she might go to Training College and qualify as a Nursery and Kindergarten teacher. She wants to do some useful service. The father objects to that most strenuously. He would rather have her go to work in an ordinary conventional office. His main argument seems to be that the neighbours will scorn him if he lets his daughter do anything so menial as to go to work for money; and even more if she does anything so modern as Nursery School Training.

That household has no religion, neither old nor new. The daughter was freely permitted to interest herself in the Church and become a Christian. There are none of the usual Buddhist tablets or Shinto ornaments in the house. Aunty has quite freely pleased herself and put a cross and picture in her own room. Because it was only fear of "what the neighbours will say" that was deciding her father's ideas she has quite determinedly set out to win her freedom. She is, in fact, so obvious about it all that I rather suspect the old man has been enjoying "playing" her. At any rate, a week ago, after exams were finished, she won his consent to go to an office job in her home town. She told me she just kept on complaining and "wailing" until he was worn out.

I asked her how long she would stick at a job I might get for her in an orphanage? It might prove very trying. She assured me that if once she got Dad's permission and started in a job she'd stick at it no matter how bad things were, rather than go home again.

She started the office job on Saturday morning and resigned Saturday afternoon! "Practically nothing to do and the boss drank sake from morning till night, so I thought I'd better leave such an odd place," said Aunty.

Now she is at home waiting for the results of the examinations to enter the Nursery Training College. In the meantime, to humour her father she has started to learn dressmaking! Aunty is fun, don't you think?

————

Plans are being made for Canon Warren to visit Izu Peninsula. He is Secretary of the Australian Board of Missions and expects to sail from Sydney on the *Changte* about March 29th. He will bring some parcels over for us and his visit will be for about two months, during which time he should be able to size up the problems here. We are looking forward keenly to his coming.

Sincerely yours,

Frank and Maida

P.S.: This reminder is not for the many readers and friends who have generously remembered the increased costs of paper, printing, and postage. Would others please let me know if they wish me to continue sending the *Newsletter*. – E.R.C.

———

Circulated by Mrs. E.R. Coaldrake, Hamilton Road, Nundah, Queensland.
[Printed] by Brisbane City Printery, Edward Street, Brisbane.

Newsletter No. 45, **April, 1952.**

NIPPON SEIKO KWAI

From – Rev. F.W. Coaldrake

[written by Maida Coaldrake with addition by Frank]

> [Address written in Japanese.]
> St. Mary's Church House
> 960 Shimouchi,
> Okaku,
> Ito-shi,
> JAPAN.
>
> April, 1952

Dear Friends,

It is difficult to believe, as I sit here and watch the afternoon sunlight streaming across the block, that only a week ago this same block was almost under water with the constant deluging rain, and that the surrounding hills of so-called sunny Ito, Riviera of central Japan, were covered in snow. It is equally difficult to believe that two days ago we stood bent against the wind on the Ito foreshore watching the waves break clean over the breakwater and jetty, and soak the men working frantically to complete some stonework. Everyone says that this has been one of the longest and coldest winters in memory. Certainly Tokyo has just had its sixteenth snowfall of the season, which we struck on our monthly ration trip up to that city. I love the look of Tokyo under snow – all the dirt and drabness of that huge city (pop. 6,000,000 at last census) is wiped out and buildings and houses take on an almost fantastic loveliness. But the incredible slush and dirt which quickly follows the constant heavy traffic soon shatters any illusion of beauty. The real beauty comes a little later when on April 4th or 5th the cherry is in full blossom and in every park and along many streets the silvery pink masses ravish the tens of thousands [of people] who come to gaze.

Our own trees planted in December are already budding and we continue to delight in the flocks of sparrows they have attracted. We are eating lettuce grown in the frames made from old Quonset Hut windows, and every day makes a difference to the look of the garden. It takes many seasons I am sure to become accustomed to the distinct line of colour which marks off one season from the other. All the long winter the landscape has been dry, withered brown, ribbed with the brilliant green of the winter wheat crop. In just a few days it always seems, the brown hills flush pink and then silver and green, and all the summer the lush richness of the fields and hills close one in. Then autumn brings its own wonderful colours, splashing the country with the reds and golds of maples and brilliance of flowers. It's little wonder that for hundreds of years the women have had special kimonos for the different seasons.

This year there is quite a change in the character of much of the countryside. Ever since the end of the war the nation has been desperately coping with the problem of hunger, and of growing enough food to meet the needs of its greatly increased population. Never a flower grew where a daikon [Japanese radish], or cabbage, or blade of rice could grow. Even along the dustiest road-side or up a most inhospitable mountain creek bed there would be the little patches of garden, someone's attempt to meet the crying need of his and his neighbour's households. What is happening today just over the hedge in our neighbour's garden is typical of what is happening all over the country. Professor Fuji has the professional gardeners in, and what yesterday was a large and flourishing vegetable patch is already showing signs of becoming a Japanese rock-garden pool, bushes, little slopes and all! The children of the gardeners are carrying off any of the vegetables they want as they are discarded. Down the Peninsula vegetable patches have given way to carnation gardens (you pay 20 to 30 yen a bloom on the Tokyo market), and every day great lorries pass our gate taking into the metropolitan areas the three products of this region – the charcoal from the mountains, the flowers from the fields, and the fish from the rich waters off the coast. (Colour Plate 11)

We rejoice that hunger in its worst forms has been banished, but we wring our hands and puzzle our heads endlessly and seemingly hopelessly over the problem of the many children in this area alone who never grow up, victims of beri-beri. Only the other morning Miyazawa-san, Frank's stalwart lay-reader and right hand vestryman, stopped in for breakfast on his way home from Sunday duties at Imaihama, and professed himself delighted and intrigued that the delicious wholemeal porridge and honey he had just enjoyed was none other than the spurned wheat he had exchanged with us for some white flour!

––––––

Lent has brought extras in the way of services, and baptisms planned for Easter Day and Easter Monday with extra instruction classes. In Ito itself the church people are using it as a time of special preparation for an advance into the community of those untouched by the church. Our big room continues to groan its agony when the 9 a.m. Sunday congregation collects. To this regular 9 a.m. service has now been added one in English at 8 a.m. for the special benefit of members of the Forces and their families who are having their leave at the B.C.F.K. (British Commonwealth Force, Korea) Leave Hotel four miles away. Sometimes nobody comes on the bus; sometimes quite a number, and always when they come they are interesting, interested, well-instructed church people – British Naval men, American Army officers, their wives and children, even a family from Texas. Their offerings go into a special fund with which one day we hope to provide a piece of furniture for the new Church.

Just overnight the previously shadowy "new Church" has become much more of a reality, for the whole of the area that it will occupy has been outlined with young azalea bushes, as a constant reminder to us all of what we are aiming at. The step between is first the re-erection of the Quonset Hut as a temporary Church and meeting place, and then the drive for more Church members and funds.

———

Our Sunday School, about which we wrote some months ago and about which so many of you have shown interest, really works. Today we can count on 15 to 20 children who are learning of the Church, and whose parents have signed a slip to say they have no objection to their children becoming baptized members of the Christian Church. That is a great step forward, as so often Sunday Schools are being used by parents who desire only that the vacuum left by discontinued "moral" teachings in the public schools should be filled. In one of our larger cottage-church centres where there is a Sunday School of 70 odd children, the mere mention of baptism and the need to tighten membership along positive lines left us with the hint that if it were done, we would have one member in Sunday School. We are still thinking out that situation.

Here in Ito where the house reasonably limits classes for the time [being], Saturday afternoon sees keen youngsters attacking lessons and catechism as they should. They write notes from the blackboard summaries, curled up on the floor. They follow the Church's year by some quite dashing posters the seniors make. They practice hymns with great gusto and very little idea of singing and altogether enjoy themselves, and the Church. Sunday service completes their attendance unit unless they have to attend day school, a not infrequent occurrence on Sundays. I wish you could have heard the chuckles of glee which came from the Nursery Class today as they prepared plasticine models for Mothering Sunday. The little ones having proudly exhibited their models, the older scholars fell on the plasticine and had a wonderful time making things themselves. We are amazed at the lack of experience in any kind of creative expression shown by these children.

———

With all the improvements going on round the block, the Rotary clothesline Frank made continues to hold pride of place in the interest and admiration of all comers. You will see the ice-man standing for a few minutes gazing at the empty lines thinking they are some kind of radio aerial. The postman never fails on washing day to stop his bike, and farmers' wives passing up the nearby path pushing their vegetable carts always pause and stare at the line whirling around.

Of course the sheets make quite a show in a country which scarcely knows what to do with a sheet. The Japanese futon usually has only a strip of linen stitched over the top of the eiderdown covering and changed very infrequently. I realised the many uses for sheets. We use them for large size tablecloths, or projector screen or cover of the travelling altar, and so on.

We took a walk the other day to the hillside above the town behind us. (Colour Plate 3) There's a large primary school accommodating hundreds of children, and also the Ito High School which houses many more – 198 seniors graduated from it last week. There is also a fine new Buddhist temple nearing completion. This is a beautiful building with the gracefully curved roof of the typical Buddhist temple, and much money and a great deal of work is going into it. About 15 years ago the old temple was burned down. Whatever the general opinion about the ancient religions of this country, they are still strong and growing, as evidenced by new shrines and temples all over the country, even if the devotion to them is of the social, community kind, rather than the religion of the heart and life. Ito is the stronghold of the Nichiren sect of the Buddhists. Nichiren [1222–1282] was a prophet and holy man, who like Isaiah exposed the scandals of a very corrupt government, and lived in Ito in exile for years – hence the strength of his following in this centre.

Though I admired the magnificent site overlooking city and sea, and appreciated the architecture of the new temple, I shivered a bit as we slipped down the hillside through the crowded burying place towards the temporary temple. The great ugly effigies guarding the entrance to the central court were grotesque and dirty. The altar within the temple was huge and golden. The steps to the temple were worn and the tatami matting rubbed from much wear, while the Buddhist nuns sitting in their little kiosk in the courtyard obviously did a good business.

———

News of our King's death struck us of the British community in Japan just as suddenly and shockingly as it reached you at home.

Most unexpectedly here in very much an outpost of the Empire we became involved in services and officialdom in a way that would scarcely have happened in Australia.

There had to be two memorial services [in Tokyo], not for reasons of rank, but owing to lack of sufficient accommodation. The first in the morning was held in Holy Trinity Church and was attended by members of the Imperial Household, S.C.A.P. and members of all the Diplomatic Legations in Japan, and many other Japanese high ranking officials. Sitting in the back, I saw a procession of nationalities such as I have never seen before. What impressed us most was their obviously real and deep feeling in what could have been a very formal affair. The order of service, which Frank and Sir Esler Dening, the British Ambassador (a good churchman) had drafted, was simple and dignified and short. We filed out into the bitter grey day, waiting for cars to move along, young men holding umbrellas against the snow, with a sympathetic and quiet crowd of Japanese passers-by looking on.

As a matter of fact that was one of the things which impressed us greatly, the personal interest and sympathy so many of our Japanese friends expressed, quite apart from the official expressions in the press and over the radio. This is a country which has a very high regard for royalty, and the depth of feeling for the hereditary head of state can best be assessed at such a time as this.

The afternoon service, repeating the morning's order, was held in the G.H.Q. Chapel for all who might wish to attend. Later, part of this service was broadcast through the Japanese national network and many Church people throughout the country heard it. Frank was variously introduced as Fr. Frank from Odawara, Pastor Coaldrake from Ito, and Bishop Coaldrake.

A widely used press photo taken in the door of Holy Trinity showing the procession entering the church had as centre the back view of the Bishop of Tokyo, present to pronounce the blessing. This cope and mitred figure was clearly marked Rev. F. Coaldrake, Australia. What a mistake!

To share in the Empire's mourning and to get to know members of the British community here in Japan, was a privilege.

———

We are continually glad about our *Newsletter* because so many people write to us about this or that, and we are kept in touch with so many in widespread places and such nice surprises happen. Sister Faith Mary, who has arrived from England to join the Tokyo House of The Epiphany for five years, said she was most anxious to meet the Australian Missionary and his wife, as she had been following our *Newsletter* and much of what she knew of Japan was from them. Then from South Africa came a letter from the widow of the late distinguished and beloved Bishop Cecil Bontflower who served some years in Japan before he went to South Africa. She was most appreciative.

We had a very happy Mothering Sunday. I baked a large spiced cake which we cut with due ceremony as a Simnel Cake and everyone went off home solemnly carrying their scrap of cake wrapped in paper, to do their bit of evangelization among the home folk. You would enjoy lots of moments like that with us I'm sure.

I am setting off to Tokyo tomorrow to do another job [to give birth]! In the meantime I will be having daily language tutoring, much to my joy. It's been impossible to have proper lessons here in Ito.

By the time this reaches you Canon Warren of the Australian Board of Missions staff, Sydney, will be with us and will spend some weeks investigating conditions here and preparing to advise the Board concerning future developments. Needless to say we are looking forward to his visit immensely.

Letters are reaching us safely and quickly at our Ito address, and I'm thinking that the joy of having a letter from any of you handed over the window sill any morning or afternoon, is very much greater than after a month of letter starvation, receiving forty in a bunch. Also there have been all sorts of useful parcels, many containing the precious powdered milk which we know is in short supply at home too. Very many thanks to each and all you dear friends.

[Frank adds:]

If I call him Harry it will do. I'd like to tell you about his problems, but I must do so in such a way that if by any chance this should be read by even his closest friends, they would not recognise him. I must safeguard his secret, but you will be more than interested in it, I think. Harry is one of the men I am now training in the Christian faith and way of life. For a long time he has been in love with the youngest daughter of a neighbouring family. All the older daughters have been married and so have gone away to become members of their respective husband's households. There are no sons in that family so the father has planned to ensure the continuity of his line by adopting a young man who, having become his son will marry his youngest daughter. To make the proposition more attractive the daughter has now been given a small shop of her own, complete with living quarters. She is now likely to get a quite eligible young man as her husband and they will carry on her father's family name, living in a fair degree of comfort as a result of the dowry she brings.

But Harry and the girl love each other with what we would describe as "true love." We would expect them to marry and settle down. This is quite impossible. Harry has considered offering himself for adoption by the father and so qualifying to be the groom. The trouble is that Harry is himself an only son and must remain in his own family so that his father may have his family line continued.

So the two of them are held apart by the old concept of Family and the child's duty to its family. They are both Christians. They both think of love as a thing hallowed by God.

What shall they do? In similar situations, and this is by no means uncommon, one method of solving the impasse is the suicide compact. These two will not do that, I think. Another method is elopement – but when the family tie is strong, as it is here, to elope is apparently a greater moral and mental strain than to commit suicide.

Harry has been in the throes of this for many months. Fortunately he is not a hasty man so there is hope that in time it will be worked out.

You see, I'm sure, that the last five years have done little to alter the relationships within either of these families. The relationship between the two young people is probably begotten of post-war conditions, but the new spark of individualism is likely to be quelled by the cold water of unemotional family duty.

Frank writes on April 5th:

The gift of a son this morn was quite a happy event for Maida in Tokyo, at St. Luke's Mission Hospital (Episcopal U.S.A.) with the Rev. Dr. Lehman attending. Both are very well, and Maida enjoying her opportunity to practise her Japanese accent on the nursing attendants.

We have chosen the names William Howard, and Canon Warren of Sydney A.B.M. has promised to officiate at the baptism of our son on May 4th. Rev. Canon

Edwards, Cheltenham, Victoria, and Ian Stewart, N.S.W., will be Godfathers, with Sister Flora, C.H.N., Victoria as Godmother.

    Yours sincerely,
        Frank and Maida

————

Circulated by Mrs. E.R. Coaldrake, Hamilton Road, Nundah, Queensland.
[Printed by] Brisbane City Printery, Edward Street, Brisbane.

Newsletter No. 46, **May, 1952.**

                                        St. Mary's Church House
                                        960 Shimouchi,
                                        Oka-ku,
                                        Ito-shi,
                                        JAPAN.

[written by Maida Coaldrake]

Dear Friends,

A brief note[37] to say all the Izu Coaldrakes are well, even if two of them are rather short of sleep at present. We hope to post enough news to fill a couple of *Newsletters* very soon. Mind you, it is all stored up in our heads, but just when we can find time to write it down we don't know.

We have unpacked parcels from many friends; some arrived during my month's absence in Tokyo. We have been overwhelmed by the generosity of each and all of you and feel so grateful, because Army Canteens are now closed to us, along with many privileges we enjoyed for years. Our spare time pre-occupation now is the fascinating game of juggling YEN to meet new prices! 100% to 150% on Australian prices now for essential commodities.

We have been ever so busy with visitors. Canon Warren has just left for KOBE and a tour with Bishop Yashiro. You will recall that they are old friends since the Bishop's Australian Journey in 1950, when the Canon was his companion and adviser. The Canon and Frank have spent hours at the table working over plans, finances and technicalities of water pumps, car springs, building methods, and the changes of the Japanese economy. For the rest they seem to have been continually arriving home after a very strenuous few days in various parts of the Mission area, or else back from Tokyo or KOFU and the mountains, where the Canon has taken more photos to show you back in Australia.

It has been so wonderful having him with us bringing Home closer, quite apart from his delightful company. Then there were all the amazing gifts from

———

37 This *Newsletter* was circulated as a single, typed page because of the pressure of events following the birth of Bill.

you all that opened out of his luggage, including springs for the Rover and a baby's bath, not forgetting a Christening Cake from Brisbane, Vita Weet biscuits, tins of milk and coffee. We enjoy the Vita Weet especially, while dates and biscuits have kept the wolf from Frank's tummy quite often when he misses getting home for meals.

Baptism Day, May 4th, was wonderful, made more so by the loving thoughts of you all. Baby C. was a cherub and lay quietly awake in his silks and laces and at 4 weeks thoroughly enjoyed the "impression" which his entrance caused. (Colour Plate 9) David Chamberlain and Gladys Smith (mission teachers) came from Kobe for the week-end, and Mrs. Wilson, an Australian friend, came from Tokyo for the day. Of course Canon Warren was there to baptize William Howard and sign him with "the sign of the Cross ... in token ..." and so on. We had a smile when it came to the place where he must, in years to come, "listen to many sermons."

Though I know next to nothing about babies Billie is very patient and we are learning! He is now 9 lbs 12 oz. at 6 weeks and very bonny, getting fairer every day, and yes, he smiles too.

Right now, as I write Frank is working on our annual balances and puzzling over cheques etc. preparing for another trip to Tokyo today. He says to mention the parcel from Moss Vale with photos included of Christ Church, St. Laurence interiors (and some food) which was opened as he travelled home from a country trip, when he had run out of food – and was it a Godsend, milk and all!

I made much strawberry jam yesterday and picked roses, rhubarb and lettuce from my garden. Also produced the first ice cream from our 1/- "army disposals" kero. frig.

Very sincerely,
    FRANK AND MAIDA

Newsletter No. 47, June, 1952.

NIPPON SEIKO KWAI

From – Rev. F.W. Coaldrake

[written by Frank Coaldrake]

St. Mary's Church House
960 Shimouchi,
Okaku,
Ito-shi,
JAPAN.

Dear Friends,

Canon Warren spent a fortnight with us and saw every corner of the peninsula. He attended our services and meetings, met people in their homes, stayed in the villages, learned to take a bath Japanese style (extremely hot) and gave us much helpful advice on many problems.

He probably found out everything necessary to make an enlightening report to the Board. Just before he arrived we were notified that we may no longer purchase supplies at B.C.O.F. canteens. This means we must buy at exorbitant prices and it was as well he should be able to go into the shops and see the articles priced at more than twice their cost in Australia, which means a very heavy drain on the A.B.M. to keep us here. The grant last year seemed a very generous one at the beginning of the year but prices rose so much that by the end of the year we had a worrying time. If it had not been for many generous parcels from friends in Australia we would not have known where to turn [for food] during the last two months.

―――

Now that the Peace Treaty has been signed with Japan I've so far seen no change in the attitude of ordinary everyday people. The May Day riots with attacks on American Army cars were quite definitely the effort of a small extremist group. I see no reason to fear any opposition, let alone violence, against other foreigners. The one thing that is happening with increasing tempo is the reversion to old customs. It is so much less bother to do the old things in the old ways. New ways are always puzzling. In religion, family life, school life, and village life in the pattern of marriage and family inheritance, the new laws of Occupation years seem to be already a dead letter. While in Australia I often spoke about the struggle between old customs and new laws, one could say almost without fear of contradiction now that the old customs are gaining the upper hand.

I see no reason to doubt that Japan's "No Armed Forces" Constitution will be evaded. The only doubt is as to how far preparations will go before the constitution is amended? It is heartening that there should still be such a large measure of opposition to the revival of armed forces from all walks of life. It shows that the Occupation has not been entirely without effect in evoking a strong and thoughtful popular opposition to a government policy. If only they don't start intimidation and assassination of leaders again everything may yet turn out alright. In the seven years Occupation there has been only one attempt at political assassination – a remarkable change from old established ways.

There is a sad, constant undercurrent to the life of Japan ... suicides. In the last year 22,300 cases of effective suicide were recorded. This is the highest ever, beating even the Depression years.

―――

There are several young women attending services and classes. They are all of such a mind that I have been expecting them one by one to ask for baptism. An older man in the group has just told me that they all hold back for the same reason. In the not distant future each will go away as a bride. The husband will be chosen by the parents and the bride will have no say in the matter. She will not expect to, nor even think that she might have an opinion as to the suitability of the man. Once married she will in due course discover what are her husband's religious affiliations and beliefs and will be expected to conform.

   Right now she desires to be baptised and become a Christian, but looking ahead to the day when her husband, who will almost certainly be a non-Christian, expresses his opposition to her Christianity, and disliking the prospect of having to give up her faith then, she wonders whether it would not be better to withdraw now.

   That is the situation at the moment. There are several possible things to do. The old man who discloses the problem to me suggests that we'll get nowhere unless we start by converting the grandparents and parents, which is pretty sound reasoning and incidentally sheds light on the limitations of any children's Sunday School programme in this country.

———

We had very good services at Easter-tide and Baptism was administered to six adults. One more was prevented on the day by family opposition. It is not so much opposition to Christianity as insistence they must continue in the traditional family patterns. I'm not able to see yet how to deal with this, though I'm meeting it everywhere. It is a matter in which the prayers of people at home could greatly help.

   The Bishop has arranged for me to have the part-time help of Fr. Toyoda from St. Mary's Hiratsuka. He will look after Mishima and its district, and come occasionally into my own area to help with problem cases. Last week I suddenly found myself with requests for four husbands for country girls!

———

Since the day our Bill arrived he rules the house and takes lots of our time, but he is now two months old and a big sturdy lad of $10\frac{1}{2}$ lbs. We no longer have the feeling that he's likely to fall apart any moment. It is really great fun having him with us despite the problems he brings and the time he takes, though I sometimes suggest to Maida we ought to spend less time with him but let him sleep. I am quite hopelessly lost when he starts waving arms and legs and trying to smile. We are quite the most doting parents there have ever been. I'm quite a good hand now at maintenance – can change his "tyre" in quick time and fill his gas tank (per bottle) without letting too much air in. But when it comes to a major overhaul I put him on the assembly line and call Maida. He takes quite kindly to the sound of services in the next room, and even hymn practice on Saturday night does not disturb him. Everybody wants to see him everytime they come to the house, and the church people have collected money to buy him a christening present. After Evensong on Sunday night last a mother and her five daughters arrived to see him and brought a very beautiful blue silk kimono with boy-style pattern on it, mostly militaristic symbols, which is traditional. Bill likes the car when we put him in it in his basket and he generally sleeps soundly the whole time, so journeys will soon be a regular part of his life. The risk of infection in the villages is too great to take him along for a while yet, as dysentery and typhus have almost reached epidemic proportions.

———

Taneko's broad grin just poked around the screen and she asked "Fuaza! Hoo-at toime is ittu neeow?" It is 6.30 p.m., and time to eat and get ready for the service in the next village tonight.

Sincerely yours,

Frank and Maida

———

P.S.: Your letters with odds and ends from various people have just arrived. Many thanks for open postal notes which we can exchange into cash at Australian Post Office in Tokyo.

Our address is now at the top of this letter, and the postage rates are the same as to any foreign country.

———

Printed by Brisbane City Printery, Edward Street, Brisbane.

Frank Coaldrake, *Izu Mission (Japan): Budget for 1952–53*, 30 June 1952.

St. Mary's Church,
Ito, Japan.

A. Superintendent   £700.0.0

B. Mission

Staff – Japanese Assistant	£300.0.0
Housekeeper	£120.0.0
Car – Operation	£400.0.0
Installments	£80.0.0
Office, literature, post, phone, insurances etc	£150.0.0
Training and Camp	£100.0.0
	£1,150.0.0
	£1,850.0.0

NOTE: Current prices of some typical commodities:

butter, 1 lb	11/6
sugar, 1 lb	2/-
tea, 1 lb	24/-
bread, 2 lb loaf	4/-
meat fresh cheap cuts, 11 lb	7/-
meat tinned, 11 lb	7/6
cheese Kraft, 12 oz tin	7/6
Nescafe, 4 oz	8/9
jam, 11 lb tin	5/6
milk powder, 11 lb tin	5/-
fish fresh, 11 lb	2/3

FINANCIAL STATEMENT FOR THE YEAR 1/6/51–31/5/52

(Converted from Yen and Sterling to Australian at official rate)

Expenditure – Budget items

ITEM	BUDGET ESTIMATE	EXPENDITURE
Assistant Priest Stipend	£250.0.0	£148.14.10
Housekeeper wages	£100.0.0	£67.10.9
Rents	£30.0.0	£18.13.10
Car – Operation	£125.0.0	£402.16.9
Car – Instalments	£270.0.0	£201.3.0
Camp staff and Training	£100.0.0	£51.4.0
Housekeeping and Personal	£425.0.0	£618.14.5
	£1,475.0.0	£1,748.16.0
Advance on 1952–53 for purchase from B.C.O.F.		
	£A1,4750.0.0	£100.0.0
Excess Expenditure	£173.18.9	£1,648.0.0
	£1648.18.9	£1648.18.9

The Excess expenditure of £173.18.9 is due to:

i. Inflationary rise in all Yen expenses, approximately 40%.
ii. Estimates were based on purchase at B.C.O.F. Canteen of many items which early became unavailable and had to be purchased elsewhere at much higher prices.
iii. B.C.O.F. prices on items which continued to be available rose as a result of inflation in Australia.
iv. The unpredicted advent of an infant.[38]

Newsletter No. 48, July, 1952.

NIPPON SEIKO KWAI

From – Rev. F.W. Coaldrake

[written by Maida Coaldrake]

St. Mary's Church House
960 Shimouchi,
Okaku,
Ito-shi,
JAPAN.

38 William Howard Coaldrake. The budget figures are exactly as they appear in the original document, even though the totals for budget estimate and expenditure are incorrect.

Dear Friends,

I feel as if the thousands of miles which lie between Izu and Australia have suddenly become a reality. It isn't only because two years have passed since we sailed from Sydney but because two Saturdays ago I stood at our gate and waved to the last of the B.C.O.F./ B.C.E.R. soldiers and their dependents on their way from Kawana Leave Hotel to Ito Station. This luxury hotel, one of the show places of the Orient, has been for some years an Army Leave Hostel, bringing a corner of Australia to our corner of Japan. Many friends from home have stayed there, and we have made many more through our Sunday morning English Communions. Sometimes we have enjoyed good beef, and talk, in the beautiful dining room. At other times we have played tennis on the courts, walked on the wonderful golf course, seen Mt. Mihara [the volcano] erupting across the water on Oshima Island, but most of all we have appreciated letters which have come quickly through its mail bag, and the privilege of sending you all news in four days for three-pence! Now it will cost us through Japanese post 1/3 d. for an air flimsy, 2/6 d. for an air-mail letter, and surface letter 9½ d. Will you please forgive us if there is a falling off in the number of letters that come from us, and there will be a six weeks' lag for many of you while surface mail letters start to bridge the gap. For the years of postal privilege, the countless parcels, papers and luxuries that have come from you to Odawara and Ito we can never thank the Army enough for the privilege, or you for your generosity.

Because there have been so many enquiries as to the ways and means of getting parcels to us, may we say that the situation is almost impossible. For some reason best known to themselves but explained as "handling" charge, the Postal authorities charge us 1/6 d. on every parcel and package from Australia before any customs duty is added. This on woollen goods is severe. Officials, challenged through newspaper columns with the matter (for it is a very live issue with foreigners at the moment), say that they must clamp down on a vicious black market circle somehow, and adopt the principle that everyone is guilty unless proved innocent.

That being the position with parcels generally either by post or ship, the one form of exemption we can get makes it even more impossible. For exemption from customs duty for second-hand goods earmarked "Relief" we must go to the Governor of the Prefecture personally before and after receipt of goods, and guarantee goods will be used for charity only. In our case it involves a 200 miles journey and soon afterwards we must also lodge a signed statement from the recipients of every single item contained in parcels, to the effect that no money will change hands on the deal. Such is sweet charity in Japan since the black market made it so. We say so reluctantly, for there are still many poor in our villages we would gladly help, but with rapidly improving conditions in Japan, most clothing goods can be had at a price locally which is not often more than we finally pay in customs and postal duties. It would now seem the best way to send help is by money paid into our banking account through A.B.M. Head Office in Sydney, which finds its way finally into most useful Yen for our use here.

All in all it has been quite a month. First of all it is the "wet" season, not the hearty wet of Australia, but misty, thick weather, which seeps into cupboards and books, and the Japanese contend, into your bloodstream as well. The only remedy for the bodily and spiritual ills which follow, they say, is to take many hot baths. So we dutifully take our hot bath each night, up to our neck in water at 42 degrees centigrade, as a routine measure, along with constant vigilance for mildew on shoes and shelves.

Sometimes there's torrential rain as well, for days on end, with the house looking like a Chinese laundry inside. But there is an unbelievable beauty about the season that is unexaggerated even by the traditional "Kaki-mono" (wall picture) – dark, misty days, clumps of new bamboo swimming ghost-like and feathery out of the mists and all the low hills draped in cloud. Beauty or no, as I look for another corner to swing nappies in, I am most grateful to the weatherman who says "only three more days" then a period of "torrid" weather.

Then midway through the month Typhoon "Dinah" hit Ito just as I was bedding down Baby Billy for the night – somewhere round 11 p.m. Frank was away in one of the other centres. We had noticed a small newspaper paragraph a few days before to say that Dinah was heading towards Kyushu – but that is hundreds of miles to the south-west of us. Typhoons are changeable (hence the distinguishing mark of a girl's name, so they say) and here was Dinah on our doorstep.

The first intimation I had that this was anything but the usual daily downpour was a sudden gust of wind which shook the house and blacked us out. Bill chuckled happily at the unexpected change in routine, while I reached for the ever-ready torch. By the time the next lash came, hot as from an oven and about 70 miles per hour, I was doing the rounds of the house wishing we were like our neighbours and sealed up hermetically with wooden shutters every night, hot or cold, wet or fine. The rain was beating against the house in parallel rods and by the time I had put up the shutters in the teeth of the wind, I was wet to the skin. I thought to check up about the possible severity, but the radio was out of commission and by this time the telephone line was down. By 12 o'clock the house was as safe as I could make it and the babe asleep in his basket, but the rooms were anything but comfortable inside with the humid heat and water dripping through the roof, and to add to discomfort, I seemed to have shut in [all] the mosquitoes surviving in Ito. Somewhere after twelve the study roof blew away with a horrid grinding and clamour, and the summer bamboo blinds outside were beating themselves to ribbons on house walls. I had given up the effort of coping with the flood in the big room, and spent the time lying on my bed with my foot against Bill's basket, wondering what was happening to the piles of timber in the grounds, whether the next gust of wind would blow in the side of the house, and hoping that Frank was not on his way home up that awful coast road. As it happened, in Ose, where he was, the typhoon was not as severe as in Ito where it was the worst ever, due to a freak tunnelling of wind down from Mt. Amagi. Nowhere else on the Peninsula did the winds reach the 100 miles per hour they did here.

In a sudden lull at the peak of the storm – that awful 15 minutes of absolute calm when you hold your breath and hope the worst is over, I heard a tiny voice at the back of the house, and rushing down the roka [corridor] I found Ikue-san (one of our church girls) and her brother, just pausing long enough to be sure all was well and then fleeing home again. The dear people, I thought, gratefully, and it being nearly 2 a.m. I went back to bed and to sleep. The rest of the typhoon blew up and away over my sleeping head.

It took us two days to set the place to rights – to dry out church records, find pieces of roof and bits of study from all over the neighbouring fields, to have trees replanted, and weep over the gladioli and tomatoes. But it had been worse elsewhere. Kawana Hotel had 58 windows broken on the coast side, and down the country there are very few vegetables of any kind at present, so scorched were they [by the wind]. The *Nippon Times* reported millions of yen worth of damage.

———

At the end of the same week another kind of "typhoon" hit us. Along with many other civilians, Embassy staffs and the like, much of our furniture had been procured during the early days of the Occupation through the Japanese government. In our case it was thanks to B.C.O.F. that we had the use of beds, carpet and wardrobe for two years. Everyone expected that it would be possible to make a bid for the furniture after the Peace Treaty had been signed and settle the whole matter happily by cheque to the Japanese. Unfortunately this was not possible so out the window went most of the movable contents of our bedroom, together with the lovely green carpet which had served so well as sitting and kneeling "zabuton" (cushions) for our church members in our large living-room, used as Chapel.

As a result Frank spent some very busy days with hammer and saw in the garage (which thus far has been used for everything but the housing of the car) and produced in addition to a cot for Bill other necessary items of furniture.

———

This cut into an already overloaded programme of preparations for the summer. Today Frank and Kubota-san and a labourer have gone off to Lake Ippeki to start on necessary alterations to the dining and cooking pavilion, and to survey the land generally. The first camp begins in two weeks, but it is impossible to make final preparations on the spot until the rains are over. Then you can see where the hillside has slipped, where the roof needs attention and where grass and fast growing shrubs must be cut.

After the Hakone Sunday School Teachers' Conference which comes at the end of the month, four lads will take up residence at the Lake and act as caretakers, general keepers of the water-pump, and airer of blankets. In the meantime a working bee of girls will go out from Ito to bring soap and water to work on the winter's dirt.

Three of the young men come from the Church in Yokohama, but the fourth is a High School lad from a neighbouring village. His mother came to Frank in much distress of mind recently asking if we might consider taking the boy into our house for the month of the summer vacation. He has got a bit out of hand lately, wants to move about the countryside with "doubtful" companions, finds the village too dull and conservative, finds his home "dark" in spirit. Even if Ito, the play centre for Tokyo-ites with its inns and girls and dozens of "pachinko" or cheap gambling dens, was the place for a lad with much spare time on his hands, we could scarcely undertake to have any more guests in the house. Gladys Smith and David Chamberlain are to come up from Kobe for six weeks and we have at least two other guests expected – withal one guest room! Frank did the next best thing and offered him a billet in the permanent team at Ippeki, and since he has often listened to the wayside preaching and dropped in at camp with some vegetables or flowers for the tables, this may not be so wide of the mark.

It interests us immensely, this desperate concern of the older generations for their youngsters. They are the first fruits of the new "democratic" way of life, the reformed educational system with its dissociation from the teaching of any religion or "morals." Speaking of that particular boy and of others whom we know are giving their parents tremendous anxiety, it seems that there is nothing new or worrying about the problem. In fact, we agree, that if young Bill in his growing up doesn't at some time get new ideas and find us stuffy and old-fashioned we shall think that a visit to the doctor is necessary! We do our best to help but we find it hard to share the anxiety except in sympathy.

––––

A scheme for providing a Library Box for each of our Cottage Churches is at last in successful operation thanks to the generosity of an S.C.M. group at Scots Prep. School in Melbourne. Ten pounds came from this group to add to the £15 already earmarked for the purpose from Mission funds. Now we have five boxes, each containing thirty books and pamphlets, with two more on order and money to buy books which are also on order. These stay two to three months in each Cottage-Church centre and the contents are read with great interest, and much discussion. Later we hope to add filmstrips to the scheme and send around a little projector to each centre in turn.

This and the Daily Bible Study notes are helping to weld the scattered Mission Church into a solid block of prayer and fellowship. In the Diocese of South Tokyo our membership is less than that of any other parish and our members – small farmers and fisher folk – are poorer. Yet our Lenten Offering was the second largest in the Diocese. In fact no other parish gave more than one quarter of our total (except for one large city church) – the evidence of the sincerity and Christian faithfulness of our people in our scattered IZU parish.

––––

In Tokyo to see doctor and dentist last week we had the pleasure of calling on the new Ambassador to Japan from Australia, Dr. E. Ronald Walker, and renewing for both Frank and myself an old friendship. Dr. Walker occupied the Economics Chair at the University of Tasmania in my student days, and Frank had often talked with him in Sydney on N.U.A.U.S. [National Union of Australian University Students] and S.C.M. matters. We had a pleasant chat and a walk round Commonwealth House to see what the carpenters and architects are making of it. The doctor is at present discovering the incredible formalities which surround the Embassy in this country and both he and his staff were just recovering from their call on the Emperor, complete with three coaches and footmen and a procession through the streets.

We stayed as usual with Neil and Geraldine Currie[39] and had a grand time swapping parental experiences. Their daughter has taken up residence since our last trip to town and now at six weeks is such a dainty blue and gold fairy that our Bill looks a huge fifteen pounder of muscle and noise beside her. We left both babes sleeping happily at home and dashed out for a breath of air as the wonderful fireworks of the Glorious July 4th celebrations turn Tokyo into a Little America, and light the sky for miles with the most splendid crackers and rockets and the like that I have ever seen, but the next morning when we set out for home in the grey dawn we had reason to be thankful to rockets and other celebrations as the customary crowd of American cars off into the country for golf and weekend holidaying hadn't as yet hit the road. We got home in record time.

————

Many letters, cards and open postal notes have come from you safely to our Ito address and we are writing our thanks as time allows. In the meantime please know how much your affection and interest has meant and how useful have been your gifts. It will be a great joy to thank you personally one day and let the menfolk speak for themselves. At the moment the younger "manfolk" is getting into true Coaldrake form and will carry on a long and most expressive harangue with any audience which offers, and gets through any day quite happily from 5 a.m. to 7 p.m. with just one hour's sleep to soothe the household's weary spirit! Needless to say he is commonly referred to as "Little Father."

　We all send our love,

　　FRANK, MAIDA and BILLY

[Black and white photograph of "Christening Day, May 1952." Frank and Maida Coaldrake with Bill. Similar to Colour Plate 9.]

————

Printed by Brisbane City Printery, Edward Street, Brisbane.

Newsletter No. 49, **August–September, 1952.**

NIPPON SEIKO KWAI

From – Rev. F.W. Coaldrake

[first section written by Frank Coaldrake, the rest by Maida]

St. Mary's Church House
960 Shimouchi,
Okaku,
Ito-shi,
JAPAN.

39 Neil Currie was Third Secretary at the Australian Embassy in Tokyo from October, 1950 until November, 1953. He served as Ambassador from 1982 to 1986.

Dear Friends,

Campers kept us more than busy from July till the end of August. We held four different camps of our own and in addition lent the camp to three groups from outside. We had smaller numbers this year and it seems to have been due to an increase in the camp fees, and to the fact that great numbers of camps have been put up throughout Japan in the last year. A real "camping craze" is starting. Our Lake Ippeki Camp was almost the first "tent camp" in Japan, and we seem to have played our part in introducing people to the joys of camp life. This year's campers were in some respects noticeably different from our first groups four years ago.

Not only were they physically more lively, but showed a much greater and spontaneous interest in games. They actually asked us for use of equipment such as for badminton, which previously we have set up ready for use but very few have even looked at it. They also showed much less of the difficulty of mixing boys and girls together in indoor recreation.

Another amusing change was noticeable at meal times. Four years ago I found it very difficult to get them to start eating. Although they were seated in front of their meal I found I could get them to start eating only if I used the customary polite Japanese patter... "I'm sorry there is nothing at all but please do eat." They would wait for the end of it then say politely, "I receive," and start eating.

This year, before I had reached the "Amen" of Grace they would all say loudly "I receive" and start eating. My guess is that these changes in attitudes have occurred everywhere. The older generations are very upset by the "boorishness" or "casualness" of the children. The children are inclined to snap their fingers at parents, accuse them of "Feudalism" and go on as usual.

The parents of a High School lad asked me to let their son come to live in our house during his summer holidays. He had become unmanageable at home and was constantly growling about the conservatism of his parents. He was asking what was the use of a High School education if he were at the end of it to come back to live in "this feudalistic village."

Eventually I arranged for him to come into camp for some time. What effect it will have is hard to say but the parents have been full of thanks – although they have not yet said a formal "thank you."

I gave the mother a lift the other day and as we rode along she said, "It was very good of you to take so much trouble with our son. I have not been to say 'thank you' yet but I intend to come very soon and make a proper 'thank you'." She will doubtless come in her best kimono to our house and with due ceremony get the matter off her mind. To thank me as we rode along together in the car would have been to insult me by being too casual as the matter of thanks is too important to be treated so lightly.

The youngest generation is, rightly or wrongly, moving away from this strict code of etiquette.

My lease of the Lake Ippeki Camp site has expired and by the end of September I must remove all our gear. This is the plan we made four years ago. Although the site is ideal in many ways we have always reckoned on moving off it this year. Our evangelism in the villages has given us enough contacts to be able to work in houses in the villages from now on. Also the Lake has become a very popular holiday resort and therefore a crowded and rowdy district. We are moving further into the Izu Peninsula for next year's camps. Near our Imaihama Cottage Church, 25 miles down the road from here, are about five possible sites. We take the gear down there next week and store it in a "go-down" until the time to prepare for camps again.

——

Maida writes:

With Bill at four months I came and went between Ito and Lake Ippeki and Bill enjoyed his first dip in the Lake over the side of the row-boat, after eating his strained vegs. outside the dining tent on the third "platform" of the hillside above the road. Like everyone else he had to stand up to the mosquito bites and another vicious little wog, the *buyu*. Our house at Ito resembled a Bus station on the road from the railway to Lake Ippeki Camp, and people called to see Bill, to shop and leave luggage, to collect books, or offer to do some gardening for us. They came in twos and threes or twenty-twos. One morning I had 22 for breakfast!

We had Gladys Smith and David Chamberlain up from Kobe Schools for seven weeks' vacation. It was grand but crowded, especially when Fr. and Mrs. Hammer from Central Theological Seminary joined us for a few days. So crowded were we that Frank and Kubota-san set to and built an extra room in one day. Our other guests for a very happy week were Neil and Geraldine Currie from Tokyo, with Deborah Margaret at three months who became a member of the Anglican faith by baptism, which was a joyous event for the Japanese congregation. Since our guests have gone I now use the extra room for sewing or laundry.

The visit of David and Gladys was a particularly happy one, for they met last summer in our House soon after David arrived from Tasmania. What more appropriate than that they should announce their engagement whilst visiting us a year later. Their marriage is very much a matter of uncertainty so far, as Gladys is under a term of service with S.P.G. and the question of her status is under discussion at present. Whatever else is uncertain the certain fact is they both want to go on serving the Church in Japan.

A little more about Bill, and again many thanks to friends everywhere for loving greetings and gifts. Each day we try to write off a note here and there, but there's never enough time in any day for all we want to write. Whether it is loving thoughts and prayers that have done it, or whether it's just the sturdy stock, Bill is now at $5\frac{1}{2}$ months and $20\frac{1}{4}$ lbs., a constant joy and amazement to all comers, particularly his doctor friend, Fr. Leeman. Two teeth appeared at 19 weeks, and his eyes remain bright blue. He is obviously meant to be a public speaker of some note if loudness of voice counts for anything! He loves his Pentavite neat out of a spoon, from the large bottle sent us by the Bishop of Bendigo, which should last over a year, with a long thank you.

One of the highlights of the Summer Tourist attractions in Ito is the Festival of the Patron Saint. For it the town dresses gaily, kimonos come out, the kiddies practice dances. The streets are garlanded, V.I.P.s visit the city and there's a super fireworks display at night. We are more than a little intrigued and amused at this Festival, for who should be the Patron Saint [so honoured] but William Adams, an Englishman, who spent a great part of his life in Japan (under compulsion or not we can never quite make out), and introduced wooden [Western-style] ship-building to Japan. He also instructed members of the Imperial Family. Bill Adams lived in Ito about 1605, and as Frank is the next Britisher to have permanent residence in Ito, naturally his photo appeared in the Press, and he spoke on the national Radio! Gladys as an Englishwoman, shared honours at the wreath-laying ceremony. It was great fun but the hottest day imaginable, and the ceremony being at noon rather took the edge off our enjoyment. Bill and I also laid a wreath on the Memorial.

In a few days we are to have elections, and the parade of trucks with their loud speakers and often with the candidate himself sitting in the back solemnly and endlessly bowing, is a regular sight. Apart from elections the Press talks much of the British Seamen Case (with tactful lack of conviction for or against), the departure of the biggest group of Russian officials to leave Japan since the refusal of the Japanese government to recognise the status of the Mission since April, and the sit-down strike in gaol of the May Day rioters who refuse to face trial, and the possible economic repercussions of the American plan to spend 750 million dollars in Japan during the next fiscal year. Here, as in Australia, there is some question as to the status and validity of passports of Japanese delegates attending the Peking Peace Conference.

On the domestic front there's a slight decrease in prices of certain essential commodities. We were able to buy some 12 oz. tins of Kraft cheese for 280 yen a tin, i.e. 6/9 d. Australian; Minced Beef in Tokyo for about 5/6 d. per lb. Bread still costs 4/9 d. a loaf, but to balance that, by the kindness of the Taxation Department, we got a refund of a little over 1,000 yen the other day [on general assessment].

_____

By one of these odd slips, parcels from Mrs. E. J. Clark at Sandgate, from Bill's Godmother, and from Keith Viney at Devonport, came in with no tax, as a result. We think of Frank thoroughly lecturing the local Post Office for charging us tax on every foreign letter, whether it was taxable or not. So effective was the lecture that for a while even legitimately understamped letters were quietly pushed into our box.

_____

I can't get accustomed to the suddenness of weather changes here. Already the nights are chilly, although we swelter at midday. During October mild, clear days will give place suddenly, ten degrees a week, to cold days, and with the mandarin crops ripening, Winter will be upon us. Already the long visibility of autumn brings Chiba Peninsula far across the Bay right on to our doorstep, and now that the corn has been cut I can see the blue rim of the sea from the windows. Out in the country the rapidly yellowing rice is rimmed with lines of red (Nerines) and if the rest of the season's typhoons miss Japan there'll be a fine rice harvest this year.

The Sunday School Teacher's Conference this year is up in the Hakone Mountains behind Odawara, our diocese being responsible for the arrangements. The weather and the accommodation in bungalows make it impossible to take the youngest Coaldrake. As it is now with solids in his diet, feeding is quite a problem. So Frank goes alone.

We hope to make a one-day visit to the Church Music School to be held next week in the mountains and at the same time explore the possibility of a site for a holiday. For it is being borne in upon us very strongly that we must, when funds permit, put up a shack somewhere away from the loud speakers of this town. Many missionaries go to Lake Nojiri across central Japan from here, but we seek somewhere closer home and the Yugawara valley with its villages, sight and sound of the sea, and hot springs attracts us as the most suitable.

We shall be writing soon again.

With every good wish and love from us all,

FRANK, MAIDA and BILL

———

Printed by Brisbane City Printery, Edward Street, Brisbane.

Letter from Frank Coaldrake to Maida Coaldrake, C/– Mrs. Neil Currie, Tokyo. Postmarked 14 September 1952 [written from Odawara].

10.00 p.m. Saturday

Darling,

This is a desolate outpost with too many reminders of you and a vast empty bed and broad empty cot – looking very nice with yen 800's worth of new mattress. I bought the mattress at Miyazawa's house. Stopped to eat the nice sandwiches in Miyazawa-san's workshop guest waiting-room with gold curtains and sofas. We reached here at 4.30 after a casual trip except for a wretched Pontiac I stopped to let pass me in Atami but when I caught him on the dirt out of Ajiro he hogged and raced. He had one near-miss with a truck on a bend and three near upsets breaking on the curves but wouldn't get out of my way so I passed him nicely in a bulldog portside on a curve and he seemed to pull up to think it over – as a result we got home quite early. You'd have enjoyed it.[40] Miyazawa seemed to sleep through it all.

---

40 Maida Coaldrake assures the reader that she would not have enjoyed it. Frank Coaldrake's driving was legendary, even infamous. It was not without reason that the first character of Kanagawa prefecture, *kami* or 'God,' was on the registration number of the jeep, leading everyone to call that particular jeep the "amen car," referring to the prayers of those who rode in it.

Newsletter No. 50, October–November, 1952.

NIPPON SEIKO KWAI

From – Rev. F.W. Coaldrake

[first half written by Maida Coaldrake, second half by Frank]

St. Mary's Church House
960 Shimouchi,
Okaku,
Ito-shi,
JAPAN.

Dear Friends,

We feel as though the events which have telescoped two months into one, may explain our long silence towards you.

First of all the Coaldrakes took a holiday! It found us on the Feast of St. Michael [29 September] already some hundred miles from home, in Hamamatsu which was hideously bombed out during the war, and Frank who visited there regularly for services early in his ministry, was unbelieving and rejoicing over the great changes that had taken place. Through the neon-lit streets with their new modern buiidings we found our way eventually to the home of Miss Grosjeans, retired S.P.G. missionary whose long and wonderful life has been spent mostly with the Church in Korea. She was very well and a delightful hostess, eager for news of the church abroad and of her friends in England and Australia. Next time we see Frank Engel[41] and his family we shall be able to confound him with tales of his youth spent in Korea!

It wasn't until we were racing along the dusty, broad No. 1 highway after leaving Hamamatsu, "Rover" fully loaded with water tank, ice-box, sleeping bags, food and, of course, Bill, that we began to feel we were on holiday. The miles of Central Honshu spread out in the hot sunlight. Bentenjima, with its fine sands and pine trees, fascinated us in its resemblance to some of the watering places in the Hawkesbury River valley. It is a small island which stands in the mouth of the outlet between a great sandy lagoon and the Pacific Ocean. Oyster beds and the frames for seaweed culture stretched along the coast for miles.

The great sprawling city of Nagoya with its heavy industries, busy port, and U.S. Security Force areas swallowed us up in the late afternoon. It was as difficult there as in most cities to get clear directions, and enquiries were made more trying by the people we asked wanting to practice their English in answering! Also there was the question of accent and local dialect, for Frank speaks with a South Tokyo accent and these central people have their own turns of consonant and phrase.

As a matter of fact, during the whole of our trip which covered a great deal of Central Japan, we noted with interest the changing accents, the different

41 A Travelling Secretary of A.S.C.M. at the same time as Frank Coaldrake.

architecture in the roof and house design and the complete change in farmers' hat styles and carts, in a short stretch of twenty miles as we crossed the prefectural boundaries.

Even babies' prams differed, moving from the inevitable baby on the back and vegetables in the pram, to a most superior high riding affair with all the family aboard that was faintly reminiscent of the original T-model Ford.

Gifu for the night – a really exciting city on the banks of a broad, swiftly flowing river, famous for paper umbrellas, elegant lanterns exported all over the world and a vast variety of textiles. Coming in through the factory area over more of the endless "road under repair" into a rather tawdry looking shopping area reeking with the smell of grilling eels, we rather wondered if we hadn't been misled into thinking we should see some of the romance of old Japan. But once over the bridge we found it all – the wonderful deep river, the hills rising straight off the banks in their thickly wooded cocked hats, and the beautiful Inns with their curved tiled roofs and green gardens. From our room at one of these Inns we saw the cormorant-fishing boats go out – flares of torchlight on the shining dark river, and I must confess I nearly fell over the balcony in excitement.

Fishing with cormorants is a very ancient sport in Japan. There are historical records of it back as far as the eighth century. And here we were in Gifu "in the season." We had arrived too late in the evening to go out to the fishing grounds, but we had read how the fish, a kind of smelt, is attracted to the torchlight and at the word from the master in each boat the birds dive in with astonishing swiftness and swallow several fish which are later retrieved by the boatmen. The next morning, in sparkling sunlight, we went down the bank and talked to the boys who were feeding their cormorants and young Bill did as much delighted squealing as did the birds.

Through Kyoto, most beautiful of cities, with its famous art treasures, pagodas, temples and shrines, and on into the flats around the great Bay which has Osaka and Kobe on its shores. Osaka has a population well over three million but like the Tokyo-Yokohama area, it is difficult to say where Osaka ends and Kobe begins. The whole plain smokes with the furnaces of great factories. Planes roar up and away every few minutes from the great air base. The road is packed with lorries, trucks, buses and motorbike trailers, but few cars. In Kobe harbour, fringed with a breakwater on the ocean side and 67 giant smoke stacks on the city side, were dozens of ocean-going vessels, both foreign and Japanese. The warehouses were full and busy and while we were in Kobe the inevitable and ever-recurring fire swept away one of the largest of these, full of bales of cotton, in a most spectacular few hours' blaze.

———

All the way down we had, as it were, a cockpit view of the Election campaign in a most significant part of Japan. We often followed along after lorries of canvassers with loud speakers blaring, or sat behind an open truck with the candidate, himself complete with huge ribbon rosette in button hole, bowing on and on, unsmiling, at the world and his dog.

The result of the elections was no surprise. But there were some very interesting points. One was the distinct split in the ranks of the Liberal Party amounting at one time to a complete rupture between the Prime Minister, Mr. Yoshida, and his rival for party leadership, Hatoyama. There has now been a working patch put over the differences. Another interesting point was the number of small parties which held a strong minority position – in our type of political scene these would all have been welded into the Opposition. A third, and very significant one, was the re-appearance of over a hundred candidates who, under the Occupation had been suspect, or "purged" from all positions in government or civil service, and a fourth interest was the complete disappearance of Communist representatives. These must either have been absorbed into one of the smaller parties under a changed colour, or else suggest a going-underground of Communist activities.

One other aspect of policy in which we are particularly interested is the complete preoccupation of the Prime Minister in all his press and public statements with trade competition between Japan and England for the markets of South-East Asia, and the problem of whether these markets can ever become a satisfactory substitute for the lost Red China trade. On the ever-present problem of over-population he states that "emigration is not a major solution. The most effective solution is to increase our foreign trade thereby providing more jobs."

———

At this point, back to Kobe for a while where we spent a week most pleasantly and busily. Kobe has a large international population of business and trades people and is the centre of training for a team of young American missionaries who are here to work with the Nippon Seiko Kwai. In addition, Kobe is Bishop Yashiro's own diocese and is therefore in many ways the centre of [Anglican] Church life in Japan. So we thoroughly enjoyed meeting people, sitting long over meals prepared from meats and vegetables unobtainable in Izu, visiting the famous Great Buddha at Nara, said to be the biggest in the world, soaking up the beauty of the ancient shrines and gardens in Kyoto and talking endlessly of Church and missionary problems in this rapidly changing context of post-occupation Japan. Bill was a huge success – six months and four teeth of him – but I must record that the first time he was surrounded by four Westerners at once he burst into tears only to be consoled when he caught a glimpse of the Japanese maid out of the corner of his eye.

So back home stopping over night on the Peninsula on which are the most famous of all shrines, those at Ise where the Emperors and rulers go to "tell their ancestors about the state of the country." For example, the young Crown Prince, Akihito [now the Heisei Emperor], proclaimed as such yesterday with great pomp and ceremony at his Coming of Age, will go in a few days to tell his great-greats especially the Emperor Meiji, what is happening and make his prayers at the shrine.

I might add that a camping holiday in this country is almost out of the question. Sometimes we drove for three hours looking for a few square yards to put our tent fly on and went as far as sixty miles off route in the search. Several times a hopeful side road led us straight into someone's back yard, but usually the problem was just that between village and village was only rice paddy, or rocky mountainside. We finished our tour by staying two nights at an Inn on the sandy wastes of Benten-jima simply because it could almost have been in Australia.

This may sound rather like a travelogue. Indeed that is what our holiday was intended to be. Working day by day in the hot-spring towns and villages, visiting farmers and small shop-keepers, worrying away at the problem of how to get at the solid citizen in this town, Ito, of 168 inns, pleasure places and "pachinko" parlours (pachinko is a particularly insidious kind of pin-ball game) we forget the great cities, the industrial man, the foreign population, the ancient Japan of beautiful buildings and even more ancient religions; and we almost forget there are other missionaries on the job, on their toes, anxious to exchange ideas and experiences. We came back tired from the whirl of people and places but on our toes too.

———

At home in Ito suddenly many plans came to a head. Our hope that Ippeki Camp material, which had to be disposed of, may continue to serve use, was fully realized. Ito Boy Scouts (Buddhist), Tokyo Y.M.C.A. and the Primary School attached to the Seiko Kwai University in Tokyo were our chief purchasers. The fruit of that came when on Sunday morning, in fine autumn sunlight, our congregation moved from the house on to the site of the new "temporary" Church for the blessing of the Foundations, and raised a most hearty "O God our help in ages past, Our Hope for years to come." Much of the money from Camp Sale will go into the Church.

Today, too, I am really typing in self-defense. There are plumbers in the roof seeking the leaks which flooded us during the last typhoon; there are carpenters switching round some windows to act as sun traps during the winter months, and, just beyond, the Church foundations are noisily being laid.

———

Frank writes:

At last after several weeks I'm in a place with a couple of hours clear for letter writing, so I'll start by catching up on lost time with your *Newsletter.* I'm sitting in an ante-room of a museum of relics of 100 years ago when the American fleet came to Japan and compelled the government to open the country to foreign trade. This port of Shimoda [at the southern end of the Izu Peninsula] was the first point of entry, and it was here that the first American Ambassador [Consul Townsend Harris] resided for his first year of office [1856]. He soon realised that he had been put off in a very isolated spot and moved off up to Tokyo, but during that year here he lived in a Buddhist temple, and after he had gone the place was preserved just as he left it. An old pipe, a knife and such things are treasured here, together with paintings of various events of the time.

The whole [place] proves to be not unattractive to Japanese holiday trippers, and they come in parties at sixpence a head to be shown around. To me the most interesting item is a model of the gaol cell in which they imprisoned the man who swam out to the American ships and begged to be taken to America to study.[42] To try to leave Japan was a capital offence and he was in due course, executed. All that happened just ninety years ago. So the things introduced then have become firmly embedded in Japanese life. Photographs, for example, were taken for the first time in Japan here in this town. That same man also "milked the cow first in Japan," a notice informs us. Cows and cameras are now thoroughly Japanese. So are guns.

Ambassador Townsend Harris was a "devout" Anglican, and used our prayer book regularly. There is no immediate obvious practical advantage in saying prayers, so it has not even yet become a regular Japanese practice. In fact I have baptised only one man here so far. He is to be confirmed before Christmas. His father runs this museum, and it is his room I am using. Perhaps we will be able to make steady progress now that we have a good solid start, but how late we are!

––––––

I've just found the first "break" in one of my most serious obstacles. I've written before about the way parents and old folk are forbidding their younger generation to receive baptism. The number of people being held back against their wishes in this matter grows steadily. Only yesterday I found that a man over fifty cannot come to be baptised because his wife and her daughter forbid it. After her first husband died, leaving her with a baby daughter, her parents adopted him so that she might marry him and continue the family name. This is a very common practice even today. The man in that position is so deprived of authority and privilege that he is always spoken of with pity, and even contempt. This particular woman says her family has always been Buddhist so he must not become a Christian. There it rests at present. But in another family the husband has been opposing his wife and child in their wish to be baptised. I had a long talk to him nearly a year ago and now it is agreed that they all be baptised in December. I am very thankful to find that it can happen, because otherwise we could make no solid progress. I know some of our friends have been praying about this, and it certainly is one of the chief things to which friends in Australia might lend their efforts.

Old things, or rather the things of the old, old days, are much venerated by the Japanese ordinary people. It is an attitude quite foreign to Australia, perhaps because we don't have such old things. In this country ancient relics

42 Frank Coaldrake was writing about the prison cell in the Townsend Harris Museum in Shimoda where Yoshida Shōin (1830–1859) was imprisoned for breaking *Sakoku* (the national seclusion policy), and from where he was taken to Edo (Tokyo) to be executed. Maida Coaldrake notes (24 May 2002): "Through Frank and this memorial I heard of Yoshida Shōin for the first time. We were later [in 1968–69] to visit his memorial statue in Shimoda as a family – and almost exactly thirty years later I was to present a successful Ph.D. thesis on his life and philosophies." See further: *Yoshida Shōin (1830–1859) and the Shōka Sonjuku*, Ph.D. Thesis, University of Tasmania, 1986, Maida S. Coaldrake.

are repaired and even replaced by good likenesses until, like the axe that had three new handles and two new heads and was still going strong after ten years, the whole thing is not really so old and venerable. We saw such things on our holiday journey through the country where Japan as a Nation came into being. Buildings and statues as originally put up over a thousand years ago now stand to be visited by holiday trippers every year. Three years ago the ancient "Golden Pavilion" in Kyoto was completely destroyed by fire. The renewal is now almost completed. In twenty years time people will not realise that it is not the original. This capacity to venerate ancient forms, should, and does, help to make the truth of Christianity appealing, but the element of life and flexibility in Christian faith and culture is a very hard thing to understand and cope with.

—

One of the really cheering things that is happening right now is the development of plans for the Youth Camps on their new site. We have moved everything from the Lake Ippeki site and have stored the necessary gear down at Kawazuhama. Apart from our own conviction that this is the best place for future camps, we have been urged by some of the people in the village to set up the camp here.

A week ago our Mission committee met leading Kawazu people and talked about their hopes and our plans. It went on for a couple of hours.

We found ourselves being asked by old and young men to bring more than a Summer camp into their village. A Centre for worship, recreation and education where the whole programme is rooted in a Living Faith is what they are asking for. None of them is yet attending our services and meetings in the next hamlet, though in some cases their sons and daughters are. More than we had realised they've glimpsed the possibilities. "Not by next year, perhaps not in five, but eventually you can help us make a new life in this village" is the way one of them urged us.

Foundation building is in progress and I have to keep an eye on it, while Bill is chewing his favourite toy – the car's spare fan belt!

Sincerely yours,
    FRANK and MAIDA

—

Circulated by Mrs. E.R. Coaldrake, Hamilton Road, Nundah.
[Printed by] Brisbane City Printery, Edward Street, Brisbane.

Maida Coaldrake, Oral History, 15 May 2002.

Kimiyo-san (Kimiyo Mutō) first joined our family towards the end of 1952 as a daily help – a lovely young girl of rare background – a Christian father, a stern and lovable umbrella maker, who had come to us in distress because, although desperately needing the small monies she could earn at age 17, he was very worried that she could find work only as a golf caddie at the R and R centre at Kawana for soldiers on leave from Korea. (Fig. 37)

Figure 37 Kimiyo Mutō standing at the Yōmeimon, Tōshōgū, Nikkō, September, 1953.

Newsletter No. 51, December, 1952 – January, 1953.

NIPPON SEIKO KWAI

From – Rev. F.W. Coaldrake

[written by Maida Coaldrake]

> St. Mary's Church House
> 960 Shimouchi,
> Okaku,
> Ito-shi,
> JAPAN.

Dear Friends,

This, almost the first opportunity we have had for any letter writing in 1953, brings you our warm good wishes for the New Year together with all the traditional Japanese "hopes" – at the front entrances of all houses and inns are placed two pine branches, three stems of bamboo, and bound in with straw rope, a spray of early plum blossom. The pine tree, because of its hardiness, denotes long life, the bamboo stems, constancy and virtue, and the plum blooming at the bitterest and drabbest time of the year, beauty in the midst of adversity, in fact the eternal silver lining.

Despite our long "official" silence through *Newsletters* for which we know you have understanding, we have had the joy through Christmas and New Year in having personal touch with many of you, as many as the purse and postal restrictions would allow. We hope Bill's laugh helped you into a joyful Christmas tide.[43] (Fig. 38)

In addition to the usual flurry of preparations for Christmas, Nativity plays, special services, gathering together of extras for parties and so on, December was made into the Red-letter month of our whole year. The foundations of the new Church, which we mentioned briefly in our last letter, grew in just six weeks into a fine Church. We call it temporary, very firmly, and had the Bishop on the very day of Dedication, turn the first sod in the area set aside for the fine stone structure of the future, but for the time we rejoice with heart and soul and voice at what is a very fine little Church, adequate for the needs of the growing Peninsula Parish.

But oh, December! Frank was foreman and chief builder, supervising plumber, electrician, transport officer, concrete mixer and the rest! I did what I could with one hand on a rapidly crawling Bill, scrubbing endless floors, turning out tea for thirty workmen two or three times a day, in fact all the things that anyone else who has helped build a Church in six weeks would know about! Everything was rather complicated by some poor concrete work which had to be done again, and by an early snowfall which set outside work back three days. The result was that

---

43 Refers to the 1952 Coaldrake Christmas bookmark with photograph of Bill sent to many friends. Also mentioned by Bishop Felix Arnott in *chapter 9*.

Affectionate
Greetings

from
Bill, Maida and
Frank Coaldrake

CHRISTMAS 1952
ITO, IZU.

Figure 38 The Coaldrake Christmas card for 1952. Bookmark which is still found in many prayer books.

we all fell over each other in the last two days, and Frank's main job became that of peacemaker between painters who wanted to paint where carpenters were working, in places where the plasterers were still patching the poor concrete up. And finally on the day that everyone came early in the morning armed to the teeth with brooms and cloths to clean and beautify for the morrow's festival, I spent a hair-greying morning finding imaginary jobs enough to keep them all happy until the floor varnish had dried sufficiently for the working bee to invade. In the late afternoon it was a case of all hands to the pump – even the Bishop already installed as a house guest, lent a hand in the form of baby sitting, and Fr. Sakurai hastily brushed up Novice-skills and worked the borrowed electric floor polisher.

But on the morning of St. Thomas' Day [21 December] the church looked beautiful – so beautiful that a church member from Mishima rushing in out of the inevitable sleet and rain, failed to discover that the nave and meeting room were built from one and a half Quonset Hut frames until she saw a photo later, for inside, the lightly-varnished walls, the darker brown pews (our Japanese congregation turns its nose up at the traditional tatami matting) and the high, light sanctuary with its lovely silver-blue dorsal curtain, are far removed from the bare hut we had some time ago in the fishing village. (Colour Plate 14. Compare Fig. 33)

When Bishop Maekawa knocked heavily on the door and was bidden to enter, more than eighty people greeted him in the packed church, people who had gathered from six centres many travelling for hours in the bitter morning cold. After the Dedication, we rejoiced mightily in the Baptism of several children and adults, and the Confirmation of eight adults. While the snow slowly coated the surrounding hills we lifted the "Church's One Foundation" to the new roof with such vigour that we didn't feel the cold any more.

Frank preached the sermon during the Holy Communion service in both English and Japanese as there were present members of the Australian Embassy staff who had come down from Tokyo for the occasion. (Colour Plate 10 and Fig. 39)

After the services came the pious festive eating, with foods of the right colours for such an occasion. The marquee lunch had to be abandoned in favour of a crowd in the meeting room, while the dignitaries, visiting priests, Mayor and the like had a buffet lunch in our big room vastly entertained by Bill Coaldrake.

Figure 39 The dedication of the temporary Church building in Itō, 21 December 1952. There were eighty people present, including the Mayor of Itō, Bishop Maekawa (front centre), and two representatives of the Australian Embassy (on right, Neil Currie later Australian Ambassador, and Raymond Percival, third from right).

For us, the Coaldrakes, the day was made perfect by a feeling of closeness to all of you at home, who by your prayers and financial support have helped us build a Church (a small brick in the vast unfinished Church). One group of friends at St. Peter's, Launceston, have provided the beautiful [crudence?] table, which gives you all a place in the Church and constantly in our prayers at the altar.

Also for us, the Coaldrakes, the day was made complete when Gladys and David Chamberlain, married the previous day in Kobe by Bishop Yashiro, arrived in a flutter of rice and confetti. Using our house as a base – they spent a fortnight on the lovely Izu Peninsula and were able to eat our home grown chickens with us on Christmas Eve. They are once more in Kobe busy with schools and in their spare time making a home.

––––––

Christmas was really joyful, the theme running behind all our thanksgiving and worship – at last a Church to worship in. The Crib looked splendid in its new setting and I'm sure Frank must have spent hours more than was strictly necessary preparing for services, just because at last he has a vestry. And in that vestry – cupboards, rows of them, and vestment drawers, enough to delight the heart of any priest. Those cupboards and drawers are made of the cheapest but most effective wood available in this district – believe it or not – camphor wood! Can anyone blame Frank for lingering? When we finally build the rectory, I shall spend every morning shut in the linen cupboard.

Christmas in Ito was a small fragment of Christmas in the Peninsula and after 8 a.m. Mass on Christmas Day following Midnight Mass, the Land Rover bounced off up the highway towards more Masses and more Plays and lots of parties. I sat at home with Bill while he bowed and smiled his thanks to many friends for a whole kennel full of stuffed rag puppies, and I began to read Christmas mail from Australia – a most happy pursuit which filled all the spare corners of a quiet day. Thank you all so much for cards and air letters and notes. We are determined to answer every one if you can wait a little while. Though we are many times tempted to do it, we have not yet descended to an acknowledgements column.

––––––

New Year passed pleasantly, with David Chamberlain and Owen O'Reilly of Sydney as guests to help us admire the beautiful kimonos worn shyly by young friends out doing the traditional New Year courtesy visiting. Our youngest Church member, standing about a head taller than Billy but his senior by two years, trotted along with her sandal bells tinkling and long coloured pins in her elaborate hair do. I was most amused to see that on the following Sunday, once more rugged up in woollies and long stockings, she still sported the same elaborate cottage-loaf style hairdo, a little worse for wear!

Yesterday Prince Chichibu, the Sportsman Prince, and younger brother of Emperor Hirohito, was buried. There has been quite a fuss concerning the non-attendance of the Emperor at the funeral, and the press is long and loud in its condemnation of the policy of the Court Chamberlains in preventing him in his desire to be present. It has created a most interesting situation in which these almost nameless personages, members of ancient Houses, are endeavouring to pull down once more the veil of semi-deity over the Emperor and be rid of all this nonsense called democracy.

The *Nippon Times* of Jan. 12th reports under the heading "Human Conflicts behind Imperial Palace Walls Force Ruler to Bow to Rigid Customs of His Ancestors." Underneath it a report described the way in which the Emperor, having ordered out the Imperial car to take him to his favourite brother's deathbed, was prevented from doing so by the Court Chamberlains, appalled at the thought of the Emperor making a midnight motor ride to another's sick bed. When the Emperor finally arrived at a more decorous hour he found the Prince had been dead since 4.30 a.m.

But for all the restrictions of his person and doings the Emperor refused to allow the will of the late Prince to be disregarded. The will made provision for a post-mortem in the interests of medical science, and a wish that he be cremated rather than buried in the Imperial tradition. However when it came to be known that the Emperor intended to be present at the funeral, the Court Chamberlains again stepped in – "An Emperor attends only the funerals of his mother and grandmother," they said, quoting 2,500 years of Imperial precedent. And that was that.

We wonder how the young Crown Prince, now preparing for attendance at the Coronation of Queen Elizabeth and a Continental "grand tour," will react to such Imperial Precedent when he ascends the throne.

One other sidelight on how much democracy means and how deeply the splendid Western ideas have not sunk in! In a press photo of the Emperor and Empress receiving New Year homage of thousands of their subjects, the Empress walks several paces behind her morning-trousered, frock-coated husband, clad in Japanese kimono, and with head bowed. At all the official functions at the Palace at which diplomats and their wives were received the men were compelled to take precedence over the women and were ostentatiously seated and served first. We had it first hand that there were some very angry wives about Tokyo on New Year's night!

———

In the last few days we have had reason to ponder once more on the rather primitive conditions prevailing in the practice of medicine, at least outside Tokyo. In many matters it is about twenty or thirty years behind that at home though every Japanese believes in the magic of some of the newer drugs. Indeed the use of the needle by all and sundry, the woman in the home, the druggist in his store, as well as the doctor in his surgery, is a matter of constant amazement. Young people, a little exhausted by the rough and tumble of a youth camp, will slip off down to the Lake Ippeki doctor to have a shot of an anti-fatigue serum. A cold in the head or a pain in the tummy, a sore fingernail, all have anti-bodies readily available at any drug store. Any pregnant woman will tell you she has just been off to have her weekly dose of calcium in the arm, and she depends entirely on such shots without altering in any way her usual daily eating or living habits. The efficacy of all this we seriously doubt. So many people have colds, pains, sores, and so many women and babies are shockingly undernourished and tardy in development.

But with regard to medical practice, mercurochrome is used generously both after operations and for any minor cut with some appalling results in the way of septic wounds, and local penicillin is given in large doses to clear up the mistakes. Last week we had reason to doubt strongly the usefulness of even that local product when it had no result at all in correcting an infection which was causing trouble.

In the same way that research lags behind world experience, the use and administration of hospitals is outdated here. Except for a few of the hospitals in the great cities, the word "hospital" usually applies to a kind of dormitory for the sick where there is provision for the camping attendance of a member of the family who cooks and generally cares for the patient. Of course this cuts down expenses greatly as nursing care consists mainly of temperature taking and wound dressing. At least the doctor has his more seriously ill patients gathered together, but from the point of view of rapid recuperation there is much to be desired. Mrs. Miyazawa's new little daughter [Hisako] was born last week in a local nursing home. When we went to visit we found that it was scarcely a nursing home by our standards, rather a midwife's home with a room to let. Mrs. Miyazawa had all her own bedding with her, much of her own food brought from home, the babe in her sole care, and three year-old Kimiko-chan, living in the room too. Kimiko didn't want to stay at home!

Plans move on for the building of a rectory and the conversion of our present semi-Japanese house into a hostel along the lines of the Hostel run by the Brotherhood in Charleville, Queensland. There are several children of our Christian families in Izu needing accommodation in Ito which is a large educational centre. If we can provide a Christian home for them and care for them in their out of school hours, we feel we have a small part of the answer to the tremendous problem of "Church schools." The present educational system provided by the Government requires children to attend at least to the end of Middle School – age 15, and is, as far as we can see, a fairly efficient system. New schools are built almost weekly throughout the nation to cope with the huge increase in scholars. Educational Reform under S.C.A.P. brought it. Church schools are hard put financially as well as on the staff side to provide anything like the same facilities. If we can have plans well advanced by the end of this present school year, April, we shall be certain of at least some young people as a start.

Today is Adult's Day – a national holiday [at the time celebrated on 15 January]. As Ito is a pleasure resort there are thousands of visitors in the town taking hot-spring baths and lounging about the pin-ball parlours in their Inn dressing-gowns. Ito isn't a nice place to live in on public holidays, especially such a day as this when all twenty year olds officially come of age together, today, and have to celebrate.

Ito is much warmer than Tokyo where we struck a snow fall all last week, even if the column-frost stands high round our house every morning. Winter is fully on us.

With warmest greetings,

Affectionately,

FRANK, MAIDA and BILL

P.S. In response to many enquiries, Postal Notes are still conveniently convertible, and the method of making gifts through any A.B.M. office direct to our personal banking account in Sydney is also a good one. Many thanks to you all.

———

Circulated by Mrs. E.R. Coaldrake. Hamilton Road, Nundah.

[Printed by] Brisbane City, Printery, Edward Street, Brisbane.

Newsletter No. 52, February–March, 1953

NIPPON SEIKO KWAI

From – Rev. F.W. Coaldrake

[written by Maida Coaldrake]

> St. Mary's Church House
> 960 Shimouchi,
> Okaku,
> Ito-shi,
> JAPAN.

Dear Friends,

Rarely it is that the "A-men" car lets the people of Ose down! But this time it has, for Frank's "Land Rover" is known throughout the Izu Peninsula as the "Amen" car and this trip there has been no rain. With their delight in play on words, it didn't take the people long to associate the downpours of rain which inevitably follow Frank's schedule each fortnight with a neat name for the well-known vehicle.

The Japanese word for rain is "AME" made possessive by the addition of "NO" slurred very readily into "AMEN..." I rejoice mightily in the spell of sunny days which presage the end of the winter but the water situation further down the coast is desperate with wells nearly dry and crops still suffering from the effects of typhoon "Dinah."

The "wet" season is still two months or more away.

Actually according to the ancient calendar, February 3rd was the beginning of Spring. So we had a snowfall to mark the event and shivered in the grip of an icy spell, which froze taps and puddles and water in the church vases. And a little later, returning from a three day visit to some of our centres, we drove up from the west coast across the mountainous backbone of Izu through passes thick with slush and melting snows, and trees dripping steadily in the mists.

As we note each year, these two coldest months bring with them a share of serious fires, and we have had three real scares lately. Two of them late on

Sunday nights, and one at high noon ravaging half a hillside were the worst in Ito, but the paper daily brings news of hospitals, schools, shops and houses blazing to nothing in a few minutes. The two Sunday night fires dragging us from our beds with the siren wailing were very close – one a timber yard a stone's throw away poured sparks over us and neighbouring houses; the other the Public Bath House, with meeting-halls above, immediately below us in the main street, was gutted in no time. We are always thankful for the patches of field which lie on either side of us and for the amazing efficiency of the fire brigade. One never knows when one's nearest neighbour's imperfect electrical wiring or carelessly covered charcoal brazier will spell disaster to the whole suburb.

———

Plans for the Hostel are progressing, dependent to a large extent on the pleasure of the officials who are holding up the Rectory plans, we suspect, because such a house has never been built in this Prefecture before. You may remember that we are living at present in a house which is half Japanese – i.e. with tatami-matting floors and sliding paper[-screen] doors, and which, with its one large all-purpose living room and Japanese style bath, will make an excellent hostel for young Church people coming to Ito to school. Pressed continually to start a "kindergarten" or a "Church school," which the community generally has come to associate with the Church, we feel that a properly conducted home away from home for some of our own young people is the answer. The Church has pioneered in these other fields and now the Government and civil authorities have taken over [these services] most adequately, but the arduous travelling conditions, and most unsuitable living quarters provided for scholars living outside educational centers, convinces us we must go ahead with our project.

The Headmaster of the Ito High School whom we visited the other day appears to agree, for he has undertaken to accept any of our Church children who pass the "Achievement" Test even though they come from outside the Ito official "sphere." Dr. Kawai's youngest daughter Tsuneko-chan [from Ose] will be one of our first residents. Until our house is finished in June we hope she and others enrolling will be billeted with church people.

———

Bill Coaldrake in his check shirts and long-uns is quite a man about the place these days. He has mastered the principle of the sliding door and as all doors and windows – not to mention cupboards – work that way there were some moments of crisis before we worked out a series of hazards. We've nicknamed him "Chanics" because of his tremendous absorption in all things mechanical.

Thank you for affectionate messages and enquiries and appreciation of his Christmas smile! Do remember him on his first birthday, April 5th, Easter Day. Isn't it a wonderful day to have one's first birthday?

Without exception our people are incredulous that his tremendous energy, growth and obvious radiant health are due to our normal methods of child care and management. That a baby should have eight teeth before he is ten months old, that he should be walking quite happily at all, and that his diet should include meat and eggs and fruit, leaves them amazed. Yet what they find most amazing of all is that he likes his bath. We are often saying how the Japanese loves his hot bath really hot between 45–48 degrees centigrade right up to his neck (you try it). But I am not sure that we've explained how the Japanese becomes accustomed to it. Easy! Baby is dunked in the family bath from earliest days and no heed is taken of the poor mite's screams and cries. Even the most enlightened parent and nurse take it for granted that a baby does not like his bath. Our lay reader's latest daughter, Hisako, was brought to us for advice on this most difficult of subjects! We said drop the bath temperature. They were most anxious she should enjoy her bath the way Bill always has but were frankly sceptical that anyone could suffer a bath at body heat or less. However they went away to experiment and later told us they did as we said by preparing a little bath of warm water, but when they put their hands in they were sure that the baby would die of cold, so they gradually increased the heat until it felt right again. So Hisako-chan took her bath crying as usual.

We haven't insisted. We are afraid to interfere. Their methods are so different and to our mind so obsolete that to alter one small aspect such as bathing would do more harm than good. Infant mortality is so high that one diversion from the old custom would be blamed for tragedy were it to occur. We feel for instance that a vitamin deficiency at present being treated by injections for the mother is a very much lesser way of treating the problem than by direct feeding of vitamins to the baby. We have neither skill nor knowledge to start a baby clinic but we have Bill and many people are beginning to ask questions.

When we tell you that Bill is often mistaken for a two-year-old you will understand why we are constantly preoccupied with the problem.

––––––

In various centres Frank is preparing small groups for Baptism at Easter.

Here in Ito four candidates are fruits of our new technique with church school scholars – i.e. keeping a limited membership and requiring parents signed approval of their children's preparation for Church membership. Every Sunday since our new Church was dedicated we have had a draft of new children come to service and we encourage them (and their parents if they enquire) to continue to come to services. They are put on a waiting list for Sunday School even if enrolment forms are returned, and the months of waiting are a good test. We sometimes suspect these kiddies are the kind we find in any town at home who do the rounds of all the Sunday Schools. Ito United Protestant Church, according to statistics, has the largest Sunday School in Japan with over two thousand scholars enrolled in several sessions. But the United Protestant Church bewails the lack of membership, especially adult membership, so we have cause to wonder and continue our cautious policy until we know this community better and where we are going.

––––––

At present we are delving deeply into the mystery of the group in the Japanese social system. When any attempt is made to formalise a loosely knit body of people and get some regular organisation going it just fades away altogether. This has happened repeatedly in our experience here even when the request for formalization has come from the group itself. There is something in the Japanese mind which seems to make it possible to work in only the most fluid medium. Please remember this when you remember the task confronting the Japanese Church and our young candidates for Baptism.

It's not always like that of course. The church school group is really a group – two classes – and even during Services you can feel them as a group carrying young Tadashi-kun [one of the Miyazawa boys] as he is gradually metamorphosed from a scrubby little boy into a composed and graceful server. As he strains to extinguish the tallest candle I'm sure every young man in the congregation is holding his arm.

Old Kubota-san from up in the mountain village has been most grateful for assistance from Australia and more recently for Frank's carrying to hospital his ailing wife. In bitter winter weather only the Land Rover could possibly negotiate the goat-track road with an invalid aboard. So he arrived on the doorstep the other day bearing two lovely Bonsai dwarf trees because he had heard I admired them. Before the war he had an amazing collection of them and is one of the few remaining teachers of the ancient art. I can sit at my desk and gaze at an unbelievably beautiful tree nine inches high with its gnarled roots twisted over a mossy rock in its pot.

Actual trees such as these grow to great age and beauty round the famous Ise shrines from whence the Crown Prince has just returned. He was making his last visit to report to his ancestors before he sets out for England and the Coronation [of Queen Elizabeth II]. It is reported that, among the many things he wishes to see and do, he is anxious to make an examination of the British Royal family system! We would be interested to watch the influence of such an examination on the Imperial household of the future.[44]

For whatever good has undoubtedly come from the Occupation, on the surface of things there is a swing towards old ways and old things. On a quick business trip to Tokyo the other day (100 miles both ways in the hot carriage with its seats so ill-fitted to Western heads and legs) I found the great department stores crowded. The two most crowded floors in all stores were the food basement and the Kimono show room. There were thousands of women around the most wonderful displays of kimono and obi cloth of every colour and design, some most beautiful. A good kimono in silk or brocade with trimmings these days costs between 20,000 and 25,000 yen (Aust. £25–£30). A working class man or clerk of little account has a monthly income of about 10,000 yen, and the farmer less. There's no question though that the kimono is a most becoming garment for the Japanese lady and she is sensible enough to realise it. Even the most stylish young lady in Tokyo lacks carriage to do justice to Western skirt or dress styles.

---

44 The present Crown Prince Naruhito undertook post-graduate studies at Merton College, the University of Oxford. Crown Princess Masako completed graduate studies at Balliol College, Oxford.

We wonder if with the kimono the whole household system is being geared up once more. About the time you are reading this we shall be hoisting up our eight feet long Carpfish [*koi-nobori* banner] to flutter in the breeze during Boys' Festival Week – a joy reserved for households which are privileged to number a son in their midst. After three years of Japan and a male predominance in the household I am beginning to wonder myself about inferiority complexes!

However there is one level on which we three are equal. Last week we went to the barber and we all came out looking alike, especially from the back. Frank looks fairly normal though there is always a slightly odd slant to a Japanese cut. Bill sporting his second man-sized hair-cut looks delicious and I – well I can hear the chuckles of my erstwhile Mr. Valentine devotees. Lady hairdressers in this country have long since proved impossible, saying themselves that they can only cut Permed hair – the strong frizzed black hair of the modern Japanese miss. Our one refuge is a barber who cut the boys during B.C.O F. Rest Hotel days at Kawana. He at least understands fine hair that curls and can cut most of it neatly off!

———

Back for a moment to more sober things – the immediate reaction in this country to President Eisenhower's sweeping denunciation of the Yalta agreement was the press statement made by Premier Yoshida the next day. What about the Kuriles and Sakhalin? If Yalta is null and void then Russia has no right to our country in the north.[45] These islands are a very raw spot constantly rubbed! We remember one man saying at the signing of the peace treaty when Yalta terms with regard to the north became official: "We feel now we have lost these islands that we have really been defeated."

And nearer at home the bitter aftermath of war – the Education Ministry's special Plea to Parents. This Spring hundreds of children of mixed parentage will reach school age. "The Education Ministry authorities are asking parents not to let their personal prejudices influence their own children's attitudes and the teachers to exert every effort in the education of these children and to avoid all discriminatory actions." Quote from the *Nippon Times*, February 11, 1953.

———

As I have been writing with budding tulips at one elbow and Bill at his endless window sliding at the other, the officials from the Building Control Office suddenly appeared to say everything was in order and signatures etc. only were required to give us the permit for the Rectory building. There had been such a delay we thought something had gone wrong.

———

In your letters there have been several references to the "humdrum" life you lead in your own parishes, to the round of ordinary things, the sparsely attended

———

45 See further: Maida S. Coaldrake, *Japan in Asia: A Dialogue in Co-Existence*, Adelaide, Rigby, 1973. These are the so-called "Northern Territories" which are still a bone of contention between Japan and Russia and are still the major reason there has never been a peace treaty signed between the two countries.

meetings, the routine services, as compared with life out here. You need never worry, for the Church at home seen from here is good and alive and so wonderfully solid and encouraging. You are the plank from which we spring and the source of so much of our own solidarity and assurance in a very unstable world. If you knew how often the thought of you moving along steadily in your routine, Communion at 8 a.m., Evensong at 7 p.m. and all in between steadies us, I am sure you would rejoice.

There are humdrum things here too: five boilings of *dai-dai* [a type of bitter orange] marmalade (some sold for enough yen to start our own Time and Talent fund for the new Church), weekday masses, Japanese on Thursday, English on Fridays, devotional hour, Saturday evenings, services Sunday, classes in any of four centres with early morning communions for the Church members Mondays and Tuesdays any week. . .and the phone and the gardens, and the rest. . .?

To those of you who are setting out for England [for the Coronation of Queen Elizabeth II] or who are already on the way, Godspeed and a wonderful time. We meant to write before but I expect we would be poor missionaries if we had time enough to keep all our correspondence up to date.

With best wishes to you all for a Happy and Holy Easter.

Yours most sincerely,

FRANK, MAIDA and BILL

[Black and white photograph of St. Mary's Church, Izu.]

Circulated by Mrs. E.R. Coaldrake, Hamilton Road, Nundah.
[Printed by] Brisbane City Printery, Edward Street, Brisbane.

Newsletter No. 53, May–June, 1953.

NIPPON SEIKO KWAI

From – Rev. F.W. Coaldrake

[written by Maida Coaldrake]

St. Mary's Church House
960 Shimouchi,
Okaku,
Ito-shi,
JAPAN.

Dear Friends,

Whenever the Izu backbone of mountains is heavily blanketed with mists cutting through the valleys and drifting right to the coast, Frank seems to have to make some special trip across it. This morning it is to say a Requiem for our faithful Mrs. Toyoda, who after fifty years of life in the Faith, died last week. She and her husband have built up a little chemist business in a township which is strongly Buddhist, but though pressure from the community was great and there has been a half-hearted attempt to put Buddhist symbols – lotus, birds and suchlike round the house, the old man stayed firmly by his decision to have Christian rites. Very often the weight of public opinion and pressure from relatives makes it impossible to carry out the wishes of the departed. But Mrs. Toyoda went to her rest with everything the Church has in its promise of immortality and comfort to the bereaved. There was even something of the special elation which attaches to Ascension Day and some of the elders and neighbours seem to be quite interested in the Christian way.

So Frank is saying a Requiem and the mists that make driving the bad roads very difficult are seeping into the house and bringing threats of mildew.

Hardly has the blue, shimmery weather of Cherry Blossom Time warmed us after the Winter, when the moist month of May creeps in. We start to turn out cupboards, wipe shoes down, sniff despairingly at blanket and "Futon" (the padded Japanese mattress) shelves, and watch the arch-enemy mildew touch books, and jam and flour stores. More than anything else it is the sudden changes in climate that beat one's energies and organisation in this country. Less than three months ago Bill and I were shouting with delight on the iced and snowy road above the town. Now the bamboo patch in the corner by the fence grows at the extraordinary pace of 2 to 3 feet a day in the moist heat.

But it's not all gloom – because the beauty of the cherry's silver pink blossoms spread over the whole countryside leaves us breathless for weeks afterwards, and the flame of the azalea does much to make one forget [the dark days]. We have some wonderful lines of vivid tangerine and mauve azalea in the church grounds, and the early roses and iris are everywhere. In our own garden a constant parade of builders and workmen make inroads on the garden beds, but as compensation, the concrete foundations of the new Rectory are giving our friends much to look at and marvel about. For the foundations themselves sit 8 feet high, Queensland style, and the main living rooms will be up where we can catch some breeze in summer.

After the successful building of the Church, Frank now has the confidence to go ahead with the house assisted only by labourers. So, despite constant parochial calls on his time, the house is moving along at a fine pace. (Fig. 40) The matchbox house in which most people live is largely put together on the ground so that it literally springs up overnight, but the solid earthquake-proof building takes much longer. Every man is a specialist – there is one to put bolts in, and one to bed the iron, and one to mix the left hand side of a tray of concrete and one on the right, and so on. A building such as ours in the normal course of affairs would move along very slowly but at all times be covered like an ant heap with busy workers. We bought a small concrete mixer and, hey presto! three men and a barrow do the work of about fifty men and a few shoulder baskets.

Spring, Easter Day and Bill's first Birthday all tumbled in on us with a number of guests as well. Bill had a pink candle on his cake to match the landscape's dazzling pinks (Colour Plate 12), and two days later, got off his knees, dusted his hands and said: "Enough of these childish things. I am a man." He now walks with great ease everywhere, especially between his two loves, the concrete mixer

Figure 40 Construction of the Itō Rectory with earthquake-proof foundations, June, 1953.

and the car horn. We do thank you all for gifts and prayers which have brought him safely to this stage of sturdy little boyhood. He has bright blue eyes still, brown hair and a wicked way of outdoing the most polite Japanese at his own bowing game. I am afraid he even bows to me when I give him his biscuit!

St. Mary's is the Church of the whole Peninsula, so though we had extra services here and kept a Vigil on Maundy Thursday night, the Three Hour Service was conducted at Imaihama, nearly 30 miles away. Easter Communions and Baptisms did seem to point to a steady growth in the spiritual life of the Church as well as in membership. But lest we sit back and grow contented, the Holy Spirit has surprising ways of pointing out the line of advance.

For a long time now Frank has been a slave to a travel schedule which the Izu Mission Committee drew up. The constant drain of energy and resources made by the system of services, and classes, and visits has been giving us all cause for alarm. But there seemed no way out of the treadmill because no Japanese priest assistant is available from the Diocese. On the other hand the church people themselves, with Japanese dependency on the person of the teacher, could not envisage meetings or services without the presence of a priest.

Ever since the reference in one of Keys Smith's newsletters about the relevance of Roland Allen's *Spontaneous Expansion of the Church* and our own reading of it, we have been much exercised over the problem of the lack of participation of the people themselves – lay and priest alike – in the evangelisation of the nation. Christianity is limited in its growth almost entirely to the ability and energy of its missionary and priestly personnel. Despite periods of persecution the Faith has been taught in Japan for more than 400 years. Yet believers amount to one-half of one per cent only. This dependency on "the teacher's person" was underlined even more when, during our Kobe stay last year, older missionaries asked after Christian families, friends of pre-war years who lived in Izu. We have been hard-pushed to find any as a matter of fact, and those we have found have failed too often to have their children and their grandchildren baptised. They say they are waiting for their children to have faith. As to their neighbours, there is no sign of responsibility. The one or two pockets of live Christianity we found quickly became "Cottage Churches" and centres of evangelism in the village.

So at the Easter Committee meeting Frank challenged our layfolk to face up to the situation of an Izu Church less dependent on the priest except for matters of priestly ministry, and left the Committee to produce such a plan. The resulting plan we work to today is very different from anything we ourselves might have devised. Though it has weaknesses, it is the People's Plan. If, after a month of working [to its stipulations], the Mishima folk show great reluctance to keep Sunday as a day apart; if the Ose Christians guarantee church attendance only on a wet day; if the Ito Children's Church and Catechism have had to go by the board for the time being, at least everybody is aware of these defects in the plan, and in themselves. But the people themselves have decided to keep the hour from 10 a.m. and 7.30 p.m. on Sundays for worship, whether together or in their homes and fields. When the priest is in the centre as he is for one Sunday a month, then there is Holy Communion, and Evensong and classes and exhorting of the faithful. When he is not, the laymen are responsible for the saying of services. In Ito we now have a 6.30 a.m. Mass every Sunday before Frank leaves and other services are conducted by the lay readers except on Ito's "special" Sunday. In time we hope and pray that a realisation of what the priestly ministry really is will come to the people – both its limitation and its tremendous importance.

In the meantime our solution of our problems – common to the whole church – is of interest to others as we found when Fr. John Sakurai was staying with us last week. Fr. Sakurai, who belongs to the Society of St. John the Evangelist, came for a most needed "rest-time" after years of too much work. In addition to his normal activities as priest in a Community with a busy House, he is in charge of a big country parish and is one of the Committee of the General Synod which is redrafting the Japanese Prayer Book. On both counts he is interested in the rural evangelism we have undertaken here and feels that it is not only the foreign missionary's problem, this inability to arouse the people to take responsibility for the growth of the Church.

On the matter of the redraft of the Prayer Book, the Committee placed the fruit of several years' work before a General Synod with neither the time nor adequate preparation to receive it. The completed draft includes such controversial issues as a revised Order of Holy Communion, and new translation of special Offices such as the Absolution of the Bier in the Order for the Burial of the Dead. The revision of the Mass has been gone into so thoroughly (and with due reference to the Prayer Books of all other sections of the Anglican Communion) that, if it is adopted as it stands, the Nippon Seiko Kwai will have the most liturgically sound Holy Communion Service in the Church. The General Synod deferred the question of its adoption for another three years and during that time copies will be sent overseas for further examination and comment, while at home various parts of the re-draft will be printed and used experimentally by the Churches. This was the most important work of the recent General Synod.

When I began to write a deluge of rain was falling but now it has given way to steamy sunlight, and I can almost see the plants in the garden growing. The mass of small aster and marigold plants under the window (sown by myself) brings to mind with a chuckle the orderliness of the seed boxes in the frames across the lawn. I asked Kubota-san to put in some seeds for me one day recently and wondered why he was just straightening his aching back two hours later! Ten days on I understood, for down the expanse of seed boxes marched row upon row of mathematically placed plants, a cornflower alternated with a poppy and on and on. There were hundreds of them, each placed carefully, one by one. And now I have realised for myself what we have always heard, that the Japanese is completely incapable of scattering seed broadcast. Rice, vegetables, everything, is sowed seed by seed and transplanted as often as three times before reaching its final location. The parable of the Sower is always met with complete lack of understanding because such waste as broadcast sowing of seed is incomprehensible. Something of this limitation has crept into the minds of the Christians for in almost any discussion of methods of evangelism, the plan of campaign usually boils down to "each one bring one" or "go after your nearest neighbour whose life already shows fruits of virtue."

Since we last wrote we have had another election and the Yoshida Government with anything but a convincing majority has taken over once more. Apart from all the criticisms and animosities and the unenviable job of governing with most of the key positions in the Diet in the hands of the opposing parties, Mr. Yoshida still holds the confidence of the majority of the people. But in these days when everyone sees a strong swing towards the old ways, it is interesting to observe that 10 out of the 18 members of the new Cabinet are all graduates of the Tokyo (Old Imperial) University. This is a sure sign that things are going back to where they were before the surrender. Before the war, graduates of this University made up the cream of Japanese bureaucracy. Civil servants who had not studied at this University had little chance of becoming Cabinet members. During the Occupation Days these Tokyo University trained leaders were purged [from government] for their wartime responsibilities. As a result, in the third Yoshida Government formed in February 1949, only three State Ministers, including the Prime Minister himself, were Tokyo graduates.

But despite this and the fact that there is a greater demand for university graduates in general employment this year than ever before, the university student himself is enjoying less and less of the liberty of mind and person so precious to the undergraduate and so essential to his full development according to our thinking. Owing to the fear of Communism, which every now and then sweeps the country in a general check up and clean out, mass meetings of students have been almost completely banned. Wherever there is a general meeting billed, police turn up on the campus. "Police" in this case is a rather loose term and often members of order and anti-riot squads belong to the National Reserve Police rather than the regular service which directs traffic and rushes to your help when you have a burglar in the house.

All these things, and the fact that the civil servant can wield an uncomfortable amount of power over the ordinary citizen whom he theoretically serves, make an interesting picture of a country swinging back into old lines.

———

It would seem that an economic crisis is not far over the horizon. Papers this week report a considerable reduction in the issue of currency. But if you were to go down into the Ito township this afternoon there would be no evidence of it. Day by day thousands of people crowd into the town from the greater cities bent on pleasure. They fill the 168 Inns and make it advisable for nearly every money-minded householder with a hot-spring connection in his family bathroom to have the housefront lifted and hang out an Inn sign.

On foot you would weave your way amongst crowds of kimono-clad merrymakers, haunting the pin-ball parlours, buying local tourist bits [and pieces], and at the same time keeping a wary eye open for a rearguard attack by one of the lads riding cafe bikes and carrying trays piled high with twelve or more loaded plates. For the local Inns do not carry huge kitchen staffs to cope with the guests. They keep standard lines such as rice and fish but send out to catering places for all the odds and ends of a meal. In a car you put your hand on the horn and get out of the streets as soon as you can, passing round and under the great tourist buses if need be.

———

Today, Ito is particularly busy as it lies directly on the route to Shimoda. Shimoda is now celebrating the "Black Ship Festival" or the arrival of U.S. Commodore Perry's Treaty Ships to break Japan's 250 years of isolation. Shimoda will be very gay with main highways running from Tokyo and the south direct to the port, accessible from any part of Japan. But we have mentioned before what an out-of-the-world place it is and how until twenty odd years ago it was only accessible from the sea through very difficult shipping channels at that. The Japanese weren't letting up much when they opened Shimoda to the Americans in 1853.

But a *Nippon Times* editorial hails the Treaty drawn up in Shimoda in 1853 as one of the great moments in history, surpassed only perhaps by the recent pact of commerce, navigation and friendship now awaiting ratification.

One interesting point about that first Treaty is the tremendous language barrier it represented. It took twelve days to write down the simplest document covering only about a foolscap page. For no one could speak English on the Japanese side as for many years it had been a forbidden language. But the

Japanese could speak a very little Dutch, and there happened to be amongst Commodore Perry's boat crew a sailor who also knew a little Dutch. So the Treaty came about. One further point of interest, it was Commodore Perry and Consul Townsend Harris [appointed in 1856] who took the first Prayer Book Christian services in Japan. Even if one questions definite diary statements containing the holding of morning and evening prayer, the sailors who lie buried in Shimoda would certainly have gone to their rest with the service from the Prayer Book read over them.

_____

When our desks are piled high with letters and there's still not more time than twenty four hours in the day then we know it's the moment for a *Newsletter*. This month there are so many letters and airflimsies that, to do them justice, there should be two letters, instead of which we find we have to telescope two months into one again. We wish it were otherwise. But please do keep writing,

Yours most affectionately,

FRANK and MAIDA

_____

Circulated by Mrs. E.R. Coaldrake, Hamilton Road, Nundah.
[Printed by] Brisbane City Printery, Edward Street, Brisbane.

Newsletter No. 54, July–August, 1953.

NIPPON SEIKO KWAI

From – Rev. F.W. Coaldrake
[written by Maida Coaldrake]

St. Mary's Church House
960 Shimouchi,
Okaku,
Ito-shi,
JAPAN.

Dear Friends,

For nearly three months the whole Japanese landscape has been drowned in rain. In the south more than one million people are homeless in the worst floods in living memory, 700 dead, about 140 billion yen damage. In the largest city of Kyushu the mud is so thick in streets and buildings, that working at the present rate, it will take sixteen years to clean it up – and Japan has never been short of manpower! These terrible floods followed a very heavy rainy season which swept through mountain areas. Rivers burst their banks, dams collapsed, huge landslides covered villages and disrupted road and rail traffic for days. The same floods also uncovered wide-spread graft and corruption in the administration of public monies allocated regularly for repairing public works. The wide, shallow river beds, dry except for a small central stream most of the year, flood very quickly after heavy rain and levees need constant maintenance. Yet in some areas there had been none for sixteen years!

Public response to the disaster has been splendid. Red Cross, United States Security Force, and local governments have worked as a team to prevent some of the worst effects in the way of disease and food shortages. But all the main newspapers suggest that the chief good that will come out of it is the cleaning up of officialdom.

In Ito we have been affected in a small way. Officially the rainy season finished with the traditional clap of thunder some weeks ago, but insofar as it rains every day and sweat pours off our bodies at every move, it is still with us.

Bill and I are fine examples of what prickly heat can be and I plan sometime to follow the lead of the little boys of the nation who have all their hair shaved off in summer. It is certainly difficult to remember that we were under snow in February. Ito has officially declared a water shortage for the first time in our four Summers and cuts off the water supply daily for five hours. Downpours of rain have obviously nothing to do with the case!

———

Floods have also affected our building programme. Everywhere the cost of timber has skyrocketed as a result of the washing out to sea of hundreds of tons of timber [stored as] logs. We are more fortunate than some since the new rectory is up to the window frame stage, but we are paying a price for our small remaining needs.

The rectory has become one of the show places of the town. Building by rule and plumbline is apparently unique for this part of the country and the resulting firm square structure is much admired. It looks like a palace amongst these build-for-a-year-or-two and for-as-many-as-possible dwellings, though it would rank as a very modest dwelling at home. The firemen who came to inspect our fire escapes were much concerned over the presence of only one entrance apart from the back door. They took some convincing on the score that we were not expecting to house twenty or more people and were quite amazed at the idea that there were separate eating and sleeping rooms. As for the boy having a room of his own – poor little fellow, how lonely! It keeps us humble that we should live so well, but we always hope it might give our neighbours an idea of other standards of living.

Typhoon warnings at the rate of two a week have slowed up the finishing of the building since a typhoon striking before the walls and windows are completely closed would be disastrous. So far all warnings have been in the nature of "wolf-wolf" but on this seaboard you can never get casual, so today we are watching weather reports on a terrific blow off Guam, which is moving north at seven miles an hour. It could reach us by Monday. However, we expect to be ready to take in our new family of Students after the summer holidays, and ourselves to be well established across the garden in the new house. Bill and I will come in for painting and floor-sanding next week.

I think there are few Australian teachers who would care much about exchanging their positions for ones in public schools in this country. All through the Summer the schools are hives of industry – extra examination coaching courses, art classes, character [*kanji*] drill, brush work, swimming practice, school cleaning and sports ground making. In addition, children up to at least middle school age, are expected to report to their teacher at school every second or third day of the holidays. The theory is that the teacher must keep in touch with the students and their health and activities, and that the children should not get out of the going to school habit! – an interesting comment on the homes. Moreover, if a child wants to travel away from the school centre, even with the family, a written certificate from the school Head must be obtained. We have just had practical experience of this as the youngest Kawai daughter, already attending school in Ito and boarding out until the Hostel is completed, had to have written permission to return home to Ose for her holidays, and we have known a young teacher to be summoned home from Lake Ippeki Camps to her home city 100 miles away to attend the funeral rites of one of her pupils – not an unusual occurrence.

You are probably wondering what of Summer camps this year. In many ways, the need that existed directly after the war for such recreation and evangelism camps has gone. Young people in our Churches are better fed and better clothed. The older ones are in permanent employment, which makes holiday periods difficult. Country people are particularly busy in the fields, and everywhere there has been an upsurge of interest in camping and youth recreation so that in a way it is no longer necessary for us to pioneer. The expiry of the lease on the Lake Ippeki land suggested we should rearrange our plans, and much camp equipment was sold and the proceeds helped to build the Church. The rest has been stored and the Izu Dendo Mission has been looking at other sites deeper in the Peninsula with a view to running evangelism camps for our own people a little later in the year.

We revisited Lake Ippeki earlier in the Summer and though the Lake and the mountains are still as lovely, there has been a mushroom growth of noisy fun parlours, drink shops, tourist bauble stalls, and above all the loud speaker system which shatters the air with the latest American hit parade tunes – not exactly a pleasant atmosphere for camping. But the storekeepers have reason to thank the Church, for before the first camps, Lake Ippeki was unknown except to the artist colony and such a thing as income from tourist trade had never been thought of. Now as a result of many people coming to camps from far away cities, the local Tourist Association has done some canny capitalising. Weekend buses thunder up the road past our gate full of holiday makers.

As I write there's a great noise of hammering from close at hand, because Bill has a hammer and an emery wheel going full speed in the shade of the bamboo screen outside this room. We have at last solved the problem of his play activity! We had been labouring under the misapprehension that 16 months old children liked balls, rocking chairs and blocks. Our Bill has a splendid pair of shoulders and arms, and stripped to the waist he is giving a display of muscle flexing that puts us all to shame. The wheel whines and the hammer bangs.

Queen Elizabeth has captured the imagination of the whole Japanese nation. Always an admirer of things British, the Japanese people gave to the [Queen's]

Coronation the enthusiastic interest one would expect to see only for their own ceremonial. Radio, newspapers, magazines, department stores and restaurants displayed flags, bunting, photographs, and everywhere the Coronation film drew packed theatres many times a day. Bishop Yashiro broadcast twice on the significance of the Coronation and the general public was very interested in the Japanese cope and mitre worn by the Archbishop of Canterbury. The Bishop felt that more could have been made of the film from an evangelistic standpoint, especially with regard to the significance of the service concerning the true relation of Church and State. He said: "As most of us know, for many years there was a close alliance between England and Japan and at every great national service held in England certain princes, admirals and generals from Japan were present. Also missionaries were friendly with Admiral Togo, General Oyama and others who were not Christians, but they came to appreciate the Established Church as a splendid arrangement by which the Government controlled the Church, and through the Church the people. When the time came, they used this experience and created Shinto as the State religion of Japan. Many of the successes and excesses of the war were the result. A system had been adopted without reference to the Spirit."

These days we find the same thing in every department of life here. We have often mentioned how every public place – station, shop, store and cafe, hangs out its Christmas lights and has its Christmas trees. One missionary was asked by a Japanese acquaintance upon refusal of an invitation owing to Christmas duties, "Oh, do you observe Christmas in the Church?"

We haven't seen the Coronation Film yet and hope that it will reach our out-of-the-way corner one day, but Mrs. Next-door, who is a member of the Prefectural Education Committee, had two documentaries on the Crown Prince's European and Canadian tour to date, and brought them in for a private showing one evening. So we caught a glimpse of processions, coaches and [Westminster] Abbey Service, together with Prince Akihito sitting among hundreds of foreign dignitaries.

————

Our concern about evangelism and the laymen's responsibility seems to be shared widely, for this summer has seen meetings in every prefecture to discuss ways and means, past accomplishment, and future plans. Laymen chaired and conducted the meetings and our representatives have returned at least stimulated into more thinking. Yesterday Frank had an interesting note from one of the city priests of our diocese asking if he might come down one day when the weather is cooler. "The laymen," he writes, "have been having some hard things to say about the priests at these evangelism meetings, and I thought I should like to have a talk about the ways we might be more effective!"

At the same time in Hokkaido, the Diocese chosen as being the most rural and smallest in membership, missionaries and Japanese clergy are having an intense evangelism campaign, working in teams in parishes and areas allocated to them by a Diocesan committee. An invitation went out to all missionaries to join in the drive, and certainly we should have loved to have gone to Hokkaido, home of the original Japanese people – Ainu – producer of butter and apples, with its wide mountain and lake districts. But apart from the time involved, each missionary had to foot his own bill. To American missionaries, paid generously and with a foreign service and cost of living allowance as well, this is as may be, but we haven't heard of many British folk going. Still we shall go to Hokkaido some day.

Two other important events in the Church world have marked the summer. One was the dedication of the renovated buildings of St. Luke's International Hospital and College of Nursing in Tokyo. This Hospital, the largest and best-equipped in the East, was taken over from the Church by the Occupation, and since the signing of the Peace Treaty has continued to be used by the Army authorities. Though unquestionably serving a very important need, it has at the same time set the St. Luke's staff the overwhelming problem of ministering to the needs of Japanese, and missionaries, to the tune of some 600 outpatients a day, in a barrack building put up after the Great Earthquake for emergency ministration only. Above the consulting rooms is a twenty bed hospital used as well for training nurses. The sheer pressure of suffering humanity crowded into those dark and most unsuitable passage-waiting rooms and the good cheer of the medical staff never varied during our necessary visits over the last three years. So it was with great pleasure we took a quick trip around the new buildings dedicated on June 15th – a beautifully appointed Chapel at the end of the main corridor and the wards able to meet the needs of 130 patients. Actually they are not new buildings, having been used by the hospital prior to the completion of the main hospital in 1943 and since then, as staff quarters. However, the sense of spaciousness and newness is apparent everywhere and there is much rejoicing. They will serve until the magnificent main building is released by the American Forces at some future date.

A little before this the new Central Theological Seminary was dedicated, complete with Chapel and staff residences. It was a most inspiring day by all accounts, but as with many of these functions in Tokyo, we were unable to make the trip. From its location in picturesque if cumbersome quarters in the historical Baron Iwasaki residence in Tokyo, the college is now housed in fine modern buildings with adequate facilities for future needs.

This is the season of the O-Bon Festival – the festival of the spirits of the departed – most widely and gaily celebrated of all the Japanese festivals, except perhaps Boys' Day. After the Buddhist prescribed prayers are said and food placed before family god-shelves everyone is given over to great dancing, feasting and singing for days on end. Lanterns are strung up in houses, shrines and cemeteries, dance platforms are put out and everyone turns out in kimono even though this dress may not be worn at other times. In Ito the O-Bon follows hard on the heels of the celebrations for Ito's favourite "patron saint," English Will Adams, who lived here about 1603. The British and Dutch Ambassadors, with their Naval Attaches, came down last Monday and we all went down to the Harbour for much speechifying and bowing and the launching of a Replica of the first wooden ocean-going ship ever built in Japan – by this same Will Adams, born in Kent and buried not far from Tokyo. The Ito Tourist Association has really worked up his life story and makes the festival one of the main attractions of this seaside resort. The other day Frank predicted the next few years should bring to light some tools supposedly used by Adams. Sure enough, on a beautifully polished table near the official table there was displayed an "ancient" axe with some "indecipherable" inscription. After the ship had been sent splashing to the water by a helpful shove or two, we went back to inspect this tool, labelled very clearly for English eyes to read "CAST STEEL." There could almost have been "Made in Birmingham" on the reverse side. At night there was a grand fireworks display to close the day's celebration.

———

The day after the Festival, David and Gladys Chamberlain left us after a short holiday en route for Kobe and Hong Kong. They have been appointed to the staff of the famous C.M.S. School, St. Stephens, near the site of the equally famous or infamous Stanley Camp. David will work mostly on the administrative side of the school organisation and Gladys will teach. We were sad to see them go, two young people anxious to serve the Church in Japan but unable to find their rightful place here. They hope that one day the way will open for their return.

Since the gaining of autonomy of the Japanese Anglican Communion and the cessation of the allocated "missionary areas" (i.e., certain dioceses and parishes given to some Overseas Church for sole staffing and administration responsibility), personnel sent from abroad and financed by Overseas Mission Boards are set to work as members of a particular diocesan staff. Frank, for instance, ranks as one of the clergy of the Diocese of South Tokyo and in all except financial matters, is responsible directly to the Bishop. In many ways this is the best in modern missionary enterprise and works well. But it does mean that often placement of personnel is not related to qualifications. David came to Japan on an understanding with the then Headmaster of St. Michael's, Kobe, to an administrative position. He was set to teaching as a temporary measure while Fr. Rex Clarke reorganised the School. Fr. Clarke, himself anxious to do parish work, returned after two years to New Zealand. School policy changed and David found himself as a teaching staff member only, in a school that could not guarantee his salary. As no other position was offered, David, as a married man, naturally accepted this most attractive billet in Hong Kong. Do pray for the Japanese Church as it struggles to cope with such problems of maturity in the days of its youth. After all it is only the exigencies of the war which brought about complete autonomy.

In the meantime we see it as a challenge of replacement of David from Australia, Fr. Clarke and family from New Zealand, and Gladys, S.P.G. England. In our Communion Fr. Clarke and David and ourselves were the only representatives from the Australian and New Zealand Churches.

At the same time do remember in your prayers Rae Campbell, recently arrived and now teaching at the International College of the Sacred Heart in Tokyo. As many of you know, Rae, after years of devoted preparations for missionary work in this country under the auspices of A.B.M., was received into the Roman Communion a year ago. She arrived in Japan a few weeks ago in the middle of the hot, wet season and began teaching the daughters of the more wealthy Japanese and foreign population in Tokyo. It is, we think, very different from the work she is capable of performing. Her enthusiasm and devotion having been thus redirected, we need someone to take her place.

Those of you who support A.B.M. so generously and, through your subscription to General Funds, help the mission in Japan, will be as delighted as we are to know that our estimated budget for 1953–54 has been approved. So, even in these days of rising costs, the work of the Izu Dendo Mission with its centre in Ito will be in no way curtailed. We do thank you all most warmly.

With every good wish,

Yours most sincerely,

FRANK and MAIDA

Circulated by Mrs. E.R. Coaldrake, Hamilton Road, Nundah.
[Printed by] Brisbane City Printery, Edward Street, Brisbane.

Maida Coaldrake, Oral History, 1 October 2001.

In late July 1953 Frank was fixing a toy with wire and what he used to cut off the wire caused a large piece to fly directly into the retina of his eye. We went to the local hospital in Ito where the doctor looked at it and said he would have to go to Tokyo to have the eye removed. This was 6 or 7 o'clock in the evening. So I faced a night of him in absolute agony. The next morning I had to take him by public transport to Tokyo for hospitalization. No-one had thought of any planning for this sort of emergency or for travelling and transportation or even for paying for the fares, all of which had to come from our basic stipend which was inadequate anyway. A.B.M. normally operated in places like New Guinea where missionaries were based at mission stations, with nurses and medical facilities as well as schools and churches. There was not adequate planning or budget for medical emergencies in the case of us in Japan. I had to suddenly take over the financial management of the parish and even had to borrow money from Miyazawa-san to pay for the train to take Frank to Tokyo because there was no money.

A man sick unto death had to travel by public transport sitting up in a train from Ito to Tokyo, a trip which took three hours. I also had the terrible worry of leaving Billy in Itō. Miyazawa-san fixed up for the train to be met by an ambulance at Yokohama, but somehow no-one told me and we went straight through to Tokyo station. We then had to walk all the way from the Izu platform across the whole width of the vast Tokyo Station to the Marunouchi exit. He was nearly dead; the pain was beyond support. Two nice young Americans took him by the elbows and more or less carried him across Tokyo Station to a taxi which then took him to St. Luke's Hospital. There he was operated upon by Dr. Hasegawa. A year later when we saw the eye specialist in Hobart he said that the operation was so skillful and sophisticated that it could not have been matched in Australia at the time. The only option would have been to remove the eyeball and replace it with a glass eye. As it was the retina was removed and a new lens inserted to leave peripheral but not direct vision.

At the time St. Luke's Hospital was the official American Episcopal hospital and had a major responsibility for military forces evacuated from the Korean peninsula. The best doctors in Japan were co-opted into service there. However the hospital itself was strictly divided into the military and civilian wings. The permanent buildings which had survived the war-time bombings were still occupied by the American military because Korean War casualties were still being treated. The civilians were relegated to rough quonset huts at the back of the hospital.

While Frank was ill the number of trips I made to the Hong Kong Shanghai Bank in Tokyo to get money was unbelievable – I had to go up to Tokyo all the way from Itō and beg them to rouse up the tellers in Australia. For us the threat of starvation was very real and there I was with a seriously ill husband and a young child, and running the Itō church as well. There was no money to pay the salary of the lay evangelist or to pay the normal bills that were coming in as always. Moreover in the hospital it was expected that relatives would look after the patient. I had to make provision to go up to Tokyo every second day, a much more difficult trip than it is today.

Postcard from Frank Coaldrake to Maida Coaldrake, 5 September, 1953 [handwritten in pencil].

Tokyo, 5 September 1953

Nurses are surging. I have had my cuppa... I'm a little tired – my lashes are growing – cause itch. Doc says "no visitors" and "quiet" signs to stay for some days yet... Op. Theatre nurse description of operation suggests my lens was not replaced but I'll ask Doc again...

P.S. Written normally with eyes closed![46]

Letter from Frank Coaldrake to Maida Coaldrake, Wednesday 12.30 [10 September 1953, handwritten in pencil].

Maida darling,

It was wonderful to hear your voice last night. But everything seemed to have landed in your lap at once! ... I've just had really tender chicken for lunch... I'm simply jumping up and down waiting to see you. But I have a nice fat letter from

46 He was blind at this stage.

my girl friend to keep me company though it's a pity I can't read it. I did open it as far as the opening line just to make sure it is a letter from you to me.

Kubota-san arrived in good order at 11.30 having been to the Bank... He has given a satisfactory account of payments he has made – so I'll let him take [50,000 yen] on to you.

> Money
> Garage [yen] 10,000
> Telephone 4,000
> Kawai trip [Dr. Kawai at Irozaki] 9,000
> Sundries 5,000
> 28,000 is what Kubota-san will need from you. Kubota-san is to give you
> the bank 50,000.

I want to go on writing and writing to you but I had better send him off.
All my love, darling,
Frank

Maida Coaldrake, Oral History, 1 October 2001.

I had to trek up and down from Ito to Tokyo every second day carrying all the food and groceries and other needs for Frank in hospital – chooks, freshly killed from our garden and bottled fruit including passion-fruit from our own trees. Miss Gardner, a retired missionary, and Miss Pond, the dietician at St. Luke's hospital, helped take care of Dad in hospital. The hospitals didn't provide any food and it was all expected to be taken care of by the family. Miss Pond in her own time turned these chickens into chicken soup, Chicken Maryland, roast chicken, and made soufflés with passion-fruit.

Letter from Frank Coaldrake to Maida Coaldrake [undated, mid-September, 1953, handwritten in pencil].

Tuesday, 9.00 a.m.

Maida darling, another day nearer you but time is very slow. I spent yesterday keeping pretty carefully wrapped up and warm because of my throat. Doctor didn't seem worried about it... Saw Miss Gardner yesterday. She has reserved the seats [to Nikkō] and wants to go at midday to pay for them.[47] She had waited to get my (or your) OK to buying a block of 4 seats – extra 400 yen to ensure room for Bill and no objectionable intruder was well worthwhile. I told her so, no

---

47 Miss Ernestine Gardner owned a house at Nikkō, some 140 kilometres north-west of Tokyo. She was a retired missionary from the U.S. Episcopal Church, herself born in Japan of American missionary parents. Her family had acquired this house as a summer retreat at some stage before the war and she generously made it available for rest and recuperation after the six weeks in hospital.

doubt, she has fixed it by this. She produced a special pack of cards, black with different colors for hearts and diamonds etc. Very easy for the eyes. I find it hard to be interested in card playing! My eye gets clearer daily. I can now make out the general outlines and colors of objects with it alone. The doctor [Hasegawa] seems pleased with the progress... How is Bill? Gosh I long to see the two of you.

2 p.m.

To the strains of *The Symphony Hour*! Dr. Hasegawa says OK to leave Thursday afternoon... I have the train tickets. Miss Gardner gave them to me this morning "in case anything should happen to her."

I have given up trying "to keep hot" [to ward off sore throat] this afternoon. It is a real swelter. Just as well you didn't come up today because this is the weather that takes it out of you. How is it in Ito? Billy will have the hose I expect – and chasing you with it. And the Dr. says it would be good to stay at Nikko a long time – even till the 14th or 15th [of October]...

Letter from Rev. Bruce McCall, Australian Board of Missions, to Maida Coaldrake, 15 September, 1953.

AUSTRALIAN BOARD OF MISSIONS,
14 Spring Street,
Sydney,
<u>N.S.W.</u>

15 September 1953

Mrs. F. Coaldrake,
St. Mary's Church House,
960 Shimonouchi,
Okaku,
<u>Ito-shi</u>,
Japan.

Dear Maida,

I should have written long ago but what prompts me now is the news of Frank's operation. Needless to say you have been very much in my prayers and I do hope that all is now satisfactory. Please give him our love and assure him of the continuance of our prayers...

Do send me some news some time. It is very hard to get news of Japan. Nobody in this office co-operates very much in those things but I am gradually cultivating Canon Warren and he has been very good lately in passing things on to me.

I loved your description of Bill out bowing to the Japanese. I expect we shall see him next year...

With all good wishes,
    Yours affectionately,
    Bruce McCall.

P.S. [handwritten] Canon Warren has just handed me your letter of September 9th. Dear Maida, I did not know your worries had been so great. Much love and prayers, Bruce.

Newsletter No. 55, September, 1953.

NIPPON SEIKO KWAI

From – Rev. F.W. Coaldrake
[written by Maida Coaldrake]

St. Mary's Church House
960 Okaku,
Ito,
JAPAN.

Dear Friends,

I little thought when I described the new section of St. Luke's International Hospital in Tokyo last *Newsletter* that, before the month was out, Frank would be a patient. A small flying piece of wire hit his left eye right in the centre. We found the scrap on the floor, visited the local eye doctor to be sure all was well, and then returned home to put up with the inconvenience of a sore spot in the pupil for a day or two. The local doctor was sure nothing was wrong. A week later after a nightmare journey over the 90 odd miles that separates us from Tokyo, Frank was admitted to St. Luke's with an advanced case of Glaucoma and all its attendant miseries, and a cataract as well, all coming from a tired hand that didn't hold a pair of pliers quite steady enough.

For the primary cause of the trouble was that the Summer has been exceptionally trying and Frank has been carrying on parish work without the necessary Assistant-priest, and physically building the new Rectory as well. Apart from our camping trip to Kobe last year which proved far from restful, we haven't had a "sit and do nothing week" since we came to Japan.

So after a most delicate operation successfully performed by one of the St. Luke's Eye Clinic specialists, Dr. Kawaihigashi, and a visiting specialist, Dr. Hasagawa, Frank is having an enforced rest, thus far amounting to four weeks of hospital bed, no visitors and a "Quiet Please" sign on the door. There is every indication that after a short period, apart from the need for glasses permanently, he will have full use of both eyes.

It's an ill wind, of course, and out of all this has come a lot of good things. Frank is getting his rest, and after he is discharged at the end of this week, we are all packing off to Nikko, famous beauty spot in the mountains, where an American missionary friend has lent us a house for as many weeks as it needs to put everyone on our feet again. In Ito we have managed to carry on with the building of the new rectory to the point of finishing the walls and painting the roof. Now the building is foursquare and solid and proof against any typhoon which might blow up during the rest of the summer, and the roof is painted a fine red.

That red, as a matter of fact, immediately marks off the buildings on the Church block from those in the rest of the town. One of the things that takes a while to digest is the uniform greyness of the Japanese houses and buildings, grey weatherbeaten wooden walls and grey tiled roofs.

That, together with the lush, rapid growth of the Summer foliage, or the plain brownness of the Wintertime, gives the landscape a uniformity during more than half of the year which can be tiring to the eye. But when Autumn suddenly flames across the land with maples alight, chrysanthemums in bloom and every second tree loaded with golden mandarins, everybody's spirits rise. And of course there's always the cherry-blossom in Spring!

Well, we got on with the building as best we could, Kubota-san and I, keeping two carpenters and three labourers busy for several weeks. The Church people had the opportunity to put into practice all the theory about the layman's responsibility in the Church and have carried on in every centre. Fr. Toyoda came down from Hiratsuka and made a quick trip round all the centres, administering the Holy Communion last weekend. So all in all, Frank has been able to rest quietly and get on with the serious job of getting his eye usable again. By November 1st the Izu Dendo Mission should have "business as usual" sign out.

———

In the meantime Bill has taken advantage of his father's absence to cut three more teeth and so get a lot more attention than usual at nights! Friend and doctor, Rev. Leeman, just before he returned to the States on furlough, looked Bill over. Most of the looking consisted in Bill's sitting on the doctor's knee (a nice man you know, wears same kind of collar as Dad!) and learning to type. When it was over Dr. Leeman declared we need have no worries about said Bill's progress – he has now flattened out nicely at height, weight and teeth of a well-developed two-year-old! Bill is not yet 18 months.

My constantly tripping back and forth to Tokyo to see Frank at one end, and care for the parish and Bill at the other, have had lots of bright spots. One of them was that I was able to go to one of the receptions arranged for missionaries to meet the Rt. Rev. Bishop Sherrill, Presiding Bishop of the American Episcopal Church. He and Mrs. Sherrill are in Japan for a quick survey of the American missionary enterprise, and their evident absorption with the work of the Church overseas was a great pick-me-up. At the particular gathering to which I was invited, held in the pleasant garden of St. Luke's Hospital, I also met many missionary friends from all over Japan of whom one sees surprisingly little. My only complaint is that American folk do not know what real tea is, or that the chilly abomination which passes under the name of "iced tea" does nothing on a hot Summer afternoon but depress the spirits of the consumer!

Then, on the day of Frank's eye operation, our good friends the Curries, of the Australian Embassy, announced the birth of twin sons, Keith and Bruce – shades of the Coaldrake twin brothers, Keith and Bruce! And on the same day news reached us from Hong Kong that the Chamberlains had safely ridden the tail of a monster typhoon and were settling in their new quarters attached to the Prep.

School of St. Stephen's College, Stanley, Hong Kong. That, by the way, is all the address needed to reach them. They will have a spare room until next month when a permanent guest by the name of Chamberlain Junior is expected.

———

Travelling up and down to Tokyo made me realise all over again how fascinating is the Izu Peninsula. From Ito to Odawara, under thirty miles in all, the train shoots through sixteen tunnels. Half-way it comes out suddenly above the beautiful hot spring resort of Atami, a town which is built almost entirely on cliff faces and on reclaimed land on the sea coast. The cliffs are covered with thickly growing plum and cherry trees, and steep paths wind in and out. Here and there you see plumes of thick steam from the hot spring pumps. At night, with festoons of millions of lights draped over the hills and reflecting in the curve of bay, it is an unbelievable fairyland. You even forget the noise of the pinball parlours, trashy shops and street stalls which amuse and tempt the thousands of daily visitors to the town. At Atami Station you move up and make more room on the seat because hundreds of overnight visitors board the train, carrying their inevitable brief case and box of souvenir sweet-meats. They are usually men (very few women travel in any but local trains) and more than likely travelling at their firm's expense on a so-called "business" trip. These business trips, paid for out of the firm's expense account, have recently become quite a national scandal, since the habit has grown up to take your business partner away to a hot spring bath, big feast and perhaps dancing to amuse you in the evening, all for a few minutes discussion which, as far as I can see, usually takes place in the train returning to Tokyo. These business men, on hot days, frequently take off their nice Western-style suits as soon as they reach their train seats and ride the rest of the two-hour journey very coolly in their underpants and singlet! This is a fact to which we are so accustomed these days that we forget our first sense of shock when we saw a whole forty of them en route from a conference, and they did just that! Rae Campbell drew my attention to it again the other day when she was staying with us and wished we had prepared her for that and many other things by writing them up more often. So please be prepared.

———

The Church and Rectory grounds are lovely at the moment. It is a pity Frank is missing them. The rather hard lines of the Quonset Hut part of the new Church (the nave) have been greatly softened and beautified by the growing sweeps of convolulus. From outside, climbing from ground to roof on bamboo poles as they do, they resemble the flying buttresses of Gothic architecture. From inside they dim out the long low windows in shaded greens and blues and mauves. At early services the Church is so lovely inside you would think we had most exquisite stained-glass windows. There are dahlias, too, and clumps of bright red and yellow canna lilies as tall as six feet, along the white walls. Great masses of zinnia which fill long beds around the house are gaudier and gayer than I ever remember them to be at home. In Japan the zinnia has the descriptive name of "one-hundred-day-flower." The rest of the garden is filled by nasturtiums growing over the rock walls, African marigolds, and the inevitable chrysanthemums. For the present, being the in-between season, the vegetable garden boasts mint and parsley only, but both are luxuries in this country.

———

The *Nippon Times* is the leading newspaper for the English-speaking foreign residents in Japan and for that reason is sometimes rather advanced in its views. Nevertheless it does mirror community attitudes. Yesterday it gave itself over to commenting on one fact that for the first time in history, Japan is host to two major international labour conferences, the first the Asian Regional Conference of the I.L.O. [International Labour Organization], and the second, the Asian Regional Conference of the International Confederation of Free Trade Unions. The Labour movement has had a very chequered career in Japan, following its shaky beginnings in the 1920s to be suppressed in 1928 by a reactionary government and finally swallowed up and debased by the later militarists. It wasn't until after the Occupation had begun that Trade Unionism gained a foothold, but today there are 6,000,000 organised workmen in the various unions. So the holding of two International labour conferences here marks the recognition of Japan's progress in this field. Moreover these conferences come at a time when it is generally recognised that the halcyon days of special procurements for the Korean War are numbered, and Japanese industry realises it must get its feet on solid ground by cutting production costs and raising the standard of products, if it is to survive in the International market competition.

That was yesterday, and now today's paper carries a strong sub-leader entitled "Danger Ahead." It draws attention to the dogmatic attitude and the secrecy with which the Education officials have put into effect a plan for changing the present schools' curriculum in that most vital subject labelled loosely "Social Studies." This subject, covering Japanese ethics, history and geography, was the basis of the pre-war state-controlled education plan by which complete control of the nation's youth was exercised. Under the Occupation reform, this was replaced by a course designed to give students in elementary as well as higher schools an opportunity to learn civics, history and the rest, in their proper relation and in line with their interests and abilities. There has been much criticism levelled against this course, quite apart from proper consideration of the aftermath of war and food shortage, on the score of the falling off in results of achievement tests, and in the increase of juvenile delinquency. Now, without warning, the Ministry of Education has issued instructions that this basic plan should be abandoned, and more definite and concentrated study made of history and geography as independent subjects, and a stronger emphasis on moral teachings, as per ancient Japanese custom. There has been a lot of controversy about the effectiveness of the Social Studies programme, but as the editorial points out, it is a pity it is taking the brunt of the attack from the reactionary elements. It concludes by saying: "It is high time we rallied our forces to remove the dominating influence of bureaucrats from the field of education."

———

Two weeks ago we had the pleasure of talking with Canon Franklin Cooper, in Japan on Air Force inspection duties. He had news of home for us and we in turn could give him a few angles on Japanese Church life which he is briefly examining. Much of his time, of course, was spent at the R.A.A.F. base at Iwakuni and in Korea, but once more we had reason to be glad Frank was in a Tokyo hospital, otherwise we may have missed him.

When we write again there should be a panorama of Japanese mountain scenery to spread before you.

Every good wish.

    Yours sincerely,

      Maida, Frank and Bill

    Circulated by Mrs. E.R. Coaldrake, Hamilton Road, Nundah.

    [Printed by] Brisbane City Printery, Edward Street, Brisbane.

Newsletter No. 56, October–November, 1953.

NIPPON SEIKO KWAI

From – Rev. F.W. Coaldrake

[written by Maida Coaldrake]

                              St. Mary's Church House

                              960 Okaku,

                              Ito,

                              JAPAN.

Dear Friends,

    We came to Nikko in the morning of a typical mountain day – rain, mists and greenness. The ancient cryptomerias were veiled in cloud for the last twenty miles, and the maples had not yet begun to redden at the tips. After miles of these ancient avenues with their history of 400 years, Nikko's one long street with its tramcars, busy taxis, bright shops and crowds of tourist parties, was a shock. We climbed away from the township up an impossible slope. The road dwindled to a lane while high rock walls and dripping-wet leaves brushed the car. Suddenly out of the green gloom sprang a red gate and behind, in the trees, was a bright red house. Its many balconies looked out on to the rocky river bed 30 feet below, and its crooked chimneys promised the luxury of a fire.

    That first brightness carried us over the discovery that the bedding had been outside in the rain for two days and that the groceries had not arrived from Tokyo, let alone that the house with its balconies and stairways inside and out seemed too large and damp ever to warm up. By the time Bill had discovered that the bright red paint rubbed off most satisfactorily on hands and clothes, there was a kettle whistling in the cavern of a kitchen and we'd found some bread and cheese. After that the house quickly diminished in size and took on the shape it was to have for six glorious weeks of mists, Autumn sun, and lots of friends coming up from Tokyo to "view" Autumn leaves, waterfalls, or Shrine processions according to their taste, while we were the happy occupants of "SHIMOAKAMON" (Lower Red Gate) House.

For Nikko, not just the town 90 miles north-west of Tokyo with its Shrines and gardens, but the whole Nikko area of mountains and water-falls, lakes and cable cars, belongs to fairytale and history-book Japan. It is the Japan you always suspect ought to be just round the corner of the crabbed and sordid existence so many Japanese live and which we must share. We didn't choose to go to Nikko, but I looked at the family purse and at the rates of charges at inns anywhere in the country. I looked at Frank and knew that, after four weeks in hospital, Ito would be no place for him for a time and I wondered what could be done? Then an American missionary friend who had been born in Japan offered us the use of her family home in Nikko for as long as we needed to set Frank back on his feet.

So we came to Nikko and though I had been reading guide books and looking up maps I was completely unprepared for the moment, when the first fortnight's rain being gone, we strolled up the mossy steps on the hillside behind the house. Until now these had been the limit of our excursions abroad, Bill's legs and Frank's strength about matching. Up the steps and down a stone path, and there we were suddenly in the midst of a crowd of tourists and pilgrims standing before the steps leading to the Temple area and the Gate of Sunlight (YOMEIMON), one of the great treasures of the Japanese nation. (Fig. 41)

In 1617 Ieyasu, the founder of the Tokugawa Shogunate, was re-interred with great dignity at Nikko, a year after his death, and by order of the Emperor he was deified under the title of "East-Illuminating-Incarnation-of-Bodhisattva." Seven[teen] years later, the construction of the mausoleum was begun by Ieyasu's grandson, Iemitsu, who was later commemorated by a similar magnificent shrine area. It is difficult to say which is more glorious – the mountain area with its huge trees and lovely views, or the perfection of the art to which 15,000 craftsmen contributed. They worked for twelve years and no expense was spared. An immense amount of gold leaf was used in the gilding so that it is estimated that the sheets of gold would cover six acres, and the timber if extended would reach 330 miles.

Both shrines are a series of buildings, joined by long, covered paths often lacquered in red or black, gold trimmed, and surrounded by exquisitely carved walls. The gates leading from court to court are masterpieces of architecture and are carved gorgeously with birds and beasts and flowers expressing a philosophy of life here and the life hereafter. One spends hours just gazing at one cornerpiece or roof beam. The whole is lacquered in whites and golds and blues and reds and guarded on either side by some monstrous god, fearsome to behold. Inside, the halls and courts are dim and quiet, though crowded with tourists moving in orderly parties with their priest-guides. Everyone takes off his shoes at the steps. My neck always had a crick in it from gazing at the ceilings and in one shrine there's a huge dragon painted the length of the hall, which is said to howl if you clap your hands under his nose. As a result the dim room full of the vague shapes of fellow sightseers resounds with sharp clapping. In another hall small panels show the same dragon in hundreds of different attitudes. But there was never time to see everything properly nor was there much sign of any religious

Figure 41 Yōmeimon, Tōshōgū, Nikkō. The "crowd of tourists and pilgrims standing before the steps," September, 1953.

feeling. You could buy prayer slips and if you were a Shinto believer (their religion embracing all religions according to the dogma of the belief) you could clap your hands before the central shrines and bow in passing. But even in the holiest of holies (the worship hall of the main shrines) it struck one forcibly that most people were only there as tourists, to buy books and click cameras and hurry on to the next beauty spot in order to catch the train home at night and boast about their visit to Nikko for years.

If you are going to object to thousands of tourists and school parties crowding out the passages and stairs and halls and souvenir shops you had better stay at home. The crowds are as much part of Nikko as are the huge Torii or stone gates which guard the entrance to the shrines (Colour Plate 13). And somehow the crowds have the storybook unreality about them. On fine days the boys in their railway-porter like suits and caps, and the girls in their sailor-collared dresses were too drab against the whites and golds and blues of the shrines and flame of the maples, but on wet days, heads and shoulders draped in brilliant coloured plastic squares, they splashed the wet roads and endless stairways with crude colour, or passed waving in their huge, crowded buses. Billy, as a resident of Nikko, felt it his social responsibility to wave to them all.

The thing that strikes you at once after even a quick glance at the Nikko Shrines is the wonderful unity of the art the architecture, the paintings, the carvings, the lacquerwork. They belong together, as indeed they should, being the work of the Momoyama period of Japanese culture during which equally famous national shrines and treasures at Kyoto and Nara were created.[48]

As for the religion, it is the disunity which strikes one – the happy-go-lucky mixture of Shinto and Buddhist. Here is a national treasure, a Shinto shrine, the god of this place a famous General who lived 400 years ago and was deified for his services to the State. But one of the most perfect gems of architecture is the Sacred Library, a treasury of Buddhist literature containing something like 7,000 volumes. Moreover, the largest building in the shrine area is the Sanbutsudo – the temple of the Three Buddhas. And here, as nowhere else, there is a spiritual atmosphere. Climbing out of your shoes you follow the crowd into the inner sanctuary and there, in a mighty high hall, are the three Kwannon – the thousand-handed Goddess of Mercy, the Amida, and horse-headed Kwannon. They are all ten feet high and sitting on their lotus flowers and, with the ineffable peace and strength on their faces, do strike religious awe into their beholders. To this temple come many pilgrims from far away places, wearing a distinguishing coloured band around their necks and anxious to have their names inscribed in the book of perpetual prayers. Incense burns, bells ring and hands clap. I went several times into this great sanctuary and watched the many genuine pilgrims at worship, and the many who just came to look. But it is an unnerving experience to watch throngs bow down and worship idols in such magnificence. One couldn't help praying that one day the temple would be torn in two and that the Holy Angels (whose festival we were keeping at that time[49]) might work with all their might against the hosts of darkness in this place.

Another contradiction of the religion of this national Shrine – all the gaudiness and brilliance and the splendour of the memorial to the Spirit of the man who had been deified, stopped suddenly short. The heart of the shrine was the

---

48 See further: William H. Coaldrake, *Architecture and Authority in Japan*, London and New York, Routledge, 1996, pp. 180–192.
49 29 September – Feast of St. Michael and All Angels.

worship hall with Shinto symbols and praying priests. But over on the edge of the first court was an arched gateway, famous only because a tiny sleeping cat dozed endlessly among his carved peonies. Behind there was a dim moss over-grown stairway half-covered in with stone walls. The stone gate at the entrance was locked and few people gave any attention to it, but one rainy afternoon we left Bill at home and climbed the hillside beyond the shrine walls. Over a high wall and we found the 207 stone steps which lead to the infinitely quiet and shadowy place where, in a bronze casket shaped like a magnificent lantern, Ieyasu's ashes rest.[50] This last court is guarded by a cast bronze door, and within are various religious symbols such as the crane and tortoise, also cast in bronze. It began to rain again while we stood in this last court and the little wisps of mist hung around the tall tree tops. Far below us were the clusters of Shrine roofs where throngs surged and stared at the memorial to a great man of history. We could hear the voices of the guides raised above the rumble of many voices while on the hilltop the rain began to fall steadily and clung to the grass growing in the cracks of the stonework.

––––

We wished many times that you might have shared all these things with us and then come home for a cup of tea and talk in front of the fire. Towards the end of our stay we weren't quite as generous with the cuppas as we might have been: having provided for three weeks and then staying six, we reached the stage of measuring tea out to cover the remaining days and finding that by adding 11 spoons of the very poor sweet tea available on the Nikko market we could just make it!

Over tea we would read our guide books again, enjoying once more some of the lovely corners we had discovered by lingering behind one party, and keeping just ahead of the next. The English in these books was often more picturesque than accurate in translation. One stated: "The Yomei-mon is indeed a collection of exquisitely carved pieces, with every corner gorgeously and delicately wrought. Admire splendid tree-peonies at both backsides." And then we have to revise our opinions in light of fact after our reading of a note on the Hanging Lantern: "Dedicated by Korean Dynasty, it easily revolves. Misdesigned by a Dutch its hollyhocks atop are set upside down." Nonetheless it is a very beautiful piece of bronze work!

One of the most interesting pieces of carving is that on the Sacred Stable. This stable is the only plain wooden building in the whole of the Toshogu Shrines, but on its transoms are seven panels with carvings of monkeys depicting the Buddhist philosophy of life. Each carving has a deep significance but the one which has captured the imagination of the world is the Hear-no-evil, See-no-evil, Speak-no-evil trio, copies of which can be had for a few yen down in the village. Other carvings of monkeys depict scenes such as a life of meditation and self-examination

50 Recent research has established that Tokugawa Ieyasu's embalmed body sits beneath the stone foundations of this bronze tabernacle.

leading to moral culture, a new life full of hope and aspiration, a life of "paramita" (Buddhist, meaning yonder shore) in the land of peace, with hope for a prosperous posterity, and so on. . . .

From the shrines we took walks and later, as Frank grew stronger, short car drives. In this way we discovered some lovely places overlooked by the majority of tourists in their haste to see all the famous places in as short time as possible. One lovely afternoon we came upon two such places – the Falling Mist Falls, trails of translucent mist flung across a high cliff face, stained by the changing reds and golds of Autumn. I will never again be able to doubt that kind of three dimensional representation so beloved of the Japanese in their kake mono (hanging pictures). Perhaps you may have seen them – trees and river, above them the first trail of clouds and further above, rocks and more water and trees, and further and above that, a kind of quiet heavenly place with clouds and more trees.

Earlier, attracted by a long maple drive, we had stumbled upon an ancient and most beautiful garden belonging to a now disused Buddhist monastery. The high-roofed gate was pure Chinese Buddhist – white plaster and simple carved wood – we sat for a long time just gazing at it, and then turned to find ourselves in one of the quietest and most beautiful places we had ever been in. (Fig. 42) Somewhere, in the long low building the small chapel which is still kept open, a tinkling bell sounded. A memorial was being said for the souls of some departed persons, and a quiet little group of elderly women entered the chapel. A tall stone Kwannon brooded over the shrubs and stone paths, and a white plaster storehouse followed the line of the gate.

Afterwards we came back often to this garden just to sit and enjoy its beauty. We saw it last splashed about with the flame-red of maple leaves, the ground sprayed with tiny white chrysanthemums. Above anything else we saw, this monastery garden would bring us back to Nikko.

———

When we said a thankful "yes" to our friend Miss Gardiner for the offer of her house, there were many blessings we hadn't anticipated. One of them was the kindness of the misty, green days which followed us to Nikko and stayed for the first two weeks. By then Frank's eyes were accustomed to being without bandages and when the clear Autumn days came he could manage quite well with the help of dark glasses only.

Another blessing was the way various friends were able to come to stay for a few days at a time, among them our friend Fr. Sakurai, who from St. Michael's Monastery at Oyama not far away, has the oversight of the parish of Nikko. The parish church at Nikko is a lovely grey stone building, beautifully proportioned, very dignified and proper to its surroundings. The St. John the Evangelist Fathers have been doing a great deal to improve the standard of music in the Church here and have lately printed two Plainsong Masses for use of the ordinary Church congregation. It was a pleasure to listen to the Nikko congregation singing the service so well and we have been inspired to take over and teach this more ambitious setting than our Ito folk are accustomed to use. We are hoping

Figure 42 Secluded temple garden at Nikkō, September, 1953. Frank Coaldrake, his injured eye still covered, accompanied by his "seeing-eye" Billy.

Fr. Sakurai might get to Ito to help us along before he leaves for his sabbatical year – covering the Pan-Anglican Conference in America and a year's study and talk in connection with his work on the new Japanese Prayer Book. Incidentally the Church in America has acclaimed him as the "Bishop Cranmer of the Nippon Seiko Kwai."

After service one Sunday we sat down to a most interesting and happy table full for lunch. Miss Gardiner, our hostess, had come up for the weekend, bringing with her Miss Pond, the dietitian from St. Luke's Hospital, who has been in

Japan since the Great Earthquake.[51] Then there was Mrs. Wilson, an Australian from Melbourne, and very good friend of the Ito Rectory, Fr. Sakurai, and two U.S. Majors just back from Korea who had also been at Church. We were greatly surprised and delighted when one of them proved to be an unknown American whose car Frank had re-directed to a safe road beyond the mountains here in Izu at the height of a typhoon five years ago. His friend in the inimitable way of the Southerner called me "Ma'am," praised everything he ate and made me feel very much a lady. Mercifully the other man of our household had his lunch early and was peacefully napping upstairs.

When we didn't feel like shrine viewing and when even the Autumn glories of the mountains and Lake Chuzenji and the Kegon Falls (a breath-taking emptying of a lake down a 360 ft. cliff) palled a little, we used to go off down the long Nikko street. There in funny musty shops we found lovely bits of woodwork or bronze lanterns and screens and old woodblock prints. One particular shop we kept for rainy days, and braved even the eternal onion soup of the lady of the establishment for the privilege of turning over her prints. Over 100 years old most of them, and afterwards when we looked once more at the modern wood block prints we had admired so much at a first-class gift shop catering for westerners, we found our taste had altered. Beautiful pictures perhaps, but the artistry and the concept of the earliest artists are incomparable.

So that was Nikko and we set off [on the return journey to] Ito all much more lively than when we had arrived, the car packed to the roof with all manner of odds and ends, some newly acquired. We had just enough money to get us to the bank in Tokyo if we had no puncture and bought only a limited amount of petrol. Cheerful in the knowledge of exactly the right money for two gallons in our community purse we drew into a service station and I asked for the necessary two. (Fig. 43) We asked in three ways, even putting up fingers. The lad dutifully put in the five gallons ALWAYS ordered by foreigners and presented the bill. When informed of his mistake he cheerfully told us it was too much trouble to draw off the extra three and accepted the money we had. The three free gallons brought us as far as Odawara on the way home from Tokyo.

———

Ito was good – the rectory clean and shiny, the grounds well cared for and the Church showing the loving care lavished on it by the daily roster. Frank was delighted with everything, including the building we had done in his absence, and everyone was delighted to see him again. When he has glasses he will be able to undertake most of his activities except for night driving on Izu roads. That will come later. We are all very thankful and know the strength your prayers have been.

———

51 Great Kantō Earthquake, 1923.

Figure 43 Caltex Service Station at Nikkō, September, 1953. (See *Newsletter No. 56*, October–November, 1953.)

Release came for our ailing Bishop Maekawa on that happiest of days – All Saints – and having attained the age of 73 in dignity and love of His Church and our Lord, we can do nothing but rejoice he has been spared further suffering. Frank was well enough to go to Yokohama for the funeral services, on the day before he welcomed into the Church the twin sons of our friends Neil and Geraldine Currie. Keith and Bruce were baptized in Holy Trinity Church Tokyo, just before setting out on the voyage home to Australia. Mrs. Dexter, their grandmother known to many of you as the wife of the late Rev. Walter Dexter of Melbourne Diocese, made a short trip to Ito before she left Japan.

And so back in Ito, writing as the early winter afternoon closes in. We have been thinking forward to Christmas and hope our Christmas mails may reach you all earlier than last year. Surface mail is a very uncertain venture. But we shall be writing again as soon as the Ito wheels have started to run smoothly.

Praise God, from whom all blessings flow.

Yours gratefully,

MAIDA and FRANK

———

Circulated by Mrs. E.R. Coaldrake, Hamilton Road, Nundah.
[Printed by] Brisbane City Printery, Edward Street, Brisbane.

Newsletter No. 57, **December, 1953 – January, 1954.**

NIPPON SEIKO KWAI

From – Rev. F.W. Coaldrake

[written by Maida Coaldrake]

St. Mary's Church House
960 Okaku,
Ito,
JAPAN.
19th January, 1954.

Dear Friends,

Just before New Year the whole of Japan cleans its house – the housewife turns out everything into the garden or street, beats "tatami," the thick straw mat floor covering, repapers sliding doors and walls, freshens up the godshelf [the family Shinto altar], makes enough of the highly indigestible, glutinous rice cake for three days' eating, and then, if she is a modern housewife, goes off to the local beauty parlor for a new "perm." Offices, factories, shops and warehouses do the same, using the same method. We fell over office furniture, desks, filing cabinets and typewriters all along the main street the day before the New Year, because, accustomed by centuries of use to folding beds and collapsible tables, the Japanese cannot clean around or under furniture. For most of the year rooms with furniture in them get the sketchiest of cleaning – a fact which we foreigners, blessed with a Japanese housegirl, know full well. Unless you take all the furniture of a room outside you cannot clean. If the "Okusan" [wife] is silly enough to insist on a room being swept and dusted every day, then for half of it she must be prepared to fall over tables and chairs standing in the passages, and carpets airing in the sun. Hence, the necessity the Occupation Army households found for employing three housegirls to a household of three or four persons, a fact which at first seemed to me to be a great extravagance. Since then I have discovered three girls would at least keep a house livable for three-quarters of the day!

But back to New Year. Like the Chinese, the Japanese prepare for weeks in advance with spring cleaning and new clothes and hairdos and cooking. Then the nation goes on holiday and everyone has a blissful time visiting around, parading gorgeous kimono, and clapping hands at the Temple on the hill. Most shrines and temples are on the top of hills, reached by climbing hundreds of steep and uneven steps through files of great trees. If the little shrine that sits on the top of the hill is a bit tawdry, why that's alright; part of the good feeling of coming to the shrine is the effort of getting so high!

It is an amazing sight to drive through the streets of a Japanese town during the New Year holidays, every door and gateway decorated with the traditional symbols of good luck, long life and prosperity – a spray of plum blossom in bud, the pine branch, the bamboo, and the one golden orange to complete it. The boys in kimono or sailor suits and long stockings (a rare sight) fly kites, and little girls with their pretty faces made up in pink and white to resemble a doll, play battledore and shuttlecock. Nowhere is any business done, and one is continually surprised to find so much walking space along the village streets. Shops all through the year overflow into the streets to such an extent that very often pedestrians and traffic have to make a detour.

We got a mountain of New Year cards in the post on New Year's Day comparable to the wonderful pile of Christmas cards and letters we received from Australia. There the similarity ended. Midnight on Christmas Eve, when in the cold damp we went across to the Church, lovely in whites and blues and candlelight to celebrate the Coming of the Christ Child, was very different from New Year's Eve. One was a tremendous outpouring of love and joyous thanksgiving in the silence of a pagan sleeping world. The other, the New Year, was marked by the long loud roll of the temple drums, on and on, like a funeral toll, beating out the one hundred and one devils who plague the lives of the people, bidding them begone for the New Year.

Christmas had been a lovely time for us all round St. Mary's, even if on the day itself the rain poured down and the wind blew freezingly across the valley. We had a grand feeling of fellowship with you at home as we practised carols, rehearsed the Nativity Play and decorated the church. It is surprisingly difficult to teach a group of twelve year olds to sing clearly and wholeheartedly, so scant is their musical background. In acting too, the simplest play becomes hard work. There is very little such self-expression in the ordinary education programme where each lesson is a loud-voiced lecture by an inadequately trained teacher to an over-large class. There are, of course, exceptions to this, but in the provinces, away from the great cities, this is the prevailing pattern. For all that, the Nativity Play in Ito was a huge success – Mary was entrancing, her expression of bliss due as much to the nursing of a sleeping doll for the first time in her life as to her religious training!

Eighty people crowded into the Church on Christmas night for this and another play, mostly parents and older brothers and sisters. We are beginning to see results of the cutting down of Sunday School membership to those whose parents are willing for them to be instructed for Baptism and who will lend their interest and support. It is so painfully easy to flood the school out with hundreds and hundreds of children with whom young teachers cannot cope and who are removed suddenly and forever when mention is made that the Sunday School is the instruction class for Christian Life and Church membership.

Christmas for me in retrospect has become a series of sounds – cold, hard rain on the roof, the delicious, mysterious rustle of cellophane in the dim dawn as Bill woke to his first real Christmas Day, the lovely new voices of our Angel-choir as it swung into "O Little Town of Bethlehem" as the Nativity Play drew to a close, and beyond, up the highway, the raucous "Jingle Bells, Jingle Bells," on the town loudspeaker bus. For truly the Japanese changes his religious sentiment at will – Buddhist in August when he celebrates the O-Bon Festival of Departed Spirits, Christian at Christmas, when he falls for the Department Store's sales talk, and Shinto at the New Year, when he enjoys Mochi rice cakes, new kimono and a long, festive walk to the shrine with his family.

Frank left early on St. Stephen's Day [December 26] for the round of the Peninsula churches Christmas Plays, children's attendance awards, Communions and long talks. For many of the church people it was a time of great rejoicing as it was their first opportunity to see for themselves that Frank's health is very much improved. As I stood at the kitchen sink and gazed at the long white radishes drying limply far up our neighbour's elm tree after the Land Rover had roared away to Imaihama, it was comforting to know that a good many people at home would be feeling as collapsed as I – Christmas over, Winter fully come, except that Radio Australia brought us up to date with news of the heat-wave that engulfed you.

Our "end-of-the-year" cleaning comes a little late, as here in the middle of this January we are up to our ears in paint, electricians and the chaos that precedes house-moving. On February 1st, Mrs. Harada, dear friend and guardian of the Imaihama cottage church for a number of years, returns with Frank to Ito to take up residence here as "House Mother" for the young students in our new Hostel. We hardly dare use the name "Hostel" because the Japanese word has rather unattractive associations. Many of the Government or locally run dormitories catering for out of town children coming into High School are dingy overcrowded places where the control is lax and the diet far from adequate for growing children. The kind of over-crowding that is possible in Japanese-style houses is quite unbelievable. The general principle followed is that a person needs just as much room as it takes to roll out the bedding "futon" at night, 3 by 6 feet Anything else is waste space.

There is often no separate dining room; baths are frequently taken at the local bathhouse and so washing facilities are the sketchiest. In Tokyo, perhaps, and Kobe, where Western influence is greater and there is more money, conditions are different. In the prefectures there is an amazing inability to think that any other scheme of living is feasible. We plan a very different Hostel for our Church children studying away from their homes.

Fire Brigade authorities came recently to inspect our new rectory and were worried over the provision of only one main staircase and back stairs (the rectory is built in Queensland style, eight feet above the ground). It took Frank some time to discover that the basis of their worry was they expected we would be sleeping at least twenty people in the house. It is not a large house, but has a study, a guest room and Bill's room in addition to the living room. They went away unconvinced that we wouldn't be sleeping rows of people in the living room, and as for the poor baby – little lonely soul sleeping by himself! It is partly economy of money and space, partly tradition and liking for living in a group that makes this situation possible.

But it does keep us humble. When we come to show friends over the rectory, we are always conscious that such a house is to them a mansion while to us it is a reasonable, well-built, but not large home. Yet on the other hand, they are often delighted to see and try to understand how foreigners live. We had a grand day last Friday when members of the Women's Auxiliary in two or three of the other centres came to visit. After Mass and "brunch" and the minor formalities of each of us standing and presenting ourselves and making a little speech about anything on our mind, we went on a grand tour. Three things struck those ladies most forcibly – one was that after living on this block we had designed a house that was so warm, and took advantage of the seascape invisible at ground level. Another was the wonderful lifting effect of coloured walls. Economising in other ways, we have really let our heads go over the colour scheme. We bought gallons of white paint and have tinted them up to our taste, with the result that Bill's room, on the cold sea-side of the house, is like the warm red glow of the fire's heart, the guest room has a lovely blue ceiling, and another room, looking into the sun, is cool green. The other thing which they kept murmuring to me and to themselves was "O Soji" – the honourable cleaning. Straw mats look clean after a vague whisk with a broom. They saw square yards of floors to be washed and polished, stairs to be wiped, beds to be made, not stuffed into cupboards. Yet to our way of thinking, it's a wonderful house for cleaning. All the wardrobes, chests and beds are built in. The kitchen is full of cupboards, there are no carpets (we can't afford them). No behinds or unders, a mop and a duster, why no work at all! So we go on learning from each other.

But there some days when I nearly burst with longing for a visit from an A.B.M. Auxiliary or a country parish Mothers' Union from Australia so that we could all purr together over the conveniences and I would neither feel wickedly wealthy, nor extravagant because my house is airy and colourful and clean.

Finally, while I am still carried away on this most important subject, the fact that Frank has supervised and to a great extent built every bit of the house with only labourer assistance leaves all our one-trade, no hobby neighbours startled and delighted. A scholar or a clerk in Japan is rather like his Chinese brother and does no manual work. Even the young schoolboys, hovering around the building, have scuttled away bothered and embarrassed because Frank has offered to let them use the floor-sander or some other mechanical device. There is much to be learnt about the dignity of labour in this country and the recreative power of hobbies. Bill can teach them something already. He knows how to use each tool in the carpenter's kit.

———

We have just had the pleasure of a visit from Sister Theodora and Sister Faith Mary of the Community of the Epiphany House in Tokyo. Sr. Theodora's many Australian friends, made during her wartime stay at the Community of the Holy Name in Melbourne, will be delighted to know how well and busy she is. It was Sr. Faith Mary's first trip into our part of Japan and the quaint fishing villages (Colour Plate 2), blue bays and stretches of ocean reminded her of the lovely English coast near Penzance. The Sisters of Nazareth, the Japanese Order which shares the same hillside and chapel as the Epiphany, is in the last stages of building a kindergarten to open shortly, with further accommodation for sisters on the second floor. The new convent building, dedicated only three years ago, is already full and there are young women waiting to test their vocation, a sign of deepening spiritual life in the Church.

———

Bishop Yashiro, in his Christmas message to the missionaries, had many interesting observations to make as a result of his recent period as parish priest in one of Kobe's city Churches. "Thinking over the new congregations," he writes, "I find them quite different from those I used to care for (i.e. in the pre-war days). Spiritually speaking the new Christian does not know how to share his new experience of Christianity with the members of his family nor his friends. It seems to me that Christian experience for them is rather more personal." We find this only too true. Time and again the new Christian stays isolated within his own group, a feeling he hates but seems unable to break down, and then when there comes the moment of decision, the marriage to be arranged, the Baptism mooted, pressure from the family or community group proves far too strong no matter what he feels deep down. He simply fades away and is often never seen again.

Do remember that when you pray for us and for the Church in Japan. It comes back time and time again to the old and ever new problem of the layman's responsibility in the Church, to his education in the Christian life, to his practice of prayer, to the availability of simple leaflets and books written in everyday language for him to understand.

There are many exceptions of course. One of our most faithful laymen [Miyazawa-san], a business man with a large family, spurred on by responsibilities arising out of Frank's long illness, has offered for full time work in the Church, if and wherever he may be used. No, he feels no calling to the ministry. He feels his is a layman's task. Pray that the Church may use him well. There is, too, the group of women who meet and pray together weekly for the expansion and strengthening of the Church, the remnant of a large church in Shimizu totally destroyed, along with 80 per cent of its members, during the war. From their prayer life has sprung the germ of a Home Mission Scheme, prayer and giving for the life and work of the Church within the Japanese community. Sometimes I think the Japanese Church has copied its Mother Missionary Churches too closely; the cutting edge and enthusiasm of youth isn't present. Pray that we may help to bring that eagerness for souls back into our part of it.

———

While Australia pants in a heat-wave we are experiencing a very mild Winter, well, less cold shall we say than last year? We are thankful about that. Fuel shortages and consequent price rises have made heating and cooking problems nightmarish. Kerosene, which in the past we have used for both, has gone up Aust. £2/5/- per 50 gallon drum in the last three months. A small bale of charcoal, everybody's staple, has gone up 75 per cent last year. There are frequently electricity shut-offs and when it does come in, it comes at 70 volts instead of 100. So you can be glad with us the weather is so co-operatingly mild (later inches of snow come).

———

At present we are very interested in two big events on the Christian Pacifist front – one the visit of Miss Muriel Lester[52] en route for China, the second the meeting

52 Muriel Lester, an Englishwoman who was one of the world leaders of the Society of Friends, the Quakers, and therefore an active Pacifist.

of a World Pacifist Conference in Japan, in April of this year. Since we are residents of Japan only at the pleasure of the Japanese Government, and though paying no taxes, have no political status, it has been difficult for Frank to understand where more than in our daily life as missionaries his contribution to pacifism may lie. In addition it is a position peculiarly fraught with difficulties to try to interpret a political scene whose background and full ramifications cannot readily be grasped by foreigners. In Japan at present, too, this question of Pacifism is of great political significance, with many non-Christian, and normally non-Pacifist organizations, deeply concerned to protect the clauses of the new Constitution which renounce arms and war as a method of settling international disputes.

The United Preparatory Committee for this World Pacifist Conference, which in Japan is responsible for the organisation, represents a most comprehensive list of organisations, from the Society of Friends, to some of the larger sects of Buddhism, and trade unions. Matters have been initiated in a most business-like way and the plan for the conference is most interesting. In order to distribute interest and arouse the public over as wide an area as possible, the Conference will travel session by session up and down the mainland, from Tokyo in the centre to Kumamoto in the south and Sendai in the north. More than 2,000 miles will thus be covered by the conference teams. Frank has been asked to attend both as the Official delegate for W.R.I. (War Resisters' International) to whose Secretariat in London our friend Tony Bishop has recently gone, and also for the Australian Pacifist Council.

The subjects could each well occupy a *Newsletter* and there will be more about them at Conference time, but they do seem to have been worked out to give a picture of the world as it is and might be, faced with the alternative of all-out war, or peace based on mutual respect and understanding. "The Korean Situation" is the subject for the first session, and "Bringing One-World Brotherhood" the fifth; between them "A-Bombs and Un-Armed Japan and Germany," "Class Hatreds" and all the rest.

"Let us advance towards a beauteous world," says the leaflet on my desk, "where there are none murdering men against their will, none using murdering tools nor any militaristic system. Is it not the right time when the whole of mankind should decide whether to perish with hatred and suspicion or to prosper with mutual respect and alliance. We should be brave enough to open the door to a new type of History. Morning is at the door. We beg you, therefore, to understand our earnest desire. We send this appeal to you on the very Twelfth Morning, beginning of Japan's entrance into war." United Preparatory Committee for The World Pacifist Conference. Japan. Dated 8th December, 1953.

This quaintly worded but sincere statement is the answer to the question, what is Japan thinking about rearmament? What do the people feel about the newly established air-arm of the National Security Force, and the rest? We don't know what Japan thinks. We know that this is how the best of Japan thinks.

We can't finish off this letter without saying to you, our friends at home, your prayers have upheld us through an exciting and difficult year. They have helped Frank back on his feet; they have helped make Billy the strong little boy he is; they have built and strengthened the Izu Church. Your letters have kept us cheerful and we do thank you.

    MAIDA, FRANK and BILL

    Circulated by Mrs. E.R. Coaldrake, Hamilton Road, Nundah.
    T.J. Higham Pty. Ltd., Printers, 14 Blackburn Road, Blackburn.

Newsletter No. 58, **March, 1954.**

NIPPON SEIKO KWAI

From – Rev. F.W. Coaldrake

[written by Maida Coaldrake]

St. Mary's Church House
960 Okaku,
Ito,
JAPAN.

Dear Friends,

From your many enquiries recently as to when we are to have furlough, I am sure you will be as delighted as we are to know that when the *Taiyuan* sails from Kobe on 28th April, the Coaldrakes will be on board and the port of destination is Sydney. Until we know the Board's wishes we cannot be very definite about plans but our time in Australia will include a rest, a period of refresher study in language, etc., and deputation visits which will happily bring us to your doorsteps.

We hope to go first to Tasmania and after that I expect you will be hearing more about our plans.

For the present, 35 days which remain on the calendar include a busy Lenten programme culminating in Baptisms at Easter. We have just had a most inspiring and heartening visit from our newly consecrated Bishop Nosse. Frank and Miyazawa-san made a special journey around the Peninsula Cottage-Churches following a wonderful Sunday of confirmations and meetings here in Ito, and came back delighted at the deep knowledge and profound interest the Bishop showed.

Last *Newsletter* was scarcely in the post before the snows came and with the snows some unfortunate happenings. The snow delayed the building work and also piled up one Sunday to a height of feet on the Mishima highway, and stopped all traffic. The Land Rover, only vehicle to make the trip right across the mountains at all, finally had to be abandoned eight miles from Ito because of a string of large trucks already snowed-in on the middle of the highway. Frank, and Fukawa-san from Mishima (who had come for the ride and was to live to regret it) walked those slippery freezing eight miles in four hours, giving me some anxious moments before they were located. In the Rover, securely locked, were all Frank's Church and personal necessities for Sunday services, and the Cinevox Movie Projector given us by the Queensland A.B.M. There were also three suitcases belonging to an American colonel returning from leave who also had to abandon his jeep and asked Frank if he might leave them in the locked Rover for safety. Three days later when the road was opened to traffic Frank was one of the first to make the journey to the snowed-up pass, only to find that the back of the Land Rover had been forced and the three suitcases were no longer in safe keeping. Neither was half the movie projector worth about £150, a cassock, alb and amice and various other odds and ends. We haven't yet solved the problem as to why a beautiful silver communion set, and offertory bag with collection, fine thermos flask, chasuble and the like were left! The only thing we can think of to explain the half-projector is that it was the speaker unit and might have been mistaken for a T.V. set. We were in no way cheered to discover that Insurance did not cover such items as were stolen.

The Ito police were much disturbed and busy and helpful. They filled in all kinds of forms and asked questions, but we haven't our projector back and we can't replace it here in Japan.

That together with money which was taken from the Church Office last summer made such a hole in our income that the most satisfactory thing which can be said for it is that we get a refund on our Income Tax![53] In this country theft and other such "natural" calamities as fires and floods, make one eligible for rebate. So does sickness and hospital expenses. Last week a nice little man from the Taxation Office of the Prefecture came to call. It looks as if we aren't going to have to pay any tax this year!

That particular snow stayed around the hills for weeks, and it had scarcely melted before another pile-up came. By this time we had moved into the new Rectory, and with the sturdy foundations and draught-proof walls to protect us, we could enjoy the view.

That was March 8th, and the last of the real winter. Today those same hills are tinged with the palest of greens and pinks and sudden warm blue days promise an early Cherry Blossom.

For the grand day of Blessing of the House and Opening of the Hostel, we had sun and winds and white clouds enough to rejoice any heart. The days before the official opening were like such days anywhere. Nothing was finished. We moved in here with doors and windows wet with paint, drawers not in, this and that not working. We also moved in complete with the Matron Harada of the Hostel, her daughter and one student, for the carpenters were repairing the Hostel, which had been our temporary residence for over a year.

What with me not knowing where anything was, and Bill turning on all the wonderful taps or upending any box he came across and then walking off with

---

53 Already on the poverty line, this all caused the Coaldrakes further severe cutbacks to food and heat in a particularly cold Winter.

the carpenters' tools,[54] three guests in the house didn't make things any easier. Japanese ladies are always so polite that it is very hard to know exactly when they want their bath, and especially what they want to eat.

A certain amount of preparation and the house looked beautiful on Sunday February 21st. In Church we had the usual 10 a.m. Mass then, in procession, went across to the Hostel, singing Psalms. The Hostel idea is to provide a home away from home for country students attending College or High School at Ito. After Harada-san had been officially introduced as the new Matron or House-mother of the Hostel we proceeded to the Rectory. By this time everyone had lost their natural embarassment at wandering through another person's house and was determined not to miss a thing. The formal Blessing over we served tea and cakes, and when Frank announced that we should welcome further inspection there was a general rush in the direction of the kitchen and pantry.

The housewives couldn't believe anything as beautiful and clean as that new kitchen could exist. As for all the space to store foodstuffs, and bottled tomatoes and jams, there just weren't any words to go round.

During the next week or two we had quite a procession of people, not all of them church members either, coming up to look around. One or two of them came back later bringing very polished and shined up husbands to whom they showed the delights of a proper kitchen and laundry. These husbands were interesting: polite but determined to give away nothing, especially anything that would involve them in a project to improve the status of their womenfolk. Their faces stayed interested and polite through the sunroom and study, and bedrooms with their wonderful built-in cupboards. They stayed polite through swing doors and hot-water system (homemade), but when the rotary cupboard in the corner of the kitchen was opened and a shiny array of pots swung into view, two of them could contain themselves no longer. Both got down on hands and knees, peered and pushed and aahed! Afterwards we discovered Ihara-san was seeing it as a fine possibility for his chemist shop! In the laundry with its copper and concrete troughs, reaction was the same, but Mrs. Wine-Merchant's efforts have not been in vain. Yesterday two workmen came up to take the measurements of everything in preparation for building her a laundry (she and her daughters-in-law and servants wash for 25 people, workboys included!) She has also paid us in advance for our Rins-and Dry (cost in Aust. when we bought it was about £6) and will take proud possession on the day we sail.

For years we have waited to find an opening into the Japanese laundry to help our neighbours in this most awful drudgery. Have I told you about their rub-and-seven-rinses all in cold water method? I could never get any Japanese women to take my invitation to drop in seriously. Now I have and we all rejoice.

---

54 In traditional Japanese carpentry apprenticeship, young children are encouraged to play at the building site until they are so overcome with curiosity that they steal and practice with tools. This is known as *nusumi-geiko* or "stolen lessons."

This week armed with soap, peg bag and all the big Church linen, I went across to the Hostel, boiled up the old familiar copper and showed Matron Harada and her daughter how to keep Church linen spotless. When it came to the ironing she insisted on standing too, for the whole of the two hours, and gave every stroke of the wrist the same attention as I give her when she is teaching me Flower Arrangement. I shall leave her our household iron, a thing unknown here in most homes. Its inside has been altered and adjusted several times to meet the different current in this part of the world.

While on purely domestic matters I can't omit my first venture into the real Japanese culture. Now that Mrs. Harada has come to stay as neighbour I have started a course in "Ikebana" or Japanese Flower Arrangement, which with "O chanoyu," Tea Ceremony, is the acme of culture for the Japanese young lady. Its limitations are obvious to anyone such as myself who comes from a land full of flower gardens, whose delight it has been to grow flowers and fill the house with their scent and colour. Though I shall never give up the large mixed bowls and the armfuls of colour which suit our style of houses so well, I am already the eager exponent of three blooms, a trail or two of leaf and a great expanse of water for a very special and restful effect.

The Flower Arrangement has been developed and taught for centuries as an art, very much as painting is taught. There are very strict rules and the rule is more important than the flower. But if one abides by the rule and has the proper container, the result in the hands of a master can be quite breathtaking. I'm not coming home as anything but an enthusiastic dabbling amateur but I am hoping that I may have some fresh ideas to pass on to you. Lessons may go on for as many years as one has desire. One may take an examination in due course, and roll out a certificate when your friends come to tea. Perhaps I shall!

———

You can't talk about O-Hana (The flower) without having a whole procession of women pass before your mind's eye. It is supremely the pursuit of women, though the best teachers are men and the art was first the pastime of courtiers. But nowadays it is as necessary to a girl to know something of the Art as to have a trousseau when the family seeks marriage for her. But O Hana reminds me that we had the inaugural meeting of the Izu Dendo Mission Women's Auxiliary last week, an interesting experience.

The time has come when everybody will benefit from a group organised with the strength of the whole body of Japanese Church women behind it. So we called a meeting, set out things to do and called for nominations for chairman and secretary. After a blushing ten minutes during which everyone (including myself for obvious reasons of absence and niceties of language) had declined office, Mrs. Harada was elected chairman and Mrs. Takashima (of great energy and organising ability at times of Church communal eatings and money raisings) was elected secretary. Both, with many gestures of apology, consented to act but both were obviously much worried by the fact that Mrs. Fujii, a woman of social standing and great community good works, had declined office and was therefore sitting "under them." The politeness and social hierarchy is a giant to be wrestled with. Both the new chairman and the new secretary have come to Frank independently since and declared it quite impossible for them to continue. We have one more meeting before we leave and after that they must battle it out for themselves. We suspect it is the thought of a possible future diocesan meeting at which they must represent the parish that really fundamentally worries them.

But whereas these women stick rigidly to convention and their "place," the women teachers throughout Japan are different. They are in the forefront of the battle the whole Federation of Teachers is waging against legislation to curtail and prevent any political activity, or opinion for that matter, by any teacher in any school. This is one of the major issues before the present session of Diet and has the whole nation nearly as jumpy as the arrival of tons of radioactive tuna fish from Bikini[55] area last week. A huge stop-work meeting, which paralyzed the nation's classes on Monday, became a further issue because many schools, especially in the Tokyo area, held compulsory Sunday sessions to keep up with their teaching schedule. Disciplinary action by educational authorities was mooted but nearly all the head teachers of all the metropolitan primary schools were involved. A bit difficult to find thirty or forty new headmasters. Designed primarily to put a stop to Communistic activities amongst the members of the Teachers' Federation, this new legislation may, if passed, do much to withdraw liberty of speech and conscience [established under the Occupation] from a most vital government service.

In the meantime, for very much the same reason, students from university campuses here and there are striking, or fighting their way through police cordons, to prevent outside action in matters of similar moment, the right to act and speak freely within the student body. There's a big uneasy movement within the masses of young thinking people these days, which heavy-handed suppressive methods, do nothing to discourage.

———

Our new rectory has attracted many callers.

The Rev. Ken Heim, senior priest of the American Episcopal Mission in Japan and therefore tremendously interested in missionary building and housing costs, paid a delightful visit in which sleep ranked as far less important than eating and talking. Sister Theodora, C.E. [Community of the Epiphany], came down soon after to get rid of a Tokyo cough, and darned all my accumulation of sox. Miss Nettie McKim, born in Japan, daughter of the famous Bishop McKim, came from Nikko, cheering with her humour and wisdom and delighting us with her experiences. She's making another visit tomorrow and bringing her sister, author of some wonderful Paper Theatre sets *[kami shibai]* teaching the Creed and the Lord's Prayer. Then there was that most delightful person, our new

55 Bikini Atoll in the Marshall Islands, where the Americans exploded an experimental nuclear bomb in March 1954. A nearby Japanese fishing ship was contaminated by radioactive fallout, thus infecting Japan's major food source for some time and causing national alarm.

Bishop, giving us wonderful recipes for anti-seasickness, enjoying our food and regaling us with anecdotes of his Kelham [theological college in the U.K.] and cricketing days. The Rev. Norman Whybray of the Church Theological Seminary in Tokyo came down for a weekend with his wife, Helene, and we are still looking forward to the visits of our Nikko hostess, Miss Gardiner with Miss Pond, the St. Luke's Hospital Dietitian. Ito hasn't any western residents to brighten our meal tables with a visit and conversation, so when visitors arrive we never stop talking, and we Coaldrakes learn a very great deal at those cheerful meal times.

That brings us once more back to our furlough, and all those wonderful known things we shall enjoy again, full-bodied Church congregational singing, thin brown bread and butter, real milk to drink, and fruit to eat, and parsnips and swedes and other vegetables I never imagined I should miss. We also dream of sausages and mash as the epitome of culture, and lamb chops and peas, and tea by the gallon. But we never wish to see a fish in any shape or form, nor chicken – roast, boiled or braised (chicken is the toughest and cheapest meat in Japan). What Bill will say to all this is difficult to imagine – he still takes a while to get accustomed to our missionary friends about the house. Their hair and eyes are the wrong colour! And what he says will be difficult to interpret anyway as he shows a bias for the Japanese language!

Looking back over these years of work around Izu, it's hard to see what we have been able to do, and where three year's work has been sunk. But only three years ago this Church "compound" was a piece of not very rich vegetable field. Now there is a Hostel for our church children, a Rectory and a lovely, well-cared for Church. Around these buildings much life moves. Now that Frank's study is on the ground floor of the house, while all the other rooms are upstairs, the Japanese drop in a lot more for advice and help. Their natural diffidence about "climbing up" into a person's house is overcome, for is not our house on the second floor? Then round the mission area there are new "Cottage-Churches." There are people attending classes for baptism, and each year a small group is presented for confirmation. In Ito, daily services and communions are attended by more devout, active Christians where a year ago there were two or three at the most. No, we haven't much to show for three years of work in some ways, but in others what has been accomplished above and beyond is breathtaking. Frank is convinced that the most important job we, as the founding missionaries in Izu, can do for the Church and the future, is to care specially and intensely for just this little flock, even if it were never to grow under our hands. For he and I are equally convinced that this is a breathing space, and that before very long the Church in Japan will be called upon to meet either or both of two crises – one aggression from the mainland of Asia, the other arising from American superficiality. To stand firm in these crises we need Christians firmly grafted into a well-organised and defined Church, deeply embedded in the Body of Christ. Remember our Christians in your prayers, isolated persons facing a pagan world, and remember that this very isolation from their fellows is the biggest burden laid upon them.

In some measure we are learning to share their isolation as we learn to live and work so far from you all, and we recognise how much it has weighed on us when we experience the tremendous lift of spirits that thoughts of furlough bring.

Our best wishes,

Yours sincerely,

MAIDA, FRANK and BILL

Circulated by Mrs. E.R. Coaldrake, Hamilton Road, Nundah.
Brisbane City Printery, Edward Street, Brisbane.

Newsletter No. 59, April–May, 1954.

NIPPON SEIKO KWAI

From – Rev. F.W. Coaldrake

[written by Frank Coaldrake]

St. Mary's Church House
960 Okaku,
Ito,
JAPAN.

Dear Friends,

This will be the last *Newsletter* for this year and we must say many thanks to those whose financial help has enabled us to send it out so widely. It is one of our strongest wishes about this visit home that we will be able to meet face to face people whom we know only through the *Newsletter*, so would you please be sure to make yourselves known to us if and when we are in your district during our travels. We leave here on April 28th by *Taiyuan* and expect to arrive in Sydney about the end of May.

Quoting from the "Geebung Polo Club," "the man who'd got a thousand and the man who'd got a pound," were as nothing to the gathering at Yokohama recently when the Church gathered to consecrate a new Bishop for our Diocese. There were 14 Bishops from every part of Japan, 50 priests of whom nearly half were from distant places, and many hundreds of laymen and women. In addition there came countless telegrams and cables from overseas people who wished they might be there. The walls of the Church could not contain the crowd and before the three-hour service had been completed everyone seemed to have felt that this act was one which could not be contained in a particular place or time. It was perhaps the more interesting to the few of us non-Japanese who were present because it was an act of the Japanese Church in its own right, conducted in Japanese by the Japanese Church. It lacked nothing of the dignity, beauty and awe that such a service has in one of the old Cathedrals of the Church elsewhere.

The new Bishop had been elected by the Synod of the Diocese some weeks earlier. That WAS an exhausting business because the method is the ancient simple process of exhaustive balloting. Everyone votes and the count is taken. Then all vote again and they count again, and so on and on until one person receives a clear two-thirds majority in both the clergy and lay votes at the same time. It took us 28 ballots to achieve the result.

The new Bishop, Isaac Hidetoshi Nosse, is very widely known and respected for his constant diligence in the care of his people's spiritual welfare. A bishop cannot be expected to have, in fact, all the abilities which his position ideally requires him to have but our new bishop will make his mark, if for nothing else, then at least for his love of his people and the Church. He is 62 and full of vigour, loves baseball, skiing, rockclimbing and hiking. When in England at Kelham for training, he played cricket with great enjoyment and still remembers the thrill of hitting boundaries off the rising ball by using baseball strokes. But "is he not a little one" would be the correct biblical description of him. He is barely five feet tall.

Soon after his consecration he came to Izu for a parochial visit. It was his first such visitation in his Diocese and he came so soon because my early departure for Australia meant it must be made now if he were to understand Izu and its problems so as to take proper care of it in my absence. The visit took five days and involved travelling 200 miles within the parish. He realized, he said, what it means to say that Izu is the biggest parish in his Diocese.

Saturday evening I met the Bishop at Ito Station. He came off a train crowded with holiday makers and as I watched at the wicket he passed without my seeing him – so small is he that he was out of sight down below the others. I found him after the crowd had dispersed. That night we spent quietly preparing for Sunday but he did inspect the just finished Font to make sure it was a worthy object. This is no ordinary factory-made Font. We found a pair of very ancient mill-stones by the roadside some time ago. They were the genuine, ancient article discarded in favour of modern mill machinery which could be driven by electricity. They had been driven by water-wheel and had ground the grain of the village for ages. After due palaver and payment they had been loaded into the car and since then had waited the moment which was now to be theirs. With one for the base, the other for the bowl and a very knobbly length of old tree trunk for the stand between, they have become a Font which the Bishop not only approved but admired. It was Os. Barnett who first drew my attention to the relevance of mill-stones to baptisms for it was in one of his talks on the meaning of Bible passages that he talked about it. His words have always remained in my mind – as so many of his words have in so many people's minds – and the sight of a pair of mill-stones by the road just meant one thing to me. We had the local stone mason hollow out a bowl in the top stone and we put a thin drain pipe down through the holes into which the grain used to run. The whole thing weighs about three hundredweight and seems to strike the Japanese artistic eyes.

———

Sunday morning service started with the Blessing of the Font. We had no baptisms then because five people are preparing for baptism later. One of these, particularly, is a cause for great rejoicing because he is an elderly man and when he is baptised the whole family will be together in the Church. After that perhaps their home will become a "Cottage-Church." As the blessing of the Font neared its conclusion Bill rounded off one of the Bishop's prayers with a smacking round "AAAAMen." He probably meant the right thing by it but lately he has been using it whenever he sees something he wants to eat!

The blessing over we moved up to the Chancel where the Bishop sat in his chair for the service of Confirmation. We had two young people and three adults. It was a joy to have these three older people join us for they have been attending services for years. They are, I am sure, the kind of people of whom it will be said in later years "they held fast to the faith." One, when asked the reason for seeking confirmation, said: "since I was fifteen I have tried to live the good life and have failed. I still want to, but I need help." Two others had been baptised in the river here in Ito about thirty years ago but had never really found a spiritual home. (One is assured that the river was cleaner in those days.) Later in the morning when drinking tea with the Bishop one of the men just confirmed, whose family have been great supporters of a Buddhist Temple here for centuries, asked the Bishop about his burial. It transpired that this had been a matter causing him to put off entry into the Church. He had been told many years ago that a Christian should not be buried in the same place as non-believers. His family vault has, of course, the earthly remains of his forbears over many centuries and his many relatives will expect that he be laid to rest there. The Bishop explained that the Prayer Book provides a prayer for the consecrating of the burial place and so the Church may bury people anywhere, even outside a Christian cemetery. He went on to advise him that, with regard to his dying, he should be sure to call in the priest that he might have the comfort and help of the Church and the grace she brings for that great event.

We had the pleasure of having as our guests that weekend, also, the Rev. Whybray and his wife. He is on the staff of our Theological College in Tokyo. He is English, his wife French. They first met on a railway station when on their way to a Student Christian Movement Conference. The Coaldrakes whooped when they heard that, it having been their own particular fate to meet first at an S.C.M. Conference. On this particular Sunday morning he acted as Bishop's Chaplain, so everything was able to be done in good order with the Churches of England, Australia and Japan combining to bring God's grace to active participation in the life of Ito. The Confirmation was followed by the Communion service with the Bishop wearing cope and mitre, not looking so small after all.

Evensong on Sunday night and an early rest, then next day we said Matins with the Hostel residents at the usual half-past seven, before boarding the Land-Rover for a three-day journey. Luggage was piled high in the back because we had to carry a full bedding outfit for two. Miyazawa-san also was making the journey. I always have my "down" sleeping bag, but the normal Japanese sleeping outfit makes a bundle too big for one person to carry. This is due to the use of cotton-wool padded quilts for mattresses and covers. We had also the altar table and all the appurtenances, our robes, and a bag of food for three men for three days. Altogether we made a snug load for the trailer. The 28 miles to that day's stop took just the hour, the bumps and curves being so bad that Miyazawa-san got car sick – he has ridden with me often and this was the first time I have known him to get that way. The Bishop takes any amount of rocking, swinging and bouncing without turning a hair. I had feared otherwise because he had given Maida a lurid prescription compounded of pickled dried plums as a cure for motion sickness, warning her that after taking it for the next ten minutes she would feel so bad she would think she was dying, but after recovering from the effect of the medicine she would have nothing more to fear.

For the past four years we have had a "Cottage-Church" at Imaihama in the house of Mrs. Harada. It has been a wonderful success among a limited circle of people. Directly as a result of it there are now three adult communicants, and three more adults and two young people waiting for Baptism and Confirmation. These numbers are, from one point of view, pitifully small but none of these people knew anything about Christianity four years ago. In addition a large number of other children and adults have been instructed. It was sound continuing work, and it was with some hesitation I asked Mrs. Harada to leave there and move to Ito to take charge of our new Church Hostel. She moved a month ago and we have had to work out new arrangements for continuing services and meetings. Beginning with the Bishop's visit we are renting a room in the "Culture House" in the heart of the village. We held our first service there with the Bishop present and that night had Evensong, Bible study and discussion. The regulars came in the morning but at night we had about ten new adults including some prominent citizens. They went away that night vowing their intention to bring 50 new people next time. Enthusiasm, the frothy kind, is very easily aroused, but the long-lasting result is likely to be more limited. It has always been so, and we need to see that there is a stiff wind to blow away the chaff, so that only the real grain remains. In these days I believe we must pay more attention to the one deeply concerned person than to the ten who are only superficially interested. Some of you may question this attitude, but I take it that my job as a missionary is to help in the development of a spontaneously growing community of Christian locals, the title of which is "the Indigenous Church." If you gave me three months notice of your visit I could whip up enthusiasm and have a thousand people in each of a dozen villages turn out to meet you. You might be impressed, but I wouldn't count on any lasting result. On the contrary, I have been told by people who went in great eagerness to hear Kagawa, that they were mightily inspired at the moment but soon afterwards were left wondering how to achieve any practical result in their own lives and in the long run sank into a deeper despair than at first. What they ask for, these people, is little-by-little practical guidance. They soon pass on what they have discovered as a real fact for themselves, to their enquiring neighbours.

The "Culture House" meeting nevertheless promises very well. It is not a "cottage church" and we are hoping to have a Christian family soon who will accept the responsibility of making their home such. But the "Culture House" is an interesting place. It was started by Japan's most famous eye-doctor, Ishihara, when he came to live nearby after retiring from practice in Tokyo.[56] He pursuaded the Village Council to devote their old office building to the service of the people when they moved to a new building. That was four years ago. A committee of elders runs the place under his general oversight. An extensive library has been built up, including some technical reference works, and is well used. In addition various classes and meetings are held there. For instance, while we held Evensong in one room the local school "Parents and Teachers Association" was meeting in the next room. During the afternoon I went to call on Dr. Ishihara to pay my respects and thank him for agreeing to our holding services and meetings there. It might easily have been that a Christian group's application be refused. He told me that he himself thought the best should be taken out of each religion but that some religion was essential. He hoped that the "Culture House" might be used to lead people to seek religious understanding and belief and for that purpose he wanted many books on religion included in the library. He had found at first that people did not have the reading habit and in order to entice them into it, the first books in the library were just ordinary novels and magazines. He was very glad to have us use the House.

Incidentally, as I passed through the room where some patients were waiting to see him – he continues his practice in a limited way – I saw an old man who used to attend our Bible Class in another village. He had reached the stage where he really believed in Christ and should soon have been baptised, but he suddenly stopped coming and we have not seen him for over a year. This day as he sat in the waiting room he was reading his Pocket Bible. We can only be praying that he may yet have the courage to throw off the bonds of his ancestors and seek baptism.

––––

Children came to "Sunday" school on their way home from school that day and sat with their eyes nearly popping out as the Bishop spoke to them. He, in turn, sat amazed as six of them almost faultlessly recited the greater part of the catechism.

In the late afternoon I took the Bishop over to see the natural wonders of hot springs where the water gushes out at boiling point. It is used to evaporate sea water and reclaim the salt. There are several such salt works nearby, the sea water being pumped two miles inland to the bore-head. Running back we took a short-cut over the mountains so that we could see some real Australian sheep on a farm that road passes. It really isn't a road – just an ox-cart track, but the Land Rover likes that sort of thing. We found the sheep and the Bishop indulged in visions of every farm having its sheepfold and family spinning and weaving their own clothing. This is actually being done in some parts of Japan and seems to be

56 Famous as a Colour Blindness expert, who was also very cultured and wrote poetry.

one real way in which the farmer can relieve his own poverty – but that is a long and exciting story I am waiting to tell you about when I meet you.

The farmer was away, which was a pity, because he too is a believer but family pressure prevents him coming into the Church. We did meet his wife. She is a dear thing but a keen Buddhist. I had not met her since my eye accident and she took the occasion to offer me solicitous words and enquire how I was. She told us that while I was in hospital she had dragged her old man every day up the hill to the little shrine and there had offered rice and prayers for my recovery.

Rae Campbell, now as you know a Roman Catholic, came to visit us the other day, and told us that while I was in Hospital the Nuns where she lives had prayed daily for my welfare. And I know that ever so many of you did too. I'm sure that I owe my sight to the loving care of all of you under God.

———

Next morning we made an early start and rolled on down through Shimoda and around to the farthest tip of the peninsula. Our destination was Ose and the "Cottage Church" at Dr. Kawai's House. (Colour Plate 5) There we said Mass and had a long conference about work in the village and arrangements during my absence. Unfortunately Osawa-san and his wife were not able to be present. They are working desperately from morning to night still repairing the damage caused by Typhoon Tess last October. Everything on his farm was burnt brown by the salt laden winds. He had to start again from seed and his most important crop, marguerite for perfume oil, has only just reached the transplanting stage. His year's income was in the oil in the great flourishing bushes spread over the hillside when the wind came. In the late afternoon we walked up the path through the hills and surprised him at work.

We also went by car in another direction up incredibly steep tracks to a plateau where war-time repatriates from Manchuria are doing what we would call "pioneering." Pacing a wilderness they are gradually encroaching on it by opening up one small patch after another in cultivation. Some of these men come to our services down in Ose and the relatives of others are coming too, so we are reckoned to have a real connection with them. One man asked me what I thought about the possibility of running sheep up there. We talked about it for a while and then Mrs. Kawai laughingly said to him "If you want to do any good with sheep you'll have to read the Bible more!" One old chap wants me to stand a big cross up alongside the pond which is the centre of their efforts there.

———

That night's service and meeting was in Mrs. Suzuki's house in Nagatsuro, the next village. There was a good turn-out of regulars and some new-comers. We think it probable that about six of the people here will be baptised soon. One problem is that I am able to get there only once a month. They are always asking for more frequent meetings but it has not been possible to arrange that so far. They are fifty miles from Ito.

We slept that night at Dr. Kawai's and left at sun-up on a long day's run. First we headed back to Shimoda. Here we were taken charge of by our one communicant member in the town, Naito-san. He acted as our Guide and showed us the places and objects connected with the stay here in Shimoda of Townsend Harris, the first American Consul-General to Japan. It is just 100 years since he lived in a temple on the shores of the bay. We know, though the local sight-seeing Association prefers to forget, that Harris was a convinced Christian gentleman who took out his prayer-book and bible every Sunday morning and read the service of Morning Prayer with his "man-servant." It was, in fact, here in this temple in Shimoda that the first Anglican services were ever held in Japan.

It was still early in the morning when we left Shimoda and headed across a range of mountains, then turned left and sped along the valley and found our way out to the sea on the west-coast peninsula. Turning up the coast we moved along nicely through rugged scenery with the Bishop remembering some of the sights he had seen when he had walked down the length of this west coast 35 years ago. The distance of a day's walk was now covered in an hour, but we were left with a clear impression that life in the villages stretched along the narrow shelf between mountain and sea was anything but easy and secure. (Fig. 22) There is so much bad weather and the coast so rugged that fishing is a very unreliable means of support. The mountains are so steep and unrelenting that only a few can make a living on them by burning [wood for] charcoal and cutting wood.

In two places the earth has relented and there are mines. One at Uguisu yields the raw material for glass making. The diggings are well up on the mountain side and an exceedingly ingenious suspension cable car system carries them round mountain shoulders and down to the barges in the bay. The gold mine is at Toi and the most notable thing about it as a gold mine is that when the pit was sunk it caused the entire Hot Spring output in the valley to dry up. You can imagine the Hotspring Inn proprietors didn't take it quietly. An echo of the fracas is heard in Ito on the other side of the peninsula whenever it is proposed to work the gold-bearing ore on the mountainside above the city. The Inn proprietors swarm like bees around the Council Chambers threatening all sorts of things if the Hot Springs of Ito are allowed to dry up for the sake of a measly gold-mine. The arguments in favour of inns as a "gold-mine" has so far won the day in Ito. There are over 400 such inns now.

———

It was easy to swoop around the coast of Izu and take in villages and hamlets at a glance, but we hadn't come that way for our pleasure. We wanted the Bishop to see that the Mission in Izu has a much bigger task in front of it than it is able to tackle all at once. To win the people for Christ and help them reclaim the land for society – it might be put like that. In any case, there must be some such second part to the statement because as the people of these villages come into the Church, the Church comes into the life of the villages. This mutual movement is naturally very limited in these early stages but we must keep an eye on the future for the best lines of development. I am quite sure we should have a stake in the west coast as soon as possible but it is so cut off from the other side, where we work, that I have not been able to include it in the programme so far despite one or two excellent openings that have occurred.

That the villages are not entirely cut off from modern ways of life was borne in on us as we sat eating our lunch. A nearby wireless entertained us with modern hits such as "Crying in the Chapel." The news told us of the return of the "radioactive" fishing boat and the dispersal of the poisonous fish through ordinary marketing channels.[57] Since the area we were in was almost entirely dependent on fishing the news was causing a great stir.

After lunch we left the west coast and headed up over the backbone of the peninsula. On the pass we stopped and gazed over the great expanse of mountain, ravine and sea with here and there a small hamlet. The Bishop seemed to have got the feel of the place for he said, "Really, our work in Izu is not only a matter of the spirit of Evangelism, it is a matter of the body too."

We reached home in time for the Bible class in Miyazawa-san's house in Ito that night, where people from the neighbourhood gather each week and it was a great privilege for them to have the Bishop to speak. These household gatherings in the towns as well as in the villages provide reticent people with an encouraging atmosphere in which to open their hearts.

Thursday morning found us moving out of Ito again at an early hour and up over yet another mountain pass. We made our first stop among the clouds in the little mountain village well known to the people of St. Peter's Launceston. We held the service of Holy Communion in the house of Kubota-san. Mrs. Kubota, who has been confined to bed with the after results of an operation throughout the very cold weather, listened to the service and made her communion from her bed. Theirs is one of twenty cottages that form the pioneering village. On this bleak plateau they are trying to make farms. Every yard of the land must be cleared of rocks and then worked up with fertilizer and compost into arable land. After five years the farms are said to yield half the normal output with twice the normal work. In one gully we found a sheepfold with four Australian sheep, all doing well.[58] This is an area where, if pasture were developed, sheep should do well.

We moved on again shortly, down the mountains and along the valley into Mishima, stopping only to pick up old Mr. Toyoda the chemist, who came with us to the Mass in Mishima at Fukuo-san's house. The faithful had gathered, and here the Bishop bade farewell to Izu, leaving Miyazawa-san and I to look up two more pioneering village men and then fight our way back to Ito through the dust and traffic.

———

[Maida Coaldrake adds:]

Although we specified no visitors in April we are to have a young Embassy couple from Tokyo for the weekend to make their Easter Communion. They

57 The radio-active contaminated fish from the *Lucky Dragon* off Bikini Atoll.
58 Given by a Christian farmer at Cressy, near Launceston, in Tasmania.

were married at Christ Church, Sydney, recently. In the midst of packing we had to have vaccinations for smallpox and cholera, which made Frank quite ill.

Our best wishes until we see you again,

Yours sincerely,

FRANK, MAIDA and BILL

————

Circulated by Mrs. E.R. Coaldrake, Hamilton Road, Nundah.
Brisbane City Printery, Edward Street, Brisbane.

Letter from the Bishop of the Diocese of South Tokyo, Isaac Hidetoshi Nosse, to the Australian Board of Missions, 18 April 1954.

Bishop's House,
235 Bluff, Naka-ku,
Yokohama,
Japan
Easter Day, April 18th, 1954

Sirs:

I was consecrated Bishop and enthroned Bishop of Tokyo Diocese on St. Matthias Day, February 24th, 1954.

During four days beginning March 13th I paid my first parochial visitation to the Izu District and witnessed the Church activities there.

I am writing this letter on the occasion of the Rev. Frank W. Coaldrake leaving for home on April 26th on furlough.

The following points called my attention during my parochial visitation to the district:

1. That house churches have come into existence at various places.
2. That the evangelism there is laying more importance on Church life rather than individual life and that the appearance of true Christians is more keenly looked forward to than the increase in their numbers.
3. That Church catechism is being well taught.
4. That converts are very pious and are filled with evangelistic spirit.

The Izu Peninsula is a mountainous district surrounded by sea and its inhabitants are mostly engaged in agriculture and fishery. Owing to the inconvenience of communication the district remains comparatively unaffected by the trend of the outside world. In an area like this only a priest of good health and energy can rush along on bad roads, officiate at the service immediately on arrival, hold a meeting and visit parishioners, and then again proceed to the next house church.

Urgent needs at present for the farming and fishing villages of Izu would be, among others, such as those enumerated below:

1. Hostels for young people.

When a rural Christian wants his young people to receive higher education, he must first send them to high schools. As most of the villages do not have high schools, the young people have to leave home and go to towns. For that purpose there must be adequate hostels where the parents can put their boys and girls in custody without anxiety. In the City of Ito, where we have Church, there is a High School. Rev. Coaldrake has already established a hostel in the compounds of the Church. I consider that great endeavour should be concentrated on the hostel so that we can expect in the near future superior clergy candidates to come out from it. It is my opinion that efforts on these lines are required in order to make churches in farming and fishing villages true native churches.

2. Two missionaries.

As the district covers a fairly wide area, another missionary in addition to Rev. Coaldrake would be welcome. If this could be realized, it would become possible to hold services at more places every Sunday. Churches in rural villages cannot become truly churchly unless they have services regularly on every Sunday.

3. Paid lay evangelist.

It would be the first experiment for the Nippon Sei-Ko-Kai but rural villages are in need of such persons, to lead in the development of better living conditions. E.g. Rural villages will become economically better off as hilly land not suitable for tilling can be utilized for pastoral purposes, and Co-operative methods of economics introduced.

I would like to ask the Australian Board of Missions to consider increasing the Izu Mission grant so that either or both 2 and 3 above, especially 3, might be carried out.

The Nippon Seiko Kwai feels greatly indebted to the Board of Mission in Australia for dispatching to the N.S.K. Rev. Coaldrake, who willingly assumed full responsibility and is showing remarkable activity to evangelize the Izu District with all his might and main. He is the pride of our Diocese. We all sincerely hope that he could devote the rest of his life to the Izu District.

The people of the South Tokyo Diocese cannot find adequate words to express their profound gratitude to Rev. Coaldrake for his enthusiastic and painstaking efforts for evangelism in spite of many difficult and unfavourable conditions. He has conquered them and acquitted himself to his credit. He has also mastered the Japanese language and has now no difficulty in his contact with Japanese people.

We earnestly hope that he will come back to us as soon as his furlough is over.

Before I finish this letter I wish to be permitted to say a few words about Mrs. Coaldrake, too. She is a modest lady and excels in virtue. I also find her to be a good leader in women and youth's groups. I learned that she possesses a special talent for organizing and guiding groups such as altar guild, too. When she returns, I intend to persuade her to engage in activities within the Diocese in works mentioned above.

Dear officials of the Board of Mission, may I ask you to remember our South Tokyo Diocese in your prayers? During the absence of Rev. Coaldrake, the clergy in the Diocese will take turns in serving the Izu District and do their utmost to maintain what he has built up there.

Now I venture to make another and last request of mine. I entreat you to be so good as to give Naoyuki Azuma, a Deacon of our Diocese, a chance to study in Australia. With regard to this matter, I have entrusted everything to Rev. Coaldrake.

With greetings for Easter at this Holy Season,

    I remain

        Yours very sincerely,

           ISAAC HIDETOSHI NOSSE

           Bishop of the South Tokyo Diocese

           N.S.K.

To: The Australian Board of Missions,
    Church of England in Australia.

7   The Campaign Against Prejudice Continues: Australia (1954–55)

The second period of furlough and deputation work in Australia was similar to the first. It should not have been. By now it was approaching ten years since the end of the war but bitterness and misunderstanding of Japan were still endemic, "an out-of-date selfish luxury" as Frank Coaldrake was to proclaim from the pulpit of St. Andrew's Cathedral in Sydney.[1] "Even in the Church there was to be found prejudice and deep-seated misunderstandings," he remarks after returning to Japan.[2]

Frank Coaldrake spent most of his time in Australia travelling and visiting parishes all over the country (some 7,000 miles by aeroplane), giving over 300 speeches and talks, not counting radio interviews and conference addresses.[3] Any time left over was used for meetings and consultations at A.B.M. Headquarters in Sydney. The Mission to Japan was re-equipped with a new Land Rover and a Rayburn slow combustion stove for the rectory, replacing the kerosene camp stove that had been the only means of cooking until then.

While Frank Coaldrake travelled and campaigned, Maida Coaldrake returned to Hobart and carried out an arduous month of deputation work in her former diocese, giving 65 talks and addresses. Young Billy attended the Lady Gowrie Kindergarten, with some limitations because he was unaccustomed to communicating in English. Margaret Elspeth Coaldrake was born in Hobart on 10 March 1955. The Coaldrake's return to Japan was delayed until she was twelve weeks old and all her compulsory inoculations could be carried out prior to departure from Sydney. Maida Coaldrake returned to Japan against doctor's orders – it was considered that conditions in Japan posed an unacceptable risk to both mother and child.

Few documents survive from this furlough. The Coaldrakes were too busy to record what they were doing. Frank Coaldrake used 16 mm black and white film and colour slides of Japan with his talks – these were something of a sensation at the time, and aroused great interest. Instead of "Coaldrake Records" we have to rely on newspaper reports, an article in *The Peacemaker*, and a paragraph in the *A.B.M. Review*, to give us a picture of this phase of the Coaldrake mission.

1 "Bitterness For Japan Criticised," *Sydney Morning Herald*, 24 January 1955.
2 *Newsletter No. 60*, April, 1956.
3 *Newsletter No. 60*, April, 1956.

"Missionary Work in Japan," *The Mercury*, Hobart, 16 October 1954.

There was a large attendance of members and friends of the Women's Auxiliary of the Australian Board of Missions at the monthly meeting in the Parish Hall, Devonport, on Tuesday, when Mrs. Frank Coaldrake, who is on furlough from Japan, was guest speaker.

Mrs. Coaldrake, who was the first Youth Organiser appointed by the Church of England in Tasmania, spoke on her work as a missionary in Japan and outlined some of the problems confronting her and her husband (the Rev. Frank Coaldrake) as the only foreign members of the staff of the diocese of South Tokio [sic].

Work among a people of a highly developed civilisation such as that of Japan, with its age-old social conventions concerning the family and marriage, public behaviour and conduct, made the life of a Christian missionary most difficult, she said. In addition, there were problems of food supplies for people unaccustomed to a rice diet, and a high cost of living. She said she was paying 25/- (Aust.) per lb. for tea and 12/- per lb. for butter before her departure for [furlough in] Australia.

But the Japanese people were as hungry for friendship as they were for rice. Beyond anything that could be accomplished in daily living among them was the fact that as representatives of the Australian people and Church, the presence of even one Christian family meant a great deal as a gesture of friendship between the two nations and between the members of the Church, both Japanese and Australian.

Although responsible to the Bishop of South Tokio [sic.], she said she and her husband were entirely supported by the Australian Board of Missions of the Church of England.

The rector (the Rev. H.A. Jerrim) presided and moved a vote of thanks to the speaker. Mrs. Coaldrake was presented with a posy by Mrs. Jerrim.

Tea hostesses for November will be Mesdames Webb, Graue and Moore.

A.B.M. Review, vol. XLIII, no. 1, 1 January 1955.

The Revd. Frank Coaldrake is doing a grand job on deputation. He is most inspiring and helpful to the missionary cause wherever he goes. His wife and Bill are in Hobart, where they will all spend Christmas together.

"Bitterness For Japan Criticised," *Sydney Morning Herald*, 24 January 1955.

"Bitterness has ruled Australia's attitude to Japan over the last ten years – bitterness which is not only sub-Christian, but is an out-of-date selfish luxury," the Rev. Frank Coaldrake said at St. Andrew's Cathedral yesterday morning.

Mr. Coaldrake has been an Australian missionary (Australian Board of Missions) in Japan since 1946 [1947] and is now on furlough. He will return to Japan shortly.

"The Japanese are ordinary human beings who have good and bad in them like the rest of us," said Mr. Coaldrake.

"We should be trying to find ways to bring out the best in them."

Mr. Coaldrake said that when relatives of war criminals sent back from Manus Island tried to send dolls to Australia to express their gratitude they were prevented from doing so.

"That is the kind of foolishness into which bitterness can lead us," he said.

"We should accept the fact that Japanese will be fishing off the Australian coast, taking proper measures to police our territorial waters. The Japanese need the fish which they have legal right to catch and which we do not need.

"We should remember that Japan's millions have not enough to eat, and also that their presence in the South Pacific may be due to the damage done to fish in the North Pacific by the Bikini atomic explosions.

NEW RELATIONSHIP

"If we gave Japan meat and bought Japanese goods so that she could afford to buy our meat, we would not be so troubled by these fishermen.

"We who dwell in plenty should remember that the Japanese are a starving people.

"We should mark the tenth anniversary of the surrender of Japan by sending her a large quantity of disaster relief/goods – food, medicine, clothes, blankets – to be stored for use when typhoon or earthquake brings disaster.

"Every year hundreds, perhaps thousands, lose their lives in disasters. Japan lives hand-to-mouth in poverty and cannot store anything for an emergency.

"We may not be able to afford to trade with her, but we could afford to give generously to feed and clothe her needy in a time of catastrophe.

"Such a gift would lay the foundation for a new relationship with Japan in the coming decade."

"Missionary Laments Antagonism Toward The Japanese," *The Standard*, Warrnambool, Victoria, 31 March 1955.

The uncharitableness of maintaining antagonism toward Japan 10 years after the end of the war was emphasised yesterday in Warrnambool by Rev. Frank Coaldrake.

Mr. Coaldrake returned recently to Australia after eight years as an Anglican missionary in Japan.

Concerning the "hang-over" of war, Mr. Coaldrake said the Japanese people should be taken on their merits.

He quoted the person who buys goods then discovers the goods were made in Japan, and promptly returns them to the shop. That, Mr. Coaldrake said, was equivalent to taking a meal from a Japanese person, for Japan needed trade to enable her to buy food for her people.

The Japanese, Mr. Coaldrake continued, could not get sufficient food. The food they had chiefly rice and vegetables, with a little meat and fish, was bulky but not sustaining.

Government objective in food was 1,800 calories a day. By contrast, the Australian minimum was 3,400 calories a day, with an average nearer 4,000 calories.

UNDER-NOURISHED

Even if the Japanese looked well fed, they were really under-nourished. This lack of nutriment was revealed in the Japanese inability to stand up to strenuous exertion.

Farmers wasted no land, and planted a new crop the day another crop was harvested.

Mr. Coaldrake gave a heartening report of the progress of the Church in Japan. He is stationed at Ito, a farming and fishing area 100 miles from Tokyo. The population of the area is 300,000, and the parish in which Mr Coaldrake works covers 3000 square miles.

"BOSS" JAPANESE

"My boss is a Japanese," Mr. Coaldrake said, meaning he serves under a Japanese bishop.

All the Church of England bishops and clergy in Japan were Japanese, Mr. Coaldrake explained. There were 270 Japanese clergy and only 20 missionaries from overseas.

The Church was working effectively to turn the people from Buddhism and Shintoism to Christianity. Membership of the Church of England in Japan had trebled since the war.

There was no limit to the expansion of Christianity. Many denominations were working in Japan to spread the Christian gospel.

Even so, the missionaries were too few to cope with all the people asking to be taught how to live the Christian life.

The best selling book in Japan since the war was the Bible in Japanese.

WRONG IMPRESSION

Typical cartoons of bespectacled Japanese gave a wrong impression, Mr. Coaldrake explained. He had found the Japanese just like ourselves.

Mothers loved their children and were devoted to their husbands. Fathers were proud of their sons and devoted to their daughters.

"It doesn't matter what language you use to speak to God," he concluded.

Yesterday morning in Warrnambool, Mr. Coaldrake addressed Anglican clergy from the rural deaneries of Camperdown and Hamilton. In the afternoon the clergy heard recorded addresses by Mr. Coaldrake.

On Tuesday night, Mr. Coaldrake lectured in Christ Church parish hall. His subject "Our Neighbours in Japan," was illustrated by coloured slides.

"Japan in the Melting Pot. Rev. Frank Coaldrake's Survey," *The Peacemaker*, vol. 17, no. 3, pp. 1 and 4.

The Rev. Frank Coaldrake, among many other things founder and first editor of *Peacemaker*, has just concluded his furlough in Australia and is ready to return to his missionary parish in the Shizuoka Prefecture, Japan.

Before leaving Australia, he addressed fellow pacifists in Adelaide and Melbourne. The following address was reported by the *South Australian Farmer* (20/5/58).

Mr. Coaldrake said that since he had been in Australia on furlough, the general elections had been held in Japan. Not one Australian newspaper had paid proper attention to the Socialist Parties in Japan when reporting the elections.

LITTLE SUPPORT FOR COMMUNISM

These Parties were quite apart from Communism, which was present in the industrial world, and which put up candidates in city and village. Communism was well organized but received little support.

Except in unions it was sponsoring (the trade union movement is new in Japan), Communism was not popular. Other trade unions were independent. It was not easy for Communism to infiltrate into non-Communist organizations in Japan.

ENLISTMENT UNPOPULAR

The Constitution stated Japan should not retain an army, and even that Japan renounced war as a sovereign right. The Government had in recent year[s] ignored that.

From the first, enlistment had been, and still was, voluntary for Japanese men.

Attractive terms were offered [to] prospective soldiers – a three year term without obligation to continue, better wages than could be earned as unskilled labourers, on retirement a bonus sufficient to pay a deposit on a house.

These were attractive conditions in a country where six million were unemployed, but the army still had to drum up recruits.

This gave the lie to the widely held belief that the Japanese were a jingoistic and militaristic people.

U.S. QUITS IN 1957

The U.S. under its Occupation terms, had agreed to protect Japan, but would withdraw in 1957. "After that you must take over," the Japanese had been told.

The U.S. had further said, "But we are afraid that by 1957 you will be unprepared. We want to see you now build up defences."

[The] Japanese answer to this had been that it could not be done; it was also uneconomical. Aid was then offered by the U.S. – goods for Japan from the U.S. and the erection of factories in Japan to manufacture articles so as to provide work in Japan.

The armed strength required of the Japanese by the U.S. in first negotiations had been 350,000 men by 1957. The Japanese went to Washington to explain that they were unable to induce men to join the army, it was also uneconomic for the nation. Compromise was reached on a strength of 240,000.

One sure indication that the Japanese men did not want to join the army was seen in the failure so far to build up the defence army to more than 100,000, said Mr. Coaldrake…

RUSSIA

Ask the average Japanese what he thinks about Russia, said Mr. Coaldrake, and he will say, "Don't forget the six days' war." Russia had declared war on Japan six days before the Second World War had ended, enabling Russia to exact reparations and to subsequently hold vast numbers of prisoners.

The war had ended in August, but Russia had been approached by Japan in April – four months before – to sue for peace for Japan with the Allies. Nothing was done. Though Russia knew of Japanese readiness to surrender, and was part of the Allies, the atom bombs were dropped on Hiroshima and Nagasaki.

Russia had taken 400,000 Japanese prisoners, but only half of that number had been sent back to Japan ten years after the war had ended. Russia replied to repeated requests for the repatriation of the prisoners that all had been returned, "except for a few thousand war criminals." But every year a few more thousand Japanese from the Russian prison camps would "turn up" on the coast returning to their own country.

The ordinary people of Japan do not trust Russia, stated Mr. Coaldrake, and do not want to have anything to do with that country. They consider Russia was backing China, also Korea.

COMMUNISTS OUTED

In 1952 the Communist Party had 50 members in the Diet. At that time an article in Russia's Pravda accused the leader of Japan's Communist Party of betraying Communism in Japan and of being a stooge to the U.S. This man had examined his ways admitted he "was a stooge," and resigned.

Next in command of the Communist Party took over and began to use force. Trains were wrecked and bombs exploded.

Reaction of the Japanese people was clearly demonstrated in the next elections – only two Communist members remained of the 50 who had formerly occupied seats...

FOOD THE KEY

The real key to the problem of Japan and the Pacific was food, claimed Mr. Coaldrake. Japan, on the whole, was close to starvation. Some folk were wealthy. Average calories per head now available were 1,800, and the necessary minimum was considered 3,400 per head. There were no food reserves in the country, and Japan was incapable of sustaining itself.

Food had to be brought in from abroad, but many countries would not trade with Japan. None was prepared to give food. Frequently, Japan had no money to buy food. The Japanese did not ask for charity, and were prepared to work for everything they received.

Food supplies from overseas were being ordered only from month to month – for a nation of 87 millions!

When people are hungry they are not always rational, reminded Mr. Coaldrake. Acute shortage of food supplies would bring hunger riots in three months – not from lack of confidence but from despair.

Japan was using 99 per cent of its food productivity, and the people knew the country could not support them. They did not look for handouts like beggars, but were a people willing and able to work.

Mr. Coaldrake said he believed Japan's salvation lay in industrialization. He believed a population of 200 million cold be held in this way, each man at his bench, but food supplies had to come from other countries.

– South Australian Farmer, 20/5/55

8 Consolidation in Japan: Izu (1955–56)

By 1955 the Japanese economy was recovering to pre-war levels. The shipbuilding industry, for example, which had been crippled by the war, began rapid expansion in 1954 and production reached second place internationally by 1955.[1] The standard of living was improving for ordinary Japanese. *Per capita* income had recovered to pre-war levels and households were starting to spend on conveniences such as refrigerators.[2] Life expectancy reached 63.60 years for men and 67.75 years for women, some thirteen to fourteen years longer than it had been in 1947 when Frank Coaldrake arrived in Japan.[3]

Living conditions were improving for the Coaldrakes as well. There was the new rectory now in full operation, with a proper hot water system provided by the Rayburn stove brought back from Australia. The Izu Mission was becoming firmly established, with the Diocese of South Tokyo recognizing it officially as a parish in 1956. There was a regular itinerary for visiting all the cottage churches in rural and coastal villages of the Izu Peninsula. Cottage industries were being established, such as sheep breeding from Australian stock. In Itō, the Coaldrakes were settling in for the long term of seeing the fruits of the hard grind of the preceding years come to fruition. There was a constant flow of visitors from Tokyo and overseas, putting strains on the limited budget. The children were growing. But it was not to last.

Extract. Copy of letter from Maida Coaldrake, 9 November 1955.

I don't know when I have been so busy, my help has been sick for 5 weeks. Frank is sad at her home conditions, so he is going with her to St. Luke's Hospital, Tokyo today.

With no second pair of hands life is packed, and you can't pass kiddies over the fence here. Frank has had to superintend the work on a new wing added to

1 Ichirō Hidaka (ed.), *New Japan*, vol. 9, 1956–57, Tokyo, The Mainichi Newspapers, 1956, p. 27.
2 Income *per capita* reached 113% of the pre-war levels 1934–39 (*New Japan*, pp. 22–23). In 1955 washing machines were owned by 12% of city dwellers (*New Japan*, p. 39).
3 *Historical Statistics of Japan*, vol. 1, Tokyo, Japan Statistical Association, 1987, p. 270.

the hostel, alterations to other rooms and lattice work going up under this house.

Autumn has come which means something I've never known in Australia – everything in the house, food, clothes, furnishings etc., has to go out in the sun for close inspection and treatment for wogs. Getting ready for winter means much alteration of clothes, washings and mendings, also I am bottling fruit as often as I can against the shortage later.

Then the church duties, and many coming and going with extra meals for the Assistant Priest Fr. Matsumoto and Servers for breakfast and so on.

Visitors: The Whitfields (Armidale) have moved onto Hong Kong and other parts of East Asia, after a month in and out here. Lovely to have them so interesting and accommodating.

Next Sunday Dean and Mrs. Roscoe Wilson (Melbourne) arrive for an indefinite stay. Alma Hartshorn (Queensland) now in Rangoon is planning a visit early in 1956. She is attached to U.N.E.S.C.O. (United Nations).

Church affairs are very healthy. Frank has a lay helper well established and his assistant priest had been accepted happily by A.B.M. and Kelham College S.A. for two years training. So Frank is working with the kind of staff he should have. There have been conferences and much travelling for Frank. He still looks forward to a few hours in his study as the height of ambition.

Newsletters haven't reached beyond the stage of notes jotted down, but today in Tokyo Frank is looking into the question of a printer.

Margaret is still sunny haired, sweet and good but very energetic, 8 months tomorrow. Billy is happiest watching his beloved carpenters working round the place.

Newsletter No. 60, April, 1956.

NIPPON SEIKO KWAI

From – Rev. F.W. Coaldrake

[written by Maida Coaldrake with "Footnotes" by Frank]

> St. Mary's Church,
> 960 Okaku,
> Ito,
> JAPAN.

Dear Friends,

"It doesn't take long to get your hand in again," I said to myself, as I killed a cockroach on the pantry floor and added it to the pile. A Tasmanian never quite gets used to the crawling and flying things that people the air and the crevices of a hot country. And certainly the summer we arrived back into on 1st. August, 1955, was the hottest ever. The rectory which we had finished just before leaving for Australia was however in very good condition, surprisingly dry and free from mildew. The Church grounds were brilliantly green and fair and the cannas blazing with colour, and the Church itself had been so swept and garnished that it was a joy to behold.

If we ever doubted that under God a great deal had been accomplished in the five years that Frank had been in charge of work in the Izu Peninsula, our homecoming this time was ample evidence of change. There was a gay welcoming crowd on Ito Station to meet us; there were the Church, and the rectory and the Hostel fully functioning. Miyazawa-san and Kubota-san were full-time laymen working on the staff of the Mission. And the following Sunday people from the cottage-church areas all over Izu came in to worship with us and rejoice at our safe return. Fr. Sammy Azuma was already in Australia at Kelham on a two-year studentship, and Frank had in his pocket a place at the same College for another young priest from this diocese.

It was nearly dusk when we said goodbye to our friends and went upstairs into the cool house. Kimiyo-san had made tea and bread and jam. We settled Margaret Elspeth into the cot from which, it seemed, Billy had climbed not long before, and left Bill to embrace old friends in his toy box. And suddenly we felt we were home.

But where is "Home"?

But what really is "home" for us? There is no "home" or "abroad" for the missionary. Once you have taken the step into the foreign field of the Church's work, it ceases to be "foreign" and you are never quite at home again even in the best and longest known places in your own country. Nor can we ever feel completely at ease where our work holds us amongst people who must always remain a little outside our understanding and experience, any more than Billy and I are at home on the breakwater of Ito harbour where the deep-sea fishing fleet anchors, though we sit there often enough. So in a way, though we have two homes both dearly loved, we yet share a little of the feeling of the great mass of homeless in the world.

So it was with us when, after four years in Japan, our ship slid quietly through Sydney Heads on the morning tide. There was a great rush of joy at the thought we were "home at last" mingled with concern lest we might be out of touch and strange to our own people. But we needn't have feared. It was wonderful to be in Australia again, to touch down at normalcy, to be Australian and ordinary, instead of "gaijin" (outside person) fascinating to the last degree of living. It was wonderful to see so many of you again, friends whom we love and with whom we could have spent our whole furlough in contentment, and very sad to miss some of you because Australia is so large. It was a joy to read a magazine that didn't have permanent waves from the post; to worship in familiar places in a familiar tongue; to look in butchers' shop windows; to borrow library books; to check on hem lines and bulbs and buttons. It was fun for me to play at being a suburban housewife with weekend shopping list and days at the beach, taking Billy day by day to the splendidly run Lady Gowrie

Pre-School Centre in Hobart. But, there's the rub, it was only playing and it ended far too quickly.

Every time we take up pen to write to you we swear that for our own sakes it must never be so long again. There is always so much clamouring to be passed on – teeming life, ideas, developments. This time it is nearly two years and two countries since we wrote a *newsletter.* New mission staff, new building projects, new angles on serving the rural population, have taken the time which might well have gone into letter writing. Then there have been welcome home meetings, Bishop's visitation, confirmation, baptisms and visitors, twenty-five of them since our return. And in the house bottling, baking and endless war on wogs, not to mention a section headed "Bringing up Bill," should all find their way into an account of how we spend our days.

Two Village Experiments

Frank has put much work into two experimental projects which have gained considerably in momentum since furlough and since Miyazawa-san has joined the staff. Miyazawa-san, you may recall, was a successful Yokohama businessman in charge of a large furniture factory who, in the prime of his life, felt he must give his full-time attention and energy to the Church's work. He is at present doing a five weeks' course in rural training at the model village centre in Shikoku conducted by the Combined Protestant Churches under the guidance and inspiration of Kagawa. Miyazawa-san's particular brief in the Izu Mission is the interpreting of the Church to the rural population. Along these lines Frank has been assisting the Government Experimental Plant station in the rugged Irozaki area in its search for suitable grasses and trees to change the pattern of life in the barren, fodderless Peninsula and generally raise the standard of living of the people.

The second project is the search for an industry which could become a regular home industry, playing a secondary part certainly in the farmer's or fisherman's scheme of work but stable enough to carry over the lean times when the crops fail or typhoons destroy farming projects. Such a project might well be the raising of sheep in small numbers. The inspiration for this stems a long way back to our discovery of one or two sheep kept as kitchen pets and to an offer made by a generous sheep owner in Cressy, Tasmania. That was five years ago. Since then we have visited another Government Experimental Station, also in Izu, where thorough-going experiments are being made in the breeding and acclimatisation of sheep and cattle.

The M.V. *Taiyuan* in its voyage of July, 1955, had not only the Coaldrakes and much luggage including a new Land Rover and Rayburn Slow Combustion Stove on board, but also some round-trippers who were very interested in the workings of the Church in Japan, and particularly in the part being played by the Australian Church. Among them were a Victorian sheep station owner and his wife who became very good friends of ours. They made a quick trip down to see us at Ito, raced by hire car to Imaihama, our Land Rover still being in the

Yokohama Customs House, looked at some sheep, taught the owner how to sit a sheep on its tail and look at its teeth, asked many telling questions, rushed back to Tokyo to catch a plane and meet their ship in Hong Kong. In parting they said: "At home we have sheep to spare for such a project." And so it transpires that as you read these words, six fortunate, or unfortunate sheep, according to the way you look at the sea, will be setting out on their journey to Japan.

From "Pig box" to Kelham

At almost the same time there will be arriving in Australia Fr. John Kanau ("Bun") Matsumoto, priest of the Diocese of South Tokyo en route to St. Michael's House, Crafers, S.A. and two years' study under the guidance of the Kelham Fathers. Fr. John doesn't know anything about sheep pens but he knows a great deal too much about "butabako" (pig-pens) as they are called, from the inside. In Tokyo during the war, he spent three months in one such 9 x 6 feet [cell] with three companions, as guest of the Secret Police. His crime? While still a deacon he insisted on continuing his ministry to his congregation after being forbidden to do so. He is 35 and has a wife and two children. His expenses and a family allowance are the care of the Australian Board of Missions which is responsible also for Fr. Azuma whom many of you will have met recently.

Australian highlights

But back to our furlough. It was a joy and a disappointment. Because Australia is so large and we saw many of you only once, you will be wondering how we fared after we left you. We found Australia wonderfully clean, spacious and friendly, and the generous open-heartedness of church people towards us and the Church we were trying to interpret was immensely encouraging. But it was a physical impossibility to do everything and go everywhere though most of our time was given to deputation. In one month alone Frank flew 7,000 miles and travelled 2,000 miles by Land Rover. In all, he spoke over 300 times, not counting broadcasts and attendances at Conferences of which there were many. Family commitments limited my movements but even so in one diocece I gave 65 talks in 4 weeks.[4] So you can gather our days were full.

One of the highlights of the tour was the much publicised Brisbane Town Hall meeting chaired by the Archbishop, which was attended by nearly 2,000 people. Another was the family fun and interest of the large gathering in Hobart early in our stay when groups stayed on talking questions until midnight. We could write endlessly of the ups and downs of a missionary deputationist's life, but we could never tell enough of the kindness we met with in the homes of people with whom we stayed, nor could we speak warmly enough of our friends in the parish of St. Thomas', North Sydney. Here, for the last month in Australia, we were

---

4 Maida Coaldrake was pregnant with her second child, born in Hobart, March, 1955.

provided with a cottage furnished by the people of the parish, making our last hectic days in Australia a pleasure.

Our best story comes from a large provincial town in N.S.W. After a brief introduction mumbled by the [local school] teacher Frank began to talk about life and people in this country, to be interrupted ten minutes later by a bright youngster who wanted to ask a question. "Did the speaker, as he seemed to know so much about Japan, happen to have come across a Rev. Frank Coaldrake there? Her Sunday School class had been sending him parcels of powdered milk." Frank says that, after that little interlude, he has never before or since had a more interested group of listeners.

Japanese War Brides

Everywhere there was plenty of interest, but even within the Church there were also to be found prejudice and deep-seated misconceptions. Questions such as "Can we trust Japan," "Do you like the Japanese?" cropped up everywhere and we felt sometimes an evening's talk had done little to get to the root of the matter. Where we could as we moved about, we visited Japanese war brides to see how they were settling into their new life and if there were anything they wanted us to do for them. Sometimes we were deeply distressed by the ostracisation which went on in a seemingly happy and often very much church-attending community. Often, of course, we found the girls happily settled and well accepted by their families-in-law; sometimes we were able to clear up some minor point of custom or language which had become an immovable mountain. This was the case in a far western township in Victoria when Frank found the 19 year old bride drowned in tears and very much wanting to go home. She simply couldn't cope with the laundry. She had attacked the family wash in the Japanese manner, taps full on, water running everywhere, and her husband had been very, very angry. There was only one rim left in the tank! Anyway, she *must* go home. If she stayed a moment longer she would surely die. There was only rain water to drink! Needless to say she couldn't speak English and her husband had no Japanese. . . .

Mud Flats, Jeepneys, Hong Kong and Wrecks

Looking back, tonight with its bitter wind and rain seems far removed from that hot August day on which we so thankfully left the ship at Yokohama. But details of the four weeks' voyage have dimmed somewhat and we remember the trip rather as a stringing out of friends across a good slice of the globe.

Fortunately for us, the Brisbane wharfies who decided to have a day or two strike when we arrived, first unloaded the Land Rover and left it sitting on the wharf, so we were able to enjoy Brisbane's glorious winter days and time with our family in comfort. We can think of several places we should rather spend our last weekend in Australia visiting than Port Alma, famous for meat loading wharfs and endless mud flats, but at least there was a racketty rail car plying between ship and Rockhampton to relieve the tedium.

Manila we found greatly changed. The scars of war are almost gone from the heart of the city. The wreck-filled harbour has been tidied up a little and we spent hours watching American soldiers using their leisure hours skimming round on water skis between hulks and great modern ships at berth. The streets are cleaner but even more crowded and full of the fascinating "Jeepneys" which act as a kind of public transport system. These gay little painted extensions of jeeps career madly around with scant regard either for traffic lights or direction. If, as we were, you are over-carried some half-mile through misunderstanding with the driver, he, with gay Spanish abandon whirls round again into the eye of the oncoming traffic and rushes you back to your destination to the tune of much encouragement from the other passengers.

Under the guidance of Helen Boyle, a charming American, who spent some of her furlough in Hobart recently, we had a grand tour of the city. Helen is secretary to Bishop Binsted of the Philippines and so could bring us up-to-date on developments in the five years since our first visit. We spent the afternoon most pleasantly chatting with the staff of the Theological Seminary and seeing over the low cool buildings spread over the crest of a hill above the city. All these, with lawns and gravelled driveways, and the beautiful uncluttered chapel, have been built recently. The separate staff houses are straight out of Home Beautiful, with their convenient living areas and cool, cane furniture. After sixteen days in the ship, Bill had a most heavenly time running barefooted on the grass with hoses playing full on him.

The Suffragan Bishop's wife, Mrs. Ogleby, has a baby the same age as Margaret (see Note 1) so we had a happy, baby free afternoon and Margaret had a luxuriously cool time in the flat at Bishopscourt with far more attention than she was accustomed to and a bath as well. Bishop Ogleby, who by the way is one of the youngest bishops in the Anglican Communion, assured us one of his chief claims to office was his length of leg which stood him so well on the long mountain treks his work involves.

We were joined later by Fr. Bruce McCall's[5] sister-in-law, Betty, at present on the staff of W.H.O. in Manila. She showed us over the famous Manila Hotel where she has an apartment and incidentally pays the equivalent of 12/6 d. to have a cotton frock laundered. This Hotel was used as an administrative centre during the Pacific Campaign by General Douglas MacArthur. To stand in those quiet empty rooms on the 8th floor which the General had used as his own suite, and look out of the low-slung windows onto the great hot sweep of city and bay, is to feel even now, that one is standing directly in history. This feeling never really leaves one, from the moment the ship catches the heavy ground swell off Corregidor, through to churches ruined by earthquake and fire and sword over centuries of other wars. And one leaves the Philippines still feeling history has other chapters in the making in those uneasy islands.

---

5 Fr. Bruce McCall was still on the headquarters staff of the A.B.M. in Sydney.

Dr. Frank and Betty (Paton) Ashton came on board at Hong Kong to greet us, and the next day being Sunday we spent many happy hours cooling off in their flat in the new wing of the Nethersole Hospital. The new wing has been completed since our last visit a year ago and is a wonderful high, airy building adding enormously to the efficiency and effectiveness of this, one of the oldest missionary hospitals in the East.

Hong Kong as always was very much a meeting of the ways. Frank [Ashton] and Betty were sailing, even before we were due to leave, bound for a brief summer holiday in Japan. So we made plans for the happy week-end we later had together showing them Ito and comparing our two worlds. David and Gladys Chamberlain, too, were leaving in a few days on the mail-boat bound for England. Their term on the staff of St. Stephen's College had been completed. David was to go before the Ordination Candidates Selection Board soon after their arrival and has since entered Cuddesdon [Theological College] to read for Holy Orders. Gladys and their two sweet children, Ian and Mary, are staying with Gladys' family.

Hong Kong was more crowded than ever, with a restless heavy feeling about its streets and business places. Han Suyin's book *Love is a Many-Splendoured Thing* reflects so truly the feeling you get in much of the East today, the tenseness and the lack of future for self as divorced from country, the terrible human need for something to prove the worth of the individual. You feel it at every turn. And in Hong Kong you never forget that the New China is just over the way with its 600 million people better fed and governed than ever before in their long history. Asia – and South-East Asia too – is no longer asking our opinion on this or that system or ideology, nor does it wait for our approval. The Church has still the only answer for the individual in this moment, but the moments are passing and there are millions and millions of individuals. The urgency of the task is beyond comprehension until you see it in terms of men, women and children, and it is beyond the salve of only a Lenten denial envelope.

Japan changes – but disasters remain

By way of contrast, Japan, especially our part of it, seemed more stable and prosperous than we had expected. Booths had become shops, shops had spread up the highway past our church gate. When the weather turned chill, people brought out overcoats – garments which have been conspicuously absent. Butter and good bread are readily available, at a price, and are much in demand. Public transport is greatly improved and there is a large increase in the number and variety of commercial vehicles on the road. National Savings have reached an unprecedented high. To commemorate the topping of the 500,000,000,000 Yen mark in Post Office Savings, a special cancellation postmark is being used this week throughout Japan (Note 2). Japanese ski teams are competing at the Austrian trials, and we have been watching some of the members of the Japanese Olympic team pacing it out up the road past here [in preparation for the 1956 Olympics]. All of which add up to the fact that, though there is a large body of unemployed both registered and unregistered, there is also more money and some prosperity in the country. Perhaps the most notable evidence of the prosperity brought about by the bumper rice crop is the fact that farmers' wives have been buying simple electric washing machines by the thousand.

But in our absence Japan hasn't become any more careful of human life. At Nagoya, our first port of call, we were greeted by news of the mass drowning of thirty young girls swimming together at a school picnic. Soon afterwards, we were horrified to read in the morning news that the presence of arsenic in a powdered milk made by the reputable firm of Morinaga had taken toll of the lives of fifty babies and caused sickness and blindness in six thousand more. More than the tragedy itself is the tragedy of public opinion which, after the first startled gasp, settled down to buy the firm's products as before. It has since been discovered that the use of inferior ingredients in the processing of the milk was responsible for the disaster. It has not yet been decided whether the Company and the staff responsible should make recompense! And on New Year's Eve at a big country Shrine such lack of provision had been made for the crowds that pressed forward to receive the festival rice cakes that the stone wall of a terrace caved in killing 128 persons. Considering three million worshippers visited the Meiji Shrine in Tokyo on New Year's Day, perhaps it is surprising that more persons do not meet their death in crowds. But that is small comfort.

Disasters usually come fast in the typhoon season but, except for a disastrous fire in Niigata City [on the Sea of Japan coast] which destroyed the whole business section of the town including the church and rectory, the typhoons were kind to us this year. We did spend several days under typhoon emergency conditions, schools closed, shops shut and so on. It's a funny feeling to spend a day in a house with the shutters up and everything movable outside lashed down, and listen to the radio progress reports on the movement of the winds, to see the sea change colour and the clouds pile up, and know from the reports that winds are screaming behind the range of mountains which divides the Peninsula; and then to have them veer away to sea and leave calm weather behind. After three such typhoon warnings in two weeks you almost wish for the real thing to relieve the tension.

Australians to stay with us

During the typhoon season we had the Eric Whitfelds of The Armidale School, Armidale, staying with us. We greatly enjoyed having friends from home to share our life and to rediscover familiar things through their eyes. The Dean and Mrs. Roscoe Wilson of Melbourne arrived soon afterwards, bringing news of home and a keen interest in everything that went on in the Church and amongst the people who are our particular care. On Harvest Festival Sunday the Dean preached a wonderful sermon, interpreted by Frank, which our people said they would never forget, not so much because of the message but because of the look on the Dean's face as he preached (Note 3).

Salvaging – "wreck"

Christmas came hard on the heels of Harvest Festival, leaving us somewhat breathless with its spate of parties, plays and Baptisms. Just before Christmas when the winds were blowing their coldest, one of our confirmation candidates arrived from Imaihama in great distress. Motherless from the age of seven she had brought up her little brother and cared for her drunken father in a wretched shack without water or electricity. Minai-chan at the age of 15 had reached the end of her tether and was generally running wild in the neighbourhood. After due consideration and talks with her father who was prepared to mend his ways, Frank and Miyazawa-san made a sudden sally. With the approval of the Neighbourhood Councillors and the grudging support of the relatives, they helped the father pull down his house and in two days build another one out of the wreck. We had Minai-chan to stay and helped as we could; a little later she attended the four-day pre-confirmation school held in the Hostel, and last Sunday with great joy was confirmed with seven other candidates at the morning service by Bishop Isaac Nosse.

And that brings us almost up to the present and to a wonderful new level of work. The fact that four of the young people confirmed last Sunday came from Christian homes, indeed two of them were fourth generation Christians, brings with it the thought of the increasing solidarity of the Church in Izu, and indeed in the whole of Japan.

Affectionate greetings to you all,
    Maida

Footnotes by Frank

1. Margaret. This delightful little female, Margaret Elspeth, joined us somewhat reluctantly on March 10th, 1955 at Hobart. She is now a sturdy, rollicking tomboy, but is already picking up the ways of the ladies. At ten months she has two chief accomplishments. She shakes her head saying "No, no, no!" and throws kisses. (Fig. 44)

2. Statistics. An Australian never gets used to the rolling on of the numbers that comprise statistics in this crowded land. 500,000,000,000 yen put away in Post Office Savings Banks deposits is worth five hundred million pounds sterling. 500,000,000 eggs are laid in Japan every month, but that means that there are only 6 eggs per month per person. 500,000,000 New Year Lottery Postcards were sold in the month of December. Stacked flat one on top of the other they would reach a height more than fifty times that of Mt. Everest.

Such reverberating totals simply echo the fact that in every minute the population of Japan increases by two. While you have been reading this one footnote some three new Japanese have arrived in the world.

3. The Dean's Face. It is a wonderful face from which to hear a sermon on Cheerfulness. I would have liked to be watching it when he heard that he had been awarded the O.B.E. in the New Year Honours List.

Figure 44 Margaret and Bill, on "Boys' Day Festival," at Itō, 5 May, 1956.

This re-awakening

Two years will almost have passed since we sent out our previous *Newsletter* in May, 1954. We hope this enlarged letter might help a little to bridge the gap. From now on we expect to post more or less regularly this simple link with friends in Australia, America, Europe, Asia and Africa.

It is interesting to recall that the first of this series of *Newsletters* was dated 20th June, 1947. It was a copy of the letter I had written my mother a week after my first arrival in Japan. My mother had the letter duplicated and sent it to friends. From then until we reached Australia on furlough in June 1954, the *Newsletter* has always been very largely my mother's responsibility. We have written to her, she has seen to the printing, proofing, wrapping and distribution. In some cities friends have accepted the responsibility of delivering copies by hand. Circulation reached a total of several hundreds.

Money for the venture has always come, a lot from some, some from a lot. That, too, has been handled by my mother.

—————

PADDY WROTE A LETTER...
Paddy wrote a letter to his Irish Molly-oh,
Saying "If you don't receive it write and let me know..."
    Please do as Paddy says so that we can bring our address list up to date.
    What about sending us the name and address of any person to whom you used to pass on the *Newsletter* by hand, and then pass it on to someone else.
"And if I make mistakes in spelling Molly dear" said he, etc. etc.

If you know the old ditty you'll know what "etc" stands for, see how relevant it might be and realise why it has to go the printer as "etc."

Beginning with this letter we are to do things differently. The job is too big now for my mother to handle without a great deal of worry. We want to include photographs and we can borrow without charge blocks which have been used locally if we print in Japan. Chiefly for these two reasons we will print the letter here and post direct to all who want to receive it.

"We will" is an overconfident word; "we will if" people want to read it and can help a little with the cost. At that point my mother will still have her hand in the matter.

Money, preferably open Postal Notes, and names and addresses of new readers should be sent to:

MRS. E.R. COALDRAKE
30, HAMILTON RD.,
NUNDAH, QUEENSLAND,
AUSTRALIA.

There is no "Subscription Rate" but if each regular reader sent us about five shillings a year we could pay the printing and posting bills for a letter at almost monthly intervals.

Printed by The Kokusai Press Tokyo, Japan.

Figure 45 "Cowboy Bill with his father at the front gate." Photograph included in *Newsletter No. 60*, April, 1956.

Letter from Frank Coaldrake to Bishop Isaac Hidetoshi Nosse, 21 October 1955.

St. Mary's Church,
960 Oka-ku,
Ito-shi,

21 October 1955

The Right Reverend Isaac Hidetoshi Nosse,
Bishop of South Tokyo,
Kugenuma.

My Dear Bishop,

Thank you for your note sent by Fr. Matsumoto concerning his appointment to Izu. I have been thinking about it ever since it arrived and I am returning it herewith.

It is most unsatisfactory.

The Izu Mission cannot agree to an appointment in such terms. The draft as a whole and the last sentence in particular obscures the fact that a promise has already been made concerning what happens four years from now.

Please send us a plain statement that the appointment of the Izu Mission from October 1st 1955 is made subject to the limitations imposed by prior agreements between the Bishop and Oiso Seiko Kwai [Oiso Anglican Church], namely:

1. From 1 October 1955 until departure for Australia Father Matsumoto is *Kanri Shisai* [Acting Rector] of Oiso Seiko Kwai [Church].
2. Upon return from Australia, [Father] Matsumoto is to be appointed *Fuku Bokushi* [lit. "Deputy Rector," but normally called "Assistant Priest"] in Izu for two years only, and that this appointment will be to Izu wholly and solely.
3. At the end of that two years in Izu, [Father] Matsumoto is to be withdrawn from Izu if, but only if, it is decided to implement the promise to the effect already made to Oiso Seiko Kwai [Church] by the Bishop before he was appointed to Izu on 1 October 1955.

Yours sincerely,
Frank W. Coaldrake

Letter [handwritten] from Bishop Isaac Hidetoshi Nosse to Frank Coaldrake, 24 October 1955.

5-6-11 Kugenuma,
Fujisawa-shi.
24th Oct. 1955

My dear Father Coaldrake,

I wish I could come and see you and talk with you. I have been very busy lately... About his [Father Matsumoto's] appointment, I shall have a talk with you when I see you next time. I will try to come to you in the middle of Nov.

Yours sincerely,
I. H. Nosse

Letter from Bishop Isaac Hidetoshi Nosse to Frank Coaldrake [dated by Frank Coaldrake upon receipt "3/11/55 at Shizuoka," handwritten in Japanese, translated by W.H. Coaldrake].

From Isaac Nosse Hidetoshi, Bishop of South Tokyo to Frank Coaldrake, Priest of the Izu Mission.

Concerning the appointment of Father Bun Matsumoto to work in the Izu Mission of the Diocese of South Tokyo:

1. From 1 October 1955 until departure for Australia in order to pursue his studies, Father Matsumoto is *Fuku Bokushi* [Assistant Priest] of Oiso Anglican Church.
2. During the same period he will be Acting Rector of the Oiso Anglican Church.
3. Upon his return from Australia, [Father] Matsumoto will work as Assistant Priest in the Izu Mission for two years. During this time he will work only for the Izu Mission. . .

[signed and sealed] Isaac Nosse Hidetoshi

Letter from Frank Coaldrake to Canon Warren, Secretary, the Australian Board of Missions, 16 January 1956.

St. Mary's Church,
960 Oka-ku,
Ito-shi,
Japan.
16/1/56

Dear Canon Warren,

Your letters of December 28th and January 8th received and full of interest. It is gratifying to know that you are available to deal with matters in Sydney. I only hope you will find it possible to work at them in a satisfying manner. It means a lot to me and I imagine to many other missionaries to have you there.

John Kanau Matsumoto:

"Bun" (the usual name because it is one way to read the character which is properly read "Kanau") will sail from Kobe January 26th via Hongkong and Tarakan to Brisbane and Sydney on the N.Y.K. Line *No. 5 Mantetsu Maru* due in Sydney on about February 12th! His English speech is not as good as Sammie Azuma's was on arrival, but he has some confidence. If you could meet him at the boat and pilot him as far as the aerodrome wicket hostess he should be alright as far as the Adelaide airport wicket hostess!

He will have all the immediate essentials but an Australian pound's worth of small change would ease his mind on arrival. You might claim any Japanese money he had as fair exchange and use it where you use all souvenirs.

"Bun" is quite a priest, too spiky to be handled anywhere else but Kelham, but unaware of his own idiosyncrasies. At heart he's a jolly good bloke and should be a useful member of society if Fr. Oddie and his boys can succeed in taking him down a peg or two.

Right now I'd like to confine our Bishop to some place for giving Bishops the "shake-down" treatment. And as for the Standing Committee of the Diocese, the best thing about it is that it has promised to resign at the time of the next meeting of Synod. A weak and faltering Bishop seems to be able to do even more harm in Japan than in Australia. For one thing, everyone who wants money for anything, clergy or lay, asks the Bishop for it. He cannot say "No" to anyone so he is always broke and runs to the Missionaries for help. His latest dream is that the A.B.M. will fill his pocket as fast as he empties it. He has just told me that he has asked the A.B.M. for money for Theological students. This he has no right to do because the American Church pays the expense of the Theological College and the Dioceses pay the College Board Yen 3,000 per month) for their students. But the Bishop wants to use the money for two fellows who were sent down from the College as unsuitable after two years. Now he wants to override the decision of the College, although as one of the House of Bishops he is one of the Trustees of the College. The trouble is he cannot say "No" to the two students who came crying and asking to be ordained. It would be a pity if the Board unwittingly helped one Bishop to subvert the work of the House of Bishops. I doubt if his request will have been submitted for the approval of the House of Bishops – the agreed procedure for any requests for help from abroad. I've just written and told the Chairman the gist of this – in more restrained language. Do you think some[one] in the right place could be given a hint that Bishop Nosse is trying to get more than he should?

The selection of Bun for this scholarship at Kelham had nothing to do with his suitability or need for such training. As it happens, it is my own personal opinion that he is the one who should have been selected on proper grounds, so I have played their game and done my part in getting him approved by the Board. But actually he was being a thorn in the flesh to Mrs. Sawada of the Elizabeth Sanders Home. You will perhaps remember her reputation as an unprincipled schemer who has been a distinct embarrassment to the Church for years J.K.M. [Fr. Matsumoto] has been standing up against her machinations so he has to be got out of her district, without any question of the justice from South Tokyo. And how fortunate that he can come back into the Izu Mission afterwards while the Diocesan watches to make sure he has forgotten all the questions he has been asking lately. They are very foolish to have forgotten that J.K.M. went to prison as a deacon under Tojo because he would not give up a ministry to which he believed he was called of God. So I'm trying to get the matter straightened out while he is on the way out. Frustration at not being free to say to the Bishop and standing committee just all the things I want to say is probably at the root of the tirade you're reading now. I'll leave it there for the present, but probably will have lots more to unburden as time goes on. But do what you can for Bun and rest assured he's worth it.

Kathleen Shima McColl:

I had not heard of this couple before. It should be quite simple to do as you suggest. I will write first to Mrs. Oglesby and ask her to find out whether Bishop Yashiro is expecting to receive £100 from me. It could so easily finish up somewhere and K.S.M. [McColl] be asked later what about it! Do I sound cynical? As to the payment of the money into my account – an amount of slightly more than that was sent me in December to use at Boatfare for J.K.M. [Fr. Matsumoto] It wasn't safe to rely on being able to get the money paid in Sydney in early January. But eventually it turned out that Japanese Government Regulations require such a fare to be paid by the sponsor in his own country and currency. So I have this money in yen in the Bank in Tokyo and could send it as soon as I hear that it is OK to do so.

Sheep:

During your leave a plan to send me half a dozen Romney Marsh sheep has matured. They are to come from a station at Terang in Victoria and the donor is to complete shipping arrangements and put them on board in Melbourne in April. The freight is to be £7 per head plus fodder which he will supply. I still haven't got clear who is to pay the freight. He thinks he can. I should have liked to have got it clear before this so as to ask the Board for help if necessary. The Donor, Mr. Neville Palmer, "Dalvui," Terang, was on the *Taiyuan* on a cruise and ventured into Izu under my guidance. On the way out he came up with the offer. We have an interested group here ready to take over the sheep and there is a government sheepbreeding centre ready to advise on the proper care of the sheep in Japan. They are to be sold for Yen 3,000 each to farmers, conditional on the lambs they will be bearing when shipped in Australia remaining our property. Offering of the "First-born"!

I don't expect to involve you in this beyond hearing this report.

At the same time I am trying to arrange the shipment on the same boat of the six Corriedales I was offered five years ago by a Cressy Tasmania station owner. There may be more difficulty there, and perhaps it will be necessary to have them come later. Mr. Baillie is on a much smaller holding than Palmer and may not feel able to do more than deliver the sheep at his front gate. Probably you will be hearing more about the Corriedales.

In general you may be interested to hear that since our return I have found my energies demanded far more than previously in more specifically priestly and pastoral work. I'm involved in all sorts of acute personal problems and propositions. Formerly, by contrast, I seem to have been working to get a mission established and oiling and adjusting the machinery. It seems to have gained a good momentum in my absence and I simply ride on it acting "conductor" to the passengers. Some quite remarkably good people getting on board too.

I had quite a field day – three days – at the Theological College last week conducting the Beginning of Term Retreat for the students. Opening the eyes of the priests of the future to the failings of the priests of the present. Dean Shunji Nishi and one of his lecturers resigned at the end of last year. The College is a much better "Institution" than it used to be but no one has been satisfied with it. And I think no one wants to take it over now. America pays the costs, the students get everything for free, the bishops are desperate for priests, every time Japanese go to a world church conference they are patted on the back as a wonderful "Younger Church" and their pride is made so much more stubborn; you said once you would like to see me go there and I didn't thank you for the idea; from some points of view I'd like to have a go at it now but I wouldn't last a week. First thing I'd do would be to make the students clean the Augeaen Stables in which they live and the flood of resentment would wash out the Dean's residence.

Maida and I are quite excited at the prospect of seeing you. Maida has come up with the idea that you should stay some months and while you are here I should fly to Australia for three months deputation work – preferably Jan–March 1957. Azuma would be back here working in Izu and you would be asked to be Acting Supt. The idea is primarily to do away with the need of rushing madly round on Deputation when we are home on furlough some time later. I wonder what you will think about it? Of course whether the Board would want me to fly home for such a deputation is another question.

With best wishes,

Letter from Frank Coaldrake to Bishop Isaac Hidetoshi Nosse, 2 February 1956.

St. Mary's Church,
960 Oka-ku,
Ito-shi.
2/2/56

The Rt. Rev. I.H. Nosse,
Bishop of South Tokyo.

My dear Bishop,

I have not been able to forget our conversation about Fr. Matsumoto while you were here for Confirmation. There are some things which I feel I must write to you.

I regret very much that I was not told clearly before Fr. Matsumoto came to Izu that the Oiso congregation would be disbanded during his absence in Australia. The action of disbanding his congregation instead of appointing a priest-in-charge shows that he is not a priest of the Diocese in normal standing. Had that fact been as clear then as it is now I would not have taken steps to secure the Scholarship at Kelham for him; and the A.B.M. would not have given money for his training. If this information were to become known in Australia it could be very difficult to persuade the A.B.M. to keep Fr. Matsumoto in Australia.

It is also very embarrassing to have as Assistant Priest on the staff of Izu Mission a priest who is not wanted anywhere else in the Diocese although there is a great shortage of priests.

The payment of Pension Dues can easily be cleared up. I think it will be found that Fr. Matsumoto has no objection in principle to paying pension dues. Did he not pay them while he was in Tokyo Diocese? There must be some purely local trouble at Oiso which could be straightened out if brought into the open. If his pension dues must be paid while he is in Australia then I am prepared to accept responsibility for them for that period because he is "Fuku Bokushi" in Izu.

I cannot agree that Fr. Matsumoto is to blame for the situation in Oiso but all three have left the position as the result of a crisis. The two previous chaplains were mature priests. The fact that such priests had to leave makes it obvious that there is some trouble there which has not been brought in to the open. They left without blame. It is a great injustice to the third priest to let him be blamed for the trouble while the first two were honourably transferred. It is also obvious that removing the third priest will not solve the problem.

If an effort is to be made to solve the problems at Oiso surely it must be done without doing an injustice to the third of the Chaplains. Also, because you have sent him to Australia as "one of the priests of the Diocese" you owe it to the A.B.M. and to Fr. Matsumoto himself to see that he is treated as "one of the priests of the Diocese". This seem to require:

1. An open settlement of the problem of pension payments.
2. The appointment of a Priest-in-charge for the Oiso congregation so long as there is a congregation comparable to other churches in the Diocese and ready to accept normal financial responsibilities.

Yours sincerely,
Rev. Frank W. Coaldrake

Newsletter No. 61, June, 1956.

NIPPON SEIKO KWAI

From – Rev. F.W. Coaldrake

[written by Frank and Maida Coaldrake]

> St. Mary's Church,
> 960 Okaku,
> Ito,
> JAPAN.

Dear Friends,

This is really Frank's story, and like all good stories ends with a wedding. But to get it from Frank's notes to you is my job because his time is very full of so many things from parish visiting right round the Izu Peninsula to taking a dog-bite case off to hospital. Though we live in a pagan society not geared normally to calling on the Christian priest, yet we are by no means free of the demands of the doorstep. Since I took a pen to write to you there has been a goat in goat-sized basket delivered on the front door mat. The fact that it wasn't our goat was the least of the complications!

When the doorbell rings we can expect anything from goats to would-be suicides. Not that the bell always rings anyway. It is just as usual for someone to open the door and call, and not getting any immediate response, to wander upstairs looking for us. I have had bread delivered to the bedroom door. In a land where a strict code of etiquette governs one's behaviour in the "genkan"[6] or entrance porch, this ministry of the doorstep is a very important one and in some ways takes the place of the normal ministry of the study at home. You may remain in the "genkan" on a cold night engaging your host in a two-hour conversation without a qualm. But should you accept his invitation to take off your shoes and climb up into the house, you are immediately swallowed up in a bog of social convention. There is a set of formal greetings to be exchanged, tea to be drunk and afterwards the exchange of presents. We have solved this problem to a large extent by building a Queensland-style house with all the living quarters upstairs, leaving study, garage and workshop only close by the front entrance. We can then persuade our reluctant visitors to step into the study for a talk with the assurance they aren't disturbing the household.

Frank did that with one of our callers, a young man who had travelled from Tokyo across to the romantic island of Oshima, not far from Ito, with the idea of jumping into the active volcano there. After he had scaled up the side of the crater and contemplated the depths, he decided it was too lonely and caught the boat back. We gave him sandwiches and talk and sent him off back to Tokyo planning to make the best of things. Another night two people turned up avowing they were husband and wife planning to seek work on Oshima the next day. Could they sleep in our church hall? Frank felt there was something odd about them because the girl did all the talking, and also because there is little work of any kind to be had on the Island. But we sent them food and blankets and left them to themselves as they seemed to wish it so, and next day they went off to catch the early boat. One never can tell, and suicide is a respectable part of the same social code of behaviour which controls conduct in the "genkan." Yesterday Oshima Island had 72 earthquake shocks. I find it hard to imagine anyone setting up home there for choice.

But this problem of suicide dogs our footsteps, turns up in all manner of forms, is present in the paper nearly every day. Runaway lovers, unhappy wives, school children who fail in examinations, sick university students, T.B. cases and on and on in a most appalling fashion, e.g., a few days ago, this brief press announcement: "Tokyo University Pediatrist Commits Suicide. Dr. Shozo Sawada, an authority on infantile tuberculosis and head of the pediatrics department of the Tokyo University Hospital's Koishikawa Clinic, committed suicide by taking poison at his office Friday afternoon. A suicide note to his family was found at his side. His thesis on the X-ray diagnosis of the chest had just come off the press." How can we get to the bottom of this rot in society other

---

6 *Genkan:* the formal house entrance or vestibule in which one takes off shoes and puts on house slippers.

than by pressing on with the work of bringing the Light of Christ to these dark places of human experience?

Which all seems to have taken us a long way from Frank's story which has a happy ending. In fact it hasn't, for if a missionary priest with a gang of young Christian campers had not taken their stand on a village street one late Summer evening and preached the Good News to farmers resting in their open houses after the toil of harvest, there might never have been the happy ending. A young man could well have been so caught in the coils of tradition that he could have found suicide the only way out. So on to Frank's notes headed:

A Wedding with a History

An eight hundred years' long family tradition was flung aside by the young man who came to our church to be married today. He is the head of the family now that his father has died and has therefore freedom enough to make the decision in many matters. In that freedom he has chosen his own wife, and then brought her to the Church to be married by Christian rites. For eight centuries the eldest son of his family has had his wife selected by the family elders in consultation with "go-betweens" and the wedding rite has been performed in the family house. The old rite is very simple. The bride and bridegroom each take three ritual sips from each of three cups of sake (rice wine). That completes the ceremony and the religious functionary standing by then recites the rite of reporting to gods and ancestors that the two have been wed. By contrast the climax of the rite in the Church comes on those words we know so well "Those whom God hath joined together let no man put asunder." This is declaring to men what God has done, while the Japanese rite declares to the gods what men have done.

The young man wanted to be wed in this way and has had his hope fulfilled. But it takes courage to be the turning point of history. He has to know his mind about those ancestors, about the present day village neighbours and relations, and the descendants who will point back to him as the one who turned the family's destiny.

The bride too had been rather daring. Dressed in the traditional gorgeous kimono and fittings up to the neck, she had dispensed with the normal headgear and draped a short, white veil over her hair held in position by a bandeau of artificial orange blossom. Gone were the Shinto gee-gaws and the broad white cotton cloth loosely draped to prevent the sudden appearance of horns turning her into a witch. She did contrive to maintain the traditional bridal decorum – an air of doleful submission. Throughout the service and the following three hour wedding feast she didn't once raise her eyes from the floor or crack the mask of apology with a smile. At the height of the fun at the feast I thought I saw signs that she was giggling but one couldn't be sure even then.

At the time of the nuptial blessing I gave them a large Family Bible to be "The Strength and the Light" of their family on the new road which they have taken.

New Ways for the Villages

A beard trimmed in bold piratical style was the only visible thing Miyazawa-san brought back from a school for village improvement. But he brought back also a great fund of new ideas and a great inspiration. The beard was unavoidable. They worked so hard from dawn to dark that he had no time to shave. That was the measure of the keenness of the twenty-eight young farmers who formed the school. Miyazawa-san of course is not a farmer. He is a business executive turned evangelist, now working full time on our staff in Izu with special concern for village projects. He needs to pick up wherever possible more detailed knowledge of farm and village life than he has so far accumulated, though that is not inconsiderable. In thinking of ways he might do this when he started with us in September, I recalled an odd incident of three years ago.

Driving down a mountain road I caught up with a man walking and offered him a lift. As we rode along I remarked on the unusual "Homespun" material of which his overcoat was made. He told me that his wife had made the coat out of tweed which they had woven in their own house from woollen thread spun by his family from the fleece of their own sheep.

Miyazawa-san wrote to that man last October and found that he was the famous Fujisaki-Sensei, one of Kagawa's notable proteges. He runs a school in his village each year in the winter for farmers, and in the summer for their wives. The school deals with every detail of farming and village life. More than twenty eminent experts attend the school to lecture on their special subjects – Folk-craft, animal husbandry, soil erosion, soil chemistry, plant introduction, butchering, cooking, diet improvement, Bible study, village economics, rural co-operative societies, family life relationships. These and many more are worked at for the month. Just about the only thing not considered is the cultivation and use of Rice! There's realism for you. Japan's rice lands are already fully cultivated. The only hope for extension of rural wealth is to move up the mountain-sides with other crops. Rice forms the bulk of the diet, but it is a very inadequate diet, and must be balanced with products from the hillsides. The rice-growing villages are strongholds of feudalism. New spontaneous developments of democratic methods in village life are needed. The rice-farmer is essentially conservative. Japan needs adventurous young farmers who will move up the hillsides, trying new crops and new methods. Such farmers need a faith that encourages adventure.

The important bearing which a change of religion has on the whole matter is made clear by a press report this week that in a certain village the elders have just banished from the village a farmer who bought a cow – it being contrary to strict Buddhist faith to breed cattle for milk or meat.

The staff of this school have almost all studied their subject abroad, and eyes are frequently turned outside Japan to countries where hill-side cultivation is practised effectively, as in Switzerland; or where village organisation is notably democratic, as in Denmark; or where homecrafts have an economic importance, as in Scandinavia.

The school has been held regularly for over twenty years. It has found that when there are five "graduates" of the school in a village they can begin to reshape the village. The founder and chief mentor of this Village School is Kagawa, and he was one of the visiting instructors.

Easter

We had a wonderful Easter. There was no difficulty in filling the roster for the twenty-four hour Watch from Maundy Thursday morning. Easter Day, which began for us at 4 a.m., was a joyful occasion. The torrents of rain which fell all day threatening the scarcely opened cherry blossom failed to dampen our good spirits. There were baptisms in three centres, and members of several cottage-church congregations joined us at St. Mary's Ito for the lovely Sung Eucharist and lunch afterwards. Our own little housegirl, Kimiyo-san, was among those baptised here in Ito. Bill insisted in standing alongside her in case she should feel shy.

Easter Monday brought an English visitor for a week's stay. He is the Rev. Dr. George Gibson, Community of St. Hilda, in Japan on a short-term lectureship at St. Paul's University, Tokyo. Later in the week, on Bill's fourth birthday, Frank went to Tokyo to meet Alma Hartshorn, who had arrived the previous night by air from Rangoon, via Bangkok and Hong Kong. She was on the first lap of a roundabout route to England which would embrace the Frank Whytes in Calcutta and a minor continental tour with May Richardson. Alma, in case some of you haven't caught up with her yet, has been working for a year with W.H.O. Technical Assistance in Burma alongside native specialists in social services.

We had a wonderful time together, and found it very difficult to drag ourselves away from talk and colour slides to get a little necessary sleep. Both George and Alma made some very strenuous trips with Frank in the Land Rover to remote parts of this mountainous peninsula, and being camera enthusiasts became quite drunk with the beauty and long lastingness of this year's cherry blossom.

Now the cherry has faded but the mountains are shaded out in every imaginable green and bronze, lit here and there with the mauves and pinks of the azalea. I have a long drawn out argument with myself each year as to which is the more beautiful, cherry or azalea. I wish you could come and see for yourselves and help me make up my mind.

Missionary Conference

Dr. Gibson left us to take a retreat for missionaries at an All-Japan Anglican missionaries Conference at Kobe. Frank went off the next night by the all-night express to one day of the conference and returned the following night. His enthusiasm on return was in no way diminished by the fact that he stood up all the way from Kobe to Atami, our nearest rail junction, ten hours flat! The train was so crowded that there wasn't even room to sit on the floor! The trains, for all except those who are fortunate enough to secure reserve accommodation in special cars, are always like that on the north-south run, another reminder that Japan is an exceedingly crowded country.

About seventy missionaries from all over Japan attended the conference, the majority being Americans. Frank found it most stimulating. The Bishop of Hong Kong was particulary arresting with his address on the Church in China.

General Synod of the Japanese Church

In the week after Easter the clerical and lay representatives of each of our ten dioceses met with the Bishops in the 25th General Synod of the Nippon Seiko Kwai. Much time was spent planning the celebrations of the hundredth anniversary of the arrival of the first Anglican Missionary in Japan in 1859. A very important, and even hazardous, step was taken in adopting the text of a Revised Prayer Book.

Newsletter *Addresses*

We've been more than delighted to receive your letters and feel we shall have to finish with an acknowledgement column each issue if we aren't careful. And we are sorry that some of you who have been getting – and using so well – several copies of [the] *Newsletter* have had to make do with one. But we ran out of copies of No. 60 owing to a greatly revised mailing list and would once more urge you to send to:

> MRS. E.R. COALDRAKE,
> 33 HAMILTON RD.,
> NUNDAH, QUEENSLAND.

your own address and those of any of your friends to whom you used to hand on a copy. And thank you for the postal notes.

> With every good wish,
>   Yours affectionately,
>   MAIDA and FRANK COALDRAKE

Newsletter No. 62, August, 1956.

NIPPON SEIKO KWAI

From – Rev. F.W. Coaldrake

[written by Frank Coaldrake]

> St. Mary's Church,
> 960 Okaku,
> Ito,
> JAPAN.
> St. Barnabas' Day [11 June]

Dear Friends,

Today is the ninth anniversary of my first arrival in Japan.

The war was everywhere obvious as I travelled across the country that day. I was taken to see Hiroshima and marvelled at the spirit of the people even then rebuilding the city that had disappeared in a flash. The noise of countless hammers was the thing that impressed me as I stood on the top of the shell of a blasted building.

On that day I learned what most of us Australians had barely been remembering then, and will have forgotten by now. It was the extent to which the Japanese cities had been treated to old-fashioned bombing. Two cities were atom-bombed. Only one city of over one hundred thousand population in the whole of the country was spared conventional bomb raids. Every city or town I passed through that day was more than half destroyed. There's nothing so completely desolate looking as an acre or two of ashes and rubble with a great smoke-stack standing orphaned in the middle.

Japan was Destroyed

Japan in those days was battered, burnt, ragged and starving. Population had been increased in one year by seven million persons because the armies and the colonists had been brought home. To feed and clothe and house the seventy million with the resources of these four small islands would be impossible at the best of times, but with those islands pulverised, the situation was hopeless. And there was a lack of hope in the people one saw standing in queues, sitting in gutters, clinging to the few trains, or feverishly padding along the streets.

American help – Australian?

The army of Occupation was very much in evidence, and I was soon to learn that this army and the help it was bringing was really the only hope for the country. Much has been written about the Occupation but the thing I remember today is that the ordinary soldiers could not resist the sight of suffering and starvation. They did what they could – but Australians back home were horrified at the thought of Australian troops fraternising with the Japanese. Consequently Australians were able to do little compared with what the Americans could do. On top of that the American government proceeded to pour relief food and clothing into Japan. They followed up with technical advisors and raw materials and enabled the Japanese to rebuild and realign their country. Much of what was inspired by the Occupation has taken a deep hold on the wills and affections of the people and is not likely to be lost, though, of course, changes have taken place.

I remember the train I rode in that day was the only train I was to see for nearly three years that had glass in the windows – I was carried by the army in one of its "specials." In fact, for the first year or more I was entirely the responsibility of the Australian Army, though in fact they never attempted to limit my freedom. Without the privilege of buying food from their canteen I would not have been able to live.

"Cholera Area" – Keep Out!

My work was to take me to many parts of the country and I soon learned to ignore not only the M.P.'s "Off limits" signs but also the Medical Corps notices advising which particular disease was loose in a particular area – "Typhoid," "Cholera." Injections seemed to have some point, until we found that the bothersome "Encephalitis" series were proved to be no use against that particular Japanese wog.

Odawara

As I travelled towards Tokyo that day my train took me through Mishima, Atami and Odawara. I was to come back to Odawara in two weeks and back through Atami to Ito and Mishima and the rest of Izu in two years. If I had known where to look I could have seen the thatch roof of the Odawara farm house that was to be my first home and to which I was to bring Maida three years later. That old thatch is still there. The nine years that I have known the house are but a day in the span of six hundred years since its great rough timbers were first erected.

Famous Exiles in Izu

If I had known where to look I could have seen the mountains of Izu, among which we now live. I had known about Izu before I left Australia. A forbidding peninsula, mountainous and inaccessible, it was the favourite place for governments to send their exiles through many centuries of Japanese history. Two of those exiles came back from Izu to effect Japan's greatest revolutions. One, political, Yoritomo [Minamoto Yoritomo, 1147–1199] in the 12th century setting up the military control over the Emperor and government which was to last until MacArthur arrived.[7] (Japanese rulers were old hands at military dictatorship before Hitler was born!) The other rebel was a Buddhist sage, Nichiren [1222–82]. He founded a new sect, and it remains to this day the only actively proselytizing Buddhist sect.

After two years of general movement around the churches of a wide area while technically being responsible for a job in the one – Odawara – I was to find myself sent by the Bishop into Izu. He assured me that I was not being sent into exile! Izu was at the hub of the Diocese but was such difficult terrain and the villagers so conservative that the church had never been able to get a footing in the area.

As I write now, I am within a stone's throw of the last remaining glade of the wood that was used by Yoritomo for his far from reputable wooing of the local baron's daughter when he was here in exile seven hundred and fifty years ago. The shrine in that wood still holds a "flirting" festival there each year commemorating the event.

---

7 This statement reflects the impact of wartime propaganda. The Tokugawa warrior shogunate was actually abolished in 1868.

First Englishman in Ito

Every morning at six we hear the boom of the great bell at the temple in which Nichiren chanted and taught seven hundred years ago.

Out of the window I can see the lights of the inns standing on the bank of the river where three hundred and fifty years ago the first Englishman to come to Japan, the ship-wrecked William Adams, taught the Japanese to build ocean-going ships. In another month or so the annual celebration of his achievements will be marked by the launching of a fifteen foot model of one of the ships he built. His ships sailed to America and the Philippines. This trim little model will sail around the bay for a week, moving among the fishing boats of today coming and going between Ito and the Coral Sea or intermediate fishing grounds. The latest Japanese fishing boats, complete with shortwave radio and radar, still incorporate lines and features taught first by Will Adams in Ito.

Will Adams' lessons of three hundred and fifty years ago were well taught. If only I might be half as effective in the building of that which has often through the centuries been called a ship – the Church.

At this moment I should like to draw a map. Perhaps there will be room for one in the next letter. I want to show you how we have effectively made inroads into the villages in this peninsula. Mountains hold no terrors for hikers and Land Rovers. In fact since we started our travelling in Izu there has been a constant opening up and improving of roads. One may travel now by Cadillac or Morris Minor to many places which at first proved too much for a jeep. In fact Izu reduced my jeep to a scrap heap and forced me to take to a Land Rover. The day when it will be possible to get to many of the villages in anything else is still far distant although main roads are improving.

State of the Mission

We have thirteen places of regular meetings or services now, and another four in the preliminary stages of development. We have a regular monthly schedule of 45 services or bible classes scattered over the whole of our 3000 square miles of parish. Some of these are conducted by lay-people and we have made appreciable progress in developing leadership among the people. Our one big handicap is shortage of staff. Money for salaries is the only thing that prevents an increase of staff! Absolutely the best thing you can do to help us is to send contributions to the Australian Board of Missions ticketted for work in Japan.

Lay Evangelist and Priest

Miyazawa-san, appointed by the Bishop and supported by a grant from A.B.M., is proving very able and industrious, especially in the village centres. The group at St. Peter's, Launceston, who gave him his sleeping bag, would be interested to see him setting off for the villages with ruck-sack on back in which he carries literature, food and sleeping bag.

A Japanese priest helps temporarily by spending three days in Izu once each month.

Committee for Self-management

A committee is elected by church members each year to help manage affairs in Izu. Training this committee to take responsibility has been one of my chief concerns. This year we have made a great step forward because the committee has adopted an "Every-member Budget." (If we keep up we will never need an "Every member Canvass"!) An income of £140 has been budgeted. This will be used for selected "token" items from the whole range of Mission expenses, bread and wine, monthly bulletin printing, Diocesan dues, and the like. Also, most significant of all, £2/10 – per **month** for clergy stipend. This is paid into my hands at the end of each month and I bank it. At the end of the year I will consult the Committee and decide how to use it. It is a necessary part of learning to run the church.

It is my plan that the Committee should move steadily towards the goal of self-management and financial independence. Next year the members will start on the very long project of building for themselves a permanent church. We are very grateful to Mr. Louis Williams of Melbourne for giving us the sketched design of a most beautiful building.

Hostel

The Hostel in Ito has been enlarged and improved with the money granted by the A.B.M. in 1954. It is fulfilling its purpose in three ways: 1. A transient Hostel for Church people on journeys through Ito. 2. A Conference House for schools for village people. 3. A Resident Hostel for Church children at school in Ito.

Relations with the Diocese

Relation of Mission to Native Church is a great subject of discussion in church circles today. We have now functioned for six and a half years as a Mission within the Diocese, responsibility for management and finance being finally in the hands of the missionary, licensed to his task by the Bishop of South Tokyo. Our membership and financial strength have increased in that time so that we now rank, in those two points, 14th in the 28 churches of the Diocese, all but two of them being older churches.

The Bishop and Standing Committee are now discussing with us the possibility of changing the "Izu Mission" into the "Anglican Church in Izu." (Fig. 46)

Yours affectionately,

Frank and Maida Coaldrake

P.S. While waiting for the page proofs of this letter we have received a most surprising cable from the Archbishop of Sydney. As President of the Australian Board of Missions he offered me the Chairmanship of the Board from January 1957. As most of you will know by the time you read this I have accepted the offer. It means leaving Izu and all the work we have in hand. As soon as possible another missionary must be sent to take our place. To leave this young church without experienced guidance at this stage would be like taking the framework away from well-poured concrete before it had hardened. We would have preferred to stay on in Japan but we believe we can see the will of God in the change even though our personal feelings were summed up by Maida's "I feel as though I'd lost a pound and found sixpence..." F.

53:560

The cost of printing and posting this *Newsletter* would be covered if readers sent us five shillings a year. We are posting to 560 persons each month. So far this year 53 have sent us this help, but some have sent double or more the amount so we are holding our own month by month.

The best way is to send an open Postal Note for 5/- to:

MRS. E.R. COALDRAKE,
33 HAMILTON RD.,
NUNDAH, QLD.

A receipt will be sent in acknowledgement.

Names of new readers and changes of address should also be sent there.

Printed by Kokusai Press, Tokyo, Japan.

Letter from Frank Coaldrake to Bishop Isaac Hidetoshi Nosse, 26 July 1956.

> St. Mary's Church,
> 960 Oka-ku,
> Ito-shi.
> 26/7/56

The Rt. Rev. Isaac H. Nosse,
Bishop of South Tokyo,
Kugenuma.

Dear Bishop,

I have just received advice from The Primate of Australia that they want me to be Chairman of the Australian Board of Missions in place of Archdeacon Robertson who is retiring at the end of this year.

The Chairman is the officer responsible to the Mission of General Synod for all the Missionary activities of the Anglican Church in Australia.

Only my sense of commitment to the work in Izu makes it a difficult matter to decide, but I have reached the conclusion that this is indeed a calling of God to work for Missions not only in Japan and I want to accept the position.

I am writing my acceptance.

I hope I may have your approval and blessing.

Shall I come and see you?

    Yours sincerely,

        Frank W. Coaldrake

Letter from Bishop Isaac Hidetoshi Nosse to Archdeacon C.S. Robertson, Chairman of the Australian Board of Missions, 28 September 1956.

DIOCESE OF SOUTH TOKYO, JAPAN

49 Shimomachi,
Mitsusawa,
Kanagawa-ku,
Yokohama,
Japan.
28/9/56

The Venerable,

The Chairman,

Australian Board of Missions,

14 Spring Street,

Sydney.

Dear Mr. Archdeacon,

It is with very deep regret that I have given my approval to Fr. Coaldrake's acceptance of the offer of the Chairmanship of the Board. His missionary service with us has been marked by several conspicuous features, notably the witness of family life and its extension in the Hostel at Ito; the constant retention of the view of the whole task in Izu Peninsula as a whole rather than in just one town; the teaching of the centrality of the church rather than the individual believer with consequent solidity of the church now established firmly in the villages of Izu; the fundamental position of worship in the life of individual and church; the importance for Japan of converting villages to Christianity; the strength of character to set a course and follow it despite indifference or opposition; and finally the strength to travel hard. We are very sorry to think that he must leave us.

I wish to ask the Board to send us another priest to take his place. The Standing Committee of the Diocese, the Izu Church Committee and the people of the Diocese are all as anxious as I am that the next priest in Izu should be a priest from Australia to continue Fr. Coaldrake's work. I hope it may be possible to send us a priest very soon, even as soon as the beginning of 1957 so that there may be no gap in the Australian ministry in Izu.

The problem of language for the new priest will be greatly lessened by the fact that first Fr. Azuma then Fr. Matsumoto are already appointed to serve as assistant priests in Izu immediately upon return from Australia. With the assured assistance of a priest able to speak English for at least the next three years the missionary will be able to serve Izu as Chief Priest from the time of his arrival while concentrating on the study of the language during the first year or two. It is indeed providential that the Board has provided study in Australia for two of our priests at this time.

The missionary priest we would like you to send should be able to take up and extend the work so well begun by Fr. Coaldrake. He is to be Chief Priest in Izu and will, if I am able to do what I hope in the near future, have a team of two Japanese priests and two theological students with him permanently. He should be capable of such leadership. He must have strength of character and be able to stand up to hard travelling. The witness of family life is so important in Japan today that we earnestly request a married priest. There is a very good house in Ito. I would hope that he had a good grip of the doctrine of the church and a willingness to love the Japanese farmers and fishermen. I should also hope to find him willing to settle down for a long period of service in Izu.

Yours very sincerely,

Izu Mission Meetings. Unofficial Minutes kept by F.W.C. [handwritten].

At Ito Hostel. 16/9/56.

<u>Present</u>: Harada, Takashima, Ihara, Osawa, Fukuo, Naito, Miyazawa, F.W.C.

... 7. Sonota [Other business]

F.W.C. reported:

F.W.C. appointed Chairman of A.B.M. from January 1957. To leave end of December. Father Azuma to arrive from Australia November 30 and take charge of Izu. Bishop Nosse will ask for another missionary from A.B.M. Probably not arrive before February at the earliest...

Izu Mission Meetings. Unofficial Minutes kept by F.W.C. [handwritten].

At Shimoda, Naito House. 20/12/56.

<u>Present</u>: Father Azuma [just arrived back from Australia], Miyazawa, Osawa, Naito, Kawai, Harada, Takashima.

Opened with prayer at 1.15 p.m.

1. Welcomed Father Azuma to Izu as Assistant Priest [and Acting Rector after Frank Coaldrake's departure]...

8. Izu After the Departure of F.W.C.:

F.W.C.: re. "Spontaneity of Church in Izu."
Duties of Priest and Laity as attached...
[Attachment] To Father Azuma and then Committee,

Post-Missionary Izu:

>   Reference: Early Minutes. First statement of danger of dependence on Priest
>   or Missionary.[8]
>
>   Query: How to make for <u>Spontaneous Expansion</u> of Church in Izu.
>
>   <u>Now</u>: C[oaldrake] going: What follows? 10 years no church?

The first duty of a Priest in Izu is:

>   Pray for and visit and care for sick and dying. N.B. dying, not died. Hence,
>   phone and phone number cards.
>
>   *Gappo* [the earnest desire for the Resurrection] quote rubric from Prayer Book.
>
>   <u>Why?</u> Baptised were by Grace made inheritors of [the] Kingdom of Heaven
>   and Church must bring comfort and grace to help prepare to enter into [this]
>   inheritance.

The second duty of Priest in Izu:

>   To maintain the schedule of services ministering to the faithful and offering
>   praise and prayer to God as our "reasonable service," *tsutomu* [lit. "work"].
>
>   The schedule in Izu has always been decided by laity representatives on [the
>   Izu Church] committee. It should not be added to or altered without
>   reference to the Committee (except in emergency).
>
>   [added in pencil] Compiling schedule should remember Priest's duty to study
>   and pray privately.
>
>   The priest will make unscheduled efforts to form new congregations and then
>   consult [the] Committee about inclusion in schedule. In Izu we have always
>   tried to remember that O.B.L. [Our Blessed Lord] called adults into the
>   Church. (not children into Sunday School.) He blessed the children but talked
>   over their heads to the adults. We do not want to start more Sunday Schools
>   in Izu, but we must baptise, instruct and care for children of the Church.

The first duty of the laity in Izu:

>   is "to assemble themselves together..." quote from card [a wall card
>   circulated for each family, not included in these records].
>
>   Hence: 1. *Reihai Jikan* [service times] and wall card which please renew in
>   every house.
>
>   Hence: 2. *Katei Kyokai* [Cottage Churches], which should aim to each hold
>   services regularly each Sunday.

The second duty of the laity in Izu:

>   is to spread the Gospel Goodnews by prayer, word and deed, like St. Andrew
>   starting with prayers for conversion of his own family, then neighbours, and
>   ultimately ["every soul" deleted] in the Izu portion of "all people who beseech

---

8 See *chapter 6: Izu Mission Meetings. Unofficial Minutes kept by F.W.C.* [handwritten]. Meeting at
   Imaihama on 2/10/50. "2. Relations between Izu Dendo [Evangelism] Mission and Diocese."

God." I have asked Father Azuma to make special efforts to help people with their own families.

Any layman is able to prepare people for *Shigwanshiki* [Admission of Catechumens], and should be prepared to serve as godparents of that person (Godparents linked from time of *Shigwanshiki*!).

The Third duty of the laity in Izu:

is to share in the financial burden of maintaining the Church's life of witness in Izu. The Izu Budget should be "a *hitori nokorazu* budget" [a budget from each person without exception].

The Third duty of the Priest in Izu:

is to help, lead and encourage the laity if they misunderstand or fail in their second duty.

Colour slide talk on Japan – notes Frank Coaldrake, c.1958.

(Fig. 46) Photograph of two Japanese Church documents. On the right: the Licence of the Bishop of the Diocese of South Tokyo to Frank W. Coaldrake as Rector of the Church in Izu. On the left: the Bishop's Certificate of Institution of

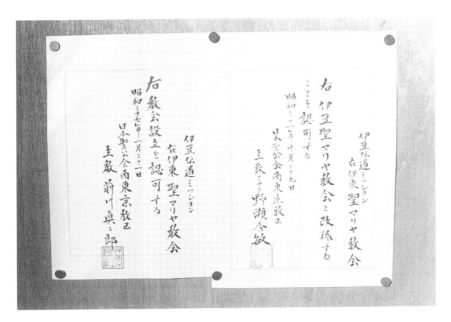

Figure 46 Left: The authorization from the Bishop of South Tokyo to establish St. Mary's Church, Izu, 21 January 1952. Right: The Bishop's Certificate of institution of St. Mary's Church, Izu as a full parish in the Diocese of South Tokyo, marking the completion of the Izu Mission, October, 1956.

St. Mary's Church, Izu in October 1956, marking the completion of the first phase of the Izu programme. Up to that time there was a "Mission" in Izu, but on that date the Diocese recognized that it had obtained the strength and experience entitling it to be instituted as a Church. The "Mission" had been instituted on St. Andrew's Day, 1949, the seven year's development as a "Mission" resulting in recognition as a Church with its own budget, its own Japanese staff and responsible for the life and extension of the Church in that area. This indicates the success of the work of the Australian Church in Izu. This is one of the "Younger Churches" within the diocese of South Tokyo. It is still weak in numbers and financial strength and still asks for continuing help from the church in Australia...

Newsletter No. 63, November, 1956.

NIPPON SEIKO KWAI

From – Rev. F.W. Coaldrake (Fig. 47)

[written by Frank Coaldrake]

> St. Mary's Church,
> 960 Okaku,
> Ito,
> JAPAN.

Dear Friends,

Our days in Japan are numbered. We wish now that we had written many more *Newsletters* so that we might have told you much more about Japan and her people. We feel that we haven't succeeded yet in bringing you to understand and appreciate these people who are most hated by Australians – the Japanese. And how Australians fear them! And how ridiculous that is, how futile. Someone else from Australia will come to Izu and will almost certainly write *Newsletters*. It is our great hope that you will continue to read about life in Izu and come to see the kind of people we are loathe to leave.

The Position in Izu

These last months are being spent tying up loose ends. There seem to be endless lines of people waiting to move a stage further along the way of Christian progress. Some who have been "hopers" for years want to become catechumens, others want to be baptised, others confirmed, others married. There are parents with problem children wanting the problems straightened out. Fishermen, with no fishing grounds wanting permits from the Australia Government, clamour for an interview. A government horticulturalist with recently discovered passionfruit wants an introduction to Cottee's and an analysis of the food composition of the fruit – never mind about its taste! The Bishop wants to increase the Japanese staff in Izu by four so they may be trained by the Australian priest!

Figure 47 Frank Coaldrake. St. Thomas' Day (21 December) 1956. The last photograph in Itō.

It seems to be quite an impossible time to be planning to leave. But there is no reason why these jobs may not be done by another. My achievement if any seems to have been to set up the work. For the next three years at least there will be an assistant Japanese priest who has just returned from Australia and can speak English. The Revd. Samuel Azuma went to St. Michael's House (Kelham) in Adelaide at the beginning of 1955 and will return to work in Izu this month. The Revd. John Matsumoto went to the same place at the beginning of 1956 and will return at the end of 1957 taking Fr. Azuma's place in Izu and continuing there for two years. Both these priests are in their thirties and after two years in Kelham should be each in his turn a tower of strength to the new missionary priest. It is a splendid situation into which to bring a new missionary and had been planned a long time ago. If we had set out to plan for my recall we could not have done better.

I am reluctantly convinced that the Lord can do very well without the Coaldrakes in Izu.

Also there are now six Romney Marsh sheep from Australia in Izu. The day they arrived we received the cable calling us home. In another month there will also be six Corriedale sheep. Mr. Palmer of Terang sent the Romneys and Mr. Bailey of Cressy the Corriedales. The arrival of these sheep marks the beginning of a long thought-of plan for the improvement of village life in Izu. Farmers have been trained beforehand in the care of the sheep and their women folk are being taught spinning and weaving. The "Izu Farmers Progress Association" has been established to carry out the project as we have conceived it. There has been just nice time to get the project established. Its future lies, not in the hands of a foreign missionary but in the hands of the farmers themselves.

The Future

Of the future we can write little but speculation. I cannot imagine how the Board could ever have dared offer the Chairmanship to Coaldrake. My own view of my past convinces me that they have made a very risky choice. But they undoubtedly had said their prayers before they decided so the only thing for me to do is to say mine now. And you too please.

It is of course a great joy to be moving into a job concerned to extend the Church ever wider and wider. I know what the Gospel can mean to people who have never known it and it is wonderful to think I might have a hand in bringing it to people in the villages of New Guinea, Borneo and Malaya as well as Australia and Izu.

We are to leave Japan by plane at noon on December 28th having celebrated Christmas in Izu. We will arrive in Sydney at 4.45 p.m. on December 29th. Qantas makes it all sound quite simple, and except for luggage it will be. The Board is providing a house which is being purchased now and will perhaps be somewhere on the North Shore Line. The Sydney office of the Board, at 14 Spring Street, will be our address and the "grindstone" for this nose for a long time to come.

Sayonara

These *Newsletters* have gone out for nearly ten years to an ever widening circle of readers. We now send 600 copies and they seem to be passed around and read at groups so that the actual number of readers is unknown. We have written for two reasons, the first being that you have so often urged us to write more. Several times it has been suggested that we publish the letters in book form. They are, however, so full of purely personal allusions that we have always put the suggestions aside. The second reason you would hardly guess. The letters have brought us wonderful sustaining encouragement in the knowledge of your interest and prayers. We have never been alone here and in times of difficulty we have been sure of being upheld by you.

For this, and also for your gifts, we cannot find type that is not too cold to express our feelings.

We could make no better bequest to our successor than your continuing friendship for Izu.

"Well then," as the customary Japanese farewell quaintly puts it, "if that is so remember honourable body's importance." ("Dewa, Sayonara, o-karada wo daiji ni.") Only because we ourselves are somewhat orientalised our nearly slanting eyes will not weep.

Frank and Maida

[Another missionary was sent, after which A.B.M. made the decision that the Izu Church should be supported by its own community. In 1995, a new church building was erected on the site of Frank Coaldrake's temporary church of 1952.]

9   Requiem (1970)

Frank Coaldrake was suddenly recalled to Australia to become Chairman of the Australian Board of Missions, the organisation which had sent him to Japan in the first place. A family photograph taken in late 1957 shows the growing children, including Kimi, born in April 1957. (Fig. 48) The Board wanted his field experience as well as his strategic thinking, even though he was not a Bishop as was more usually the case. He was reluctant to leave Japan, but accepted the position because it was the key strategic position for the "mission" of the Anglican Church of Australia, with responsibility for overseas missions throughout the Asia and Pacific, including Papua New Guinea, and Australian missions to Aboriginals and Torres Strait Islanders. Some of his later ideas are set out in collected papers entitled *Flood Tide in the Pacific: Church and Community Cascade into a New Age.*[1]

For the next thirteen years he was to work to professionalise mission training, and move mission into the post-colonial era, emphasizing partnership and collaboration with the emerging churches of the Asia-Pacific. He was to help draft the key strategic document of the Anglican Church on mission at the Anglican World Congress in Toronto, 1963, the document called *Mutual Responsibility and Interdependence* which rejected colonialism and stressed partnership and equality of member churches. Both Frank and Maida Coaldrake were delegates at this Congress. Frank Coaldrake helped draft the epochal document which stated in relation to the church's mission that a "single mission holds us together in one Body. To use the words 'older' or 'younger' or 'sending' or 'receiving' with respect to Churches is unreal and untrue in the world and in our Communion. Mission is not the kindness of the lucky to the unlucky; it is mutual, united obedience to the one God whose mission it is. The form of the Church must reflect that."[2] The experience and example of the Coaldrake

---

1 Stanmore, N.S.W., Australian Board of Missions, 1963.
2 See: E. R. Fairweather (ed.), *Anglican Congress 1963. Report of Proceedings*, Toronto, Editorial Committee Anglican Congress, 1963, pp. 120–121. See also Michael Challen, *Holy Persons – Frank Coaldrake*, text of Sermon given by the Right Reverend Michael Challen, [then] Executive Director, The Brotherhood of St. Laurence, St. Paul's Cathedral, Palm Sunday, 5 April 1998, Evensong Lenten Series, p. 7.

Figure 48 The Coaldrake Family, Sydney, Christmas, 1957. Kimi was born in April of that year.

mission of reconciliation to Japan lay behind Frank Coaldrake's contribution at Toronto.[3]

He was to feel constrained from commenting publicly on issues of social justice, pacifism and Australia-Japan relations out of concern that it might compromise the work of the A.B.M. He declined the offers of several episcopacies, on the grounds that he had come back from Japan only to pursue the work of the A.B.M. in the broader mission context.

He drove himself hard, both as an administrator, and in extensive field trips throughout Asia, the Pacific and Australia. He was elected Archbishop of Brisbane on 10 July 1970, a bold recognition by the Anglican Church of one of its radical figures. He died suddenly just twelve days later of a heart attack, before he could be installed as Archbishop. His title at the end of his life was thus "Archbishop Elect of Brisbane and Metropolitan Elect of Queensland."[4] He was the first Australian

3 On one occasion at another international conference on mission he was interrupted during a speech by an Asian or African delegate who accused him of being a white colonial who spoke no language but imperial English. The rest of the speech was immediately delivered in Japanese.

4 Section 17 of the *Constitution of the Province of Queensland* (of the Anglican Church), as it stood in 1970, stated: "When an election has been confirmed or an appointment made by the authority in or to whom the same is vested or delegated, as the case may be, the Bishop so elected or appointed shall be the Metropolitan and Bishop of the Metropolitan See, and shall be entitled to exercise the functions of such Metropolitan, as from the date of his enthronement in the Cathedral Church of the Metropolitan See." Possession of the office of Archbishop, including the title "Archbishop Elect", therefore dated from election while exercize of the office would have dated from enthronement. Letter from Dr. Phillip Aspinall, Archbishop of Brisbane, 12 July 2002.

and the first Queenslander to be elected Archbishop of Brisbane. It was highly unusual for a priest not already a bishop to be chosen as an archbishop. The nearly unanimous vote for him on the first ballot represented a new recognition and acceptance of his leadership in mission and in reconciliation both within Australia and in the Asia-Pacific region.

The two documents in this chapter are extracts from the euologies of the two Requiem Masses of 1970. One is by an Australian bishop, the other by a Japanese bishop. The first is from the Eulogy delivered by Bishop Felix Arnott at Frank Coaldrake's Requiem Mass, at Christ Church St. Laurence in Sydney. Bishop Arnott was to be elected Archbishop of Brisbane a month later. Bishop Arnott had married Frank and Maida Coaldrake at the same church in 1949. The second document comprises extracts from the Eulogy preached by Bishop Isaac Hidetoshi Nosse at the Requiem Mass at St. Mary's Church, Izu, the church founded by Frank Coaldrake. Bishop Nosse was Bishop of the Diocese of South Tokyo (later Yokohama) from 1953, during the later three years of the Coaldrake mission.

Eulogy by Bishop Felix Arnott at the Solemn Requiem at Christ Church St. Laurence, Sydney, for Frank William Coaldrake, Chairman of the Australian Board of Missions and Archbishop Elect of Brisbane, on Friday, 24 July 1970.

(Reprinted from *A.B.M. Review,* vol. 60, no. 5, Oct.–Nov. 1970, pp. 8–10, with permission.)

John 5:35: "He was a lamp, a light and shining, and for a time you were content to enjoy the light that he gave."

... In Frank Coaldrake there was much of the spirit of John Baptist. All his life he was a burning and shining light to many, and we rejoice in his light. He was a leader in every respect, a man of courage, one who had a prophetic vision, and above all a man of God.

For 10 years he was in Japan. He was the only European in the Diocese of Yokohama [formerly South Tokyo]. It was a difficult age, that post-war age. He went into the district of Izu, an isolated and mountainous district of over a quarter of a million people, in fishing and farming communities. He was very happy there.

He returned to Australia in 1956 to become Chairman of A.B.M. He was a great Chairman and a great missionary statesman. He travelled to mission stations throughout New Guinea and the Pacific. He became an acknowledged leader both of the missionary movement and of the ecumenical development. He was one of the figures to be reckoned with at the Toronto Conference, and the M.R.I. [*Mutual Responsibility and Interdependence*] document owed a good deal to him.

The qualities of leadership he had shown made him the obvious choice for Brisbane when Sir Philip Strong retired and, as I have said, his appointment inspired universal joy. He was looking forward to it. I know how happy those twelve days were but God had other work for him to do, and God consecrated him in his own particular way, quietly, as he slept into his presence. He was a burning and a shining light, a John. He was a man who had the courage of a prophet.

It is rather hard, looking back over 30 years, to understand what it meant to be a pacifist in the years before and during the war. Frank Coaldrake was an unashamed pacifist of a very creative kind, who edited a pacifist newspaper in his spare time. His conscience was outraged by all that went on in the war. It cost breaks with many of his friends and great suffering. He felt all the agony. He was a great Australian, but like Jeremiah he felt his protest must be made and he did not spare himself. It was because of that background that he felt called to go to Japan, and he broke with much of the past and many attractive offers that could have been made to him here. This to him was a real Christian attempt to live out the life of reconciliation between enemies to which he had devoted so much of his youth and energy...

"He was a burning and shining light." I have said a lamp must be lit, but the lamp of Frank's life was surely lit by God. He was convinced of it, for he was a man of deep personal religion and a sense of vocation that communicated itself to all his friends. Like John he was more than a prophet. He was truly a man of God, one who in his preaching and all his work and every department of his life proclaimed the way of the Lord.

... The Old Testament day begins at evening and ends with the going down of the sun. The day of the New Testament Church begins with the break of day and ends with the dawning light of the next morning. It is the time of fulfillment, the resurrection of the Lord. At night Christ was born, a light in the darkness. Noon turned to night when Christ suffered and died on the Cross, but in the dawn of Easter morning, Christ rose in victory from the grave... At the break of the day the Church remembers the morning on which death and sin lay prostrate in defeat and new life and salvation were given to mankind.

In the same faith, on this lovely morning, and in the early mornings to come, we will remember Frank Coaldrake, and thank God that in him he gave us a shining light.

Eulogy by Bishop Isaac Hidetoshi Nosse, retired Bishop of South Tokyo, 3 September 1970, at St. Mary's Church, Izu. [Translated by Bishop Nosse.]

[The Requiem vestments made by the Izu Women's Guild were worn.] (Fig. 49)

In this church that he built we wish to remember Father Coaldrake today, and think about what he has done with all our heart and sorrow and gratitude.

Father Coaldrake dedicated his whole life to God, and worked actively as a servant of God, always lead by the far-reaching vision and always walking at the

Figure 49 Requiem vestments made by the Izu Women's Guild in 1958.

head of us. At the age of 58 he was elected Archbishop of Brisbane, which is his hometown, and Metropolitan of Queensland, which is a very vast area. And twelve days afterward, on July 22nd, he was called back by God and passed away to his heavenly home.

Not only the grief of his family but of the whole of Australian Seikōkai, especially that of the Diocese of Brisbane, was great; they had been in the midst of their joy to have the first Brisbane-born Archbishop because the preceding archbishops were all British-born. Telegraphs and letters of congratulations, radios and televisions were whirling all about him; everybody all over Australia was elated and pleased and was expectant because he would surely breathe fresh air into the Australian Seikōkai and the outcome would be bright and soaring up high. Father [Coaldrake] laughed when a university friend who is a confirmed atheist sent him a telegram which said, "It is the proof of wisdom that flows deep down in the river of Church of England that you were elected Archbishop."

... [in 1947] he came up to Japan, sent by the Australian Seikōkai. He was the first civilian who came to Japan from Australia after the war.

He lived like a hermit in a detached room that belonged to the house of the Murotas in Odawara. He called young people together and lived with them, sleeping on bare floors and worked for their training. He sometimes had camps for boys. Kubota, Kimata, Sato, Ishikawa, Kakiuchi, Yamazaki and others helped Father at those camps and have all dedicated themselves for priesthood. Fr. Coaldrake's sincerity and straightforwardness as a servant of God made people around him earnest and sincere.

Studying Japanese at Odawara and getting to know Japanese people more and more, he thought it right to follow the advice of a bishop who told him that the Gospel for fishermen and farmers is more important than the town people, and displayed his unique missionary work on the Izu Peninsula and propagated his mission. If someone was looking out of a window of a farmer's cottage, he would raise his voice and talk about the word of God. If fishermen were sitting about the boats that had been pulled up on to the beach, he would go near to them and told them earnestly about the Gospel. Sheep would suit the hilly regions of the Izu, he thought. And they were imported and prospered over the hills of the Izu. For kindling wood the eucalyptus and the acacia which are quick to grow would be good, he thought, and they were transplanted from Australia. Now they are growing profusely everywhere in Izu district. Everybody was charmed by his unique sweet eyes and the earnest and active way he always carried himself. At the time the roads from Ito to Shimoda were very bad and usually it took two hours to cover. But for Father it was 40 minutes' drive in his flying jeep. In this jeep he did his visiting and he took people to their homes. He built a Church and a rectory in Ito and held Holy Communion every Sunday and the morning and evening services every day, and an orderly atmosphere prevailed which was the result of his love of order. He associated with people of different classes, and in this church he received and was called upon by many people.

The Australian Seikōkai sent word to him and reminded him that Australian mission covers all the areas of the Pacific, and requested him to become the chairman of the Australian Board of Missions. Father declined, saying that his mission was in Japan. However, they insisted that, since he was dedicated to God, their wish was for him to display his mission for the sake of the whole Pacific area and that it was the request of the whole of the Australian Seikōkai. Father succumbed and was appointed to this important post. Just as was expected, he invigorated the missionary work of the whole Pacific area and left his footprints on Pacific islands and on Korea... Father Coaldrake had a habit of biting his pipe. It is well known that there are marks of deep tooth bites on his pipe. When discussions became hot and his opinion did not seem to be accepted, he first bit his pipe with a cutting sound and then stood up and smiled and said that he would succumb to other opinions. His admirers say that the visions he saw always materialised in due time... Father was a candid and sincere man who did what he said. Anything he could do he did and he would not let other people do it for him. He never wasted time. He made this church and the rectory with his own hands like a carpenter... Many things he left for Japan. One is Rev. Miyazawa. He was a businessman. Like Father he was candid and honest. The first service of Father's work for Izu was held at Miyazawa house, officiated by Bishop Maekawa. Mr. Miyazawa, who was at the head of a big family, was greatly influenced by him. By the noble character of Father Coaldrake whose words and deeds always went together and who told the Gospel easily Mr. Miyazawa was gradually lead to offer his life for the work of God...

Father Coaldrake always walked on the so-called skyline rather than on the plain.... He came over to Japan as the first missionary after the war and worked actively at the head of us. He became the Chairman of the Board of Missions of the whole of the Pacific area. Not only was his leadership superb but his learning and self-discipline was first-rate, acquired by his own ability and effort. He was chosen as Archbishop and we find ourselves guided by him without our being conscious of it. He certainly walked on the skyline at the head of us.

The Coaldrakes after Frank

After Frank Coaldrake's death in 1970, Maida Coaldrake continued volunteer work for the church in missionary training as Lecturer in Pacific History at the A.B.M.'s House of the Epiphany for a number of years, at the same time bringing up a family of three children. Suddenly widowed at age fifty-one with three teenagers, she had to take over sole financial as well as parental responsibility for the family, pursuing an academic career establishing courses in Japanese history at the University of Sydney and later at the University of Tasmania, and as Dean of Students at Christ College, until ostensible "retirement" in 1984. She was instrumental in establishing the Sister City Relationship between Hobart and Yaizu, the fishing port city which was the home of the ill-fated *Lucky Dragon*, contaminated by nuclear fallout from the Bikini Atoll U.S. testing in 1954.

Her lectures and publications for teachers, under the auspices of the History Teachers' Association of New South Wales, changed the standard of Higher School Certificate Asian History in N.S.W. These addressed such central issues to the understanding of Australia-Japan relations as "Japan in the Twentieth Century: Modernisation and Militarism."[5] Her book *Japan in Asia* called attention to the legacy of the war with the continuing U.S. occupation of Japanese territories in Okinawa and by the Soviet Union of the "Northern Territories" adjacent to Hokkaidō.[6] She contributed energetically to the work of the Japanese Studies Association of Australia, writing a chapter on Izu and social change for one of its

5 Maida S. Coaldrake, Number 2 in Modern History, The History Teachers' Association of N.S.W. Pamphlet Series, Rosebery, N.S.W., 1971 (39 pp.); "Japanese Socialism – An Historiographical Approach," *Teaching History*, Journal of the History Teachers' Association of NSW, vol. 8–3 (November 1974), pp. 4–16; *Aspects of Modernisation in China and Japan in the Nineteenth Century*, Number 1 in Modern History. The History Teachers' Association of N.S.W. Pamphlet Series, Rosebery, N.S.W., 1971 (40 pp.); *Meiji Restoration: An Introduction to Select Documents from Japanese History*, Number 9 in Modern History, History Teachers' Association of N.S.W., Sydney, 1974. See also: M.S. Coaldrake and N.K. Meaney, *Select Documents from American and Japanese History*, Marrickville, N.S.W., Science Press, 1974; *The West and the World*, N. K. Meaney (ed.), Marrickville, N.S.W., Science Press, 1973. Chapters on China and Japan (required textbook for Higher School Certificate, New South Wales).
6 Maida S. Coaldrake, *Japan in Asia: A Dialogue in Co-Existence*, Rigby Topics in Modern History Series, Adelaide, Rigby Ltd, 1973.

first books,[7] and organising the biennial conference held at the University of Tasmania in 1982.

She spent each northern summer for twenty-two years, from 1974 until 1996, as Visiting Professor at the Summer School of Asian Studies at the prestigious Jesuit-founded Sophia University in Tokyo. From 1985 until 1992 she returned to Japan as Senior English teacher at St. Hilda's Anglican Girls' School in Tokyo. Her scholarly distinction and service to Australia-Japan relations were recognised with the award of the Doctor of Letters (*Honoris Causa*) in 1997 by the University of Tasmania. This followed on from her own doctorate awarded in 1985 in the field of Japanese intellectual history.[8] In 1997, her service to Australia-Japan relations and education was recognized by the Emperor and people of Japan with the conferral of The Order of the Precious Crown – Wistaria (*Hōkanshō*), one of Japan's highest imperial orders, becoming only the second Australian woman to receive this award.[9]

The Coaldrake "children," perhaps through conditioning, perhaps from personal proclivity, all entered the "family business" of Japan, each from a different angle. All learned Japanese or brushed up their childhood fluency. Margaret Elspeth Coaldrake, who had left Japan as a two-year old, completed her honours degree in Japanese and anthropology at the University of Sydney, followed by a master's degree in museum studies at the University of Leicester in the U.K. She was instrumental in the creation of the Powerhouse Museum, Sydney, and the National Museum of Australia in Canberra. Margaret served for two terms as a member of the Board of the Australia-Japan Foundation and as Deputy Chair of the Australian National Commission for U.N.E.S.C.O.

Angela Kimi Coaldrake, the youngest child born just three months after the Coaldrakes returned to Australia, received her B.A. from the University of Sydney, followed by a scholarship from The East-West Center for her master's degree in Asian Studies from the University of Hawaii. She completed her doctorate at The University of Michigan in Ethnomusicology and Japanese Music while on a Fulbright Postgraduate Scholarship and Center for Japanese Studies Prize Fellowship. She obtained professional performance qualifications in Japan in the traditional school of *koto* (13 string zither) receiving the performance name of Reiku Hirowakyō. She has performed at the Sydney Opera House and the National Theatre, Tokyo. Kimi is Associate Professor at the University of Adelaide and the author of *Women's* Gidayū *and the Japanese Theatre Tradition*.[10]

William Howard Coaldrake undertook the course in Asian Studies at the Australian National University. He received both a Knox and a Fulbright Fellowship

---

7 Maida S. Coaldrake, "From Exile's Retreat to Businessman's Resort: The Changing Face of the Izu Hantō, in Harold Bolitho and Alan Rix (eds.), *A Northern Prospect. Australian Papers on Japan*, Canberra, Australian National University Press, 1981, pp. 34–52.

8 *Yoshida Shōin and the Hagi Sonjuku*, Ph.D. Thesis, the University of Tasmania, 1985.

9 The first was Joyce Ackroyd, who had been Frank Coaldrake's tutor in Japanese at the University of Sydney in 1946, and later Professor of Japanese at the University of Queensland.

10 Nissan Institute, Routledge Japanese Studies Series, London and New York, Routledge, 1997.

in 1976, enabling him to pursue doctoral studies in the history of Japanese art and architecture at Harvard University. He took courses in Japanese history, language and art with such great scholars as John M. Rosenfield, Edwin O. Reischauer, John K. Fairbank, Albert Craig and Donald Shively, forming enduring friendships and scholarly networks.

After completing his doctorate, he taught Japanese art and architectural history for three years at Harvard. He became a member of the Kyoto Guild of Traditional Master Builders in 1980, spending extended periods of field work at heritage building sites in Japan. He returned to Australia in 1988 to the Research School of Pacific Studies at the A.N.U., Canberra. In 1992 he was appointed to the newly created Foundation Chair of Japanese at the University of Melbourne. He is the author of several books on Japanese architecture, including one on "his beloved carpenters" (see *Letter from Maida Coaldrake, 9 November 1955*).[11] Today his fourth floor office at the University of Melbourne overlooks Fitzroy and Brunswick where Frank Coaldrake began planning his mission to Japan sixty years ago. It is a constant reminder that much has been accomplished in Australia-Japan relations in those sixty years, but much remains to be done.

11 William H. Coaldrake, *Japanese Castles*, translation and adaptation, Japanese Arts Library, Tokyo, New York and San Francisco, Kodansha International and Shibundo, 1986, (originally published in Japanese as *Shiro*, by Motoo Hinago, Nihon no Bijutsu series no. 54, 1970); *The Way of the Carpenter: Tools and Japanese Architecture*, Tokyo and New York, Weatherhill, 1990; *Architecture and Authority in Japan*, Nissan Institute, Oxford, Japan Studies Series, London and New York, Routledge, 1996.

Select bibliography

Guide to archival resources

Anglican Board of Mission–Australia (formerly the Australian Board of Missions)

State Library of New South Wales,
Macquarie St, Sydney,
N.S.W. 2000, Australia.
"Australian Board of Missions, 1873–1978."

Brotherhood of St. Laurence

Library,
67 Brunswick Street,
Fitzroy,
VIC 3065, Australia.

Coaldrake Family Records

C/- Professor William H. Coaldrake, Foundation Professor of Japanese,
Melbourne Institute of Asian Languages and Societies,
The University of Melbourne,
VIC 3010, Australia.

National Archives of Australia

PO Box 7425, Canberra Mail Centre,
A.C.T. 2610, Australia.
Letter, 21 April 1943, F.W. Coaldrake to the Australian Minister for External Affairs and 5 May 1943 reply to the above. Series number A989/1, Item 1943/700/48.
ABC radio presentations by Rev. Frank Coaldrake: 1. Ex-Enemy Villages, 2. Secrets of the Sacred Mountain. Series number SP369/1, Items C/48 and C/49.
Talks by F.W. Coaldrake: Department of Information–Broadcasting Division (February 1941) transcripts.

National Library of Australia

Canberra,
A.C.T. 2600, Australia.
"Australian Student Christian Movement, records 1895–1986."

ScreenSound Australia (National Screen and Sound Archive)

McCoy Circuit, Acton,
A.C.T. 2601, Australia.
Film: *Coaldrake Collection Compilation: first consignment*, title number 41366.
Film: *Coaldrake Movies Collection: compilation second consignment*, title number 43548.
Film (1948–1949): *Coaldrake Movie Collection: The Anglican Church in Japan as Seen by the Australian Missionary Frank Coaldrake*, title number 526742.

The University of Melbourne

Baillieu Library and Archives,
VIC 3010, Australia.
"The Peacemaker, An Australian Venture in Reconstruction," 1939–1971, microfilm: UniM Baill MIC/o 6353.
"Frank Coaldrake Papers," Archive accession numbers: 80/156 and 101/19.

Secondary sources

The following is a selected bibliography of additional sources used to prepare the introduction, chapter commentaries and text notes. It is not intended as a comprehensive bibliography of Australia-Japan relations, the Occupation period in Japan or the history of the Anglican Church in Japan.

Carter, I.R. (1967) *God and Three Shillings, The Story of the Brotherhood of St. Laurence*, Melbourne, Landsdowne Press.
Cortazzi, Hugh (ed.) (2001) *Japan Experiences. Fifty Years, One Hundred Views, Post-war Japan Through British Eyes*, Japan Library Series, Surrey, England, Curzon Press.
Dobson, Jill (2001) *Modernisation and Christianity: Australian Missionary Views of Japan, 1912–1939*, in: Paul Jones and Vera Mackie (eds.), *Relationships: Japan and Australia, 1870s–1950s*, Melbourne, History Department, the University of Melbourne.
Dore, R. P., (1959) *Land Reform in Japan*, London, New York, Toronto, Oxford University Press.
Dower, John W. (1986) *War Without Mercy: Peace and Power in the Pacific War*, New York, Pantheon Books.
Foreign Affairs Association of Japan, The (1949) *The Japan Year Book, 1946–48*, Tokyo, The Foreign Affairs Association of Japan.
Hirai, Kiyoshi (ed.) (1957) *The Japan Christian Year Book, 1957*, Tokyo, The Christian Literature Society (Kyo Bun Kwan).
Ishii, Ryōsuke (1980) *A History of Political Institutions of Japan*, Tokyo, The Japan Foundation. Originally published in Japanese in 1972 by the University of Tokyo Press.

Nippon Seikōkai Yokohama Kyōku rekishi iinkai (ed.) (1998) *Mina ni yorite. Yokohama Kyōku hyakunijūgonen no ayumi, (In His Name. A History of the 125 years of Yokohama Diocese)*, Tokyo, Seikōkai shuppan.

Nippon Seikōkai Yokohama Kyōku Izu Mariya Kyōkai (ed.) (1998) *Izu Mariya Kyōkai no gojūnen (The 50 years of St. Mary's Church, Izu)*, Itō.

O'Brien, Laurie (1966–(2000)) "Coaldrake, Frank William (1912–1970)," in John Ritchie *et al., Australian Dictionary of Biography*, Melbourne, Melbourne University Press, vol. 13, pp. 451–452.

Ritchie, John, *et al.*, (1966–(2000)) *Australian Dictionary of Biography*, Melbourne, Melbourne University Press.

Rodd, L. C. (1972) *John Hope of Christ Church St Laurence*, Sydney, Ambassador Press.

Shorrock, Hallam C., and Joseph J. Spae (eds.) (1968) *The Japan Christian Year Book, Meiji Centennial Issue, 1968*, Tokyo, The Christian Literature Society (Kyo Bun Kwan).

Vories, W. M. (1940) *The Ōmi Brotherhood in Nippon: A Brief History of the "Ōmi Mission" founded in Ōmi-Hachiman, Japan, in 1905*, Ōmi-Hachiman, Japan, The Ōmi-Hachiman Brotherhood Book Department. Fifth edition, June. First published in 1934.

Index

F.W.C. refers to Frank William Coaldrake. Page numbers in **bold** refer to illustrations and captions in the text. Page numbers with the suffix n refer to footnotes on the page. Numbers prefixed by P refer to colour plates and captions.